# Texas Politics

## With Coverage of Mexican-American Politics

### Tenth Edition

Richard H. Kraemer| Charldean Newell | Fernando Pinon

*What Incident brought the demise of Ben Barnes?*

D1304260

CENGAGE
Learning™

Australia • Brazil • Japan • Korea • Mexico • Singapore • Spain • United Kingdom • United States

CENGAGE
Learning™

**Texas Politics: With Coverage of Mexican-American Politics, Tenth Edition**

Richard H. Kraemer| Charldean Newell | Fernando Pinon

Executive Editor:
 Maureen Staudt
 Michael Stranz

Senior Project Development Manager:
 Linda de Stefano

Marketing Specialist:
 Sara Mercurio
 Lindsay Shapiro

Production/Manufacturing Manager:
 Donna M. Brown

PreMedia Supervisor:
 Joel Brennecke

Rights & Permissions Specialist:
 Kalina Hintz
 Todd Osborne

Cover Image:
 Getty Images*

© 2009 Cengage Learning

ALL RIGHTS RESERVED. No part of this work covered by the copyright herein may be reproduced, transmitted, stored or used in any form or by any means graphic, electronic, or mechanical, including but not limited to photocopying, recording, scanning, digitizing, taping, Web distribution, information networks, or information storage and retrieval systems, except as permitted under Section 107 or 108 of the 1976 United States Copyright Act, without the prior written permission of the publisher.

For product information and technology assistance, contact us at
**Cengage Learning Customer & Sales Support, 1-800-354-9706**

For permission to use material from this text or product, submit all requests online at **cengage.com/permissions**
Further permissions questions can be emailed to
**permissionrequest@cengage.com**

ISBN-13: 978-0-495-83310-9

ISBN-10: 0-495-83310-X

**Cengage Learning**
5191 Natorp Boulevard
Mason, Ohio 45040
USA

Cengage Learning is a leading provider of customized learning solutions with office locations around the globe, including Singapore, the United Kingdom, Australia, Mexico, Brazil, and Japan. Locate your local office at: **international.cengage.com/region**

Cengage Learning products are represented in Canada by Nelson Education, Ltd.

For your lifelong learning solutions, visit **www.cengage.com/custom**

Visit our corporate website at **www.cengage.com**

Printed in the United States of America
1 2 3 4 5 6 7 12 11 10 09 08

# Contents

Preface viii

---

**CHAPTER 8**

# The Governor    235

---

**CHAPTER 9**

# The Administrative State    266

---

**CHAPTER 10**

# The Judiciary    303

# Preface

*exas Politics* has now been published for more years than many of its readers have lived. Since 1979, the government and politics of Texas have changed a great deal. The state now has more than 23 million people—more than double the 1980 figure—and is second only to California in population. The Republicans have evolved from a decidedly minority political party into the dominant party, especially in statewide politics. Oil and gas revenues now fuel only 2.5 percent of the state budget, which has increased from $16.8 billion at the time of the first edition of this book to over $150 billion. Citizens find it easier to register to vote and cast their ballots. One elective office—that of state treasurer—has disappeared, and the governor has gained considerable power over state agencies and the state budget.

Other aspects of government and politics have not changed appreciably. The Texas Constitution is still a patchwork of detailed provisions and numerous amendments—in fact, more each year—rather than a streamlined document. The judicial system still consists of a hodgepodge of courts with overlapping jurisdictions. Business and economic interests continue to be the dominant influence on the legislature. The executive branch remains confusing because of the myriad boards and commissions that dominate state administration. The growth of local governments has slowed, with the number of municipalities increasing faster than special districts for a change. Council-manager government remains the favorite of home-rule municipalities. Change and the lack of it are part of what makes studying Texas politics interesting.

The reader will encounter three basic themes in *Texas Politics*, tenth edition. In each case, the authors are describing reality and challenging the readers to make their own assessment. In doing so, we often rub against long-held political notions and biases. First, the overriding theme is a comparison of the reality of Texas government and politics to the democratic ideals of participation, majority rule, minority rights, and equality before the law. Throughout, the authors raise the question of whether a particular political decision meets the test of being good for society as a whole or whether only special interests are served. This discussion is set in the context of the state's individualistic–traditionalistic political culture. As political scientists, the authors are trained to be analysts, not merely observers, of politics. Our mission is not to offer a defense or an apology for the present system but to identify the differences between governmental practices and the sense of fair play and equity expected in a democratic system. Thus, we point out where the system works well, but we also examine the faults of the system and suggest needed changes. The study questions that end each chapter often ask the reader to make the same analysis and agree or disagree with the suggested changes, and the "You Decide" feature incorporated into each chapter outlines a debate in which the reader can engage with other students.

A second theme is increasing conservatism even in a state that has always been conservative. The Democrats have long been divided into liberal and conservative wings, with the term *conservative* mainly meaning protection of business interests and a paternal attitude toward ethnic minorities and the poor. The Republicans seem destined to a division between economic conservatives and social conservatives.

Third, because political ideologies are so different among the various political factions and because the ethnic and racial composition of the state is changing rapidly, we introduce a theme of conflict. We particularly call attention to conflicts among the rich, the poor, and the middle class; among and between Anglos, Mexican Americans, and African Americans; between ideologies; and between religious traditions. In addition, the state now displays sharp distinctions between the two major political parties, a secondary indication of racial, ethnic, and cultural differences.

This edition brings with it a new look, with full-color production and more photographs and other artwork to pique students' interest. Major updates include

- Chapter One: An update on the latest economic trends and latest demographic estimates

- Chapter Two: Constitutional amendments through mid-2007; updates of comparison of Texas and other state constitutions

- Chapter Three: Updates on lobbying in the 2007 legislature. Discussion of the recent victories and losses of some of the state's major interest groups, especially conservative Christian groups

- Chapter Four: Discussion of the 2006 Republican and Democratic state party platforms; updates on party organizational developments through mid-2007; discussion of third-party success, and lack of success, in 2006

- Chapter Five: Analysis of the results of the 2006 election; discussion of the arguments surrounding the effort of Republicans to pass "anti-voter fraud" legislation in the 2007 legislature; discussion of 2006 voter turnout

- Chapter Six: Crisis of leadership in recent legislative sessions, with emphasis on the attempts to overthrow the speaker of the House; changes in committee structure for the Eightieth Texas Legislature

- Chapter Seven: Dynamics of recent legislative sessions, including a summary of the accomplishments—and failures—of the 2007 session

- Chapter Eight: Emphasis on the Rick Perry gubernatorial years, including his skirmishes with the Texas Legislature and his efforts to extend executive power

- Chapter Nine: Changes in agencies headed by elected officials and in other major state agencies

- Chapter Ten: Update on the structure of the court system through 2006; update of the way the state pays jurors; update on crime statistics; update on U.S. Supreme Court rulings pertaining to state judicial campaigns

- Chapter Eleven: Discussion of recent developments in regard to the issue of religious expression; update of actions by 2007 legislature concerning the right to bear arms; discussion of 2007 Attorney General's opinion on doctors' criminal culpability for performing illegal abortions; recent developments in school finance

- Chapter Twelve: Developments in Texas local government, including the quest for funding and the slowing of growth in the number of special districts

- Chapter Thirteen: Analysis of the fiscal years 2008–2009 budget, including the use of the surplus to balance the budget rather than any reform of state taxes

- Chapter Fourteen: Updates on selected policy issues, including business policy, poverty, the environment, and transportation, featuring the state's continuing failures to address the needs of poor people, its seeming inability to move away from being a major polluter, and struggles over the Trans-Texas Corridor

- Chapter Fifteen: Recent changes in the economy and what they suggest about the future; discussion of trends in population and their political implications; recent state and local actions in regard to defending the state against terrorism

Each chapter invites readers to visit the companion site for this book: http://academic.cengage.com/polsci/Kraemer/TexasPolitics10e. There, the reader can gain access to the online research guide and many helpful learning aids as well as find a 2010 edition update to critical aspects of politics and finance. Faculty members can use the Web site to access the Instructor's Manual, PowerPoint presentations, and other teaching aids. These resources and a well-crafted Test Bank can also be found on the PowerLecture for Texas Politics, Tenth Edition CD-ROM. Adopters may also request a copy of *ABC News: Texas Political Theatre* on DVD or VHS, which offers a collection of important news stories, interviews, and other video clips to stimulate class discussion and students' interest in Texas politics. Because the Dallas County Community College District has adopted *Texas Politics* for its telecourses, individuals with access to DCCCD programming on public television may find the content familiar.

Many people have helped in the preparation of the tenth edition of this book. The authors would like to thank the instructors who reviewed the text with their careful reading of the ninth edition and the many useful suggestions they made: Lee Almaguer, Midland College; John N. Barbour, Angelo State University; Mary E. Barnes, Blinn College; Vida Davoudi, Kingwood College; Robert Glen Findley, Odessa College; Sharon A. Navarro, University of Texas at San Antonio; Theron Waddell, Galveston College; Mark A. Cichock, University of Texas at Arlington. Our colleagues at the University of Texas at Austin and the University of North Texas also offered constructive criticism and helpful hints. Sometimes we agreed with the reviewers but were unable to comply with their suggestions because of page limitations. Nevertheless, many changes in this edition are due to their comments and the comments of colleagues across the state who called our attention to points deserving coverage or correction. We are similarly indebted to students who raised provocative questions and pointed out places where greater clarity would be appreciated.

In addition, many other individuals offered valuable assistance in helping us to find specific information or documents. They include librarians and other faculty members, graduate students, legislative and state agency staff members, and journalists. We particularly want to thank the staff of the chief clerk's office in the Texas House of Representatives. We are especially grateful to two people who

have been endlessly helpful to us over the course of many editions of this textbook: Ben Sargent, who makes his editorial cartoons from the *Austin American-
Statesman* available to us, and Anne Cook, librarian of the photo library at the
Texas Department of Transportation, who has helped choose the photographs
that have adorned the covers of these books. We also gratefully acknowledge the
work of Mark Shomaker of Blinn College, who prepared the instructor's materials for this edition of *Texas Politics*.

Of course, any errors of fact or interpretation are ours alone.

*Richard H. Kraemer*
Emeritus Professor of Government
The University of Texas at Austin

*Charldean Newell*
Regents Professor Emerita of Public Administration
University of North Texas

*David F. Prindle*
Professor of Government
The University of Texas at Austin

# The Context of Texas Politics

The San Jacinto Monument near Beaumont commemorates the 1836 battle in which Texans won their independence from Mexico.

If I owned Hell and Texas, I'd rent out Texas and live in Hell.

GENERAL PHILIP H. SHERIDAN, FORT CLARK, 1855

So what is Texas? The simplest answer is that it
is America on steroids.

THE ECONOMIST, A BRITISH NEWSWEEKLY, 2003

All government is bad, including good government.

EDWARD ABBEY, THE JOURNEY HOME, 1977

# Introduction

Much has changed in Texas between the era in which General Sheridan made his oft-quoted evaluation of the state and the era in which the editors of *The Economist* made theirs. In 1855, Texas was poor and sparsely settled and offered few civilized comforts to a soldier assigned to garrison an outpost against Native American raids. Today, Texas is the nation's second most populous state, with four-fifths of its population living in cities or suburbs, and the state leads the country in consuming energy and producing semiconductors, among other distinctions. Yet, as we shall see, in some ways the state has changed little since Sheridan's time. Texas is a constantly evolving mix of old and new.

Old habits of thought and behavior evolved to meet the problems of the nineteenth century, when Texas was settled by Americans of western European background. They persist today, despite serious new problems created in the latter decades of the twentieth and first decade of the twenty-first centuries. As Texans prepare themselves to meet the challenges of the future, they have to ask themselves if the habits and institutions they have inherited are up to the job.

In this chapter, the first topic is a summary of the history of Texas, with an emphasis on important political events and the development of the economy. Some of the most basic principles of democratic theory are then discussed, along with an explanation of why it is vital to understand them, and a brief look at one of democracy's problems. Two discussions then situate Texas within the American federal system and the international arena. The focus then shifts to

Texas's political culture and some historically crucial social and political attitudes. The next subject is the economy of Texas and the way it interacts with the state's political system. As an introduction to some discussions later in the book, the origin and distribution of the state's population are then considered. Finally, there is a brief outline of the agenda for the rest of the book.

# Texas History: A Chronology

## THE EARLIEST DAYS

The history of Texas is as exciting as that of any region in the nation, and our mythmakers have embellished it a little more than in most states. Texas has existed under six flags: those of Spain, France, Mexico, the Republic (and state) of Texas, the Southern Confederacy, and the United States. Texas has seen the administration of thirty-seven Spanish governors, fifteen Mexican governors, five presidents of the Republic, and forty-eight state governors.[1]

Humans have inhabited Texas for much longer than there has been such a thing as a state. Skull fragments found near Midland (dubbed "Midland Minnie") and a complete female skeleton discovered near Leander have been dated at 10,000 to 13,000 years old; a larger Clovis period (10,000–9,000 B.C.) site has been excavated in Denton County. At the time of the first European exploration in the sixteenth century, perhaps 30,000 to 40,000 Native Americans inhabited what is now Texas, and some estimates run as high as 130,000. Among the major groups were the Caddo tribes of North and East Texas, Tonkawas in Central Texas, Karankawas along the coast, Coahuiltecans from the Rio Grande river to what is now San Antonio, Lipan Apaches and Comanches in West Texas, and Jumanos in the Trans Pecos region. Determined to keep their lands, they violently resisted European settlement. Westward advancement in Texas cost seventeen White lives per mile. One can only guess at the cost to the Native Americans, although it was probably much higher.

As early as 1519, just twenty-seven years after the European discovery of the New World and a century before the English Pilgrims landed at Plymouth Rock, Spanish explorer Alonzo Alvarez de Pineda mapped the entire Gulf Coast. Several expeditions followed, but Spanish activity was not extensive until 1685, when the French explorer Rene Robert Cavaliere de Sieur La Salle built a small fort in what is now South Texas. This threat of competition from their imperial rivals spurred the Spanish to establish a series of missions beginning in 1690. The purposes of these missions were to extend the sphere of Spanish domination and civil law and to convert Native Americans to Christianity. Spanish influence extended across South Texas from Louisiana to New Mexico, and by the time of the American Revolution in 1776, about 2,300 Native Americans had been baptized.

But Spanish power was already waning as a result of economic and military factors. After one abortive attempt, Mexico achieved independence from Spain in 1821. What followed for Texas was a period of freebooters, privateers, and filibustering expeditions. Several American and Mexican adventurers led private invasions in unsuccessful attempts to establish control over Texas, and pirates—notably the Frenchman Jean Lafitte—operated out of Galveston Island, preying on Spanish shipping.

Despite the centuries of Spanish influence, at the time of Mexican independence in 1821, there were only three permanent European settlements in Texas—San Antonio, Nacogdoches, and Goliad—and the European population had declined to 7,000 during the previous thirty years. Although their numbers were relatively small, Spaniards and Mexicans left rich and indelible influences on Texas through their language, law, religion, and culture.

## ANGLO-AMERICAN COLONIZATION

Colonization from the south did not succeed in Texas because of shortsighted economic policies. The Spanish government exploited the few settlers by paying poor prices for their cattle and other products and at the same time charging them high prices for trade goods. As a result, few moved to the giant province.

Texas was potentially much more attractive to settlers from the neighboring United States. There, frontier land was sold to would-be settlers, but in Texas, land was free if one could get a government grant. Because the Spanish government had failed to persuade Mexican citizens to colonize the area, it was nervous about expansionist impulses in the United States. Spain decided to gamble that it could acculturate Anglo settlers and use them to protect Mexican interests against the growing, rambunctious democracy to the north.

Moses Austin, a native of Connecticut, abandoned his unsuccessful business activities in Missouri and turned his attention to Texas. Moses died after filing a formal application for settlement with the viceroy of Mexico in 1819. He was succeeded by his son Stephen F. Austin, who received a generous land grant as well as permission to bring in 300 families for colonization. The first settlements were at Columbus on the Colorado River and at Washington-on-the-Brazos. As **impresario**, or agent, Austin had wide powers over his colony to establish commercial activity, organize a militia, and dispense justice.

Other colonies quickly followed, and the non-Native American population jumped from 7,000 to more than 35,000 between 1821 and 1836. The great majority of the settlers came in good faith, intending to take the oath of allegiance to Mexico and be good Mexican citizens. But the cultural differences they encountered made this difficult. Not only was Spanish the official language, but the colonists, mostly Protestant, were required to accept Roman Catholicism. Some also continued to keep Black slaves, although this practice was illegal in Mexico.

Furthermore, the new Mexican nation was suffering from violent political instability, and policy toward Texas was both inconsistent and made 800 miles away in Mexico City by men who knew little about conditions in the area. Moreover, Anglos tended to regard themselves as culturally superior to Mexicans, and vice versa. Alienation between Texas and Mexico grew, much as alienation between the colonists and the British had grown prior to the American Revolution two generations earlier.

## REVOLUTION

The Mexican government now feared further Anglo-American settlement and acted to curtail it. The settlers responded with demands for concessions, including the right to use the English language in public business and the separation of Texas from the state of Coahuila. Austin was imprisoned in Mexico City for a time, and conditions degenerated. What followed is known to virtually every

The Alamo in San Antonio symbolizes the state's colorful political history.

schoolchild in the state: Texas's war for independence. The most celebrated engagement was the battle in San Antonio during March 1836 in which a few Anglos and Texas-Mexicans held the Alamo against a much larger Mexican force for eleven days before being massacred. Nevertheless, although it makes a stirring story, the Alamo was not a decisive engagement. That distinction belongs to the Battle of San Jacinto, which took place between the new Texas army, led by Sam Houston, and the Mexican army, led by General Antonio Lopez de Santa Anna, on April 21.

Surprising the Mexicans while they took a siesta in the afternoon, the Texans routed them in a mere eighteen minutes, captured Santa Anna, and ordered him to sign a document agreeing to their independence or be executed. Santa Anna signed, but repudiated the treaty as soon as he was safely across the border. Texans, however, considered themselves independent, and the Republic of Texas became a reality.

The history of the republic was eventful but short. Independence brought sudden growth, with the population rising rapidly to about 140,000. But the Mexicans invaded twice, capturing San Antonio both times. Resistant Native Americans continued to cause severe problems as well. The new nation soon found itself in debt and with a depreciating currency. Sentiment for annexation by the United States had always been strong, and on December 29, 1845, the U.S. Congress voted to admit Texas into the Union as the twenty-eighth state. This was one of those rare events in history in which an independent nation gave up its sovereignty and became part of another nation. Unlike other states, Texas retained the title to all of its public lands when it accepted statehood.

★ ★ ★ ★ ★ ★ ★ ★ ★ ★ ★ ★ ★ ★ ★ ★ ★ ★ ★ ★ ★ ★ ★ ★ ★ ★ ★ ★ ★

### *How Many Heroes?*

Although Texans are certain that the men who gave their lives at the Alamo were heroes, they are not quite sure how many of them there were. For most of the twentieth century, the Daughters of the Republic of Texas maintained a roster of "Heroes of the Battle of the Alamo" that contained 183 names, mainly Anglo. Over the decades, a few Spanish-surnamed defenders were added, so that by the early 1990s the "official" number of heroes was 189.

Recent scholarly research, however, has suggested that the victorious Mexican army counted as many as 257 Texan bodies after the battle. Because of the incomplete nature of the Mexican records, it may be impossible to come up with a definitive number.

★ ★ ★ ★ ★ ★ ★ ★ ★ ★ ★ ★ ★ ★ ★ ★ ★ ★ ★ ★ ★ ★ ★ ★ ★ ★ ★ ★ ★

SOURCE: David McLemore, "160 Years Later, Historians Ask: Who Died at the Alamo?" *Austin American-Statesman*, March 12, 1996, B6.

## EARLY STATEHOOD

A final peace treaty with Mexico had never been signed, and the Mexican government still considered Texas merely a rebellious province. Annexation of the area by the United States precipitated the Mexican War. This conflict was short and decisive. The first engagement took place at Palo Alto, near present-day Brownsville, on May 8, 1846, and Mexico City fell just four months later, on September 14. Under the Treaty of Guadalupe Hidalgo, the defeated nation relinquished all claim to Texas and, in return for $15 million, ceded all territory west of Texas and south of Oregon to the United States. One can only wonder what the value of this vast tract is today.

Acceptance of Texas into the Union was not without controversy. At the time of her independence in 1836, Texas contained about 5,000 Black slaves.[2] Because Texas permitted slavery, annexation was supported by the slave states and opposed by the states where slavery was illegal. The Whigs, soon to be succeeded by the Republicans, were generally opposed to slavery and to the admission of Texas. Democrats were generally in favor.

No political parties, as such, existed in the Republic of Texas. Sam Houston, the hero of the battle of San Jacinto, was the dominant political figure, and political debate generally divided along pro-Houston and anti-Houston lines. But for the reasons outlined, to the extent that Texans thought about national politics, most were Democrats.

By joining the United States, however, Texas plunged into the political controversy over slavery. That issue simmered at higher and higher temperatures until it boiled over with the election of an antislavery Republican, Abraham Lincoln, as president in 1860. Fearful that Republican control would mean a federal effort to emancipate their slaves, the southern states withdrew from the Union. Texas seceded in February 1861 and joined the new Confederacy in March.

Texans fought at home, on an expedition into New Mexico, and in large numbers in West Virginia, Tennessee, and elsewhere during the Civil War. Southern troops and southern generals were usually superior to their northern counterparts and won many battles. The agricultural South, however, was outgunned, outmanned, and outsupplied by the industrial North, and southern political leadership was inferior to Lincoln's. The U.S. president issued the Emancipation Proclamation, freeing the slaves, on January 1, 1863, an act that persuaded European powers not to enter the war on the South's behalf. As a consequence, the North ground down the South's ability to wage war over four years until the Confederacy fell apart in the spring of 1865. With the defeat of the rebellion, federal troops landed at Galveston on June 19, 1865, proclaiming the freedom of the state's 250,000 slaves. "Juneteenth" is still celebrated by African American Texans as Emancipation Day.

## POST-CIVIL WAR TEXAS

Confusion and bitterness followed the war. Despite President Lincoln's stated policy of "with malice toward none, with charity for all," the reaction in Texas, as in other parts of the South, was to continue to oppose national policy even though the war was over. Confederate officials and sympathizers were elected to state and local office; Black Codes that severely restricted the activities of the former slaves were passed by state legislatures. This defiance by the defeated South strengthened the position of the Radical Republicans in Congress and caused a hardening of policy, and Lincoln's assassination prevented him from moderating their desire to punish the states of the defunct Confederacy for their rebellion. During the period known as Reconstruction, military government was imposed on the South, and former Confederate officials and soldiers were largely excluded from voting and from holding public office.

These actions by the federal government intensified the hostility with which most White Texans viewed the Republican Party. African Americans, as one might expect, voted for the Republicans, giving White Texans even more reason to support the Democrats. Political activity by the freed slaves also gave rise to the Ku Klux Klan in Texas and throughout the South. Klan members met in secret, bound themselves by oath, and frequently wore hoods to conceal their identities. Their purpose was to keep African Americans in a position of great inferiority. Their methods included intimidation, violence, and sometimes murder.

The best remembered governorship of this Reconstruction period was that of E. J. Davis, one of a number of Texans who had fought for the Union during the war. A Republican, Davis held office from 1870 to 1874. Using the substantial powers granted by the Constitution of 1869, Davis acted like a true chief executive and implemented policies consistent with the philosophy of the Radical Republicans in Washington. To his credit, Davis reformed the penal system and greatly improved public education. To his discredit, during his tenure, state indebtedness increased considerably, and there were allegations of financial impropriety. But whatever the merits of his administration, to White Texans he was a traitorous agent of the hated Yankees.

In 1873, after political restrictions against former Confederate officials and soldiers were removed, a Democrat, Richard Coke, defeated Davis in his reelection bid by a two-to-one margin. Davis contested the election, and the pro-Republican state Supreme Court invalidated it on a technicality. The Democratic legislature, however, declared Coke the winner. For a time, the capital city of Austin was a battleground. Coke and the legislature occupied one part of the capital, and Davis, surrounded by loyal state police, held another. Davis left office in 1874 only after President Grant refused his request for assistance. For years, Texas Democrats used the Davis administration as a frightening example of what would happen if voters ever again strayed from the fold and voted Republican. Indeed, it was more than a century before another Republican governor was elected in Texas.

More important than the ouster of Davis, however, was the repudiation of the Constitution of 1869 and its replacement with Texas's current basic law, the Constitution of 1876. The adoption of this document represented the end of Reconstruction and a substantial return to the traditional principles of the Jeffersonian Democrats, including very limited government and low taxes.

## THE LATE NINETEENTH CENTURY

Texas did not suffer the physical destruction that burdened other Confederate states, and economic recovery and development came quickly after the Civil War. The Hollywood version of this era in Texas is one of cowboys, cattle drives, and range wars. There is some basis for the mythical view of post–Civil War Texas as a land of ranches and trail drives, for between 1866 and 1880 four million cattle were driven "north to the rails."[3] Nevertheless, the actual foundation of the state's economy was King Cotton. In East Texas, the fields were worked largely by African Americans, and in West Texas, by Mexican Americans. Cotton remained the cash crop and principal export well into the twentieth century. However, in terms of the self-image of Texans, the myth of cow culture has been far more important than the reality of cotton farming.

★ ★ ★ ★ ★ ★ ★ ★ ★ ★ ★ ★ ★ ★ ★ ★ ★ ★ ★ ★ ★ ★ ★ ★ ★ ★

For many years, Galveston permitted gambling and the sale of mixed drinks, despite state laws prohibiting these practices. State and local authorities looked the other way—probably because they were bribed—until the 1950s. The common explanation in Texas was that "Galveston was discovered by pirates and has been run by them ever since."

★ ★ ★ ★ ★ ★ ★ ★ ★ ★ ★ ★ ★ ★ ★ ★ ★ ★ ★ ★ ★ ★ ★ ★ ★ ★

Texas has few navigable rivers, and transportation was a major problem. Because of the size of the state, thousands of miles of railroad track were laid. In 1888, railroad construction in Texas exceeded the total for all of the other states and territories combined. In 1881, embarrassed officials discovered that the state legislature had given the railroads a million more acres of land for rights of way than were available, and the land-grant laws were repealed. In all, more than 32 million acres of land were given to the railroads, thus establishing early on the easy relationship between the state government and large corporations.

Race relations were difficult statewide, but particularly in East Texas. "Jim Crow laws" severely limiting the civil rights of African Americans began to make their appearance, and in East Texas, violence against the former slaves was common and often fatal. Between 1870 and 1900, an estimated 500 African Americans died as a result of mob violence, much of it led by the Ku Klux Klan. Race relations and equality of treatment for all citizens continue to be problems today.

Throughout most of the final quarter of the nineteenth century, conservative Democrats maintained control of the state. Their rule was based on White supremacy and the violent emotional reaction to the Radical Republican Reconstruction era. But other political parties and interest groups rose to challenge them.

With the penetration of the state by railroads and the increase in manufacturing came organized labor. Most notable were the militant Knights of Labor, which struck the Texas & Pacific Railroad in 1885 and won concessions. Another strike a year later, however, turned violent. Governor John Ireland used troops, ostensibly to protect railroad property, and the strike was broken. The union was severely criticized. In the optimistic and growing economy of the 1880s, labor unions were even less acceptable in the South than elsewhere. In Texas, they were viewed as "Yankee innovations" and "abominations." Although a combination of capital was called a corporation and given approval by the state to operate under a charter, combinations of labor, called unions, were frequently labeled restraints of trade by the courts and forbidden to operate. Laws and executive actions also restricted union activities. These biases in favor of capital and against organized labor are still common in Texas.

More important than early labor unions was the agrarian movement. By the 1870s and 1880s, many of those who worked the land in Texas—whether White, African American, or Mexican American—were tenant farmers. Having to borrow money for seed and supplies, they worked all year to pay back what they owed and rarely broke even. Money and credit were scarce even for those who owned land, and railroad rates were artificially high.

The National Grange, or Patrons of Husbandry, was founded in 1867 in Washington, D.C., to try to defend farmers against this sort of economic hardship. The first chapter was established in Texas in 1872, and the organization quickly grew. Grangers were active in local politics, and the state organization lobbied the legislature on issues relevant to farmers. The Grange not only was influential in establishing Texas Agricultural & Mechanical College (now A&M University) and other educational endeavors but also played a significant role in writing the Constitution of 1876. About half of the ninety delegates to the constitutional convention were Grangers, and they left their mark on the charter, writing provisions for a figurehead governor, restrictions on taxation and indebtedness, and provisions for the regulation of railroads. Despite hundreds of amendments, the constitution is still essentially the narrow, restrictive document created by disgruntled farmers more than a century ago.

James S. Hogg, representing a new breed of Texas politician, was elected governor in 1890 and 1892. The first native Texan to hold the state's highest office, Hogg was not a Confederate veteran. He presided over a brief period of reform that saw the establishment of the Railroad Commission, regulation of monopolies, limitations on alien ownership of land, and attempts to protect the public by regulating stocks and bonds. Unfortunately, it was also an era that saw the enactment of additional Jim Crow laws, including the requirement for segregation of African Americans from Whites on railroads.

Both major political parties were in turmoil, and in the 1890s, opposition to the Democrats in southern states was most effectively provided by the new People's, or Populist, Party. The Populists represented the belief that ordinary people had lost control of their government to rich corporations, especially the banks and railroads. Populists advocated monetary reform, railroad regulation, control of corporations, and other programs aimed at making government responsible to the citizens. Populists reached their peak strength in Texas in 1894 and 1896 but failed to unseat the Democrats in statewide elections. The dominant party, as it had done with the Greenbackers, adopted some Populist programs, and most farmers returned to the Democratic fold. However, Populism, although not the dominant sentiment, is still influential in Texas. Texans who are usually political conservatives can sometimes be roused to vote for candidates who argue that government is making policy at the behest of wealthy insiders rather than ordinary people. The Populist streak makes Texas politics less predictable than it might otherwise be.

Jim Hogg left the governorship in 1895, and the brief period of agrarian reform waned, due in large measure to changes in the membership of the legislature. In 1890, about half the representatives were farmers, but by 1901, two thirds were lawyers and businessmen. The representation of these professions is similarly high today.

## THE EARLY TWENTIETH CENTURY

Seldom has a new century brought such sudden and important changes as the beginning of the twentieth century brought to Texas. On January 10, 1901, an oil well came in at Spindletop, near Beaumont. Oil had earlier been produced in Texas, but not on such a scale. In 1900, the state had supplied 836,000 barrels of oil—about 6 percent of the nation's production. The Spindletop field exceeded that total in a few weeks, and in its first year gushed out 3.2 million barrels.

At first, Texas competed with Oklahoma and California for oil production leadership. But with the discovery of the huge (6 billion barrels) East Texas field in 1930, the Lone Star State became not only the nation's leading producer but the world's. Oil's abundance and low price led steamship lines and railroads to abandon the burning of coal and

A cluster of oil derricks close together in the Spindletop field during the early boom of the 1900s near Beaumont.

convert to oil. Petroleum created secondary industries, such as petrochemicals and the well service business. Thousands of farm boys left home and took jobs as manual labor "roughnecks." A few became wildcatters (independent explorers), and some of these earned fortunes. More large fields were discovered in every part of the state except the far western deserts and the central hill country. Oil, combined later with gas, replaced cotton and cattle as the state's most important industry. Severance (production) taxes became the foundation for state government revenue.

The rise of the oil industry created considerable conflict as well as prosperity. Texans were determined to prevent the spread of the Standard Oil Company's monopoly into the state. Beginning in 1889, the Texas attorney general began bringing "antitrust" suits against local companies affiliated with Standard Oil. After Spindletop, attorneys general were even more energetic in trying to repel the expansion of the monopoly. By 1939, the state had brought fourteen antitrust actions against oil companies.[4] People in other states often see Texas as dominated by the oil industry. In reality, as this brief summary illustrates, the state has had an ambivalent relationship with the industry. Texans generally celebrate small, independent firms, especially wildcatters. But they are suspicious of the major corporations, and state politicians sometimes reflect that suspicion. It is one expression of the Populist tradition in state politics.

The agrarian movement had ended, but the spirit of progressivism was not completely dead. In 1903, the legislature passed the Terrell Election Law, which provided for a system of primary elections rather than the hodgepodge of practices then in use. The legislature also curtailed child labor by setting minimum ages for working in certain industries. National child labor legislation was not passed until thirteen years later. Antitrust laws were strengthened, and a pioneer pure food and drug law was enacted. Farm credit was eased, and the legislature approved a bank deposit insurance plan, a program not adopted by Washington until the 1930s.

Running counter to this progressive spirit, however, was the requirement that a poll tax be paid as a prerequisite for voting. Authorities differ as to whether African Americans, Mexican Americans, or poor Anglos were the primary target of the law, but African Americans were hit especially hard. Their voter turnout, estimated to be 100,000 in the 1890s, dropped to about 5,000 by 1906.

Even this small number was too many for the advocates of White supremacy, however. In 1904, the legislature permitted, and in 1923 it required, counties to institute the "White primary," which forbade African Americans and Latinos to participate in the party contest to nominate candidates for the general election. In that era Texas was a one-party Democratic state (see Chapter 4), so the winner of the Democratic primary was always the winner in the general election. Thus, even if minority citizens managed to cast a ballot in November, they could only choose among candidates who had been designated by an all-White electorate in April.[5]

Early efforts to ensure conservation of the state's natural resources enjoyed little success. Few attempts were made to extract oil from the ground efficiently. A large majority of the oil in most reservoirs was never extracted, and some of the recovered oil was improperly stored so that it ran down the creeks or evaporated. Many improperly drilled wells polluted groundwater. The "flaring" (burning) of natural gas was commonplace into the 1940s. Fifteen million acres of virgin pine trees in East Texas were clear-cut, leading to severe soil erosion. By 1932, only a million acres of forest remained, and wood products had to be imported into the state. Conservation and environmental protection are still uphill battles in Texas.

# WARS AND DEPRESSION

World War I, which the United States entered in 1917, brought major changes to Texas. The state became an important military training base, and almost 200,000 Texans volunteered for military service. Five thousand lost their lives, many dying from influenza rather than enemy action.

America's native hate-mongering organization, the Ku Klux Klan, flourished in the early 1920s. Originally founded to keep African Americans subjugated, after the war the Klan expanded its list of despised peoples to include immigrants and Catholics. Between 1922 and 1924, the Klan controlled every elective office in Dallas, in both city and county government. In 1922, the Klan's candidate, Earle Mayfield, was elected to the U.S. Senate. Hiram Evans of Dallas was elected imperial wizard of the national Klan, and Texas was the center of Klan power nationwide.

When Alfred E. Smith, a New Yorker, a Roman Catholic, and an anti-prohibitionist, was nominated for the presidency by the Democrats in 1928, Texas party loyalty frayed for the first time since Reconstruction. Texans voted for the Republican candidate, Herbert Hoover, a Protestant and a prohibitionist. Because of such defections from the formerly Democratic "Solid South," and because of the general national prosperity under a Republican administration, Hoover won.

Partly because the state was still substantially rural and agricultural, the Great Depression that began in 1929 was less severe in Texas than in more industrialized states. Further, a year after the stock market collapsed, C. M. "Dad" Joiner struck oil near Kilgore, discovering the supergiant East Texas oil field. This bonanza directly and indirectly created jobs for thousands of people. Houston became so prosperous because of the oil boom that it became known as "the city the Depression forgot."

The liquid wealth gushing from the earth in East Texas, however, also created major problems. So much oil came from that one field so fast that it flooded the market, driving prices down. The price of oil in the middle part of the country dropped from $1.10 per barrel in 1930 to $0.25 a year later, and some lots sold for as little as $0.05 a barrel. With their inexpensive overhead, the small independent producers who dominated the East Texas field could prosper under low prices by simply producing more. But the major companies, with their enormous investments in pipelines, refineries, and gas stations, faced bankruptcy if the low prices continued. The early 1930s was therefore a period of angry conflict between the large and small producers, with the former arguing for production control and the latter resisting it.

The Railroad Commission attempted to force the independents to produce less, but they evaded its orders, and millions of barrels of "hot oil" flowed out of the East Texas field from 1931 to 1935. There was confusion and violence before the state found a solution to the overproduction problem. After much political and legal intrigue, the Railroad Commission devised a formula for "prorating" oil that limited each well to a percentage of its total production capacity. By restricting production, this regulation propped up prices, and the commodity was soon selling for more than a dollar a barrel again.

As part of this system of controlling production and prices, in 1935 Texas Senator Tom Connally persuaded Congress to pass a "Hot Oil Act," which made the interstate sale of oil produced in violation of state law a federal crime.

The major companies thus received the state-sanctioned production control upon which their survival depended. Meanwhile, the Railroad Commission was mollifying the independents by creating production regulations that favored small producers. For four decades, the Railroad Commission was in effect the director of the Texas economy, setting production limits, and therefore price floors, for the most important industry in the state. Because Texas was such an important producer, the commission's regulations exerted a powerful effect on the world price of oil. The commission's nurturing of the state's major industry was a major reason the Depression did not hit Texas as hard as it had many other states.

Most Texans were thus able to weather the Depression, but there were still many who were distressed. Unemployment figures for the period are incomplete, but in 1932, Governor Ross Sterling estimated that 300,000 citizens were out of work. Private charities and local governments were unprepared to offer aid on this scale, and in Houston, African Americans and Hispanics were warned not to apply for relief because there was only enough money to take care of Anglos.

The state defaulted on interest payments on some of its bonds, and many Texas banks and savings and loans failed. A drought so severe as to create a dust bowl in the Southwest made matters even worse. Texans, with their long tradition of rugged individualism and their belief that "that government is best which governs least," were shaken and frustrated by these conditions.

Relief came not from state or local action but from the national administration of the new liberal Democratic president, Franklin D. Roosevelt. Texas Democrats played prominent roles in Roosevelt's New Deal (1933–1945). Vice President John Nance Garner presided over the U.S. Senate for eight years, six Texans chaired key committees in Congress, and Houston banker Jessie Jones, head of the Reconstruction Finance Corporation, was perhaps Roosevelt's most important financial adviser and administrator. The New Deal poured more than $1.5 billion into the state in programs ranging from emergency relief to rural electrification to the Civilian Conservation Corps.

★ ★ ★ ★ ★ ★ ★ ★ ★ ★ ★ ★ ★ ★ ★ ★ ★ ★ ★ ★ ★ ★ ★ ★ ★ ★ ★ ★

## The Silver Lining

During the Depression, an incident occurred that is of particular interest to students in Texas politics classes. Dr. Caleb Perry Patterson, chairman of the Department of Government at the University of Texas, was faced with the prospect of a greatly reduced budget and a consequent loss of teaching positions in the department that would force him to fire several of his colleagues. Patterson convinced the legislature to make the six-semester-hour course in American Government a required class in all Texas colleges receiving public funds. He thus saved the jobs of his colleagues by imposing a degree requirement that accounts for many of the readers of this book. The History Department was not able to convince the legislature to pass a similar requirement for the American history course until twenty years later, in 1957.

★ ★ ★ ★ ★ ★ ★ ★ ★ ★ ★ ★ ★ ★ ★ ★ ★ ★ ★ ★ ★ ★ ★ ★ ★ ★ ★ ★

In spite of the Depression, companies moved to Texas to take advantage of its cheap energy supplies, and manufacturing grew at a rate of more than 4 percent per year between 1919 and 1939. On the eve of World War II, Texas stood on the threshold of becoming one of the nation's major industrial states.

As it had during the first global conflict, Texas contributed greatly to the national effort during World War II from 1941 to 1945. The state was once again a major military training site; several bases and many out-of-state trainees remained after the war. More than 750,000 Texans served in the armed forces, and thirty-two received Congressional Medals of Honor. Secretary of the Navy Frank Knox claimed that Texas contributed a higher percentage of its male population to military service than did any other state.

## POSTWAR TEXAS

By 1950, profound changes had occurred in Texas society. The state's population had shifted from largely rural to 60 percent urban in the decade of the 1940s, the number of manufacturing workers had doubled, and Texas had continued to attract outside capital and new industry. Aluminum production, defense contracting, and high-technology activities were among the leaders. In 1959, Jack Kilby, an engineer employed by Texas Instruments, developed and patented the microchip, a tiny piece of technology that was to transform the state, the nation, and the world.

Texas politics continued to be colorful. In 1948, Congressman Lyndon B. Johnson opposed former Governor Coke Stevens for a vacant U.S. Senate seat. The vote count was very close in the primary runoff which, with Texas still being dominated by the Democratic Party, was the only election that mattered. As one candidate would seem to pull ahead, another uncounted ballot box that gave the edge to his opponent would be conveniently discovered in South or East Texas. The suspense continued for three days, until Johnson finally won by a margin of eighty-seven votes. Historical research has left no doubt that the box that put Johnson over the top was the product of fraud on the part of the political machine that ruled Duval County. Among students of American politics, this is probably the most famous dirty election in the history of the country. The circumstances surrounding the election have attracted so much attention because "Landslide Lyndon" Johnson went on to become majority leader of the U.S. Senate, vice president, and then in 1963, the first Texan to attain the office of president of the United States.

After the war, the state's politics was increasingly controlled by conservative Democrats. As a former slave state, Texas was one of twenty-two states that had laws requiring racial segregation. The 1954 U.S. Supreme Court decision (*Brown* v. *Board of Education*, 347 U.S. 483) declaring segregated public schools unconstitutional caused an uproar in Texas. State leaders opposed integration, just as their predecessors had opposed Reconstruction ninety years earlier. Grade-a-year integration of the schools—a simple and effective solution—was rejected. Millions of dollars in school funds were spent in legal battles to delay the inevitable.

After World War II, Texas again experienced an influx of immigrants. Immigration in the nineteenth century had been primarily from adjacent states, Mexico, and west, central, and southern Europe. Today, immigrants come not only from all fifty states but from all of Latin America and a variety of other areas, including those of the Middle East and Asia.

# GRADUAL POLITICAL CHANGE

Since the 1950s, Texas has become increasingly diverse politically as well. Politicians such as U.S. Senator Ralph Yarborough (1957–1971), Commissioner of Agriculture Jim Hightower (1987–1991), and Governor Ann Richards (1991–1995) demonstrated that liberals could win statewide offices. Republicans also began winning, first with U.S. Senator John Tower (1961–1984) and later with Governor Bill Clements (1979–1983 and 1987–1991). Furthermore, candidates from formerly excluded groups enjoyed increasing success, especially after the passage of the Voting Rights Act of 1965. Morris Overstreet was the first African American elected to statewide office, gaining a seat on the Court of Criminal Appeals in 1990. That same year, Mexican Americans Dan Morales and Raul Gonzalez were elected attorney general and justice of the supreme court, respectively. Kay Bailey Hutchison broke the gender barrier in statewide elections to national office by being elected U.S. Senator in 1993.

# CONTEMPORARY TEXAS

Texas entered a period of good times in the early 1970s. As worldwide consumption of petroleum increased dramatically, the demand for Texas oil outstripped the supply. The Railroad Commission removed market-demand production restrictions in 1972, permitting every well to produce any amount that would not damage ultimate recovery. The following year, the Organization of Petroleum Exporting Countries (OPEC) more than doubled world oil prices and boycotted the American market. Severe energy shortages developed, and the price of oil peaked at more than $40 per barrel. Consumers, especially those from the energy-poor Northeast, grumbled about long lines at gas stations and high prices, but the petroleum industry prospered and the state of Texas enjoyed billion-dollar treasury surpluses.

The 1980s, however, were as miserable for Texas as the previous decade had been agreeable. High oil prices stimulated a worldwide search for the black liquid, and by 1981, so many supplies had been found that the price began to fall. The slide was gradual at first, but the glut of oil was so great that in 1985 the price crashed from its peak of over $40 a barrel in the 1970s to under $10. As petroleum prices plunged, so did Texas's economy: For every $1 drop in world oil prices, 13,500 Texans became unemployed, the state government lost $100 million in revenue from severance taxes, and the gross state product contracted by $2.3 billion.[6] Northern consumers smiled as they filled the gas tanks of their cars, but the oil industry and the state of Texas went into shock.

The oil depression reverberated throughout the state. As its economy contracted, Texas found itself badly overbuilt in both residential and commercial construction. Because no one was buying land or buildings, developers went out of business, and the banks and savings and loans that had financed their projects died with them. In 1988, 113 banks failed. Property foreclosures set new state records in 1987 and 1988. Former Governor John Connally and former Lieutenant Governor Ben Barnes were among the thousands of Texans forced to declare bankruptcy.

Economic poverty was only one of the miseries that visited Texas in the 1980s. The state's crime rate shot up 29 percent.[7] Most of the crimes committed were related to property and were probably a consequence of the demand for illegal drugs, which constantly increased despite intense public relations and interdiction efforts at the national level. Texans insisted upon better law enforcement and longer sentences for convicted criminals just as the state's tax base was contracting. The combination of shrinking revenues and growing demand for services forced Texas politicians to do the very thing they hated most: increase taxes. In 1984, the legislature raised Texas taxes by $4.8 billion. Then, faced with greatly reduced state income, it was forced to act again. First came an increase of almost $1 billion in 1986, and then in 1987, there was a boost of $5.7 billion, the largest state tax increase in the history of the United States up to that time. The system of raising revenue, relying even more heavily on the sales tax, became more regressive than ever. To make matters worse, the increase came just as Congress eliminated sales taxes as a deductible item on the federal income tax. By the end of the 1980s, Texans were battered, frazzled, and gloomy.

But the situation reversed itself again in the 1990s. As the petroleum industry declined, entrepreneurs created other types of businesses to take its place. Computer equipment, aerospace, industrial machinery, and scientific instruments became important parts of the economy. The state began to export more goods. Despite the fact that Texas oil production reached a fifty-year low in 1993, by the mid-1990s the economy was booming, even outperforming the nation as a whole. The boom continued to the end of the century, at which point the state had the eleventh largest economy in the world. The entry into a new economic era was underscored by the fact that by 1997 more Texans were employed in high-tech industries than by the oil industry.

Prosperity brought another surge in immigration, and in 1994, the Lone Star State passed New York as the second most populous in the country, with 18.4 million residents.[8] Even the crime rate was down. The election of the state's governor, George W. Bush, to the presidency of the United States in 2000 seemed to guarantee a rosy future for Texas.

The new century contained many surprises for Texans and Americans, however, and some of them were unpleasant. The national economy began to stagger during the spring of 2001. Soon the media were full of revelations of gigantic fraud in the accounting practices of many apparently successful corporations. The news sent the stock market into a tailspin, and the high-tech sector so important in Texas was hit particularly hard. As high tech went into a recession, Texas lost thousands of jobs.[9]

Economic troubles were joined by political disaster on September 11, when radical Muslim terrorists highjacked four jet planes, flying two into, and in the process destroying, the World Trade Center in New York, flying another into the Pentagon building in Washington, D.C., and crashing another into farmland in Pennsylvania. The national grief and outrage over the 3,000 murders were accompanied by many economic problems as the United States struggled to spend money to prevent such attacks in the future, and by sundry political difficulties as Congress and the president, Republicans and Democrats, argued over what new policies and institutions to create in light of the newly realized challenge of terrorism. Although not a direct target of the attacks, Texans were as much involved in their consequences as the residents of other states. Efforts to guard borders and protect buildings were hugely expensive, and conflicting ideas about the ways to interdict terrorists while protecting the civil liberties of loyal citizens were as intense in Texas as elsewhere. The new era in American history guaranteed a new era in Texas politics.

In addition, Texas continued to face some old problems. More than 17 percent of its population lived in poverty in 2005, the fifth highest among the states.[10] Although the overall crime rate was lower, the tide of drugs coming into society showed no signs of abating. And as will be discussed in this book, Texas still had major problems with its society and political system. Whether its traditional political attitudes will be adequate to deal with the challenges of the new era is a question that will be considered in the course of the discussion.

# Texas as a Democracy

In this book, one of the major themes will be the concept of **democracy** and the extent to which Texas approaches the ideal of a democratic state. A democracy is a system of government resting on the theory that political legitimacy is created by the citizens' participation. **Legitimacy** is the belief people have that their government is founded upon morally right principles and that they should therefore obey its laws. According to the moral theory underlying a democratic system of government, because the people themselves (indirectly, through representatives) make the laws, they are morally obligated to obey them.

Complications of this theory abound, and a number of them are explored in each chapter. Because some means to allow people to participate in the government must exist, free elections, in which candidates or parties compete for the citizens' votes, are necessary. There must be some connection between what a majority of the people want and what the government actually does; how close the connection must be is a matter of some debate. Despite the importance of "majority rule" in a democracy, majorities must not be allowed to take away certain rights from minorities, such as the right to vote, the right to be treated equally under the law, and the right to freedom of speech.

In a well-run democracy, politicians debate questions of public policy honestly, the media report the debate in a fair manner, and the people pay attention to the debate and then vote their preferences consistently with their understanding of the public interest. Government decisions are made on the basis of law, without anyone having an unearned advantage. In a badly run or corrupt democracy, politicians are dominated by special interests but seek to hide the fact by clouding public debate with irrelevancies and showmanship, the media do not point out the problem because they themselves are either corrupt or lazy, and the people fail to hold either the politicians or the media accountable because they do not participate or because they participate carelessly and selfishly. Government decisions are made on the basis of special influence and inside dealing. A good democracy, in other words, is one in which government policy is arrived at through public participation, debate, and compromise. A bad democracy is one in which mass apathy and private influence are the determining factors.

All political systems that are based on the democratic theory of legitimacy have elements of both good and bad. No human institution is perfect—no family or church or government—but it is always useful to compare a real institution to an ideal and judge how closely the reality conforms to the ideal. Improvements come through the process of attempting to move the reality ever closer to the ideal. Although many of them could not state it clearly, the great majority of Americans, and Texans, believe in some version of the theory of democracy. It is therefore possible to judge our state government (as it is also possible to judge our national government) according to the extent to which it approximates the ideal of a democratic society and to indicate the direction that the political system must move to become more democratic. Chapters in this book will frequently compare the reality of state government to the ideal of the democratic polity and ask readers to judge whether they think there is room for improvement in Texas democracy.

As indicated, one of the major causes of shortcomings in democratic government, in Texas as elsewhere, is *private influence over public policy*. Ideally, government decisions are made to try to maximize the public interest, but too often, they are fashioned at the behest of individuals who are pursuing their own special interests at the expense of the public's. This book will often explore the ways that powerful individuals try to distort the people's institutions into vehicles of their own advantage. It will also examine ways that representatives of the public resist these selfish efforts to influence public policy. Part of the political process, in Texas as in other democracies, is the struggle to ensure that the making of public policy is truly a people's activity rather than a giveaway to the few who are rich, powerful, and well connected.

# Texas and American Federalism

This book is about the politics of one state. Just as it would be impossible to describe the functions of one of the human body's organs without reference to the body as a whole, however, it would be misleading to try to analyze a state without reference to the nation. The United States has a **federal system.** This label means that its governmental powers are shared among the national and state governments. A great many state responsibilities are strongly influenced by the actions of all three branches of the national government.

Education, for instance, is primarily a responsibility of state, not federal, government. Yet the president and Congress often influence Texas education policy by sponsoring and enacting many laws that direct the state to govern the schools in a certain way or that promise money in return for taking some action. For example, in 2001 Congress enacted, and in 2002 President Bush signed, the No Child Left Behind Act. This law imposed many requirements on states, including a mandate that they administer an achievement test to every child in grades three through eight and that they impose sanctions on schools whose students failed to live up to a set of national standards. In preliminary trials of this test in 2003, Texas students scored so poorly that there was panic in the state Board of Education. Faced with the prospect of losing federal money from the U.S. Department of Education, the board voted to "dumb down" the test by decreasing the number of questions that had to be answered correctly to pass.[11]

Similarly, the U.S. Supreme Court has often forced Texas schools to stop something they were doing—prayers in the classroom, for example. It has also made it necessary for them to do things they did not want to do—integrate racially, for example.

Education is only one of the state policy spheres in which the federal government is a constant and important influence. Washington, D.C., also makes an impact on Texas government in areas such as

1. **Federal grants (see Chapter 12), which provide a significant portion of state revenue each year**

2. The U.S. Supreme Court overseeing the actions of the state government and, historically, forcing Texas to make many changes in its behavior, especially with regard to civil rights and liberties (see Chapter 11)

3. Congress allocating many of the "goodies" of government, such as military bases, veterans' hospitals, highways, and so on, which have a crucial impact on the state's economy

4. Congress also mandating the state government to take actions, such as making public buildings accessible to people with disabilities or instituting background checks on gun purchasers, that force the Texas legislature to raise and spend money

5. Congressional policymaking and budget decisions shaping sensitive state issues such as the response to poverty (Medicaid policy, for example), and protection of the environment (requirements for clean water and air, for example)

6. When Congress declares war, or the president sends troops to a foreign conflict without a declaration of war, Texans fight and die. The war on terrorism that began with the 9/11/01 attacks has imposed particular burdens on Texas. In its efforts to seal national borders from infiltration, the federal government has slowed the traffic between the United States and Mexico, which has inevitably damaged commerce between that country and Texas. Efforts to protect buildings, dams, bridges, and water supplies from future attacks have required expenditures of large sums of money by state and local authorities. Campaigns to train "first responders" such as police, fire, and medical personnel to react quickly and competently to potential terrorist incidents have put further strain on local and state budgets. Policies by the federal Department of Justice to identify terrorists by gaining access to information about all residents of the United States have raised fears, in Texas as elsewhere, that ordinary citizens will lose many of their civil liberties.

7. The many discretionary powers of the president, such as cutting tariffs on imported goods or releasing federal disaster-relief funds, leave their mark, for good or ill, on the state's economy.

8. The raising or lowering of interest rates by the Federal Reserve Board constricts or stimulates Texas's economy along with the economies of the other forty-nine states. The changes thus created powerfully affect both the amount of money the state legislature has to spend and the demands on its allocation of resources.

Texas politics is thus a whole subject unto itself and a part of a larger whole. Although the focus of this book is on Texas, there are frequent references to actions by national institutions and politicians.

# Texas in the International Arena

Despite the fact that the U.S. Constitution forbids the individual states to conduct independent foreign policies, Texas's shared border with Mexico has long exercised an important effect on its politics. Not only are many Texas citizens of

Mexican (and other Latin) background, but the common border of Texas and Mexico, the Rio Grande, flows for more than 800 miles through an arid countryside, a situation that almost demands cooperation over the use of water. Furthermore, with the passage of the North American Free Trade Agreement (NAFTA) in 1993, Texas became important as an avenue of increased commerce between the two countries. Interstate Highway 35, which runs from the Mexican border at Laredo through San Antonio, Austin, the Dallas/Fort Worth Metroplex, and on north to Duluth, Minnesota, has become so important as a passageway of international trade that it is sometimes dubbed "the NAFTA highway." As a result of their geographic proximity, Mexico is an important factor in the Texas economy and Texas politics, and vice versa.

One of many possible examples from the early years of the twenty-first century illustrates the interconnections of Texan and Mexican politics. The example is drawn from the criminal justice system, which at first glance might seem to be a matter of wholly internal interest to Texas. On the contrary, even such a subject as the state's execution of a murderer can have an international impact.[12]

In 1988, Javier Suarez Medina shot to death a Dallas police officer while the officer was conducting an undercover drug sting. There was no doubt about Medina's guilt, as he was immediately apprehended by other police officers—the perfect open-and-shut, smoking-gun-in-the-hand arrest. But things were not as simple as they appeared at first. Medina, as became clear later, had been born in Mexico. Because of his foreign nationality, under the Vienna Convention of Consular Relations of 1963, ratified by the United States and 169 other countries in 1969, local authorities were supposed to notify the Mexican consul and allow that country to assist Medina with his defense. However, Medina gave conflicting and confusing statements as to his nationality, claiming at various times that he came to El Paso when he was three years old, when he was seven, or that he was born in that city. Partly because of their confusion as to his nativity, and partly, no doubt, because of their intense desire to punish a cop killer, neither the Dallas police department nor the state ever contacted the Mexican consulate. Medina was tried, convicted of murder, and sentenced to die by lethal injection.

While Medina sat on death row, however, his case came to the attention of Mexican officials. They launched a campaign to persuade the state to retry him, this time complying with the requirements of the consular treaty. Part of the conflict was caused by the fact that except under unusual circumstances, such as crimes under military law or during wartime, Mexico does not execute criminals. The case became a patriotic cause in Mexico, with all that country's politicians feeling bound to try to make Texas officials reverse the conviction or at least commute Medina's sentence to life in prison.

In 2002, Mexican President Vicente Fox made a personal crusade of the Medina case. He appealed to the Texas Board of Pardons and Paroles, Governor Rick Perry, and President George W. Bush to stop or postpone the execution. Fox had been the most pro-U.S. (and pro-capitalist) president in Mexico's history. In numerous visits to this country, and to Texas, he had attempted to forge personal and institutional bonds that would allow the United States and Mexico to overcome their historical suspicion of one another. He thus had good reason to think that his intervention might sway some important person to rethink Medina's scheduled execution. If he had been able to affect the decisions of Texas's government in such a visible way, it would have enormously helped his own popularity within Mexico. In turn, his enhanced power would have been a good

# YOU DECIDE

## Should Texas Have a Foreign Policy?

As the world has become more integrated, and especialy as economies have become globalized, Texas leaders have attempted to establish institutions for dealing with foreign governments. Their efforts in this area have been particularly enthusiastic in regard to Mexico. The state opened a trade office in Mexico City in 1971, helped establish the Border Governors' Conference in 1980, began the Texas–Mexico Agricultural Exchange in 1984, has participated in the Border States Attorneys General Conference since 1986, and established the Office of International Coordination to deal with the problem of retrieving child support payments from fugitive fathers in 1993. Texas governors now have special advisers on the economy and politics of foreign countries, and they take trips to visit foreign politicians in the hopes of increasing commerce between their state and foreign countries.

In its attempts to establish regular relationships with foreign countries, Texas comes close to having a state "foreign policy." But is it wise for a state, as opposed to the United States national government, to be so deeply involved in foreign affairs?

| PRO | CON |
| --- | --- |
| ▲ The Constitution does not forbid states to enter into voluntary, informal arrangements with foreign governments, and the Tenth Amendment declares that anything not forbidden to the states is permitted. | ▼ A major reason that the independent states came together to form the union in 1787 was so they could stop working at cross-purposes in foreign policy and present a united front to the world. That is why Article I, Section 10 of the Constitution says that "No state shall . . . enter into any Agreement or Compact . . . with a foreign Power . . ." |
| ▲ Most state foreign policy initiatives, such as Texas's trade agreements with Mexico, deal with friendly relations, not disputes. | ▼ The Logan Act of 1799 prohibits U.S. citizens from "holding correspondence with a foreign government or its agents, with intent to influence the measures of such government in relations to disputes or controvies with the United States." |
| ▲ Since when is competition a bad thing? If citizens want to keep labor unions strong and the environment clean, they should vote for candidates who will support such policies. | ▼ If states (and cities) are allowed to compete for business with foreign countries, their rivalry will cause them to lower standards of labor and environmental protection. |
| ▲ As the example of Javier Suarez Medina illustrates, Texas's domestic actions already have an impact on relations with foreign countries. It would be better to acknowledge this fact frankly and make state policy with the conscious intent of furthering the state's interests. | ▼ If all fifty states have independent relations with foreign countries, it will cause confusion and chaos between the federal government and those countries. |

SOURCE: Julie Blase, "Has Globalization Changed U.S. Federalism? The Increasing Role of U.S. States In Foreign Affairs: Texas–Mexico Relations," PhD dissertation, University of Texas at Austin, 2003.

thing for the United States in general and Texas in particular. Nevertheless, all national and state individuals and institutions politely ignored Fox. Medina was executed on August 14, 2002.

Fox was scheduled to visit Texas, and President Bush at his ranch in Crawford, in late August of that year. However, the Mexican president's inability to affect the Medina case was, from his point of view and the point of view of his country, an insult that could not be ignored. Fox canceled the visit. His office issued a statement that "it would be inappropriate to carry out this trip to Texas given these lamentable circumstances." Relations between the two countries, on the upswing after decades of hostility, immediately turned around and became tenser.

In January 2003, the Mexican government filed a complaint before the International Court of Justice (ICJ; known informally as the World Court) in the Hague, Netherlands, alleging that fifty-four Mexican nationals, several of them in Texas, were currently on death row even though the Mexican consulate had not been notified of their arrest and trial. The next month, the ICJ issued a decision telling Texas and Oklahoma to postpone three executions until it had time to investigate the cases. The ICJ has no authority in the United States, and both states ignored its "order." The Mexican government obviously hoped to use the publicity the World Court's decision generated to bring moral persuasion to bear on American state governments. So far, it has had no success in this area, but the fact that it is trying is an indication of how seriously Mexicans take the issue.

Fox and Perry eventually decided that the interests of their two polities were too important to ignore, and they agreed to disagree. In November 2003, Fox returned to Texas as the governor's guest.

In 2006, the United States Supreme Court held in two other cases, one from Oregon and one from Virginia, that foreign-born convicted criminals did not have the right to be re-tried because their states had failed to notify their native countries of their arrest. The Justices did not squarely address the issue of whether individuals are entitled to rights under the Vienna Convention, or whether that treaty refers only to diplomacy between nations. No matter how the Court ruled, of course, it was too late to save Medina, or to undo the damage between Mexican and Texas/United States relations.

Nevertheless, despite the legal ambiguity, and despite the two leaders' rapprochement, the point had been made that the actions of Texas's criminal justice system have repercussions on relations between the United States as a whole and a foreign country. The political choices Texans make have consequences far beyond their own government.

# The Texas Political Culture

Like the other forty-nine states, Texas is part of a well-integrated American civil society. It is also a separate and distinctive society with its own history and present-day political system. Culture is the product of the historical experience of a people in a particular area. Our political system is the product of our political culture. **Political culture** refers to a shared system of values, beliefs, and habits of behavior with regard to government and politics. Not everyone in a given political culture accepts all of that culture's assumptions, but everyone is affected by the beliefs and values of the dominant groups in society. Often, the culture of the majority group is imposed on members of a minority who would prefer not to live with it.

Texas's political culture is unusual partly because of the state's great size, its geographic isolation until the twentieth century, and the historical fact that it was an independent republic before joining the United States. Partly, it is also distinctive because it is a mixture of the Old South and the West of the frontier.

Texas shares with other southern states its history as a society that formerly held slaves and one that was defeated in a civil war and then occupied in a humiliating fashion by victorious northern troops. In common with other White southerners after the end of Reconstruction, Anglo Texans attempted to deny full citizenship to African Americans. Because of the Lone Star State's proximity to Mexico, the Anglos further tried to suppress the citizenship of Latinos. The historical heritage of White people in Texas is thus one of extreme cultural conservatism. This conservatism has extended not only to attitudes on civil rights for minority citizens but to a hostility toward labor unions and to liberal political programs in general.

Mixing with and reinforcing the southern cultural conservatism has been an intense individualism deriving from the myth of the frontier. Anglo Texans have always seen themselves as ruggedly independent, as self-sufficient pioneers who need no help from anyone and are not obligated to support other people with their taxes. This hostility toward collective action, especially on behalf of the weak, has dovetailed perfectly with southern cultural conservatism to strengthen public opposition to liberal, activist government in Texas.

Political scientist Daniel Elazar and his associates have extensively investigated patterns of political culture across the fifty states. Elazar identifies three broad, historically developed patterns of political culture.[13] Although every state contains some elements of each of the three cultures, politics within states in identifiable regions tend to be dominated by one or a combination of two of the cultures.

In the **moralistic** political culture, citizens understand the state and the nation as commonwealths designed to further the shared interests of everyone. Citizen participation is a widely shared value, and governmental activism on behalf of the common good is encouraged. This culture tends to be dominant across the extreme northern tier of American states. The states of Washington and Minnesota approach the "ideal type" of the moralistic culture.

In the **individualistic** political culture, citizens understand the state and nation as marketplaces in which people strive to better their personal welfare. Citizen participation is encouraged as a means of individual achievement, and government activity is encouraged when it attempts to create private opportunity and discouraged when it attempts to redistribute wealth. This culture tends to be dominant across the "middle north" of the country from New Jersey westward. Nevada and Illinois approach the ideal types of the individualistic culture.

In the **traditionalistic** political culture, citizens technically believe in democracy but emphasize deference to elite rule within a hierarchical society. While formally important, citizen participation is not encouraged, and the participation of disfavored ethnic or religious groups may be discouraged. Government activity is generally viewed with suspicion unless its purpose is to reinforce the power of the dominant groups. This culture tends to be dominant in the southern tier of states from the east coast of the continent to New Mexico. The ideal types of states with traditionalistic cultures are Mississippi and Arkansas.

**TABLE 1-1**
## The Three Political Cultures

| Type | Moralistic | Individualistic | Traditionalistic |
|---|---|---|---|
| **Attitude toward Participation** | Encouraging | Encouraging | Supports if on behalf of elite rule; otherwise, opposes |
| **Attitude toward Political Parties** | Tolerant | Strong party loyalty | Discouraging |
| **Attitude toward Government Activity** | Supports if activity is on behalf of the common good | Supports if on behalf of individual activity; opposes if on behalf of redistribution of wealth | Supports if on behalf of elite rule; otherwise, opposes |
| **Attitude toward Civil Liberties and Civil Rights** | Strongly supportive | Ambivalent; support rights for themselves but indifferent to rights of others | Indifferent |
| **Religious Groupings Most Commonly Supporting** | Congregationalists, Mormons, Jews, Quakers | Lutherans, Roman Catholics, Methodists | Baptists, Presbyterians, Pentacostals |
| **Geographic Area of Strongest Impact** | Northernmost tier of states plus Utah and Colorado | Middle north tier of states | Old South plus New Mexico |

NOTE: These are descriptions of general historical patterns only. They do not necessarily apply to the behavior of any specific family, individual, or group.

SOURCE: Daniel J. Elazar, *American Federalism: A View from the States,* 3rd ed. (New York: Harper & Row, 1984), 109–173; Ira Sharkansky, "The Utility of Elazar's Political Culture: A Research Note," in Daniel J. Elazar and Joseph Zikmund II, eds., *The Ecology of American Political Culture: Readings* (New York: Thomas Y. Crowell, 1975), 247–262; Robert L. Savage, "The Distribution and Development of Policy Values in the American States," in *Ibid.,* 263–286, Appendices A, B, and C.

Table 1-1 collates the three political cultures as they are manifested across a number of important political and social dimensions. It is important to understand that the general tendencies displayed in the table permit many exceptions. They only report broad patterns of human action; that is, they summarize the way many people in the groups have often behaved through history. They do not describe everyone, nor do they prescribe a manner in which anyone must behave in the future.

The research that has been done on Texas places it at a midpoint between the traditionalistic and individualistic political cultures.[14] Historically, the state's experience as a slave-holding member of the Confederacy tended to embed it firmly in traditionalism, but its strong business orientation, growing more important every decade, infused its original culture with an increasingly influential individualistic orientation. Many of the political patterns discussed in this book are easier to understand within the context of the Texas blend of cultures.

Not all Texans have shared the beliefs and attitudes that will be described here. In particular, as will be discussed in more detail in Chapter 5, African

Americans and Mexican Americans have tended to be somewhat separate from the political culture of the dominant Anglo majority. Nevertheless, both history and present political institutions have imposed clear patterns on the assumptions that most Texans bring to politics.

There is one sense in which Texas has a well-earned reputation for uniqueness. All visitors have testified to the intense state patriotism of Texans. Whatever their education, income, age, race, religion, gender, or political ideology, most Texans seem to love their state passionately. Whether this state patriotism is due to the myth of the Old West as peddled by novels, schools, and Hollywood, or to the state's size and geographic isolation, or to its unusual history, or to something in the water is impossible to say. This patriotism has little political relevance because native Texans show no hostility toward non-natives and have elected several non-native governors. But woe to the politician who does not publicly embrace the myth that Texas is the most wonderful place to live that has ever existed on the planet! As scholars rather than politicians, the authors of this book intend to look at the state through a more analytic lens.

Part of the larger American political tradition is a basic attitude toward government and politicians that was most famously expressed in a single sentence attributed to President Thomas Jefferson: "That government is best which governs least." As the quote from Edward Abbey at the beginning of this chapter attests, Jefferson's philosophy has a powerful presence in the United States in contemporary times. The name usually given to that philosophy is **conservatism,** and it has dominated Texas politics since the end of the Civil War.

★ ★ ★ ★ ★ ★ ★ ★ ★ ★ ★ ★ ★ ★ ★ ★ ★ ★ ★ ★ ★ ★ ★ ★ ★ ★ ★

## Rhetoric and Reality

In practice, laissez faire in Texas has often been **pseudo** (false) **laissez faire.** Entrepreneurs don't want government to regulate or tax them, and they denounce policies to help society's less fortunate as "socialism." But when they encounter a business problem that is too big to handle, they do not hesitate to accept government help.

A good example is the city of Houston. Its leaders praise their city as the home of unrestrained, unaided free enterprise. In fact, however, Houston has historically relied on government activity for its economic existence. The ship channel, which connects the city's port to the sea, was dredged and is maintained by government. Much of the oil industry, which was responsible for Houston's twentieth-century boom, was sustained either by state regulation through the Railroad Commission or by the federal government selling facilities to the industry cheaply, as occurred with the Big Inch and Little Inch pipelines. Billions of dollars of federal tax money have flowed into the area to create jobs in the space industry (the Johnson Space Center and NASA).

Houston's business leaders have not resisted such government action on their behalf—quite the contrary. It is only when government tries to help ordinary people that the business community upholds the banner of laissez faire.

★ ★ ★ ★ ★ ★ ★ ★ ★ ★ ★ ★ ★ ★ ★ ★ ★ ★ ★ ★ ★ ★ ★ ★ ★ ★ ★

SOURCE: Joe R. Feagin, *Free Enterprise City: Houston in Political-Economic Perspective* (New Brunswick, N.J.: Rutgers, 1988).

The term *conservatism* is complex, and its implications change with time and situation. In general, however, it refers to a general hostility to government activity, especially in the economic sphere. Most of the early White settlers came to Texas to seek their fortunes. They cared little about government and wanted no interference in their economic affairs. Their attitudes were consistent with the popular values of the Jeffersonian Democrats of the nineteenth century: The less government the better, local control of what little government there was, and freedom from economic regulation, or **laissez faire** (a French word loosely translated as "leave it alone"). Conservatism is, in general, consistent with the individualistic political culture on economic issues (welfare, for example) and consistent with the traditionalistic political culture on social issues (civil rights, for example).

Texas conservatism minimizes the role of government in society in general and in the economy in particular. It stresses an individualism that maximizes the role of businesspeople in controlling the economy. To a Texas conservative, a good government is mainly one that keeps taxes low.

Consistent with the emphasis on laissez faire is a type of **social Darwinism:** the belief that individuals who prosper and rise to the top of the socioeconomic ladder are worthy and deserve their riches, while those who sink to the bottom (or having been born there, stay there) are unworthy and deserve their poverty. Social Darwinists argue that people become rich because they are intelligent, energetic, and self-disciplined, whereas those who become or remain poor do so because they are stupid, lazy, and/or given to indulgence in personal vices. Socioeconomic status, they argue, is the result of natural selection.[15]

Of course, a person's success in life frequently is the result of his or her behavior and qualities of character. But it also depends on many other factors, such as education, race and ethnicity, proper diet and medical care, the wealth and education of the person's parents, and luck. Nonetheless, social Darwinism continues to dominate the thinking of many Texans. They strongly resist the idea that government has an obligation to come to the aid of society's less fortunate.

This resistance to government aid to the needy has resulted in many state policies that mark Texas as a state with an unusually stingy attitude toward the underprivileged. For example, among the fifty states, in the middle years of the first decade of the twenty-first century, Texas ranked forty-fifth in its weekly payments to the mothers of poor children (TANF) and forty-fourth in its spending on Medicaid for poor people who needed healthcare.[16]

Pseudo laissez faire economic doctrine and social Darwinism lead to a **trickle-down theory** of economic and social development. If business flourishes, so the theory goes, prosperity will follow and benefits will trickle down to the majority of Texans. In other words, if government caters to the needs of business rather than attempting to improve the lives of the poor, everyone's economic situation will improve. To a degree, the trickle-down theory does work, but only to a degree, since about 18 percent of the state's citizens existed at or below the poverty level in 2005.[17]

There is another general attitude toward government, called **liberalism,** that accepts or even endorses government activity as often a good thing. Although conservatives have dominated Texas politics through most of its history, liberals have occasionally been elected to public office, and liberal ideas have sometimes been adopted as state policy. The conflict between liberalism and conservatism underlies much political argument in the United States. The way these two ideologies have formed the basis for much of Texas politics will be explored in Chapter 4.

# Economy, Taxes, and Services

In 1855, when General Sheridan made his harsh evaluation of Texas found in the chapter-opening quotation, the state was poor, rural, and agricultural. As summarized earlier in this chapter, however, in the twentieth century, its economy was transformed, first by the boom in the oil industry that began with the new century and then by its diversification into petrochemicals, aerospace, computers, and many other industries. Metropolitan areas boomed along with the economy, and the state became the second most populous in the nation.

The state's political culture, however, has not changed as rapidly as its population and its economy. Texas's basic conservatism is evident in the way the state government treats business and industry. In 1996, a private firm conducted a nationwide survey to determine how favorable a "business climate" each of the states had created. North Carolina was found to have the most favorable business climate, with Texas second.[18] In 2003, *Forbes* magazine ranked Austin as the best business city in the country, with Dallas number nine and Houston number fifteen.[19] Using a different set of measures in 2005, *Congressional Quarterly* evaluated Texas as the state with the tenth greatest "economic momentum."[20]

But while in the short run a favorable business climate consists of low taxes, weak labor unions, and an inactive government, in the long run these policies may create a fragile economy. Other observers are less admiring of the Texas economy and less optimistic about its future.

For example, the Corporation for Enterprise Development (CED) is a private organization that grades each state in terms not only of its economic health at any one time but also its capacity for positive growth. In 2002 and again in 2006 the CED flunked the Texas economy as a whole, giving it Ds in "earnings and job quality" and "resource efficiency," and Fs in "equity," and "quality of life." The CED commented in 2002 that "a theme of inequality throughout the state . . . the disparity between the wealthy and the poor . . ." augured poorly for Texas's future. In contrast to Texas, the CED reported that its "honor roll" states of Colorado, Connecticut, Maryland, Massachusetts, Minnesota, New Jersey, Virginia, and Wisconsin were pursuing public policies that ensured them a brighter economic outlook.[21]

Part of the substance of this textbook will be discussions of the way the politics of Texas reflects "a theme of inequality." Some chapters will analyze the sources of unequal politics; some will portray its consequences in terms of public policy. Always, the implications of inequality for democratic legitimacy will be a major topic.

Because of the Jeffersonian conservative philosophy underlying much of the activities of Texas government, it generally does little, compared to the governments of other states, to improve the lives of its citizens. As Table 1-2 illustrates, on several measures of state services, Texas ranks near the bottom. The state spends comparatively little on education, health, welfare, the environment, and the arts. Furthermore, it raises the relatively small amount of revenue it does spend in a "regressive" manner; that is, in a manner that falls unusually lightly on the rich and unusually heavily on the poor. The philosophy that dominates Texas politics holds that if government will just keep taxes low—especially on its wealthier citizens—and stay out of the way, society will take care of itself.

The available evidence, however, suggests that Texas's laissez faire ideology

**TABLE 1-2**

## Texas's Rank among States in Expenditure and Taxation

| Category | Year | Rank |
|---|---|---|
| a. Per-capita state income | 2004 | 32 |
| b. State government per-capita spending | 2003 | 48 |
| c. Spending per school pupil | 2005 | 39 |
| d. Average teacher salary | 2005 | 32 |
| e. Per-capita Medicaid spending | 2004 | 44 |
| f. Average monthly benefit, Women, Infants and Children (WIC) | 2004 | 45 |
| g. Average monthly payment, Temporary Assistance to Needy Families (TANF) | 2004 | 45 |
| h. State spending on arts agency | 2005 | 46 |
| i. Per-capita spending on water quality | 2002 | 47 |
| j. Progressivity of state and local taxes | 2004 | 43 |

SOURCES: a from Legislative Budget Board, *Texas Fact Book 2006* (Austin, LBB, 2006), p. 18; b, c, d, e, f, g, h, and j from Kendra A. Hovey and Harold A. Hovey, *CQ's State Fact Finder 2006* (Washington, D.C.: Congressional Quarterly, 2006), pp. 187, 218, 219, 255, 307, 311, 91, and 170; i from the document "Texas on the Brink: How Texas Ranks Among the 50 States," on the Web site www.bayareanewdemocrats .org/files/texasrankings.

may have had a pernicious effect on its quality of life. As Table 1-3 emphasizes, Texas ranks relatively low on measures of air cleanliness, the general health of its population, its freedom from crime, the educational status of its citizens, and other measures of civilized living. Texans as a group are so patriotic that it is difficult for them to believe that their state is a comparatively undesirable place to live. But the evidence is consistent.

Texas state government is therefore faced with serious problems in preparing its citizens and society for the future. So far, it has demonstrated only a lukewarm inclination to deal with them. The greatest accomplishment of Texas state government through the twentieth century was to keep taxes low. As Texans proceed through the twenty-first century, they have to wonder if low taxes are enough of an achievement.

# The People of Texas

In many ways Texas is the classic American melting pot of different peoples, although it occasionally seems more like a boiling cauldron. The state was originally populated by various Native American tribes. In the sixteenth and seven-

**TABLE 1-3**
## Texas's Rank in Measures of Quality of Life

| Measure of Quality of Life | Year | Rank |
|---|---|---|
| a. Crime rate | 2004 | 6 |
| b. Number of prisoners | 2004 | 1 |
| c. Incarceration rate | 2004 | 2 |
| d. Poverty rate | 2005 | 5 |
| e. "Condition of children" index | 2005 | 37 |
| f. Drinking water quality | 2004 | 32 |
| g. Air pollution emissions | 2001 | 1 |
| h. SAT scores | 2005 | 23 (out of 24) |
| i. High school graduation rate | 2003 | 35 |
| j. State health ranking | 2005 | 39 |
| k. Percentage of population obese (25.7%) | 2004 | 8 |
| l. Percentage of households "at risk for hunger" | 2004 | 1 |
| m. Percentage of workers without health insurance | 2005 | 1 |
| n. "State livability index" | 2006 | 43 |
| o. "Chance For Success Index" for children | 2006 | 48 |

SOURCES: a, b, c, e, f, g, h, j, and k from Kendra A. Hovey and Harold A. Hovey, *CQ's State Fact Finder 2006* (Washington, D.C.: CQ Press, 2006, pp. 268, 274, 276, 309, 95, 97, 207, 242, 247; d from Suzannah Gonzales and Corrie MacLaggan, "Texas is Fifth-Poorest State, Data Show," *Austin American-Statesman*, August 30, 2006, B1; i from Jason Embry, "Study Ranks Texas 35th in Rates of Graduation," *Austin American-Statesman*, June 21, 2006, B1; l from "Texas Leads Nation in Households at Risk for Hunger," *Austin American-Statesman*, October 29, 2005, B5; m from Paul Krugman, "A Private Obsession," *New York Times*, April 29, 2005, A27; n from the Web site: www.morganquitno.com/sr06mlrnk.htm; the "livability index" is a composite score created by combining a number of indicators of well-being; in 2006 the "most livable" state was New Hampshire, while the least livable was Louisiana; o from study by Pew Center for the States, "From Cradle to Career: Connecting American Education from Birth to Adulthood," based on thirteen indicators of various stages in life that are correlated with future achievement, reported by Bob Dart, "Study: Texas Kids Start Out Behind," *Austin American-Statesman*, January 4, 2007, B1.

teenth centuries, the Spaniards conquered the land, and from the intermingling of the conquerors and the conquered came the "mestizos," persons of mixed Spanish and Native American blood. In the nineteenth century, Anglos wrested the land from the heirs of the Spaniards. They often brought Black slaves with them. Soon waves of immigration arrived from Europe and Asia, and more mestizos came from Mexico. After a brief outflow of population as a result of the oil price depression of the late 1980s, the long-term pattern of immigration resumed and brought many more thousands during the 1990s and beyond.

## THE CENSUS

At the end of each decade, the national government takes a census of each state's population. The census itself is a hot political topic because it is the basis for distributing money from many federal programs and also for allocating seats in both the U.S. House of Representatives and the state legislatures. Critics of the census charge that it misses millions of poor people, especially those for whom English is not the first language. Local authorities claimed that the population of Texas was undercounted by several hundred thousand people in 1980 and 1990 and again in 2000. Whether these complaints are justified or not, the bureau publishes official figures that are available in libraries and over the Internet. Table 1-4 shows the official Texas numbers for 1980 to 2000. The increase in population indicated in the table entitled Texas to three additional seats in the U.S. House in 1990 and two more in 2000, bringing the state's total to thirty-two.

Between the decade markers, the Census conducts more informal surveys. In late 2006 it released a preliminary estimate that Texas had been the fastest-growing state from the period spanning July 1, 2005 to July 1, 2006, gaining 579,275 people in those twelve months. State demographer Steve Murdock re-

**Cartoonist Ben Sargent illustrates the consequences of Texas's traditionally stingy policies toward its poorer citizens.**

*Courtesy of Ben Sargent.*

## TABLE 1-4
## The Texas Population, 1980, 1990, and 2000

| Ethnic Group | 1980 | 1990 | 2000 | 2000 Percent of total |
|---|---|---|---|---|
| Anglo (Non-Hispanic White) | 9,350,299 | 10,291,680 | 10,933,313 | 52.4 |
| African American | 1,710,175 | 2,021,632 | 2,404,566 | 11.5 |
| Hispanic or Latino* (of any race) | 2,985,824 | 4,339,905 | 6,669,665 | 32.0 |
| Other | 200,528 | 378,565 | 844,276 | 4.1 |

*The great majority of Hispanics in Texas are Mexican American or Mexican.

SOURCES: For 1980 and 1990, *1992–93 Texas Almanac and State Industrial Guide* (Dallas: A. H. Belo Corp., 1991); for 2000, the United States Census Web site, www.census.gov/.

ported that if the state continued to grow at the anticipated pace, by 2010 its population would be 25 million.[22]

Besides the overall increase in population of 22.8 percent in the final decade of the twentieth century, the most significant fact revealed by the 2000 census was the rapid increase in Texas's Hispanic population. Whereas Hispanics, the great majority of whom, in Texas, are either Mexican or Mexican American, constituted 21 percent of the state's population in 1980 and 26 percent in 1990, by 2000 they totaled 32 percent, and their percentage continues to grow. The other important minority group, African Americans, comprised 11.5 percent of the state's citizens, a percentage that has not changed appreciably since 1980.

Meanwhile, the non-Hispanic White population (Anglos), which used to be a large majority, had dropped to 52.4 percent in 2000. The inevitable consequence of the increasing trend-line of the Latino population arrived in 2005, when the Census Bureau announced an estimate that Texas's population consisted of 50.2 percent Black plus Latino.[23] In other words, there is now no "majority" ethnic group in the state; every group constitutes a minority of the population. If present population growth rates continue, however, a majority of Texas's population will be Hispanic by 2030.[24]

The distribution of population in Texas shows evidence of three things: the initial patterns of migration, the influence of geography and climate, and the location of the cities. The Hispanic migration came first, north from Mexico, and to this day is still concentrated in South and West Texas. Likewise, African Americans still live predominantly in the eastern half of the state. As one moves from east to west across Texas, annual rainfall drops by about five inches per 100 miles. East Texas has a moist climate and supports intensive farming, while West Texas is dry and requires pumping from underground aquifers to maintain agriculture. The overall distribution of settlement reflects the food production capability of the local areas, with East Texas remaining more populous. Cities developed at strategic locations, usually on rivers or the seacoast, and the state's population is heavily concentrated in the urban areas.

# THE POLITICAL RELEVANCE OF POPULATION

Our division of the Texas population into Anglos, Mexican Americans, and African Americans reflects political realities. All citizens are individuals, form their own opinions, and have the right to choose to behave as they see fit. No one is a prisoner of his or her group, and every generalization has exceptions. Nevertheless, it is a long-observed fact that people in similar circumstances often see things from similar points of view, and it therefore helps clarify political conflict to be aware of the shared similarities.

In this book Anglos, Mexican Americans, and African Americans will often be discussed as groups, without an intent to be unfair to individual exceptions. Historically, both minority groups have been treated badly by the Anglo majority. Today, the members of both groups are, in general, less wealthy than Anglos. For example, according to the 2000 census, the mean household income of both Latinos and Blacks was about 62 percent of the figure for Anglos in the state. On the one hand, this represents a narrowing of the income gap between minorities and Anglos that existed in 1990. On the other hand, the difference in wealth is still very substantial and large enough to cause economic conflict.[25]

Political differences often accompany economic divisions. As will be discussed in Chapters 3, 4, and 5, Mexican Americans and African Americans tend to hold more liberal political opinions than do Anglos and to vote accordingly. This is not to say that there are no conservative minority citizens and no liberal Anglos. Nevertheless, looked at as groups, Mexican Americans, African Americans, and Anglos do display general patterns of belief and behavior that can be discussed without being unfair to individual exceptions. As a result, as the minority population increases in size relative to the Anglo population, its greater liberalism is likely to make itself felt, sooner or later, in the voting booth. Furthermore, Texans of Asian background are a relatively small but growing proportion of the population. As their population becomes larger, they may exert

★ ★ ★ ★ ★ ★ ★ ★ ★ ★ ★ ★ ★ ★ ★ ★ ★ ★ ★ ★ ★ ★ ★ ★ ★ ★ ★ ★ ★

## Que Pasa?

The 2000 census portrayed a Texas in transition. Among other revelations was the fact that only 62 percent of its population had been born within the state. A continuing influx of immigrants, diluting its traditional Old South culture, had many ramifications for Texas, some of them political and others not. Among the latter was the decline of traditional Texas dialects, from the deep-South drawl of the piney woods of the east to the nasal "twang" of the residents farther west. Although many older citizens continue to speak in a "Texas" accent, more and more residents of the state come from somewhere else and sound like it. In fact, nearly a third of Texans speak a language other than English at home. Spanish is by far the most common non-English language spoken, but about 7 percent speak Vietnamese, Chinese, Hindi, or some other Asian language.

★ ★ ★ ★ ★ ★ ★ ★ ★ ★ ★ ★ ★ ★ ★ ★ ★ ★ ★ ★ ★ ★ ★ ★ ★ ★ ★ ★ ★

SOURCES: Terry Wallace, "Could the Urban Influx of Outsiders Take the Twang Out of Texas?" *Denton Record-Chronicle*, March 24, 2002, A6; "Portrait of Our Nation," *Austin American-Statesman*, June 9, 2002, E1; Gaiutra Bahadur, "Census Survey Confirms Texas' Growing Diversity," *Austin American-Statesman*, August, 7, 2001, A1.

an independent influence on the political process. Texas's changing mix of population is therefore constantly changing the state's politics.

# The Agenda

The following chapters will examine the ways Texans organize and behave politically to attempt to deal with their social and economic problems. There will also be a cautious attempt to assess the state's future prospects. Every chapter will contain a comparison of the reality of Texas politics to the democratic ideal and a discussion of how defensible the reality is. The topics to be considered are, in order, the Texas Constitution, the state's important interest groups, the activities of political parties, and the individual voter within the context of campaigns and elections. Next, the focus will shift to the institutions of state government—the legislature, the executive branch, and the judiciary. An examination of local government will follow and then analyses of state public policy; first is a discussion of how the state raises and spends its money and then an examination of other representative issues. Finally, an attempt is made to suggest some challenges the state will face in the future.

## Summary

This chapter began with an overview of the history of Texas, with emphasis on important political events and the development of the economy. The discussion then shifted to the topic of democratic theory, which holds that the legitimacy of a government rests upon the citizens' participation, and to the topic of Texas's place in the American federal system and the international arena. The focus then moved to the state's conservative political culture.

As a result of its political culture, ran the argument, there is a preference in Texas for an individualistic worldview, a less-government-is-better approach, pseudo laissez faire, social Darwinism, and the trickle-down theory of economic and social development. The twin results are an inactive government and a relatively poor quality of life compared to that in many other states. Texas has a large and diverse population that is always growing and changing. Insofar as the future can be predicted, it seems that the population will continue to grow, with an increasingly large non-Anglo, and especially Hispanic, component.

## Glossary Terms

| | |
|---|---|
| conservatism | liberalism |
| democracy | moralistic political culture |
| federal system | political culture |
| impresario | pseudo laissez faire |
| individualistic political culture | social Darwinism |
| laissez faire | traditionalistic political culture |
| legitimacy | trickle-down theory |

## Study Questions

1. Can you see anything in Texas's history that might account for the fact that Texans tend to have an unusually intense state patriotism?

2. Could a king or queen be legitimate? According to what theory?

3. Describe the basic features of the moralistic, individualistic, and traditionalistic political cultures. Would you say that your family's values are well described by any of the three? Do your own values differ in a significant manner from those of your parents or grandparents?

4. Describe the basic features of political conservatism and liberalism. How do conservatism and liberalism relate to moralism, individualism, and traditionalism?

5. How do you think the Texas political culture differs from the political culture of the United States as a whole?

6. In general, what has been Texas's historical policy toward business (the economy)? Toward taxes? Toward education? Toward welfare? Toward environmental protection?

7. Would you say that the evidence supports the opinion that Texas is a better place to live than other states?

8. In another ten to twenty years, present-day minority groups may constitute a majority of the Texas population. What effects might this change have on the state's politics and government?

## Surfing the Web

Readers are urged to visit the companion site for this book:

**http://academic.cengage.com/polsci/Kraemer/TexasPolitics10e**

# The Constitutional Setting

Representative Betty Brown sponsored a bill in the Eightieth Legislature in 2007 to prevent voter fraud by requiring citizens to present additional identification to vote. The proposal was very unpopular with senior citizens, minorities, and women. The bill failed.

Constitutions should consist of only general provisions;
the reason is that they must necessarily be permanent, and that
they cannot calculate for the possible change of things.

ALEXANDER HAMILTON, AMERICAN STATESMAN AND ONE OF THE AUTHORS OF
*THE FEDERALIST PAPERS* URGING ADOPTION OF THE U.S. CONSTITUTION

All political power is inherent in the people, and
all free governments are founded on their authority,
and instituted for their benefit.

ARTICLE I, TEXAS CONSTITUTION

# Introduction

Since its ratification in 1789, the U.S. Constitution frequently has been used as a model by emerging nations. State constitutions, however, seldom enjoy such admiration. Indeed, the constitution of the state of Texas is more often ridiculed than praised because of its length, its obscurity, and its outdated, unworkable provisions.

Such criticism of state constitutions is common. The political circumstances that surrounded the writing of the national Constitution differed considerably from those that existed at the times when many of the fifty states—especially those of the old Confederacy—were writing their constitutions. State constitutions tend to be very rigid and include too many specific details. They do not follow the advice of Alexander Hamilton cited above. As a result, Texas and many other states must resort to frequent **constitutional amendments**, which are formal changes in the basic governing document.

In federal systems, which are systems of government that provide for a division and sharing of powers between a national government and state or regional governments, the constitutions of the states complement the national Constitution. Article VI of the U.S. Constitution provides that the Constitution, laws, and treaties of the national government take precedence over the constitutions and laws of the states. This provision is known as the "supremacy of the laws" clause. Many states, including Texas, have constitutional and statutory provisions that conflict with federal laws, but these are unenforceable because of Article VI. Although the U.S. Constitution is supreme, state constitutions are still important because state governments are responsible for many basic programs and services, such as education, that affect citizens daily.

A **constitution** is the basic law of a state or nation that outlines the primary structure and functions of government; thus, the purposes of all constitutions are the same. This chapter examines those purposes as well as outlines the development of the several Texas constitutions. It elaborates the principal features of the state's current document, briefly traces the movement for constitutional reform in Texas, and provides an overview of constitutional politics.

*Gregg Abbot*

# Purposes of Constitutions

## LEGITIMACY

The first purpose served by a constitution is to give legitimacy to the government. Legitimacy is the most abstract and ambiguous purpose served by constitutions. Legitimacy derives from agreed-upon purposes of government and from government keeping its actions within the guidelines of these purposes. The constitution contributes to this legitimacy by putting it down on paper. A government has legitimacy when the governed accept its acts as moral, fair, and just and thus believe that they should obey its laws. This acceptance cuts two ways. On the one hand, citizens will allow government to act in certain ways that are not permitted to private individuals. For example, citizens cannot legally drive down a city street at sixty miles an hour, but police officers may do so when in the act of pursuing wrongdoers. Proprietors of private schools cannot command local residents to make financial contributions to their schools, but these same residents pay taxes to support public schools.

On the other hand, citizens also expect governments not to act arbitrarily; the concept of legitimacy is closely associated with limiting government. If the police officer sped down a city street at ninety miles an hour just for the thrill of doing so or if citizens were burdened with confiscatory school taxes, these acts probably would fall outside the bounds of legitimacy.

What citizens are willing to accept is conditioned by their history and their political culture. In Texas and the remainder of the United States, democratic practices including citizen participation in decision making, and fair processes are a part of that history and culture. Even within that broad acceptance of democratic principles, legitimacy varies from nation to nation and even from state to state. In England, for example, most police do not carry weapons; in California, pedestrians have absolute right of way in crossing streets. The traditionalistic/individualistic political culture that predominates in the South is even more dedicated to limiting government than the moralistic political culture; thus, southern constitutions as a group tend to be very restrictive.

## ORGANIZING GOVERNMENT

The second purpose of constitutions is to organize government. Governments must be organized in some way that clarifies who the major officials are, how they are selected, and what the relationships are among those charged with basic governmental functions. Again, to some extent, the American states have been guided by the national model. For example, both levels incorporate **separation of powers**—that is, a division into legislative, executive, and judicial branches. Also following the national Constitution's lead, the states have adopted a system of **checks and balances** to ensure that each separate branch of government can be restrained by the others. In reality, separate institutions and defined lines of authority lead to a sharing of powers. For example, passing bills is thought of as a legislative function, but the governor can veto a bill.

★ ★ ★ ★ ★ ★ ★ ★ ★ ★ ★ ★ ★ ★ ★ ★ ★ ★ ★ ★ ★ ★ ★ ★ ★ ★ ★ ★ ★ ★ ★ ★

## Is It Legal?

Public regard for what is legal is dynamic. For example, traditionally, Texans were unable to carry a concealed weapon legally, although police detectives could do so. However, the 1995 legislature passed a "right to carry" bill allowing ordinary citizens who had passed certain requirements and paid a fee to carry concealed weapons.

★ ★ ★ ★ ★ ★ ★ ★ ★ ★ ★ ★ ★ ★ ★ ★ ★ ★ ★ ★ ★ ★ ★ ★ ★ ★ ★ ★ ★ ★ ★ ★

Each state has an elected chief executive. Each state except Nebraska has a legislative body composed of two houses, usually a house of representatives and a senate. Each state has a judicial system with some sort of supreme court. Just as the U.S. Constitution includes many provisions that establish the relationship between the nation and the states, state constitutions include similar provisions with respect to local governments. Specific organizational provisions of state constitutions vary widely and invariably reflect the political attitudes prevalent at the time the constitutions were adopted and various amendments added. In Texas, the traditionalistic and individualistic political cultures have dominated the constitutional process.

## PROVIDING POWER

Article I, Section 8 of the U.S. Constitution expressly grants certain powers to the national government and implies a broad range of additional powers through the "necessary and proper" clause. This clause, also known as the "elastic clause," enables Congress to execute all its other powers by giving it broad authority to pass needed legislation. Thus, granting specific powers is the third purpose of constitutions. The Tenth Amendment reserves for the people or for the states powers not explicitly or implicitly granted to the national government. As the U.S. Constitution has been developed and interpreted, many powers exist concurrently for both the federal and the state levels of government—the power to assess taxes on gasoline, for example. Within this general framework, which continues to evolve, the Texas Constitution sets forth specific functions for which the state maintains primary or concurrent responsibility. Local government, criminal law, and regulation of intrastate commerce illustrate the diversity of the activities over which the state retains principal control.

A combination of factors has reduced the power of state officials, however. For example, the federal government's widespread use of its interstate commerce powers has limited the range of commercial activities still considered strictly intrastate. The **incorporation** of the **Bill of Rights**—the first ten amendments to the U.S. Constitution—has compelled changes in the criminal justice systems of the states. Incorporation means making the national protections, for example, the right to a fair and speedy trial by a jury of one's peers, applicable to state and local governments. In addition, the ability of individual states to deal with many socioeconomic matters such as energy use, civil rights, and urbanism is now seriously impaired. Thus, they are increasingly viewed as a responsibility of government at the national level. Nevertheless, the fundamental law of the state spells out many areas for state and local action. Which, if any, of the broad problems the national government addresses depends on the prevailing Washington political philosophy, the party that controls Congress, the national administration, and who sits on the U.S. Supreme Court.[1]

## LIMITING GOVERNMENTAL POWER (Reflects Checks and Ballance and Sep of power)

American insistence on the fourth purpose of constitutions—limiting governmental power—reflects the influence of British political culture, our ancestors' dissatisfaction with colonial rule, and the extraordinary individualism that characterized national development during the eighteenth and nineteenth centuries.

*Started to limit Davis EJ*

In Texas, the traditionalistic-individualist political culture resulted in a heavy emphasis on limiting government's ability to act. For example, the governor has only restricted power to remove members of state boards and commissions, particularly those appointed by a predecessor, except by informal techniques such as an aggressive public relations campaign against a board member. This belief in limited government continues to wax strong in the new millennium. Citizens usually want less government regulation and more controls on spending.

Chief among the guarantees against arbitrary governmental action is the national Bill of Rights. It was quickly added to the original U.S. Constitution to ensure both adequate safeguards for the people and ratification of the Constitution. The Texas Bill of Rights, included as Article I in the Texas Constitution, resembles the national Bill of Rights.[2] Later amendments to the national Constitution have extended guarantees in several areas, especially due process and equal protection of the laws, racial equality, and voting rights. In Texas, reactions to post–Civil War Reconstruction rule were so keen at the time the current constitution was written that the document contains many specific and picayune limitations. The creation of certain hospital districts and the payment of pensions to veterans of the war of independence from Mexico are examples. Such specificities have made frequent amendments necessary and have hamstrung legislative action in many areas.

# Texas Constitutions

The United States has had two fundamental laws: the short-lived Articles of Confederation and the present Constitution. Texas is currently governed by its sixth constitution, ratified in 1876.[3] The fact that the 1876 constitution had five predecessors in only forty years illustrates the political turbulence of the mid-1800s. Table 2-1 lists the six Texas state charters.

**TABLE 2-1**

## Constitutions of Texas

| Constitution | Dates |
|---|---|
| Republic of Texas | 1836–1845 |
| Statehood | 1845–1861 |
| Civil War | 1861–1866 |
| Reconstruction | 1866–1869 |
| Radical Reconstruction | 1869–1876 |
| State of Texas | 1876–present |

Having been formally governed by Spain for 131 years and by Mexico for 15, Texans issued a declaration of independence on March 2, 1836. This declaration stated that "the people of Texas, do now constitute a Free, Sovereign, and Independent Republic, and are fully invested with all the rights and attributes which properly belong to independent nations." After a brief but bitter war with Mexico, Texas gained independence on April 21 after the Battle of San Jacinto. Independence was formalized when the two Treaties of Velasco were signed by Mexican President Antonio López de Santa Anna and Texas President David Burnet on May 14, 1836. By September, the Constitution of the Republic of Texas, drafted shortly after independence was declared, had been implemented. Major features of this charter paralleled those of the U.S. Constitution, including a president and a Congress, but the document also guaranteed the continuation of slavery.

The United States had been sympathetic to the Texas struggle for independence. However, admission to the Union was postponed for a decade because of northern opposition to admission of a new slave state. After ten years of nationhood, Texas was finally admitted into the Union. The Constitution of 1845, the Statehood Constitution, was modeled after the constitutions of other southern states. It was regarded as one of the nation's best at the time. The Constitution of 1845 not only embraced democratic principles of participation but also included many elements later associated with the twentieth-century administrative reform movement and was a very brief, clear document.[4]

The Constitution of 1845 was influenced by Jacksonian democracy, named for President Andrew Jackson. Jacksonians believed in an expansion of participation in government, at least for White males.[5] Jackson's basic beliefs ultimately led to the spoils system of appointing to office those who had supported the winning candidates in the election ("to the victors belong the spoils"). Jacksonian democracy also produced long ballots, with almost every office up for popular vote, short terms of office, and the expansion of voting rights. Thus, while participatory, Jacksonianism was not flawless.

When Texas joined the Confederate States of America in 1861, the constitution was modified again. This document, the Civil War Constitution of 1861, merely altered the Constitution of 1845 to ensure greater protection for the institution of slavery and to declare allegiance to the Confederacy.

Texas was on the losing side of the Civil War and was occupied by federal troops. President Andrew Johnson ordered Texas to construct yet another constitution. The 1866 document declared secession illegal, repudiated the war debt to the Confederacy, and abolished slavery, although it did not provide for improving conditions for African Americans. In other words, the state made only those changes that were necessary to gain presidential support for readmission to the Union.

Radical postwar congressional leaders were not satisfied with these minimal changes in the constitutions of the southern states. They insisted on more punitive measures. In 1868–1869, a constitution that centralized power in the Texas state government, provided generous salaries for officials, stipulated appointed judges, and called for annual legislative sessions was drafted. It contained many elements that present-day reformers would like to see in a revised state charter. Because the constitution was forced on the state by outsiders in Washington and by *carpetbaggers*—northerners who came to Texas with their worldly goods in a suitcase made out of carpeting—White southerners never regarded the document as acceptable. They especially resented the strong, centralized state government and the powerful office of governor that were imposed on them. However, because all former rebels were barred from voting, the Constitution of 1869 was adopted by Unionists and African Americans. Ironically, this constitution least accomplished the purpose of legitimacy—acceptance by the people—but was the most forward looking in terms of power and organization.

The popular three-term governor Elisha Pease resigned in the fall of 1869 after the radical constitution was adopted. After a vacancy in the state's chief executive office lasting more than three months, Edmund J. (E. J.) Davis was elected governor and took office at the beginning of 1870. The election not only barred the state's Democrats and traditional Republicans, both conservative groups, from voting but exhibited a number of irregularities. Davis was an honest man, but the radical state charter, Davis's radical Republican ties and his subsequent designation as provisional governor by President Ulysses Grant combined to give him dictatorial powers.[6]

# The Present Texas Constitution

Traditionally Democratic as well as conservative, Texans began to chafe for **constitutional revision**—changes to reform or improve the basic document—when the Democrats regained legislative control in 1872. An 1874 reform effort passed in the Texas Senate but failed in the House. This constitution would have provided flexibility in such areas as how tax dollars could be spent and terms of office. It also would have facilitated elite control and a sellout to the powerful railroads, which were hated by ordinary citizens because of their pricing policies and corruption of state legislatures.[7] The legislature called a constitutional convention, and ninety delegates were elected from all over the state. The convention members were overwhelmingly conservative and reflected the "retrenchment and reform" philosophy of the Grange, which was one of several organizations of farmers.[8] This conservatism included a strong emphasis on the constitutional purpose of limiting government and a tolerance for racial segregation shared with other institutions of the time. As noted in Chapter One, southern farmers were determined to prevent future state governments from oppressing them as they believed they had been oppressed under Reconstruction.

★ ★ ★ ★ ★ ★ ★ ★ ★ ★ ★ ★ ★ ★ ★ ★ ★ ★ ★ ★ ★ ★ ★ ★ ★ ★ ★ ★

## Independence Now and Then

Because Texas was an independent republic when the United States annexed it, the annexation agreement reflected compromises by both the state and national governments. For example, Texas gave up its military property but kept its public lands. The national government refused to assume the state's $10 million debt. Texas, however, can carve four additional states out of its territory should the state want such a division.

In the 1990s, a radical group calling itself the Republic of Texas contended that because Texas had been illegally annexed in 1845, it remained a nation. Pursuing this belief, members of the movement harassed state officials in a variety of ways, including filing liens against the assets of public agencies and regularly accusing state officials of illegally using their powers. Several of these individuals are still in prison for their violent actions.

★ ★ ★ ★ ★ ★ ★ ★ ★ ★ ★ ★ ★ ★ ★ ★ ★ ★ ★ ★ ★ ★ ★ ★ ★ ★ ★ ★

Accordingly, the new constitution, completed in 1875, curbed the powers of government. The governor's term was limited to two years. A state debt ceiling of $200,000 was established. Salaries of elected state officials were fixed. The legislature was limited to biennial sessions, and the governor was allowed to make very few executive appointments.

When this document went to the people of Texas for a vote in February 1876, it was approved by a margin of 136,606 to 56,652; 130 of the 150 Texas counties registered approval. All the ratifying counties were rural areas committed to the Grange and would benefit from the new constitution. The twenty counties that did not favor the new charter were urban areas that were heavily Republican, where newspaper criticism of the proposed document had been severe.[9]

## GENERAL FEATURES

*[handwritten: Voted mostly by urban areas]*

The Texas Constitution of today is very much like the original 1876 document in spite of 440 amendments by the middle of 2007 and some major changes in the executive article. It includes a preamble and sixteen articles, with each article divided into subsections (see Table 2-2).[10] When the Texas Constitution was drafted over a century ago, it incorporated protection for various private interests.

It also included many details of policy and governmental organization to avoid abuse of government powers. The result is a very long, poorly organized document that does not draw clear lines of responsibility for government actions. As an example of details that might be contained better in legislation than in constitutional law, Article V, Section 18 spells out procedures for electing justices of the peace and constables. These provisions have been amended four

Cartoonist Ben Sargent pokes fun at the fact that the Texas Constitution had been amended 440 times by the mid-point of 2007 and that, in recent years, voters have had to familiarize themselves with as many as twenty-eight amendments in a single election.

*Courtesy of Ben Sargent.*

times; one amendment is so specific that it allows Chambers County the flexibility to have between two and six justice of the peace precincts. Besides having its own amendment, Chambers County (county seat: Anahuac) is best known for being one third under water.

The Texas Constitution reflects the time of its writing, an era of strong conservative, agrarian interests and of reaction to carpetbagger rule. Changes in the U.S. Constitution, both by amendment and by judicial interpretation, have required alterations of the state constitution, although provisions that conflict with federal law remain. These unenforceable provisions, along with other provisions that are so out of date that they will never again be enforced, are known as deadwood. Both the Sixty-fifth Legislature in 1977 and the Seventy-sixth Legislature in 1999 undertook to clean up the constitution by removing deadwood provisions through the formal amending process.

The public had voted on 617 proposed amendments by the middle of 2007, resulting in the addition of 440. These amendments have produced a state charter that is poorly organized and difficult to read, much less interpret, even by the

**TABLE 2-2**
## Articles of the Texas Constitution

I.      Bill of Rights

II.     The Powers of Government

III.    Legislative Department

IV.     Executive Department

V.      Judicial Department

VI.     Suffrage

VII.    Education [and] the Free Public Schools

VIII.   Taxation and Revenue

IX.     Counties

X.      Railroads

XI.     Municipal Corporations

XII.    Private Corporations

[XIII. Spanish and Mexican Land Titles—deleted by amendment in 1969]

XIV.    Public Lands and Land Office

XV.     Impeachment

XVI.    General Provisions

XVII. Mode of Amending the Constitution of the State

*Takes a 2/3 vote in legislates* (handwritten)

*Last amendment to be defeated was gay marriage* (handwritten)

courts.[11] Yet the amendments are necessary because of the restrictiveness of the constitution. In recent years, voters have tended to approve all proposed amendments. They approved all forty-two voted on in the 2001–2003 period.

The Lone Star State can almost claim the record for the longest constitution in the nation. Only the constitution of Alabama contains more words than the 90,000 plus in the Texas charter.[12]

## SPECIFIC FEATURES

The Texas Constitution is similar in many ways to the U.S. Constitution, particularly the way in which the purposes of organizing and limiting government and legitimacy are addressed. Each government has executive, legislative, and judicial branches. Both are separation of powers systems; that is, they have separate institutions that share powers. Both include provisions against unequal or arbitrary government action, such as restricting freedom of religion. The two documents are less alike in terms of the purpose of providing power to government. The national Constitution is much more flexible in allowing government to act than is the state document. Texas legislators, for example, cannot set their own salaries.[13]

## BILL OF RIGHTS

Like the national Bill of Rights, Article I of the Texas Constitution provides for equality under the law; religious freedom, including separation of church and state[14]; due process for the criminally accused; and freedom of speech and of the press. Among its thirty protections, it further provides safeguards for the mentally incompetent and provides several specific guarantees, such as prohibition against outlawing an individual from the state. It includes an equal rights amendment for all Texans.

Citizen opinion generally supports the U.S. and Texas Bills of Rights. However, just as the public sometimes gets upset with the U.S. Bill of Rights when constitutional protections are afforded to someone the public wants to "throw the book at"—an accused child molester, for example—Texans sometimes balk at the protections provided in the state constitution. A 1992 Texas poll revealed that, if given a chance to vote on the Texas Bill of Rights today, "a significant number of Texans would balk at several sweeping protections including the rights to assemble and protest, to hold unpopular beliefs, and to bear arms."[15] Nevertheless, modern efforts toward constitutional revision have left the provisions intact.[16]

Following the terrorists' attack on the World Trade Center in New York City in 2001, many Americans have been willing to sacrifice some protections to help prevent further acts of terrorism, a willingness that has engendered national debate on the conflict between homeland security and civil rights and liberties. Support for such intrusions on basic civil liberties has been dwindling, however.[17] Because homeland security issues involve racial and ethnic profiling, Texas, with its very diverse population, could be affected more than some other states. In a few Texas cities such as Farmers Branch, efforts to restrict non-citizen immigrants occurred in 2006. These actions reflect a national concern over illegal immigration and impatience with the lack of a federal immigration bill. Chapter Eleven discusses rights and liberties in greater detail, including interpretations of the right to keep and bear arms.

## SEPARATION OF POWERS

Like the national Constitution, the state charter allocates governmental functions among three branches: the executive, the legislative, and the judicial. Article II outlines the separation of powers, including the "departments"—as the branches are labeled in the state constitution—of government. The national government divides power between the nation and the states as well as among the three branches. Providing for a sharing of power should keep any one branch from becoming too powerful. Article II outlines the separation of institutions, and the articles dealing with the individual departments develop a system of checks and balances similar to those found in the national Constitution. Often, the same checks found in the U.S. Constitution are established in the state constitution.

A check on power results from assigning a function commonly identified with one branch to another. For example, the House of Representatives may impeach and the Senate may try—a judicial function—elected executive officials and judges at the district court level and above.[18] The governor has a veto over acts of the legislature and an item veto over appropriation bills—a legislative proceeding. The Texas Supreme Court may issue a writ of mandamus ordering an executive official to act—an executive function. These examples are applicable at the national as well as the state level and illustrate that powers are not truly separated but overlapping and shared.

## LEGISLATIVE BRANCH *Strongest branch*

The Texas legislature, like the U.S. Congress, consists of a Senate and a House of Representatives. The legislative article (III) establishes a legislative body, determines its composition, sets the qualifications for membership, provides its basic organization, and fixes its meeting time. All these features are discussed in Chapter Six. The article also sets the salary of state legislators. Although a 1991 constitutional amendment provided an alternative method to recommend salaries through the Ethics Commission, the commission has never made a salary recommendation, and legislative salaries remain frozen at a surprisingly low $7,200 a year.

Rather than emphasizing the positive powers of the legislature, the article spells out the specific actions that the legislature cannot take, reflecting reaction to the strong government imposed during Reconstruction. For example, the U.S. Constitution gives Congress broad powers to make any laws that are "necessary and proper." In contrast, rather than allowing lawmaking to be handled through the regular legislative process, the Texas Constitution sometimes forces state government to resort to the constitutional amendment process. For example, an amendment is needed to add to the fund maintained by the state to help veterans adjust to civilian life by giving them good deals on the purchase of land. Another example is the need for an amendment to change the percentage of the state budget that can be spent on public welfare.

The state constitution also provides the following limitations on legislative procedure:

1. The legislature may meet in regular session only every two years.

2. The number of days for introduction of bills, committee work, and floor action is specified. To permit early floor action, the governor can declare an emergency.

3. Salaries and the per diem reimbursement rate are described. Historically, this degree of specificity made an amendment necessary for every change in these figures. Although the Ethics Commission has made no recommendations about salaries, it has upgraded the per diem rate.

4. The legislature cannot authorize the state to borrow money. Yet, Section 23-A provides for a $75,000 payment to settle a debt to a contractor for a building constructed at the John Tarleton Agricultural College (now State University) in 1937.

5. The legislative article, not the municipal corporations article, includes provisions for municipal employees to participate in Social Security programs.

6. In spite of a stipulation that the legislature cannot grant public monies to individuals, exceptions are made for Confederate soldiers, sailors, and their widows.

*When a state official leaves office, where do the $ for his campaign go?*

These examples are taken only from the legislative article. A list of all similar idiosyncratic provisions in the constitution would be massive because limitations on legislative action are scattered throughout the constitution, especially in the General Provisions. Such detailed restrictions tie the hands of legislators and make it necessary for them to take many issues to the voters that are seemingly of little significance. Still, the legislature is the dominant institution in the state.

## EXECUTIVE BRANCH

Little similarity exists between the provisions for the executive branch in the state charter and those in the national Constitution. The U.S. Constitution provides for a very strong chief executive, the president, and creates only one other elected official, the vice president, who since 1804 has run on a ticket with the presidential candidate. Tradition is that the presidential candidate selects the running mate, usually in an effort to pick up votes where the top candidate is weak. Article IV provides that the governor will be elected statewide and will be the chief executive of the state. However, the state constitution requires that the following individuals also will be elected statewide:

1. The lieutenant governor, who presides over the Texas Senate

2. The comptroller (pronounced con-TROL-ler) of public accounts, who collects the state's taxes and determines who keeps the state's money on deposit

3. The commissioner of the General Land Office, who protects the state's environment and administers its vast public lands

4. The attorney general, who is the state's lawyer

5. Members of the Texas Railroad Commission, who regulate intrastate transportation and the oil, gas, and other mining industries.

*Elected statewide*

Furthermore, statutory laws require that the commissioner of agriculture and members of the State Board of Education be elected. Thus, quite unlike the president, who appoints most other key federal executives, the governor is saddled with five other elected executives and two key elected policymaking boards. He or she has no formal control over these individuals. Thus, Texas has a **plural executive,** with the result that the executive branch is "disintegrated" or "fragmented." Each elected executive is independent of the other. The governor must contend with about 250 state agencies, most of which receive policy direction from an administrative board or commission. The governor also has little power to reorganize executive agencies.

*Special sessions can only last 30 days and can only be called on by the governor*

Thus, the executive article, like the legislative one, is overly specific and creates roadblocks to expeditious governmental action. Government cannot act when faced with too many restrictions, even when citizens need a fast response. More than the other articles, Article IV reflects the period of its writing—the extreme reaction in the 1870s to the excesses of Reconstruction Governor E. J. Davis. In a 1999 rating of institutional powers of the governor, the Texas governor was rated just slightly below the mean when the number of separately elected officials, tenure, appointments, budget authority, veto power, and control of party were all considered.[19] The governor was weakest on the factors of separately elected officials and statutory budget authority. This ranking is far higher than previous ones, which tended to look only at constitutional factors.

Governors have also learned how to use what constitutional powers they have. For example, through control of special sessions and through the veto power, the governor retains significant legislative power. There is also no restriction on the number of terms that a governor may serve. Additionally, two modern amendments have strengthened the governor's position. In 1972, the governor's term of office was lengthened from two years to four years. In 1980, gubernatorial removal powers were strengthened by an amendment to Article XV. This amendment allows governors to remove, with the advice and consent of the Senate, individuals they have appointed. Legislation approved in 1993 further strengthened the office by giving the governor greater control over major policy boards such as those dealing with insurance regulation and public education.

★ ★ ★ ★ ★ ★ ★ ★ ★ ★ ★ ★ ★ ★ ★ ★ ★ ★ ★ ★ ★ ★ ★ ★ ★ ★ ★

## The Succession Amendment

The Seventy-sixth Legislature in 1999 proposed seventeen amendments to the Texas Constitution. One of the most interesting ones was Proposition 1, which established a procedure for succession to the lieutenant governor's office. Amid wide speculation that Governor George W. Bush might be the next U.S. president, the state wanted to ensure an orderly procedure if Lieutenant Governor Rick Perry moved up to the governor's office. The amendment established a procedure whereby the members of the Senate would elect one of their own members as acting lieutenant governor. The individual would remain a member of the Senate. Even before the vote on the amendment, political speculation began about which senator might be catapulted into the very powerful position of lieutenant governor and, thus, presiding officer of the Senate.

★ ★ ★ ★ ★ ★ ★ ★ ★ ★ ★ ★ ★ ★ ★ ★ ★ ★ ★ ★ ★ ★ ★ ★ ★ ★ ★

## JUDICIAL BRANCH

The national judicial system is clear-cut—district courts, appeals courts, the U.S. Supreme Court—but the Texas judicial system is not at all clear. Like so many other articles in the constitution, the judicial article has various specific sections. These range from the requirement for an elected sheriff in each county to the restricted right of the state to appeal in criminal cases.[20]

Article V, the judicial article of the state constitution, has three distinctive features. First, the constitution establishes a rather confusing pattern of six different types of courts. Further complicating the picture is the fact that Texas (along with Oklahoma) has two supreme courts, one each for civil (Supreme Court) and criminal (Court of Criminal Appeals) matters.

Second, each level of trial courts has concurrent, or overlapping, jurisdiction with another level; that is, either level of court may hear the case. Additionally, trial courts established by statute have different jurisdiction from those established by the constitution. For example, in civil matters, constitutional county courts have concurrent jurisdiction with justice of the peace courts in civil cases involving $200 to $5,000. County courts at law overlap district courts in civil matters involving up to $100,000. Although the legislature can adjust the jurisdiction of statutory courts, the authority of constitutional courts can be altered only by constitutional

*How Much money from Arte gas tax is taken for every gallon*

amendment. Furthermore, the minimum dollar amounts stated in the constitution reflect economic values of the nineteenth century. In an area of multimillion-dollar lawsuits, having a district court—the chief trial court of the state—hear a case in which the disputed amount is $1,000 or less hampers the more significant trial work of that court. The courts are fully discussed in Chapter Ten.

Third, qualifications for Texas judges are so stated as to allow those with no legal training to be eligible for a trial court bench.[21] The resulting confusion increases the likelihood that someone without legal experience will be elected as a justice of the peace or county judge. The problem of judicial qualifications is aggravated by the fact that judges are elected in Texas so that, on occasion, vote-getting ability may be more important than the ability to render fair judgments.[22] The tradition of elected judges reflects the nineteenth-century passion for long ballots. In the national government, the president appoints all judges.

## LOCAL GOVERNMENT

*general flexible*

Local governments in Texas fall into three categories: counties, municipalities (cities and towns), and special districts. The state constitution, through Articles III, IX, and XI, gives these governmental units varying degrees of flexibility.

Counties, which are administrative and judicial arms of the state, are most restricted. They are saddled with a commission form of government that combines executive and legislative authority and is headed by a judge. The powers vested in the county governments and the services they offer are fragmented. An amendment of some 2,000 words was passed in 1933 to allow larger counties to adopt a home-rule charter, but the provisions were so restrictive as to be inoperable.

*Given the option of toll roads*

**Home rule** allows a government to write its own charter and make changes in it without legislative approval. Had it been workable, this provision would have allowed counties to choose their own form of government and have more flexibility in day-to-day operations. The provision was deleted in 1969.

In contrast, cities enjoy a workable home-rule provision. Those with populations of more than 5,000 may become home-rule units of government. General-law cities, which are those without home-rule charters, must operate under statewide statutes. Cities, towns, and villages, whether operating under a home-rule charter or general law, are fairly free to provide whatever services and create whatever policies the citizens and governing bodies want, as long as there is no conflict with constitutional or statutory law. The major constitutional difficulties for cities are the ceilings imposed on tax rates and debt and limitations on the frequency of charter amendments.

Special districts are limited-purpose local governments that have taxing authority. The legislature generally authorizes the creation of special districts, although constitutional amendments have created some water and hospital districts. School districts are the best-known type of special district, but there are literally dozens of varieties. Because these types of government provide a way around the tax and debt limits imposed on cities and counties, they continue to proliferate.[23] (Chapter 12 discusses local government in detail.)

## SUFFRAGE

The provisions on voting and the apportionment of legislative bodies are interesting because many of them have clearly conflicted with federal law, which itself continues to evolve as the legal/political philosophy of federal judges changes. As a result, Article VI has been subject to frequent amendments to catch up with changes such as the nationally established voting age and to allow participation in bond elections by voters who did not own property. The suffrage section of the constitution is shot through with "temporary transition provisions" to bridge the gap between state and federal law.

## AMENDMENTS

The framers of a constitution cannot possibly anticipate every provision that should be included. Consequently, all constitutions specify a procedure for amendment. Unlike eighteen other states—most notably California—which allow citizens to initiate constitutional amendment proposals by petition or the forty-one states that provide for a constitutional convention (see Table 2-3), Texas has only one way to propose an amendment.

In Texas, proposals for amendments may be initiated during a regular or special session of the legislature, and an absolute two-thirds majority—that is, one hundred House and twenty-one Senate members—must vote to submit the proposed changes to the voters. The governor cannot veto a proposed amendment. The legislature also specifies the date of the election at which an amendment is voted on by the public. At least three months before the election, a proposed amendment must be published once a week for four weeks in a newspaper in each county. Whenever possible, amendments are placed on the ballot in general elections to avoid the expense of a separate, called election. Only a simple majority—that is, half plus one—of those citizens who choose to vote is needed for ratification, making it rather easy to add amendments. The governor officially proclaims the passage or rejection of amendments.

Texas's 440 constitutional amendments are vivid proof that the amendment process in the state has occupied considerable legislative time and that citizens have frequently confronted constitutional propositions at the polls. Another sixteen proposals were scheduled to be voted on in November 2007. Table 2-4 points out the relentlessness of the amendment phenomenon and the increasing reliance on amendments as a way to get something done in government. Forty-five percent of the amendments were added between 1980 and 2003. Some streamlining of the state charter ensued from a constitutional amendment passed in November 1997 that called for an elimination of duplicate numbers

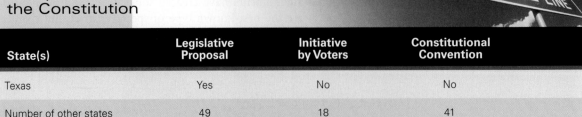

**TABLE 2-3**

## Comparison of State Provisions for Amending the Constitution

| State(s) | Legislative Proposal | Initiative by Voters | Constitutional Convention |
|---|---|---|---|
| Texas | Yes | No | No |
| Number of other states | 49 | 18 | 41 |

SOURCE: *The Book of the States, 2006 Edition*, vol. 38 (Lexington, Ky.: Council of State Governments, 2006), 11–15.

TABLE 2-4
Texas Constitutional Amendments, 1879*–2003

| Decade | Proposed | Adopted | Cumulative Total |
|---|---|---|---|
| 1870s–1880s | 16 | 5 | 5 |
| 1890s | 15 | 11 | 16 |
| 1900s | 20 | 10 | 26 |
| 1910s | 35 | 9 | 35 |
| 1920s | 26 | 12 | 47 |
| 1930s | 45 | 34 | 81 |
| 1940s | 35 | 25 | 106 |
| 1950s | 43 | 33 | 139 |
| 1960s | 84 | 55 | 194 |
| 1970s | 67 | 44 | 238 |
| 1980s | 99 | 88 | 326 |
| 1990s | 80 | 64 | 390 |
| 2000s through 6/07 | 52 | 50 | 440 |
| Total through 6/07 | 617 | 440 | 440 |

*The first amendment to the 1876 Texas Constitution was adopted in 1879.

SOURCE: Complied by C. Neal Tate and Charldean Newell.

in the Texas Constitution and of obsolete provisions. However, most observers thought that the amendment did not provide sufficient clout to take care of all the needed cleanup, an opinion reinforced by the forty-two amendments already passed in the twenty-first century.

# Constitutional Revision

## OVERVIEW OF THE NEED FOR REFORM

The framers of the U.S. Constitution were wise enough to provide only the essential structure of national government and to consign broad powers to governmental agents. The flexibility inherent in this approach has made possible

The Texas Secretary of State's office posted this sample ballot on his Web site prior to the May 12, 2007, constitutional amendment election. This site, www.sos.state.tx.us, is always a source of the latest proposed amendments.

No. 0000

**CONSTITUTIONAL AMENDMENT ELECTION** *(ELECCIÓN SOBRE ENMIENDAS A LA CONSTITUCIÓN)*
*(Condado de)* SAMPLE COUNTY, TEXAS
MAY 12, 2007 *(12 de mayo de 2007)*
**SAMPLE BALLOT** *(BOLETA DE MUESTRA)*

INSTRUCTION NOTE: *(NOTA DE INSTRUCCIÓN)*
Place an "X" in the square beside the statement indicating the way you wish to vote. *(Marque con una "X" el cuadro al lado de la frase que indica la manera en que quire usted votar.)*

No. 1

_ **For** *(A Favor)*

_ **Against** *(En Contra)*

"The constitutional amendment authorizing the legislature to provide for a reduction of the limitation on the total amount of ad valorem taxes that may be imposed for public school purposes on the residence homesteads of the elderly or disabled to reflect any reduction in the rate of those taxes for the 2006 and 2007 tax years."

*"Enmienda constitucional que autoriza a la legislatura para disponer la reducción del monto total de impuestos al valor que, siendo para fines de las escuelas públicas, puedan establecerse sobre los hogares residenciales de ancianos o discapacitados, de modo que se refleje cualquier reducción de la tasa tributaria correspondiente a los ejercicios fiscales de 2006 y 2007".*

the country's transition from a nation whose government was mainly concerned with fending off "hostile" Native Americans and delivering the mail to one whose government now shoulders the burdens of world leadership and myriad socioeconomic policies. State constitutions, on the other hand, tend to reflect the concerns of vested interests. These interests prefer the "security blanket" of constitutional inclusion to being left at the mercy of legislatures with changing party alignments, political persuasions, and political concerns.

The ratification dates of state constitutions provide a clue as to what to expect in the way of content. The two newest states—Alaska and Hawaii—have workable, sound constitutions that were modeled in part on the ideal document proposed by the National Municipal League[24] and have clearly profited by the mistakes of others. Unless they have been updated, older state charters tend to be more problematic.

During the bicentennial celebration of the U.S. Constitution (1987–1989), Americans were proud that their fundamental law had been amended only twenty-six times (a twenty-seventh amendment was added in 1992) and that ten of the amendments—the Bill of Rights—were added almost immediately after ratification. At the national level, the admonition of Alexander Hamilton that opens this chapter has been heeded. In contrast, by the beginning of 2006, the average state constitution has been amended 133 times. The champions of amendments are Alabama (with 766), California (513), and South Carolina (485). Texas comes in fourth with its 440. The next closest states (Maryland, Nebraska, New York, Oregon, and South Dakota) are all in the lower 200s. In contrast, five state constitutions revised in the modern era—those of Illinois (1971), Michigan (1964), Pennsylvania (1968), Montana (1973), and Virginia (1971)—have only 11, 25, 30, 30, and 40 amendments, respectively. In contrast, Louisiana, with a 1975 constitution, already has 129 amendments. Louisiana also has had 11 constitutions, more than any other state. Whatever the primary method of proposing amendments in a given state, the result can be few or many charter changes depending on how good the basic document is.[25]

Advocates of reform urge Texas to follow Hamilton's prescription by adopting a new document that is general, flexible, and streamlined in place of the specific, rigid, complicated constitution that hampers its government now.

Reformers are not all of one mind and frequently differ on the details of their proposals. Nevertheless, reform advocates tend to agree on fundamentally important changes that should be made in the current constitution, as follows:

1. **The biennial legislative session:** As state politics and finance become more complex, the short legislative sessions held only every other year become more of a problem to developing long-range public policy.

2. **The judicial system:** The Texas judicial system, as previously discussed, is characterized by multiple layers of courts with overlapping jurisdictions. Many reform advocates would like to see the establishment of a stream-lined, unified judicial system.

3. **The plural executive branch:** The executive branch has many elected officials and two policymaking boards. Reformers suggest an executive branch modeled on the national executive—that is, a single elected official and a series of executive departments responsible to that official to avoid the disintegrated, fragmented nature of the present structure.

4. **County government:** Especially in urban counties, the structure of county government and its lack of power to pass ordinances (local laws) mean that the counties cannot respond readily to urban problems. Reform advocates suggest that county government be streamlined and given at least limited ordinance power.

5. **Detailed provisions in the constitution:** For example, each time more funding is needed for welfare payments or the veterans' land program, a constitutional amendment must be passed. Thus, another area for reform is removing from the constitution details that are better left for statutory law, which can be changed more readily as situations demand.

★ ★ ★ ★ ★ ★ ★ ★ ★ ★ ★ ★ ★ ★ ★ ★ ★ ★ ★ ★ ★ ★ ★ ★ ★ ★ ★ ★ ★ ★

### *Security Blankets: Why Constitutional Change Is Difficult*

One Texas example of a "security blanket" is the provision authorizing workers' compensation insurance for state and local government employees. Another example is the section that benefits veterans by providing funds for land purchases. A third benefits homeowners, who receive a partial tax exemption for their primary residence (homestead).

★ ★ ★ ★ ★ ★ ★ ★ ★ ★ ★ ★ ★ ★ ★ ★ ★ ★ ★ ★ ★ ★ ★ ★ ★ ★ ★ ★ ★ ★

## RECENT REFORM EFFORTS

Attempts have been made to modernize the Texas Constitution from time to time since its adoption in 1876. Serious interest in constitutional reform/revision was evident in 1957–1961, 1967–1969, 1971–1974, and to some extent, 1991–1993 and 1999. The only reform effort that resulted in an opportunity for the electorate to decide on a new document came in 1975.

## 1971–1974

The 1971–1974 effort was important for two reasons. First, it clarified a long-standing concern about whether the legislature had the constitutional right to convene itself as a constitutional convention. A 1972 constitutional amendment authorized the Sixty-third Legislature to convene itself as a constitutional convention. This constitutional convention was quickly labeled the "Con-Con." Second, the Texas Constitutional Revision Commission, created by the same amendment, provided a detailed study of the state constitution that served as the basis for new constitutions proposed in 1974 and 1975. The proposal drafted by the constitutional convention was defeated when two issues—parimutuel (that is, racetrack) betting and right to work, which is an antiunion provision—were introduced that became the red herrings for foes of reform. (Red herrings are diversions intended to draw attention away from the main issues.) They brought opposition from Bible Belt conservatives and organized labor. The proposal died before ever reaching the voters.

## 1975

Interest in constitutional reform remained high. When the Sixty-fourth Legislature convened in January 1975, constitutional revision was a principal issue. Senate Joint Resolution 11 (with amendments) emerged as the vehicle for accomplishing constitutional change. Although the legislature did not adopt all the changes suggested by the 1973 revision commission, legislators did draw heavily on that work.[26] Highlights of SJR 11 included annual legislative sessions, a streamlined judicial system, and modernization of county government. SJR 11 eliminated such details as the welfare ceiling. It gave more power to the governor coupled with a limit of two terms. It also provided for property tax relief and a tax on petroleum refining.

Powerful interests lined up on both sides of this proposed constitutional reform, with vested economic interests and emotionalism acting as important components of the struggle for ratification of the document. In spite of the efforts of most state officials to convince voters of the worth of the proposed state charter, voters defeated the entire proposal by a two-to-one margin on November 4, 1975. Governor Dolph Briscoe, fearful of higher taxes and government expansion, and county officials, concerned for their jobs, helped to bring about defeat. A combination of interests worried that the "equal educational opportunity" provisions would upset the scheme of funding public schools helped convince citizens to vote against the proposal. Texans clearly preferred the old, lengthy, familiar document to one they saw as possibly promoting more spending and allowing greater governmental power.

## 1976–1991

Little interest in constitutional revision was evident in the fifteen years following the defeat of the proposed new state constitution. Too many problems demanding immediate solutions filled the recent legislative sessions. Legislators did not have time to give consideration to constitutional change beyond proposing more amendments. Besides, virtually every group with interests protected by the current constitution, from veterans to the University of Texas and Texas A&M systems to county commissioners, was anything but encouraging of constitutional change.

## 1992 AND BEYOND

Following the 1991 legislative session, Senator John Montford drafted a joint resolution that proposed a new constitution for consideration in 1993. The Montford proposal included such features as:

- Six-year terms for senators and four-year terms for House members

- A limit of two consecutive terms for a senator and three for a House member

- A sixty-day budget session of the legislature in even-numbered years

- Empowerment of the legislature to meet to reconsider bills vetoed by the governor

- The only elected executives to be the governor, lieutenant governor, and comptroller, each with a limit of two terms

- Simplification of the court system and provision for nonpartisan elections

- Creation of five regional university systems, each of which would share in the Permanent University Fund (PUF)

- Ordinance power for counties, subject to local voter approval[27]

As is so often the case, immediate problems such as the budget shortfall, school finance, and a prison system unable to cope with the volume of state prisoners crowded out constitutional revision in 1993. When Senator Montford prepared

From 1989 to 2006, the legislature wrestled with the thorny issue of public school finance, trying various funding schemes to rectify the objections of state courts that the Texas public education system did not provide "efficient and effective" education for all students. At the "eleventh hour" in 2006, the legislature produced a funding scheme meeting a court-ordered deadline that could otherwise have resulted in shutting down the schools.

*Courtesy of Ben Sargent.*

the draft constitution, he was one of the most powerful state senators in Texas, but even he had other issues to address in 1995. Subsequently, he left the legislature to become head of Texas Tech University. Without a champion, constitutional revision was not considered by the 1997 legislature.

After the 1997 legislative session, Representative Rob Junell, chair of the powerful House Appropriations Committee, expressed interest in constitutional reform. Junell liked some of the Montford ideas, particularly reducing the number of elected officials, including making judges subject to gubernatorial appointment. He was joined by Senator Bill Ratliff, chair of the equally powerful Senate Finance Committee. Their proposal included the following:

- Six-year terms for senators and four-year terms for House members
- Limiting the elected executives to the governor, lieutenant governor, comptroller of public accounts, and attorney general
- Providing for an executive department that would consist of specified department heads, excluding elective officials and reporting to the governor
- Simplification of the court system, with judges to be appointed by the governor
- Establishing the possibility of a veto session for the purpose of reconvening to consider whether to override the governor's veto

Known as HJR 1 and SJR 1 in the Seventy-sixth Legislature in 1999, the Junell-Ratliff proposal was withdrawn from committee in late April when the sponsors realized that their resolution had no chance of being considered by the full House or Senate. Opposition was widespread among both the Democratic and Republican state party organizations, the Texas AFL-CIO, and various other interest groups. Longtime political reporter Sam Attlesey characterized the demise of the proposal as due to "a lack of interest, excitement or crisis in state government."[28]

Although three powerful legislators took an interest in constitutional reform in the 1990s, nothing came of their efforts. Neither other legislators nor citizens had much interest in constitutional revision. Both were more concerned about the issues that regularly beset the Texas political system—education, healthcare, highways, air quality, and so on. Moreover, a pressing concern for constitutional reform is more likely to arise from a moralistic political culture than the traditionalistic-individualistic culture that characterizes Texas. Most Texans are politically conservative and prefer the basic governing document that they know to one that could cause social-political-economic changes that they might not like. Consequently, Texas has continued to use a patchwork approach to its basic document, relying on constitutional amendments and statutory law to alleviate some of the shortcomings of the constitution. The 1999 amendment that authorizes removal or rewording of outdated and repetitive parts of the state constitution is illustrative of the amendment approach to constitutional patching. Modifying the election code to ensure that the qualifications for voting in Texas conform to national requirements is one example of a statutory fix.

Twenty-nine states have constitutions newer than Texas's, and twelve have state charters written since 1950. Yet in spite of the occasional difficulty of governing under the present state charter, only the League of Women Voters has shown a long-term concern for constitutional revision, joined by sporadic media interest in reform.[29] Recent sessions of the legislature have faced too many problems demanding immediate solutions to allow legislators to give any consideration to a new constitution. Furthermore, many citizens fear that change may be for the worse rather than for the better, and special interests want to preserve what they already have embodied in the state charter. This conservative stance, reflecting once again the state's traditionalism, is encouraged by the major economic forces in the state.

# Constitutional Politics

Making a constitution, like other lawmaking processes, is highly political. Whether the issue is general constitutional reform or an individual amendment, changing a constitution will benefit some groups and disadvantage others. Because the requirement of a two-thirds legislative vote plus public approval makes constitutional change more difficult than ordinary lawmaking, the political stakes are greater when alteration of a state's fundamental charter is an issue.

## SOMETHING FOR EVERYONE

Various special interest groups attempt to embody their political, social, economic, and/or moral viewpoints in the constitution by either advocating a particular change or working against it. If a group can embed its particular policy concern in the constitution, the issue is likely to remain there, perhaps forever. In other words, it is easier to "amend in" a provision than to "amend it out." The relative ease of amending the state charter contributes to this attitude of using the constitution as a security blanket. The constitution has become a political "goody" store that contains something for everyone.

One strategy used by these groups is to seek an authorizing provision in the constitution that will result in economic gains for the group. For example, a set of 1985 amendments about funding for water supply benefits small cities, farmers, and ranchers, all of whom vigorously advocated passage of the proposals.

Similarly, tax relief has been a frequent subject for constitutional amendment since 1978. Almost everyone got something from the amendments and the accompanying legislation. Farmers and ranchers thought they had been shortchanged by 1978–1980 amendments when other economic groups gained substantial advantages. Consequently, a 1981 amendment exempted livestock and poultry from all taxation, much as lumber interests had earlier managed to get trees excluded. By 1987, after four years of economic difficulty, oil producers sought their share of tax relief and managed to secure an amendment exempting from taxation certain kinds of offshore drilling equipment that was not in use. A 1997 amendment authorized the legislature to cap increases in residential property tax appraisals and school districts to permit an elderly person to transfer a property tax freeze (already a benefit) to a different residence.

Sometimes a group tries to prohibit a state from taking, or being able to take, a particular action. When the foes of parimutuel betting helped to destroy the efforts of the 1974 constitutional convention, their goal was to prevent the constitutional authorization of gambling in Texas. As noted in the previous section, this issue was a political red herring dragged in by general opponents of constitutional reform and illustrates tactics that were used to defeat change. The proposed constitution did not specifically provide for parimutuel betting, but it did not prohibit it. Opposition to parimutuel betting has since lessened, and in November 1987, voters approved it in a referendum held at the time of a constitutional amendment election. A 1991 amendment authorized more gambling through a state lottery.

The strategy of getting something for everyone by opposition to particular policies has more recently focused on various proposed amendments that would prohibit a state income tax. In 1993, voters overwhelmingly approved an amendment that mandates a voter referendum if the legislature should ever pass an income tax. The amendment also requires that at least two thirds of the revenue from an income tax be pledged to reduce property taxes that support public schools, with the remainder to go to support education. The importance of this provision became apparent in 2004 when the legislature sought ways to fund Texas public schools.

At other times, a group seeks to advance some special interest that is already the subject of a constitutional guarantee. The periodic amendment of the legislative article on the Veterans Land Board is an example. This constitutional provision authorizes the state to sell bonds both to purchase land for veterans and to underwrite low-cost loans for home purchasers. It must be amended each time an authorization for more bond sales is needed.

A similar case is the periodic introduction of amendments to the welfare section of the legislative article to provide funds to pay for aid to the state's needy citizens. Mainly a device for limiting the amount of money that can be spent for welfare, the constitutional provision about welfare has not been a political "plum" or guarantee for the state's poor people. Still, a 1982 amendment authorized the legislature to provide funds for this purpose up to a maximum of 1 percent of the state budget, beginning in 1983–1984. There is still a ceiling on welfare expenditures, but the 1982 provision is somewhat more generous than the old provision and is elastic—that is, the amount available for welfare goes up as the budget goes up.

Another example of the politics of constitution making concerns branch banking, which the Texas Constitution prohibited before a 1986 constitutional amendment. Larger banks wanted branch banking because they wanted to establish branches in other parts of a city or even in other cities. Smaller, independent banks, fearing the competition that a change would permit, opposed the practice. From 1987 through 1990, Texas banks and savings and loans suffered many failures. Because branch banking had been legalized, finding purchasers for the failed Texas financial institutions was easier. Larger, more stable banks both in Texas and in other states could acquire the troubled banks and make them branches. In 1997, financial institutions were major advocates of a proposal that would allow Texas homeowners, like the citizens of all other states, to take out a second mortgage on their residence. Voters, viewing home equity loans as a type of easy credit, went along with the banks and savings and loans.

Private interests are not always the only ones seeking constitutional change. Sometimes elected officials want changes in the constitution to enhance their power, but such ideas often do not fly with the general public. In 1980 and 1981, for example, the governor tried to gain greater control over the state's budgeting and spending processes through constitutional amendment, but the public defeated both of the proposed amendments. In 1999, voters defeated a proposal that would have allowed state employees who serve on local government boards to be paid the same as other compensated board members. Public officials also may try to prevent constitutional change through fear of losing powers. Members of the Texas Association of County Officials (TACO) were a potent lobbying force against the proposed 1975 constitution. They were afraid of losing political control if county governments were modernized.

★ ★ ★ ★ ★ ★ ★ ★ ★ ★ ★ ★ ★ ★ ★ ★ ★ ★ ★ ★ ★ ★ ★ ★ ★ ★ ★ ★ ★

### *Using Amendments Instead of Statutes*

The constitutional amendment election of November 2005 illustrates that the amendment process is often used instead of legislation, is highly political, and focuses on the specific.

Nine proposals were advanced concerning railroad finance, a ban on gay marriage, economic development not constituting debt, conditions for denying bail, defining rates for commercial loans, altering the membership of the State Commission on Judicial Conduct, lines-of-credit with reverse mortgages, land title relinquishments in Smith and Upshur Counties, and easing the length of terms on regional mobility commissions. The proposals concerning interest rates and terms on mobility commissions failed. The others passed. All of these joint resolutions focused on issues that, in most states, would have been matters of statutory law, not constitutional law.

One issue overshadowed the others: the provision that marriage consists only of the union of one man and one woman and prohibiting any subdivision from altering that status. The so-called "gay marriage" proposal was very controversial. Because it was badly drafted, it may well affect other relationships and could deter some highly skilled people from wanting to work in the state if, for no other reason, than its intent is clearly to discriminate against one category of people. Moreover, it was redundant because a ban on same-sex marriage already existed in statute. Conservative Texas, however, was caught up in the national frenzy of reaction against more liberal states attempting to provide for marriage among same-sex couples.

★ ★ ★ ★ ★ ★ ★ ★ ★ ★ ★ ★ ★ ★ ★ ★ ★ ★ ★ ★ ★ ★ ★ ★ ★ ★ ★ ★ ★

## THE POLITICAL PROCESS

The political process involved in constitutional change is essentially the same as other activities designed to influence public policy. Elected officials, political parties, special interests and their lobbyists, and campaigning are all involved. A brief illustration of the process is provided by a situation that began in 1979 and was initially resolved by an amendment approved by the voters in 1984—namely, the issue of building funds for the state's universities. The University of Texas at Austin and Texas A&M University at College Station, through provisions in Article VII of the state constitution, were the sole beneficiaries of the Permanent University Fund (PUF). The PUF was worth over $10.7 billion in 2005, and an improving stock market would have made that value grow. These funds can be used for buildings, other permanent improvements, and enrichment activities. The PUF gets its money from the proceeds of the oil and gas leases on a million acres of public land granted to the two universities and from investment

of these proceeds. Seventeen other state universities originally received money for buildings directly from the legislature and then, beginning in 1947, from a dedicated fund fed by the state property tax. Institutions created after 1947 were dependent on legislative appropriations.

In 1979, as part of a general tax-relief movement, the legislature reduced the rate for the state property tax to almost zero. In the 1979 and 1981 sessions of the legislature, a variety of proposals to establish an alternative to financing college building programs were introduced. Neither the legislators nor the universities could agree on a proposal. The legislature subsequently proposed a constitutional amendment to abolish the state property tax altogether, and the voters approved the amendment in late 1982. Also in 1982, the universities received some building funds in a special legislative session to tide them over until the larger issue could be decided.

The 1983 legislature then had to deal with the issue of funding university construction. The legislators agreed on a basic plan that provided PUF coverage for other institutions in the UT and A&M systems and established a separate fund to cover the other state institutions. This separate fund would cover repairs and renovations, new construction, library and equipment purchases, and land acquisitions. They also agreed on a special infusion of funds to the two predominately African American institutions in the state, Texas Southern University and Prairie View A&M. The UT and A&M representatives wanted to ensure that the PUF was not opened to other universities. They feared a significant reduction in the funds available to the two flagship institutions. Their willingness to include their branch campuses in the PUF avoided the need to include these branch campuses in the new construction fund. At the same time, UT and A&M also gained the agreement of the other universities not to seek inclusion in the PUF.

From the beginning, wrangling among the Texas Higher Education Coordinating Board, which oversees the fund, the universities eligible to receive funds, and lawmakers arose as to the proper amount. Initial funding was finally set at $50 million a year, and at times, the funding grew to almost $90 million annually. The institutions that participated in the Higher Education Fund were greatly aided by it, especially so in lean appropriation years when the institutions would have been hard-pressed to fund the purchase of library books or to make building repairs from the regular funding.

In 2001, the legislature changed the system to begin reducing the amount of appropriated funds that went into the Higher Education Fund, and the difference was deposited in a new fund called the Texas Excellence Fund to spur research. No appropriation was made to the permanent Higher Education Fund for fiscal years 2004–2005. The Seventy-eighth Legislature in 2003 then dictated that the Texas Excellence Fund and a University Research Fund would be repealed as of September 1, 2005. At that point, yet another fund, the Research Development Fund, would be created.

The saga of university construction has involved many people. Legislators themselves have diverse interests. Some come from districts with one or more state universities. Others are budget conscious; still others are strong alumni supporters of the institutions they had attended. Different governors have been more or less supportive of the needs of higher education. The state's universities have different needs and different growth rates and often have difficulty agreeing on a strategy to pursue with the legislature. Taxpayers want assurance that tax increases will not be necessary to fund college construction. The Coordinat-

## YOU DECIDE

### Should Texas Convene a Constitutional Convention?

The Texas Constitution was ratified in 1876. By mid-2007, it had been amended 440 times and is more than 90,000 words in length. The average for all fifty states is 133 amendments and 35,278 words. The only state with a population larger than that of Texas, California, has a constitution with 513 amendments and 54,645 words. The constitution of New York, the third largest state, has 291 amendments and 51,700 words.

| PRO | CON |
|---|---|
| ▲ Texas should convene a constitutional convention to draft a new state charter. The present state constitution<br>• is antiquated<br>• is in conflict with the national Constitution<br>• protects special interests<br>• reflects agrarian interests<br>• is far too specific<br>• needs frequent interpretation<br>• poorly organizes government thus, does not meet the needs of an urban state | ▼ The state constitution should not be revised to avoid<br>• mistaking newness for quality; the U.S. Constitution is 89 years older than the Texas Constitution<br>• increasing partisanship that could create a political disaster<br>• a process likely to be an expensive exercise resulting in stalemate<br>• "fixing something that ain't broke"<br>• giving more authority to counties, which are already inefficient<br>• giving government, especially the governor, too much power<br>• removing protection against arbitrary governmental action from those groups protected by the charter |

ing Board has to ensure a balance of all needs, not just those associated with libraries and physical facilities. Business and industrial interests are also part of this complex funding issue: Information-based firms depend on research, but business in general does not want to get stuck with the whole bill for building universities. Ethnic minorities continue to press for special funding because of historical discrimination.

In 1984, the issue of university construction was seemingly resolved as part of a broad solution to financing *capital* improvements (those of long-term duration). In 2003, a more conservative group of legislators faced with a $10 billion deficit pulled back general capital funding in favor of dollars designed to attract outside research funding. The issue of capital funding provides a portrait of how many varied interests can become involved in constitutional change. Different constitutional change issues have different casts of characters, of course, but they all are fraught with similar complex political relationships.

This shift in emphasis to research-only funding has a major effect on every university student outside the University of Texas and Texas A&M systems. Because of the elimination of the special pot of funding for construction, repairs, libraries, equipment, and land that was not specially tied to external research funding, students found themselves saddled with the costs for these items in the form of assessments such as special library fees and higher tuition that was in part pledged to construction bonds. At the same time, the PUF institutions were pointing out that they did not have adequate dollars to take care of all their building repair needs and that they were under similar pressures to emphasize their research missions.

## Summary

Constitutions have four purposes: legitimacy, organizing government, providing power, and limiting governmental power. The six Texas constitutions have embodied these purposes in varying degrees. Texans were so unhappy with Reconstruction government that, given the opportunity to draft and ratify a new constitution in 1876, they concentrated their attention on legitimacy and limiting government. The intent of the framers was to curb governmental power.

Thus, they largely ignored the importance of assigning sufficient power to government officials. Also, they subverted the purpose of organizing government by creating a fragmented set of institutions and offices designed to diffuse authority. Although this approach limits government, it also makes citizen participation more difficult because state government is confusing to most people. Partisans of democracy are frustrated because the state constitution makes the people's ability to govern themselves more difficult. Yet the current constitution reflects the traditionalistic-individualistic political culture of the state.

Lacking the farsightedness of the framers of the U.S. Constitution, the authors of the Texas charter produced a restrictive document that today sometimes impedes the development and implementation of needed policies and programs. By the middle of 2007, lawmakers and citizens had resorted to amending the Texas Constitution 440 times to make possible programs that otherwise would have been consigned to legislative dreamland. In one sense, the element of democratic theory that holds that public input into policy is important is satisfied by such a practice, but policies are very hard to modify once they are written into the constitution. Dynamic public issues such as funding for water quality, welfare, and public education could be handled more smoothly without the necessity of proposing and ratifying a constitutional amendment. Now, if a policy proves to be ineffective, only another amendment can solve the problem.

The most cumbersome and/or unnecessarily restrictive provisions in the 1876 constitution and their consequences are the following:

1. The governor, although held responsible by the public for overall state leadership and the action of state agencies, in reality has limited direct control over most major policymaking offices, boards, and commissions.

2. The legislature is caught between the proverbial "rock and a hard place." While constantly being criticized by the citizenry for poor legislative performance, it nev-

ertheless must operate within the constraints of poverty-level salaries, short and infrequent sessions, and innumerable restrictions on legislative action.

3. Texas judges are well aware of the lack of cohesiveness in the judicial system, but they are virtually powerless to provide simpler, more uniform justice because of the overlapping and parallel jurisdictions of the state's courts and the lack of effective supervision of the whole judicial system.

4. County governments, even when county commissioners are progressive in attitude, are restricted by their constitutional structure and scope.

5. The 440 amendments exacerbate the poor organization of the charter, making it even more difficult for the layperson to read.

Twice in the 1990s, powerful legislators showed an interest in constitutional revisions. Whether similar efforts will succeed in the future is uncertain. The electorate still lacks sufficient understanding of the shortcomings of the present constitution to be receptive to increases in governmental power. Citizens are far too concerned about state taxes, public education, social services, crime and punishment, and many other pressing issues to give constitutional revision much attention. Although the current constitution "creaks and groans," the state still takes care of its business.

In addition, special interests have found it easy to amend the current document by influencing key legislators and then mounting serious campaigns to elicit voter support. They prefer the protection of a constitution to more easily changed statutes. Thus, a successful revision effort may have to wait not only until the citizens of Texas are more aware of the pitfalls of the present document but also until powerful special interests can be persuaded to work for, not against, constitutional reform. Article I of the Texas Constitution as quoted at the beginning of this chapter is ironic: The emphasis has come to be more on the phrase "political power" than on the intended phrase "inherent in the people." For now, "if it ain't broke, don't try to fix it" prevails.

## Glossary Terms

Bill of Rights

checks and balances

constitution

constitutional amendment

constitutional revision

home rule

incorporation

plural executive

separation of powers

## Study Questions

1. What are the four purposes of constitutions? Which ones are most reflected in the Texas Constitution? Which ones are least reflected?

2. How many constitutions has Texas had? Why have there been so many? Do you think there needs to be another one? Why or why not?

3. Why is the Texas Constitution so frequently amended? What types of interests are involved when constitutional change is advocated?

4. Why do you think the constitution, the legal framework of a state, is so important?

5. What similarities and differences do you see in the U.S. and Texas Constitutions?

6. Texas seems to govern itself despite the criticisms of the state constitution. Consequently, constitutional reform is unnecessary. Do you agree or disagree with this statement? Why?

7. Consider the short list of features of the Montford and Junell-Ratliff proposals for a new constitution provided in this chapter and whatever other knowledge you have. Neither proposal was adopted. Speculate on why the proposals failed. Who do you think was for and against them?

8. Do you think you, personally, could get interested in constitutional revision? Why or why not?

## Surfing the Web

Readers are urged to visit the companion site for this book:

**http://academic.cengage.com/polsci/Kraemer/TexasPolitics10e**

# Interest Groups

**3**

The Capitol building in Austin is the focus of attention for many interest groups.

As soon as several of the inhabitants of the United States have taken up an opinion or a feeling they wish to promote in the world, they look around for mutual assistance; and as soon as they have found each other out, they combine. From that moment they are no longer isolated men, but a power seen from afar, whose actions serve for an example, and whose language is listened to.

ALEXIS DE TOCQUEVILLE, *DEMOCRACY IN AMERICA*, 1835

Money doesn't talk, it swears.

BOB DYLAN, "IT'S ALRIGHT, MA (I'M ONLY BLEEDING)," 1965

# Introduction

Politics is concerned with the making of *public* policy, but a great many of its actions have *private* consequences. When government imposes a tax, begins to regulate an industry, or writes rules about the behavior of individuals, it makes an impact not just on the public in general but on citizens in particular. Human nature being what it is, people often tend to judge the action not so much on the basis of its value to their community as on the basis of its utility to themselves. Seeking to obtain more favorable policies, people organize to try to influence government. When they do, they create a problem for democracy. As citizens, we want our government to take account of the impact of its laws on individuals, but we do not want the special wishes of some people to be more important than the shared needs of us all. To the extent that public policy is made or modified at the behest of private interests, democracy is impaired.

In Texas as elsewhere in the United States, special organized interests are always busy trying to influence what government institutions do. Citizens have to decide whether these groups are merely presenting their point of view to public authorities or whether instead they are attempting to corrupt the process of self-government.

In this chapter, the discussion first focuses on the definition and classification of interest groups. The chapter then describes and analyzes their activities and moves on to consider some efforts that have been made to regulate lobbying. There is then an examination of the history and recent activities of some of the major interest groups in Texas. The interest-group system in Texas is evaluated in the light of democratic theory.

# Interest Groups

## DEFINITION

An interest is something an individual or individuals have that has value and is therefore worth defending. It can be economic, religious, ethnic, or indeed, based on almost anything. People who produce oil have an interest, as do Catholics and fans of Harry Potter novels. Interests affect politics in two general ways. One topic of Chapter Four will be the manner in which they form the basis for much of the battle between political parties. In this chapter, the subject is the direct effect of interests and interest groups on Texas government.

In the broad sense, an **interest group** is a private organization of individuals who have banded together because of a common cause or role. The focus here, however, is on **political interest groups,** those that try to influence politicians to make public policy in line with their preferences. When people join these groups, they exercise their right guaranteed by the First Amendment to the U.S. Constitution to "assemble" and "petition" the government.

Interest groups can be usefully contrasted with political parties. The focus of a party is broad, encompassing many different interests, whereas the focus of a group is narrow, comprising just one interest. Parties attempt to gain power by running candidates in elections, whereas groups try to affect power by influencing officeholders. Therefore, while parties are forced to appeal to the citizenry to marshal support, groups may work entirely behind the scenes. By joining groups, people gain the ability to affect government decisions beyond what they achieve with just their vote.

## CLASSIFICATION

Interest groups may be classified according to the types of interests they defend.

1. **Economic groups,** such as manufacturers' associations or labor unions. These represent the most common type of interest group and also, in general, the type with the most resources. Within this large category, there are many more specialized groups representing specific types of industries or occupations. An example of the former would be banking and financial organizations, represented by the Texas Bankers Association, among others. Examples of the latter would be professional associations, such as the Texas Bar or the Texas Medical Association. Like labor unions, these groups represent people who share a type of livelihood. Unlike most labor unions, they are composed of people who are generally well-educated and relatively wealthy.

2. **Spiritual groups,** such as church organizations or pro-life and pro-choice associations. These groups unite people who may be otherwise very different but who share a faith or a public policy position derived from their faith.

3. **Artistic or recreational organizations,** such as the local Symphony League or the Texas Association of Bass Clubs. This type of group includes people who share a hobby or other type of pastime.

4. **Ethnic groups,** such as the League of United Latin American Citizens (LULAC) or the National Association for the Advancement of Colored People (NAACP).

★ ★ ★ ★ ★ ★ ★ ★ ★ ★ ★ ★ ★ ★ ★ ★ ★ ★ ★ ★ ★ ★ ★ ★ ★ ★ ★

Although many Texas public universities include an elected student representative on their governing board, no formal organization exists to represent the interests of students, in the United States in general or Texas in particular. There is, however, such an organization in the United Kingdom, named the National Union of Students. The NUS provides a range of services, from welfare advice and information to clubs and societies, bars, shops and catering services, student community action projects, and charity fundraising events. It also attempts to represent students' views within the institution. Students' union officers sometimes sit on the board of governors of the college or university, and the organization helps to support students in their academic appeals.

★ ★ ★ ★ ★ ★ ★ ★ ★ ★ ★ ★ ★ ★ ★ ★ ★ ★ ★ ★ ★ ★ ★ ★ ★ ★ ★

SOURCE: NUS Web site: www.nusonline.co.uk/about/

5. Associations of local governments, such as the Texas Municipal League and the Texas Association of County Officials.

6. Public interest groups, such as Common Cause or the League of Women Voters. These groups try to pursue their understanding of interests common to all citizens rather than the individual interests of their members. The members of these groups can disagree about what constitutes the "public interest"—they can have opposed positions on whether school vouchers would be a good thing for education, for example—but their positions are based on their differing understanding of the broad-based needs of all citizens rather than on their own personal needs.

# Interest Groups in the Political Process

## WHO IS ORGANIZED?

The two most important points to understand about interest groups are that not all people who share an interest are organized and that organized interests are much more powerful than unorganized interests. Although the famous quotation from Alexis de Tocqueville at the beginning of this chapter might lead us to believe that every potential interest spawns an interest group, in fact some interests are far more likely to be organized than others. Those that are organized are relevant to policymaking; those that are not organized are usually irrelevant.

For example, oil and gas producers are well organized and politically powerful in Texas. Oil and gas consumers, however, are not organized, except insofar as general consumers' groups (which theoretically represent everybody but never have a very large membership) include petroleum among the many products of interest to them. As a result, unless the price of gasoline at the pump rises steeply as it did in 2006 and 2007, thus creating public anger, petroleum consumers are not usually of much concern to policymakers. Under ordinary conditions, government policymakers are likely to pay much more attention to petroleum producers.

There are three general rules of interest-group formation. First, economic-producing groups are more likely to be organized than are consuming groups (as in the previous oil and gas example). Second, regardless of the type of group, people with more education and income are more likely to join than are people with less education and income. Third, citizens who join groups out of personal involvement as opposed to economic stake tend to feel very strongly about the particular issue that is the group's reason for existence. They are therefore much more likely to contribute money, write letters, attend rallies, and in other ways engage in actions that get the attention of government officials. Consequently, because they are more likely to be organized, producers tend to exert more political influence than consumers, the middle and upper classes more influence than the working classes, and passionate believers more influence than citizens who are less emotionally involved.

## FUNCTIONS

Interest groups attempt to persuade both the public and individual government officials to take a particular point of view on specific public policies. In trying to be persuasive, they perform six important functions in the political process.

1. They furnish information to officeholders in all branches of government. This activity includes both communicating their collective opinion on public policy and supplying policymakers with their version of the facts.

2. They politicize and inform members of their groups as well as others.

3. They mediate conflict within their groups.

4. They engage in electioneering, especially the contribution of money to candidates, and possibly in other interventions in the governing process, such as filing lawsuits.

5. By disseminating information supporting their own policy stands to citizens, they help to form public opinion.

6. By providing institutions other than political parties that help people to participate in the process of governing, they help their members to become more involved democratic citizens.

## ACTIVITIES

Interest groups therefore enhance democratic government by supplying information to citizens, contributing to debates about issues, getting people involved in politics, and shaking up the established order by influencing institutions. But because they often attempt to skew the process of government to benefit themselves, these groups also can be a corrupting influence. A closer look at their activities will show the extent to which they deflect public policymaking into private channels.

### ELECTIONEERING

One of the most common ways interest groups try to ensure that their future efforts at persuasion will be more effective is by supporting candidates for public office. Interest groups that have helped elect a politician can be confident that they will not be forgotten when the politician enters government.

Usually, the most effective way to help candidates is to give them money. Because campaigning demands the purchase of advertising in expensive media, all candidates but the few who are personally rich need to beg wealthy individuals and groups for large amounts of money. In this regard, one of the important developments of recent decades has been the rise of **political action committees** (PACs) and their influence on elections.

A PAC is a committee formed by an organization, industry, or individual for the purpose of collecting money and then contributing that money to selected political candidates and causes. Because PACs coordinate and concentrate the financial clout of multitudes of individuals with a single interest, they can influence public policy far more effectively than can most ordinary, isolated citizens. Some states, such as Minnesota, Maine, and California, limit the amount of money that PACs can contribute in state elections, but in Texas, these groups may give as much as they wish. Both the politicians and the contributors understand, if only tacitly, that what the interest groups expect is an exchange: The groups give the candidates money, and if they win, the candidates give the groups public policy.

Individuals, not just organizations, can contribute large amounts of money during campaign cycles. Table 3.1 details some of the contributions made by the

**TABLE 3-1**

## Partial List of Political Contributions by Bob Perry to Organizations and Candidates, 2005–2006

| Organization | Amount Donated | | |
|---|---|---|---|
| Republican Party of Texas | $780,000 | | |
| Texans for Lawsuit Reform | $601,000 | | |
| Hillco Partners Political Action Committee | $545,000 | | |

| Candidate | Candidate For | Won? | Amount Donated |
|---|---|---|---|
| Rick Perry | Governor | Yes | $380,000 |
| Greg Abbott | Attorney General | Yes | $320,265 |
| David Dewhurst | Lieutenant Governor | Yes | $285,000 |
| Susan Combs | Comptroller | Yes | $250,000 |
| Patrick Rose | House of Reps | Yes | $15,000 |
| Ben Bentzin | House of Reps | No | $70,000 |
| Bill Welch | House of Reps | No | $65,000 |

Total contributed to organizations and candidates: $6,700,000

SOURCE: Laylan Copelin, "Big Political Spender Outdoes Himself in '05–'06," *Austin American-Statesman*, December 6, 2006, A1.

most politically generous Texan, Bob Perry (no relation to governor Rick Perry) during the 2005–2006 campaign season. Some of the $6.7 million he poured into the political process went directly to candidates. Some of it went indirectly to candidates through such intermediaries as Hillco Partners, a lobbying firm that represents Perry. Not all of the candidates he supported won their races, but most did, and the winners can be expected to be very attentive to Perry's policy requests in the coming years.

There is no point in criticizing the integrity of public officials for being willing to accept large amounts of cash from groups and individuals that are pushing a narrow agenda. It is the reality of electoral financing, not personal dishonesty, that makes politicians overly sensitive to private, as opposed to public, interests.

## LOBBYING

To **lobby** means to attempt to influence policymakers face to face. Everyone has the constitutional right to try to make an impact on what government does, and it is obvious that a personal talk with a government official has more impact than one anonymous vote. Because of the rules of interest-group formation, however, some groups are much more likely than others to be able to afford to lobby. It is corporations and trade organizations that employ the most **lobbyists**—people whose profession is to try to influence government. Wealthy special interests may have good or bad arguments for their positions, but in either case, they employ the most people to make sure that their arguments are heard.

**Who are the Lobbyists?** During the 2007 legislative session, there were 1,151 lobbyists registered with the Texas Ethics Commission—more than six for each of the 181 members of the legislature.[1] Lobbyists vary as much in their experience and competence as do the legislators they are trying to influence. Top-flight freelance lobbyists can make over $1.5 million per session; there were thirty of these professional stars during the 2005 legislature, according to a study by Texans for Public Justice.[2]

People do not have to be professionals to exercise their rights to freedom of speech and freedom to petition the government. Concerned citizens who want to express their views to government, especially to the legislature, can do so as individuals or as members of a group (see box on the following page). Citizens who are willing to get organized, inform themselves, and spend the time talking to politicians can sometimes have an important impact on policy. This principle is illustrated by the story of Senator Jeff Wentworth (R–San Antonio) and bicyclists during the 2001 legislative session. Wentworth, concerned about traffic safety in rural areas, filed a bill (SB 238) to forbid cyclists from riding in large groups on farm and ranch roads. The law, if passed, would have required all bicyclists on two-lane roads without a shoulder to ride single file and wear a "slow moving vehicle" triangle sign on their backs.

But it turned out that bicyclists were organized, felt intensely about their hobby, and were willing to play political hardball. Members of the Texas Bicycle Coalition (TBC) were extremely displeased with the proposed statute. They argued that it would stamp out charity rides and hinder tourism. They began a statewide effort to convince Wentworth of the error of his ways.

"Oh, I was inundated," Wentworth told journalist Dave McNeely. "I had more emails and letters and phone calls on that bill than on all the other bills

I'd filed combined. And nearly all the communication was in opposition to the bill." The TBC also staged a demonstration at the capitol building to remind legislators that there were lots of bicyclists and that they were willing to vote on this issue.

★ ★ ★ ★ ★ ★ ★ ★ ★ ★ ★ ★ ★ ★ ★ ★ ★ ★ ★ ★ ★ ★ ★ ★ ★ ★ ★ ★ ★

## *The Beginning of Lobbying*

I n the nation's earliest days, members of the national Congress did not have offices. They lived in hotels or boardinghouses near their legislative chambers and worked "out of their hats." Petitioners hoping to enlist their aid in legislation waited for them in their hotel lobbies; hence the term lobbyist. In Texas, it was not until 1865 that all legislators had offices in the capitol.

★ ★ ★ ★ ★ ★ ★ ★ ★ ★ ★ ★ ★ ★ ★ ★ ★ ★ ★ ★ ★ ★ ★ ★ ★ ★ ★ ★ ★

Faced with massive opposition, Wentworth chose the prudent course and backed down gracefully. He agreed to a watered-down version of the bill, which would have left it up to county officials to decide if some of their roads were so dangerous that they required special regulations for cyclists. The weaker version of the proposed law, however, was still not acceptable to the TBC. SB 238 never got out of committee.[3]

Although examples such as the Texas Bicycle Coalition are numerous, most of the time on most issues it is wealthy special interests that have the resources to hire the best lobbyists and thus have the most influence. Table 3-2 provides a partial list of the clients and earnings of two of Austin's best-known lobbyists, according to the reports they filed with the Texas Ethics Commission (TEC) after the legislative session of 2005.

Many of the most successful lobbyists are former state legislators or executives. These individuals are able to parlay their knowledge of the governmental process and their friendship with many current officeholders into a personal influence that is rentable. One of the lobbyists registered with the TEC, for example, is Gib Lewis, a former speaker of the Texas House of Representatives. In December 1990, Speaker Lewis was indicted by a Travis County grand jury for accepting and failing to report a gift. Under a plea bargain made with the district attorney, Lewis pled guilty to two misdemeanors, was fined $2,000, and agreed not to run for reelection. Out of office, he promptly formed a lobbying firm, accepting money legally to influence the members of the institution over which he used to preside. As he described his five-member lobbying team, Business Partners Ltd., to a journalist in 2003, "Our expertise is direct contact with members of the legislature."[4]

Not all lobbyists come from the ranks of the people they are hired to persuade, not all serve special economic interests, and not all earn fortunes from their work. Some "public interest" lobbyists serve their conception of the common good and take home a modest salary for their efforts. But the biases in the interest-group system mean that most of the people doing most of the lobbying will be serving narrow, wealthy interests.

**TABLE 3-2**

Two Important Texas Lobbyists and Their Clients, 2006 (Partial List)

| Lobbyist | Client | Maximum Value of Contract |
|---|---|---|
| Russell (Rusty) Kelley | AT&T | $100,000 |
| | Aetna | $150,000 |
| | City of Amarillo | $50,000 |
| | General Motors | $100,000 |
| | San Antonio Spurs | $50,000 |
| | Texas Beverage Association | $150,000 |
| | Texas Association of Mortgage Attorneys | $100,000 |
| Mignon McGarry | Capitol One Services | $50,000 |
| | Centerpoint Energy | $50,000 |
| | Hospital Corporation of America | $150,000 |
| | Honda North America | $50,000 |
| | Pepsico | $100,000 |
| | Texas Orthopedic Association | $25,000 |
| | Recording Industry Association of America | $25,000 |

SOURCE: Texas Ethics Commission Web site, www.ethics.state.tx.us/.

**What Lobbyists Do and How They Do It** The best lobbying technique is direct personal contact. Lobbyists try to see as many legislators as possible every day, buying a lunch, chatting for a few minutes, or just shaking a hand. Most lobbyists are able to get on a first-name basis with each legislator they think might be sympathetic to their goals. The speaker of the House and the lieutenant governor are key figures in the legislature, and lobbyists try, above all else, to ingratiate themselves with these two powerful officials.

*Contributions or Bribery?* The best way to ensure personal access to politicians is to give them money or the equivalent. This money is contributed in a variety of ways. Groups spend some of it entertaining legislators and executives at parties, taking them to lunch, giving them awards, and attracting them to similar events that give lobbyists the chance to cultivate personal relationships and apply the arts of individual persuasion.

Another more direct way in which groups funnel money to politicians is by giving them campaign contributions. Few lobbyists are as brazen as East Texas chicken magnate Lonnie "Bo" Pilgrim, who, during a fight over a new workers' compensation law in 1989, simply handed out $10,000 checks on the floor of the Senate.[5] (Although the bad publicity from the 1989 incident persuaded Mr. Pilgrim to be less visible in his use of money, he still actively attempts to influence legislators. The Pilgrim's Pride Corporation, according to TEC records, reported spending between $45,000 and $110,000 as the client of four different state lobbyists in 2005.) But the state capital is thronged at all times, and especially when the legislature is in session, by representatives of interest groups who are eager to use money in a less public manner in the hope that their largesse will be rewarded with favorable laws, rulings, and interpretations.

★ ★ ★ ★ ★ ★ ★ ★ ★ ★ ★ ★ ★ ★ ★ ★ ★ ★ ★ ★ ★ ★ ★ ★ ★ ★ ★

Ordinary citizens—those not employed by an interest group—who feel the need to influence legislation have every right to journey to the Capitol in Austin to lobby representatives. During the 2003 legislative session the *Austin American-Statesman* published some rules that amateur lobbyists should remember when trying to make a persuasive argument. During the 2005 session, the *Dallas Morning News* published an article containing similar rules. Here is the combined list.

1. **Be persistent, outgoing, and friendly.**

2. **Be informed about the process of lawmaking and the party and policy position of individual legislators. The Legislature's Web site is a good place to acquire basic facts.**

3. **Forget the form letters. Many lawmakers refuse to read them.**

4. **Explain your position and situation as clearly and briefly as possible.**

5. **Be personal; tell individual stories that help lawmakers understand your perspective.**

6. **Have available brief, clear, written details.**

7. **Be flexible; committee hearings often run long or late.**

8. **Citizens who have a specific new law in mind should approach legislators as much as a year before the start of the next legislative session.**

★ ★ ★ ★ ★ ★ ★ ★ ★ ★ ★ ★ ★ ★ ★ ★ ★ ★ ★ ★ ★ ★ ★ ★ ★ ★ ★

SOURCES: Dave Harmon, "Texans Mobilize to Fight Cuts in Their Lifelines," *Austin American-Statesman*, March 24, 2003, AB5; Katherine Goodloe, "Capitol Ideas," *Dallas Morning News*, April 10, 2005, E1.

The ongoing saga of the Texas Association of Business (TAB), Texans for a Republican Majority (TRM), its political action committee (TRMPAC), and former U.S. House majority leader Tom DeLay provide a contemporary example of the intersection and mutual reinforcement of money, private interests, and public power in Texas and elsewhere.[6] By 2001, Republicans were in office in the White House and the U.S. House of Representatives and were soon to be a majority in the U.S. Senate. They controlled the Texas governorship and the state senate, and had their sights on the state house of representatives. Tom DeLay, U.S. Representative from Sugar Land, and in line to become the majority leader in the House, conceived the idea of creating an organization that would use state and federal Republican Party organizations to bring the money of national corporations to bear on elections to the state house of representatives in Texas. Once Republicans controlled all three branches of the state government, they could then re-draw the district lines for the national House of Representatives, resulting in still more Republicans being elected to Congress (see Chapter 6 for more on this redistricting plan). Presumably, the corporations would then benefit from Republican policies within the state as they had already benefited at the national level.

There was, however, an obstacle to the Republican plan. Under a law passed in 1903, Title 15, Chapter 251 of the Texas Election Code made it illegal for corporations to contribute money to candidates for public office. The reason for the law is clear. Elections, especially those of a relatively low level such as those for the state house of representatives, are partly decided on which candidate can afford to buy the most advertising. Corporations are concentrations of great wealth. If corporate money is not divided among many candidates in a race, but concentrated on one, it can be the deciding factor on election day. If allowed to use their resources, corporations can easily outspend millions of ordinary citizens and can dominate elections. Government will cease to be of the people, by the people, and for the people. By outlawing corporate campaign contributions in 1903, legislators were attempting to preserve democracy in Texas.

Part of the effort of the 1903 law was to define the nature of corporate involvement. It is legal for corporations to state general positions on issues of public policy. This is, indeed, their constitutional right under the First Amendment's guarantee of freedom of expression for American citizens. But they are not permitted to expressly advocate voting support for particular candidates or parties.

Representative DeLay's plan was an attempt to evade the purpose of the 1903 law. Although not all the details are known, and the nature of DeLay's control of TRMPAC is under dispute, the general outlines of the plan have been exposed by journalists and Travis County District Attorney Ronnie Earle. In brief, TRMPAC received $2.5 million in corporate contributions from, among others, Sears, AT&T, Bacardi, and several insurance companies; the contributions were coordinated by TRM. During the 2002 election campaign TRMPAC sent the money, minus some administrative expenses, to the Republican National Committee (RNC) in Washington, then separately forwarded the names of certain Republican candidates for the state house. A short time later, the National Committee contributed the same amount of money to those candidates. TRMPAC and the RNC, in short, engaged in a money-laundering scheme designed to circumvent the state election law. All the Republican candidates favored in this way defeated their Democratic opponents, and Republicans became the majority party in the state house. Whether the Republican candidates would have lost without the laundered corporate cash is impossible to say, but it certainly did not hurt them.

Also during the 2002 election campaign, the Texas Association of Business was using some of the same corporate money to send out direct mailings to potential voters attacking the same Democratic candidates targeted by TRMPAC, and recommending support for Republican candidates (see Table 3-3). Although the mailed flyers did not use the specific words "oppose" or "support," or the phrase "vote for," they strongly implied such a partisan message. Later, Judge Mike Lynch concluded that the flyers engaged in "what most non-technical, common-sense people (i.e. non-lawyers) would think of as clear support for specific candidates."

Some of the Democrats defeated in the 2002 balloting suspected the outlines of the scheme and filed a civil suit in state court. District Attorney Ronnie Earle launched a three-year criminal investigation. In September 2005 the Travis County Grand Jury indicted DeLay and several of his associates in TRMPAC, as well as TRM, on conspiracy and money laundering charges. An indictment, of course, is not a conviction. That the purpose of TRMPAC's and TRM's actions was to evade the law seems clear, but that fact does not mean that specific individuals were guilty of crimes.

In the spring of 2006 DeLay resigned his seat in the U.S. House and declined to run for reelection. (Later that year the voters in his former district elected a Democrat to represent them in Congress.) The legal maneuvering, however,

**TABLE 3-3**

## Corporations Donating to Texas Association of Business for Four Million Mailers Attacking Democrats and Praising Republicans, 2002

| Corporate Donor | Amount Contributed |
| --- | --- |
| Alliance for Quality Nursing Home Care | $300,000 |
| AT&T | $300,000 |
| U.S. Chamber of Commerce | $131,573 |
| Aetna | $100,000 |
| Blue Cross of California | $100,000 |
| Humana | $100,000 |
| Pacificare | $100,000 |
| State Farm Mutual Automobile Insurance | $25,000 |
| Boeing Aircraft | $5,000 |

NOTE: Partial list.

SOURCE: Laylan Copelin, "Lobbyist Added To Campaign Lawsuit," *Austin American-Statesman*, September 7, 2006, A1.

continued. In June of 2006 district judge Mike Lynch threw out two of the three charges against Texans for a Republican Majority, holding that even though the TV ads sponsored by that organization were perfectly clear in intent, the Terrell election law was so vague it could not be applied in the case of the 2002 election. There were still civil suits pending against TRM, as well as the criminal cases against DeLay and TRMPAC. In November of 2006 a Travis Country grand jury re-indicted TRM on another charge of illegally spending corporate money on campaign advertising after the accusation it had been re-written to meet the judge's objections. As this book went to press, the eventual outcome of the conflict was unknown.

Not all interest groups use money so unashamedly as the Texas Association of Business. Some that employ lobbyists to represent relatively poor groups rely on persistence, information, and the passion they feel for their cause. They sometimes score important victories. Nevertheless, despite the occasional influence of such public-oriented groups as Public Citizen (see box), the power of money, day in and day out, to capture the attention of lawmakers makes wealth one of the great resources of politics and ensures that rich interest groups, over the long run, will tend to prevail over poor ones.

The power of money in the interest-group system brings up uncomfortable questions about democracy in Texas. Simply giving money to a politician for personal use is bribery and is illegal. Bribery is a danger to democracy because it sub-

A small organization with a small budget, Public Citizen, has worked to reform state law and practice on consumer safety, pollution, sustainable energy, access to the courts, government ethics, and campaign finance. The organization's rule to not accept contributions from corporations, professional associations, or government agencies has had two consequences. First, it has freedom of action to follow its principles, regardless of whose toes it may step on in the process. Second, it will never be rich. It relies on the dues and contributions of its 5,300 individual members in Texas to keep it running, and on the dedication of its staff.

Despite its relative poverty, Public Citizen has had a series of modest successes over the years. Its influence stems from its skill at marshaling publicity. Whenever journalists need to get a quotation expressing the pro-consumer, pro-honesty-in-government, anti-special-interest point of view, Public Citizen is one of the organizations they call. Upon occasion, such publicity influences the public to pressure government policymakers to take some action that they would otherwise have avoided. Thus, Public Citizen was instrumental in the creation of the Texas Ethics Commission, the passage of a new "lemon law" to protect the buyers of used cars, and the imposition of safety improvements by the South Texas and Comanche Peak nuclear power plants. In 2002 it raised such a clamor over Public Utility Commission Chairman Max Yzaguirre's conflicts of interest (his ties to the crooked energy-trading corporation Enron, which frequently did business before the Commission) that Yzaguirre resigned.

"Most Texans are surprised at how open our government is to input from our citizens," opined Tom Smith, director—and therefore chief lobbyist—for Public Citizen Texas in 2005. "Too few of them take advantage of it." By devoting a great deal of time and energy to lobbying on behalf of ordinary Texans, Smith and the employees of similar public-interest groups hope to make up for the majority's lack of direct influence on state government.

★ ★ ★ ★ ★ ★ ★ ★ ★ ★ ★ ★ ★ ★ ★ ★ ★ ★ ★ ★ ★ ★ ★ ★

SOURCES: Information about Public Citizen Texas comes from its Web site, www.citizen.org/texas/, especially two press releases, "Public Citizen Celebrates 20 Years In Texas" from October 5, 2004, and "Public Citizen Applauds Yzaguirre's Decision to Resign" from January 17, 2002; Smith quoted in Katherine Goodloe, "Capitol Ideas," *Dallas Morning News*, April 10, 2005, E1.

stitutes money for public discussion in the making of public policy. When policy is made at the behest of a few rich interests working behind the scenes, then government is **plutocratic** (that is, government by the wealthy), not democratic. The disturbing fact is that the line between outright bribery (illegal) and renting the attention of public officials with campaign contributions, entertainment, gifts, and speaking fees (legal) is a very thin one. Money talks, and those with more of it speak in louder voices, especially in a state characterized by low legislative salaries and no public campaign finance.

*Information* Thousands of bills are introduced in the Texas legislature every session, and legislators can have no more than a passing knowledge of most of the policy areas involved. Even those legislators who may have specialized knowledge need up-to-date, accurate information. Therefore, in Texas as in other states, information is one of the most important lobbying resources. The information furnished is biased because it represents the group's viewpoint, but it also must

## YOU DECIDE

### Should Corporate Political Action Committees Be Banned?

A political action committee (PAC) is an organization that collects voluntary contributions from citizens—generally, those who are affiliated with a particular organization such as a corporation, church, or labor union, or who believe in a particular cause—and distributes them to candidates. Reformers have often called for government to forbid corporations to form PACs.

| PRO | CON |
|---|---|
| ▲ Although "money talks," money is not speech. The First Amendment to the U.S. Constitution should not be interpreted so as to protect the power of money. | ▼ The First Amendment protects individual freedom of expression, and citizens should be able to express themselves by contributing money to candidates or organizations. |
| ▲ It is bad enough that individuals are able to corrupt the process of government by renting the allegiance of politicians with campaign contributions; it is much worse that corporate interests are able to do so. | ▼ A PAC is merely an organization that permits individuals with a shared interest to coordinate their political activity; shared economic interests are just as worthy of representation as religious, ideological, ethnic, or any other kind of interest. |
| ▲ Corporations already possess a great political advantage over ordinary citizens because of their ability to hire lobbyists and buy media advertising; the presence of PACs makes that advantage even more lopsided and unfair. | ▼ The supposed political advantage possessed by corporations is a fiction in the mind of so-called reformers. In fact, corporations are over-taxed and over-regulated. They should have more political influence, not less. |
| ▲ The political power of corporations has resulted in public policies that have contributed to the growing inequality of wealth in the United States; in order to permit the reversal of those policies, corporate power must be curtailed. | ▼ Growing inequality of wealth has been caused by economic trends that are independent of government policies. Besides, differences in material equality reflect differences in merit, and are therefore good, not bad. |

be accurate. Getting and keeping a reputation for providing solid information are among the most important assets a lobbyist can develop.

Information is a tool of influence not only in dealing with the legislature but also in dealing with the bureaucracy. State executive agencies have a constant need for information and sometimes no independent means of finding it. They may come to rely on lobbying groups to furnish them with facts. For example, since 1996, the state insurance commissioner has relied on the Texas Insurance

Lobbyists crowd outside the entrance to the Texas House of Representatives on the last day of this session for the House to pass bills, Thursday, May 12, 2005 in Austin.

Checking Office (TICO) to gather the data the commission uses to regulate insurance rates. The Checking Office is a subsidiary of an insurance industry lobbying group. An industry group is therefore supplying the information used to regulate the industry it represents. Consumers might suspect that such data will not show that insurance companies are charging too much.[7]

**Regulation of Lobbying** It would be a violation of the constitutionally protected rights of expression and association for government to *prevent* individual citizens from organizing to influence the political process. However, government has the authority to *regulate* the manner in which citizens attempt to exercise their rights. This distinction is especially apt in regard to the use of money, where the proper freedom to state one's case can easily evolve into an improper attempt to corrupt the system.

Nevertheless, aside from laws of general application regarding such crimes as bribery and conspiracy, Texas makes little attempt to regulate the activities of interest groups except in the area of lobbying. Early attempts at regulation in 1947, 1973, and 1981 were weak and ineffective because no state agencies were empowered to enforce the laws.

In 1991, however, the legislature passed a much-publicized Ethics Bill, which limited the amount of food, gifts, and entertainment lobbyists can furnish legislators and required lobbyists to report the name of each legislator on whom they spend more than $50. Most important, it created an Ethics Commission that could hold hearings on complaints of improper behavior, levy fines, and refer violations to the Travis County district attorney for possible prosecution. Texas seemed at last to have a lobbyist regulatory law with teeth.

The 1991 law was less forceful than it appeared, however. It failed to require legislators to disclose sources of their outside income and also neglected to ban the use of campaign contributions for living expenses. A three-quarters majority is required on the Ethics Commission for some important actions, which limits its activities. Finally, while the members of the commission are appointed by the governor, lieutenant governor, speaker of the House, and chief justice of the Texas Supreme Court, those who are chosen must come from a list of candidates furnished by the legislature.

By 2003, pressure was again building for a reform of the state's ethics laws. That year's legislature passed a new bill that made a variety of changes. Among the amended ethics law's provisions are the following:[8]

1. It requires candidates for public office, whether they win or not, to disclose cash balances in their campaign accounts and report the employer and occupation of larger donors.

2. Legislators who are lawyers now have to disclose when they are being paid to try to delay trials during a legislative session and their referral fees. Also, they are forbidden to represent a paying client in front of a state agency.

3. Candidates must file campaign finance reports via the Internet unless they raise or spend less than $2,000 a year and do not use a computer to keep their records.

4. Local officials in cities of more than 100,000 population and school districts with more than 5,000 students must file personal financial statements like those filed by other state officials.

Information is a useful resource in a democracy, and the 2003 Ethics Bill, because it ensures that more information will be available to the public, is a good thing. Furthermore, the provision that forbids legislators/attorneys to practice before state agencies is genuine reform that will make the outright buying of influence more difficult. Nevertheless, the new law does no more than previous "ethics" bills to dilute the impact of private influence on public affairs. The TRMPAC scandal illustrates the fact that politicians often devise creative ways to circumvent the laws that are supposed to keep their behavior within ethical boundaries. Without public determination to change the very basis of the political exchange of policy for money, wealth will continue to exercise exorbitant influence over Texas politics. As long as legislators' salaries remain below the poverty line, as long as private money dominates public elections, and as long as private information is used to make public policy, the prospects for effective control of lobbying are poor.

## PERSUADING THE PUBLIC

Although most interest-group energy is expended in lobbying government directly, some groups also attempt to influence government policy indirectly by "educating" the public. Sometimes they operate by buying television commercial time to argue their public policy case to citizens, who, they hope, will then pressure their representatives to support the groups' agendas. Sometimes they operate by attempting to persuade citizens to vote a certain way on a referendum.

The 2005 legislative sessions were good ones for observing the efforts of interest groups to persuade the public on behalf of their private causes. Especially noteworthy was a public-relations battle between giants SBC and Verizon Communications on one side and cable companies in alliance with Texas cities on another.[9]

Not so long ago, the telephone and television industries were separate entities. Telephones transmitted private conversations over lines owned by the phone company. Television sets received entertainment that had been broadcast over the airwaves via large transmitters owned by different corporations. Although both industries were partially regulated by government agencies—the Federal Communications Commission in Washington and the Public Utility Commission in Austin—in each case the industry was under the authority of a different set of laws.

With the advent of personal computers in the 1980s, however, the phone business and the television business began to meld into one telecommunications industry. By 2005 most consumers watched television programs that had not been broadcast but had arrived at their homes over coaxial cable, and the cable companies were planning to begin offering telephone services At the same time, telephone companies, having already merged with computer companies, were planning to get into the video industry, offering phone and television over the Internet. All these plans, however, were often impeded by communications laws that had been written during an earlier era, and all of them brought the two previously distinct industries into conflict.

During the regular and special 2005 legislative sessions two phone titans, SBC and Verizon Communications, attempted to persuade politicians to write a new set of regulations that would help them get into video and thereby compete with cable companies. The law ordered a cable company to negotiate franchise agreements with each city it served. The cities, for their part, exacted concessions from the cable companies, requiring them to carry a variety of public-access channels and to pay a fee to the city each year. Because the cable companies enjoyed a virtual monopoly in the provision of clear video programming, they could charge high prices for their services. The arrangement was a win-win situation for both the companies and the municipal governments. Verizon and SBC asked the legislature to exempt their Internet video services from the requirement that they negotiate separate deals with each city. These phone companies lobbied legislators to pass a law allowing them to apply for a single statewide franchise that would enable them to pick and choose the cities, or neighborhoods within cities, where they would offer their new services.

The cable companies cried foul and launched their own lobbying effort in alliance with the Texas Municipal League (whose member cities stood to miss out on a fortune in franchise fees if cable lost this battle) to defeat the phone company bill. The two contending coalitions also conducted a sustained public-relations campaign, each side trying to convince members of the public that their version of telecommunications policy was in the public interest. At first, cable companies attempted to bar the telephone companies' ads attacking them, but soon gave up that fight. The public was treated to an ill-tempered video brawl, with ads accusing the other side of being selfish, mean-spirited, and untruthful, and extolling their own side as being paladins of consumer interests. Meanwhile, various observers and spokespeople wrote op-ed pieces for the newspapers, arguing with their version of relevant arguments and evidence that one choice or the other should be the pick of good citizens in Texas. For a technical issue involving difficult questions of technology, economics, and law, it was a remarkably loud and unavoidable controversy on the state's television screens.

Cable and the cities prevailed in the regular session of the legislature, but in the second special session, the tide turned. Mired in indecision over school finance, legislators managed to pass a telecom bill that handed SBC and Verizon total victory. It is impossible to say whether this outcome was significantly affected by public opinion, was the result of lobbying, or illustrates the triumph of an idea whose time had come.

On September 7, Governor Perry signed the bill into law. That was not the end of the telecom saga, however. The next day, cable firms filed suit in federal court, asking that the state law be tossed out. Not deterred, in October SBC filed an application for a statewide video franchise with the Public Utilities Commission. In January 2006, the cable industry filed another suit in state court, attempting to forbid the Public Utility Commission to implement the law. Meanwhile, starting a business strategy to protect themselves in case they lost in court, cable companies were forming partnerships with telephone companies to offer both phone and video services via the Internet to consumers. As this book went to press, the political, economic, and legal outcomes of the cable vs. phone companies competition were all unknown.

From the standpoint of democratic theory, the efforts of wealthy special interests to create public support through such public campaigns have both reassuring and troubling aspects. On the one hand, by expending their resources on propaganda aimed at ordinary citizens, interest groups greatly expand the amount of information available to citizens. Many thousands of people who would otherwise have not considered the issue of cable franchises were moved to think and act by the noisy campaign. Because an informed citizenry is a democratically competent citizenry, such campaigns are worthy additions to public debate. On the other hand, the arguments presented in the ads reflect a private, one-sided viewpoint. The cable and telephone industries could choose to express their positions on television, but no one can afford to buy television time to speak for the general public interest. On balance, such campaigns probably do more good than harm, but it is a close call.

## INFLUENCING ADMINISTRATORS AND CO-OPTING AGENCIES

The executive branch of government also is an interest-group target. All laws are subject to interpretation, and most laws allow the administrator substantial leeway in determining not only the intent of the lawmakers but also the very meaning of their words. Interest groups attempt to influence the interpretation of laws that apply to them.

As society has become more complex, each individual has become less and less able to provide for her or his own needs. Where once people grew their own food, most must now buy it from large corporations. How can they be sure that it is pure, honestly labeled, and sold at a fair price? The wave of illness and death that swept the nation in 2006 as a result of the consumption of bagged spinach contaminated with *E. coli* bacteria illustrates the problem of protecting public health in a large, complicated society in which people must have faith in the food they purchase. There are similar problems in many other areas of life.

Where once people traveled by horses or mules raised on the family homestead, they now drive expensive vehicles that also are supplied by large corporations. How can they be sure that these are safe and honestly advertised?

Where once they drew water from a local well or river, they now hold a glass under a faucet at home and turn the tap. How can they have confidence that the water is safe to drink?

To protect people's interests in those areas in which they cannot protect themselves, administrative agencies, or bureaus, have been created in the executive branch of government. Although many agencies provide public services, many others are regulatory. Their function is to protect the public interest by regulating various narrow, private interests. The concern here is with the regulatory agencies created to ensure that a particular industry provides good services at fair prices. Unfortunately, the history of these agencies is that, over time, they lose their independent role and become dominated by the interest they were created to control. This transition from guardian of the public interest to defender of private interests—called **co-optation**—has several causes.

First, people who serve on regulatory agencies tend to come from the industry being regulated and return to it after their stint in government is over. This oft-observed activity is called the **revolving door.** Members of the Federal Communications Commission, for example, usually have spent their work lives in the broadcasting industry. As a result, regulators tend to have the perspective of the industry, to sympathize with its problems and share its values.

Second, it is almost impossible for even the best-intentioned regulators to remain independent from the interest to be regulated because they come to have cordial personal relationships with the people in the industry. Even if they had no connection with the petroleum industry before their election, for example, railroad commissioners soon gain many friends in the industry. It becomes more and more difficult for commissioners to interpret public policy problems differently from their buddies in oil and gas.

Third, although a serious problem may cause an initial public outcry demanding regulation of a private interest—railroads, meat packers, or insurance companies, for instance—once regulatory legislation is passed, the public tends to lose interest, and the spotlight of publicity moves elsewhere. From that point on, only the regulated industry is intensely interested in the activities of the government agency. Regulators find that representatives of the industry are constantly in front of them in person, bringing information, self-serving arguments, and the force of personality, while there is no one to speak up for the public. When the Texas Department of State Health Services is creating hospital regulations, for example, it is frequently visited by spokespersons for the health industry. In such situations, it is only human to be more influenced by personal persuasion than by an abstract conception of the common good.

This co-optation of government regulators in Texas is well illustrated by the history of the state's relationship with the insurance industry. Insurance is a mammoth business that produces $3.5 trillion a year in revenue nationwide. Within Texas, the more than 2,200 insurance companies employed 222 lobbying entities during the late 1990s.[10]

The need for government to regulate the insurance industry in order to protect consumers is evident from the nature of the business. As J. Robert Hunter, former Texas insurance commissioner, testified before the Committee on Commerce, Science, and Transportation of the U.S. Senate in 2003,

> insurance is not a normal product like a can of peas or even an auto. One cannot "kick the tires" of the complex legal document that is the insurance policy until a claim arises . . . a consumer pays money today

for a promise that may not be deliverable for years. That promise must be secured from many threats, including insolvency and dishonesty.[11]

Texas began to regulate the industry in the late 1800s to try to protect consumers from unscrupulous practices. By the late 1980s, however, the board was notorious among consumer representatives for always taking the side of the insurance industry in any dispute with customers. In 1991, the Travis County grand jury issued a report on its investigation of the insurance industry and the board. The grand jury reported that it was "shocked by the size of the problem, frightened by what it portends for our future economic health, and outraged by the ineffective regulation of the State Board of Insurance. . . . The potential exists for a . . . disaster in the insurance industry . . . we see embezzlement and self-dealing by insurance company insiders and regulators who are asleep at the switch." The report went on to say that "fraud in the insurance industry is widespread and deep and it is covered by falsified documents filed with the State Board of Insurance."[12]

Partly because of this report, by 1993, the board's practices were so notorious that it had become a political issue. That year, the legislature abolished the three-member board, giving its former powers to a single commissioner, transferring some of its power to other state agencies, and renaming the agency the Texas Department of Insurance. Politicians and citizens hoped that because the new commissioner would have clear responsibility for promulgating and enforcing rules, he or she would be more easily held accountable to the public.

The fact that there was one person, as opposed to three people, responsible for regulating the insurance industry in the public interest, however, did not change the fact that a wealthy special interest still had all the tools necessary to imprint its private desires upon public affairs. The new institutional structure did nothing to reduce the resources the industry could pour into lobbying, nor did it alter the 16 percent of state legislators with personal financial ties to the industry.[13] J. Robert Hunter, appointed by Governor Ann Richards as the first insurance commissioner, later reported that when he took the job he had known that the influence of the industry was large. "But until I went and became an insurance commissioner I had no clue as to how big." According to Hunter, several members of the legislature, at least one of whom was an insurance agent, harassed him on a regular basis, demanding that he fire certain employees whose actions had displeased them, and threatening to cut his budget if he resisted their direction. Hunter ignored their demands, but he lasted only a year at his job, resigning after Richards's defeat in 1994.[14]

By 2002, the actions of the insurance industry had again made it a political issue.[15] Ninety-five percent of homeowner insurance policies were unregulated by the state. Premiums had been rising steadily, and many people had lost their coverage. Moreover, one huge company, Farmers Insurance, was discovered to have engaged in some creative accounting in regard to the documents it filed with the Texas Insurance Commission. While claiming to the state that it had to raise premiums because it was losing money, Farmers submitted other documents to the federal Securities and Exchange Commission asserting that it was extremely profitable.[16]

With citizens in an uproar over their insurance rates, the state's politicians responded. In August 2002, Attorney General John Cornyn filed suit against Farmers, alleging violations of the Texas Insurance Code and the law against deceptive trade practices. Governor Perry participated in the press conference at which Cornyn announced the suit. Shortly thereafter, Insurance Commissioner Jose Montemayor ordered Farmers to stop a variety of its business practices, although he pulled his punch considerably by giving the company a ninety-day grace period, during which it could continue its behavior undisturbed.[17]

The reaction of the insurance industry to this political onslaught was not surprising to people familiar with Texas politics. In anticipation of the attorney general's lawsuit, and trouble with the legislature during the 2003 session, in July 2002, five of the state's biggest insurers (excluding Farmers) had joined forces to found the Texas Coalition for Affordable Insurance Solutions, an association devoted to applying more influence to the political system. The association quickly hired Public Strategies, Inc., a top Austin public relations and lobbying firm, to represent its interests.[18]

Despite the amount of lobbying power arrayed against change in the power of companies to operate unhindered, in 2003 the legislature passed insurance reform bills that required companies to disclose more information and gave the state insurance commissioner the authority to review homeowners' premiums and order reductions where warranted. Quickly after the end of the legislative session, Insurance Commissioner Montemayor ordered twenty-four of the companies that operate in Texas, including the three biggest, Allstate, State Farm, and Farmers, to cut their homeowners' rates an average of 13.4 percent. The Department of Insurance estimated that the cuts would save consumers more than $510 million. The companies complained and threatened to leave the state, but Montemayor stuck by his guns and the companies backed down. The insurance crisis was over, at least for the moment. The episode provided two useful lessons in Texas politics. First, even in a state with powerful lobbies, an aroused and attentive public can prevail against concentrated private influence. And second, administrative agencies are not always captured by the industries they regulate.[19]

Nevertheless, by 2007 consumers' representatives had judged the 2003 reforms to be at best a partial success. The rates charged by the companies for home insurance in Texas had inched down, but were still the highest in the nation. "We were all told that our rates would come back down," commented Alex Winslow, director of the consumer advocacy group Texas Watch. "What actually happened was they went up and stayed up."[20]

Whether the insurance reform surge of 2002 and 2003 will have meaningful long-run consequences cannot be confidently predicted. Nevertheless, the episode underscores the point that the history of insurance and politics in Texas is a story of cycles. For long periods, companies are successful in co-opting government regulation, and in the regulatory vacuum they induce, they are free to get away with almost anything. After enough abuses accumulate, the public becomes enraged and demands action. At that point, there is a spasm of political activity that may, for a time, rein in the behavior of the companies. After the short period of reform, however, the public's attention shifts to other outrages, and the quiet, relentless power of money reasserts itself. In a sense, the relationship of the insurance industry and the political system is a template for the Texas interest-group system as a whole.

Because groups representing narrow private interests do not always win in Texas, scholars who compare interest group power in the states classify the Lone Star State in the "dominant/complementary" category, as illustrated in Table 3-4. The five states in the "dominant" category are those in which interest groups,

## TABLE 3-4

## Classification of the Fifty States According to Overall Impact of Interest Groups, 2002

| Dominant | Complementary | Dominant Complementary | Subordinate |
|---|---|---|---|
| Alabama | Alaska | Colorado | Michigan |
| Florida | Arizona | Connecticut | Minnesota |
| Montana | Arkansas | Delaware | South Dakota |
| Nevada | California | Hawaii | |
| West Virginia | Georgia | Indiana | |
| | Idaho | Maine | |
| | Illinois | Massachusetts | |
| | Iowa | New Hampshire | |
| | Kansas | New Jersey | |
| | Kentucky | New York | |
| | Louisiana | North Carolina | |
| | Maryland | North Dakota | |
| | Mississippi | Pennsylvania | |
| | Missouri | Rhode Island | |
| | Nebraska | Vermont | |
| | New Mexico | Wisconsin | |
| | Ohio | | |
| | Oklahoma | | |
| | Oregon | | |
| | South Carolina | | |
| | Tennessee | | |
| | **Texas** | | |
| | Utah | | |
| | Virginia | | |
| | Washington | | |
| | Wyoming | | |

SOURCE: Clive S. Thomas and Ronald J. Hrebenar, "Interest Groups in the States," in Virginia Gray and Russell L. Hanson, eds., *Politics in the American States: A Comparative Analysis*, 8th ed. (Washington, D.C.: Congressional Quarterly, 2004), 122.

according to investigators, are the "overwhelming and consistent influence on policymaking." Groups in the middle category, "complementary," tend to work in conjunction with other institutions, especially political parties, the executive branch, or other groups. Texas is one of the twenty-six states in the category between these two, meaning that groups here are very strong but not completely dominant.[21]

## INTEREST GROUPS AND THE COURTS

Like the legislative and executive branches, the judicial branch of government also makes policy by interpreting and applying laws. For this reason, interest groups are active in the judicial arena of politics. Groups representing important economic interests make substantial contributions during judicial campaigns, hire lawyers to influence judges with legal arguments, and file suits. Money talks in courtrooms as well as in legislatures and the executive branch.

Nevertheless, courts also can be an avenue of success for interest groups that have been unsuccessful in pressing their cases either through electoral politics or by lobbying the other two branches of government. An outstanding example is the National Association for the Advancement of Colored People (NAACP). Not only has this organization won such profoundly important national cases as *Brown* v. *Board of Education* (347 U.S. 483, 1954), in which segregated schools were declared unconstitutional, but it also has won vital victories at the state level. In *Nixon* v. *Herndon* (273 U.S. 536, 1927), the U.S. Supreme Court held that a Texas law excluding African Americans from the Democratic primary was unconstitutional. The Texas legislature attempted to nullify this decision by writing a new law authorizing party leaders to make rulings to the same effect, but this was struck down in *Nixon* v. *Condon* (286 U.S. 73, 1932). Later, in *Smith* v. *Allwright* (321 U.S. 649, 1944), the Texas NAACP won still another victory when the Court held that racial segregation in party primaries on any basis whatsoever is unconstitutional. Thus, although groups representing dominant interests may win most of the time, the history of the NAACP in Texas proves that any interest group can sometimes prevail if it organizes and knows how to use the court system.

# Major Interest Groups in Texas

Interest groups want publicity for their programs and goals, but they tend to hide their operations. Political scientists have not done extensive research on interest groups in Texas, and the activities of such groups and the precise nature of their influence are difficult to discover. Nevertheless, we will try to describe some of the major interest groups in the state, explain their general success or weakness, and chart how their influence has changed over time.

## TEXANS FOR LAWSUIT REFORM

Scholars who study interest groups have identified "General Business Organizations" as the most influential types of lobbying groups in state capitols.[22] It is easy to see why business is so powerful: Business is by definition organized and normally has more resources to put into politics than any other sector of society.

But as the example of insurance in 2002 and 2003 illustrates, the effectiveness of business lobbying varies with the situation. Not every business interest gets what it wants every time. Nevertheless, many business interests dominate policymaking much of the time.

A good example of a business group that has been spectacularly successful in Texas since 1994 is Texans for Lawsuit Reform (TLR). The group was formed by business leaders determined to change what they perceived as "Texas' Wild West Litigation Environment" by altering the state's tort laws. Torts are wrongful acts; the loser of a civil lawsuit concerning such an act can be forced to pay an amount of money to compensate a victim and may be required to pay an extra amount as punishment (see the discussion of "tort reform" in Chapter 11).

TLR proceeded along two paths. First, it forged alliances with other groups attempting to make it harder to file and win "frivolous" lawsuits in the state, most notably the Texas Medical Association. Second, it used its deep pockets to earn the gratitude of lawmakers in the state, most of them Republican. In total, TLR contributed $1,208,032 to candidates in 2002, most of whom won. TLR is an important reason that Republicans now control both houses of the state legislature, and members of the party are well aware of it.[23] Further, TLR has attempted to maintain its influence by sustaining its campaign generosity. During the 2006 election cycle, for example, it distributed $3.8 million to Texas candidates, 95 percent to candidates for the legislature.[24]

In 1994, George W. Bush ran for governor partly on a platform stressing tort reform. A law passed the 1995 legislature, but because the institution was then dominated by Democrats, it was a much-compromised, milder version of the bill than partisans of TLR hoped to see. In the intervening years, TLR kept spreading the campaign money to Republican candidates, and by 2003, with that party's accession to majority status in both houses of the legislature as well as the state house, its moment had arrived. The 2003 reforms gave the TLR about everything it wanted. As of 2003, it became much harder to sue anybody for anything in Texas. "Texas will be a better place to live," stated TLR president Richard Trabuisi Jr. triumphantly, "to raise a family, and work for a living once this historic legislation goes into effect."[25] Indeed, in 2006 the TLR bragged on its Web site that a report from the Pacific Research Institute (which, on its own Web site identifies itself as a "free market think tank") had ranked Texas "best in the nation" on its "U.S. Tort Liability Index."[26]

Others, of course, had contrary opinions. But for the moment, Texans for Lawsuit Reform was king of the mountain among interest groups.

## DOCTORS

Sitting on the top of that mountain of influence with business is the Texas Medical Association (TMA).[27] Founded in 1853, the state's major doctors' interest group paid scant attention to state politics for most of its history. Its attitude changed in 1987 when, in the first battle of a fifteen-year war, it attempted to persuade the legislature to put a cap on damage awards in medical malpractice cases. Because such a limit would have cut into the income of plaintiffs' attorneys, it was opposed by the Texas Trial Lawyers Association (TTLA). With ten times the membership of the TTLA (38,000), the TMA was nevertheless soundly whipped in legislative infighting. Doctors then decided to pay more attention to politics.

The TMA turned its attention to acquiring political influence with great intelligence. It contributes large amounts of money to legislative and judicial candidates. One study determined that the organization's PAC contributed almost $600,000 in the two years prior to the 1998 elections. Another concluded that "Physicians Associations and Clinics" gave $1,554,017 to politicians during the 2002 election cycle. Furthermore, TMA suggests to doctors that they lobby their patients on bills the TMA deems important. Its Web site offers physicians supplies of political posters, lapel stickers, and cards to pass out to "staff, patients, family and friends." It allies itself with other interest groups, joining forces with business tort reformers and even cooperating with its traditional rival, the Texas Trial Lawyers Association, on some lobbying efforts when the interests of doctors and lawyers ran parallel in 2001. Most important, it jumped on the bandwagon of history, allying itself with the Republican Party just as the GOP was poised to take over Texas politics.

As a result, the TMA is now one of the most effective political interest groups in the Lone Star State. According to the association's figures, it has succeeded in passing as much as 90 percent of the legislative agenda items it has sponsored. In 1999, it successfully persuaded the legislature to pass a law exempting doctors from antitrust laws and permitting them to negotiate fees and policies with health maintenance organizations (HMOs). This accomplishment was particularly noteworthy because the HMO bill was opposed by business and insurance companies, traditional stalwarts of the Republican Party.

Doctors have been similarly effective in exerting their influence over the courts. According to the consumer group Court Watch, doctors and hospitals won 86 percent of their cases before the Texas Supreme Court from 1994 to 1999—the highest success rate of any interest group.

The TMA has not always been perfect in its political choices, however. After the 2001 legislature, when Governor Perry vetoed a bill requiring HMOs to pay medical claims promptly, doctors were furious. In retaliation, the group endorsed Democratic gubernatorial candidate Tony Sanchez in 2002. Perry's big victory (see Chapter 5) introduced considerable awkwardness between the governor and the association, and the TMA had to mend its fences. It fired its chief political strategist and began giving even more money to Texas politicians, especially the governor. These efforts were successful. When Governor Perry staged a public signing of a new "prompt-pay bill" in June 2003, he was flanked in front of the news cameras by the TMA's board of directors. Perry made it clear he wanted bygones to be bygones. "Whether it's doctors or hospital administrators or any of a host of other individuals who are involved in the delivery of health care in Texas, we are very much open to bringing them back into the tent, so to speak," said the governor.

During the 2006 special session of the legislature, in which elected leaders labored under an ultimatum from the state supreme court (see Chapters 6 and 7), the TMA worked to lessen the impact of the proposed new business tax. As the organization informed its members on its Web site shortly after the close of the session,

> The tax bill that is on its way to Governor Perry's desk will impose new taxes on businesses in the service industry, including many physician practices in Texas. Thanks to the efforts of the Texas Medical Association . . . however, those taxes will not be nearly as onerous as they could have been. For many specialists . . . the tax savings will be $1,000 or more.[28]

Taxes that doctors do not have to pay, of course, must be paid by someone else, either in a positive sense—other industries must shell out more to make up the difference—or in a negative sense—citizens must do without some government service that otherwise would have been provided. The changes in the 2006 tax bill are thus a measure of the TMA's lobbying clout in relation to other interests.

And so the Texas Medical Association, having strayed from the majority party coalition, has now bought its way back in. Thus do many interest groups acquire influence in Texas.

## LAWYERS

As Texans for Lawsuit Reform and the Texas Medical Association are good examples of interest groups that have risen in importance, the Texas Trial Lawyers Association is the premier example of an interest group that has declined.

Like other occupational groups, attorneys have interests.[29] Lawyers have a great advantage not available to the members of other occupations, however: Many legislators and all major court judges share their profession. Lawyers therefore have an automatic advantage in arguing their positions on public policy to legislatures or courts, as they will frequently be addressing people with similar values and point of view.

For this reason, combined with the customarily generous political giving of its members, the Texas Trial Lawyers Association was for a long time a powerful force in the state's politics. Until the late 1980s, the association was able to block all legislation that threatened the income of attorneys. As mentioned, in 1969, against the opposition of doctors, the TTLA dominated efforts to reform the workers' compensation system in Texas, thereby preserving it as a fountain of employment for its members.

By the 1990s, however, the TTLA's influence was on the wane. Attorneys were a traditional part of the Texas Democratic Party's coalition, and their power declined with their party's. On the other hand, business, the traditional ally of the Republican Party, grew in power as the GOP's star ascended in Texas. In the 1995 legislature, business made a determined push to overhaul the state's tort system. Tort reform is an excellent example of an issue that pits well-organized, well-funded groups against each other. People in business, and doctors, hate such lawsuits because of their costs in time, legal fees, and sometimes punitive damages, while lawyers love them because they constitute the stuff of their livelihood. Thus the TTLA, along with many Democratic representatives and many consumer groups, fought tort reform.

But Republican Governor George Bush, riding a tremendous national and state victory by his party in the 1994 elections and aided by wealthy pro-business interest groups such as Texans for Lawsuit Reform, pushed through important changes in Texas's tort laws. These made it more difficult to win punitive damages against a business, lowered the maximum amount of damages that could be awarded, decreased the percentage of an award that one company among many defendants could be forced to pay, limited the ability of attorneys to "shop around" for a sympathetic judge, and made other similar changes.

As Democrats have retreated into an embattled minority, the TTLA has fought ineffectively to reverse their fortunes and its own. In 1997 and 2003, the legislature limited lawsuits even more. Democratic officials have been swept from statewide office and lost their majorities in both houses of the legislature.

Republican candidates now routinely run against "greedy trial lawyers" as much as their Democratic opponents. Lawyers have found themselves so unpopular that they have become a stealth interest group, using their money to finance more respectable spokespeople while keeping themselves invisible. During the 1997 session, when lawyers backed a bill to allow medical malpractice claims against health maintenance organizations, they supported it furtively, almost secretly.

Similarly, during a fight over Proposition 12—which capped maximum medical malpractice awards at $750,000—in 2003, lawyers' contributions financed the "Save Texas Courts" campaign that urged citizens to vote against the proposition, but lawyers were nowhere to be seen or heard in the public controversy. Business in general, and doctors in particular, were just as generous in supporting the "Yes on 12" campaign, but did not feel the need to conceal their participation. In fact, much of the pro-12 advertising consisted of contrasting symbolic images of doctors (who presumably enjoy high public esteem) with symbolic images of lawyers (who are proverbially seen by the public as sharks).

In the end, Proposition 12 squeaked to passage by a 51-to-49 percent margin. The voter turnout of 12 percent of the state's registered voters was high for a special election, and suggested that all the expensive campaigning had spurred unusual interest among Texas's citizens.[30] The outcome suggested that attorneys were almost as unpopular with the public as they had become in the legislature.

The Texas Trial Lawyers Association therefore looks to be a giant in eclipse. Unless the Democratic Party finds a way to reverse its decline in public support, the attorney's organization faces a hard future.

## THE CHRISTIAN RIGHT

In the late 1970s, a number of national organizations arose, calling for a return to "Christian values," as they defined them, in American government and in society.[31] The groups' purposes were to inform religious, politically conservative voters of a candidate's positions on certain issues and to persuade them to participate more actively in local politics. By the 1990s, these groups were a formidable presence at virtually every level of American politics. They have been especially important in the South.

Although Christian Right groups do not all place the same emphasis on each individual issue, they share a cluster of strongly conservative positions on important political issues. As Texan Tom DeLay, Republican former majority leader of the U.S. House of Representatives (and discussed earlier in this chapter), told an interviewer in 1999, the choices facing the United States are, "Will this country accept the worldview of humanism, materialism, sexism, naturalism, postmodernism, or any of the other 'isms'? Or will we march forward with a biblical worldview, a worldview that says God is our creator, that man is a sinner, and that we will save the country by changing the hearts and minds of Americans?"[32] Members of the Christian Right understand "a biblical worldview" to require them to be pro-life on the abortion issue, to oppose homosexual marriage, to fight against tax policies they view as subversive to families, to support school vouchers allowing public money to fund private schools, and to endorse a constitutional amendment that would permit organized prayers in public schools.

During the 1990s, the Christian Right made a vivid impact on Texas politics and society. Whereas the power of such interest groups as Texans for Lawsuit Reform rests on their ability to provide large quantities of money to campaigns, the power of the Christian Right rests on its ability to strongly influence the voting decisions of millions of citizens and to mobilize thousands of activists to capture control of political organizations at the grass roots. Members of the Christian Right are concerned citizens in the best sense, organizing to pursue the public interest as they understand it.

The most dramatic flexing of the Texas Christian Right's muscles occurred in its capturing of the state Republican Party machinery in 1994 and its domination of the GOP's conventions through 2006. These events are discussed in detail in the next chapter.

The 2007 legislature offered a good opportunity for observing the reach, and the limits, of Christian right influence in Texas politics.[33] When Governor Perry issued an executive order providing for public schools to vaccinate young women for HPV, a sexually transmitted virus that sometimes causes cervical cancer, social conservatives objected. They believed that knowing that they were protected against the virus would encourage young women to engage in premarital sexual activity. Christian Rightists persuaded their Republican allies in the legislature to pass a law overturning the governor's order.

Another successful bill sponsored by the representatives of the Christian right doubled the cost of a marriage license, to $60, unless the intending couple took an eight-hour marriage counseling course. In a third victory for the movement, the house and senate passed rules that will result in posting the motto "In God We Trust" in their chambers.

The Christian Right did not get everything it wanted from the 2007 legislature, however. A bill that would have forced state high schools to offer elective courses on the Bible was amended to make the offering optional. Another bill that would have banned funding for stem cell research—which Christian conservatives believe to be experimentation on an unborn child—did not pass. A third bill, introduced in the senate, which would have had the state pay pregnant women planning to have an abortion $500 if they instead had the baby and then gave it up for adoption, never made it out of committee.

In general, the 2007 session showed that the Christian Right was still very powerful, but not absolutely dominant, in Texas politics. In particular, conservative Christians appear to be the most successful when they advocate symbolic actions that do not attack anyone else's interests—posting "In God We Trust" in the legislative chambers, for example. They appear to have more trouble when they try to influence state policy to take a direction that impinges on other interests, especially when those interests are part of the Republican Party coalition. For example, business interests often support stem cell research, because it brings science-based industry, and federal research money, into the state. When the Christian Right attempted to ban state funding of such research, they came up against another powerful part of their own coalition.

Because the future promises to supply many examples of both kinds of issues, the Christian Right is certain to be active in state politics for many years to come.

# THE OIL AND GAS INDUSTRY

As befitting its historical status as the most important sector in the Texas economy, the oil and gas industry has a close working relationship with state government and is well represented by several interest groups. Principal among these are the Texas Oil and Gas Association (TOGA), which represents the industry as a whole but is dominated by the large producers, and the Texas Independent Producers and Royalty Owners (TIPRO), which is dominated by the smaller producers and royalty owners.

TOGA, TIPRO, and other groups keep track of the voting records of members of the legislature, contribute generously to the campaigns of representatives who are friendly to their interests, and are tireless in providing information to the legislative staff on conditions within the industry. Because oil and gas production is widely distributed within the state, and oil and gas business offices are even more widely distributed, petroleum's interest groups have a great deal of influence over a large majority of legislators, whether they are liberal or conservative on other issues.

This influence was demonstrated in the 1999 legislative session. Reacting to a depression in the business caused by a slump in worldwide oil prices, lawmakers passed a law giving small producers a $45 million tax break. Critics pointed out that world copper prices were also depressed, but the legislature did not offer tax relief to the small copper industry in the El Paso area. Copper simply did not have the organizational or financial clout of petroleum in Texas.[34] As the world price of oil trended upward in 2005 and 2006 the Texas petroleum industry experienced boom times and had no more need of special help from the state legislature. Oil politics were therefore quiet. Nevertheless, TOGA and TIPRO will continue to be powerful groups in state government for many years to come.

# ORGANIZED LABOR

Many Texans think of organized labor as a powerful interest group that has great influence on state policy, but there is little evidence to support this assumption. The primary explanation for this lack of power is cultural. As discussed in Chapter One, the conservative political culture that dominates most of the southern states is hostile to labor unions. Texas is no exception. In 2005, 12.5 percent of the national workforce was enrolled in labor unions, but only 6.2 percent of the Texas workforce. Forty-three states had a higher proportion of their workers unionized. Texas had fewer than one-fourth as many union members as New York, despite having nearly 1.5 million more wage and salary employees.[35]

Politically, unions have traditionally allied themselves with the Democratic Party nationally and with the liberal wing of that party within the state. But the relative weakness of liberals in Texas has meant that labor unions are even less powerful than their membership figures would suggest. Their weakness is reflected in the relatively anti-labor nature of Texas's laws. Workers' compensation insurance, unemployment insurance payments, and other benefits are lower than those of most other industrial states, and the laws regarding unions are restrictive rather than supportive. Unions are forced to make public disclosure of virtually all their major activities. This is not, of course, true of corporations. There are prohibitions against secondary boycotts, check-off systems for union dues, and mass picketing and other such activities, and the "right-to-work" law prohibits the closed shop and the union shop.[36] In addition to these debilitating regulations on organized labor in the private sector, Texas joins Georgia as the state with the most restrictive legislation dealing with public sector unions.

Organized labor would like nothing better than to get rid of this array of restrictions, but it lacks the political power to do so. Although the state umbrella labor group, the American Federation of Labor-Congress of Industrial Organizations (AFL-CIO) political action committee, puts money into political races, the rise of the traditionally pro-management, anti-labor Republican Party to unchallenged power has given the workers' organization a set of discouraging alternatives: It can continue to give money to Democrats, who lose continuously, or it can give money to Republicans, who will, once elected, vote against its interests anyway.

The year 2003 was a good one in which to observe the futility of labor's political efforts in Texas. The AFL-CIO put its energies into three political causes. It tried to dissuade the legislature from passing a bill that would increase the governor's power and reorganize much of the state bureaucracy (see Chapter 9). It opposed the drawing of new redistricting maps that would favor Republican candidates for the U.S. House of Representatives (see Chapter 6). And it joined the coalition attempting to persuade voters to defeat Proposition 12, discussed earlier. Its defeat in each campaign simply underscored its ongoing irrelevance to the state's politics.

Nationally, organized labor made a political comeback in 2006. The Democrats won both houses of Congress with a strong push from the national AFL-CIO and its allied unions. Union citizens comprised 5.6 million of the 6.8-million vote margin enjoyed by Democratic candidates. As a result, labor looked to have much more influence over national policymaking in 2007 and 2008.[37] In Texas, however, with Republicans staying firmly in control of the state political machinery, organized labor could only anticipate continuing futility.

# LEAGUE OF UNITED LATIN AMERICAN CITIZENS

The most venerable of the Hispanic organizations, the League of United Latin American Citizens (LULAC), was formed in Corpus Christi in 1929.[38] Its founding members were much concerned about discrimination against Mexican Americans, especially in public education. In its first three decades, LULAC pursued the goal of equal education as both a private charitable organization and a public crusader. Privately, LULAC formed local self-help organizations to advance Latino education. Its "Little School of the 400" program of the 1950s, for example, which taught Spanish-speaking preschoolers the 400 English words they needed to know in order to survive in first grade in public schools, was so successful it inspired the national program Head Start. Publicly, the organization persuaded the U.S. Supreme Court to forbid Texas to segregate Mexican Americans in public schools in 1948.

Branching out to other issues, in 1953 LULAC won another suit against Texas's practice of excluding Mexican Americans from juries. Then, in 1959, it persuaded the state legislature to sponsor its program to teach Latino preschoolers English. Soon the Texas Education Agency was paying up to 80 percent of the program's funding. LULAC may have represented a struggling minority, but it had become part of the state's political establishment; it was a success.

Into the 1970s, LULAC continued to be the standard bearer for Mexican American aspirations for full citizenship in the United States in general and Texas in particular. But in that decade, it began to falter. As an organization dispensing millions of dollars in foundation grants, it attracted members who were more interested in advancing themselves than in advancing their ethnic group. Beginning in the mid-1970s, LULAC was rocked by a series of financial scandals. The worst of these occurred in 1994, when the president, José Velez, together with three Taiwanese gangsters, was indicted by a federal grand jury on charges of collecting millions of dollars in a scheme to smuggle Asians and Hispanics into the United States illegally. Not only was the organization troubled by scandal during the 1990s, but it was also racked by internal power struggles. Individuals and different Latino groups fought each other—Mexican Americans versus Puerto Ricans, for example—so that the organization no longer seemed to be a league of *united* Latin American citizens.

The cumulative effect of LULAC's troubles had a devastating effect on its prestige and membership. Once capable of mobilizing a quarter of a million citizens nationally, by the late 1990s, the organization could count on no more than 50,000 active members. At its 1999 national convention in Corpus Christi, there were few people in the audience for its workshops and fewer corporate sponsors. Whereas, in 1987, eight national presidential candidates had addressed its delegates, not a single one showed up in 1999. Younger, better-run organizations such as La Raza and the Mexican-American Legal Defense Fund (MALDEF—created by LULAC itself in 1968) seemed to be on the verge of taking over the mantle of most respected Hispanic organization.

But LULAC is on its way back. Even while the leadership was faltering, the grass-roots activists who worked in its local chapters always comprised a reservoir of good citizenship, available for mobilization. During the late 1990s and early 2000s, several honest and competent presidents put the organization's finances in order and then expanded and reorganized its staff.

Just as important, LULAC's leadership has been engaging in creative political activity. It has forged a political alliance with the most respected African American organization, the NAACP. In July 2002, LULAC's president, Hector Flores, addressed the NAACP's national convention, the first time a person in his position had given a speech to that organization. His remarks cemented an agreement of cooperation that had been working for a year, featuring a joint and bilingual voter mobilization project. LULAC was also exploring alliances with non-minority but liberal groups. During the early and middle years of the twenty-first century, the organization was attempting to create partnerships with others concerned with the environment, women's issues, and police-community relations.

LULAC's leadership was also pursuing an evident strategy of speaking out on general issues of social justice, without caring too much about their specific relevance to Latinos. For example, the organization held a panel discussion on child labor during its seventy-fourth annual convention in 2003. The same year, its national president, Hector Flores, lobbied Congress not to pass President George W. Bush's proposed tax cuts (they passed despite his efforts). During the 2003 Texas legislative session, the state organization brought busloads of high school seniors to Austin to try to persuade representatives not to cut funding for higher education (these measures also passed despite the students' lobbying).

In 2005, the Texas state LULAC organization threw its support behind Congressional ratification of the Central American Free Trade agreement (it passed, early the next year).

LULAC's leadership thus seems to have broadened its focus and thereby revitalized the organization. The path of the future for LULAC appears to lie in an expansion of its purposes from advocacy of the interests of Latin Americans in particular to advocacy of liberal causes in general. Whatever the success of this strategy, the organization seems to have regained its vigor.

## TEACHERS

*Fundamentally Democrat*

In a 2002 ranking of the forty most successful interest groups in the fifty states, two political scientists judged teachers to be the second most influential after business.[39] Teachers do not, like business, possess the resource of wealth, for nowhere are they very well paid. Instead, teachers resemble the Christian Right in illustrating the power that can come from use of another resource: organization. In some states, a high percentage of public school teachers belong to a union or some other advocacy organization, and many belong to several. Teachers can usually be counted on to march, rally, write letters, contribute to political action

**TABLE 3-5**

## Comparison of Four Largest Texas Teacher Organizations, 2000 and 2006

**TSTA:** Texas State Teachers Association (Affiliated with National Education Association)
**TFT:** Texas Federation of Teachers (Affiliated with AFL-CIO)
**TCTA:** Texas Classroom Teachers Association
**ATPE:** Association of Texas Professional Educators

|  | TSTA | TFT | TCTA | ATPE |
|---|---|---|---|---|
| Membership, 2006 | 65,000 | 51,000 | 50,000 | 106,000 |
| Membership, 2000 | 80,000 | 85,000 | 40,000 | 110,000 |
| Endorses candidates? | Yes | Yes* | No | No |
| Supports pay raises? | Yes | Yes | Yes | Yes |
| Supports collective bargaining? | Yes | Yes | No | No |
| Supports publicly funded vouchers for private schools? | No | No | No | No |
| Lobbies legislature? | Yes | Yes | Yes | Yes |

*Indirectly, through a political action committee.

SOURCE: Compiled by David Prindle in August 2000 and October 2006 from organization Web sites and interviews with organization officers.

committees, and vote in an informed manner. It is because they are such good citizens, willing to put in the time and trouble to act together, that teachers are generally so effective in advancing their interests.

In Texas, however, the effectiveness of teacher participation is weakened by a number of cultural and political difficulties. The traditionalistic political culture that has been so important in Texas history has never been particularly friendly to public education, and the state generally places in the lower ranks of educational funding. In 2005, for example, it stood thirty-ninth among the states in spending per pupil, and thirty-second in average teacher salary.[40]

Politically, Texas's teachers are marked more by disorganization and competition than by coordination and cooperation. Like Texas's other white-collar workers, many of the state's teachers resist unionization, and many belong to no professional organization. As Table 3-5 illustrates, the membership of three of the four largest organizations declined noticeably in the period from 2000 to 2006. Those teachers who are members of organizations are divided among seven statewide and dozens of local groups, all fiercely competitive and sometimes recommending different strategies to their members.

Moreover, teachers share with lawyers the current disadvantage of being members of the Democratic Party coalition. This problem does not arise only from a mistake in coalition building. A high percentage of teachers are ideologically liberal (see Chapter 4). They have become a favorite rhetorical target of conservatives, who love to blame teachers for the poor quality of some American schools and blame teachers' unions for opposing some of the conservatives' favorite proposed reforms, especially school vouchers. The teachers organizations are therefore fundamentally at odds with the state's current power structure.

As Eric Hartman, legislative director for the Texas Federation of Teachers, told a reporter after the 2003 legislative session, "We're getting tired of this 'kick-the-teacher' legislation."[41] Similarly, Mary Ann Whiteker, president of the Texas Association of Mid-Size Schools, remarked to another reporter in 2005 that "The difficult thing is not to take this personally. You just walk through the Capitol thinking, 'Why do they hate me so much?' "[42] Therefore, when teachers' lobbyists attempt to persuade Texas legislators to back their policy proposals, they tend to get a mixed reception. They start from a position of weakness but can manage to make some headway by using information intelligently and by reminding politicians, however tacitly, that teachers are knowledgeable voters.

The actions of the legislature during the 2006 special session illustrate the equivocal influence of teachers' organizations. On the one hand, as part of House Bill 1, the education-finance law passed under threat of a judicial takeover of the schools, legislators gave all public-school teachers a raise of $2500. On the other hand, teachers are deeply suspicious of the general law (discussed in Chapter 11), believing that it will be financially destructive in the long run, and that it forces teachers to place too much emphasis on standardized testing. As Donna New Haschke, president of the Texas State Teachers Association, wrote in the organization's magazine, HB 1 is

a school finance fix almost certain to become a long-term headache for Texas schools . . . Obviously, the folks who wrote House Bill 1 haven't spent much time in a classroom.[43]

Teachers groups are therefore in a dangerous but not necessarily fatal political environment in modern Texas. They face difficult obstacles, some of their own making, but they also possess important political resources that they often use skillfully.

# Conclusion

Political interest groups present a dilemma to partisans of democratic government. By giving people a channel of input to government in addition to the one vote possessed by each citizen, such groups broaden and intensify the people's participation and are therefore good for democracy. But by creating a means by which some individuals can be much more influential than others, these groups often allow private perspectives to dominate public policymaking and are therefore bad for democracy. In Texas, where interest groups are powerful, the negative qualities of the interest-group system often dominate.

## Summary

Interest groups are very influential in American and Texas politics because they provide two indispensable ingredients: money and information. Groups are active in every

**Ben Sargent laments the fact that interest groups with many resources, especially those representing business, have disproportionate influence over politicians.**

*Courtesy of Ben Sargent.*

phase of politics: They engage in electioneering, lobby government officials, co-opt agencies, litigate in the courts, and attempt to persuade the public to support their point of view. Private interests thus frequently dominate the making of Texas public policy.

Although many efforts have been made to regulate lobbying, the results have not been encouraging. The Texas political system provides a friendly setting for maximizing interest-group influence. The most powerful groups tend to be those that represent major economic interests and especially those that have allied themselves with the dominant Republican Party. Groups that are traditional allies of the Democrats have fared less well.

Interest groups are good for democracy in that they enhance debate about public policy and encourage citizens to participate in politics. But they also damage democratic government by substituting private influence for public deliberation in the creation of government policy. Interest groups are powerful in Texas, where the negative qualities of the interest-group system often dominate.

## Glossary Terms

co-optation                     political action committee
interest group                  political interest group
lobby                           revolving door
lobbyist

## Study Questions

1. What is meant by the terms interest group, lobby, and lobbyist? Are interest groups and lobbies the same thing? If you write a letter to your legislator, are you lobbying?

2. What functions do interest groups perform? How do they perform them?

3. From the perspective of democratic theory, what is good and what is bad about the power of interest groups in Texas?

4. What general point is illustrated by the story of Jeff Wentworth and the Texas Bicycle Coalition? What point is illustrated by the story of Texans for a Republican Majority?

5. What interests tend to be organized? What is the difference in political influence between organized and unorganized groups?

6. How can an interest group attempt to influence public opinion? What is good and what is bad about such efforts?

7. Why are teachers, lawyers, and organized labor generally less influential in Texas politics of the 2000s? Why are Texans for Lawsuit Reform, doctors, and the oil and gas industry generally more effective?

## Surfing the Web

Readers are urged to visit the companion site for this book:

**http://academic.cengage.com/polsci/Kraemer/TexasPolitics10e**

# Political Parties

**4**

*The Houston skyline and a cowboy in rural Texas symbolize the vast differences in life styles that political parties must try to bridge.*

The political parties created democracy and modern democracy is unthinkable save in terms of the parties . . . The parties are not therefore merely appendages of modern government; they are the center of it and play a determinative and creative role in it.

E. E. SCHATTSCHNEIDER, *PARTY GOVERNMENT*, 1942

A political party is an organization that takes money from the rich and votes from the poor under the pretext of protecting the one from the other.

ANONYMOUS

# Introduction

Both Schattschneider's favorable assessment of **political parties** and the anonymous cynical disparagement of their value are justified. Parties are, indeed, the only organizations capable of holding together many fractious interests so that governing is possible. At the same time, in Texas and elsewhere, parties frequently serve democracy badly.

This chapter opens with a discussion of ideology and interests, the two bases for much party conflict. It proceeds to a brief history of the state's political parties, an examination of the major functions of parties, and an outline of party organization in Texas. The "four-faction system" that has recently emerged, and which can make the Texas two-party system confusing, is then explained, followed by a discussion of the state's occasional third-party efforts. At several points, the reality of Texas's party politics is contrasted with the democratic ideal.

# Ideology

In Texas as elsewhere, party rivalry is often based on differences in ideology. **Ideology** is a system of beliefs and values about the nature of the good life and the good society, about the relationship of government and the economy, about moral values and the way they should be achieved, and about how government is to conduct itself. The two dominant, and contesting, systems of beliefs and values in American and Texas life today are usually referred to as "liberalism" and "conservatism."

## CONSERVATISM

*Free enterprise*

The basic principle underlying **conservatism**, at least in economic policy, is laissez faire. In theory, conservatives prefer to allow free markets, not government, to regulate the economy. In practice, conservative governments often pursue **pseudo laissez faire** in that they claim to cherish free markets but actually endorse policies that deeply involve government in helping business to overcome problems in the marketplace. Nevertheless, at the level of ideology, and certainly at the level of their argument with liberals, conservatives believe that economies run best if governments leave them alone. When contemplating economic problems such as poverty, pollution, unemployment, or healthcare, conservatives argue that government has caused most of them through over-regulation and that the best way to deal with them is for government to stop meddling and allow the market to work. For example, local land developers don't want a city to tell them how high a sign should be or what kind of landscaping is required to hide ugly buildings or old junk cars. It is common to speak of conservatives as being on the "right wing" of the political continuum.[1]

## LIBERALISM

**Liberalism** is the contrary ideology. Liberals are suspicious of the workings of unregulated markets and place more faith in the ability of government to direct economic activity. When thinking about economic problems, they are apt to blame "market failure" and suggest government activity as the solution. To continue the development example used with conservatism, a liberal would want a city government to protect the environment and would work for sign ordinances and landscaping policies. It is common to speak of liberals as being on the "left wing" of the political spectrum.

All this is relatively clear. When dealing with issues of personal belief and behavior, such as religion, sexual activity, or drug use, however, liberals and conservatives often switch sides. Conservatives are generally in favor of more government regulation; liberals are in favor of less. Liberals oppose prayer in school, whereas conservatives favor it; liberals oppose laws regulating sexual behavior, whereas conservatives endorse them; and so on. An exception to this rule would be the issue of private gun ownership. Conservatives generally want less regulation of guns; liberals want more.

Finally, on foreign policy issues, liberals and conservatives tend to follow partisan rather than ideological cues. That is, liberals tend to endorse whatever a

Democratic president wants to do and oppose the wishes of a Republican president, while conservatives support Republicans and oppose Democrats.

Since the 1960s, there has been a slight tendency among liberals to emphasize "human rights" in foreign policy and a slight tendency among conservatives to emphasize military force, but these long-term positions are easily scrambled by short-term partisan struggle. For example, liberals generally supported, and conservatives generally opposed, Democratic President Bill Clinton's air attack on Iraq in 1998, but liberals generally opposed, and conservatives generally supported, Republican President George W. Bush's ground invasion of the same country in 2003.

In summary, American ideological arguments are often confusing because liberals usually favor government activity in the economic sphere but oppose it in the personal sphere, whereas conservatives usually oppose government activity in the economic sphere but favor it in the personal sphere. Confusing or not, this ideological split is the basis for a great deal of rhetorical argument and many intense struggles over public policy (see Table 4-1).

## IDEOLOGY IN TEXAS

As discussed in Chapter One, Texas has historically been dominated by a combination of the traditionalistic and individualistic political cultures. The particular mix of those cultures within the state has generally produced an ideology that has been hostile to government activity in general and especially in regard to providing help for society's poorer and less educated citizens. The basic attitudes associated with cultural values have thus translated, in the Texas case, into an ideology of political conservatism.

The distribution of opinion in the present-day population suggests that, when it comes to ideology, not much has changed in Texas since frontier days. A survey conducted in 2006 reported that only 14 percent of Texas adults were willing to label themselves liberals, while 32 percent called themselves moderates, and 49 percent claimed the label "conservative."[2] The meaning of these simple self-reports is not completely clear because, by calling themselves conservative, people might be referring to economic issues, social issues, foreign policy issues, or all three. Moreover, national public opinion research over many years has shown that a significant percentage of American citizens label themselves conservative in general but endorse many specific liberal government domestic programs. Still, the self-reported percentages are sufficiently dramatic to emphasize the weakness of the liberal ideological tradition in the Lone Star State.

In Texas as elsewhere, the contradictory nature of political ideologies—sometimes recommending government activity, sometimes opposing it, and not always in a logically coherent manner—often makes the arguments of politicians and journalists difficult to understand. Nevertheless, ideologies form the basis for much of the party battle. In general, the Democratic Party is controlled nationally by liberals, and the Republican Party is controlled by conservatives. In Texas, however, the picture is more complicated. Both common observation and scholarly research lead to the conclusion that, historically, both the Democratic and Republican Parties in Texas have been unusually conservative.[3] The Democrats are more liberal because they, unlike the Republicans, harbor a large and active liberal faction. To understand how this situation has come about, it is helpful to have some knowledge of the way ideologies are learned and of the history of Texas as a southern state.

## TABLE 4-1
## Policy Differences between Liberals and Conservatives

| Issue | Conservative Position | Liberal Position |
|---|---|---|
| **Economic Issues** | | |
| Taxation | As little as possible, and when necessary, regressive taxes such as sales taxes* | More to cover government spending; progressive preferred* |
| Government spending | As little as possible, except for military and anti-terrorism | Acceptable to provide social services or homeland security |
| Nature of government regulation | More in personal sphere; less in economic | Less in personal sphere; more in economic |
| Organized labor | Anti-union | Pro-union |
| Environment | Favors development over environment | Favors environment over development |
| **Social Issues** | | |
| Crime | Supports more prisons and longer sentences; opposes gun control | Favors social policies to attack root causes; favors gun control |
| Abortion | Pro-life | Pro-choice |
| Affirmative action | Opposes | Supports |
| Prayer in public schools | Favors | Opposes |
| Homosexual marriage | Opposes | Favors |
| **Foreign Policy Issues** | | |
| Human rights as large component of foreign policy | No, although the "Bush Doctrine" favors democracy | Yes |
| Free trade | More likely to favor | Less likely to favor |
| Military spending | More | Less |
| U.S. military intervention abroad | More likely to favor** | Less likely to favor** |

* A progressive tax is one that increases proportionally with income or benefit derived, such as a progressive income tax. A regressive tax, such as the sales tax, is a flat rate—the same for everyone. It is termed "regressive" because it places proportionately less of a burden on wealthy taxpayers and more of a burden on those with lower incomes.
**However, liberals tended to support the U.S./NATO bombing war against Serbia in 1999, while conservatives tended to oppose it; the ideologies reverted to form in regard to the invasion of Iraq in 2003.

NOTE: Two words of caution are in order. First, this table presents only a brief summary of complex issues, and thus, some distortion is inevitable. Second, it would be inaccurate to assume that every liberal agrees with every liberal position or that every conservative agrees with every conservative position. Even the most devout ideologues have inconsistencies in the beliefs and hitches in their logic.

# Political Socialization

As analyzed in Chapter One, the attitudes and values of the traditionalistic/individualistic political culture that dominates Texas results in ideological conservatism: a basic hostility to government action, pseudo laissez faire, social Darwinism, and the trickle-down theory of economics. How is this ideology perpetuated? How is it transmitted from one generation to another?

The process by which we teach and learn our political knowledge, beliefs, attitudes, values, and habits of behavior is called **political socialization**. In this process, we are influenced by many things—peer groups, political leaders, and a variety of experiences—but the basic agents of political socialization seem to be family, schools, churches, and the media. An extensive discussion of the process of socialization is beyond the scope of this book, but some attention should be paid to these four agents, particularly as they operate in Texas.

## FAMILY

The family is the most important agent of socialization. The first things a child learns are the basics: attitudes toward authority, others, oneself, and the community outside the family. Although scholarly studies of the process of political socialization in Texas are rare, it is fair to say that most parents in the state pass along their attitudes and philosophy to their children. Parents transfer political ideas along with religious beliefs and attitudes toward other people almost unconsciously as their children hear their conversations and observe their behavior throughout the many hours of association at home. As heirs to the Texas political culture, the attitudes most parents transmit to their children are conservative and antigovernment. By the time other social institutions begin to "teach" children consciously, they have already learned fundamental attitudes. For this reason, basic political orientations are difficult to alter, and the ideas of the population, in Texas as everywhere else, change only slowly.

## SCHOOLS AND CHURCHES

The public school system, and in some cases the churches, can be very influential in shaping political attitudes and beliefs. Again, the influence is strongly conservative.

Many Texans regularly attend religious services, and most houses of worship teach acceptance of religious theology, an acceptance that often spills over to include acceptance of prevailing social and political institutions as well. Among Whites, the religious establishment is probably more conservative than most, because the type of Protestantism that dominates Anglo religion in the state stresses the responsibility of individuals for their own fate rather than the communitarian (government) responsibility of everyone for everyone else.

Other religious traditions are also important in Texas, most notably Roman Catholicism among Mexican Americans. The Catholic Church has historically been more encouraging of government activity on behalf of society's underdogs than have Protestant churches. However, Protestantism, the dominant religion among the historically dominant social group, has been associated with attitudes that reinforce political conservatism.

The overall influence of churches, however, may not be as intense or pervasive as that of the public schools, where students spend six or more hours a day, five days a week, for up to twelve years. There is little indication that schools in Texas educate children about politics or encourage them to participate in the political process in any way other than voting.

The essence of politics is conflict, but Texas public education does not recognize this. Instead, the schoolchild is taught to value the free enterprise system but not to be aware of its potential deficiencies, to be patriotic, and to respect authority. The nature of politics is distorted. The child is educated to passivity rather than to democratic participation.

In the most thorough study of socialization by public schools in Texas, anthropologist Douglas Foley spent sixteen months in a small South Texas town (which he called "North Town") during 1973 and 1974; he then returned during the summers and some weekends in 1977, 1985, 1986, and 1987. After interviewing students, teachers, administrators, politicians, and townspeople, and observing many activities, including sporting events, classroom teaching, social dating, and ethnic confrontations, Foley came to definite conclusions about the sorts of ideas passed along by North Town's schools.

> After a year in North Town . . . I came to see that the school simply reflected the general conservatism of the community. The town's social and political environment did not demand or encourage a highly open, imaginative, critical curriculum. North Towners did not want their children reading avant-garde literature or critiques of corporation polluters or revisionist accounts of President Johnson's political corruption. They wanted their schools to discipline and mold their children into hardworking, family-oriented, patriotic, mainstream citizens.[4]

North Town is only one small place in a big state, but Foley's conclusions are consistent with common observations about Texas schools in general. The conservatism he found in North Town, while not found in every classroom or every school district, is generally representative of Texas public education.

# MEDIA

As with other institutions in the state, most of the mass media in Texas are conservative. Most newspapers and TV and radio stations are profitable businesses that depend on other economic interests for their advertising revenues. Consequently, there is a tendency among the media to echo the business point of view on most issues. As Everett Collier, former editor of the *Houston Chronicle*, used to put it, "We are not here to rock the boat."[5]

In the two decades, a new media force has appeared on the political scene: talk radio. Its superstar, Rush Limbaugh, offered his listeners a mixture of energetic conservative argument, personal attack, misinformation, comedy, and egotism that has proven enormously popular. By the early 1990s, he was playing to an estimated radio audience of 20 million people each day and, according to surveys, was the main source of political news for 26 percent of the population, or almost 70 million.[6] Limbaugh's success spawned a host of imitators. The national and state airwaves are now full of talk-show hosts offering polemical analyses of public policy, almost all from the right-wing point of view.

★ ★ ★ ★ ★ ★ ★ ★ ★ ★ ★ ★ ★ ★ ★ ★ ★ ★ ★ ★ ★ ★ ★ ★ ★ ★ ★ ★ ★ ★

## *The Realities of Change*

While Texans continue to be strongly conservative in a political sense, their efforts to teach their children about social attitudes have undergone a major transformation since the 1960s. This evolution of socialization strategy is well illustrated by scholarly investigations of Texas history. As David Montejano documents, inculcating attitudes of Anglo superiority and Mexican American inferiority was an explicit part of the Texas socialization process during the nineteenth and first half of the twentieth centuries, impressed upon young people through laws, words, and political customs. Montejano writes of the system of practices he terms the "catechism of segregation," thusly: "This meaning was taught to them in countless lessons—the Mexican school was physically inferior, Mexican children were issued textbooks discarded by Anglo children, Mexican teams were not admitted to county athletic leagues, Mexican girls could not enter beauty contests, and so on." Such raw and ugly socialization is almost inconceivable today, except in a few small-town backwaters. Today, the conflicts between Anglos and Hispanics tend to be at the level of economic class, as illustrated by the fight over school funding begun by the 1987 *Edgewood* v. *Kirby* court decision discussed in Chapter Eleven. In terms of socialization, Texas schools now attempt to teach human equality, and history textbooks, starting at the elementary level, make a great effort to include all major ethnic groups in their subject matter.

★ ★ ★ ★ ★ ★ ★ ★ ★ ★ ★ ★ ★ ★ ★ ★ ★ ★ ★ ★ ★ ★ ★ ★ ★ ★ ★ ★ ★ ★

SOURCE: David Montejano, *Anglos and Mexicans in the Making of Texas*, 1836–1986 (Austin: University of Texas Press, 1987), 230, passim; an informal survey of Texas history textbooks conducted during the 1990s by David Prindle.

In the middle of the first decade of the new century liberals created their own radio network, "Air America," to compete with Limbaugh and his imitators. The new network struggled at first, suffering a dearth of sponsors and enduring organizational problems. Whether it will survive, and whether it will ever make a difference to Texas public opinion, are questions that cannot yet be answered. For the moment, therefore, there is no credible alternative to conservative radio in the Lone Star State.

## EVALUATION

After reviewing the socializing effects of families, schools, churches, and the media, one might wonder how any view other than the conservative ideology exists in Texas. It does exist, however, for several reasons: Some people adopt a personal point of view that is contrary to the opinion-molding forces around them; liberal families, churches, schoolteachers, and news outlets do exist in Texas, although they are in the minority; the national, as opposed to local, news media often display a liberal slant; and millions of non-Texans have moved to the state in the last few decades, bringing different political cultures with them. Political conservatism continues to dominate, but as the Texas population increases and becomes more diverse, the ideology is being challenged and modified by competing cultural values.

Ideology, however, is not the only basis for political party support. Equally important are people's interests and the way parties attempt to recruit citizen loyalty by endorsing those interests.

# Interests

An **interest** is something of value or some personal characteristic that people share and that is affected by government activity—their investments, their race, their jobs, and so on. When there is a question of public policy on which political parties take differing positions, people often line up behind the party favoring their interests, whether or not their political ideology is consistent with that party's. Moreover, parties often take positions that will attract the money and votes of citizens with clashing interests. Thus, parties put together **coalitions** of interests to attract blocs of voters and campaign contributions. Party positions are therefore almost always much more ambiguous and confusing than they would be if they were simply based on ideology.

For example, in recent years, Republican Party candidates in Texas have tended to criticize the state's tort laws—the statutes that allow people who believe that they have been injured by someone else to sue for damages. Republicans have argued that the state makes it too easy to file "frivolous" lawsuits and allows juries to award damages that are too large to injured parties. They have supported "tort reform" by the state legislature. On the other hand, Democrats have tended to side with plaintiffs in lawsuits, arguing that injured people should have easy access to the courts and should be entitled to large amounts of money as compensation for injuries. They have usually opposed tort reform.

As a result, the types of people who tend to be the target of tort lawsuits (doctors and business owners, for example) have been inclined to support Republican candidates. Those who tend to benefit from such suits (plaintiff's attorneys, for example) have tended to side with Democrats. This alignment has very little to do with ideology and a great deal to do with who gets what from government. (This subject is also discussed in Chapters 3 and 11.)

Not all interests are economic. Since the 1960s, for example, Mexican Americans and African Americans have tended to support the Democratic Party because they have perceived the Republicans as less tolerant of ethnic diversity.

Whether an interest arranges people in a politically relevant manner depends on what sorts of questions become issues of public policy.

Interests and ideologies tend to combine in different ways in different people, sometimes opposing and sometimes reinforcing one another. For example, a Latino doctor in Texas would be drawn to the Republicans by her professional interest and drawn to the Democrats by her ethnic interest. She might have had trouble making up her mind about how to vote in the 2006 election. On the other hand, an Anglo oil company executive or a Black labor union president would probably have experienced no such conflict. In each case, the citizen's personal ideology may either reinforce or contradict one or more of his or her interests. The way interests and ideologies blend and conflict, and interact with candidates and parties, is one of the things that makes politics complicated and interesting to study.

Interests thus help structure the party battle. They are politically important for other reasons as well. See Chapter Three for a detailed discussion of the organizing and lobbying efforts of interest groups.

## From Issue to Non-issue

Interests do not always follow party lines. Sometimes, they are "cross-cutting," that is, they create internal tensions within each major party. An example from contemporary political debate is the issue of illegal immigration. Both the Republican and Democratic parties contain large groups who favor major efforts to guard the southern border with Mexico more closely. Both parties, however, also contain large groups who oppose such enforcement efforts. When a cross-cutting issue surfaces in a legislature, the tensions within each party often result in paralysis.

The fate of the immigration issue in the 2007 Texas legislature is a good example. In October 2006 a group of social conservatives within the ruling Republican Party, the Texas Conservative Coalition Research Institute, published a report advocating stringent new anti-illegal-immigrant laws. Among their proposals were new laws denying birthright citizenship to children of undocumented immigrants, and penalizing employers who hired the undocumented. A group of Republicans was ready to pass such laws during the 2007 session.

But another group of major Republican campaign contributors represented industries that often employ undocumented Mexican immigrants. For example, Bob Perry, in home construction, and Lonny Pilgrim, in chicken processing, both run businesses that keep costs down by hiring these workers. Republican legislators responsive to such contributors made a coalition with the Mexican American Legislative Caucus, all of whose members are Democrats, to suppress the issue. Working together, these disparate groups managed to squelch the debate on immigration before it ever got started. The issue was not mentioned during the 2007 session.

★ ★ ★ ★ ★ ★ ★ ★ ★ ★ ★ ★ ★ ★ ★ ★ ★ ★ ★ ★ ★ ★ ★ ★ ★

SOURCE: Megan Headley, "Northward Ho! How the Immigration Debate Left Texas," *Texas Observer*, March 23, 2007, 12.

The partisan coalitions that have characterized recent Texas politics are summarized in Table 4-2. It is important to understand that not every person who has an interest agrees with every other person with the same interest, and so citizens who share interests are not unanimous in their partisan attachments. For example, although most of the people in the computer business who contributed large amounts to a political party during the 1990s and 2000s gave to the Republicans, not all did. Similarly, although the great majority of African American voters supported the Democrats, thousands did not. Table 4-2 describes how interests lean in general, not how every person with that interest behaves.

Politics would be fascinating enough if, once ideologies and interests had arranged themselves into a party coalition, they stayed that way. In fact, however, the party battle evolves as history changes the way people live. A hundred years ago, the Democratic Party was the more conservative party and dominated Texas almost completely. Today, the Republican Party is more conservative and has achieved at least temporary dominance over the Democrats.[7] It is not too much of an exaggeration to say that the history of Texas is written in the story of the two major parties.

## TABLE 4-2
### Interests Generally Supporting the Two Major Parties

| Type of Interest | Democrats | Republicans |
|---|---|---|
| Economic class | poor, lower middle | wealthy, upper middle |
| Economic structure | workers, esp. labor unions | management |
| Professions | plaintiff's attorneys, public employees | physicians, business entrepreneurs |
| Development vs. environment | environmentalists | developers, rural landowners |
| Industry | entertainment | oil and gas, computers |
| Ethnicity | African American, Mexican American | Anglo |
| Religion | Catholic, Jewish | Protestant, esp. evangelical |

# Texas Political Parties: A Brief History

Prior to joining the Union, Texas had no political parties. In the early days of settlement, the free spirits who came to Texas were happy to leave government and politics behind them. During the period of the Texas Republic (1836–1845), Texas politics was dominated by Sam Houston, the hero of the war for independence from Mexico. Although there were no political parties, pro-Houston and anti-Houston factions provided some discussion of public policy.

Texas entered the United States in 1845 as a slave state. Nationally, the Democrats were proslavery, while their opponents, the Whigs, ignored the issue. Moreover, the Democrats had endorsed the admission of Texas to the Union in the 1844 election, whereas the Whigs had waffled. Thus, most Texans were Democrats.

Party divisions became intense after the Civil War ended in 1865. The Republican administration of Abraham Lincoln had defeated the Confederacy, of which Texas was a member, and freed the slaves. Reconstruction, or federal government occupation, settled on all the southern states. White southerners found themselves under the rule of northerners, the military, and African Americans. Rightly or wrongly, they believed themselves to be subject to tyranny by a foreign conqueror. They identified this despotic occupation with the Republican Party. In this emotionally searing experience, southern politics of the next century was forged. The Democratic Party became the vehicle of southern resistance to northern domination and of White opposition to full citizenship for African Americans.

*[handwritten note in left margin:]* The republicans at the time were really more like the conservative democrats

As a result, when Reconstruction ended in 1874, Texas, like the other former members of the Confederacy, was a solid one-party Democratic state. It kept the **one-party system** until the 1970s, with telling effects on politics and public policy.

At the national level, the United States has a competitive two-party system. For example, between 1928 and 2004, the Republicans and Democrats each won ten presidential elections. Competitive party systems are characterized by a great deal of public dialogue between the parties. Although personal attacks are made and inaccurate statements are common, intelligent discussion and genuine debate also occur. Emerging groups of voters—African Americans, Latinos, and women, for example—and emerging issues such as the environment and abortion find receptive ears in one or more of the competitive parties. In this way, these concerns become known throughout the political system.

Citizens are relatively active in a two-party system, and voter turnouts are therefore fairly high. A one-party system is very different, and Texas furnished a good example in the first three quarters of the twentieth century. Because there was no "loyal opposition," elections were decided in the Democratic primary, and nominees usually ran unopposed in the November general election. The party label is the most important guide the American voter has at election time, but in Texas, it was of no value. Texas's voters usually had a choice of several candidates for each elective office, but they all ran as Democrats. There was some debate on public policy between liberal Democrats and conservative Democrats, but only a little.

Without party competition to foster debate and spur voter interest, most White citizens (in most areas of the state, minorities were prevented from voting) were apathetic, and voter turnout was very low. Candidates of all ideological persuasions, from Ku Klux Klansmen to liberals, ran as Democrats.

Traditional party functions such as recruiting, financing, and conducting campaigns were performed not by the party but by informal, unofficial organizations, campaign committees, and other groups. Voters were uninformed about these groups and knew little, if anything, about who controlled them or what their goals were.

One result was that when voters elected Democrats to the offices of governor, lieutenant governor, attorney general, treasurer, and so on, they were not sending a Democratic "team" to Austin. They were sending independent officials who were frequently rivals and had little in common except personal ambition and a Democratic label. The parties acted to emphasize, not overcome, the fragmentation of power created by the state constitution.

Under these conditions of splintered power, because there was no unified team, there was no unified program. Each politician went his or her own way. The act of holding together disparate interests, which is the basis for E. E. Schattschneider's praise of parties at the beginning of the chapter, was not performed.

In other words, one-party politics in Texas was really no-party politics. Instead of the vigorous debate and citizen involvement that characterize well-run democracies, confusion and apathy reigned.

The transition to two-party politics in Texas, as in most of the South, occurred gradually. Beginning in 1928, Texans sometimes voted for Republican presidential candidates. In 1961, Republican John Tower cracked the Democratic monopoly at the state level by winning a special election for a U.S. Senate seat. Republicans began to win a few local elections in Dallas and Houston soon thereafter, but conservative Democrats continued to dominate state politics into the 1970s.

In 1978, Bill Clements beat John Hill for the governorship and became Texas's first Republican governor in 104 years. But Clements could not win reelection in 1982, in spite of spending a record $13.2 million during his campaign.

Republican President Ronald Reagan's landslide reelection in 1984 seemed to have finally broken the Democrats' hold on Texas. Dozens of Republican candidates rode Reagan's coattails to victory in local elections, as did Phil Gramm, the Republican candidate for U.S. senator. Some of the local officeholders subsequently lost their reelection bids, but by then, Texas could no longer be considered a Democratic monopoly.

Seen against this historical background, the election of 1994 appears to be truly a watershed. Republicans defeated an incumbent Democratic governor, retained a second U.S. Senate seat, pulled almost even in the state Senate, and saw hundreds of local offices fall to their candidates.

By 2006, Texas could just barely be considered a two-party state. Every statewide elective official, including all eighteen members of the two top courts, was Republican, as were both U.S. senators and majorities in both houses of the state Legislature. Moreover, Texans gave decisive majorities of their major-party vote to Republican presidential candidates in 1992, 1996, 2000, and 2004. The last Democratic bastion—the party's slim majority in the state's thirty-two-member delegation to the U.S. House of Representatives—had been destroyed by the legislature's redistricting bill in 2003. If the voting trends of the past two decades continue, Texas might become as much a one-party state in the twenty-first century as it was in the twentieth but with a different party in command.

★ ★ ★ ★ ★ ★ ★ ★ ★ ★ ★ ★ ★ ★ ★ ★ ★ ★ ★ ★ ★ ★ ★ ★ ★ ★ ★ ★ ★ ★

## The Loyal Opposition

A different way of organizing party competition is found in Great Britain, where the minority party—the party out of power—is referred to as "the loyal opposition." Its leader is on the government payroll, and his or her function is to criticize the ruling party. This institutionalized opposition voice provides the British with an alternative perspective, competing policy choices, and the robust debate that is essential in making democratic government work. The system does not guarantee that British democracy never produces foolish choices, but when bad policies arise, they stem from some cause other than inadequate discussion.

★ ★ ★ ★ ★ ★ ★ ★ ★ ★ ★ ★ ★ ★ ★ ★ ★ ★ ★ ★ ★ ★ ★ ★ ★ ★ ★ ★ ★ ★

Table 4-3 displays the growth in the number of Republican officeholders in Texas from 1974 to 2006.

Patterns in Texas's voting history over the past two decades are underscored by public opinion research. In a survey taken in late 2004, 46 percent of the state's citizens described themselves as more-or-less regular supporters of Republicans, while only 36 percent were regular supporters of Democrats. Even if the 12 percent of the population who described themselves as independents chose to support Democratic candidates in a given election, those candidates would still not have a majority.[8]

Together, the voting and survey data suggest that, during the last two decades of the twentieth century, Texas went through a political **realignment**—a change in

**TABLE 4-3**
## Growth of Republican Officeholders in Texas

| Year | U.S. Senate | Other Statewide | U.S. House | Texas Senate | Texas House | Other | Total |
|------|-------------|-----------------|-----------|--------------|-------------|-------|-------|
| 1974 | 1 | 0 | 2 | 3 | 16 | 53 | 75 |
| 1982 | 1 | 0 | 5 | 5 | 36 | 270 | 317 |
| 1990 | 1 | 6 | 8 | 8 | 57 | 722 | 802 |
| 1994 | 2 | 13 | 11 | 14 | 61 | 958 | 1059 |
| 1998 | 2 | 27 | 13 | 16 | 72 | 1397 | 1527 |
| 2002 | 2 | 27 | 15 | 19 | 88 | 1815 | 1966 |
| 2004* | 2 | 27 | 21 | 19 | 87 | 2010 | 2166 |

* Republican officials declined to return numerous phone calls in 2006 and 2007 seeking to update these totals.

NOTE: Neither the Republican Party nor the Texas secretary of state keep track of the total number of electoral offices within Texas. As a result, it is impossible to express the above raw numbers in percentage terms.

SOURCE: Republican Party of Texas, October, 2005

the partisan identification (psychological affiliation resulting in a standing decision to vote for a given party)—of its citizens. Until the 1980s, enough Texans had adopted a standing decision to vote for Democrats that the party's candidates could count on winning most of the time. By the twenty-first century, however, enough Texans had changed their psychological affiliation so that Republicans were normally victorious in statewide, although not necessarily local, elections. Once solidly Democratic, Texas had realigned to be generally Republican.

The growth of two-party competition in Texas has been good for democracy. Instead of the confused jumble that characterized Texas politics when Texas was a one-party state, in recent years there has been robust debate between the parties on many issues of importance to the citizens. Whether the democratic dialogue can last if the Republicans continue their statewide dominance is another question.

The public debate is so loud because policy differences between the parties are quite substantial. Table 4-4 displays some summary statements from the state Democratic and Republican Party platforms of 2006. As the table illustrates, the differences between the activists who write these platforms are of two kinds. First, on some issues—for instance, abortion, the minimum wage, and labor unions—party activists are clearly and firmly on opposing sides. Second, the parties are concerned about different issues and therefore talk about different subjects. For example, the Republicans, but not the Democrats, talk about the right to gun ownership, whereas the Democrats are the only party to mention the responsibility of government to provide affordable childcare. And third, the parties occasionally agree completely on an issue. Both, for example, clearly oppose the Trans-Texas Corridor.

**TABLE 4-4**

## 2006 Texas State Political Party Platforms

| Issue | Republican | Democratic |
|-------|-----------|-----------|
| Abortion | We affirm our support for a human life amendment to the Constitution . . . We urge the reversal of *Roe* v. *Wade*. | Texas Democrats . . . trust the women of Texas to make personal and responsible decisions about when and whether to bear children. |
| Affirmative action | We oppose affirmative action. | Texas Democrats support innovative approaches to ensure diversity in every Texas institution of higher education. |
| Childcare | We oppose any government regulations that will adversely affect the availability, affordability, or the right of parents to choose childcare. | Texas Democrats support child care initiatives that will encourage the private sector and non-profit providers to expand the availability of quality child care programs. |
| Church and state | America is a Christian nation, founded on Judeo-Christian principles . . . We . . . oppose any governmental action to restrict, prohibit, or remove public display of the Decalogue or other religious symbols. | We believe . . . entangling government with religion is dangerous to both government and religion . . . we must never use the power of government at any level to impose our personal religious observances on others. |
| Environment | We oppose the Endangered Species Act. | We support the adoption, the immediate implementation, and the strong enforcement of clean air plans by State officials . . . the implementation of aggressive water conservation and reuse practices. |
| Evolution | We support the objective of teaching and equal treatment of scientific strengths and weaknesses of scientific theories, including Intelligent Design. | Not mentioned. |
| Guns | The Party calls on the Legislature and the Congress to . . . repeal all . . . laws . . . that infringe on the right to keep and bear arms. | Not mentioned. |
| Hate crimes | We urge the immediate repeal of the Hate Crimes Law. | Texas Democrats support . . . strong enforcement of the James Byrd, Jr. Memorial Hate Crimes Act. |
| Healthcare | We support market-based, private sector initiatives to improve the portability, quality and affordability of healthcare. | Texas Democrats support comprehensive reform to provide guaranteed access to affordable healthcare for all Texans. |
| Homosexual marriage | We believe that traditional marriage is a legal and moral commitment between a natural man and a natural woman. | Not mentioned. |

*(continued)*

**TABLE 4-4**

(*continued*)

| Issue | Republican | Democratic |
|---|---|---|
| Labor unions | An individual should have the freedom to work in the job he/she desires without being forced to join or pay dues to any organization. | All employees, public and private, must have the right to organize, collect dues . . . and negotiate collectively with their employers . . . (We support) the repeal of the Texas right to work law. |
| Minimum wage | We believe the Minimum Wage Law should be repealed. | We believe the minimum wage must be increased meaningfully to make up for lost purchasing power. |
| Public school vouchers | We encourage the Governor and the Texas Legislature to . . . allow maximum freedom of choice in public, private, or parochial education. | . . . many Republicans seek to siphon off public education funds for inequitable, unaccountable voucher and privatization schemes. . . |
| Stem cell research | We commend the President for banning most government funding of human embryo stem cell harvesting. | Texas Democrats strongly and unconditionally support research into stem cell therapies and state funding of research into stem cell therapies at state public universities. |
| Transportation | We urge the repeal of the Trans-Texas Corridor legislation. | We oppose the proposed Trans-Texas Corridor. |
| Welfare | We support welfare reforms designed to break the cycle of dependency by requiring welfare recipients to work. | Not mentioned. |

SOURCES: 2006 Democratic and Republican state platforms, downloaded from the state party Web sites.

# Functions of Political Parties

Following this summary of the history of the two parties in Texas and their ideological and interest bases, it would be helpful to list the useful tasks that parties can perform. From the perspective of activists and candidates, the basic purpose of parties is to win elections and thus gain the opportunity to exercise control over public policy. While pursuing this goal, however, they often fulfill several functions that make them valuable institutions from the perspective of democratic theory. These functions include:

- Involving ordinary people in the political process, especially persuading them to vote and teaching them the formal and informal "rules of the game"

- Recruiting political leaders and persuading them to restrain their individual ambitions so that the party can achieve its collective purposes

- Communicating to the leaders the interests of individuals and groups

- Adding factual information and persuasive argument to the public discussion of policy alternatives

- Structuring the nature of political conflict and debate, including screening out the demands of certain people and groups (usually fringe individuals or groups that represent very small minorities)

- Moderating differences between groups, both within the party and in the larger society

- Partially overcoming the fragmented nature of the political system so that gridlock can be overcome and coherent policy made and implemented

Political parties in any democracy can be judged according to how well or badly they perform these functions. How do Texas parties measure up?

# Party Organization

All parties are organizations, but they follow many different patterns of structure. In general, we can say that American parties, compared to those in foreign democracies, are weakly organized. They are not structured so that they can function easily as a cohesive team. The parties in Texas are especially weak in an organizational sense. As a result, they often do not perform the function of overcoming gridlock and making coherent policy very well, nor do they structure conflict to make it sensible to most ordinary citizens. A review of state party organization will suggest why this is so.

Figure 4-1 shows that in Texas, as in most states, parties are divided into a permanent organization and a temporary one. The **permanent party organization** consists of little more than a skeleton force of people who conduct the routine but essential business of the party. The party's primary purpose of winning elections requires far more people and much greater activity. The party comes alive in election years in the form of a **temporary party organization** geared to capturing power.

## THE TEMPORARY PARTY ORGANIZATION

The temporary party organization is focused on the spring primary and the fall general election. It attempts to choose attractive candidates and mobilize voters to support them.

In Texas, party membership is determined by the act of voting; there are no permanent political party rolls. When citizens vote in the Democratic Party primary, for example, they are considered "affiliated Democrats" until the end of the calendar year. They may vote only in the Democratic runoff, if there is one, and participate only in Democratic conventions. The next year, they may legally change their affiliation and participate in Republican Party activities.

### PRECINCT AND COUNTY CONVENTIONS

In the 254 counties of Texas, there are more than 6,000 precincts, each having from 50 to as many as 3,500 voters. Each voter is entitled to have a voice in choosing the precinct chairperson and proposing and voting on resolutions that will establish party policy, but voter participation in party affairs is low. Normally,

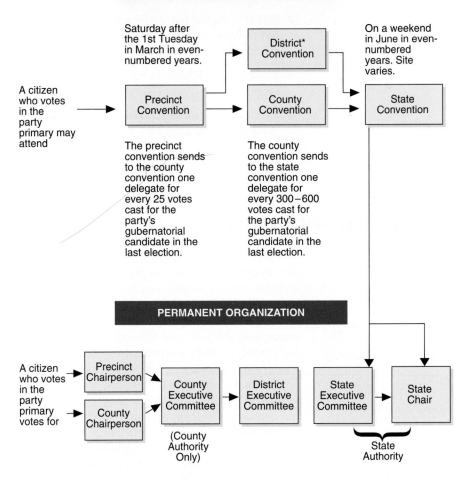

**FIGURE 4-1: Major Party Organization in Texas**

SOURCE: State Democratic and Republican headquarters.
*District conventions are held in counties with more than one senatorial district.

only a small fraction of those who vote in the primaries—who are themselves only a fraction of the total number of registered voters and a smaller fraction of the citizens of voting age—participate in conventions or other party affairs.

The main function of the precinct convention is to select delegates to the county convention, which is the next echelon of the temporary party organization.[9] The main function of the county convention is to select delegates to the state convention. Both precinct and county conventions can be either short or long, peaceful or filled with conflict, productive of resolutions or not.

## THE STATE CONVENTION

Both major parties hold their state conventions on a weekend in June during even-numbered years. The party state executive committee (SEC) decides when and where the convention is to be held. Depending on the year of the election cycle in which it occurs, the June convention performs some or all of the following activities:

1. It certifies to the secretary of state the party nominees for the general election in November.

2. It writes the party platform.

3. It selects the members of the SEC.

4. It names the Texas committeeman and committeewoman to the national party committee.

5. During presidential years, it selects the "at-large" delegates to the national party convention (who are not committed to supporting any particular candidate, as opposed to the "pledged" delegates who are sworn to support specific candidates and whose identity depends on the support candidates received in the March primary election).[10]

6. It selects a slate of presidential electors to serve in the national electoral college in the event the party's candidates for president and vice president win in Texas.

Party conventions have tended, over the past several decades, to travel in opposite directions—the Democrats from argument to harmony and the Republicans from agreement to disharmony. Until the 1980s, the liberal and conservative wings of the Democratic Party often fought viciously over party planks and leadership positions. In the 1990s, however, the party came to be dominated more and more at the organizational level by the liberal faction. In conventions, the delegates now tend to adopt liberal platforms—at least in regard to social issues—and save their criticisms for the Republicans. In contrast, when the Republicans were a small minority, they rarely argued over policy in their conventions. As their influence in the state grew, however, Republicans generated greater and greater internal disagreement, especially between social and economic conservatives.

Activists in both major political parties argue constantly about what policy positions they should adopt. One of the common arguments, illustrated here, is that the party should be ideologically pure—that is, completely and uncompromisingly liberal or completely and uncompromisingly conservative.

*Courtesy of Ben Sargent.*

Members of the Texas delegation break out in song before the start of the evening session at the Republican National Convention in Madison Square Garden Thursday, Sept. 2, 2004 in New York.

The new pattern was set in 1994, when delegates from the Christian Right dominated the convention. They easily elected Tom Pauken, their favored candidate, as state chair of the party, beating Joe Barton, the candidate of the business establishment, and Dolly Madison McKenna, who represented Republicans who were moderate on social issues. They adopted a party platform that was far more conservative, especially on social issues, than many of the party's candidates for public office wanted. Among other provisions, the Republicans supported federal and state initiatives to outlaw abortion under all circumstances and recommended that the public schools teach "creation science" in biology classes. The socially conservative platform and the convention's choice of a party chair sparked vigorous but futile opposition from delegates who were economically conservative but more moderate on social issues.

The success of this 1994 grass-roots takeover of the Republican Party organization shows that dedicated citizens who are willing to spend time can have a large impact on party machinery. There are probably many liberal groups who are planning to have a similar impact on the Democratic Party in the future.

From 1994 to 2006, the Christian Right dominated Republican state conventions. In 1994, 1996, and 1998, Republican state platforms began with the words, "We believe in you! We believe that you are a sacred being created in the image of God." By 2000, those Republican delegates who were economic conservatives but social liberals had stopped making hopeless objections to Christian Right positions at the state convention, although the intra-party battle continued to rage on other fronts.

Although events in the Democratic and Republican state conventions engender much publicity, their importance should not be exaggerated. Because can-

Delegates wave signs in support of Texas House Democrats, known as the "The Killer D's" as they speak on stage during the Texas State Democratic Convention in Houston, Saturday, June 19, 2004. The representatives fled the state the year before in protest of a Republican redistricting plan.

didates for public office in Texas are nominated in primaries rather than in caucuses or conventions (see Chapter 5), and because candidates typically raise their own campaign funds independently of the party, the state convention and platform are of little importance to what nominees say and do. Candidates typically run to gather support from the large number of potential voters, not the tiny number of party activists who write the platforms.

In 1994, the two most important Republican candidates, George W. Bush, running for governor, and Kay Bailey Hutchison, running for U.S. Senate, pointedly ignored the state Republican platform and dissociated themselves from its abortion plank. Bush distributed his own "platform" that disagreed with his party's at several points and strongly differed from it in emphasis. In 1996, Governor Bush publicly disagreed with party Chair Tom Pauken on campaign strategy. In 2002, Governor Rick Perry publicly opposed twenty-three of forty-six planks in his party's platform, distanced himself from sixteen others, and endorsed only seven.[11] By 2002, social conservative delegates to the Republican convention were so frustrated with the economic conservative officeholders they termed "RINOs" (for "Republicans in Name Only") that they sponsored Rule 43 as a floor amendment to the platform. This "RINO Rule" would have denied party funds to any candidate who refused to swear to endorse and attempt to implement every party plank if elected. Party Chair Susan Weddington, presiding at the convention, managed to squelch the Rule 43 movement, but disappointed Christian Right delegates promised to persevere at future party gatherings.[12] Although the equivalent of Rule 43 was not adopted in 2004 or 2006, the 2006 state party platform did contain the declaration that "We strongly expect the SREC (State Republican Executive Committee) Candidate Resource Committee to consider candidates' support of the Party platform when granting financial or other support."[13] Because candidates raise most of their own campaign funds and thus do not rely on the official party organization, however, proclamations tend to be threats.

In summary, if students want to know what candidates plan to do if elected, they may want to ignore platforms and instead pay attention to the positions of the candidates themselves. The platform positions and rhetoric reproduced in Table 4-4 are good indications of the values and beliefs of the major party activists as groups but are not reliable guides to the issue positions of candidates as individuals.

# PERMANENT PARTY ORGANIZATION

## PRECINCT CHAIRPERSONS

The citizen who votes in the primary has an opportunity to participate in the selection of the precinct and county chairpersons of his or her party. The precinct chairperson is the lowest ranking permanent party official. Elected for a two-year term, he or she is expected to be the party leader at the precinct level, recruiting candidates, arranging for the precinct convention, getting out the vote, and in general, beating the drum for the party.

## COUNTY EXECUTIVE COMMITTEE

Together, the precinct chairs form the county executive committee, which is charged with two major responsibilities: (1) conducting the party primary elections and (2) conducting the county convention. It is presided over by the county chairperson, the most important official at the local level. Elected for two years to a demanding job, this official is unpaid, although some receive private donations.

County chairs are compensated by the state for the expense of conducting their party's primary elections. After the primary election has been held, the county executive committee canvasses the vote and certifies the results to the state executive committee.

## DISTRICT EXECUTIVE COMMITTEE

The Texas Election Code also provides for district executive committees. Their membership varies according to the number of counties and sections of counties that make up the senatorial district. These committees are supposed to perform party primary duties related to the district. In practice, however, few district executive committees are functional. Most district duties are performed by county executive committees.

## STATE EXECUTIVE COMMITTEE

The highest permanent body in the state party is the state executive committee, and the highest state party official is the party chair. Both are elected by the state convention. If the party controls the governorship, the chair of this party is likely to be a friend and political ally of the governor. Normally, the governor and the party chair work together to advance the party campaign during an election year.

The Republicans in 1996 and 1998 were a notable exception. The rancor between social conservatives, as represented by Tom Pauken, the party chair, and economic conservatives, as represented by Governor George Bush, caused a split in campaign duties. Bush ran the fund-raising and campaign efforts for GOP presidential candidate Bob Dole in 1996 and congressional candidates both years, while Pauken oversaw money-raising efforts for "downballot" state candidates.[14] With the departure of both Bush and Pauken by 2000, harmony returned to the Republican camp. Governor Perry and party chair Susan Weddington cooperated smoothly in the early years of the new millennium.

In a similar fashion, the chair of the state committee of the party out of power usually has a close relationship with the party's top leaders. By law, the executive committee of each party is responsible for staging the state convention, for certifying the party's candidates, and for coordinating a general party campaign over and above the efforts made by each individual candidate.

## THE (UN)IMPORTANCE OF PARTY ORGANIZATION

American political parties are not "responsible parties"—that is, they have neither centralized control over nominations and financing nor the power to impose the party platform on members. In Texas, parties are especially weak because it is in fact the primary election, not the party organization, that is important in determining who is nominated to office. Furthermore, candidates normally rely on their own fund-raising and organizing ability more than they rely on their party to help them get elected.

As a result, when candidates succeed in capturing an office, they mostly have themselves and the individuals and groups who contributed to their campaign fund to thank for their achievement. They therefore have very little loyalty to the party; they are more likely to feel beholden to some wealthy interest group. Officeholders are often ideologically friendly with others of the same party, but they are not obligated to cooperate with one another. The parties have no discipline over them.

Texas party organizations have some ability to fashion a "party attitude" on public policy because they are centers of information flow and personal interaction, but they are incapable of forging a disciplined governing team. Therefore, the party platforms summarized in Table 4-4 are in fact largely irrelevant to candidates' positions. They are a good indication of the sentiments of the party activists as a group, but they say little about the policy stands of candidates as individuals.

The unimportance of party organization in Texas is illustrated by the fact that the GOP was victorious in elections from 1994 to 2004 despite its internal squabbling. In a similar fashion, the Democratic Party won elections in the Lone Star State in previous decades despite the fact that it was internally divided.

The consequence of their organizational weakness is that Texas parties often fail to perform many of the functions that make parties elsewhere useful to democracy. By and large, they cannot recruit political leaders or overcome the fragmented nature of the political system by forming officials into disciplined organizations. Instead of thinking of parties in Texas as two stable, cohesive teams, it would be more realistic to imagine them as two (or as discussed in the next section, three or even four) loose confederations of citizens, interest groups, and officeholders that sometimes cooperate because of occasional ideological agreement and temporary parallel interests.

Lack of party cohesiveness also has important consequences in the legislature. Scholarly research has established the importance of party organization in state lawmaking bodies. According to Gerald Wright and Brian Schaffner, when the legislature has parties structured into two teams, political conflict is ordered so that issues tend to fall on either side of a clear, stable, voting cleavage in the legislature. Under such conditions, citizens are able to make sense of the political struggle. When Republicans and Democrats have no institutionalized divisions and organization, "It seems almost as though each bill is considered anew rather than in the context of established sides and coalitions."[15] In these circumstances lawmaking is confused and confusing, and citizens have difficulty holding politicians accountable for their actions.

Traditionally, Texas's weak parties have been reflected in the disorganization of its legislature. All through the 1990s and until 2007, the presiding officers (see Chapter 6) appointed members of both parties to chair important committees. The parties did not even caucus as separate groups until 1989, and afterward, those caucuses met only rarely during the legislative session.[16] Even in 2005, after the bruising and bitter partisan gerrymander of 2003, Republican Speaker Tom Craddick appointed Democrats to chair ten of forty-three House committees, and Republican Lieutenant Governor David Dewhurst chose Democrats to chair six of the fifteen Senate committees.

Political scientists expect that this lack of partisan organization is likely to change as Texas's parties become more ideologically opposed. Over the past several decades, parties in the U.S. Congress have become more ideologically polarized and less cooperative.[17] As Texas parties travel in the same direction, the historical pattern of bipartisan cooperation in the state legislature is likely to traverse a similar path. Future legislatures will probably witness fewer minority party appointments to committee chairs, stronger legislative party organizations and much more cohesive party voting. Such changes will undoubtedly produce more stress for legislators, but they might be good for democratic politics because the functioning of state government will be more coherent and responsible.

★ ★ ★ ★ ★ ★ ★ ★ ★ ★ ★ ★ ★ ★ ★ ★ ★ ★ ★ ★ ★ ★ ★ ★ ★ ★ ★ ★ ★

## Both Sexes But Only One Profession

As party interests and ideologies evolve through history, so does their leadership. Texas passed some sort of a milestone in the late 1990s when both parties, for the first time, elected women as leaders. Republican Susan Weddington was a former businesswoman from San Antonio. Democrat Molly Beth Malcolm was a former teacher and drug counselor from East Texas. Malcolm was a rarity in modern Texas politics—a former Republican who became an important Democrat.

Weddington and Malcolm each resigned as party chairs in 2003. The Republican Party retained its female leadership, as Tina Benkiser replaced Weddington. Democrats also acquired new chairs, but both were male. Charles Soechting was elected party chair in 2003, and was replaced by Boyd Richie in 2006. Clearly, in the twenty-first century the sex of a politician is of much less importance than it was in earlier times. The three recent party chairs do share a profession, however; all are lawyers.

★ ★ ★ ★ ★ ★ ★ ★ ★ ★ ★ ★ ★ ★ ★ ★ ★ ★ ★ ★ ★ ★ ★ ★ ★ ★ ★ ★

The new, more party-conscious Texas political environment was on display in the primary election of 2004. Democrat Ron Wilson, an African American from Houston, had been conspicuously independent of his party's organizational needs since his election to the state House of Representatives in 1976. His

# YOU DECIDE

## Should Texas Have Responsible Parties?

I n 1950, the American Political Science Association (APSA) sponsored a report entitled "Toward a More Responsible Two-Party System," in which it stated its organizational position that democracy would work better in the United States if the country's parties were more disciplined and coherent. In 2002, there was a movement within the ranks of the Texas Republican Party to force its candidates to endorse every plank in the party platform, on the theory that democracy would work better if Republicans, at least, were disciplined and coherent. Both APSA in 1950 and many Republican activists in 2002 endorsed the idea that disciplined party teams are better for democratic governance than the disorganized, candidate-centered system that prevails in both the United States and Texas.

Should such disciplined parties be the Texas institutions of the future?

| PRO | CON |
|---|---|
| ▲ When different candidates from the same party take differing positions on issues, it confuses the voters. If candidates were all forced to stand for the same things, citizens would be more able to understand the choices available to them, which would make for more intelligent voting. | ▼ Election campaigns are often confusing because politics itself is complicated and ambiguous. The solution to confusion is for citizens to better inform themselves, not for parties to impose a false clarity in voting choices. |
| ▲ Many foreign democracies have disciplined, responsible parties. Probably because politics in those countries makes sense, those typically have higher voter turnout than the United States and still higher turnout than Texas. | ▼ Almost all those foreign democracies have multi-party systems, so citizens have more choices on election day. There is no evidence that any of those countries is better governed than the United States or Texas. |
| ▲ Disciplined parties would prevent wealthy special interests from secretly buying the loyalty of candidates. Once candidates got into office, there would be no betrayals of the public's trust. | ▼ If wealthy special interests were denied access to candidates, they would simply corrupt parties. The problem is the power of money, not the lack of party discipline. |
| ▲ Once candidates were forced to endorse a single set of principles in order to run, they would form a cooperating team when in office, and public policy would be both easier to enact and more self-consistent. | ▼ One of the major reasons that candidates vary in their policy positions is that constituencies vary from place to place. Any party that forced its candidates to say the same thing everywhere would soon discover that most of its candidates lost. Losers do not enact public policy. |

SOURCES: "Toward a More Responsible Two-Party System: A Report of the Committee on Political Parties. American Political Science Association." *American Political Science Review*, vol. 44 (September 1950), 15; Austin Ranney, *Curing the Mischiefs of Faction: Party Reform in America* (Berkeley: University of California, 1975); Jake Bernstein, "Elephant Wars: The Christian Right Flexes Its Muscles at the Republican Convention," *Texas Observer*, July 5, 2002, 8-9.

willingness to vote with Republicans had made Wilson one of the few Democrats who retained internal power in the legislature as the party balance changed. He publicly supported the election of the new House speaker, Tom Craddick, and received many favors in return, being one of the minority-party representatives that Craddick appointed to chair a committee.

Wilson's lack of party loyalty was for many years of no concern to his constituents, who regularly reelected him by large margins. But by completely deserting the Democrats and endorsing the Republican redistricting plan in 2003, he went too far. In the March 2004 Democratic primary, Wilson was challenged by Alma Allen, a professional educator, member of the state board of education, and incidentally, also a Black candidate. During the primary campaign, Allen steadily pounded Wilson for his support of redistricting as well as his vote for Republican budget cuts. State Democratic leaders, including party chair Charles Soechting, publicly backed Allen. The voters got the message and nominated Allen by an eleven-point margin (because there was no Republican candidate running in this largely African American district, a victory in the primary ensured election in November). They made it clear that, in the new world of Texas politics, party loyalty mattered.[18]

# Two Parties, Three Factions (or Perhaps Four)

## REPUBLICANS

Ideologically, the Texas Republican Party tends to be strongly conservative, usually opposing government involvement in the economy but sometimes endorsing such involvement in personal life. Although the party holds two recognizable factions, the social conservatives (most of whom are members of the Christian Right) and the economic conservatives, it is not appropriate to speak of two opposed groups within the Republican Party. Many Republican officeholders manage to embody both wings of the party as they endorse social conservatism in their *intangible*, symbolic public statements but concentrate on passing *tangible* conservative economic policies while in office.

A good example is governor Rick Perry, who took office in 2000 when governor Bush resigned to run for president, and was elected on his own in 2002. In 2006, looking toward another re-election campaign, he publicly endorsed the teaching of "intelligent design" (a euphemism for Christian creationism) rather than the scientific theory of evolution by natural selection in the state's public-school biology classes. Because "intelligent design" is a religious doctrine, it would be unconstitutional to teach it in public schools, as courts have held several times.[19] There is consequently very little chance that such a doctrine could be taught in the state's biology classes. Even if such an unlikely event came to pass, the governor would have virtually nothing to do with it because his office does not have the power to set school curriculum for the state. By endorsing the teaching of "intelligent design," therefore, Perry was not making a genuine proposal for a realistic policy option. He was expressing symbolic solidarity with Christian conservatives.

Meanwhile, during his tenure in office, Perry had concentrated on urging the legislature to pass tangible, business-oriented policies such as tort reform, tax relief, and lightening of regulation. He had thus managed to appeal to both halves of his party's coalition, the social conservatives through symbolism and the economic conservatives through policies. As long as Republican politicians such as Perry are able to thus combine both sides of the party in their individual persons, Republicans will not be split into identifiable factions.

## GEOGRAPHIC DISTRIBUTION

Because the Republicans are the clearly dominant party in Texas, it is easier to describe the areas where they are weak than the areas where they are strong. They are weakest in the areas of the state where Mexican Americans are in the majority or nearly so—along the Rio Grande. They are also less dominant in central Texas, in the "Golden Triangle" of cities in the extreme southeastern part of the state, and in a few counties in the piney woods near the Louisiana border. As a rule, they are less important in the central cities (where minorities are numerous) than in the suburbs or small towns. Everywhere else, their advantage ranges from decisive to overwhelming.

## SOCIOECONOMIC AND ETHNIC DISTRIBUTION

GOP activists come from a relatively narrow socioeconomic and ethnic base. Most candidates and party activists are Anglo, middle or upper class, businesspersons or professionals. Since 1994, they have tended to be evangelical Protestants, although Tom Pauken, the party chair whose battles with Governor Bush have already been described, was Catholic. A sprinkling of African Americans and Latinos can be found among active Republicans (such as Railroad Commissioner Michael Williams, who is Black), but the party has not appealed to significant numbers of minorities since the 1960s. Furthermore, the party's traditional opposition to policies such as welfare and job-training programs aimed at helping the poor has generally ensured that its activists and voters would be fairly wealthy.

## CONSERVATIVE DEMOCRATS

Despite the fact that Texas has a "two-party system," it has for several decades actually offered its citizens three voting options, for the Democrats historically have been split into two factions. This "three-faction system" has the advantage of making more choices available to voters and the disadvantage of making Texas politics more confusing and chaotic than it might otherwise be.

Conservative Democrats are the representatives of habits of thought and behavior that survive from when Texas was part of the Old South. This traditionalist culture is very conservative on social issues but tends to be conflicted and inconsistent on economic issues. Many southerners are normally conservative economically but can be aroused to a fervent belief in the ability of government to protect the little people of society from wealthy individuals and corporations—an attitude that has historically been known as **populism**. The Populist (People's) Party was strong in Texas during the 1890s, and candidates who make populist-type appeals, such as Jim Ferguson (governor from 1915 to 1917) and W. Lee "Pappy" O'Daniel (1939–1941), have sometimes been elected. This populist streak makes the Old South part of Texas hard to predict on economic issues.

At the level of the party activists and officeholders, the conservative faction of the Democratic Party is slightly less devoted to laissez faire than Republicans but much more so than the liberal faction. It tends to be conservative on social issues, although conservative Democratic candidates have been known to bend to the left on social issues in an attempt to persuade minority citizens to vote for them. During the 2002 campaign, three of the Democrats' major candidates, Tony Sanchez (governor), Ron Kirk (U.S. senator), and John Sharp (lieutenant governor), were so conservative that they were virtually indistinguishable from their Republican opponents on economic issues, differing from the GOP candidates primarily by being more liberal on such social issues as affirmative action and abortion. Chris Bell, the party's candidate for governor in 2006, however, was clearly a liberal on most issues.

## GEOGRAPHIC DISTRIBUTION

The historical base of conservative Democrats is the piney woods of East Texas, where the traditionalist political culture is strongest. As Republicans have made major inroads among White conservatives, this base has shrunk considerably.

Small cities and rural areas in other parts of the state sometimes remain conservative Democratic in their affiliation, although they are steadily evolving toward greater Republican strength. Conservative Democratic candidates now have to court Hispanic voters to have any hope of success, a necessity that causes them to moderate their issue positions, especially on social issues.

## SOCIOECONOMIC AND ETHNIC DISTRIBUTION

Representing the historically dominant wing of the party, until recently conservative Democrats drew support from all classes in Texas, but that pattern is changing as Republicans continue to increase their support among the wealthy. Like the Republicans, they have historically been popular among the Anglo middle and upper classes, business and professional people, and white-collar workers. Unlike the Republicans, they also drew substantial support from workers, especially those in rural areas and small cities. Again, this pattern may be changing as the Republicans grow in popularity.

# LIBERAL DEMOCRATS

Liberals usually recommend policies that depend on government's being active in economic affairs, especially on behalf of those who have less wealth and power. They tend, however, to oppose government intervention in personal life. Former Governor Ann Richards (who died in 2006) and former mayor of San Antonio (and also former U.S. Secretary of Housing and Urban Development) Henry Cisneros are good examples of Texas liberal Democrats. The most famous and successful of all Texas Democratic politicians, Lyndon Johnson, was mainly, although somewhat inconsistently, a liberal. While a member of the U.S. House of Representatives, from 1937 to 1949, he sided with the left wing of the national party. While U.S. senator, from 1949 to 1961, he leaned more toward the conservative side. As president, from 1963 to 1969, however, he provided vigorous liberal leadership to the country.

## GEOGRAPHIC DISTRIBUTION

In recent elections, liberal Democrats have been most successful in the areas of Texas where Hispanics are most numerous, in southern and far western areas of the state along and near the border with Mexico. Liberals are also strong where labor unions are a factor: in far East Texas, in East Central Texas, and along some of the Gulf Coast. Liberals can usually rely on doing well in Austin, the Beaumont–Port Arthur–Orange complex, Corpus Christi, and El Paso. They are few and weak in all of North Texas, the Panhandle, and the south plains; they win very small percentages of the vote in the Metroplex, Amarillo, Lubbock, and Midland–Odessa.

## SOCIOECONOMIC AND ETHNIC DISTRIBUTION

Identifying the socioeconomic components of liberal Democratic strength in Texas is more complex than in the case of Republicans or conservative Democrats. Liberals form, at best, an uneasy coalition. While it can be said that liberal strength comes mostly from labor unions, African Americans, Mexican Americans, and certain educated Anglos, the mix is a volatile one that does not make for stable cooperation. White middle- and upper-class liberals can support African Americans and Mexican Americans in their quest for equal treatment, but labor unions have sometimes been cool in this area. African Americans and Mexican Americans usually give little support to reform legislation—of campaign spending and lobbying, for example—or to efforts to protect the natural environment, issues that energize Anglo liberals. Many Mexican Americans have sometimes been reluctant to vote for African American candidates, and vice versa.

Liberal leadership comes largely, but not exclusively, from the legal, teaching, and other professions. In earlier years, union officials provided leadership for the liberal faction, and in some areas, they still do. But officials of the state unions, like their national counterparts, have become more conservative in recent years. Leading the liberal Democrats is an uncertain business, especially after the electoral disasters the party has experienced since 1994.

# THE FUTURE OF THE THREE-FACTION SYSTEM

The future does not look bright for Texas conservative Democrats. They are being drained from the right and squeezed from the left. The national party long ago became dominated by a moderate-to-liberal philosophy. Within Texas, Republicans steadily draw away conservative voters, while liberals continue to dominate the party organization. In 2002, the Democratic party offered a "dream team"— a slate of economically conservative candidates for governor, U.S. senator, and lieutenant governor—that differed from its Republican opposition not so much in ideology as in diverse ethnicity. This strategy of running a conservative but multicultural team failed badly, as all three Democrats lost. In 2006, the Democrats nominated a White liberal, Chris Bell. This strategy also failed. In contemporary Texas, therefore, it may seem that the candidates and issues endorsed by Democrats are irrelevant, because in statewide races they are a hopeless minority.

Yet, as Texas evolves toward a population in which minorities constitute the majority, Democrats are almost certain to continue to nominate many Mexican American and African American candidates. Predictions are always risky, but it is possible to imagine Democratic Party strategists concluding from the 2002 and 2006 election results that the only way to challenge Republican dominance in the future is to keep running ethnically diverse, albeit liberal, candidates.

It may be realistic, therefore, to foresee a day in the not-too-distant future when Texas has only a conservative Republican Party and a liberal Democratic Party. If voter turnout rates continue to favor conservative Anglos (see Chapter 5), then this arrangement along the ideological spectrum will ensure that Republicans will dominate the state for a long time. If liberal-leaning minorities begin to turn out to vote at higher rates, however, they will alter the party balance decisively. One of the few predictions that can confidently be made about party politics in Texas is that things will change.

## Third Parties in Texas

Texas has had its share of **third parties.** The Know-Nothing Party, representing those who objected to Roman Catholics and immigrants, made a brief appearance before the Civil War. After the Civil War, the Greenback Party, which advocated inflation of the dollar, made an equally brief visit.

More important was the Populist (People's) Party, which reflected widespread discontent among farmers and other "little people." The Populists advocated an extensive program of government regulation of big business and economic policy reform. In particular, the party's 1892 national platform recommended government ownership and operation of railroads, confiscation of all land owned by corporations "in excess of their actual needs," and an

**Anemia is a disease associated with physical weakness. Here cartoonist Ben Sargent uses anemia as a metaphor for the state Democratic Party's seeming inability to field strong statewide candidates against the dominant Republicans in the 2006 election year.**

*Courtesy of Ben Sargent.*

income tax for individuals.[20] The fact that the Populist candidate for president drew 100,000 votes in Texas in 1892—almost 20 percent of the votes cast—illustrates the point that Texas's normal political conservatism can be credibly challenged.

New parties cannot get on Texas ballots by simply announcing their intention to run candidates. To allow every splinter group to call itself a party and thereby grab a line on the ballot would make for confusing, chaotic elections with dozens of candidates running for each office. In addition, of course, the major parties are not eager to make it easy for upstart competitors to grab the attention of voters. As a result, every democratic country, and every American state, has laws that discriminate in some manner against new parties.

Texas has some of the toughest ballot access laws in the nation. A person nominated for statewide office by one of the major parties is automatically accorded a spot on the ballot. But in the days following the April primary runoffs, an independent candidate must collect signatures totaling 1 percent of all the votes cast in the last gubernatorial election. These signatures must come from registered voters who did not participate in a primary or runoff that year. All signatures must be accompanied by the voter's registration identification number. The rules vary somewhat for candidates for federal offices and local offices, and for parties as opposed to individuals, but none of them are permissive. If a party manages to collect enough signatures to get its candidates on a ballot, it can ensure itself a place for the next election by garnering 5 percent of the vote for any statewide office or 2 percent of the gubernatorial vote.

Needless to say, these rules prevent most independent and third-party candidates from ever getting on the ballot. The Reform Party, riding the popularity of its first presidential candidate, Texan Ross Perot, managed to make the ballot in 1992 and 1996 but has since faded.

Libertarians have qualified for the ballot in every election since 1986. In 1998, the Greens were able to attract enough signatures so that their candidates qualified. The Greens occupied the ultraliberal end of the ideological spectrum, demanding a much more active government to regulate business on behalf of workers and the environment. Libertarians were the consistent antigovernment party, opposing any regulation of the economy (which made them more conservative than the Republicans on economic issues) and equally opposing regulation of personal life (disapproving of the war on drugs, for example, which made them more liberal than the Democrats on social issues). Although their candidates attracted only a small percentage of the vote in any given election, the leaders of both these parties had hopes of becoming major forces in the future.

Generally, candidates must be the nominees of some party in order to even think about running for statewide office. After 1859, when Texas revolutionary hero Sam Houston, running on his own ticket, beat Democrat H. R. Runnels for the governorship, there were no significant statewide independent candidates for almost a century and a half. In 2006, however, with the two already tiny third parties fading, citizens disgruntled with the major parties were offered two candidates who were independent of all party backing.

The first 2006 independent, comptroller Carole Keeton Strayhorn, exemplified the dilemma of the "tweeners," the people who are more-or-less in the middle of the ideological spectrum. During the early 1980s, she had been the conservative Democratic mayor of Austin. In 1985 she became a Republican and ran successfully for a series of offices. Always more liberal than most Republicans but more conservative than the typical Democrat, she was as uneasy in her new party as she had been in her former party. As the Republicans consolidated their grip on state government in the early 2000s, she grew increasingly vocal in her criticisms of the policies pursued by her party, especially in regard to education and welfare. In 2006 she obtained the 45,540 signatures (from registered voters who did not vote in either major party's primary) necessary to put her on the November ballot as an independent candidate. She came in third in the election for governor.

The other 2006 independent was difficult to describe in ordinary political language. A musician, novelist, and humor columnist, Kinky Friedman had had very little to say about politics his entire life when he decided to run for governor in 2005. His campaigning did not do much to dispel the mystery of where he stood on issues, for his "speeches" consisted mainly of comedic one-liners interspersed with clever insults of ruling Republicans. He seemed to appeal mainly to people who were generally disgusted with politics in Texas or to liberals who despaired of voting for a forthright Democratic candidate. He brought a lightness of tone, but no realistic political alternatives, to the campaign of 2006, and only managed to come in fourth.

African Americans have never established a separate political party in Texas, although their main interest group, the National Association for the Advancement of Colored People (NAACP), often functions as a sub-faction of the liberal Democrats. Mexican Americans have established several well-known political organizations aimed at improving the lot of Spanish-speaking Texans. In 1929 (see Chapter 3), an interest group called the League of United Latin American Citizens (LULAC) was formed to try to overcome ethnic discrimination and to encourage Mexican American participation in civic affairs. The American GI Forum came into being to fight ethnic discrimination during World War II, and Viva Kennedy clubs and the Political Association of Spanish-Speaking Organizations (PASSO) were active in the 1960s. In the 1970s, Mexican Americans formed a true political party called La Raza Unida (*la raza* means "the race"), which won some local elections—notably in Crystal City—and even ran candidates for governor and other state offices. But infiltrated by the FBI for alleged radicalism and beset by personal and factional feuds, the party was out of existence by the early 1980s. Mexican Americans in Texas are currently represented by a number of interest groups, including LULAC and the Mexican American Legal Defense and Educational Fund (MALDEF), and by two organizations within the Democratic Party, Mexican American Democrats (MAD), and Tejano Democrats. What organizational patterns future Mexican American politics will take is not clear, but it seems certain that Mexican Americans will be of growing importance in Texas politics, as they form an increasingly large percentage of the state's population.

## Summary

Ideology is one of the most important bases for political parties everywhere, but in Texas, where parties have historically been weak, ideology has usually been more important than party affiliation. The major ideological conflict has been between conservatives and liberals. Liberals tend to favor government regulation of the economy but oppose it in personal life, whereas conservatives tend to favor regulation of personal life but oppose it in the economy. These basic differences lead to differences in many areas of public policy, from taxation to abortion. The Texas Republican Party is consistently strongly conservative, but the Democratic Party is split, at least temporarily, into a conservative and a liberal faction.

Parties appeal to interests, as well as to ideology, to mobilize voter support and campaign contributions. In attempting to form winning coalitions by putting together groups of voters and contributors, they sometimes reinforce their ideological leanings and sometimes violate them.

From 1874 to the 1970s, Texas was a one-party Democratic state. One-party states are characterized by an absence of party competition, inadequate debate about public policy, low voter turnout, and usually conservative public policy. For a while in the 1980s and 1990s, Texas appeared to have established vigorous two-party competition, but in retrospect, those decades witnessed a transition to what may be one-party Republican rule.

Texas's political parties have both temporary and permanent party organizations. Nominations are made in primaries, and party leaders have no control over candidates or officeholders. Thus, party organization is much less important than ideology and interests in explaining the politics of the state. This lack of organizational strength means that Texas's parties are not "responsible" and are incapable of fulfilling some of the functions that they would perform in an ideal democracy. Nevertheless, in today's political situation, there is at least robust and spirited debate of public policy. Furthermore, the increasing partisan intensity in the legislature that accompanied the war over redistricting in 2003 may be a sign that Texas's parties are about to become more organized, disciplined, and coherent.

Texas has given birth to a number of third parties, none of which achieved permanence but several of which influenced public policy in the state.

## Glossary Terms

coalition

conservatism

ideology

interest

liberalism

one-party system

permanent party organization

political party

political socialization

populism

realignment

temporary party organization

third party

## Study Questions

1. What are the basic ideological differences between liberals and conservatives? What are the more important policy differences between them?

2. Are you a liberal or a conservative? Are there any policy areas in which you disagree with what would otherwise be your ideological tendency?

3. What were you taught about democracy and Texas politics in elementary and high school? Was your instruction adequate?

4. Can you think of any interests you have that are better represented by one party or the other? Do your interests tend to clash with or reinforce your ideology?

5. What are the functions of political parties? How well do Texas parties perform them?

6. Describe briefly the temporary and permanent party organizations in Texas. What political institution renders both of them relatively unimportant in determining the activities of the parties?

7. The three party groups—Republicans, conservative Democrats, and liberal Democrats—draw their support from different geographic areas and sections of the population. Describe the typical support base of each group.

8. Are you a Democrat, a Republican, or an independent? Why?

## Surfing the Web

Readers are urged to visit the companion site for this book:

**http://academic.cengage.com/polsci/Kraemer/TexasPolitics10e**

# Voting, Campaigns, and Elections

**5**

The 2006 gubernatorial candidates shaking hands before a televised debate illustrates the peaceful competition for power that underlies democracy.

Suppose they gave an election and nobody came?

BUMPER STICKER FROM THE 1960S

Politics has got so expensive that it takes lots of money to even get beat with.

WILL ROGERS, AMERICAN HUMORIST, 1931

# Introduction

Nothing is more basic to the concept of democratic government than the principle of elected representatives freely chosen by the majority of the people, with each person's vote counting equally. In an ideal democracy, election campaigns are contests conducted by rival candidates for the people's support. Candidates debate public policy rather than engaging in a competition of personal insult and insinuations. On the official voting day, citizens cast their ballots on the basis of their evaluation of the debate, with almost everyone participating. On the other hand, in a bad democracy, election campaigns deal in trivialities, evasions, and slanders, candidates pay more attention to the wants of special-interest contributors than to the needs of the public, and very few citizens bother to participate on election day.

Is Texas close to or far from the democratic ideal of campaigns and elections? It is the overall purpose of this chapter to provide readers with information that will allow them to begin to answer this question for themselves. The chapter begins with a consideration of the reasons that voting is important to democracy. The topics that follow include the history of the suffrage (the right to vote) in Texas, the state's registration procedures, and its disturbingly low voter turnout. The focus next turns to election campaigns, with special attention given to the impact of money on the outcome. Afterward, the various types of public elections in Texas are described. Next, the election campaigns and voting results of 1994 through 2006 are chronicled. Last comes a comparison of the reality of Texas elections with the democratic ideal and an argument that there is much room for improvement.

# Voting

## WHY VOTE?

As is the case with many important questions, the answer to this one is, "It depends." It depends on whether voting is viewed from the perspective of the individual voter, of the candidates, or of the political system.

From the perspective of the individual voter, there may seem to be no logic in voting, for public elections are almost never won by the margin of a single vote, except perhaps in small towns and special districts. The individual voter has very little hope of affecting the outcome of an election. Why, then, do so many people bother to register and vote? The main reason is that people do not think of voting in completely logical terms. Like other political behavior, voting is governed not only by reason but also by personal loyalties, ideological fervor, custom, and habit. Most people vote primarily because they have been taught that it is their duty as citizens (as in fact it is). And even though a single vote is unlikely to affect the outcome of an election, participation in the governing of the community is important to the self-development of each individual.

From the perspective of the candidate, voting is extremely important. There is a saying among politicians that "votes are counted one by one by one." It expresses the insight that although citizens may seem to be part of a mass, it is a mass of individual personalities, each with his or her own motivations, ideology, interests, and hopes for the future. Politicians who forget that each potential supporter is an individual soon find themselves forcibly retired.

From the perspective of the political system, elections are crucial. In democratic theory, it is the participation of the citizens that makes government legitimate (that is, morally right and worthy of support). When large numbers of citizens neglect or refuse to vote, this raises questions about the most basic underpinnings of political authority.

Voting also performs other functions in a democratic society. The act of participating in an election decreases alienation and opposition by making people feel that they are part of the system. Further, the electorate does have an effect on public policy when it chooses one set of candidates who endorse one set of policies over another. Although one vote is unlikely to determine the outcome of an election, groups of like-minded citizens who vote the same way can be decisive.

Finally, large-scale voting has the added virtue of helping to prevent corruption. It is relatively easy to rig an election when only a few people bother to go to the polls. One of the best guarantees of honest government is a large turnout on election day.

So, despite the fact that one vote almost never matters, democracy depends on each citizen acting as if it does. When people take their right to vote seriously and act as responsible citizens, the system works. When they refuse to participate and stay home on election day, they abdicate control over government to the elites and special interests who are only too happy to run things. We can at least partly judge the extent to which a country or state has a legitimate government by the level of voter turnout among its citizens. How does Texas stack up? This question will be addressed shortly. First, however, must come a look at the legal context of the voting act. The most important parts of that context are suffrage and the system of registration.

# SUFFRAGE

One of the most important historical developments in American politics has been the expansion of the **suffrage**—the right to vote. The writers of the U.S. Constitution delegated to the states the power to determine voter eligibility in both national and state elections. At the time the Constitution was written, each state decreed the qualifications for voting within its boundaries, and limitations on the suffrage were widespread. Generally, states restricted the suffrage to adult White male property owners who professed a certain religious belief, which varied with the state. As a result of these restrictions, only about 5 percent of the 3,939,214 persons counted in the first national census in 1790 were eligible to vote. An even lower percentage actually went to the polls.

Since that era, a series of democratic reform movements has slowly expanded the suffrage. In the 1820s and 1830s, church membership and property ownership were removed as qualifications for voting in most elections. After the Civil War, the Fourteenth and Fifteenth Amendments to the Constitution were enacted in an attempt to guarantee full political rights to the freed slaves. At first, African Americans voted in substantial numbers. But the southern states, including Texas, retaliated with a series of legal and informal restrictions that succeeded in withdrawing the suffrage from African American citizens in most parts of the old Confederacy by 1900. (It is partly because of persistent southern resistance to Black suffrage that the region is said to have a "traditionalistic" political culture.) It was not until 1965, when Congress passed the Voting Rights Act, that the federal government began to enforce the right of African Americans to vote. In subsequent years, federal court decisions expanded the protection of Black suffrage. Women were enfranchised with the ratification of the Nineteenth Amendment in 1920, and in 1971, the Twenty-sixth Amendment lowered the minimum voting age to eighteen.

Several points stand out in this two-century evolution of the right to vote. First, it is not exclusively Texan but part of a national, even a worldwide, movement toward expanded suffrage. Within the United States, suffrage has been substantially nationalized. States still enact laws, but they do so within guidelines set down by the Constitution, Congress, and the Supreme Court and enforced by the federal Justice Department.

Second, an important part of the story of the struggle to include all citizens in the suffrage has been the fact that well into the 1970s, Texas and other southern states attempted to evade and obstruct the post–Civil War amendments and, later, the Voting Rights Act. They came up with various gimmicks such as poll taxes, White-only primaries, literacy tests, and more to keep African Americans from exercising the franchise.[1] These obstructions also successfully discouraged many Mexican Americans and poor Whites from voting. As a result, voter turnout in the South was far below the levels prevailing in the North.

Third, however, an equally important part of the story is that the federal government, supported by concerned citizens in both the North and South, gradually defeated these anti-democratic schemes, so that by the mid-1970s, all adult Americans had the legal right to vote. As will be discussed shortly, not all of them exercised that right, but at least state governments were no longer preventing them from going to the polling booth. The legal battle for democratic suffrage has been won.

# REGISTRATION

Every democratic political system has a **voter registration** procedure to distinguish qualified voters from those who are ineligible because of immaturity, lack of citizenship, mental incapacity, or other reasons. In most countries, registration is easy; in some nations, the government goes to great lengths to make sure that all citizens are registered before every election.

Like the other former slaveholding states of the old Confederacy, however, for most of its history, Texas used a series of legal devices to deliberately limit registration and thus voting. The most effective and longest lasting of the anti-registration schemes was the poll tax. This was a $1.50 fee that served as the state's system of registration during the first part of the twentieth century. Those who paid it by January 31 were registered to vote in that year's elections. It discouraged less affluent citizens from registering, for back before inflation had eroded the value of the dollar, the fee represented a substantial portion of a poor person's income. Because people had to be registered in order to vote, this tax was a convenient way for the more affluent to ensure that they would not have to share power with their fellow citizens. Moreover, because minority citizens were usually poor, this device had the deliberate effect of keeping the ballot box a White preserve.

★ ★ ★ ★ ★ ★ ★ ★ ★ ★ ★ ★ ★ ★ ★ ★ ★ ★ ★ ★ ★ ★ ★ ★ ★

## *Anti-fraud or Anti-Democrat?*

In both the 2005 and 2007 legislative sessions, Republican representatives introduced legislation, which, if they had passed, would have required citizens to show a photo ID, such as a driver's license, before they could be issued a ballot at a polling booth on election day. Both years the bills passed the House of Representatives over Democratic objections, but were killed by Democratic parliamentary maneuvers in the Senate. Before being defeated, however, they sparked lively debates between the parties, both in and out of the legislature.

Republicans argued that under the present system of voter identification, fraud was too easy and had become too common. People needed a driver's license to rent a movie on a DVD, they argued, and it was at least as important to prevent dishonest voting as to prevent dishonest film renting. Democrats countered that there was no evidence of widespread voter fakery, and that the real purpose of the measure was to disenfranchise people who tended not to have photo identification—older, minority citizens who tend to vote Democratic. The voter ID bill, they charged, was actually a new form of poll tax.

★ ★ ★ ★ ★ ★ ★ ★ ★ ★ ★ ★ ★ ★ ★ ★ ★ ★ ★ ★ ★ ★ ★ ★ ★

SOURCES: Mark Lisheron, "A Dewhurst Promise, and Voter ID Bill Dies," *Austin American-Statesman*, May 24, 2007, B7; Tom Aldred and Brent Connett, "ID Rule Will Bolster Integrity of Elections," *Austin American-Statesman*, May 1, 2007, A7; Nathanael Isaacson, "Call ID Rule What It Is—A New Kind of Poll Tax," *Austin American-Statesman*, April 28, 2007, A21; Mark Lisheron, "Bill Says You Must Show ID to Vote," *Austin American-Statesman*, April 19, 2005, B1; Tina Benkiser, "Democrats Are Blocking a Bill to Halt Voter Fraud," *Austin American-Statesman*, May 16, 2005, A13; Leticia Van de Putte, "Texans Shouldn't Need Driver's Licenses to Vote," *Austin American-Statesman*, May 18, 2005, A11.

In 1964, the nation adopted the Twenty-fourth Amendment to the Constitution, outlawing the poll tax. Two years later, the U.S. Supreme Court threw out Texas's tax. The state legislature then devised a new system of voter registration.

The easier it is to vote, the more poor, uneducated citizens are able to exercise their democratic rights, but the easier fraud becomes. The harder it is to vote, the less we must worry about fraud, but the fewer poor and uneducated citizens will vote. In this cartoon, Ben Sargent takes his stand with making voting easy, and against Republican bills that would, if passed, have made it harder in the name of preventing fraud.

*Courtesy of Ben Sargent.*

Although no tax had to be paid, the period of annual registration was identical: October 1 through January 31. Because most poor people (especially minorities) had little education, they were not apt to follow public affairs as closely as those with more education. By the time they became interested in an upcoming election, they had often missed their chance to register. The new law, then, was another ploy to reserve the ballot box for the White and wealthy.

In January 1971, a federal district court struck down this registration law as a violation of the **Equal Protection Clause** of the Fourteenth Amendment to the U.S. Constitution.[2] Declaring two provisions of the law—the annual registration requirement and the very early deadline for registration—to be discriminatory, the court expressed the opinion that 1.2 million Texans were disenfranchised by them. Later that year, the legislature responded with a new law that made registration much easier. Its major provisions, as amended, are as follows:

1. **Initial registration.** The voter may register either in person or by mail. A parent, child, or spouse who is registered may register for the voter.

2. **Permanency.** The voter remains registered as long as he or she remains qualified. A new voter registration card is issued every two years.

3. **Period of registration.** Voters may register at any time and may vote in any election, provided that they are registered thirty days prior to the election.

   To vote in Texas today, one must:

   a. Be a United States citizen eighteen years of age by election day.

b. Be a resident of the state and county for thirty days immediately prior to election day.

c. Be a resident of the election precinct on election day.

d. Have registered to vote at least thirty days prior to election day.

e. Not be a convicted felon, or, if convicted, have finished serving one's sentence.

# Texas Turnout

## GOVERNMENT BY THE PEOPLE?

Despite the fact that registration has been relatively easy in Texas for more than three decades, **voter turnout,** while climbing erratically, is still below national levels. Voter turnout means the proportion of the citizens eligible to vote who actually cast ballots —not the proportion of those registered, but the proportion of adult citizens.

Table 5-1 shows that the percentage of Texans voting in both presidential and off-year congressional elections is considerably lower than the percentage voting nationally. An average of 46.6 percent of eligible Texans turned out

**TABLE 5-1**

### Percentage of Voting-Age Population Voting in National Elections, 1972–2006

**Presidential Elections**

|        | 1972 | 1976 | 1980 | 1984 | 1988 | 1992 | 1996 | 2000 | 2004 |
|--------|------|------|------|------|------|------|------|------|------|
| **U.S.**   | 55.5 | 54.3 | 51.8 | 53.1 | 50.2 | 55.2 | 50.8 | 52.2 | 60.3 |
| **TEXAS**  | 45.4 | 47.3 | 44.7 | 47.2 | 44.2 | 49.0 | 43.0 | 45.0 | 53.4 |

**Off-year Congressional Elections (House of Representatives)**

|        | 1974 | 1978 | 1982 | 1986 | 1990 | 1994 | 1998 | 2002 | 2006 |
|--------|------|------|------|------|------|------|------|------|------|
| **U.S.**   | 36.1 | 35.1 | 38.0 | 36.4 | 35.0 | 38.9 | 37.6 | 39.0 | 39.5 |
| **TEXAS**  | 18.4 | 24.0 | 26.2 | 29.1 | 26.8 | 35.0 | 28.0 | 32.0 | 30.1 |

SOURCES: *Statistical Abstract of the United States*, 101st ed. (Washington, D.C.: U.S. Department of Commerce, Bureau of the Census, 1980), 517; 106th ed. (1989), 259; Federal Elections Commission, Washington, D.C., "Political Intelligence," *Texas Observer*, November 27, 1992, 8; "Voter Turnout Higher Than in '98, Survey Says," *Dallas Morning News*, November 7, 2002, A15; Walter Dean Burnham, Department of Government, University of Texas at Austin; George Mason University voter turnout Web site: http://elections.gmu.edu/Voter_Turnout_2004.htm

for presidential balloting in the three-plus decades since the new registration law went into effect, and an average of 27.7 percent turned out for off-year congressional elections. In the 2004 presidential balloting Texas voter turnout was about seven percentage points below the turnout level in the country as a whole, and in the 2006 congressional contest it was about nine points below. In only the most recent presidential election did the state's turnout rise as high as 50 percent—although the trend line is comforting in this regard.

Turnout for state offices is usually even lower than for these national elections, and turnout for local offices is poorer still. Many mayors have been elected with the votes of fewer than 10 percent of their city's electorate.

In other words, government in Texas is never "by the people." At best, it is by a smidgen more than half the people; often, it is by a quarter of the people or even fewer.

## WHY DON'T TEXANS VOTE?

Americans in general are not known for high voter turnouts, but Texans seem to vote even less than the residents of many other states. Why?

Texas is a rather poor state with a very uneven distribution of wealth. (In 2006 the U.S. Census Bureau estimated that it had the fifth highest rate of poverty among all the states, and a median income more than four thousand dollars below the national average.)[3] The poverty rate is important because the poor and less educated, in the absence of strong parties to persuade them to go to the polls on election day, have a tendency to stay home. When the poor don't vote, the overall turnout rate is low.

The differences between rich and poor citizens are strongly related to differences between turnout rates for ethnic groups. Consider, for example, the national voter turnout rates for Hispanics, Anglos, and African Americans in the 2000 presidential and 2002 congressional elections in Table 5-2.[4]

As in the nation as a whole, minorities in Texas tend to go to the polls at lower rates than Anglos. As a result, the low overall state turnout rate is at least partly caused by the tendency of its Black and Latino citizens to stay home on election day. Thus, those who vote tend to be richer, better educated, and White; those who abstain tend to be poorer, uneducated, and minority. This does not mean that all Anglos vote, or that all minorities stay home on election day. But in democratic politics, statistical probabilities have major consequences.

**TABLE 5-2**
## Self-Reported Voter Turnout, 2000 and 2002

|  | Anglo | Hispanic (any race) | African American |
|---|---|---|---|
| 2000 | 56.4% | 27.5% | 53.57% |
| 2002 | 44.1% | 18.9% | 39.7% |

# THE CONSEQUENCES OF NONVOTING

The participation differences between ethnic groups in Texas have an important impact on public policy. Minority citizens tend to have more liberal opinions about what government should be doing, at least partly because they are more likely to be poor than Anglos. When they fail to go to the polls, however, their views become irrelevant. Because the more conservative White citizens vote at higher rates, their preferences usually determine which candidates win and therefore which policies are pursued by government.

Low minority turnout is thus one of the major explanations for conservative public policy in Texas.

For example, minorities as a whole are far more Democratic than are Anglos. According to a 2006 survey, only 26 percent of the state's Anglos identified themselves as Democrats, as opposed to 53 percent of Hispanics and 72 percent of Blacks.[5] Nothing is permanent in politics, and rising incomes or some other circumstance may change the balance of party identification among ethnic groups in the near future. But for the present, when minorities don't vote, it hurts Democrats.

Furthermore, it is not just any Democrats who suffer from low minority turnout. The liberal wing of the party needs minority support to win. As Tables 5-3 and 5-4 illustrate, African Americans and Hispanics often hold views on public policy that are clearly more liberal than the opinions of Anglos. Once again, the future may differ from the past and present. For now, however, it seems clear that if African American and Hispanic Texans had higher turnout rates, liberal Democrats would win elections much more often. Such an outcome would mean that government policy in Texas would be more liberal. As it is, the liberals rarely go to the polls, so state government remains conservative.

The crucial part played by different turnout rates is illustrated for the 2002 U.S. Senate race in Table 5-5. Blacks and Mexican Americans voted overwhelmingly for the Democratic candidate Ron Kirk, while Whites supported Republican candidate John Cornyn by a substantial margin. If members of each of the three major ethnic groups had gone to the polls at the state average of 32 percent, Kirk would be one of Texas's senators today. Because Whites turned out to

★ ★ ★ ★ ★ ★ ★ ★ ★ ★ ★ ★ ★ ★ ★ ★ ★ ★ ★ ★ ★ ★ ★ ★ ★ ★ ★ ★

## *Participation Is Easy*

Voting turnout tends to be low among students. Nevertheless, it is very easy for students to register and vote if they want to. Campus political clubs often hand out voter-registration forms, school newspapers frequently list polling areas in advance of election day, and schools themselves commonly provide venues for early voting. Individuals can also access voter registration information by logging on to the state Secretary of State's office. Go on the Web to www.sos.state.tx.tx.us/ and click on the "Elections and Voter Information" icon at the top left of the page.

★ ★ ★ ★ ★ ★ ★ ★ ★ ★ ★ ★ ★ ★ ★ ★ ★ ★ ★ ★ ★ ★ ★ ★ ★ ★ ★ ★

TABLE 5-3
## U.S. White and African American Public Opinion, 1989–2005

| Issue | Percent Agreeing Among | |
| --- | --- | --- |
| | White | African American |
| Think that government should do something to reduce differences between rich and poor (those most willing to redistribute): 1989 | 29 | 47 |
| Favor government health insurance: 1996 | 35 | 53 |
| Support capital punishment: 2000 (Texas only) | 81 | 44 |
| Support school vouchers: 2001 | 53 | 46 |
| Agree that the federal government should ensure everyone a job and a good standard of living: 2004 | 26 | 45 |
| Agree that the federal government should cut services and spending: 2004 23 | 23 | 7 |
| Support affirmative action programs: 2005 | 44 | 72 |

SOURCES: Top item from National Opinion Research Center surveys, *An American Profile: Opinions and Behavior*, 1972–1989 (New York: Gale Research, Inc., 1990), 572; second item from 1996 National Election Study, reported in William Lasser, *American Politics: The Enduring Constitution*, 2nd ed. (Boston: Houghton Mifflin, 1999), 184; third item from Christopher Lee, "Majority Think Innocent Have Been Executed," *Dallas Morning News*, June 22, 2000, A1; fourth item from Karen O'Connor and Larry J. Sabato, *American Government: Continuity and Change* (New York: Pearson, 2004), 411; fifth and sixth items from *The ANES Guide to Public Opinion and Electoral Behavior*, Ann Arbor, Michigan, University of Michigan, Center for Political Studies, accessed on the Web on October 1, 2006: www.umich.edu/~nes/nesguide; seventh item from *The Gallup Poll: Public Opinion 2005* (New York: Rowman and Littlefield, 2007), 314.

vote at higher rates than minorities, however, Cornyn won, and Texas has two Republican senators instead of one from each party.

The importance of different ethnic turnout rates compels the conclusion that the description of trends in Texas party success in Chapter Four must be modified. Chaptevr Four presented a portrait of a state undergoing a "realignment" from a normal Democratic majority to a normal Republican majority. Now it can be seen that the realignment scenario depends on a continuation of ethnic differences in voter turnout. Further, Texas's Latino population is rapidly growing (see Chapters 1 and 15), and because Mexican Americans generally vote Democratic when they do participate, they present the Democratic Party with a so-far-unrealized potential to resume its majority status among Texans. In the near future, it can be said with some confidence that the Republicans will continue to dominate Texas *as long as its minority citizens continue to stay away from the voting booths.* The Republican trend, which seems so solid when viewed from the perspective of election results since 1994, is actually quite fragile and could easily be upset if only the Democrats learned how to inspire their partisans to vote.

**TABLE 5-4**

## U.S. Anglo and Hispanic Public Opinion, Early 1990s to 2001

| Question | Anglos | Hispanics |
|---|---|---|
| **GOVERNMENT SPENDING SHOULD INCREASE ON: (1990)** | | |
| Programs to help Blacks (percent agreeing) | 23.5 | 53.7 |
| Programs for refugees and legal immigrants | 16.4 | 41.3 |
| English should be the official language (strongly agree) | 45.6 | 13.7 |
| **The basis of job hires and college admissions should be: (1990)** | | |
| Government quotas | 1.7 | 19.4 |
| Strictly merit | 52.0 | 29.3 |
| Are you satisfied with the way immigrants are treated? Percent saying yes: (2001) | 58 | 36 |
| Support school vouchers: (2001) | 53 | 44 |

SOURCES: First five items from Rudolfo O. de la Garza, Louis DeSipio, F. Chris Garcia, John Garcia, and Angelo Falcon, *Latino Voices: Mexican, Puerto Rican, and Cuban Perspectives on American Politics* (Boulder, Col.: Westview Press, 1992), 91, 97, 110; sixth item from *The Gallup Poll 2001* (Wilmington, Del.: Scholastic Resources, 2002), 158; seventh item from Karen O'Connor and Larry J. Sabato, *American Government: Continuity and Change* (New York: Pearson, 2004), 411.

# Election Campaigns

Democracies do not hold elections unannounced. There is a period of time before the voting day in which the candidates attempt to persuade potential voters to support them. This period is the **campaign**. In Texas, would-be officeholders run initially during the spring primary campaign. Those who win nomination in the primary then campaign to win the November general election.

## CAMPAIGN RESOURCES

### PEOPLE

Whatever their strategies, candidates must have two essential resources: people and money. The people who are needed are both professionals and volunteers. The professionals plan, organize, and manage the campaign, write the speeches, and raise the money. Volunteer workers are the active amateurs who distribute literature, register and canvass voters, attend the phone banks, and transport

## TABLE 5-5
### Projected Vote in 2002 U.S. Senate Race, Assuming Ethnically Equal Voter Turnouts

| Ethnicity | % of Population | % of Vote for Kirk | % of Vote for Cornyn | Projected Kirk Vote at 32% Turnout | Projected Cornyn Vote at 32% Turnout | Projected % for Kirk (D) | Projected % for Cornyn (R) |
|---|---|---|---|---|---|---|---|
| White | 52 | 30 | 69 | 705,624 | 1,622,935 | | |
| Black | 11.5 | 97 | 3 | 500,715 | 15,486 | | |
| Hispanic | 32 | 66 | 33 | 948,014 | 474,007 | | |
| Asian | 2.7 | 67 | 33 | 81,201 | 39,994 | | |
| Total Vote | | | | 2,235,554 | 2,152,422 | | |
| Total % | | | | | | 50.1 | 49 |

SOURCES: Calculations by Brian Arbour from exit poll data supplied by Daron Shaw and Mike Baselice. We are grateful to all three for their help.

supporters to the polls on election day. No major election can be won without competent people who are brought together early enough to plan, organize, and conduct an effective campaign or without a sufficient number of volunteers to make the personal contacts and get out the vote.

The act of volunteering to work on a campaign not only is useful to the candidate but also is of great importance to the volunteers and to the democratic process. People who work on a campaign learn about the stupendous exertions, the difficult choices, and the painful blunders that make up public life in a free society. They learn tolerance for other points of view, how to argue and evaluate the arguments of other people, and why the media are important. Finally, they learn that when they win, the faults of the republic are not all corrected and that, when they lose, civilization does not collapse. They learn, in other words, to be good citizens. In Texas as elsewhere, political campaigns are the most intense means of creating the truly participatory society.

Professional and voluntary participation, the first major resource of campaigns, is thus entirely uncontroversial. Everyone endorses it. But about the second resource, money, there is great controversy.

## MONEY

Except in many municipal elections, where volunteers are most important, money is the most important campaign resource. Politicians need money to publicize their candidacies, especially over television. Table 5-6 illustrates the costs of buying advertising in major media outlets in 2004. The need to buy campaign advertising in many such media repeatedly over a period of months makes the

**TABLE 5-6**

## Costs of Political Advertising in Selected Texas Cities, 2004

| (Television) City | Station | Cost of 30-Second Spot* | Cost of 10-Second Spot |
|---|---|---|---|
| Dallas | KDFW (Fox) | $14,000 | $7,000 |
| Houston | KHOU (CBS) | $5,000 | $2,500 |
| Austin | KXAN (NBC) | $2,500 | $1,250 |
| Lubbock | KCBD (NBC) | $400 | $240 |
| (Newspaper) City | Paper | Cost of Full-page, Black & White Ad** | Cost of Full-page, Color Ad** |
| El Paso | *Times* | $8,369.90 | $9,601.92 |
| Amarillo | *Globe-News* | $5,127.75 | $5,822.75 |
| San Antonio | *Express-News* | $22,206.28 | $24,009.24 |
| Fort Worth | *Star-Telegram* | $16,905.45 | $18,953.48 |

*Prime time, popular show.
**Monday through Saturday; advertising is more expensive on Sunday.

SOURCE: Compiled by David F. Prindle, Professor of Government, University of Texas at Austin, in January 2004.

cost of running for office in Texas formidable. For example, Tony Sanchez spent more than $67 million (62 percent of it for television advertising) attempting to defeat Rick Perry and win the governorship in 2002, while Perry spent almost $28 million (73 percent of it for TV) successfully defending his hold on the office. The two major-party candidates for lieutenant governor, David Dewhurst and John Sharp, spent about $12 million between them, while the major-party candidates for attorney general, Greg Abbott and Kirk Watson, spent roughly $4.5 million.[6]

This money must come from somewhere. Very few candidates, such as H. Ross Perot, who tried to win the presidency as an independent in 1992 and 1996, and Sanchez, are so rich that they are able to finance their own campaigns. The great majority of candidates must get their money from a source other than their own pockets.

Except at the presidential level, the United States is one of the few democracies that does not have **publicly funded campaigns**. In many other countries, the government gives the parties tax money to cover part of the expenses of campaigning.

This means that the parties, if their candidates are successful, are relatively free of obligation to special interests. In the United States at every level except the presidency, however, we rely on **privately funded campaigns.** Candidates and parties must persuade private citizens to part with checks, or their campaigns will fail.

The candidate with the most money does not win every election. In 1990, for example, Republican gubernatorial candidate Clayton Williams outspent Democratic candidate Ann Richards two to one and still lost, and in 2002, Tony Sanchez paid out more than two-and-a-half times Rick Perry's total, yet failed to defeat him.[7]

But the best financed candidate does win most of the time. And just because a victorious candidate spent less than the loser does not mean that money was unimportant to his or her campaign. Ann Richards's expenditure of more than $10 million in 1990 and Rick Perry's expenditure of $28 million in 2002 are large chunks of cash by anyone's accounting. Further, scholarly research has established that financial share is positively correlated to vote share, or in other words, the more money candidates spend, the more votes they tend to attract, especially in primary elections.[8] In sum, although money may not be a *sufficient* resource to ensure political victory, it is still a *necessary* resource. People who are willing to contribute large amounts of money to campaigns, therefore, are extremely important to candidates.

**Where Does the Money Come From?** Most of the money contributed to candidates comes from wealthy donors who represent some sort of special interest. For example, of the four major gubernatorial candidates in 2006, Democrat Chris Bell received a quarter of his contributions from people who wrote checks for $25,000 or more; Kinky Friedman received 30 percent of his contributions from checks of the same size, Carole Keeton Strayhorn relied on such contributions for 45 percent, and Rick Perry for 47 percent.[9] In all state campaigns in 2006, 140 Texans contributed at least $100,000, for a total from those contributors of $52 million.[10] Employing such large contributions, people and organizations with wealth or access to wealth are able to rent the gratitude of candidates by helping to fund their campaigns. Ordinary people who have to worry about paying their bills are not able to contribute nearly as much and therefore cannot ensure candidates' attention to their concerns. In this way, private funding of campaigns skews public policy in favor of special interests.

Therefore, when it comes to money and political campaigns in Texas, the following summary seems justified: Money is very important, but it is not the only resource. Volunteers, imagination, ideology, partisanship, and personality also play a part, as do such things as the state of the economy and the presence or absence of a scandal. The 1994 elections demonstrated that on those unusual historical occasions when the voters are particularly angry at the incumbent party, money is relatively unimportant. Nevertheless, because economic wealth is so unequally distributed, it seems particularly dangerous to democratic government. It gives a very few citizens access to a very large political resource. For that reason, journalists and textbook authors are always worrying about its potential power.

As a rule, politicians dislike the system of private campaign financing, finding it time consuming and demeaning. Many retired officeholders have written

# YOU DECIDE

## Should Texas Have Publicly Funded Campaigns?

Although there is a system of public financing in place for presidential campaigns, and for state legislative campaigns in Maine and Arizona, most of the states permit their elections to be financed entirely from private sources. In Texas, candidates must either pay their own way or accept contributions from private individuals and organizations. There have been many suggestions, over the years, for some sort of plan (generally modeled on the federal system) for Texas to use tax money to support the campaigns of at least the major-party candidates in whole or in part.

| PRO | CON |
|---|---|
| ▲ State support of candidates would free them from dependence on special interests. | ▼ Unless all private contributions were outlawed, candidates would still feel beholden to those who contributed. If all private contributions were prohibited, then all candidates would become dependent on state largesse. The state would not be able to resist making "regulations" that would inevitably either favor one party or suppress vigorous debate. |
| ▲ As with the federal income-tax check-off system, a state program would devise a means of ensuring that participation in the system was voluntary. | ▼ Use of tax money to support candidates would mean that the coerced contributions of citizens were being used to subsidize candidates whose views many of them might abhor. |
| ▲ Granted that the program should be limited to general elections, are we going to refuse to clean up part of Texas politics because we cannot clean up all of it? | ▼ State contributions would almost certainly be limited to candidates in the general election. This would leave candidates in primaries still dependent on wealthy special interests. If the program were extended to primaries, then dozens of candidates would have an incentive to enter, and the costs would grow huge. |
| ▲ As with ballot-entry laws, some test of a party's appeal in the previous election could be applied to for state support. Besides, perhaps a few fringe parties arguing their "extremist" views might be a good thing for Texas | ▼ If the program were to be limited to candidates of the two major parties, it would suppress the expression of alternative political opinions. If it were expanded to all parties, it would provide incentives for small fringe parties to claim tax subsidies to publicize their extremist views. |

SOURCES: Elizabeth Daniel, "Public Financing: Making It Work," *The National Voter*, June/July 2001, 8–14; Jim Hightower, "The Hard and the Soft," *Texas Observer*, July 18, 2003, 15; Center for Governmental Studies, *Investing in Democracy: Creating Public Financing of Elections in Your Community* (Los Angeles: Center for Governmental Studies, 2003); Public Campaign Web site, accessed October 2, 2006: www.publicampaign.org/; Cato Institute Web site, accessed October 2, 2006: www.cato.org/campaignfinance/.

in their autobiographies that they hated having to ask people for money, both because it made them feel humiliated and because they would rather have been working at crafting public policy. A survey of Texas candidates taken by Common Cause in 1990 revealed that 65 percent of them supported public financing of campaigns.[11] Yet the opposition of the special interests who benefit from the current system has thus far stymied efforts to introduce reform.

**Control of Money in Campaigns** The power of money in campaigns disturbs partisans of democracy because it seems to create an inequality of citizenship. Everyone has only one vote, but some people are multimillionaires. Those with more money to contribute seem to be "super citizens" who can wield influence denied to the rest. For this reason, many people have for decades been trying to control the impact of money in both state and national races. Their success at both levels is spotty at best.

In Texas, several laws have been passed to control the use and disclosure of the money collected by candidates. These laws have been made steadily tougher over the years, but they still allow wealthy individuals to purchase more political influence than is available to their fellow citizens.

*The Revenue Act of 1971* This is a federal law intended to broaden the base of financial support and minimize the dependence of candidates on large donations from a few contributors. It provided that taxpayers may stipulate that $1 of their U.S. income tax ($2 on a joint return) be put into the Presidential Election Campaign Fund to provide for the partial public funding of these national campaigns. The amount that taxpayers can contribute has since been raised to $3 for an individual and $6 for a joint return.

*The Federal Election Campaign Act of 1972* This law applies only to campaigns for federal offices—president, vice president, and members of Congress. It establishes a Federal Election Commission, requires candidates to make periodic reports of contributions and expenses, and places certain limits on contributions. Individuals may donate up to $1,000 in each primary or general election and a maximum of $25,000 in a given year. Groups may contribute up to $5,000 per candidate.

*The Texas Campaign Reporting and Disclosure Act of 1973* As amended, this act outlines procedures for campaign reporting and disclosure. It appears to strengthen the election code in several areas where previously it was deficient. As amended, the act's major provisions are:

1. Every candidate for political office and every political committee within the state must appoint a campaign treasurer before accepting contributions or making expenditures.

2. Contributions exceeding $500 by out-of-state political committees can be made only if the names of contributors of $100 or more are disclosed.

3. Detailed financial reports are required of candidates and managers of campaign committees. They must include a list of all contributions and expenditures over $50.

4. Violators face both civil action and criminal penalties.

The 1973 law sounds like a genuine attempt to force public disclosure of the financial sponsors of candidates. Its great flaw, however, was that it contained no provision for enforcement. Because laws do not enforce themselves, the public reporting of private contributions was at best a haphazard affair. Moreover, the law failed to impose any limits on the amount that individuals or organizations could contribute to campaigns; as long as they reported the amount, they could attempt to buy as much influence as they could afford.

*1991 Ethics Law* In 1991, the legislature passed another ethics bill designed to regulate and moderate the impact of private wealth on public policy in campaigns and at other levels of Texas politics. This law created an Ethics Commission that could hold hearings on public complaints, levy fines, and report severe violations to the Travis County (Austin) district attorney for possible prosecution.

Again, however, the law failed to place limits on campaign contributions. Furthermore, it required a "supermajority" of six of eight commissioners for important actions, a provision that was practically guaranteed to prevent the vigorous investigation of violators. As John Steiner, the commission's executive director, stated publicly, "There's very little in the way of real enforcement . . . in most of the laws we administer. It's just an unenforced statute except that if people don't [obey the law], it gets some bad press."[12]

In 1995, the legislature imposed some changes on the financing of judicial campaigns but defeated proposals for broader reforms. In 2003, legislators amended the ethics law to make it apply more rigorously to lobbying but did not change the provisions that applied to campaigning. See Chapter Three for a discussion of the details of the new provisions of this law.

When the Sunset Commission (SC) began evaluating the Texas Ethics Commission (TEC) in 2002 (see Chapter 7 for a discussion of the SC), the supposed ethics watchdog itself came in for some bad publicity. Journalists reported that in its decade of existence the TEC had never issued a subpoena, audited a file, or referred a complaint for criminal prosecution. Further, the commission cannot compel targets of an investigation to respond, and therefore, campaign organizations have little incentive to provide complete information. Indeed, members of the public are unable to discover if financial disclosure reports are accurate because the TEC does not thoroughly check the reports that are filed.[13] Journalists, students, and scholars will go on consulting the information in the TEC database because it is the only source of campaign contribution information. Its value as an accurate view of the money trail in Texas politics, however, is limited.

In summary, there is virtually no control over, and very little effort to ensure the public disclosure of, the influence of money in Texas political campaigns. As a consequence, people with money have more influence over politicians than do ordinary citizens. For observers who take democratic theory seriously, this situation is the single most disturbing fact about Texas politics.

*Hard v. Soft* The Federal Election Campaign Act (FECA) of 1972 originally set limits on the amount of money individual candidates could contribute to their own campaigns. But in the case of *Buckley* v. *Valeo* (424 U.S. 1, 1976), the U.S. Supreme Court held that these limits were unconstitutional suppressions of the freedom of speech guaranteed by the First Amendment. It is this decision that allowed Texas billionaire H. Ross Perot to spend millions of dollars of his own money to finance his independent candidacies for the presidency in 1992 and 1996.

STUFFED.

BEN SARGENT
©1999 The Austin American-Statesman
Universal Press Syndicate

Cartoonist Ben Sargent points out that there is more than one way to corrupt democratic government.

*Courtesy of Ben Sargent.*

*Buckley* v. *Valeo* also extended the right of free speech to political action committees (PACs) for "party building" at the national level. PACs were permitted to spend unlimited amounts on political activities such as get-out-the-vote campaigns or to contribute as much as they wanted to the party organizations, as long as these contributions were not directly coordinated with an individual candidate's election campaign. In the jargon of campaign financing, contributions that go directly to a candidate are "hard money," while those that go to parties, and therefore presumably benefit candidates only indirectly, are "soft money." The effect of *Buckley* v. *Valeo* was not limited to federal elections. Shortly after the case was decided, the attorney general of Texas ruled that the decision voided similar provisions in the state's 1973 campaign finance law as well (Texas Attorney General Opinion H864, 1976). As a result, Clayton Williams and Tony Sanchez were able to spend millions of dollars of their own wealth in their runs for governor in 1990 and 2002, and corporate, labor, and trade association PACs were permitted to contribute whatever they wished to state campaigns.

During the 2007 legislature, there were a few attempts to impose more controls on campaign contributions, but they went nowhere.[14] In summary, at the national level, and even more so in Texas, there is very little control over the ability of rich individuals and interests to buy influence over candidates.

## NEGATIVE CAMPAIGNING

In addition to the influence of money, another disturbing characteristic of contemporary campaigning is the use of personal attacks on candidates by their opponents, generally in television spots. Candidates are accused of everything from drug addiction to mental illness to marital infidelity to financial dishonesty to Satanism. Mainly, they are accused of being liars.

People being imperfect creatures, some of these charges are bound to be true. If anyone's past conduct is scrutinized closely, episodes of untruthfulness, unkindness, sexual misbehavior, or financial impropriety can usually be uncovered. Candidates can therefore almost always dig up some dirt on each other. Because politicians believe that such attacks are effective, they are placing more and more emphasis on the exposure of each other's personal flaws to the exclusion of other strategies. Their television advertising attempts to blow up ordinary human weaknesses into evidence of monstrous immorality and to frighten citizens into believing that their opponents are not just mistaken, but hateful.

Personal attacks now dominate the airwaves during election years. According to a study by the Center for Responsive Politics in the Annenburg Public Policy Center at the University of Pennsylvania, 80 percent of the TV campaign spots aired during the fall of 2006 by the Republican and Democratic campaign committees of the U.S. House of Representatives were negative.[15]

Negative campaigning has a corrosive effect on democracy for four reasons. First, some elections are decided on the basis of inaccurate or irrelevant charges. Second, discussions of public policy and how to solve national or state problems are shunted aside in everyone's eagerness to throw mud. Third, many good people may decide not to enter political life so that they can avoid becoming the targets of public attack. Fourth, negative campaigning disheartens citizens, who are thus more apt to stay home on election day. Research by political scientists has concluded that such campaigns may depress voter turnout by as much as 5 percent.[16]

Texas has had its share of negative campaigns and, thus, its share of damage to the democratic ideal. A large part of the gubernatorial race in 1990, during both the Democratic primary and the general election, consisted of accusations of illegal drug use by Ann Richards (who won both races despite the charges). The gubernatorial races in 1994 and 1998 were relatively clean, but some of the other contests were savage. The campaign of 2002, to be discussed shortly, broke all records for viciousness and distortion. Negative campaigning in Texas seems no worse than it is in most states, but that is bad enough.

# Public Elections

A public election is the only political activity in which large numbers of Texans (although, as we have seen, usually not a majority) are likely to participate. The state has three types of elections: primary, general, and special elections.

## PRIMARY ELECTIONS

A **primary** is an election held within a party to nominate candidates for the general election or to choose delegates to a presidential nominating convention. It is because primaries are so important in Texas that parties are weak. Because they do not control nominations, party "leaders" have no control over officeholders and so, in reality, cannot lead.

Under procedures begun in 1988, the primary election in Texas occurs on the second Tuesday in March in even-numbered years, prior to the general election. The Texas Election Code provides that any political party whose candidate for governor received 20 percent or more of the vote in the most recent general election must hold a primary to choose candidates for upcoming elections. Parties whose candidates polled less than 20 percent may either hold a primary or choose their candidates by the less expensive method of a nominating convention. In effect, Republicans and Democrats must hold primary elections, while smaller third parties may select their candidates in conventions.

Under Texas law, a candidate must win the nomination with a majority vote in the primary. If there is not a majority winner, as there frequently is not if there are more than two candidates, the two leading vote getters meet thirty days later in a general runoff election.

## TEXAS'S "OPEN" PRIMARY

There are three types of primary election:

1. A **blanket primary,** used in only two states, is like a general election held before the general election. All candidates of all parties run on one list, and any registered voter can participate.

2. An **open primary** is one in which any registered voter may participate in any party's primary.

3. A **closed primary** is one in which only registered members of a party may participate in that party's primary.

Technically, Texas laws provide for a closed primary. In practice, however, voters may participate in any primary as long as they have not already voted in the primary of another party during the same year. The only realistic sense in which Texas has a closed primary is that once voters have recorded their party affiliation by voting in one party's primary, they cannot participate in the affairs of the runoff primary or the convention of another party during that year.

Aspiring candidates obtain a place on the primary ballot by applying to the state executive committee for statewide office or to the county chairperson for local office. Drawings are held for position on the ballot, and filing fees (discussed in Administration and Finance section) must be paid before the ballot is printed.

## WHEN HELD

For most of the twentieth century, Texas and many of the other southern states held primaries in May. Several small northern states, most famously New Hampshire, held their primaries very early in a presidential year—often in January. Both candidates and the media concentrated on these early primaries. As a result of the importance of the early contests in the small northern states, in recent decades the presidential nominating campaigns have often been nearly over by the time southern primaries were held. In the Democratic Party, this could mean that candidates whom many Texas conservatives considered too liberal—George McGovern in 1972 and Walter Mondale in 1984, for example—had wrapped up the nomination before Texans had a chance to register their opinions.

For some years, there was talk among conservative leaders about establishing an early presidential primary in Texas so that candidates would be forced to cater more to the state's voters. By 1986, ten southern states had moved to adopt a southern regional "super primary," to be held the second week in March beginning in 1988. In a surprise move, the Texas legislature adopted the new primary date during a special session in the summer of 1986. Texas primaries, both regular and presidential, are now held on the second Tuesday in March, with the primary runoff elections on the second Tuesday in April.

## ADMINISTRATION AND FINANCE

In Texas, primary elections are administered entirely by political party officials in accordance with the provisions of the Texas Election Code. The process is decentralized. Most of the responsibilities and work fall on the shoulders of the county chairperson and the members of the county executive committee. They must arrange for the polling places, provide the voting machines and other equipment, print the ballots, and determine the results. The election is supervised by a presiding judge and an alternate appointed in each precinct by the county chair, subject to approval by the county committee. The presiding judge appoints two or more clerks to actually conduct the election—checking registration rolls, issuing ballots, and settling occasional disputes.

Conducting a primary election is expensive, especially in a state as large as Texas. Clerks are paid a salary, albeit a modest one. Polling places and voting machines must be rented, ballots printed, and other expenses paid. Prior to 1972, the costs were met by charging each aspiring candidate a filing fee. Texas was the only state in which primary elections were financed entirely by the candidates themselves.

In 1973, the Sixty-third Legislature enacted a permanent primary election finance bill, which provides for a combination of state and private funding. Filing fees are still in use, but the amounts are reasonable, ranging, in 2006, from a high of $5,000 for U.S. senator to $75 for county surveyor.[17] Expenses beyond those that are covered by the filing fees are paid by the state. County political party chairs pay the costs of the primary and are then reimbursed by the secretary of state.

## GENERAL ELECTIONS

The purpose of a **general election** is to choose state and national executives and legislators and state judges. General elections are held in even-numbered years on the Tuesday after the first Monday in November. In 1974, Texas joined the group of states that elect their governors and other state officials in the "off year," the even-numbered year between presidential election years. At the same time, the state adopted a constitutional amendment that extended the terms of office for the governor and other state officials from two to four years.

Unlike primary elections, general and special elections are the responsibility of the state. The secretary of state is the principal election officer, although the election organization is decentralized and most of the actual work is performed at the county level. The county commissioners court appoints election judges, chooses the method of voting—paper ballots or some type of voting machine—and pays the bills. The county clerk conducts absentee balloting and performs many of the functions charged to the commissioners court.

Nominees of established parties are placed on the ballot when they win a party primary or are chosen by a party convention. New parties and independent candidates get on the general election ballot by presenting a petition signed by a specified number of qualified voters who have not participated in the primary election of another party. The number of required signatures varies with the office. At the local level, it may be no larger than 500; at the state level, it is 1 percent of the votes cast in the last gubernatorial election.

There is no standard election ballot in Texas. Primary ballots vary from party to party, and general election ballots vary from county to county. Whatever its form, the ballot lists the offices to be filled, beginning with the president (in an appropriate year) and proceeding down to the lowliest local position. Candidates' political party affiliations are listed beside their names, and candidates of the party that polled the most votes in the most recent gubernatorial election are listed first. Other parties' candidates appear in descending order of that party's polling strength in the preceding election. A space is provided for write-in candidates. Constitutional amendments, if any, are listed separately, usually near the bottom of the ballot, followed by local referendum questions.

A somewhat different form of the general election is held in cities. Elections for mayors and city councils are usually held in the spring, and are always technically nonpartisan. Party labels do not appear beside the candidates' names, and no party certification is needed to get on the ballot. It is custom abetted by city charter provisions, not state law, that prevents partisan politics at the local level (see Chapter 12). By denying the voters the guidance provided by a party label, nonpartisan elections are even more confusing for them than are general elections, and voter turnout tends to be even lower.

Ben Sargent expresses the growing suspicion of the reliability and honesty of electronic voting (see box)

*Courtesy of Ben Sargent.*

# SPECIAL ELECTIONS

In Texas, a number of special elections are held in addition to primary and general elections. They may be called at the state level to fill vacancies in Congress or in the state legislature or to vote on proposed constitutional amendments. Because special elections are held at irregular times, they, like municipal contests, generally feature very low voter turnout. A special election held in September 2003, in which the voters were asked if they wished to ratify Proposition 12, which capped medical lawsuit awards at $750,000, generated a barrage of op-ed newspaper columns, and engaged such wealthy interest groups—doctors vs. lawyers—that spending on television spots and mailed flyers topped $13 million. Yet all the loud publicity managed to persuade only about 13 percent of the eligible citizens to go to the polls. (Proposition 12 passed narrowly). Thus do small fractions of the population often determine state policy through special elections.[18]

# ABSENTEE OR EARLY VOTING

While voters who register their preferences in the conventional manner must get to a polling place between 7 A.M. and 7 P.M. on election day, Texas citizens may vote absentee in any election. Voting may be done for a period of two weeks before the election at the county clerk's office or at a variety of polling places throughout the county. In the past, one needed a reason to vote absentee, such as a planned trip from the county or illness. In 1987 the legislature removed the restrictions, and anyone can now vote early. As many as half the voters cast early ballots during the first decades of the twenty-first century in Texas.[19]

★ ★ ★ ★ ★ ★ ★ ★ ★ ★ ★ ★ ★ ★ ★ ★ ★ ★ ★ ★ ★ ★ ★ ★ ★ ★ ★ ★ ★

## An Electronic Fix?

Because there is no standard ballot in Texas, the manner in which voters record their choices varies from place to place and changes with the evolution of technology. Since 2002 some counties have been experimenting with the eSlate, a minicomputer that permits citizens to record their partisan choices electronically. In theory, voters in the areas where the eSlate is in use can find their preferred candidates on an electronic screen and then record their choices by pressing an Enter button at the bottom of the screen. The voters' choices are stored in cyber-memory. After the polls close, the units are delivered to a tabulation center, where the votes are counted. Its advocates argue that this type of voting is more efficient and less subject to fraud than traditional paper balloting.

In practice, the new technology, like the old technology, has proved to be imperfect. In 2002 and 2004, a variety of glitches and mistakes, and perhaps efforts to manufacture results, sparked embarrassment, charges of vote tampering, and threats of lawsuits. Although there were only minor problems with Texas voting in 2006, there was major trouble with the eSlates in Ohio, Pennsylvania, Florida, and Maryland. Moreover, a chorus of criticism of the eSlate by computer scientists has lent authority to skepticism about

*(continued)*

★ ★ ★ ★ ★ ★ ★ ★ ★ ★ ★ ★ ★ ★ ★ ★ ★ ★ ★ ★ ★ ★ ★ ★ ★ ★ ★ ★ ★

(continued)

computer voting. Researchers at Cal Tech, MIT, and Stanford have concluded that the traditional low-tech paper ballots were *less* likely to be lost or fraudulently miscounted than the new e-ballots. Without actual physical ballots that can be observed and stored, electronic ballots offer an opportunity for manipulation of the results through hacking and other means available to cyber-criminals.

While paper ballots have never deterred dishonest politicians from attempting to steal elections, the problems with the eSlates underscore the point that no technology is fool- and fraud-proof. The solution to ballot fraud will remain the same with computer voting as it has been with previous means of recording citizen preferences: eternal vigilance by a suspicious public. There is no technological cure for the ills of democracy.

★ ★ ★ ★ ★ ★ ★ ★ ★ ★ ★ ★ ★ ★ ★ ★ ★ ★ ★ ★ ★ ★ ★ ★ ★ ★ ★

SOURCES: Ed Housewright and Victoria Loe Hicks, "County Democrats Say Early Votes Miscounted," *Dallas Morning News*, October 23, 2002, A1; "Votescam in the Electronic Age," *Texas Observer*, December 20, 2002, 12; Erika Jonietz, "Valid Voting?" *Technology Review*, February 2004, 74; Ian Urbina, "Electronic Voting Machines Are Making Officials Wary," *New York Times*, September 24, 2006, A19; Ian Urbina and Christopher R. Drew, "Experts Worry as Poll Problems Resist Overhaul," *New York Times*, November 26, 2006, A1.

# Elections of 1994 through 2000

The political realignment toward which Texas had been inching since the 1960s finally arrived in 1994. Republicans successfully defended a U.S. Senate seat, picked up two seats in the U.S. House of Representatives, increased their representation in the Texas legislature, and garnered more than 900 local offices. They won both vulnerable railroad commission seats and captured minorities on the state Supreme Court and the state board of education. George W. Bush defeated incumbent Democrat Ann Richards to become Texas's governor. Until 1984, Texas had been a one-party Democratic state. After 1994, it increasingly looked like a one-party Republican state.

The Republican victory was based on a clear pattern of ethnic and economic class cleavages and on differences in voter participation. Democratic candidates drew support from lower-income Anglos, Mexican Americans, and African Americans. Republicans were supported by the wealthy in general and wealthy Anglos in particular. Because voter turnout was higher in the areas and among the people who tend to support Republicans, they were the winners.

It was perhaps at the level of the judiciary that the Republican Party made the most significant gains in 1994. GOP candidates won every seat they contested on the state Court of Criminal Appeals and Supreme Court, gaining their first majority on the latter since the days of Reconstruction. Republicans captured nineteen local judgeships from the Democrats in Harris County alone. The major long-term result of the Republican court victories was to replace plaintiff-oriented, prolawsuit judges with business-oriented, antilawsuit judges.

The fact that the 1994 results inaugurated a lasting pattern rather than a temporary perturbation was illustrated by the results of 1996, 1998, and 2000. Republicans continued to win every statewide electoral contest as well as all of Texas's electoral votes for president.

# Election of 2002

Both the campaigns and the results of the 2002 election illustrated important trends and concepts in Texas politics. At the beginning of the contest, Democratic prospects did not look entirely hopeless. Unlike its weak efforts during the 1998 and 2000 campaigns, the party in 2002 had a strategic plan and the money with which to implement it, or so its leaders believed. If the problem with Democrats was that their natural base of Blacks, Hispanics, and Anglo liberals was failing to turn out on election day, then it seemed to party leaders that the solution was to nominate candidates who energized the base.

The party, therefore, with some difficulties in the primaries, managed to nominate an African American, Ron Kirk, as its candidate for U.S. Senate, a Mexican American, Tony Sanchez, as its standard-bearer for governor, and an Anglo, John Sharp, as its aspirant for lieutenant governor. The Democratic leadership hoped that each candidate would draw voters of his own ethnic group, all of whom would vote for the other candidates of the party. Moreover, by persuading multimillionaire Sanchez to be the nominee, Democrats hoped to overcome the absence of funding that had sunk Gary Mauro, their gubernatorial candidate in 1998.

Sanchez came through with the funding, contributing more than $60 million to his own campaign, but otherwise, the Democratic "dream team" flopped. As Table 5-7 illustrates, ethnic and economic voting followed familiar patterns, with Democrats capturing large majorities of minority voters and those lower on the income scale, and Republicans commanding the allegiance of Anglos and those with higher incomes. The Democratic strategy depended on their dream team inspiring a large turnout among its supporters. In fact, although turnout in some Latino and African American districts was up slightly from previous off-year elections, it did not rise nearly enough to offset the overwhelming advantage all Republican candidates enjoyed with Anglo voters. GOP candidates not only won every statewide office—executive, legislative, and judicial—but captured control of the state House of Representatives for the first time since Reconstruction.

As far as the tone of the 2002 campaign was concerned, all observers agreed that it was the sleaziest, the most vicious, and the least democratically informative contest that anyone could remember. With almost all Texas candidates relatively conservative in policy stance, there were few issues to disagree about. Democrats accused Republican incumbents of failing to deal with the state's insurance crisis (see Chapter 3), but Republican incumbents' actions against Farmers Insurance during the summer seemed to defuse that issue. Republicans tried to tar their opponents with the label "liberal," but such accusations were not credible, given the public records of Sanchez, Kirk, and Sharp. Instead of a wholesome democratic dialogue over differing views of public policy, citizens were treated to what one journalist, borrowing a term from football, termed "smash-mouth politics." [20]

Texas Gov. Rick Perry with his wife, Anita, at his side, is shown casting his ballot at an electronic voting machine during early voting Thursday, Nov. 2, 2006, in Austin.

TABLE 5-7

## Economic and Ethnic Voting in 2002 Gubernatorial Election: Exit Survey Data

TEXAS STATE LINE

| Group | % Sanchez (D) | % Perry (R) |
| --- | --- | --- |
| **Ethnicity** | | |
| White, Caucasian | 24 | 70 |
| African American, Black | 93 | 7 |
| Latin, Hispanic | 60 | 35 |
| **Annual Household Income** | | |
| $8,000 to $11,999 | 74 | 26 |
| $15,000 to $19,999 | 59 | 36 |
| $20,000 to $24,999 | 44 | 53 |
| $35,000 to $39,999 | 32 | 60 |
| $100,000 and above | 28 | 68 |

SOURCE: Republican party exit polls, conducted immediately after 2002 balloting. We are indebted to Daron Shaw and Mike Baselice for making this information available to us.

The most deplorable contest among a host of negative campaigns was the one between Sanchez and Perry for the governorship. Sanchez's TV ads were tough, mean, and personal, but at first, they at least dealt with public policy. They blamed Perry for the state's troubled schools, ridiculed him for accepting contributions from energy and insurance interests, and mocked him for being an unelected governor. Toward the end of the contest, however, still behind in the polls, Sanchez made an attack on Perry that was unconnected to any issues before the electorate. Perry's chauffeur had been stopped for a traffic violation by a police officer one day in 2001 as he drove the governor to the capitol building. Not aware that there was a camera and voice recorder on the hood of the police car, Perry had gotten out of the limousine and said to the officer, "Why don't you just let us get on down the road?" Sanchez's campaign got hold of the tapes and played them frequently in television ads, adding: "Rick Perry. Why don't we just let him get on down the road?"

It was unfair and unworthy of a hopeful public servant, but it was not the bottom of the barrel. That was supplied by Perry's campaign. For months, Perry had been running ads informing the electorate that, during the 1980s, one of Sanchez's banks had been discovered to have been knowingly laundering illegal drug money from Mexico. Although the federal judge who had been in charge of the case was happy to tell anyone that he had found that Sanchez had not known about the source of the money, the Perry campaign ignored the facts and kept running the misleading ad.[21]

This was bad enough. But after Sanchez's embarrassing "get on down the road" ad, the Perry campaign retaliated with what was perhaps the most noxious spot in the history of negative advertising. Perry put on camera two former federal Drug Enforcement Administration agents, who insinuated that Sanchez had somehow been involved in the slaying of DEA agent Enrique "Kiki" Camarena in 1985. There was neither evidence nor reasoning to support the charge. If Sanchez had not known about the drug laundering, he certainly could not have known of the drug traffickers' intention to kill an undercover agent. But the Perry campaign played the ad over and over in every media market anyway. Although candidates have asserted many reprehensible things about one another over the years, this was probably the first time that one has accused another of being a murderer. The fact that the charge was a fiction made it all the more indefensible.[22]

The campaign and voting of 2002, therefore, fell far short of constituting a good democratic election. By and large, candidates failed to inform the electorate by debating issues, contenting themselves with spending their money on misleading personal attacks. For their part, many citizens failed to live up to their responsibilities by staying home on election day. Democracy in Texas has a long way to go.

# Election of 2004

There were no contests for governor or U.S. Senator in Texas on November 2, election day 2004, but interest was high anyway. Texas former governor, Republican George W. Bush, was being challenged for reelection to the nation's presidency by Democratic Senator John Kerry of Massachusetts, and many seats for the U.S. House of Representatives and the state legislature were being hotly contested.

Bush, who had narrowly lost the popular-vote margin in 2000, managed to raise his share of the popular vote by 1.6 percent, which was enough to eke out a slim 51 to 48 percent victory, accompanied by a decisive 286 to 252 electoral vote margin. Republicans picked up five seats in the U.S. House of Representatives. Their successful struggle to redraw the Lone Star State's Congressional boundaries—described elsewhere in this book—resulted in the defeat of four of the five Democratic representatives who had been "targeted." Republicans also picked up four U.S. Senate seats

Republicans lost one seat in the state house of representatives, but retained their majority of 87 to 63. They defended their 19 to 12 advantage in the state senate, and kept their locks on the Railroad Commission and court system.

Texas, like the nation, would remain conservative and Republican for at least the next two years.

# Election of 2006

Since 1994 Texas had generally tracked with the rest of the country in its electoral politics. That is, both the state and the nation moved in a Republican direction. In 2006, however, Texas diverged wildly from the pattern evident in the United States as a whole.

Nationally, 2006 was a "throw the rascals out" election, with citizens furious at the Republican Congress for defending the unpopular war in Iraq and seeming to countenance corrupt governance. Republican President George W. Bush was a particular target of voter ire, as about six in ten respondents in ballot-box exit polls reported that they disapproved of the way he was handling his job. Although Bush himself was not running for anything, independent citizens in particular (those who did not identify with either party) voted against Republican candidates to show their opposition to his foreign policy.[23] The Democrats won both the U.S. House of Representatives and the Senate for the first time in twelve years.

The results in Texas were very different. As they had since 1994, Republican candidates won every statewide office, electing or reelecting candidates to the governorship, lieutenant governorship, railroad commission, attorney general, comptroller, agriculture commissioner, land commissioner, and U.S. Senator, plus eight judgeships on the supreme court and court of criminal appeals. They kept their majority among the state's 32-member delegation to the U.S. House of Representatives, although Democrat Nick Lampson did defeat a Republican write-in candidate to capture a seat from the 22nd Congressional district, previously represented by scandal-tarred Tom DeLay, and Ciro Rodriguez ousted seven-term Republican representative Henry Bonilla in the 23rd district. Democrats gained five seats in the state house of representatives, but they still did not come close to commanding a majority in that body. In a single geographically based district race for one of the seats on the state board of education, Democrat Rick Agosto managed to defeat Republican Tony Cunningham. Otherwise, Republicans continued their domination of the state's political structure.

The most interesting and unusual race was for governor, in which incumbent Rick Perry staved off the campaigns of Democrat Chris Bell, independent Carole Keeton Strayhorn, independent Kinky Friedman, and Libertarian James Werner to win reelection with 39 percent of the vote. Bell, who came in second with 30 percent, won a few counties in areas that have come to be "normally" Democratic—those along the Rio Grande and a handful in central and east Texas. Strayhorn won majorities in a small number of widely scattered counties in the process of collecting 18 percent, while Friedman, whose eccentric persona had attracted national attention to his campaign, managed to garner only 12 percent and did not win a single county. Werner received the support of only 1 percent of the voters. Perry gained support from every area of Texas and won the great majority of the state's counties.

A trend that continued, in both Texas and the nation as a whole, was negative and misleading campaign advertising. One journalist described the national tone of campaign television spots in 2006 as "the sorriest, sleaziest, most disheartening and embarrassing in memory."[24] This may have been an exaggeration when applied to Texas, for no candidate stooped so low as to accuse his or her opponent of being a murderer in a TV ad, as Rick Perry had accused Tony Sanchez in 2002. Still, the tone of much television advertising in 2006 was laden with innuendo and contempt for truth, let alone good taste. It was not the worst, but it was bad enough.

There were a few local Democratic wrinkles in the statewide Republican triumph. Austin continued to give its votes to the now-minority party. More surprisingly, Dallas county experienced a strong Democratic surge. Democrats won every countywide office they contested, including 42 judgeships. In the most significant contest, Craig Watkins defeated Toby Shook to become the county's first African American district attorney. In Harris County (Houston), Republicans continued to dominate, but their margin of victory was smaller than in the past. The GOP's judicial candidates had won by an average of 9 percentage points in 2002. In 2006, their winning margin was down to 4 points. Political scientists attributed the trends in the state's two largest cities to continuing demographic changes. Minorities, especially Latinos, have been moving to those cities, while Anglos have been moving to the suburbs in outlying counties. Because minorities tend to vote Democratic, the Democratic vote in the cities is increasing. Whether the 2006 results marked a partisan tipping point in Dallas and the writing-on-the-wall for Houston, however, is a question that will only be answered in hindsight.[25]

★ ★ ★ ★ ★ ★ ★ ★ ★ ★ ★ ★ ★ ★ ★ ★ ★ ★ ★ ★ ★ ★ ★ ★ ★ ★ ★ ★ ★ ★ ★ ★

## What's In a Name?

Among the unusual aspects of the gubernatorial campaign of 2006 was the candidates' reliance on nicknames. Independent "Kinky" Friedman had been born with the first name Richard, but had adopted the odd moniker decades before, and written books under that name. Independent Carole Keeton Strayhorn wanted the voters to identify her as "Grandma." Democratic candidate Chris Bell had been born Robert Christopher Bell. Republican Governor Rick Perry's actual first name was James.

Libertarian candidate James Werner, unable to generate much publicity for his own minor-party candidacy, decided that the problem was that he lacked a nickname. He conducted an Internet contest in which Texans were invited to log on to his Web site and suggest a nickname. The winning entry was "The Libernator." It did not help Werner win the governorship.

★ ★ ★ ★ ★ ★ ★ ★ ★ ★ ★ ★ ★ ★ ★ ★ ★ ★ ★ ★ ★ ★ ★ ★ ★ ★ ★ ★ ★ ★ ★ ★

SOURCES: "Under the Dome," *Austin American-Statesman*, October 7, 2006, E2; Libertarian Web site www.nametheguv.com/suggestions/listtop10/.

# Conclusion

All in all, a survey of voters, campaigns, and elections in Texas is not very encouraging to people who take democratic theory seriously. If the legitimacy of government in a democracy depends on the participation of citizens, then the very low voter turnout in state elections raises serious questions about the legitimacy of Texas government. Moreover, the great disparity in turnout between ethnic groups most certainly biases public policy away from the patterns that would prevail if all citizens voted. Looking beyond voting, the great impact of money on political campaigns and elections suggests the possibility, if not the certainty, that wealthy elites control the policy process, rendering whatever citizen participation exists irrelevant. A cynical view of democracy finds much support in Texas electoral politics.

There is, however, some cause for optimism. The old barriers to participation that kept people from exercising their citizenship are gone, and in fact voter turnout has been rising slowly and unsteadily in recent decades. It is possible that time and education will bring more people to fulfill their potential as citizens.

Further, the gubernatorial campaigns of 1990 and 2002 proved that money is not the only thing that counts in Texas politics, and the Republican surge of 1994 demonstrated that the electorate is capable of making informed choices in the polling booth.

The system, then, is imperfect but not completely depraved. For anyone trying to make a better state, there are both many flaws to try to correct and some reason to hope that they may be correctable.

## Summary

Voting, campaigning, and elections are important to study because in a democracy the legitimacy of the government depends on the people's participation. Thus, despite the fact that single votes almost never determine the outcome of elections, voting is important to the individual, the candidate, and the political system.

Consistent with its traditionalist history and culture, Texas until recently attempted to suppress voting by all but wealthy Whites. Today, voter turnout is still below the national average, which is itself comparatively low. Turnout of African Americans and Mexican Americans is generally lower than the turnout of Anglos. This disparity makes public policy more conservative than it would be otherwise.

In campaigns, candidates attempt to persuade voters to support them. To do so, they are forced to spend large amounts of money, which means that they become dependent on wealthy special interests that contribute to their cause. This dependence has consequences for public policy. Money is not absolutely decisive in campaigns, however, and candidates who are outspent by their opponents sometimes win.

There are three kinds of elections in Texas. Primary elections are held to choose candidates for general elections. In general elections, the electorate determines who will serve in public office. Special elections are held when they are needed between general elections, often to either fill unexpected governmental vacancies or to ratify constitutional amendments.

One of the more disturbing trends in election campaigns is the prevalence of negative personal attacks in television advertising. Recent historical experience is somewhat mixed in regard to negative campaigning. On the one hand, the gubernatorial campaigns of 1990 and 2002 were paradigms of sleazy viciousness. On the other hand, several of the most important state campaigns in the 1990s were fought cleanly, which gives some reason to hope that future elections may be more issue oriented than those in the past.

A comparison of the reality of Texas electoral politics with the ideal of the democratic polity thus suggests that Texas falls very far below the ideal but offers some reason for optimism.

## Glossary Terms

campaign

closed primary

election

Equal Protection Clause

general election

open primary

primary

privately funded campaigns

publicly funded campaigns

suffrage

voter registration

voter turnout

# Study Questions

1. In the days when Texas deliberately suppressed the voter turnout of everyone but wealthy Whites, was its government legitimate?

2. What are the consequences of differences in turnout among ethnic groups in Texas?

3. What effects does money have on campaigns? Are these good or bad for democratic government?

4. Suppose Texas were to adopt a system of publicly funded electoral campaigns. What effects might this change have on candidates, political parties, campaigns, and public policy?

5. Why have Texas's laws so far largely failed to curb abuses of private campaign financing?

6. If negative campaigns get results, why is there any concern about them?

7. What are the consequences for public policy of the importance of primary elections in Texas?

8. In what ways did the general elections of the 1990s through 2006 in Texas conform to the state's historical pattern of voting? In what ways did they depart from the state's historical pattern?

# Surfing the Web

Readers are urged to visit the companion site for this book:

**http://academic.cengage.com/polsci/Kraemer/TexasPolitics10e**

# Organization of the Texas Legislature

The Senate Room of the Texas Capital is seen here from the gallery where spectators sit.

They are often criticized, rarely understood, complain about being unappreciated and yet are never ignored. They serve under the banner of the public good and usually view their career choice as an opportunity to effect change. And when one of their own stumbles, the whole profession suffers.

GENE ROSE, *STATE LEGISLATURES*, JUNE 1999

The speaker is the facilitator of making the process work. You're never going to remove his ideas. But it should be a process where everybody can have their say, and the speaker doesn't have an agenda.

JAMES "PETE" LANEY, SPEAKER OF THE TEXAS HOUSE OF REPRESENTATIVES, 1993–2003, QUOTED IN *STATE LEGISLATURES*, JULY/AUGUST 2002

# Introduction

Early in the history of the United States, the legislative body was seen as not only the most important branch of government but also as the part of government that truly represented all elements of the population (or at least, the elements deemed worthy of representation in those days). In short, the prevailing concept was of a "citizen legislature." Legislatures are particularly important in democratic theory because they institutionalize the people's choices and translate the people's wants into public policy. In many American states today, the citizen legislature concept can still be seen—great diversity in the professions of the members, short terms, short sessions, little or no pay for serving in government, and few amenities such as staff or offices. Idaho and Wyoming, for example, boast of their citizen legislatures.[1] An existing reform movement targets the U.S. Congress as needing to shed itself of its reliance on elitism and special interests in favor of being a citizen legislature.[2]

Thus, legislative bodies are meant to represent the people and to reflect the differing views of a community, state, or nation. However, at the same time, they are meant to enact public policy, to provide funds for government operations, and to perform a host of other functions on behalf of the people who elected them. Carrying out the public policy function in a twenty-first century context requires time to deliberate, staff to assist in researching issues, and other elements of professionalism that go beyond the concept of a citizen legislature.

As this chapter demonstrates, the Texas state legislature reflects both the traditional citizen legislature concept and the more modern professional concept. It also alludes to the great negative of modern legislatures: dominance by special interests.

The Texas legislature is still not completely representative of the state as a whole, but especially from the mid-1980s on, it has increased its diversity along ethnic and gender lines, its members come from many different career backgrounds, and it includes both major political parties. Achieving greater diversity helps the state more nearly meet the most fundamental tests of democratic government: representation and fairness.

Texas's **biennial** legislative sessions are the focal point of the state government. Biennial means that the regular legislative sessions occur every other year. In these sessions, legislators must wrestle with important economic and social issues, define public morality and provide methods to enforce it, and also attend to strictly political chores, such as redistricting. They are burdened in these endeavors, however, by a number of structural weaknesses in the legislative system and by a historic lack of public confidence and support. As Gene Rose's quote cited above describes, the life of a legislator is not an easy one. However noble their motives, even the best legislators are subject to criticisms and jests.

This chapter examines the functions of legislative bodies, characteristics of members of the Texas legislature, and legislative compensation. It describes the constitutional, statutory, and informal aspects of legislative structure and the politics of redistricting. It outlines the internal organization of the two houses, including presiding officers, committees, and staff. It then suggests reforms to improve the organizational aspects of the legislature. Chapter Seven reviews the legislature in action, making public policy.

# Functions of Legislative Bodies

If asked what legislators do, most people probably would answer, "Make laws." This answer is correct but incomplete. Legislative bodies have several other functions as well, most of which arise from the separation of political institutions and the system of checks and balances that underlie our system of government. Lawmaking, **reapportionment** and **redistricting,** and the constituent function of proposing constitutional amendments are all activities traditionally associated with legislative bodies. Americans also deem it appropriate for a legislature to help shape the political agenda.

In contrast, activities such as overseeing the administration or doing **casework**—favors—for constituents may at first blush seem to belong to the executive rather than to the legislative branch. Similarly, when the activity at hand is accusations and trial (impeachment), the details of court organization or procedures, or the settling of disputes such as those over elections, one may think first of the judiciary. Educating and informing the electorate may seem to be a function well suited to the schools or to private groups. In fact, the legislature is involved in all these functions.

# FORMAL FUNCTIONS

## LAWMAKING AND THE POLITICAL AGENDA

The most obvious legislative activities are those that involve the making of public policy through the passage of legislation. Although many other people—the governor, bureaucrats, the courts, lobbyists, and citizens—are involved in the process of making laws, the basic prerogative for writing, amending, and passing them belongs to members of the legislature. Legislators may gather facts and opinions through investigations and hearings. They also need to represent the views of their constituents—especially if their districts have a reasonable degree of consensus on an issue—in their proposals and their votes.

In the process of lawmaking, especially, legislators help shape and fix the political agenda for Texas. That is, they have a major voice in determining what the state's policies will be in such important areas as education, welfare, and the environment. They set up priorities by how they appropriate money, and the state constitution gives the legislature the dominant role in the budgetary process. Legislators also determine whether the political climate in Austin will be one of cooperation or competition with the executive branch and between Republicans and Democrats. Will there be one state agenda for political action, or will there be separate agendas such as the legislature's and the governor's or the Republicans' and the Democrats'?

Legislative priorities also offer a good measure for testing the dominant political culture of the state. What is the tone of proposed legislation? Does it focus on promoting the interests of the few and treating politics as an extension of the business world (individualistic culture)? Does it strive to maintain the existing social order and balance of political power (traditionalistic)? Does it strive to address the common good (moralistic)?

## REAPPORTIONMENT/REDISTRICTING

Reapportionment and redistricting could be considered a part of the general lawmaking function, but they have occupied so much legislative time and attention in recent years that they deserve a separate discussion. Every ten years, following completion of the federal census of population, the legislature must reapportion itself—that is, decide which parts of the state get more members of the legislature and which lose membership—by drawing boundary lines for the state senatorial and representative districts as well as for the Texas congressional districts. Between census reports, the legislature makes districting adjustments as needed or, more likely, as forced by litigation. *Redistricting*—the redrawing of the electoral lines—is a source of intense political activity. The case study presented later in this chapter concerning redistricting in 2003 illustrates the importance—and the partisanship—of this function.

## THE CONSTITUENT/AMENDMENT FUNCTION

A body empowered to create or amend a constitution is described as having a constituent function. State legislatures are involved in the ratification of amendments to the national Constitution. They also propose amendments to state constitutions and pass statutes that "make do" until constitutional change can be brought about. When amendments to the U.S. Constitution are proposed, the ratification method is always a vote by the state legislatures. In Texas, which lacks a statewide initiative to propose constitutional amendments, *only* the legislature can suggest an amendment to the state constitution. As we saw in Chapter Two, Texas legislators are continually engaged in this function.

## THE JUDICIAL FUNCTION

Just as legislators are not the only people involved in lawmaking, judges are not the only ones involved in judicial matters. Whenever the House formally accuses—impeaches—a judge or executive branch official and the Senate tries the person accused, or whenever the legislature passes laws dealing with courts and court procedures, the judicial function comes into play. Legislative bodies also control the number, jurisdiction, and general organization of the judiciary through the lawmaking power.

## THE ELECTORAL FUNCTION

Although it is infrequently exercised, the electoral function of the legislature is important. When necessary, election disputes are settled by the legislative body. In addition, the House makes the official declaration of the winners of the state executive offices after election results are tabulated.

## THE ADMINISTRATIVE FUNCTION

Legislative bodies traditionally serve as executive bodies by supervising state administration—the process of **legislative oversight.** This supervision is exercised through the standing committees of each house, which hold hearings and request state agency administrators to testify and answer questions about their programs, rules, and expenditures. The oversight function of the Texas legislature was strengthened with the passage of the Sunset Act of 1977 and the establishment of the Sunset Advisory Commission to review administrative agencies and make recommendations to the legislature about their continuance or reorganization. (See Chapter 9 for details.) It was further strengthened in 1981 when a statute was passed that allowed the legislature to review rules and regulations of administrative agencies. Also included in the oversight function is the legislative audit of state expenditures, which serves to determine whether appropriated monies have been spent legally.

    The relationship between state agency personnel and legislative supervisors, however, often is less that of the watched and the watchdogs than of program advocates and their supporters. When special interests and the press rally around a certain agency, that agency's so-called watchdogs generally become a friendly link to the larger assembly of legislators on the floor. Approval of executive appointments, removal of state officials, and some aspects of budget preparation are other administrative duties of the legislature, as are those housekeeping activities designed to ensure its own smooth operation.

## THE INVESTIGATORY FUNCTION

The relationship between state administrators and their overseers in the legislature is not always mutually beneficial. Legislators may perceive, sometimes with the assistance of representatives of special interests, that a state agency or set of state agencies is not doing its job properly or is not acting in the public interest. There may even be suspected *malfeasance*—illegal conduct—in office. An investigation may ensue by the committee that has jurisdiction over that agency, by the House General Investigating Committee, or by an ad hoc or interim committee created for the purpose; the committee may decide to recommend action to the appropriate house. The investigatory function is called into play less often in Texas than in other states where conflict-of-interest laws are stronger and special interests have less influence. However, a widely publicized example was the joint Select Committee on the Organization and Management of the Texas Youth Commission, which addressed concerns about the multiple abuses identified in the youthful offender penal system in the state in 2007.

Today, all public agencies undergo constant, intense scrutiny through the efficiency review program directed by the Legislative Budget Board (this review function was transferred from the comptroller's office in 2003) and through increased legislative demand for **privatizing** public functions—turning them over to private businesses or individuals. The beginning assumption is not illegal conduct but suspected inefficiencies.

# INFORMAL FUNCTIONS

## CASEWORK

One informal function performed by the legislature—that is, one that is not spelled out in law—is casework: troubleshooting or problem solving on behalf of a constituent. Casework stems directly from the formal function of representation. Being a state senator or representative does not just mean representing an abstract number of people living in a voting district, nor does it mean merely reflecting the views of the district when voting on legislation. Membership in the representative body also involves helping a constituent who is having difficulty getting a welfare check from the Texas Health and Human Services Commission or providing information for someone who wants to know how to apply for a job with the Department of Public Safety.

State legislators spend less time at this activity than do members of Congress, who serve on a full-time basis. Nevertheless, the attention of state legislators is often diverted from policy matters to the problems of their constituents. Lawmakers also spend virtually every weekend during the session in their districts, giving their constituents an opportunity to talk about pending legislation.[3]

## EDUCATION AND INFORMATION

A second informal function of legislators is to provide information to constituents and educate them on public issues of the day. This task may be performed in a low-key manner, such as by issuing a newsletter at regular intervals. It can be performed by giving speeches at meetings of the hometown Rotary, Kiwanis, or Business and Professional Women's Club. It includes interviews with media reporters.

Other sources of information are the House Media Service and the Senate News Office, which provide audio and video clips, photographs, and news releases to increase understanding of the legislative process and to perform a

Congress approved 2 seats to Congress. One to Columbia and the other to...

service for small and medium-size media outlets that cannot afford to keep a crew stationed in Austin during the legislative session. Along the same lines, online computer access to bills and resolutions under consideration by the legislature was made available to the public beginning in 1995. For the half of the population that has ready access to computers, the state's Web sites offer a great deal of information. Since 2003, responsibility for e-government reports for Texas belongs to the Legislative Budget Board.

# Structure of the Legislature

## SIZE, ELECTIONS, AND TERMS

With the exception of Nebraska, which has a unicameral (single-house) legislature, the American states have patterned themselves on the **bicameral** model of the U.S. Congress. Article III of the Texas Constitution stipulates that the legislature is composed of a Senate and a House of Representatives.

The two houses have approximately equal power, but the Senate has more prestige and is considered the upper house. One reason is its smaller size. Another is that each senator represents nearly five times as many citizens as does a member of the House. Still another factor is the Senate's control over executive appointments. In addition, the Senate's presiding officer, the lieutenant governor, is elected by the entire state. The Senate's less formal procedures permit more extended—and sometimes highly publicized—debate than in the House, and a senator's term of office is longer than that of a member of the House. Traditionally, the Senate's national counterpart, the U.S. Senate, has been considered the more prestigious national legislative chamber. At both the state and national levels, when a member of the House seeks and wins a Senate seat, this achievement is regarded as a political promotion.

The average state senate has 40 members; the average lower house, 112. The Texas Constitution fixes the number of state senators at 31 and the maximum number of representatives at 150. The U.S. Congress has 100 senators and 435 representatives.[4] In the national government, the number of senators is determined by the number of states; the number of members of the House, by statute (legislation). Among the fifty state legislatures, only the term *senate* is used consistently; the lower house is known variously as the assembly, house of representatives, and general assembly.[5] While the terms *house* and *senate* are used by both national and state governments, and the term *legislator* refers to a lawmaker at any level, *Congress* and *congressman/woman* are exclusively national.

Key features of the system for electing legislators include

1. Selection in the November general election in even-numbered years

2. Election from **single-member districts**

3. Two-year terms for House members and four-year staggered terms for senators, without limit as to the number of terms that can be served[6]

4. A special election called by the governor to fill a vacancy caused by death, resignation, or expulsion from office

★ ★ ★ ★ ★ ★ ★ ★ ★ ★ ★ ★ ★ ★ ★ ★ ★ ★ ★ ★ ★ ★ ★ ★ ★ ★ ★ ★

## *Term Limits*

The issue of term limits was hotly debated during the 1990s, although interest seems to have waned in the twenty-first century. Twenty-one states initially set legislative term limits, but, by 2007, only fifteen states still had them. The Texas legislature considered but rejected a variety of term limit bills during the 1990s. The U.S. Supreme Court in 1995 struck down efforts by states to limit the terms of members of the U.S. Congress, holding that the federal Constitution preempted the question of the number of times that members of Congress could serve. Republican members of Congress made term limits part of the campaign promises in their "Contract with America" in 1994, although in 1995 they failed to get enough votes to propose a constitutional amendment limiting their own terms. Many municipal charters in Texas and elsewhere do have limits on the number of terms the mayor and council can serve.

Proponents of term limits see them as a way to try to regain public confidence in legislative bodies that increasingly have been regarded as remote and lacking in understanding of public wishes. Opponents are concerned about such matters as a possible lack of policy expertise on the part of legislative leaders and arbitrarily jettisoning a popular legislator because of artificial term limits. They contend that, "We have term limits now. Just ask any incumbent defeated in the last election." The greatest criticism of term limits, however, is that they are inherently undemocratic because they rob voters of free choice in an election. Thus, democracy today is seeking to limit democracy tomorrow.

★ ★ ★ ★ ★ ★ ★ ★ ★ ★ ★ ★ ★ ★ ★ ★ ★ ★ ★ ★ ★ ★ ★ ★ ★ ★ ★ ★

SOURCES: Summary of "Coping with Term Limits,: A Practical Guide" (Denver: National Conference of State Legislatures, 2007), available at http://www.ncsl.org/programs/legismgt/ABOUT/Termlimit.htm. For background on this issue, see Keith B. Hamm and Gary F. Moncrief, "Legislative Politics in the States," in Virginia Gray and Russell Hanson, *Politics in the American States,* 8th ed. (Washington, D.C.: Congressional Quarterly Press, 2004), 167–169; B. Drummond Ayres Jr., "Term Limit Laws Are Transforming More Legislatures," *New York Times,* April 28, 1997, A1, A14; Karen Hansen, "The Third Revolution," *State Legislatures,* September 1997, 20–28; Tim Storey, "2002 State Legislative Elections," *The Book of the States,* 2003, 81.

*Dewhurst*

*lt. govenor*

Newly elected legislators take office in January. Whenever reapportionment to establish districts of approximately equal population size occurs—at intervals of no more than ten years—all senators are elected in the same year. They then draw lots to determine who will serve for two years and who will serve the full four-year term. This phenomenon occurred in 2001, when the legislature redrew district lines, and in 2002, when elections reflecting the new lines were held.

If a vacancy occurs because of death, resignation, or expulsion from office, the governor calls a special election to fill it. The most common reason for a vacancy is resignation, usually occurring when a representative runs for higher office. In 2003, two longtime senators resigned. Bill Ratliff decided to reenter private life, and Teel Bivins became ambassador to Sweden. Expulsion is unusual because it requires a two-thirds majority vote in the legislator's house. Death is also rare among members of the legislature. However, deaths do occur: Representative Ronny Crownover was replaced by his wife, Myra, after he died of leukemia in 2000. She was subsequently re-elected in her own right.

# SESSIONS

only

## REGULAR SESSION

The constitution provides for regular biennial sessions, beginning on the second Tuesday in January of odd-numbered years. These sessions may run no longer than 140 calendar days. Six other states (Arkansas, Massachusetts, Montana, Nevada, North Dakota, and Oregon) also have biennial sessions; the rest have either annual or continuous sessions or the authority to divide a biennial session across two years.

The truncated biennial legislative session accentuates all the formal and informal factors that influence legislation in Texas. For example, insufficient time for careful consideration of bills heightens the power of the presiding officers, the lobbyists, and the governor. Also, the short biennial session prevents issues from being raised in the first place so that the state sometimes delays dealing with problems until a crisis occurs. Although there have been a number of changes in the specifics of the legislative sessions over the years, voters have consistently rejected amendments providing for annual sessions. They fear increased governmental power and spending, in part, a reflection of the antigovernment attitude implicit in a conservative political culture and, in part, an acknowledgment of the $20 million price tag for a regular session.

## SPECIAL SESSIONS

*Can't exceed the 140 day session rule*

The governor can call the legislature into special session for a maximum of thirty days. The governor determines the agenda for this session. If a legislator wishes to add items to the agenda for a special session, the governor must agree. Thirty-two other state legislatures have mechanisms for calling themselves into special session. In Texas, only in the extraordinary situation that resulted in the impeachment of Governor Jim "Pa" Ferguson in 1917 for suspected corruption has the legislature ever convened a special session on its own. The Senate, under the 1999 succession amendment to the constitution, can meet as a committee of the whole to elect an acting lieutenant governor.

The governor may call one special session after another if necessary. However, because the voting public has rejected annual sessions several times, Texas governors usually try to avoid calling numerous special sessions that might appear to function as annual sessions. The average price tag—about $1.7 million per special session—is another disincentive. Nevertheless, governors sometimes have little choice about calling a special session because too much legislative business—often including the state budget—is unfinished. For example, Governor Bill Clements called two special sessions in 1989 and four in 1990 to deal with school finance and workers' compensation. Governor Ann Richards called two special budget sessions in 1991 and a school finance session in 1992. No special sessions were called from 1993 through 2002. Governor Rick Perry called seven special sessions between June 2003 and April 2006, including three controversial sessions to force congressional redistricting in 2003 and four sessions from 2004 to 2006 to deal with school finance.

# LEGISLATIVE DISTRICTS

*The average size of each US Congressional district*

## MECHANICS

Only one senator or representative may be elected from a particular district by the people living in that district. Although some districts are 300 times larger than others in geographic size (see Figures 6-1 and 6-2 for examples of districts), each senatorial district should have approximately 737,418 residents, and each house district should have approximately 152,700 as of 2005.[7] Achieving equally populated districts does not come easily, however, because the task is a highly political one carried out by the legislature, and the Texas population continues to grow.

If the legislature fails to redistrict itself, the Legislative Redistricting Board (LRB) comes into play. The LRB is composed of five *ex officio* state officials; that is, they are members by virtue of their holding another office. These five are the lieutenant governor, the speaker of the House, the comptroller of public accounts, the general land commissioner, and the attorney general. If both the legislature and the LRB fail in the reapportionment and redistricting task, the matter goes to the federal courts for resolution. Also, the redistricting handiwork of the legislature and the LRB is always subject to review by the U.S. Department of Justice because Texas, as a state that formerly discriminated against ethnic minorities in the voting process, is subject to the Voting Rights Act of 1965.

## HISTORY

Prior to the mid-1960s, legislative districts were a hodgepodge based partly on population, partly on geography, and largely on protecting rural interests. Members of the Senate have always been elected in single-member districts, but in the past, those districts reflected land area, not population. Indeed, the Texas Constitution once prohibited a single county, regardless of population, from having more than one senator. House districts were constitutionally based on population but with limitations that worked against urban counties.[8] In addition, **gerrymandering**—drawing district lines in such a way as to give one faction or one party an advantage—was the norm. (*Gerrymander* is pronounced with the sound of "g" as in gate, not "g" as in gentry.)

The federal courts changed the ability of the state to artificially limit representation from urban areas and forced the drawing of legislative districts according to population. In 1962, in *Baker* v. *Carr*[9]—the one-person, one-vote case—the U.S. Supreme Court overturned a legislative districting system that gave one group substantial advantages over another. In 1964, in *Reynolds* v. *Sims*,[10] the Court laid down its first guidelines on conditions that would necessitate redrawing district lines, including a mandate that the membership of both houses be based on population. The Texas House of Representatives continued to use multimember legislative districts[11] until the courts forced some counties to abandon them in 1975 and others volunteered to do so.[12]

Citizens in urban areas, Republicans, and ethnic minority groups have all been prominent in redistricting suits. As Table 6-1 shows, the predominant ethnic minorities in Texas—African Americans and Hispanics—have made some gains through population-based districting. Ethnic minority groups made up 21.6 percent of the legislature in 1987; the percentage had risen to 30.4 percent

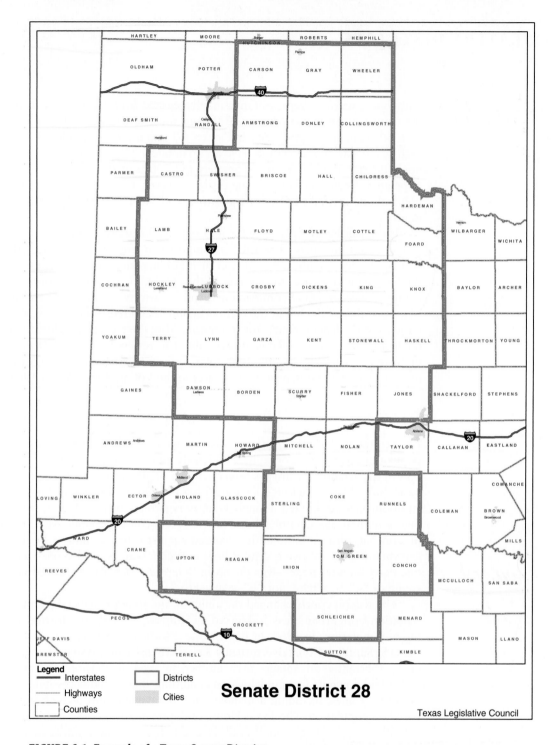

**Senate District 28**

Texas Legislative Council

**FIGURE 6-1  Example of a Texas Senate District**

*Although it includes two metropolitan areas, San Angelo and Lubbock, Senator Robert Duncan's district nevertheless encompasses forty-six counties.*

SOURCE: *Texas Legislative Council.*

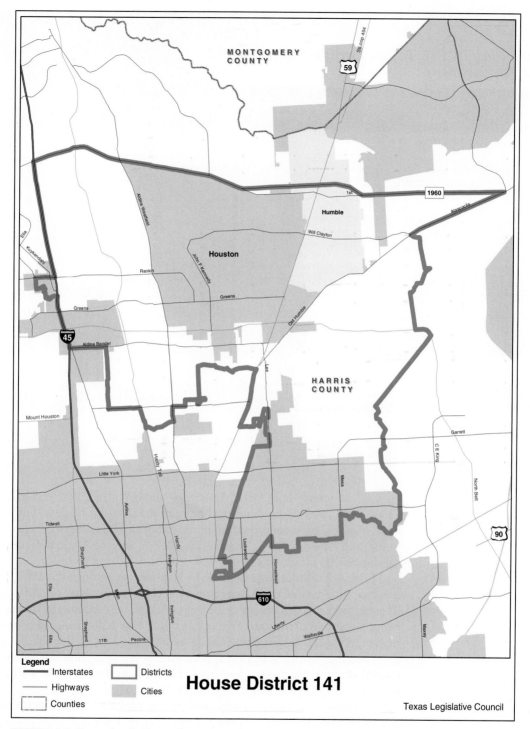

**House District 141**

Texas Legislative Council

**Legend**
- —— Interstates
- —— Highways
- ☐ Counties
- ☐ Districts
- ▨ Cities

**FIGURE 6-2  Example of a Texas House District**

*Representative Senfronia Thompson's district includes both part of Houston and part of unincorporated Harris County.*

*SOURCE: Texas Legislative Council.*

## TABLE 6-1

### Ethnicity in the Texas Legislature, 1987–2007, by Percentage

| Year | Anglo | Hispanic/Mexican American | African American | Asian American |
|------|-------|---------------------------|------------------|----------------|
| 1987 | 78.5%* | 13.3% | 8.3% | 0% |
| 1989 | 77.9 | 14.4 | 7.7 | 0 |
| 1991 | 78.5 | 13.3 | 8.3 | 0 |
| 1993 | 73.5 | 17.7 | 8.8 | 0 |
| 1995 | 72.4 | 18.8 | 8.8 | 0 |
| 1997 | 73.0 | 18.5 | 8.4 | 0 |
| 1999 | 71.8 | 19.3 | 8.8 | 0 |
| 2001 | 71.8 | 19.3 | 8.8 | 0 |
| 2003 | 69.6 | 21.0 | 8.8 | .6 |
| 2005 | 68.5 | 21.0 | 9.4 | 1.1 |
| 2007 | 69.6 | 21.0 | 8.9 | .5 |

*Percentages do not always equal 100 due to rounding.

in 2007, counting one Asian American member. The 2005 census estimates added Texas, at 50.2 percent non-Anglo, to the short list of states with a majority of its population comprised of ethnic minorities (the others are Hawaii, California, and New Mexico). However, in 2007, it was the Anglo percentage of the legislature that increased slightly.[13]

Table 6-2 shows the gains made by Republicans through the 2007 legislative sessions, with most of these gains coming in urban areas. After the 2002 elections, Republicans held both houses of the legislature, all the executive offices, and all the major judgeships of the state. Democrats briefly kept a slight edge in congressional seats until the 2003 redistricting effects were felt at the polls. Republicans in Texas have benefited not only from reapportionment but also from the national trend toward conservative politics and from the steady evolution of the state's politics from one-party Democrat to two-party and then to Republican dominance.

In addition to ethnic, party, and urban pressures, legislators have to be concerned with the federal Voting Rights Act of 1965 and with producing redistricting plans that the governor will not veto. Moreover, the federal courts continue to monitor redistricting efforts.[14] With all these competing demands, it is no wonder that the legislature usually fails to produce a plan that pleases everyone. Because redistricting is so controversial, even to the point of dominating the legislative session in which it occurs, the legislature often fails to get the maps drawn or finds that it must do the task more than once.

**TABLE 6-2**

## Political Party Membership in the Texas Legislature, 1977–2007, Transitional Years and Most Recent Years

| Year | Senate (N = 31) | | House (N = 150) | | Both Houses (N = 181) | |
|------|----------|------------|----------|------------|----------|------------|
| | Democrat | Republican | Democrat | Republican | Democrat | Republican |
| 1977 | 90.3% | 9.7% | 87.3% | 12.7% | 87.9% | 12.1% |
| 1987 | 80.6 | 19.4 | 62.7 | 37.3 | 71.3 | 28.7 |
| 1997 | 45.2 | 54.8 | 54.7 | 45.3 | 53.0 | 47.0 |
| 2003 | 38.7 | 61.3 | 41.3 | 58.7 | 40.9 | 59.1 |
| 2005 | 39 | 61 | 42 | 57 | 41.7 | 58.3 |
| 2007 | 35.5 | 64.5 | 45 | 55 | 44.2 | 55.8 |

Reapportionment is always highly partisan, and Texas Democrats were never more sure of that fact than after legislative redistricting in 2001 and congressional redistricting in 2003. This Ben Sargent cartoon parodies the many "Survivor"-type reality shows popular on television in the early 2000s.

*Courtesy of Ben Sargent.*

After the 1990 census, districts were redrawn in 1991, adjusted in 1993, and redrawn again in 1996. However, redistricting disputes of the 1990s were comparatively mild compared to the disputes following the 2000 census. The legislature failed to agree on a redistricting plan, leading to the Legislative Redistricting Board's coming into play for only the third time since the procedure was established in 1951. The LRB effort subsequently was altered by a three-judge federal court. All of the plans favored the Republicans, who were the majority party, but the GOP was feuding with itself as well as with Democrats.[15] The biggest redistricting fight of the early 2000s occurred over congressional districts in 2003. The Democrats had already lost all the executive offices and their legislative majority and were focused on holding their U.S. House majority. The result was a nasty, intensely partisan series of special sessions in 2003, as described in the accompanying box. Senate efforts to prevent such disputes in the future by establishing a bipartisan commission to oversee congressional redistricting died in the lower house.

★ ★ ★ ★ ★ ★ ★ ★ ★ ★ ★ ★ ★ ★ ★ ★ ★ ★ ★ ★ ★ ★ ★ ★ ★ ★ ★ ★ ★

## Redistricting: Battleground Texas

Reapportionment and redistricting are always highly partisan issues. The dominant party always claims to be righteous in its efforts to seek equity according to how voters spoke in the last election. The minority party always claims that its constituents have been disenfranchised by the latest electoral scheme. In Texas, these claims reached new highs—or perhaps, new lows—in 2003 when congressional redistricting resurfaced late in the regular session of the Seventy-eighth Legislature.

Governor Rick Perry and Speaker of the House Tom Craddick, apparently heavily influenced by then-U.S. House Majority Leader Tom DeLay of Sugar Land and a national GOP strategy of trying to increase the number of Republican members of Congress through midterm redistricting in key states, called for a redrawing of congressional lines. At the time, Texas had seventeen Democratic members of the U.S. House of Representatives and fifteen Republicans. (Both Texas members of the U.S. Senate were Republicans.) Based on their electoral successes in 2000 and 2002, the Republicans thought they could gain as many as seven additional seats in the 2004 elections, thereby creating a probable twenty-two to ten split. A stronger Republican majority in Congress was seen as a way to solidify the GOP's 2002 gains and to increase the likely success of President George Bush's legislative package. Thus, the stakes were high indeed. The unusual aspects of the situation were that legislators traditionally do not redistrict between censuses when they are not compelled to do so by the courts, the openly partisan agenda for redistricting, and the targeting of incumbent members of Congress.

House Democrats fended off the congressional redistricting attempt in the regular session when fifty-three of the sixty-two Democrats left the state and set up shop at the Ardmore, Oklahoma, Holiday Inn. Their absence meant that insufficient numbers of House members were present to constitute the necessary quorum for legislative action. The Democrats successfully killed the bill because the legislature had to abandon redistricting and move on to other business to finish the regular session. However, doing so only made the Republican leadership angrier and more determined. The public was confused, and the media labeled the AWOL Democrats the "Killer D's." Republicans had another name for them: the "Chicken D's." Legislators had walked out in protest before, including the Republicans in 1993 and the Democrats in 1979. In 2003, the House Democrats stressed that they were fighting with the only tool available to them to prevent a redistricting that did not legally have to occur again until 2011 and that was not designed to correct underrepresentation of minorities or unequal population but explicitly to benefit one political party. The Republicans asked for help from the federal Homeland Se-

*(continued)*

★ ★ ★ ★ ★ ★ ★ ★ ★ ★ ★ ★ ★ ★ ★ ★ ★ ★ ★ ★ ★ ★ ★ ★ ★ ★ ★ ★ ★

(continued)

curity Department to locate the absent Democrats and help bring them home, a move that backfired in terms of public relations. (Why bring in the federal government when supposedly the bill was to get rid of the influence of the federal courts on redistricting?) Rhetoric was heated on both sides.

The governor called a special session to begin June 30, saying that legislators, not the federal courts, should draw district maps. A variety of proposed maps was produced, and hearings were held across the state. Participation in the hearings was heavily orchestrated by Democrats so that public sentiment on the proposed maps was largely negative. Rural Texans were especially vocal in the negative effects on their representation that were reflected in the drafts. Republicans in the meantime promised more minority districts and worked to split the Democratic ranks by appealing to African American and Hispanic members of the legislature. House members yielded and approved a congressional redistricting bill. Senate Democrats relied on the two-thirds rule, which requires the approval of two thirds of the members (twenty-one) to allow a bill to be debated. A bloc of eleven Democrats and one Republican held firm, and the Senate did not produce a redistricting bill.

The governor called a second special session for July 28, lambasting the minority for blocking the redistricting bill and preventing effective work on some cleanup financial issues. Lieutenant Governor David Dewhurst who, up until this point, had stuck with Senate tradition, indicated that he would set aside the two-thirds rule. While the Democrats called this move "unprecedented," in truth the two-thirds rule had been set aside in previous special sessions by Democratic lieutenant governors. Eleven Democratic senators then followed the lead of their House counterparts and fled the state to Albuquerque, New Mexico, to prevent a Senate quorum. The politically supercharged atmosphere got even more heated when Republican senators levied $57,000 in fines against the absent Democrats and ultimately withdrew cell phone privileges and even blocked the Democratic staff members from parking at the capitol. The Democrats held firm, and the second called session ended. Finally, Senator John Whitmore of Houston broke the stalemate by returning to Austin to protest the overturn of the two-thirds rule and to provide an in-state voice for his party's frustrations with the stifling of minority party opinion. Many of the absentee Democrats were highly critical of his return to the state.

The saga continued into September when the governor called a third special session. The Democrats continued to shout "partisan, waste of money, unfair." The Republicans continued to retort that "it's time to get down to work." The governor was eager not only to resolve the redistricting issue but also to complete an attack on the powers of the comptroller (a potential rival) by stripping powers from that office and giving them to legislative staff officers. The remaining Democrats gave in to the inevitable; Congressional redistricting passed; and the Democrats vowed immediate challenges via the Justice Department and the courts. However, the Justice Department and subsequently a panel of three federal judges approved the plan. Very simply, there is no prohibition against redistricting for purely partisan grounds, and there was insufficient evidence that minority interests were damaged by the redistricting scheme to bar it on those grounds. The end of the story, at least, in advance of the 2004 elections, was the party switch by longtime conservative Democrat Ralph Hall. The Republican establishment welcomed him with a recognition of all his Congressional seniority and a big endorsement in the primaries. As of 2007, the Republicans held nineteen seats, and the Democrats held thirteen.

(continued)

(*continued*)

Two important aspects of this struggle are evident. One is a reiteration of the fact that all reapportionment and redistricting is political, yea partisan. The other one, with more serious implications for the legislature itself, is the bitter divisiveness that characterized the struggle.

SOURCE: The media in Texas ran the redistricting story as a front-page/lead item for weeks. A few of the more useful sources are these: Pete Slover and Matt Stiles, "Majority of AWOL Lawmakers Where You'd Least Expect: Oklahoma," and Christy Hoppe and Gromer Jeffers, Jr., "Angry Over Redistricting, State Reps Deny Quorum," run as companion pieces under the banner "Democrats Disappear," *Dallas Morning News*, May 13, 2003, 1A, 11A; Patricia Kilday Hart, "The Unkindest Cut," *Texas Monthly*, October 2003, 44–52; Lee Hockstader, "Caught in the Crossfire," *Washington Post Weekly Edition*, October 6–12, 2003, 14.

The Democrats return from exile after trying to block congressional redistricting in 2003 by fleeing the state.

## PARTY AND FACTIONAL ORGANIZATION

Historically, until the late 1970s, Texas was a one-party—Democratic—state. In the legislature, unlike the situation in the U.S. Congress and many other state legislatures, political party organization did not exist. As a one-party state, Texas saw factionalism within the Democratic Party replace the party differences that characterized other legislative bodies.

Political party affiliation and party organization have grown in importance as Texas briefly became a two-party state, then as it moved into being a Republican-

# YOU DECIDE

## Should Redistricting Occur More Frequently Than Every Ten Years?

The redrawing of state legislative and congressional district lines must occur every ten years after each federal census to reflect changes in population. In Texas, congressional lines were redrawn in 2001 and then again in 2003. In 2007 the legislature debated new methods of congressional redistricting. Should redistricting occur more frequently than the year following each decennial census report?

| PRO | CON |
| --- | --- |
| ▲ Districts should be drawn frequently to reflect changes in Texas's growing population. | ▼ The population changes daily; it is impossible to "keep up" with the population on a yearly or biennial basis. |
| ▲ Although the law does not require equity in political party distribution, lines should be redrawn to reflect changes in party preference. | ▼ The legal requirements are only for equality in population size and for an absence of racial discrimination. |
| ▲ The legislature should always redraw lines if otherwise the most recent lines were set by the courts, not by legislators. | ▼ If the courts have drawn the lines, the legislature has already failed once. Why should it change lines that the courts have approved? |
| ▲ The state legislature should be sensitive to the desires of the political party in the majority nationally. | ▼ The U.S. Constitution gives state legislatures the power to determine district lines. |

dominant state. As Table 6-2 shows, Republican representation in the legislature has grown from minuscule in 1977 to a majority in the Texas Senate since 1997 and in the Texas House since 2003. Beginning in 1983, party members in the House designated floor leaders. In the 1989 session, House Republicans formed a formal caucus for the first time since Reconstruction, and today, they regularly select a party whip—the person designated to line up votes on behalf of the official party position. House members, particularly, reported more intensely partisan disagreements beginning with the 1997 session when the Democratic majority narrowed substantially and especially with the coming of the Republican majority and the change in the speaker's position in 2003.

Although the Senate has been Republican-majority since 1997, most of the time—redistricting notwithstanding—the Senate has continued a longstanding tradition of operating with less partisanship than the House. The Senate presiding office has continued to deal with members on an individual basis. The Texas House has grown to look more like the U.S. Congress, which is organized strictly along party lines.

Even with the party alignment shifting and with partisanship increasing, the minority party did continue to receive significant committee appointments, and the presiding officers often relied on their assessment of and ties to individual legislators more than party affiliation in working through legislative business. However, Democrats have received fewer plum House committee chairmanships in recent years, while Senate chairmanships are allocated proportionately to the party membership in the upper chamber. For example, in 2007, only ten of the forty (25%) House committees were chaired by Democrats though the Democrats constituted about 44 percent of the membership. In the Senate, where Democrats held only 35.5 percent of the seats, they still held five of the fifteen committee chairmanships (33%).

The liberalism or conservatism of a legislator is often more important than the party label. Liberals versus conservatives and urban versus rural/suburban interests are typical divisions. These differences cut across party lines and are most evident on issues such as taxation, spending, and social welfare programs. The Texas legislature thus displays some tendency toward issue orientation. However, discussion of legislative procedure in Chapter Seven will indicate that the minority party often has a hard time being heard, especially in the House.

## COMPENSATION

Since 1975, members of the Texas legislature have received a salary of $7,200 each year; this figure was established by constitutional amendment. (Texas is one of only six states that set legislative salaries by constitution.) Legislators also receive a per diem (daily) allowance when the legislature is in regular or special session to cover lodging, meals, and other expenses; for the Eightieth Legislature in 2007–2008, the per diem rate was $139. In contrast to salary, the per diem rate is among the highest in the nation. When they serve on a state board or council or conduct legislative business between sessions, legislators also are entitled to per diem expenses for up to twelve days a month. In addition, they receive a $0.445 mileage allowance. The presiding officers receive the same compensation and are also entitled to apartments provided by the state.

As Figure 6-3 shows, as of 2005, California, the largest state in population, paid legislators $110,900 a year, more than fifteen times what Texas, the second largest state, pays.[16] The Texas legislative stipend is not even half the federal minimum for a family of four to be above the poverty level! The low level of Texas salaries, which voters have repeatedly refused to change, makes legislators simultaneously more susceptible to lobbying tactics—at $7,200, a free lunch is important—and more likely to divert their attention to finding ways to earn a decent living. The latter task has become more difficult with the increase in committee work between legislative sessions and occasional special sessions.

Under a 1991 state constitutional amendment, the Ethics Commission can convene a citizen advisory board to recommend changes in legislative salary; the proposal must then be submitted to the voters. However, as of 2007, no such

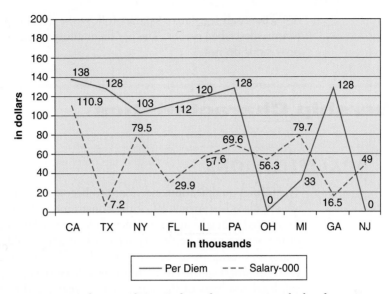

NOTE: The Michigan and New York per diem rates are calculated.

FIGURE 6-3  Legislative Salaries, Per Diem in Ten Largest States, 2005

*SOURCE: The Book of the States, 2006 Edition,* vol. 38 (Lexington, KY: Council of State Governments, 2006), 84–87.

board had been formed. The Ethics Commission also is empowered to increase the per diem expense money and has done so regularly.

The "bottom line" on legislative compensation is that the salary is very low, especially for a high-population state with a complex legislative agenda. The fringe benefits" are rather generous, however. Some legislators have manipulated salary, the per diem, and travel reimbursements to bring in more than $75,000 during a regular session year. On average, a legislator receives about five times the stipulated salary when all forms of compensation are considered. The fundamentally undemocratic aspect of legislative compensation is that citizens have authorized only the $7,200 salary and might be surprised at the total compensation package. Nevertheless, the reality that confronts Texans is that only Texas, Alabama, and New Hampshire have not increased legislative salaries for more than thirty years.

Legislators also receive an allowance for operating an office both during the session and in the interim between sessions. In 2007, the monthly allowance during the regular legislative session was $37,000 for both regular members and committee chairs. At the conclusion of the legislative session, the allowance dropped to $36,000 per month during the interim, on the assumption that fewer temporary staff members would be needed between sessions. These allowances compare favorably with those granted by other states. Texas was fourth nationally in the rankings of legislatures with the most staff as of 2003.[17] Additionally, legislators are entitled to retirement benefits if they serve at least twelve years if the retirement age is under 50 or eight years if the age is 60 or over. Joining the retirement system is optional; participants have 8 percent of their monthly salaries deducted. The retirement is based on the annual salary of a district judge, which was $125,000 in 2007. A major controversy in 2005 was the legislative decision to raise judges' salaries, in effect granting themselves a handsome retirement increase.

The small legislative salaries follow the general principles of the citizen legislature described earlier. The per diem allowances, staff budgets, and retirement provisions do not.

# Membership Characteristics

## FORMAL QUALIFICATIONS

The **formal qualifications** necessary to become a member of the Texas legislature are stipulated in Article III of the constitution. They are those commonly listed for elected officials: age, residency, U.S. citizenship, and voting status. Members of the Senate must be twenty-six years of age or older, qualified voters for five years, and residents of the senatorial district from which they are elected for one year. Members of the House must be at least twenty-one years old, qualified voters, legal residents of the state for two years, and residents of the district from which they are elected for one year.

## PERSONAL CHARACTERISTICS

The formal qualifications are so broad as to make a substantial portion of the Texas citizenry eligible to run for legislative office. However, individuals with certain types of personal characteristics tend to get elected more readily than individuals who lack the characteristics. These characteristics reflect political, social, and economic realities and traditions and confirm the state's conservative political tradition. That they exist does not mean that they are desirable. Indeed, they indicate that certain groups may be underrepresented in the Texas legislature.

In general, Texas legislators tend to be middle-aged, White, male Protestant lawyers or businessmen who are married, have college educations, belong to a number of civic organizations, have considerable personal money as well as access to campaign funds, and have the support of the local media. Not every legislator has all of these personal characteristics, but an individual elected without having any of them would be extraordinary indeed. Trends in ethnicity and party membership are shown in Tables 6-1 and 6-2. Selected characteristics are shown in Table 6-3.

★ ★ ★ ★ ★ ★ ★ ★ ★ ★ ★ ★ ★ ★ ★ ★ ★ ★ ★ ★ ★ ★ ★ ★ ★ ★ ★

### *Students as Legislative Staffers*

House members in particular are always seeking additional staff assistance because their office budgets are often less than those of senators. Students often volunteer and frequently become very responsible members of a legislator's staff, either in Austin or in the home district. Some become paid staffers.

★ ★ ★ ★ ★ ★ ★ ★ ★ ★ ★ ★ ★ ★ ★ ★ ★ ★ ★ ★ ★ ★ ★ ★ ★ ★ ★

**TABLE 6-3**

## Selected Characteristics of Members of the 80th Texas Legislature, 2007–2008

| Category | Senate = 31 | House = 148–150 |
|----------|-------------|-----------------|
| Republicans/Democrats | 20/11 (64.5%–35.5%) | 82/68 (54.6%–45.4%) |
| Ethnicity | 7 Hispanic, 2 African American (29% minority) | 33 Hispanic, 14 African American, 1 Asian American (32% minority) |
| Women | 27 men, 4 women (12.9% women) | 118 men, 31 women (21.3% women) |
| Oldest/Youngest | 66/36 | 83/28 |
| Professions | 15 different ones, led by law, fields of business | 25 different ones, led by law, business, ranching |
| Tenure | 26 returning, 5 Freshmen (16.1% turnover) | 122 returning, including 4 who began in 2006, 28 Freshman (18.7% turnover) |

SOURCE: By count, using official records of the House and Senate.

## WHITE, MALE

Race, ethnicity, and gender are all factors in politics. Both ethnic minorities and women are considerably underrepresented in the Texas legislature in terms of numbers, though not necessarily ideologically. Although Texas's total minority population exceeds 50 percent, minority membership in the legislature in 2007 was only 31 percent. The first Asian American member was elected in 2002; no Native American is a member. Although there are about 100 women for every 97 men in society, slightly less than 20 percent of the Eightieth Texas Legislature were women. An important contextual fact about ethnic representation is that most ethnic minority members are Democrats, and the Democrats have been the minority party in both houses since the 2002 elections.

## LAWYERS AND BUSINESSPERSONS

Legislators tend to be white-collar professionals and businesspersons. Other fields such as farming and ranching also have fairly strong representation, given their small numbers in the general population. Law traditionally has been seen as preparation for politics. In fact, aspiring politicians often attend law school as a means of gaining entry into politics. The result is that attorneys, who make up less than 4 percent of the state's total population, hold about one third of Texas legislative seats. Their numbers have been waning in recent years, reflecting a national trend away from lawyers as legislators. The most frequent business fields

## TABLE 6-4

## Occupations and Professions Represented in the Texas Legislature, 2007–2008

| | | |
|---|---|---|
| Advertising | Engineering | Oil and gas |
| Architecture | Farming | Pharmacy |
| Business | Finance, banking, and investments | Public safety |
| Civics/government/public service | Food service/hospitality | Ranching/cattle and/or horse breeding |
| Communications and public relations | Insurance | Real estate |
| Computing/information technology | Law | Retired (unspecified) |
| Construction/development | Medicine/health professions | Sales and marketing |
| Consulting | Military | Veterinary medicine |
| Education | Ministry | |

SOURCES: Official House of Representatives biographies, www.house.state.tx.us/members/pdf/biodata.pdf; Senate Fact Sheet, www.senate.state.tx.us/80r/Senate/Facts.htm.

are real estate, insurance, finance, and various forms of consulting. Table 6-4 shows the wide variety of occupations represented in the Eightieth Legislature.

### FIFTYISH

In 2007, the median age group of members of both houses of the Texas legislature was 50 to 59, compared to the state median age of 32.3. Only twenty-four House members and one senator were under 40 (22.7 percent, as compared with 77.4 percent of the total population). Forty-one House and six Senate members were 60 and over (26 percent as compared with 9.3 percent of the total population). Thus, the growing numbers of young adults are especially underrepresented, but the statistics are a bit misleading because two thirds of those under 40 are children. Senior citizens are somewhat overrepresented, a fact that may reflect the reality that the paltry salary of legislators dictates that most individuals wait until they are financially secure to consider running for office.[18]

### OTHER FACTORS

*Education, marital status, religion, organization, money,* and the *media* are additional factors in legislative elections. Since the late 1970s, virtually all members of the legislature are college educated, and slightly over half hold more than one degree—especially in law or business. The preponderance of legislators are married, although each year more members decline to state whether they are married. In 1991, the legislature had its first acknowledged gay man as a member.

Legislators no longer include religious preference in their biographical information, and it is increasingly difficult to find current information about the religious preferences of Texas citizens. This reality may reflect a greater sensitivity to religious freedom in the state. The most recent information is from the 1990s, when about two thirds of both houses were Protestant, a little over a quarter of each house was Roman Catholic, a small number of Jews were members, and several members provided no information about their religion. Those preferences were roughly in keeping with the preferences of the state's residents as a whole, and one can assume that legislators continue to look a great deal like the general public in their religious preferences. The Texas legislature rarely deals with issues that have a basis in religion, although someone's religious views may influence thinking about issues such as school vouchers or parental consent for teenage abortions. However, in 2007, the House considered a number of bills that would infuse religion into public policy,[19] one of a number of areas that reflected sharp differences in Senate and House policy preferences.

Legislators also tend to be members of the "right" groups. Membership in civic associations, business and professional groups, and social clubs all help convince voters that the candidate is a solid citizen. Such memberships also provide contacts with potential campaign donors. Campaigning for office is expensive.

In 2006, the lowest amount of campaign funds raised by a winning candidate for the Texas House of Representatives was $3,573, while the highest amount was $2,735,806. In the Senate, the range of funds raised by winning candidates was $532,709 to $1,7741,045.[20] The amounts raised, especially in the House, reflect whether the district is considered "safe," making election/re-election easy, and who the candidate is (the most dollars went to the powerful speaker of the House). Also, unexpended funds can be held over and used for a variety of purposes that must be only vaguely related to the role of state legislator.[21] (See Chapter 5 for a discussion of campaigns and elections.) Generally, candidates with some personal money are better able to attract financial support than those of ordinary means, in part because they move in "money" circles. Favorable media exposure—news coverage and editorial endorsements by newspapers, magazines, radio, and especially television—is of tremendous importance during a campaign. The media decide who the leading candidates are and then give them the lion's share of free news space. Texas media tend to be conservative and to endorse business-oriented candidates.

## EXPERIENCE AND TURNOVER

**Seniority** has long been of great importance in the committee structure of the U.S. Congress, and Texas voters in many districts were accustomed to reelecting members of the Texas congressional delegation, at least until new district lines were drawn in 2003. Rapid **turnover** of 20 to 25 percent has traditionally characterized the Texas legislature, with the result that state legislators have been accused of being inexperienced and amateurish. However, the turnover rate has been inching down. After the 2006 elections, both houses had a turnover rate of less than 20 percent. Moreover, a typical freshman senator is likely to have had prior governmental experience in the House, and a typical freshman House member may have served on a county commissioners court, city council, or school board.

What causes legislative turnover? Running for higher office, retirement, moving into the more profitable private sector, and reapportionment/redistricting are among the causes. So also are tough urban reelection races, changing party alignments, and voter perception—correct—that seniority is not as important in the state legislature as it is in the U.S. Congress. Nevertheless, seniority is important. Not only does it increase the probability that a legislator will be knowledgeable about policy issues, but it also means that the legislator will understand how the system works. In the Senate, especially, the more senior members tend to chair committees.

# Internal Organization of the Legislature

## THE PRESIDING OFFICERS

The presiding officers of any legislative assembly have more power and prestige than do ordinary members. In Texas, however, the lieutenant governor and the speaker of the House have such sweeping procedural, organizational, administrative, and planning authority that they truly dominate the legislative scene.

Although most state legislatures have partisan leadership positions analogous to the majority and minority leaders in the U.S. Congress, this is not yet the case in Texas because of the historical one-party tradition, the tendency to have bipartisan leadership, and the domination of the presiding officers. The committee chairs hold the secondary positions of power, after the presiding officers. Chairs are appointed by the presiding officers and thus do not offer any threat to the power of either the speaker or the lieutenant governor.

### LIEUTENANT GOVERNOR

The lieutenant governor is elected independently by the citizenry, serves as president of the Senate but is not a member of it, and does not run on the ticket with the gubernatorial candidate. The lieutenant governor rarely performs any executive functions and is chiefly a legislative official. The term of the office is four years.

Twenty-seven other states use the lieutenant governor as the presiding officer of the upper house. But these states (usually) also look to the governor for policy recommendations; their chamber rules are such that the lieutenant governor, far from exercising any real power, is generally in a position similar to that of the vice president of the United States—neither an important executive nor a legislative force. Such is not the case in Texas, where the lieutenant governor is a major force in state politics and the dominant figure during legislative sessions.

The lieutenant governor orchestrates the flow of legislation in the upper house. Republican David Dewhurst, a wealthy businessman and former CIA agent who served a single term as commissioner of the General Land Office as his only previous public office, was elected as lieutenant governor in 2002. His was the closest major race in the state, with popular former Comptroller John Sharp, a Democrat, running as his opponent. By 2006, his reelection victory was more decisive. Dewhurst apparently did his homework before the 2003 session, sought the advice of experienced senators, organized the Senate for business quickly, and appointed committee chairs from both parties, a precedent begun thirty years earlier by Lieutenant Governor William P. (Bill) Hobby. During the partisan battles over redistricting in the summer of 2003, Dewhurst originally held firm and tried to maintain the neutrality and calm of the Senate. Ultimately, he yielded to party pressures and forced the redistricting issue by setting aside the traditional two-thirds rule. Dewhurst apparently tried to seek the high road on issues such as school finance and child protection legislation, but he and his House counterpart, as well as the governor, seemed to go in different directions.[22] In 2007, his interest in the governorship was apparent, and many senators thought Dewhurst failed as a legislative leader.

Dewhurst's immediate predecessors were both Republicans. Bill Ratliff, a Senate powerhouse, was selected by his colleagues to act as presiding officer for the 2001 session. Lieutenant Governor Rick Perry, who presided over the 1999 session, had moved up to the governor's mansion in late 2000 following Governor George W. Bush's election to the U.S. presidency. Ratliff chose to return to the Senate rather than run for lieutenant governor and subsequently resigned from office after the rancorous redistricting battles of 2003. Ratliff rued the end of civility in his beloved Senate and thought that it no longer played the important moderating role it long had in tempering the actions of the more passionate and more fractious House.[23] These two short-term presiding officers followed two long-term presiding officers, both Democrats. Bob Bullock ruled the Senate from 1991 until 1999, and Bill Hobby presided over the Senate from 1973 until 1991.

★ ★ ★ ★ ★ ★ ★ ★ ★ ★ ★ ★ ★ ★ ★ ★ ★ ★ ★ ★ ★ ★ ★ ★ ★ ★ ★ ★ ★

## *An Unusual Succession to Office*

With a 1999 constitutional amendment confirming his right of succession, Rick Perry became governor on December 21, 2000, following George W. Bush's resignation to become the U.S. president. The Senate then met on December 28 as a committee of the whole to elect one of its own members as acting lieutenant governor and presiding officer for the 2001 session and until the 2002 elections. Senate President pro tempore Rodney Ellis presided over the election, laying out the ground rules of a series of secret ballots until one of the six candidates (five Republicans, one Democrat—the Senate had a one-vote Republican majority) emerged with a majority. Although the media tried to block the secret ballots, the state Supreme Court upheld the senators' right to vote in private. Bill Ratliff defeated David Sibley by a vote of sixteen to fifteen; both finalists are Republicans, but Ratliff received more support from the Democratic minority.

Under the terms of the amendment to Article III, Section 9, the person elected to serve as presiding officer until the next election for lieutenant governor must remain a senator. Although Ratliff continued to serve as a senator, he did give up his role as a committee chair.

★ ★ ★ ★ ★ ★ ★ ★ ★ ★ ★ ★ ★ ★ ★ ★ ★ ★ ★ ★ ★ ★ ★ ★ ★ ★ ★ ★ ★

## SPEAKER OF THE HOUSE

The speaker of the Texas House of Representatives is an elected member of the House who is formally chosen as speaker by a majority vote of the House membership at the opening of the legislative session. The results of the election are rarely a surprise; by the time the session opens, everyone knows who the speaker will be. Candidates for speaker begin maneuvering for support long before the previous session has ended. And during the interim between sessions, they not only campaign for election to the House in their home districts but also try to secure from fellow House members written pledges of support in the race for speaker. If an incumbent speaker is seeking reelection, usually no other candidates run.

It is important for legislators to know whether the speaker is seeking reelection because they must decide whether to back the incumbent or take a chance on supporting a challenger. The decision is crucial: The speaker rewards supporters by giving them key committee assignments—perhaps even the opportunity to chair a committee—and by helping them campaign for reelection to the legislature. A House member who throws support in the wrong direction risks legislative oblivion.

Until 1951, speakers traditionally served for one term; between 1951 and 1975, they served either one or two. The House seems to have abandoned the limited-term tradition, however. Billy Clayton served four terms as speaker (1975–1983), and his successor, Gib Lewis, served five (1983–1993). James E. (Pete) Laney, a West Texas cotton farmer, bested eight other House members to become speaker in 1993 and was elected to a fifth term in 2001.

Representative Jim Pitts learned in 2007 what it means to challenge the speaker. He went from chair of the powerful Appropriations Committee in 2005–06 to vice chair of the Government Reform Committee in 2007.

*Courtesy of Ben Sargent.*

When a majority of Republicans was elected to the House in 2002 for the first time since Reconstruction, Tom Craddick, a longtime Midland legislator, quickly secured the necessary votes to become speaker in 2003. Controversy surrounded him instantly because his staff was filled with former insurance industry lobbyists at a time when insurance reform was likely to be a significant item in the forthcoming legislative session; he seemed to be going against the admonition in the chapter-opening quotation of not having his own agenda. It is not unusual for legislative leaders or state executives to appoint prominent lobbyists to their staffs; mainly former legislators, the lobbyists tend to be very wise in the ways of state politics. In Craddick's case, though, there were clear ties to the insurance lobby as well as allegations that he had shown favoritism in the previous legislative session toward interests represented by his daughter, a lobbyist. Craddick added fuel to the proverbial fire because he also did away with seniority appointments on the all-important budget-writing Appropriations Committee, loosened controls over House committee spending, and was slow in making committee appointments. Democrats were concerned that the minority voice would be stifled and alleged that Speaker Craddick had loaded important committees with ultraconservative ideologues.

Craddick's more ideological, if not outright more partisan, approach was bound to draw complaints because Democrats were in the minority for the first time in 130 years. A major factor was simply the contrast between Craddick's style and that of his predecessor, Laney, whose approach was lower key and reformist. However, Craddick's subsequent behavior as leader made it clear that his approach was, as a popular expression states, "my way or the highway." The media, political analysts, and other observers, including Republicans concerned about the public schools, grew increasingly critical of the speaker's stranglehold on the House and his relentless defense of his positions.[24] In the modern era, speaker styles have run the gamut from that of reform (Laney and Price Daniel Jr.) to partisanship and even ethics violations (Lewis), but the point about Craddick is that he seems to stay embroiled in one controversy after another.

A bitter fight for the speakership in 2007 led to the demotion of Appropriations Chair Jim Pitts, in spite of promises by the speaker of "no retaliation," and tarnished the reputations of some Democrats who opted to support the speaker rather than oppose him, although he often squelched their voices in the lower chamber. Thereafter, the speaker was heavily criticized for letting the House drift during the 2007 regular session, and a coup against the speaker was threatened toward the end of the session. Sixty members even walked out briefly in protest of Craddick's heavy-handed leadership. By session's end, seven House members—Fred Hill, Delwin Jones, Jim Keffer, Brian McCall, Jim Pitts (all Republicans), Senfronia Thompson, and Sylvester Turner (both Democrats)—had already announced that they would run for speaker in January 2008.[25]

## PRO TEMPORE POSITIONS

*Pro tempore* ("for the time being") positions are largely honorific in Texas. At the beginning of the session, the Senate elects one member to serve as president pro tempore to preside when the lieutenant governor (president of the Senate) is absent or if the lieutenant governor's office becomes vacant. At the end of the session, another individual is elected to serve as president pro tempore during the legislative interim; this person is usually one of the senior members. House rules also provide for the speaker to appoint someone to preside over the House temporarily or to appoint a speaker pro tempore to serve permanently. Whether to select anyone at all and who the individual will be are options left to the speaker.

## LEGISLATIVE COMMITTEES

Legislative bodies in the United States have long relied on committees to expedite their work because the alternative is trying to accomplish detailed legislation, planning, and investigation by the whole house. These committees are critical to the legislative process. This chapter offers only a general outline of Texas legislative committees; a more detailed discussion of their powers can be found in Chapter Seven. The presiding officers appoint committee members. The five basic types of committees in the state legislature are listed here. Note that these categories are not mutually exclusive.

1. **Standing committees** are established by the rules of the two houses as permanent committees. They deal with designated areas of public policy.

2. **Subcommittees** are subdivisions of standing committees. They consider specialized areas of their standing committees' general jurisdiction.

3. **Conference committees** are formed for the purpose of arriving at acceptable compromises on bills that have passed both houses but in different forms. These temporary committees include members from both houses; a selected number of members of the standing committees that originally had jurisdiction over the bills in question are usually members of the conference committee. Sometimes the main proponents of the two versions can work out a compromise, and the conference committee does not have to meet.

4. **Ad hoc committees** are temporary and are appointed to consider specific issues or problems; they resemble special and select committees in the U.S. Congress. Conference committees are a type of ad hoc committee.

5. **Interim committees** continue the work of the legislature after the session ends, to study a particular problem and/or to make recommendations to the next legislature. Interim committees are frequently joint committees— that is, they have members from both houses.

### STANDING COMMITTEES

Before Speaker Daniels's reform legislation of 1973, Texas lawmakers had to contend with forty-six House committees and twenty-seven Senate committees. All legislators served on at least four committees. The lines of committee jurisdiction were hazy; determining which committee had jurisdiction over a bill was much like trying to fit together a jigsaw puzzle. In 1973, however, the number of standing committees was reduced to nine in the Senate and twenty-one in the House.

By 2007, the House had forty standing committees, plus six standing subcommittees. The Senate had fifteen standing committees, plus five standing subcommittees (see Table 6.5). These numbers go up and down slightly with different sessions, but the trend is certainly growth in numbers. Senators usually serve on three committees, and House members usually serve on two.

**TABLE 6-5**

# Standing Committees of the Eightieth Legislature, 2007–2008

| Fifteen Senate Committees (Plus Five Standing Subcommittees) | Forty House Committees (Plus Six Standing Subcommittees) |
|---|---|
| Administration | Agriculture & Livestock |
| Business & Commerce | Appropriations |
|   SC on Emerging Technologies & Economic |   SC on Criminal Justice |
|   Development |   SC on Education |
| Criminal Justice |   SC on General Government |
| Education |   SC on Health & Human Services |
|   SC on Higher Education |   SC on Regulatory |
| Finance |   SC on Special Issues |
| Government Organization | Border & International Affairs |
| Health & Human Services | Business & Industry |
| Intergovernmental Relations | Calendars |
|   SC on Flooding & Evacuations | Civil Practices |
| International Relations & Trade | Corrections |
| Jurisprudence | County Affairs |
| Natural Resources | Criminal Jurisprudence |
|   SC on Agriculture, Rural Affairs & Coastal Resources | Culture, Recreation & Tourism |
| Nominations | Defense Affairs & State-Federal Relations |
| State Affairs | Economic Development |
| Transportation & Homeland Security | Elections |
| Veteran Affairs & Military Installations | Energy Resources |
|   SC on Base Realignment & Closure | Environmental Regulation |
| | Financial Institutions |
| | General Investigating & Ethics |
| | Government Reform |
| | Higher Education |
| | House Administration |
| | Human Services |
| | Insurance |
| | Judiciary |
| | Juvenile Justice & Family Issues |
| | Land & Resource Management |
| | Law Enforcement |
| | Licensing & Administrative Procedures |
| | Local & Consent Calendars |
| | Local Government Ways & Means |
| | Natural Resources |
| | Pensions & Investments |
| | Public Education |
| | Public Health |
| | Redistricting |
| | Regulated Industries |
| | Rules & Resolutions |
| | State Affairs |
| | Transportation |
| | Urban Affairs |
| | Ways & Means |

In 1973, a modified seniority system was introduced in the Texas House of Representatives. Under this system, a representative may ask for appointment to a desired committee slot on the basis of seniority—that is, the number of terms the legislator has served in the House.[24] If less than half the committee's membership has been selected according to seniority, the member's request is granted. The speaker then appoints the remainder of the committee members, including the committee chairperson and vice chairperson. Speaker Craddick, however, eliminated seniority appointments from the Appropriations Committee so as to centralize his control more.

In the Senate, the presiding officer—the lieutenant governor—appoints all committee members and the committee chairpersons and vice chairpersons. A modified seniority rule applies as follows: For committees of ten or fewer members, three must be persons who have served on that committee in the last session; for committees of more than ten members, four must have served on that committee during the last session. A senator may serve as chairperson of only one standing committee during any one session. Ironically, while reformers at the federal government level have worked hard and with some success to gain a relaxation of the seniority rule in Congress, reformers at the state level have sought to introduce seniority into the Texas legislature. The reason proposed for introducing seniority into the Texas system is the same as that for originally instituting the system in Congress: to mitigate some of the power concentrated in the hands of the presiding officers. At the national level, however, U.S. House Speaker Dennis Hastert, (1999–2007) began appointing committee chairs without regard to seniority in some cases. In the U.S. Senate, seniority remains inviolable.

Although seniority can discourage capable young legislators, it does assure that those who play a significant part in conducting legislative business have experience and possibly some degree of expertise. The experience factor is important. Legislative committees control the flow of legislation in both houses, and the method by which their members are selected generally influences the outcome of public policy in the state.

## OTHER COMMITTEES

The standing subcommittees in the Senate are also appointed by the lieutenant governor. Other subcommittees in both houses are named by the committee chairpersons, who are unlikely to act contrary to the wishes of the presiding officers. Ad hoc and conference committees are creatures of the speaker and lieutenant governor. Interim committees are somewhat different. Their members *may* include a combination of appointees of the presiding officers and the governor, including citizen (nonlegislative) members. The 1961 Legislative Reorganization Act directed standing committees to study matters under their jurisdiction during the legislative interim, but in many cases, special interim committees are appointed instead. Often, these committees are support-building devices for legislation that failed during the previous session. Such committees are not mandated to deliver a report back to the legislature. Of course, if the speaker or lieutenant governor is interested in the study, the likelihood of a full report increases substantially. Although legislative staff is available to assist either standing or special committees between legislative sessions, interim committees often are created without a staff and/or funds.

A modern device is the select committee, which includes legislators and governor's appointees. The Select Committee on Public Education created by the Sixty-eighth Legislature (1983–1984) had the support of the leadership and the governor; consequently, it is an example of a well-funded, highly publicized study committee. Another example is the Select Committee on Tax Equity in 1987–1988, created by the Seventieth Legislature. The Joint Select Committee on Public School Finance, which served in 2003–2004, is an example of a significant interim committee intended to produce recommendations for legislative action on an important topic. Its job was to recommend a way to fund public schools in the state. In 2007, the Select Committee on the Operation and Management of the Texas Youth Commission had the important function of producing legislation that would result in the reorganization of a corrupt, abusive agency.

## LEGISLATIVE STAFF

Although Texas legislators enjoy better office budgets and staff allowances than their counterparts in many other states, they still must rely on information furnished by outside groups. For example, the Texas Research League, a private business-oriented group, performs numerous studies and makes recommendations to the legislature. The Legislative Budget Board (LBB), an internal agency of the legislature, makes recommendations on the same appropriations bills that it helps to prepare. The Legislative Reference Library, while a valuable tool, is limited to maintaining a history of legislation in Texas and furnishing information on comparable legislation in other states.

Legislative committees also have limited budgets and professional staff, although a presiding officer may give his favorite committees liberal spending privileges. Accordingly, committees often must rely on assistance from the institutional staff of the legislature, such as the LBB, and from other state agencies, such as the attorney general's office or the comptroller's office. In addition, from time to time, legislators with compatible views form study groups to work on issues.

The lack of adequate staffing is of major importance to Texans. It means that legislators, in committee or individually, cannot easily obtain impartial, accurate information concerning public policy. Nonetheless, citizen interest in supporting larger budgets for legislative operations seems to be nil. Indeed, some Texans see any move on the part of legislators to eliminate their dependence on private groups and state administrators for information as a ploy to "waste" more tax money. This attitude, fully encouraged by lobbyists, keeps staffing low although the National Conference of State Legislatures notes that the strength of a legislative body rests with its staff.[25]

However, a major change occurred in the third called session of 2003 when the LBB, the most powerful staff agency, was given even more power at the expense of the state comptroller's office.

The creation of the Texas Legislative Council (TLC) in 1949 was a major step toward providing research and technical services to Texas legislators. But the TLC has never been adequately funded to provide full-time bill-drafting and research services, and its small staff receives more requests for information than it can handle. The LBB, composed of the presiding officers and other legislators, prepares the legislative budget. Its staff, heavily influenced by the presiding officers, is in an awkward position to make independent recommendations. And the other auxiliary organization of the legislature, the Legislative Audit Committee, is composed of the presiding officers and certain ex officio legislators. Its professional staff, headed by the state auditor, who serves at the pleasure of the committee, also is heavily influenced by the presiding officers.

House Bill 7, third called session, 2003, made several changes in these staff agencies. The E-Texas reports, the public school reviews, and the state agency efficiency reviewers were removed from the comptroller's office and given to the LBB. The comptroller remains the responsible official for certifying that sufficient funds exist to fund the state budget. The presiding officers were designated as joint chairs for all three staff agencies, and the membership and quorum for the TLC were changed to give less advantage to House members.

Other political appointees assist members individually but their major responsibilities are to the House or Senate as a body. These include the secretary of the Senate, the chief clerk of the House, their assistants, the sergeants-at-arms, the pages, and clerical staff.

# General Criticism and Suggested Reforms

## CRITICISM

Extensive efforts to revamp state legislative structures have been made by organizations such as the National Legislative Conference, the Council of State Governments, the Citizens Conference on State Legislatures, and the National Municipal League. This last organization even produced a Model State Constitution as a "companion piece" for its Model City Charter. But state legislatures have been universally noninnovative. As Alexander Heard observes, "State legislatures may be our most extreme example of institutional lag. In their formal qualities, they are largely 19th-century organizations, and they must, or should, address themselves to 20th- [and now 21st-] century problems."[26]

The Texas legislature seems caught in the proverbial vicious circle. Low salaries and short terms force legislators to maintain other sources of income, a necessity that leads to inattentiveness to legislative business, especially between sessions. On salary alone, a legislator would be far below the federal poverty line. However, the generous $139 a day allowance, plus mileage allowance, helps raise the total compensation to over $30,000 for the average legislator during a legislative year. That sum is not as munificent as it sounds, as living away from home in Austin for five months consumes most of the per diem allowance. Indeed, legislators often have roommates to share expenses, just like college students.

The electorate, on the other hand, views the legislature as a group whose members work only 140 days every two years (many citizens forget about interim committee assignments) but get paid every month. Most citizens probably do not realize—and may not care—that legislators make only $600 a month in salary. They would probably care more if they realized that most of a legislator's compensation comes from the per diem allowance. In 1984, voters explicitly refused to allow legislators more than $30 a day in expense money. The $139 figure came about through the discovery of a loophole in the statute setting per diem payments.

Yet citizens are not very consistent in their views. While they are reluctant to vote for decent legislative salaries, they seem to find little difficulty in entrusting a multibillion-dollar budget to an inexperienced and poorly paid group of legislators whom they view as amateurs at best and scalawags at worst.[27] Furthermore, they seem oblivious to the detrimental effect on legislation caused by inadequate salaries for both legislators and their staffs and the resulting dependence on special interests or on "gamesmanship" to maximize the per diem payments.

## SUGGESTED REFORMS

### SESSIONS

The institution of annual legislative sessions has been a major reform proposal in all recent constitutional revision efforts. Annual sessions would allow legislators time to familiarize themselves with complex legislation, permitting them, for example, to bring a little more knowledge to the chaotic guessing game that produces the state's biennial budget. Annual sessions would virtually eliminate the need for special sessions when a crisis arises between regular sessions. They would allow time for the continual introduction of all those special resolutions, such as declaring chili the official state dish, that have negligible importance for the general public but take up so much valuable legislative time. They also would provide an opportunity for legislative oversight of the state bureaucracy. Coupled with adequate staff support, annual sessions would allow legislators to engage in more long-range planning of public policy.

The legislature also needs to be empowered to call itself into special session. At present, if legislative leaders see the need for a special session and the governor is reluctant to call it, the legislature is helpless. In thirty-two other states, legislators can initiate a special session either independently or in conjunction with the governor, and efforts to gain that privilege for Texas legislators continue to be pressed. At a minimum, legislators need more freedom to add to the agenda of special sessions. Even though a session is called for a specific purpose, other significant items could be entered on the agenda and dispensed with, thus reducing the clutter of the next regular session's agenda.

The restrictions on both regular and special legislative sessions result in a high concentration of political power. The presiding officers dictate the flow of business during regular sessions, and the governor dominates special sessions. The next chapter more fully examines this concentration of power and its effects.

### SIZE AND SALARIES

Some advocates of reform have recommended that the Texas House be reduced in size to 100 members. Others have suggested that, because both houses are now elected on the basis of population distribution, one house should be eliminated altogether and a unicameral legislature adopted. But tradition strongly militates against such a change. The physical size of the state poses another risk to reducing the size of the legislature. As population and thus district size continue to grow, citizens will increasingly lose contact with their representatives. A reduction in the number of legislators would be a trade-off between legislative efficiency and representativeness. Although efficiency is important to citizens, so is being represented by someone from a small enough geographic and population area to understand the needs of the people in the district.

More serious are recommendations for salary increases. The $7,200 salary is insufficient to allow legislators to devote their full energies to state business. A salary in the range of the average among the nine other largest states—$61,000— would not, of course, guarantee that legislators would be honest and conscientious and devote all of their working time to the business of the state. A decent salary level, however, would ensure that those who wished to could spend most of their time on state business. Moreover, it might also eliminate the retainer fees, consultant fees, and legal fees now paid to many legislators. In addition, it would guard against only the rich being able to run for public office. However, a livable wage for legislators also flies in the face of the fiction that the state has a citizen legislature filled with individuals serving only because of their civic-minded nature.

## TERMS OF OFFICE

If Senate members had staggered six-year terms and House members had staggered four-year terms, legislators could be assured of having time to develop expertise in both procedures and substantive policy. Moreover, the virtually continuous campaigning that is required of legislators who represent highly competitive urban districts would be greatly reduced, leaving them more time to spend on legislative functions. Less campaigning also might serve to weaken the tie between legislators and the lobbyists who furnish both financial support for campaigning and bill-drafting services.

## Summary

In many ways, the Texas legislature is typical of state lawmaking bodies: its large size (181 members), its domination by Anglo males, its somewhat limited professional staff, its relatively short terms of office for its members (two years in the House and four in the Senate), and its reliance on legislative committees as the workhorses of the legislative process. Nevertheless, the following distinctive features of the Texas legislature are atypical, especially when it is compared with the legislatures of other large urban states:

1. The legislature is restricted to one regular session of 140 days every two years.

2. Legislators are paid only $7,200 a year, although they receive a generous per diem payment for expenses.

3. The presiding officers—the speaker of the House and the lieutenant governor in the Senate—are preeminent in the legislative process. If either presiding officer is inclined to be arbitrary, democracy suffers.

4. A sometimes high turnover rate and the shifting memberships of the large number of committees make it difficult for legislators to develop expertise in specific areas of legislation.

5. Special interests have an extraordinary influence on both the election and the performance of legislators. This dominance raises the issue of when and how constituent voices are heard.

Texas legislators face the biennial task of developing sound public policy for a major state without jeopardizing the support of the presiding officers or the special interests crucial to their reelection. Moreover, they operate in the highly constrained environment of both structural handicaps and lack of public confidence. They must spend much of their time tending to casework, sitting in committee meetings, or running for office. As Chapter Seven will show, they succeed better than one might expect, given the many difficulties they face. Nevertheless, changes in legislative organization would help promote legislative independence and allow more time for planning and policy development. Recommendations for reform include the following:

1. Annual sessions

2. Higher salaries, approximately $60,000–$61,000

3. Four-year terms for House members and six-year terms for senators

4. Reduction in the number of legislative committees

## Glossary Terms

| | |
|---|---|
| bicameral | privatizing |
| biennial | reapportionment |
| casework | redistricting |
| constituent function | seniority |
| formal qualifications | single-member districts |
| gerrymandering | turnover |
| legislative oversight | |

## Study Questions

1. What are the differences between a regular and a called legislative session?

2. What does "one person, one vote" mean? What have been its implications for Texas? Is this concept responsible for the increases in ethnic minority representation in the legislature? Why or why not?

3. What are the characteristics of the average Texas state legislator? Is it significant that the legislature is in fact likely to underrepresent important groups in the state's population? Why?

4. What are the problems caused by a biennial legislative session?

5. Should Texas legislators be paid more? Why or why not?

6. Besides making laws, what other functions do legislators perform?

7. Should the number of terms that a legislator can serve be limited? Why or why not? If you support term limitation, indicate how many terms you would have senators and representatives serve. Also, would you keep the terms at their present length? Discuss.

8. Do you prefer that the Texas legislature remain as it is or that it be more like the legislatures of other big urban states such as California and New York? Discuss.

## Surfing the Web

Readers are urged to visit the companion site for this book:

**http://academic.cengage.com/polsci/Kraemer/TexasPolitics10e**

# The Legislative Process

Speaker of the House Tom Craddick looks relieved at the close of the 2007 regular session, having barely survived being removed from his leadership position.

What lobbyists can dream, lobbyists can do.

STEVE WOLENS OF DALLAS, *FORMER REPRESENTATIVE,* 1995

Legislative bodies seldom live up to what the public expects of them.

*TEXAS MONTHLY,* 2003

# Introduction

In January of odd-numbered years, 31 senators and 150 representatives gather in Austin to try to work their way through more than 10,000 legislative proposals of various kinds. Texans can predict that prisons, education, utilities, and tax reform will be headlined in the state's newspapers, but the process by which these and other issues are resolved can be a confused jumble to the layperson. If they think of it at all, citizens often consider the legislative session a biennial free-for-all.

One reason for this seeming confusion is that complex rules are a basic part of the legislative process. The larger the assembly, the more necessary are the parliamentary procedures that facilitate working through the agenda.

Another reason is that the legislative process consists of several stages. To judge the fate of a particular proposed piece of legislation known as a **bill**, one must know which stage the bill is in. Is it in committee? On the floor for debate? In a **conference committee**? In the governor's hands? Discussion, changes, votes, approvals, and disapprovals occur at various stages. Those who wish to follow the process of a piece of legislation through newspaper accounts must read carefully to determine whether votes taken are on the bill itself, an amendment to an amendment, a substitute motion, or a motion to table the bill or return it to committee. Indeed, to the uninitiated, it may seem that the same bill is being voted on over and over again.

A third reason is the growing complexity of the issues that legislators face. Juggling the need for services with revenue sources is a frequent source of dismay.

Although their powers were somewhat limited by the modest seniority rules adopted by both houses in 1973 and described in the previous chapter, the presiding officers basically control the flow of legislation in Texas. Their power over public policy in Texas is tremendous. However, many who are not legislators—a supporting cast that includes the governor, the lobbyists, the state bureaucrats, legislative staffers, and sometimes the public—are also involved in making legislative policy. Representative Wolens's comment at the opening of the chapter expresses his frustration at the brazenness of the business lobby during the 1995 session.

This chapter describes the important influences on legislation, how a bill becomes a law in Texas, and lawmaking outside the legislature.

# Power of the Presiding Officers

By constitutional mandate, the presiding officer in the Senate is the lieutenant governor, and the presiding officer in the House of Representatives is the speaker of the House. The powers that the holder of each of these positions enjoys are derived from the rules of the legislative body over which he presides and are of two basic sorts. The first has to do with the organization of the legislature and legislative procedure. In varying degrees, all presiding officers exercise this power of the chair. The second sort of power is institutional, and it has to do with the maintenance of the legislature as a vital organ of government.

A reform-oriented House or Senate can limit the powers of the presiding officers. Also, politics can dictate a change anytime when there is a new leader. However, tradition and the realities of politics ordinarily militate against an overthrow of the powerful legislative leadership during the session. So also does the legislative amateurism that results from short sessions, low pay, and high turnover in membership. The Eightieth Legislature in 2007 proved to be an exception, with efforts to oust the speaker occurring at both the beginning and the end of the session, and announcements in May of 2007 that multiple candidates would challenge Tom Craddick in January of 2008.

From time to time, the leaders themselves have a reform bent. One reason for the introduction of modified seniority in 1973 was that one-term reform Speaker Price Daniel Jr. insisted on some controls over lobbyists. In 1993, Speaker Pete Laney blunted the power of the speaker and made the House more democratic.

Often, though, powerful leaders are a convenience, albeit sometimes a tiresome or costly one. The significance of some of the specific procedural and

Lieutenant Governor David Dewhurst celebrates his reelection with supporters in November 2006.

institutional powers of the lieutenant governor and speaker of the House is discussed in the following sections.

# PROCEDURAL POWERS

Legislative committees have life-or-death power over a **bill**, the way in which legislation is introduced. Legislators' appointments to major committees, especially as chairperson or vice chairperson, largely determine their influence with the legislature as a whole. Presiding officers can thus use their powers of appointment to reward friends and supporters with key positions on important committees and to punish opponents with nonleadership positions on minor committees.

## COMMITTEE MEMBERSHIP

Although seniority does play a role in the formation of House committees, the speaker still effectively determines their composition. The seniority appointments are made after the speaker appoints the chairpersons and vice chairpersons of the committees. The speaker always has some choice because several representatives often have the same amount of seniority in the House. The power of an individual speaker is illustrated by the 2003 actions of Speaker Tom Craddick when he eliminated the seniority appointments from the Appropriations Committee to ensure that its makeup would reflect his conservative ideology.

Senate rules stipulate only that a minority of members must have prior service on a particular committee. Thus, the lieutenant governor, as presiding officer of the Senate, dominates those committee selections.

Special-interest representatives, as well as legislators, are frequently involved in the bargaining that eventually determines who will fill committee slots. Members of interest groups, wanting friends on committees, frequently make suggestions to the presiding officers about member selection. The only committee appointments not made by the presiding officers are those few appointments to special-interest study committees that the governor might make. And even in these cases, the legislature has the power to approve or disapprove nonlegislative appointments to the interim committee.

## CONFERENCE COMMITTEES

A major bill seldom passes both houses in identical form. Each time one fails to do so, a conference committee may be appointed to resolve the differences. Before 1973, conference committees could, and frequently did, produce virtually new bills. Beginning in 1973, the House adopted a rule effective at the beginning of each session limiting the conference committee to ironing out differences in the two versions of a bill. Resolving these differences often means adding new material to the bill at the conference stage. Five members from each house are appointed to conference committees by their respective presiding officers. Each house has one vote on the conference committee report; in other words, three members on each house's team of five must agree on the conference version of the bill before the bill can be reported back to the House and Senate. The conference report must be accepted or rejected, without change, by each house. This procedure makes conference committee members key figures in the legislative process. Most conference reports, or versions of the bill, are accepted because of time limitations.

Appointees to conference committees usually share the viewpoints of the presiding officers on what should be done with the bill in question. Representatives of special interests often become involved in conference committee deliberations in an attempt to arrange trade-offs, or bargains, with the presiding officers, making one concession in exchange for another. However, sometimes the main proponents of the two versions of the bill are able to work out a compromise without the committee even meeting.

## COMMITTEE CHAIRPERSONS

The standing committees control legislation, and their chairpersons not only specify the committee agenda, subcommittee jurisdiction, and assignments but also control the committees. Lobbyists for special-interest groups work hard to influence the selection of chairpersons and vice chairpersons of committees. A lobbyist's year is generally successful if his or her choice is appointed to chair a committee crucial to the lobbyist's special interests. However, if a lobbyist must deal with an unfriendly chairperson, the session may seem long and trying.

The reward-and-punishment aspect of committee appointments is especially evident in the appointment of chairpersons, for it is through them that the presiding officers control legislation. True seniority is relatively unimportant in determining chairmanships, but some experience is useful. Obviously, political enemies of the lieutenant governor or the speaker are not likely to chair standing committees.

As noted in Chapter Five, Democrats and Republicans are increasingly sharing power in the legislature. Although sessions from 2003 on have been branded as highly partisan, the presiding officers continued to operate to an extent on a nonpartisan basis by blessing the members of both parties with committee chairmanships. This approach helps avoid the gridlock that is common in Congress, where each party has traditionally put up roadblocks against the favored legislation of the other party. It thus allows the Texas legislature to set public policy in spite of a very short legislative session. Taking a nonpartisan approach to legislation has worked well, as the partisan alignment in the legislature has gone from Democratic domination to Republican ascendancy.

In 2003, the divisiveness in the legislature was partially along party lines but even more because the extremists in both parties dominated their colleagues. Rather than steering toward the middle, or slightly to the right of the middle, as had been the tradition in the state, the Seventy-eighth Legislature saw clash after clash of right versus left. As a result, ordinary civility was a casualty to the legislative wars.[1] Out-and-out rudeness and hostility were openly displayed, particularly on the floor of the House of Representatives. Especially in the House, elements of that partisanship have continued, though the Senate has returned to a somewhat less partisan style.

## REFERRAL

Because of the large number of committees, which committee has jurisdiction over a particular legislative proposal is ill defined by the Texas legislature. Unlike the U.S. Congress, where committee jurisdictions are relatively clear, jurisdictional ambiguities are pervasive in the Texas committee system. The large number of standing committees—forty in 2007—in the House and the absolute silence of Senate rules on committee jurisdiction create these ambiguities. The committee system in Texas thus allows the presiding officers to use their referral power to determine the outcome of a bill. In other words, if the speaker or lieutenant governor favors a bill, the bill will be referred to a committee that will act favorably toward it. If the presiding officer opposes the proposed legislation, it will be assigned to an unfriendly committee. However, the referral powers of the Senate's presiding officer were curtailed somewhat by the 1973 reform of the committee system and by Senate rules that can force a change in referral.

Some of the factors considered by the presiding officers when assigning bills to committees include: (1) the positions of their own financial supporters and political backers on the bill; (2) the effect of the bill on other legislation, especially the availability of funding for other programs; (3) their own ideological commitment to the bill; (4) the past record of support or nonsupport of the bill's backers, both legislators and special interests; and (5) the bargaining in which the bill's backers are willing to engage, including promises of desired support of, or opposition to, other bills on which the presiding officers have strong positions as well as a willingness to modify the bill itself.

The state struggled with public-school funding, children's health, and other issues from 2003 on, but the legislature focused on political questions such as redistricting instead of pressing policy needs. This Ben Sargent cartoon sums up legislative and executive leadership during the period as an empty gas tank.

*Courtesy of Ben Sargent.*

CHAPTER SEVEN: THE LEGISLATIVE PROCESS

# YOU DECIDE

## Should Seniority Determine Committee Chairs in Texas?

Seniority is extremely important in the Congress of the United States. The seniority rule for determining congressional committee chairs is that the chairmanship goes to the member of the majority party with the longest continuous service on that one committee in that one house of Congress. Senators or U.S. representatives in their party caucuses can bypass this rule but seldom do. In Texas, a committee chair may be of either political party and the presiding officers determine all the chairs and vice chairs regardless of seniority.

| PRO | CON |
|---|---|
| Texas should select legislative committee chairs by a predominately majority party-seniority procedure because: | Texas should not use the majority party-seniority procedure favored by the U.S. Congress because: |
| ▲ The speaker of the House and the lieutenant governor would not be so all-powerful. | ▼ The short legislative session cries out for tight control by the presiding officers. |
| ▲ The party that the voters prefer would dominate the policy process. | ▼ The majority party did not get all of the votes, and the Texas system allows both parties to have some voice in public policy. |
| ▲ The chair would always be someone knowledgeable about the committee and its work. | ▼ The most senior person is not the only legislator in the House or Senate who knows procedure or understands the work of the committee. |
| ▲ The chair would fully understand the legislative process. | ▼ Learning legislative process demands paying attention, not passing time. |

## SCHEDULING/THE CALENDAR

In all legislative bodies, bills are assigned a time for debate. This scheduling—placing the bill on a legislative calendar—determines the order of the bill's debate and vote. In Congress, the majority leader controls the two Senate calendars, although the informality of the Senate reduces the importance of the calendars; the Rules Committee of the House assigns bills to one of five calendars.

In Texas, the two calendars committees control placement of bills in the House; both are controlled by the speaker. In the Senate, the members control the agenda by being able to take bills out of order with a two-thirds vote. However, the lieutenant governor controls efforts to change the order of debate by making legislators publicly state their intentions.

Scheduling is more important in Texas than in some other states or in Congress because of the short biennial legislative session. A bill placed far down on the schedule may not come to the floor before the session reaches its 140-day mandatory adjournment. In addition, items on the calendars are called in order, and some calendars do not allow debate. For example, in the House, it is highly advantageous to have a bill placed on the Local, Consent, and Resolutions Calendar, which is used for uncontested legislation. The timing of debate may well determine the outcome of the vote. Legislative strategies include trying either to delay the call of a bill until negative votes can be lined up or to rush a bill through before opposition can materialize. Another factor to be considered in Senate scheduling is the possibility of a **filibuster**. It is much easier to shut off attempts to "talk a bill to death" early in the session than when only a few days are left for action. (The filibuster is discussed under "Step Three: Floor Action" later in this chapter.)

★ ★ ★ ★ ★ ★ ★ ★ ★ ★ ★ ★ ★ ★ ★ ★ ★ ★ ★ ★ ★ ★ ★ ★ ★ ★ ★ ★ ★ ★

## Three Ways to Block a Bill

### The Filibuster

Former Senator Bill Meier, who talked for forty-three hours straight in 1977, holds the Texas and world records for filibustering. More recently, in 1993, Senator Gonzalo Barrientos stopped just short of eighteen hours in an unsuccessful effort to protect Austin's Barton Creek and its popular swimming hole.

### The Technicality

One of the most bizarre events in the history of the Texas legislature occurred in 1997, when conservative Representative Arlene Wohlgemuth, angry at the blockage of a bill regarding parental notification before girls under eighteen could get an abortion, raised a point of order about the calendar for May 26. The effect was to kill fifty-two bills that were scheduled for debate because the point of order concerned the calendar itself. Her fellow legislators referred to the incident as the "Memorial Day Massacre" and were irate that months of work, including the delicate negotiations between House and Senate members to achieve compromise bills, apparently had been for nought. After tempers cooled, legislators found ways to resurrect some of the bills by tacking them onto other bills that had not been on the calendar for Memorial Day and by using resolutions.

### Pocketing

The presiding officers can also block bills by pocketing them; that is, they can decline to send a bill to the floor for debate even though a committee has given it a favorable report. Often, a presiding officer will pocket a bill because it virtually duplicates one already in the legislative pipeline or to keep an unimportant bill from cluttering up the agenda near the end of the session when major legislation is pending.

★ ★ ★ ★ ★ ★ ★ ★ ★ ★ ★ ★ ★ ★ ★ ★ ★ ★ ★ ★ ★ ★ ★ ★ ★ ★ ★ ★ ★ ★

In the House, the powerful Calendars Committee and, to a lesser extent, the Local, Consent, and Resolutions Calendars Committee control the placement of bills on one of the House calendars. The speaker's powers are indirect through the appointment of the committees and their chairpersons and vice chairpersons.

A member essentially goes "hat in hand" to one of these gatekeeper committees—usually the Calendars Committee, because it deals with major legislation—to try to get her or his bill on the calendar. However, if any committee member objects to the bill, the bill is never scheduled. Moreover, these committees meet in secret. House members can challenge a ruling by the committee, but because a two-thirds vote is required to pry the bill from committee and other members fear reprisals as they try to get their own bills out of committee, attempts to force a scheduling of debate are very rare.

The calendar system in the House is somewhat confusing. There are four calendars (see Table 7-1): the Daily House; the Supplemental House; the Local,

**TABLE 7-1**

## A Comparison of the Legislative Calendars in the Texas Legislature and the U.S. Congress

| Texas Legislative Calendars | |
|---|---|
| **Senate** | **House** |
| Senate | Daily House |
| Intent | Supplemental House |
| | Local, Consent, and Resolutions |
| | Congratulatory and Memorial |
| | Categories for grouping legislation on the Supplemental House Calendar, which is the major calendar, are: emergency; major state; constitutional amendments; general state; local, consent, and resolutions; resolutions; and congratulatory and memorial resolutions |
| **Congressional Calendars** | |
| **Senate** | **House** |
| Senate | House |
| Executive | Union |
| | Consent |
| | Private |
| | Discharge |

Consent, and Resolutions; and the Congratulatory and Memorial. The most significant of these is the Supplemental House Calendar because it incorporates the daily calendar as well as any carryover business. Compounding the confusion is a series of categories—which overlap the names of the calendars—used to group legislation on the calendars and rules about differential treatment of House and Senate resolutions.

For example, well-publicized bills will find their way to the Supplemental House Calendar under the category of Major State unless an emergency exists (such as authorizing repairs to the capitol after a fire). The Local, Consent, and Resolutions Calendar deals with business involving one part of the state (for example, the creation of a new special district in a single county) and with noncontroversial proposals. Placement of a bill on that calendar signifies no opposition, although the bill can be withdrawn and placed on a different calendar if opposition develops later.

No calendars committee exists in the Senate, and technically, the main calendar—the Senate Agenda—is simply called in numerical order. However, bills virtually never come up in order because of motions to take up other bills out of order. A motion to take up a bill out of order requires a two-thirds vote. Moreover, if a senator intends to ask for consideration of a bill out of order, he or she must file an intention to do so with the clerk, stipulating the date on which the motion will be made and asking for a place on the Intent Calendar. When Bill Hobby was lieutenant governor, he formalized the Intent Calendar as a way of forcing the members to reveal their plans in advance to avoid surprising the presiding officer. All other business not on the Intent Calendar can then be placed on the Senate Calendar.

A legislator has two ways to improve the chances that a bill will be placed high enough on a calendar to ensure floor debate on it. First, members may pre-file bills as soon as the November elections are completed. Early filing does not ensure that the presiding officer or the chair to whose committee the bill is referred will be favorably disposed toward the proposed legislation, but obtaining a low number because of quick filing may at least ensure that the bill is referred to committee early in the session. Second, if the bill is one in which the governor has a keen interest, the governor can declare an emergency to force speedy consideration of the proposal.

## RECOGNITION

One of the prerogatives of the presiding officer of any assembly is the recognition of individuals who wish to speak. In legislative bodies, with the occasional exception of presiding officers who are simply arbitrary, the recognition power is traditionally invoked in a fair and judicious manner. Recent speakers and Senate presidents have followed this tradition, although Speaker Craddick allowed some heckling in 2003 and seemed to lose interest in maintaining control in 2007. In Texas, the Senate procedures for scheduling legislation—that is, the Intent Calendar—give the presiding officer extraordinary power. The lieutenant governor must recognize a bill's sponsor before the sponsor can move the bill for consideration, and the sponsor needs the presiding officer's support to achieve the necessary two-thirds vote of the legislation. Effectively, eleven senators who oppose a bill can block it, because the sponsor cannot then hope to achieve a two-thirds majority.

## PROCEDURES

At the beginning of each regular session of the Texas legislature, each house adopts the rules of procedure that will govern that session's legislative process. Procedures can change considerably, as was evidenced by the 1973 reforms and the 1983 and 2003 House changes giving the speaker more control over appropriations, members' office budgets, and committee jurisdictions. However, many rules are carried over from one session to another or are only slightly modified.

Numerous precedents determine how the rules will be applied, and of course, all parliamentary rules are subject to interpretation by the chair. Thus, the presiding officers greatly influence the outcome of policy deliberations by their acceptance or rejection of points of order, their decisions as to whether a proposed amendment is germane, their announcement of vote counts, and so forth.

In summary, procedural interpretation, recognition of those wishing to speak, determination of the timetable for debate, referral of bills, and the appointment of committees and their chairpersons all combine to make the presiding officers truly powerful. While none of these powers is unusual for a club president, they take on greater significance when we realize that they are used to determine the outcome of policy struggles within the government of a major state.

★ ★ ★ ★ ★ ★ ★ ★ ★ ★ ★ ★ ★ ★ ★ ★ ★ ★ ★ ★ ★ ★ ★ ★ ★ ★ ★

### Can Presiding Officers Vote?

The presiding officer of the Senate has limited voting powers, because the lieutenant governor is not a member of the Senate. He can vote when a tie on a bill occurs and during debate when the Senate sits as a committee of the whole. The speaker is a member of the House and can vote, although he rarely does so. However, if he does vote, and there is a tie, he cannot vote again to break it. A tie is considered a failed vote at that point.

★ ★ ★ ★ ★ ★ ★ ★ ★ ★ ★ ★ ★ ★ ★ ★ ★ ★ ★ ★ ★ ★ ★ ★ ★ ★ ★

SOURCE: One of the speakers who did occasionally vote was Ben Barnes, whose autobiography is a rich summary of Texas politics in the 1960s. See Ben Barnes, *Barn Burning, Barn Building: Tales of a Political Life, from LBJ to George W. Bush and Beyond* (Albany: Bright Sky Press, 2006).

## INSTITUTIONAL POWERS

The presiding officers also appoint the members of three important arms of the legislature: the Legislative Budget Board, the Texas Legislative Council, and the Legislative Audit Committee. Each of these bodies exists to serve the legislature as a whole, providing policy guidelines at the board level and technical assistance at the staff level. As discussed in Chapter Six, the third called session of the legislature in 2003 made a number of changes affecting the organization and jurisdiction of these three agencies. One change was that the presiding officers now serve as joint chairs of each board.

## LEGISLATIVE BUDGET BOARD

At the national level, in most states and even in most cities, the chief executive bears the responsibility for preparing the budget. In Texas, both the governor and the legislature prepare a budget, and state agencies must submit their financial requests to each. The legislative budget is prepared by the Legislative Budget Board (LBB), a ten-member Senate–House joint committee that operates continually, whether the legislature is in session or not. In addition to the presiding officers, there are four members from each house appointed by the presiding officers. By tradition, these include the chairpersons of the committees responsible for appropriations and finance. Because of the importance of these "money" committees, their chairpersons sometimes develop power bases within the legislature that are independent of the presiding officers.

A professional staff assists the board in making its budget recommendations and then often helps defend those recommendations during the session. The staff recommendations on state agency requests are crucial to an agency's appropriations. Executives in administrative agencies therefore work closely with LBB staff in an effort to justify their spending requests. Additionally, the staff assists the legislature in its watchdog function by overseeing state agency expenditures and agency efficiency. This function increased in importance during the long period of budget "crunches" from 1985 through 1995 so that the LBB and the Governor's Office of Budget and Planning now oversee agency planning and monitor agency performance in meeting state goals and objectives. The agency's power to assess the efficiency of other state agencies was significantly enhanced in 2003 at the expense of the state comptroller, who retained the responsibility to certify that revenues are adequate to support the state budget.

## TEXAS LEGISLATIVE COUNCIL

The membership of the Texas Legislative Council was modified in 2003 to reduce the domination by the House of Representatives. Today, its fourteen members consist of the speaker and the lieutenant governor, who each appoint six additional members from the House and six members from the Senate.

The council oversees the work of the director and professional staff. During the session, the council provides bill-drafting services for legislators; between sessions, it investigates the operations of state agencies, conducts studies on problems subject to legislative consideration, and drafts recommendations for action in the next session. In short, it is the legislature's research office, similar to the Congressional Research Service.

## LEGISLATIVE AUDIT COMMITTEE

In addition to the presiding officers, the other four members of the Legislative Audit Committee are the chairpersons of the Senate Finance, House Ways and Means, House Appropriations, and Senate State Affairs committees. The state auditor, appointed by the committee for a two-year term subject to two-thirds confirmation of the Senate, heads the professional staff. This committee oversees a very important function of all legislative bodies, namely, checking that agencies properly spent money budgeted to them (the *postaudit*). The auditor and the auditor's staff also check into the quality of services and duplication in services and programs provided by state agencies. The highly detailed work of the pro-

★ ★ ★ ★ ★ ★ ★ ★ ★ ★ ★ ★ ★ ★ ★ ★ ★ ★ ★ ★ ★ ★ ★ ★ ★ ★ ★ ★ ★ ★ ★ ★

### Presiding Officers' Powers of the Chair: A Summary

#### Procedural Powers

1. Appointing half or more of the members of substantive committees and all members of procedural and conference committees (the House reserves half of the positions for seniority appointments; the Senate requires only that some members have prior experience)

2. Appointing the chairs and vice chairs of all committees

3. Determining the jurisdiction of committees through the referral of bills

4. Interpreting procedural rules when conflict arises

5. Scheduling legislation for floor action (especially important in the Senate, which lacks a complex calendar system)

6. Recognizing members who wish to speak or not recognizing them and thus preventing them from speaking

#### Institutional Powers

1. Appointing the members of the Legislative Budget Board and serving as the cochairs thereof

2. Appointing the members of the Texas Legislative Council and serving as the cochairs thereof

3. Appointing the members of the Legislative Audit Committee and serving as the cochairs thereof

★ ★ ★ ★ ★ ★ ★ ★ ★ ★ ★ ★ ★ ★ ★ ★ ★ ★ ★ ★ ★ ★ ★ ★ ★ ★ ★ ★ ★ ★ ★ ★

fessional staff involves a review of the records of financial transactions. In fact, the larger state agencies have an auditor or team of auditors assigned to them practically year-round.

# Limits on Presiding Officers

It may seem as if the presiding officers are nearly unrestrained in their exercise of power. There are several personal and political factors, however, that prevent absolute power on the part of the speaker of the House and the lieutenant governor.

## PERSONALITY AND AMBITION

Although there is always the danger that presiding officers may become arbitrary or vindictive and thus abuse their office, they are usually so powerful that they do not need to search for ways to gain influence other than through persuasion, compromise, and accommodation. Arbitrariness is a function of personality, not of the office. Former Lieutenant Governor Bill Hobby of Houston, who served eighteen years and seemed content to play a statesmanlike role rather than seeking higher office, was the epitome of fair play, as was Bill Ratliff, who was elected by his colleagues to serve as presiding officer when Rick Perry became governor.

Also, speakers or lieutenant governors with political ambitions—at least six have become governor—generally avoid angering special interests and thus cutting themselves off from potential financial campaign support or business credit. They also prefer not to anger other state officials who may be instrumental in furthering their political plans. Not making enemies is also the rule for presiding officers contemplating lucrative business positions when they leave office.

## LEGISLATORS

State senators and representatives have their own power bases, without which they probably would not have been elected. Longtime members not only have supporters across the state, including influential special interests, but also have the advantage that seniority brings within the legislature itself. If they have served as the chairperson of a major committee for more than one session, legislators are especially likely to have their own power bases as well as the support of the presiding officers.

Furthermore, the presiding officers are limited in their leadership responsibilities to legislators. The speaker of the House, especially, spends considerable time trying to organize and manage 149 colleagues, their pet bills, and their requests. The lieutenant governor is more of a statewide public figure. He is elected independently of the governor and is in demand as a speaker and goodwill ambassador. In addition, the House has more complicated legislative procedures than does the Senate. The president of the Senate can frequently bring about consensus behind the scenes and prevent disruption on the Senate floor.

It may appear that the membership always follows the lead of the presiding officers. In many cases, basic agreement on ideological positions already exists among the majority because the leadership and most legislators are usually conservative. In other instances, members will go along with the leadership in the hope of later being able to act independently on matters of importance to them or to their districts. Finally, the powers of the presiding officers are largely granted by House and Senate rules. A totally arbitrary leader whose abuse of the system became intolerable could be stripped of much power by changes in those rules. Such action is highly unlikely. However, the Eightieth Legislature in 2007–08 served as an example of member control, especially in the House, which challenged the speaker in January and continued to threaten challenges through the regular session. Senators groused a bit about the lieutenant governor's control of legislation but did not act on the complaints.

## INTEREST GROUPS AND STATE ADMINISTRATION

Over the past fifty years, as the number of state governmental agencies and bureaucrats has increased, an alliance has developed between private and public interests. These coalitions and the presiding officers often share the same political viewpoint, making confrontations unlikely. The public is seldom considered by these alliances, especially when some of the more powerful special interests of the state, such as oil and gas, insurance, banking, and real estate, are involved. An example of a bureaucracy–private interest alliance is the Department of Banking and financial institutions.

★ ★ ★ ★ ★ ★ ★ ★ ★ ★ ★ ★ ★ ★ ★ ★ ★ ★ ★ ★ ★ ★ ★ ★ ★

## *Whose Bill Is It, Anyhow?*

An Austin lawyer-lobbyist remarked on his twenty years as a legislator by noting, "Here at the legislature, if you ask the question, 'Whose bill is it?' what you mean is, which lobby wrote it. If you want to know which legislator is sponsoring the bill, you ask, 'Who's carrying the bill?' That'll give you some idea of how influential lobbyists are."

★ ★ ★ ★ ★ ★ ★ ★ ★ ★ ★ ★ ★ ★ ★ ★ ★ ★ ★ ★ ★ ★ ★ ★ ★

## THE GOVERNOR

Constitutionally, the governor is a weak chief administrator—hence, the alliance between state bureaucrats and the lobbyists, not the chief executive. Even so, the governor is by no means a weak chief legislator. The governor's veto power is almost absolute because the legislature often adjourns before the governor has had time to act on a bill.

A governor who wants a particular piece of legislation enacted can threaten the legislature with a special session if the legislation seems to be in jeopardy. Because special sessions are costly to state legislators in terms of both time and money, such a threat can be a powerful tool for the governor. The governor must be prepared to make good on such a threat, as, for example, Bill Clements did when he called a special session on tort reform—that is, changes in the basis of civil lawsuits—in 1987 after failing to get action from the 1987 legislature. Rick Perry's three special sessions in 2003 to force redistricting are another example. Such threats, however, do not always work, particularly if the legislature perceives that the governor is usurping legislative authority, as was the case in 2007 when Governor Perry tried to create state policy by executive order, leading to legislative rebellion (see Chapter 8).

Another of the governor's strengths lies in the strong ties a conservative (usually the political orientation of the Texas governor) has to the same interest groups as the legislators. These ties often make it possible for the governor to call on these interests to support a position that is in conflict with that of the legislature.

## THE ELECTORATE/THE CONSTITUENTS

Legislative bodies were created to be the people's voice in government, although only about one third of the eligible voters bother to vote in legislative elections. Citizens are likely to find it challenging and perhaps difficult to exert as much influence over the leadership and members of the Texas legislature as do state officials and private interests. One reason for this situation is the strength of special interests. Another is the lack of knowledge on the part of most citizens in Texas and other states about what goes on in the state capital. Citizens focus on issues affecting them directly, such as drunken driving, but the ordinary day-to-day legislative events do not stir the interest of most Texans. Furthermore, powerful special interests work hard to avoid stirring up the citizens. One exception in 1995 involved an impressive show of solidarity by women who believed that symptoms they were experiencing resulted from breast implants as the legislature was debating a measure that would make it difficult to sue for such problems. They were a vocal lobby and deflected the legislation for that session. In 2007 the religious right helped to bring down the governor's proposal to mandate that all sixth-grade girls be inoculated with a vaccine designed to prevent a type of sexually transmitted cervical cancer.

# How a Bill Becomes a Law in Texas

The Texas Constitution specifies that a bill be used to introduce a law or a change in a law. Bills that pass both houses successfully become acts and are sent to the governor for his or her signature or veto. In addition to bills, there are three types of resolutions in each house:

1. **Simple resolutions are used in each house to take care of housekeeping matters, details of business, and trivia. Examples include procedural rules adopted by each house—serious business, indeed—and trivia, such as birthday greetings to a member.**

2. **Concurrent resolutions are similar to simple resolutions but require the action of both houses. An example would be their use for adjournment.**

3. **Joint resolutions are of major interest to the public because they are the means of introducing proposed constitutional amendments. They require no action by the governor.**

Each bill or resolution is designated by an abbreviation that indicates the house of origin, the nature of the legislation, and a number. For example, S.B. 1 is Senate Bill 1; S.J.R. indicates a joint resolution that originated in the Senate.

Bills may originate in either house or in both simultaneously, with the exception of revenue bills, which must originate in the House, according to the Texas Constitution. During a typical session, legislators introduce more than 6,000 bills and joint resolutions, of which only 25 to 30 percent are passed.[2] After each census, when the legislature must also deal with reapportionment and redistricting, the number is reduced by several hundred as a concession to the time redistricting will take. Because lawmakers must consider so many proposals in such a limited time, originators of a bill often mark a bill "By Request" and drop it in the hopper—the traditional legislative "in-basket." This is their way of indicating that they were asked to introduce the legislation but do not expect it to receive serious consideration.

Table 7-2 summarizes the procedural and structural differences in the two houses. Structural differences in the two houses were discussed in Chapter Six. The major differences in the procedures of the two houses are:

1. **The House has more than twice as many committees as the Senate; therefore, the speaker has a greater choice in determining where to refer a bill.**

TABLE 7-2

## A Comparison of the Texas House and Senate

| Feature | House | Senate |
|---|---|---|
| Size | 150 | 31 |
| Term | 2 years | 4 years |
| Committees | 40 | 15 |
| Limits on debate | usually 10 minutes | none |
| Calendars | 4 | 2 |
| How presiding officer selected | elected by constituents in a single-member district, then elected by fellow members of the House as speaker | elected statewide as lieutenant governor of Texas |

2. The calendars are different (as explained earlier in this chapter).

3. Debate is unlimited in the Senate, whereas House debate is usually limited to ten minutes per member and twenty minutes for the bill's sponsor.

To be enacted into law, a bill must survive as many as four legislative steps and a fifth step in the governor's office (see Figure 7-1). Because the smaller size of the Senate enables it to operate with less formality than the House, we use the Senate to trace the path of a bill through the legislative process.

## STEP ONE: INTRODUCTION AND REFERRAL

Every bill must be introduced by a member of the legislature, who is considered the sponsor. If a bill has several sponsors, so much the better because its chances of survival will be greatly enhanced. There are two ways to introduce bills: (1) the member, after being recognized by the lieutenant governor as president of the Senate, may introduce it from the floor, or (2) the member may deposit copies of the bill with the secretary of the Senate (in the House, with the clerk), including prefiling a bill in November. The secretary assigns a number to the bill that reflects the order of submission. The reading clerk then gives the bill the first of the three readings required by the constitution. The first time, only a caption is read, which is a brief summary of the bill's contents. The second method of introducing bills is the one more commonly used. Legislation can only be introduced in the first sixty days of the session; as the deadline draws near, the number of bill filings increases exponentially.

The lieutenant governor (in the House, the speaker) then refers the bill to a committee. If the bill is to survive, it must be assigned to a friendly committee. The bill's sponsor will have been on "good behavior" in the hope that the lieutenant governor will give the bill a favorable referral.

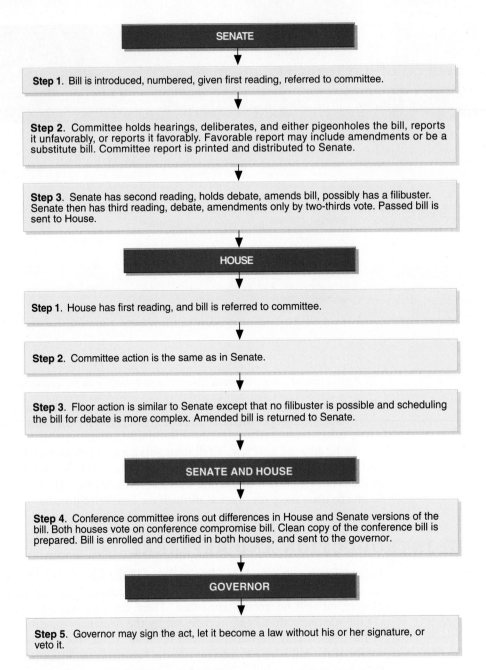

**FIGURE 7-1  How a Bill Becomes a Law in Texas**

*This figure traces the passage of a bill that originated in the Senate. Steps 1 to 3 for the Senate and House would be reversed if the bill originated in the House. The example presumes the need for a conference committee.*

# STEP TWO: COMMITTEE ACTION

Standing committees are really miniature legislatures in which the nitty-gritty of legislation takes place. Legislators are so busy—particularly in Texas, with the short, infrequent sessions—that they seldom have time to study bills in detail and so must rely heavily on the committee reports. A bill's sponsor, well aware of the committee's role, will do everything possible to ensure that the committee's report is favorable. It is particularly important to avoid having the bill *pigeonholed* (put on the bottom of the committee's agenda, with or without discussion, never to be seen again) or totally rewritten, either by the committee or, if the bill is referred to a subcommittee, by the subcommittee. If the bill can escape being pigeonholed, its sponsor will have a chance to bargain with the committee in an effort to avoid too many changes in the bill.

The standing committees hold hearings on proposed legislation. Major bills will generate considerable public, media, and lobbyist interest. The large number of committees—especially in the House—and the volume of proposed legislation sometimes mean that these hearings are held at odd hours, such as 11 P.M.

A senator, but not a representative, can **tag** a bill, indicating that the lawmaker must get forty-eight hour's written notice of the hearing. If the senator does not receive notice or if the bill was not posted publicly seventy-two hours in advance, a senator can use a tag to object to the bill and delay the committee hearing. Tagging is sometimes an effective practice to defeat a bill late in the legislative session.

The committee may report the bill favorably, unfavorably, or not at all. An unfavorable report or none at all will kill it. Unless there is a strong minority report, however, there is little reason for the committee to report a bill unfavorably; it is easier to pigeonhole it and avoid floor action completely.

# STEP THREE: FLOOR ACTION

Once reported out of committee, a bill must be scheduled for debate. The Senate Calendar is rarely followed; instead, senators list their bills on the Intent Calendar, which in essence is a declaration of intent to ask for a suspension of the rules to take up a bill out of order. As with any motion to suspend the rules, two thirds of those present and voting must vote yes on the suspension. Before filing an intent to ask for a suspension, the bill's sponsors generally get an assurance from the presiding officer that they will be recognized and thus given an opportunity to make the motion.

When the bill receives the necessary two-thirds vote, it can proceed to its second reading and debate. (If the second reading has not occurred by the time the legislature is within seventy-two hours of adjournment, the bill dies.) The sponsor is relieved because only a simple majority of votes is required for passage. (In the House, the Calendars Committee establishes a schedule for debate.) Abandonment of the two-thirds vote procedure during the second called session in 2003 sparked a huge controversy (see Chapter 6).

Senators have unlimited privileges of debate: They may speak as long as they wish about a bill on the floor. Sometimes senators use this privilege to filibuster—that is, to try to kill a bill by talking at length about it and anything else that will use up time. By tying up the floor and preventing other bills from being considered, the senator or group of senators hopes to pressure enough of the membership to lay aside the controversial bill so that other matters can be debated. The filibuster is most effective at the end of the legislative session when time is short and many bills have yet to be debated. Shutting off debate, however, requires a simple majority vote. Despite their potential effectiveness, filibusters do not occur frequently because so much Senate business is conducted off the Senate floor in bargaining sessions. The presiding officer, incidentally, has the power to ask the intention of a member when the member is recognized for debate and thus knows when a filibuster will occur. Tradition also dictates that a member who plans to filibuster notify the press of the forthcoming event.

If a bill is fortunate enough not to become entangled in a filibuster, debate proceeds. During the course of debate, there may be proposed amendments, amendments to amendments, motions to table, or even motions to send the bill back to committee. However, if a bill has succeeded in reaching the floor for discussion, it is usually passed in one form or another. A vote is taken after the third reading, again by caption, of the bill. At this stage, amendments require a two-thirds vote. It is more or less routine for four fifths of the Senate to vote to suspend the rules and proceed immediately to the third reading.

# IN THE HOUSE: STEPS ONE THROUGH THREE REPEATED

If it was not introduced in both houses simultaneously, a bill passed in the Senate must proceed to the House. There, under its original designation (for example, S.B. 341), it must repeat the same three steps, with the exceptions noted earlier. It has little chance of passing if a representative does not shepherd it through. (This situation is true in reverse also, when a bill passes the House and is then sent to the Senate.) In addition, the Laney reforms of 1993 included a series of deadlines concerning the final seventeen days of a legislative session, and a bill must comply with those House rules. For example, after 135 days of a regular session, the House cannot consider a Senate bill except to adopt a conference report, reconsider the bill to remove Senate amendments, or override a veto; the deadlines for various types of House bills are earlier.[3] The following explanation assumes that the bill being followed passes the House but with one amendment added that was not part of the Senate's version.

# STEP FOUR: CONFERENCE COMMITTEE

Because the Senate and House versions of the bill differ, it must go to a **conference committee,** which consists of ten members: five appointed from each house by the presiding officers. If the House and Senate versions of the bill exhibit substantial differences, the conference committee may attach several amendments or rewrite portions of it. It may even be pigeonholed. On a bill with only one difference between the versions passed by the two houses, the single vote of the committee members from the Senate and the single vote of those from the House may be obtained without too much wrangling.

The bill is then reported back to the Senate and the House for action in each chamber. The report of the conference committee must be voted on as it stands; neither house can amend it. It must be accepted, rejected, or sent back to the conference committee. If it fails at this stage—or indeed, at any stage—it is automatically dead. No bill can be introduced twice during the same session, although a bill can be rewritten and introduced as a new piece of legislation.

If the bill receives a majority of the votes in each house, the engrossing and enrolling clerk prepares a correct copy of it, first for the house where the bill originated, then for the other house. Its caption is read a final time, and it is signed by the presiding officers, the House chief clerk, and the Senate secretary. The vote of passage is certified, and the engrossed (officially printed) bill, now an act, is sent to the governor for action. A record of these steps is printed in the journal of each house.

## STEP FIVE: THE GOVERNOR

The governor has ten days (excluding Sundays) to dispose of enacted legislation. If the legislature adjourns, the ten-day period is extended to twenty days. The governor has three options available to deal with an act. The first is to sign it, thus making it law.

The second is to allow the act to become law without signing it. If the governor does not sign it, an act becomes law in ten days if the legislature is in session and in twenty days if it is not. By choosing this rather weak course of action, the governor signifies both opposition to the legislation and an unwillingness to risk a veto that could be overridden by a two-thirds vote of both houses or that would incur the disfavor of special interests supporting the bill.

Third, the governor may veto the act. Although it is possible for the legislature to override a veto, the governor often receives legislation so late in the session that the act of vetoing or signing it can be deferred until the session has ended. A veto then is absolute, because it must be overridden during the same legislative session in which the act was passed and the legislature cannot call itself into special session. At any time, the legislature may have difficulty mustering the two-thirds vote necessary to override a veto. Because recent legislative sessions have been faced with one crisis after another and have had too little time to deal with issues, the governor's powers have been strengthened through use of the veto and threats of a veto.

If the governor chooses to veto, the veto applies to the entire act, except in the case of appropriations bills. On an appropriations act, the governor has the power of **item veto**; that is, specific items may be vetoed. This is a powerful gubernatorial tool for limiting state spending, but in recent years, the legislature has blunted this tool by making lump-sum appropriations to agencies such as colleges and universities.

When the governor signs an act, it becomes one of the few proposals that manage to survive. It is entered in the statute books by the secretary of state. If it contains an emergency clause, it becomes effective as law either immediately or whenever designated in the bill. If it does not, it becomes effective ninety days after the session ends. Again, there are special circumstances for appropriations acts. They always become effective September 1 because the state's **fiscal year** (its budget period) is from September 1 through August 31 of the following year.

# Legislative Dynamics

The public often thinks that the legislature accomplishes very little, as the chapter opening quotation from *Texas Monthly* notes. It is in fact amazing that the legislature accomplishes as much as it does, given the limitations under which the institution must labor. The forces influencing legislation are complex and varied: interest groups, the powers of the presiding officers, the governor, constitutional limitations, political parties, the role of committees, short and infrequent sessions, inadequate salaries, and the prerogatives of individual members.

## HANDICAPS

Consideration of thousands of bills and resolutions each session means the legislative workload is very heavy. Very few of these proposals are substantively important, and many are trivial matters that could more easily be left to administrative agencies. Less than one third of them are passed. Nevertheless, in the short 140-day session, legislators must acquaint themselves with the proposals, try to push their own legislative programs, attend to a heavy burden of casework, spend countless hours in committee work, meet with hometown and interest-group representatives, and hear the professional views of state administrators who implement programs. Although many legislators are personally wealthy, those who are not must also try to avoid going into debt because their salaries are inadequate and their personal businesses or professions cannot be attended to when the legislature is in session.

Lenient lobbying laws, lack of public support for adequate information services for legislators, and the need for continuous campaigning make the average legislator easy prey for special interests. On many issues, the interests of a legislator's district and of special-interest groups often overlap and are difficult to distinguish. Even when the interests are not so closely aligned, legislators may

The end of a legislative session is always chaotic, with bills of high interest to the public falling by the wayside as time runs out. The 2007 session was especially frantic because of the House revolt against the speaker.

*Courtesy of Ben Sargent.*

have to depend on lobbyists for much of their information. Certainly, they depend on them for campaign help.

The legislators' frustrations are especially evident when the biennial budget is considered. Appropriations are the major battleground of legislative sessions. There are always more programs seeking support than there is money available to support them. Power struggles over money continue because each individual who promotes a program—be it for highways, public schools, higher education, utilities rates, environmental protection, lending rates, law enforcement, or welfare administration—believes in either its moral rightness or its economic justification. Who wins the struggles is determined not only by the power and effectiveness of the groups backing a program but also by the political preferences of the legislators. Furthermore, the winners largely determine public policy for the state, because few government programs can operate without substantial amounts of money. Chapter Thirteen examines the politics of the budgetary process in detail.

Lack of public understanding and support is another handicap for legislators. The public often criticizes politicians for being unprincipled and always willing to compromise. But the role of compromise in the political system, and especially in legislative bodies, is undervalued by the citizens. Caught in all the cross-pressures of the legislative system, members rarely have the opportunity to adhere rigidly to their principles. Those who watch closely what happens in the legislature are not the electorate back home but campaign supporters, lobbyists, and influential citizens. Members must satisfy these people if they are to have any chance of getting their own proposals through the legislature or in fact of being reelected for another term.[4]

Legislators may have to vote for new highways that they view as superfluous to get votes for issues important to them and their home districts. They may have to vote in favor of high interest rates on credit cards to gain support for tighter regulation of nursing homes. They may have to give up a home-district

★ ★ ★ ★ ★ ★ ★ ★ ★ ★ ★ ★ ★ ★ ★ ★ ★ ★ ★ ★ ★ ★ ★ ★ ★ ★ ★ ★

## *Frivolity Forever*

State legislatures are somewhat notorious for wasting time on frivolous matters, and Texas and California are among the worst. Examples of frivolous issues that are not the stuff of major public policy include:

- An accolade to actor Ed Asner for his work in the Mary Tyler Moore television show

- Naming the Pleurocoelus the official state dinosaur

- Naming the chiltepin the official pepper, the sweet onion the official vegetable, and the guitar the official musical instrument

- Designating the Texas red grapefruit as the state fruit, the Texas blue topaz as the official gem, and the horned lizard as the official reptile

- Designating the following "capitals": Waxahachie, crape myrtle; Weslaco, citrus; and Knox City, seedless watermelon

★ ★ ★ ★ ★ ★ ★ ★ ★ ★ ★ ★ ★ ★ ★ ★ ★ ★ ★ ★ ★ ★ ★ ★ ★ ★ ★ ★

SOURCE: Charles Mantesian, "The Official Waste of Time," *Governing*, September 1997, 18, and http://www.infoplease.com/ipa/A0108277.html. The legislature also designated rodeo as the official sport.

highway patrol office to obtain funds for needy children. Just as legislators who hope to be successful must quickly learn the procedural rules, they must also learn the art of legislative compromise.

## CHANGING ALIGNMENTS

Recent sessions of the legislature have been especially interesting because of the shifting alliances within it. The transitional nature of the state, and thus of the legislature, serves to substantiate the adage that "politics makes strange bedfellows." Thus, an additional difficulty legislators face is adjusting to the shifting trends within the legislature. Long dominated by rural, Democratic conservatives, in recent years the legislature has become more urban and more Republican. When urban issues are at stake, temporary bipartisan alliances among big-city legislators sometimes are formed. However, the 2003 legislative session brought to the forefront a growing problem for the Texas legislature, namely, its sharp division between liberals and conservatives—effectively, a sharp division between Democrats and Republicans—that threatens the state lawmaking body with the same sort of gridlock that characterizes the U.S. Congress.

Compounding the problem of party and geographic transition is the fact that the two houses have not changed in the same way. Although Republicans are the majority in both houses, the degree of partisanship, the sharpness of the ideological divisions, and the traditions surrounding the operation of the two houses are quite different. The Senate periodically provides glimpses of moralistic thinking; the House appears frozen in the state's individualistic-traditionalistic political culture.

In the Senate, as previously discussed, eleven members can prevent a measure from reaching the floor for debate. In 2007, one Democratic senator was even brought in from his sick bed to become the eleventh, blocking vote on a bill to force Texans to provide additional identification other than a voter registration card to be able to vote. Most of the time, the Senate continues to operate as a chamber characterized by civility and a lack of hard-edged partisanship. Only when really partisan issues are at stake does the Senate minority gain its way by preventing consideration of the bill.

The alliance of conservative Democrats and Republicans gave the House a distinctly conservative flavor beginning in the mid-1980s. Liberal–conservative skirmishes nevertheless were plentiful in the late 1990s and promised to continue regardless of which party was in the majority. The Texas House of Representatives temporarily seemed to draw strength from the Laney reforms, which brought a higher sense of ethics as well as fairer procedures to the lower chamber. However, splits along party lines have worsened, and blatant partisanship often arises in the House.

★ ★ ★ ★ ★ ★ ★ ★ ★ ★ ★ ★ ★ ★ ★ ★ ★ ★ ★ ★ ★ ★ ★ ★ ★ ★ ★ ★ ★ ★ ★

### *Legislative Activity*

The Texas legislature provides up-to-the-minute information on its Web page: www.capitol.state.tx.us.

★ ★ ★ ★ ★ ★ ★ ★ ★ ★ ★ ★ ★ ★ ★ ★ ★ ★ ★ ★ ★ ★ ★ ★ ★ ★ ★ ★ ★ ★ ★

# Evaluation and Reform

## ASSESSING THE LEGISLATURE

At the close of each legislative session, a number of organizations assess the session and evaluate the membership. Many of these rankings merely reflect how closely the members adhered to the position favored by the organization, so it is difficult to use these lists except as measures of, say, probusiness or prolabor votes. The press also joins in the rating game but reflects publishers' viewpoints—for example, the liberal viewpoint of the *Texas Observer*'s annual legislative assessment. One effort to judge legislators on grounds other than political philosophy, however, is that of *Texas Monthly*, which includes both liberals and conservatives of both urban and rural persuasions in its biennial list of ten best and ten worst legislators.[5] The criteria used by *Texas Monthly* are also suitable for use by the public in its evaluation, as follows:

> A good legislator is intelligent, well prepared, and accessible to reason; because of these qualities, he is respected by his colleagues and effective in his work. He uses power skillfully and to its maximum without abusing it, and without exception his integrity is beyond reproach. On issues of statewide importance, he wears no parochial blinders; he is both faithful to, and broader than, his district.
>
> SOURCE: "THE TEN BEST AND THE TEN WORST LEGISLATORS," TEXAS MONTHLY, JULY 1977, COPYRIGHT 1977 BY MEDIATEX COMMUNICATIONS CORPORATION. USED BY PERMISSION.

The session as a whole is even more difficult to evaluate. One's own political viewpoint and interest in specific issues can bias one's view of the actions of legislators. It is necessary to consider the bills and the votes as well as the people. A sample of general criteria for such an assessment would include these questions:

1. Did the legislature deal with major issues facing the state or mainly with trivial issues?

2. Did the appropriations bill reflect genuine statewide concerns or only the interests of the large lobbies?

3. Did the leadership operate effectively, forcing the legislature to give attention to major issues and arranging compromises on stalled bills, or did it cater to the lobbyists or the personal agendas of the presiding officers?

4. Was the effect of current legislation on future social, economic, and physical resources considered, or did the legislature live for today?

A brief evaluation of the legislatures in the 1990s and 2000s reveals changes in that branch of government over time.

■ The Seventy-second Legislature (1991–1992) was characterized by rancorous debates over issues such as redistricting and the quest for new revenues while avoiding the "I" word (income tax).

- The Seventy-third Legislature (1993–1994) streamlined the penal code and began the withdrawal of support for state regulation of business that characterized the Seventy-fourth Legislature in 1995–1996.

- In 1997–1998, the Seventy-fifth Legislature rediscovered its social conscience a bit in areas such as healthcare and school bus safety and used the surplus to help provide minor property tax relief in local school districts.

- The Seventy-sixth Legislature in 1999–2000 was focused on making Governor George W. Bush look good for his presidential run in 2000; accordingly, it emphasized public education, tax cuts, and getting tough on crime.

- In 2001–2002, the Seventy-seventh Legislature was dominated by increasing partisanship tied to the decennial redistricting battle and the need to undo some of the legislation of the previous session that made Bush look good but created problems for state government.

- In 2003–2004, the Seventy-eighth Legislature consolidated health and human services agencies, focused on redistricting through three special sessions, and gave more power to legislative staff agencies at the expense of the comptroller.

- In 2005–2006, the Seventy-ninth Legislature finally dealt with school finance, but only after a last-minute special session, stabilized teacher retirement, and overhauled the workers' compensation system. See the boxed sampler for the 2007–2008 legislature.

★ ★ ★ ★ ★ ★ ★ ★ ★ ★ ★ ★ ★ ★ ★ ★ ★ ★ ★ ★ ★ ★ ★ ★ ★ ★ ★ ★ ★

## Public Policy, Legislative Style: A 2007 Sampler

The Eightieth Legislature in 2007–2008 had a big surplus; thus, it had to decide how to enhance the public schools, whether to provide more social services, and the direction to take on many issues involving the regulation of citizens' behavior. The Eightieth Legislature passed bills that included

- a $152.5 billion biennial budget that relied on the surplus to avoid tax increases

- an overhaul of the Texas Youth Commission

- blocking of the governor's executive order that mandated that all sixth-grade girls had to be vaccinated against a cancer caused through sexual intercourse

- stricter requirements for renewing a driver's license for individuals 85 years of age and older

- a "silver alert" for missing senior citizens, similar to the familiar "Amber alert" for children

- establishing a Castle Doctrine allowing Texans to defend their homes, workplaces, and cars with deadly force

*(continued)*

★ ★ ★ ★ ★ ★ ★ ★ ★ ★ ★ ★ ★ ★ ★ ★ ★ ★ ★ ★ ★ ★ ★ ★ ★ ★ ★ ★ ★

★ ★ ★ ★ ★ ★ ★ ★ ★ ★ ★ ★ ★ ★ ★ ★ ★ ★ ★ ★ ★ ★ ★ ★ ★ ★ ★ ★ ★

*(continued)*

- replacing the Texas Assessment of Knowledge and Skills exam with end-of-course exams

- broadening enrollment criteria for the Children's Health Insurance Program to allow 127,000 more beneficiaries

- amendments to fund cancer research and record individual lawmakers' votes on final passage of bills

The failures of the 2007 legislature included

- providing flexibility in the mandate to all public universities to accept all students in the top 10 percent of their high school graduating class

- voter ID, requiring additional identification beyond a voter registration card

- measures to lower electric rates

- expansion of state-authorized gambling

★ ★ ★ ★ ★ ★ ★ ★ ★ ★ ★ ★ ★ ★ ★ ★ ★ ★ ★ ★ ★ ★ ★ ★ ★ ★ ★ ★ ★

SOURCES: Emily Ramshaw and Robert T. Garrett, "Water Plan Passes; Electric Bill Doesn't," *Dallas Morning News*, May 29, 2007, 1A, 8A; Christy Hoppe, "Touching Your Life in Little Ways," *Dallas Morning News*, May 29, 2007, 1A, 9A; Karen Brooks, "House Works Through Tension," *Dallas Morning News*, May 29, 2007, 8A; "The Session Scorecard," *Dallas Morning News*, May 29, 2007, 8A; "Winners and Losers," *Dallas Morning News*, May 29, 2007, 9A; Associated Press, "An Accounting of Notable Issues of the 2007 Legislature," *Austin American-Statesman*, available at http://www.statesman.com/news/content/gen/ap/TX_XGR_Did__Didnt.html?COXnetJSessionIDbuild36=
r1hnGhyclLgGkyLj8GkTqhCMkBGBPnprJpz5hd2KLNGI2P9w45bT!-176393930&UrAuth=%60N
_NUOcNVUbTTUWUXUVUZTZUTUWUbUbUZU%60U_UcTYWYWZV&urcm=y .

## SUGGESTED REFORMS

In the previous chapter, ways to improve the formal structure for the legislature were suggested. Improvements are also needed in legislative organization and procedures, especially in the areas of committees and ties to lobbyists.

### COMMITTEES

The twenty-one House standing committees of 1973 had grown to forty for the 2007 session. The Senate managed to operate with only nine standing committees from 1973 until 1985 but had fifteen in 2007. These numbers do not count subcommittees or select committees in either house. Thus, both houses need to be wary of further committee expansion.

Having substantially fewer committees would result in less ambiguity over committee jurisdiction. In addition, both houses could make more use of joint committees instead of submitting every issue for separate study and hearings. A joint budget committee is particularly needed. Fewer committee meetings would give legislators more time to familiarize themselves with the issues and the contents of specific bills.

Fewer committees might also increase the chance for adoption of uniform committee rules throughout the two houses. Better meeting facilities for

In 2007 the House considered a number of bills that, if passed, would have infused public policy with religious preferences. This cartoon jabs at the potential legislation that failed to keep religion out of politics while pointing out how hard it is to "vote against God."

*Courtesy of Ben Sargent.*

committees and more professional committee staff are also needed. Currently, chairs can hire staff or elect to use their own, so that independence is also a political issue.

## THE LOBBY

Until legislators are able to declare their independence from lobbyists and state administrators, it will be impossible for the legislature to be truly independent of all interests but the public interest. Such a change depends on many factors: citizen attitudes such as public willingness to allow adequate legislative sessions, pay, and staff support for legislators; public financing of election campaigns; and a commitment on the part of legislators to give up the social and economic advantages of strong ties to the lobby. The likelihood of total independence from the lobby is not high: All legislative groups everywhere have some ties to special interests. At a minimum, however, Texas needs to abandon such blatant practices as allowing lawyer-legislators to accept retainer fees from corporations that subsequently send lobbyists to Austin to influence these same legislators. A starting point in reform was Speaker Laney's rule prohibiting members of his own staff from accepting a job as a lobbyist for a year after leaving the speaker's office. That rule, however, is not binding on the staff members hired by other speakers.

# CONCLUSION

The Texas legislature is improving its ethnic representation and probably reflects the increasing Republicanism of the state. However, in this century, the strident ideology and partisanship displayed over issues such as redistricting and social programs made the legislature more nearly resemble the U.S. Congress. Such a resemblance is not a good thing because fragmentation of power makes coherent public policy virtually impossible at the national level. In Texas, the tone is set by the powerful presiding officers in Texas, who can seek to bring about consensus and make the development of coherent public policy highly likely or who can opt to push their own personal agendas. Thus, for all its problems, the Texas legislature can be highly effective if the leadership is so inclined. Because the Texas legislature is centralized, it is capable of translating public preferences into policy.

Because so few Texans vote, however, it often translates the preferences of the richer and better educated minority into policy. Although liberals then criticize the content of public policy, they cannot deny that the process is effective and that it is rational from the standpoint of most Texas voters, if not of all citizens.

# Nonlegislative Lawmaking

The responsibility for lawmaking was intended to rest with the legislature; however, executive, administrative, and judicial officials also make public policy that has the force of law. This overlap of functions, rather than being described as a separation of powers, should more correctly be defined as a separation of roles and institutions with a sharing of powers.

# LAWMAKING BY THE GOVERNOR

The governor is involved in lawmaking in two ways. First, by presenting messages to the legislature giving actual recommendations on legislation, the governor influences its outcome. The governor may also rally the support of political cronies and lobbyists for or against a bill. Besides vetoing bills, the governor can threaten to veto and so force changes in appropriations and other bills.

Second, the governor can indirectly influence how, or even if, legislation will be administered through appointments to state boards and commissions. Because the bureaucracy interprets general legislation and thus determines how it is to be applied in specific instances, gubernatorial appointees may have tremendous influence on how the public does (or does not) benefit from state laws. Often, though, the ties between an agency's permanent bureaucracy and legislators are so strong that the board members appointed by the governor have only limited influence.

The governor also influences legislation indirectly by being the major liaison between Texas and other states and between Texas and the federal executive establishment. In this capacity, the governor can affect interstate and federal–state relationships and policies.

# LAWMAKING BY THE ADMINISTRATION

In addition to the governor and lieutenant governor, the state executive branch includes four other elected executives and two elected state boards. There also are dozens of policymaking boards and their staffs. As noted earlier, the administration (or bureaucracy) has a tremendous effect on how legislation is carried out. Because statutes are written in rather general terms to avoid unnecessary rigidity and specificity, administrative policies, rules, and regulations are a must. Each board policy made and each staff rule or regulation written supplement the statutes enacted by the legislature and constitute lawmaking.

Individual administrators also interpret statutes, an action that is a type of lawmaking. In addition, by functioning as expert advisers to members of the legislature during the session, administrators can directly influence the outcome of bills. Indeed, they often use their bureaucratic skills in conjunction with special-interest groups that are concerned with similar issues. Perhaps no executive agency is as influential as the attorney general's office, which can issue opinions on the constitutionality of legislation. These opinions have the force of law unless they are successfully challenged in court.

# LAWMAKING BY THE COURTS

The judiciary, too, has a role in lawmaking. The courts are frequently asked to determine whether a statute is in conflict with higher law. Both federal and state courts can review legislative acts that have been challenged on the grounds of unconstitutionality. Federal and state judges also spend considerable time hearing challenges to administrative interpretations of laws. In fact, most of the civil dockets of the courts are taken up with administrative matters—for example, whether an agency has jurisdiction over the matter at hand or whether an administrative interpretation is correct.

## Summary

Understanding the legislative process in Texas involves some knowledge of parliamentary procedure and an appreciation for the role of the presiding officers. To become a law, a bill must survive numerous parliamentary and political obstacles. Most bills never become laws. Important features of the Texas system are

1. The presiding officers control both the composition of legislative committees and the appointment of committee chairpersons.

2. The speaker of the House and the lieutenant governor in the Senate—the presiding officers—decide whether a friendly or unfriendly committee will consider a bill.

3. The presiding officers indirectly determine when and if a bill will be debated.

4. The presiding officers decide who will speak for and against a bill once it reaches the floor, and the lieutenant governor can even use this power of recognition to allow a filibuster to develop.

5. The staff agencies designed to assist the legislature have relatively low budgets and are dominated by the presiding officers.

6. Even if a bill passes both houses, it may still be killed by a conference committee or a governor's veto.

Legislators face many pressures, and evaluating their work is more difficult than it might seem. Sometimes they are blamed for lawmaking that is really the handiwork of the governor, the state bureaucracy, or the courts. Changes in legislative organization and procedure would help improve legislative efficiency and independence. Recommendations for reform include the following:

1. Reducing the number of committees, especially in the House, and then in turn providing adequate funds for a professional and independent committee staff

2. Evaluating continually the method of selecting committee chairpersons

3. Reducing the influence of the lobby.

Reforms in the day-to-day operation of the legislature are unlikely, however, unless some of the changes suggested in the previous chapter, such as higher pay, better staff support, and annual sessions, are instituted.

Nevertheless, despite its obstacles, the Texas legislature is able to produce laws that are in keeping with the political sentiments of a majority of Texas voters. Legislative bodies are the manifestation of representative government. While elected executives must represent the whole, diverse state of Texas, individual legislators represent smaller and presumably more homogeneous districts. Thus, they can more easily discern the wishes of their constituents and try to enact those wishes into law. Although any given individual may not like the public policy developed by the legislature, careful observers must admire the legislature's ability to conduct business under the pressure of a short session. The gridlock for which the U.S. Congress has been criticized traditionally has not usually been a problem in Texas except in years when redistricting dominates, although the state is on the precipice now as to whether gridlock will become the rule on many issues. For the moment, one can conclude that the Texas legislature serves its democratic purpose of enacting the will of the public—or at least, the will of the fraction of the public that votes—into statutory law. The following chapters turn to an examination of the executive branch.

## Glossary Terms

| | |
|---|---|
| bill | fiscal year |
| conference committee | item veto |
| filibuster | tag |

## Study Questions

1. In what ways are the presiding officers of the legislature extremely powerful? Why do you think this situation exists?

2. Trace the process by which a bill becomes a law in Texas.

3. You are a member of the Texas House of Representatives and are sponsoring a bill. What kind of people—inside and outside the legislature—would you hope to line up in support of the bill? Why?

4. You are a member of the Texas Senate and are opposed to a bill that has been introduced. What strategies do you have available to defeat the bill at various stages in the legislative process?

5. If you could change any one aspect of the Texas legislative process, what would you change? How would you change it? Why do you think this reform is the most important?

6. Legislators are supported by the LBB, the State Auditor's Office, and the Texas Legislative Council but still also depend on lobbyists. Why? What do you think should be the minimum ground rules for the behavior of a lobbyist? How does this dependence detract from democratic principles?

7. In Texas, the legislature dominates state politics. As a student of democratic political theory, discuss whether this domination results in the most democratic government the state could have.

8. Having studied how the Texas legislature is organized and how it functions, do you think you would ever want to run for the legislature? Why or why not?

## Surfing the Web

Readers are urged to visit the companion site for this book:

**http://academic.cengage.com/polsci/Kraemer/TexasPolitics10e**

Governor Rick Perry delivers the 2007 State of the State address before the Eightieth Texas Legislature.

Why does anyone want to be governor of Texas? The governorship is like the super-super gift in the Neiman-Marcus Christmas catalog—something for the man who has everything and absolutely unique!

ANONYMOUS POLITICAL SCIENTIST

Let's fight for the Texas we aspire to, the Texas that can be, the Texas that can lead the world.

GOVERNOR RICK PERRY
STATE OF THE STATE ADDRESS, 2007

# Introduction

Democratic theory pays much more attention to the legislature than to the executive. Nevertheless, because chief executives and administrative agencies are important components of government, they too deserve to be measured against the ideal of democracy. In Texas, the legislature has been the dominant branch of state government through most of the state's history. Indeed, Texas is often cited for the weaknesses associated with the governor's office. However, a Texas governor with ideas and boldness can capture the support of the public and greatly enhance the limited constitutional and statutory powers of the office. Bargaining skills and persuasive ability rather than the formal powers of the governorship are the keys to gubernatorial leadership. Moreover, the formal powers of the office have grown over time through constitutional amendment and legislative action. The legislature increased those powers significantly in 2003.

This chapter first examines the basic structure of the governor's office, the formal qualifications for the office and personal characteristics of those who are typically elected to it, the roles that the governor plays, and the limitations on those roles, including the **plural executive** system. It is a portrait of a well-paid, prestigious state office hampered by a restrictive state constitution, a legislature that defied history in 2003 to give the governor more power than at any time since 1876, and a state administration that is largely independent of the governor's control. It is also a portrait of individuals who have overcome the constitutional weaknesses of the office through their political skills and personal magnetism; indeed, in 2007, Governor Rick Perry used the executive order in new ways to expand his power, albeit with mixed results.

# Basic Structure of the Governor's Office

## ELECTION, TERM OF OFFICE, AND TENURE

### ELECTION

In Texas, the governor is chosen in a statewide election held during "off years"—that is, even-numbered years when there is no presidential election. The candidates are selected in party primaries held earlier the same year (see Chapter Five). Gubernatorial elections are held in the off year so that national issues won't overshadow state issues. However, election contests for the Texas governor's office often focus on personalities, not issues, so that the importance of the off year is lost, and its main effect is that fewer people vote because they don't have the presidential election as a drawing card. In fact, voter turnout reached a modern low of 16 percent of registered voters (roughly 10 percent of eligible citizens) during the 1994 primaries. The lieutenant governor is selected in the same manner but runs independently of the governor.

### TERM

In 1974, when a 1972 constitutional amendment went into effect, the governor's term of office was extended from two to four years. There is no constitutional limit on the number of terms a governor may serve in Texas. Table 8-1 summarizes some characteristics of the governor's office compared with those

**TABLE 8-1**
## The Texas Governor among the States

| Texas Provision | Number of Other States with the Provision | Beyle's Ranking of Institutional Power |
|---|---|---|
| Four-year term without restrictions on number of terms or number of consecutive terms* | 12 | 5 (high) |
| Public election of five or more state executives | 29 | 1 (low) |
| No provision for any executive cabinet arrangement | 7 | 1.5 (low)** |
| 2006 salary of $115,000 or more | 25 | |
| Shares responsibility for budget preparation | 14 | 2 (fairly low) |
| Item veto over appropriations | 42 | 5*** (high) |

*Only Vermont and New Hampshire have a two-year term.
**Beyle's ranking was of appointment power over major functional areas of state government.
***Beyle's ranking was of the whole veto power, including the Texas governor's advantage because of the short legislative session.

SOURCES: *The Book of the States, 2006,* vol. 38 (Lexington, Ky.: Council of State Governments, 2006), 151–169; Thad Beyle, "The Governors," in Virginia Gray, and Russell L. Hanson, eds., *Politics in the American States: A Comparative Analysis,* 8th ed. (Washington, D.C.: CQ Press, 2004), 212–213.

of other states. The table shows the number of other states that share a particular characteristic with Texas as well as the ranking of the Texas governor on a national scale of institutional power. The Texas governor, overall, ranks in the middle, but the ranking does not reflect the most recent exercises of power.

## TENURE

Until World War II, Texas governors were routinely elected for two terms.[1] During and after the war, this precedent was supplanted by a trend to three terms, as indicated in Table 8-2. The precedent was broken when Governor Preston

**TABLE 8-2**
## Texas Governors and Their Terms of Office, under 1876 Constitution

| | | | |
|---|---|---|---|
| Richard Coke* | 1874–1876 | Miriam A. Ferguson | 1933–1935 |
| Richard B. Hubbard | 1876–1879 | James V. Allred | 1935–1939 |
| Oran M. Roberts | 1879–1883 | W. Lee O'Daniel* | 1939–1941 |
| John Ireland | 1883–1887 | Coke R. Stevenson | 1941–1947 |
| Lawrence S. Ross | 1887–1891 | Beauford H. Jester* | 1947–1949 |
| James S. Hogg | 1891–1895 | Allan Shivers | 1949–1957 |
| Charles A. Culberson | 1895–1899 | Price Daniel | 1957–1963 |
| Joseph D. Sayers | 1899–1903 | John Connally | 1963–1969 |
| S. W. T. Lanham | 1903–1907 | Preston Smith | 1969–1973 |
| Thomas M. Campbell | 1907–1911 | Dolph Briscoe | 1973–1979 |
| Oscar B. Colquitt | 1911–1915 | William (Bill) Clements | 1979–1983 |
| James E. Ferguson† | 1915–1917 | Mark White | 1983–1987 |
| William P. Hobby | 1917–1921 | William (Bill) Clements | 1987–1991 |
| Pat M. Neff | 1921–1925 | Ann Richards | 1991–1995 |
| Miriam A. Ferguson | 1925–1927 | George W. Bush | 1995–2000 |
| Dan Moody | 1927–1931 | Rick Perry | 2000– |
| Ross Sterling | 1931–1933 | | |

*Coke and O'Daniel resigned from the governorship to enter the U.S. Senate. Jester died in office.
†Ferguson was impeached and convicted.

SOURCE: Adapted from "Governors of Texas," prepared by the Texas Legislative Council and available at http:/www.lrl.state.tx.us/legis/leaders/govbio.html.

Smith, trying for a third term in 1972, was among the many state politicians who were swept out of office on the wave of public reaction to the Sharpstown Bank scandal.

Modern governors serving four-year terms have had mixed results in being reelected, in part due to the shifting party preferences of Texans. Bill Clements (Republican) lost to Mark White (Democrat) in 1982, but White lost to Clements in 1986. Ann Richards (Democrat) then served a single term after her 1990 election. On the other hand, George W. Bush (Republican) won a second term by an overwhelming majority, although he resigned to become president of the United States. Rick Perry (Republican) was also elected to two full terms after serving out Bush's unexpired term so that, if he completes the term begun in 2007, he will be Texas's longest-serving governor. The long-term likelihood is that most governors will serve no more than two full terms. Intra- and interparty competition as well as the difficult and controversial problems governors face suggest somewhat limited service. In addition, because Texas is the second most populous state in the Union, Texas governors will often be in the spotlight as future presidential or vice presidential candidates. Such was the case with Bush, who became president in 2001. Perry made no secret of his interest in being nominated for vice president in 2008. Indeed, the chapter-opening quote from his 2007 State of the State Address reflected his efforts to place Texas into the largest possible context.

# IMPEACHMENT AND SUCCESSION

## IMPEACHMENT

In Texas, a governor may be removed from office only through an **impeachment** proceeding. Impeachment is similar to a grand jury indictment; that is, it is a formal accusation. The state constitution is silent on what impeachable offenses are.[2] By implication and by the precedents set in the impeachment of Governor James E. Ferguson in 1917, however, the grounds are *malfeasance, misfeasance,* and *nonfeasance* in office—in other words, official misconduct, incompetence, or failure to perform.[3]

The impeachment procedure in Texas is similar to that at the national level. The House of Representatives, by a majority vote of those present, must first impeach the executive. Once the formal accusation is made, the Senate acts as a trial court; a two-thirds vote of the senators present is necessary to convict. Penalties for conviction are removal from office and disqualification from holding future governmental offices in the state. If there are criminal charges, they must be brought in a regular court of law.

## SUCCESSION

If a governor is removed from office by impeachment and conviction, dies in office or before taking office, or resigns, the constitution provides that the lieutenant governor shall become governor. A 1999 constitutional amendment further stipulated that, should the governor become disabled, the lieutenant governor would carry out the duties of the office; should the governor die or otherwise be unable to return, the lieutenant governor would become governor for the rest of the term of the governor who had vacated the office. If the lieutenant governor is unable to serve, the president pro tempore of the Senate would carry out the duties. Once the lieutenant governor becomes governor, the lieutenant governor's position is vacant. The vacancy would be filled within thirty days by the election of a member of the Senate to serve as presiding officer and to fulfill the duties of lieutenant governor until the next general election. The amendment clarified some issues previously addressed by statute, such as whether one person could be governor and lieutenant governor simultaneously (not possible), but some ambiguity in the wording still exists. The executive article states that the senator who is elected as presiding officer is also the lieutenant governor. The legislative article is more ambiguous because it states "perform the duties of the Lieutenant Governor." The language of this amendment is confusing!

★ ★ ★ ★ ★ ★ ★ ★ ★ ★ ★ ★ ★ ★ ★ ★ ★ ★ ★ ★ ★ ★ ★ ★ ★

## *Gubernatorial Succession*

The last governor to die in office was Beauford Jester in 1949, who was succeeded by Allan Shivers. The impetus for the 1999 amendment was to ensure a smooth transition in the event that Governor George W. Bush was elected president before his term expired in January 2002. The Bush run at the presidency also intensified Senate elections set to occur in 2000 because control of the Senate might mean not only control of redistricting (see Chapter 6) but also control of the all-powerful presiding officer's selection. The national election results of 2000 confirmed the need for the amendment.

★ ★ ★ ★ ★ ★ ★ ★ ★ ★ ★ ★ ★ ★ ★ ★ ★ ★ ★ ★ ★ ★ ★ ★ ★

## COMPENSATION

A 1954 amendment allows the legislature to determine the salary of the governor and other elected executives. The legislature provided generous increments for many years, raising the governor's salary from $12,000 in 1954 to $99,122 in 1992–1993. Then the state budget allowed no raises for state employees for five years. The salary was raised to $115,345 for fiscal year 2001 (FY 01), and the salary of other state executives was increased to $91,217. These salaries remained the same through FY 07. Once second only to New York, by 2006, the Texas governor's salary had slipped to twenty-sixth and was continuing to go down in the national rankings as other states awarded pay raises to governors.[4] The lieutenant governor is paid as a legislator—$7,200 a year plus a per diem—although he or she receives a salary supplementation for acting as governor whenever the governor leaves the state.

The governor also receives numerous fringe benefits. The constitution provides an official mansion, and other benefits include a travel and operating budget, a car, the use of state-owned aircraft, bodyguards furnished by the Texas Department of Public Safety, and offices and professional staff. These benefits compare favorably with those of other governors.

★ ★ ★ ★ ★ ★ ★ ★ ★ ★ ★ ★ ★ ★ ★ ★ ★ ★ ★ ★ ★ ★ ★ ★ ★ ★ ★ ★ ★ ★ ★

## Show Me the Money

Although well paid, particularly in comparison to legislators with their $7,200 salaries, the Texas governor is by no means the best-paid executive on the state payroll. Top-dollar honors belong to some of the larger universities in the state—University of Texas at Austin, Texas A&M University, the University of Houston/Main Campus, the University of North Texas, and Texas Tech University, all of which are the hub institutions of systems. The chancellors of the university systems and the presidents of the largest institutions receive base salaries of several hundred thousand dollars. Beyond that, they get all sorts of perquisites, such as houses and cars, that substantially increase their compensation. In addition, some large institutions pay bonuses for successful fund-raising, and some chancellors receive supplemental pay from individual institutions in the system—particularly medical schools. Dollars raised from local funds are used to supplement rather modest state-appropriated salaries. These large salaries often are matters of contention when university appropriations are discussed—and, for that matter, among faculty when the president gets a raise but faculty members do not. In 2006, for example, when David Smith resigned as chancellor of the Texas Tech University System, the university still paid him $716,000 as salary and $371,000 in deferred compensation.

However, even these salaries pale when compared to those of the football and basketball coaches at UT-Austin and Texas A&M. Following the Longhorns' national championship in 2006, Coach Mack Brown's salary was raised from just under $2.2 million to $2.55 million. When UT-Austin hired Gail Goestenkors from Duke in 2007 to be the women's basketball coach, her base salary plus incentives was over $1 million; the salary of Rick Barnes, the men's basketball coach, was raised to $2 million in 2007. His nearest competitor in the state was Mark Turgeon at Texas A&M, with a $1.2 million salary. Even in high schools, big 5-A school coaches earn in excess of $100,000, far more than the principal or teachers. If salaries are a measure of priorities, then Texans must value football first; education, second; and general government, third.

★ ★ ★ ★ ★ ★ ★ ★ ★ ★ ★ ★ ★ ★ ★ ★ ★ ★ ★ ★ ★ ★ ★ ★ ★ ★ ★ ★ ★

SOURCES: "Paid to Quit: Smith's $1.1 Million Deal," KCBD-TV, February 23, 2006; "Texas' Brown Getting Hefty Pay Raise," http://sports.espn.go.com/ncf/news/story?id=2310990, January 29, 2006; Chip Brown, "Women's Coach Set to Cash in at Texas," *Dallas Morning News*, April 5, 2007, 5C; and Mark Rosner, "Barnes Becomes $2 Million Man," *Austin American-Statesman*, April 17, 2007, 1C, 5C.

## STAFF AND ORGANIZATION

Like other chief executives, the governor alone is unable to perform all the functional and ceremonial tasks assigned to the governor's office. Assistance in fulfilling these obligations comes from a personal staff and from the professional staffs of the divisions that make up the Office of the Governor. Certain staff members are assigned to act as legislative liaisons—in effect, to lobby for the governor's programs—and often it is through them that the governor makes known an impending threat to veto a particular piece of legislation. Other staff members are involved in recommending candidates for the hundreds of appointments the governor must make to state boards, commissions, and executive agencies. The governor's aides also prepare the executive budget, coordinate the various departments and activities of the governor's office, and schedule appointments and activities. Overall, in addition to handling routine duties and occasional emergency situations, the governor's staff must provide assistance in performing the specific tasks assigned to the office by law and in formulating political moves to promote the enactment of the governor's programs.

As of 2006, Governor Rick Perry's office had 266 staff members, more than any governor other than Florida's.[5] This number appears low when one considers that Governor Ann Richards had a staff of almost 400. The comparison is somewhat deceiving because the Richards payroll was significantly less than the Perry payroll. The Richards approach was Jacksonian in nature, creating "many jobs for the people," although the pay was modest. That approach was in keeping with her overall **populist** approach—a populist appeals to ordinary citizens. Governors George W. Bush and Rick Perry followed a traditional businesslike approach of appointing fewer people but at much higher salaries.

★ ★ ★ ★ ★ ★ ★ ★ ★ ★ ★ ★ ★ ★ ★ ★ ★ ★ ★ ★ ★ ★ ★ ★ ★ ★

## *Governor's Office Staffing*

How do the big-population states compare in the number of gubernatorial staff members? Florida leads with 278; Texas has 266; California, 185; New York, 180; Illinois, 130; Pennsylvania, only 68. Whether the state has a cabinet and how many functions have been temporarily assigned to the governor's office both play a role in determining staff size.

★ ★ ★ ★ ★ ★ ★ ★ ★ ★ ★ ★ ★ ★ ★ ★ ★ ★ ★ ★ ★ ★ ★ ★ ★ ★

Each governor organizes the office somewhat differently. Commonly, new program initiatives begin under the governor's auspices and then become independent or move to other agencies. More than anything else, the configuration of programs makes the difference in organization. As of 2007, the governor's office consisted of the following elements:[6]

- **The Appointments Division, which assists the governor in making nominations for boards, commissions, and advisory committees**

- **The Budget, Planning, and Policy Division, which prepares the executive budget, including coordination of requests from state agencies and cooperation with the Legislative Budget Board to prepare a state strategic plan and monitor the development and implementation of the plans of individual agencies**

- **The Criminal Justice Division (CJD), which provides funding to local, regional, and statewide projects for making the state safer**

- **Governor's Committee for People with Disabilities, which serves a rather general advocacy function on behalf of people with disabilities**

- **The Division of Economic Development and Tourism, which markets Texas and promotes opportunities for everything from vacationing to business relocation**

- **Texas Film Commission, which encourages moviemaking in the state by providing support for such activities as finding locations and accommodating production needs**

- Human Resources Division, which provides information about employment in the governor's office

- Texas Military Peparedness Commission, which works to prevent base closures and assists defense-dependent communities

- Texas Music Office, which is an information clearinghouse and promotion agency for the music industry

- Press Office, which issues all press releases and announcements on behalf of the governor and works with the media

- State Grants Team, which alerts agencies and local governments about funding opportunities

- Governor's Commission for Women, which seeks to improve the personal and professional status of women and which performs an advocacy role

- Texas Workforce Investment Council, which is responsible for planning and evaluation activities in conjunction with the development of a well-educated, skilled workforce

- Texas Review and Comments System (TRACS), which is the intergovernmental review system

★ ★ ★ ★ ★ ★ ★ ★ ★ ★ ★ ★ ★ ★ ★ ★ ★ ★ ★ ★ ★ ★ ★ ★ ★ ★ ★

## *Texas Version of Foreign Affairs*

One of the surprising consequences of the end of the Cold War between the United States and the former Soviet Union has been the assertion of American state activity in international affairs. Although Article I, Section 10 of the U.S. Constitution forbids the states to enter into any agreement or compact with a foreign power, both California and Texas seem to have been pursuing their own foreign policies for several years.

California has opened ten trade offices in foreign capitals, including Mexico City, London, and Tokyo. The 2003 Texas legislature moved the economic development function into the governor's office in an effort to end corruption in the former Department of Economic Development, and Governor Rick Perry was quick to pursue international business connections. He created controversy with a 2004 trip to Italy to meet with industries there because business interests financed the trip. He generated more controversy in 2007 while pushing the Trans Texas Corridor highway system, signaling an intent to award operation of new toll roads to foreign corporations. He also joined a number of other southern border-state governors in active involvement in immigration issues. There also is a Division of Border and Mexican Affairs within the Secretary of State's Office to craft agreements with Mexico dealing with trade, environmental management of the Rio Grande, and immigration.

★ ★ ★ ★ ★ ★ ★ ★ ★ ★ ★ ★ ★ ★ ★ ★ ★ ★ ★ ★ ★ ★ ★ ★ ★ ★ ★

SOURCES: Julie Blase, "The Evolution of State Influence on U.S. Foreign Policy as Illustrated by Texas-Mexico Relations," unpublished paper, Department of Government, University of Texas at Austin, December 1, 1997; Dave Lesher, "Golden and Global California," *Los Angeles Times*, January 8, 1998, A; Don Melvin, "Perry: Italy Trip Good for Texas Jobs," *Dallas Morning News*, March 10, 2004, 3A; and Christy Hoppe, "Governor Uses Religious Themes to Call for Compassion in State Government," *Dallas Morning News*, January 17, 2007, 1A, 9A.

Although they are not listed as formal divisions of the office, the governor's staff also includes individuals who advise on public policy, help to work policy initiatives through the Texas legislature, and provide legal advice. In addition, the governor's office has taken primary responsibility for strategic planning in homeland security for the state.

# Qualifications for Governor

## FORMAL QUALIFICATIONS

As is true of the qualifications for members of the legislature, the formal qualifications for governor are so broad that several million Texans could legally run for the office. Article IV of the constitution stipulates that the governor must be at least thirty years old, be a citizen of the United States, and have been a resident of Texas for the five years immediately preceding the election. These qualifications also pertain to the lieutenant governor. Article IV also mandates that the governor "shall be installed on the first Tuesday after the organization of the Legislature, or as soon thereafter as practicable." Article III gives the legislature the responsibility for settling any election disputes that might arise concerning the governor.

## PERSONAL CHARACTERISTICS

Formally qualifying for the governorship and actually having a chance at being considered seriously as a candidate are two very different matters. The social, political, and economic realities of the state dictate that personal characteristics, not stated in law, help determine who will be the victors in gubernatorial elections. Some of these personal characteristics are based on accomplishments, or at least positive involvement, of the gubernatorial aspirant. Others are innate traits that are beyond the control of the individual.

These characteristics are similar to but even more stringent than those for members of the legislature. In short, unless something unusual occurs in the campaign, tradition dictates that the successful candidate for governor will be a White Anglo-Saxon Protestant (WASP) male who is politically conservative, involved in civic affairs, and a millionaire. More than likely, but less inevitably, this individual will have held some other office, often that of attorney general or lieutenant governor, although being a professional politician is sometimes a liability among voters with a penchant for electing "good ol' boys."

The most atypical governor in more than a half century was Ann Richards (1991–1995), a populist Democratic female (see Chapter 4 for a discussion of populism in Texas). Richards took strong stands against concealed weapons and environmental destruction and urged reform of selected state agencies, such as the Insurance Commission and Department of Commerce, that had strong ties to business. Rick Perry, a Republican, is very much in the conservative mainstream of Texas political belief and served as a member of the Texas House, as agriculture commissioner, and as lieutenant governor before ascending to the governorship in late 2000. He is distinguished perhaps by representing rural West Texas rather than an urban area. The chapter-opening quote from his State of the State

George W. Bush served as governor from 1995 until 2000, when he resigned after being elected president of the United States.

speech in 2007, however, reflected his new political thinking when proffered a world leadership role for Texas, a concept in keeping with the widely held belief that he was running for the Republican vice presidential nomination in 2008.

## CONSERVATIVE

Traditionally, a gubernatorial candidate had to be a conservative Democrat. E. J. Davis, a much-maligned Republican governor during Reconstruction, was the only Republican governor until Bill Clements was elected in 1978. The state has now evolved from one-party Democrat to two-party to Republican ascendant. Today, because of the growth of the Republican Party, the governor is likely to be a conservative Republican for the foreseeable future. It will be difficult for a Democrat to win the governorship in the immediate future, particularly until the voter apathy described in Chapter Five is overcome.

In the 1990 Ann Richards–Clayton Williams race, Richards's self-proclaimed Democratic populism did not win the race for her. Rather, Clayton Williams's "open-mouth-put-foot-in" rhetoric lost the election for him. He seemed particularly adept at insulting women and ordinary taxpayers. In the first instance, he opined that rape was like bad weather so that, "If it's inevitable, [a woman should] just relax and enjoy it." In the second, Williams, a multimillionaire who financed much of his own campaign, bragged about not paying federal income taxes. Richards was the most recent Democratic governor.

In the previous race, between Clements and Mark White in 1986, White—the conservative Democrat—lost because of a faltering economy that he neither caused nor could fix and because of the education funding issue. White had taken a strong stand for school reform and the tax increase necessary to finance it, noting at the time that he probably had forfeited his own second term. Indeed, during the 1986 campaign, White was portrayed as a high-tax, free-spending liberal.

George W. Bush entered the race in 1994 as a mainstream Republican, concerned with state control over state policy, the integrity of the family, the quality of education, and the rising incidence of juvenile crime. He and Richards differed little on those issues. He reflected more of a national Republican position in wanting to cut welfare and in openly advocating a freer operating climate for business, especially by placing many restrictions on lawsuits for such activities as professional malpractice and faulty products. Significantly, however, he talked about his conservatism, not his party affiliation.

The Tony Sanchez–Rick Perry gubernatorial race in 2002 was costly and mean spirited, a signal of the 2003 legislative session yet to come. Perry claimed education, healthcare, transportation, water, and border affairs as priorities but

★ ★ ★ ★ ★ ★ ★ ★ ★ ★ ★ ★ ★ ★ ★ ★ ★ ★ ★ ★ ★ ★ ★ ★ ★ ★ ★ ★ ★ ★ ★

## Good Ol' Girl

Ann Richards wanted to ensure that Texans understood the difference between her people's campaign (populism) and run-of-the-mill liberalism. She went to some lengths to look like a good ol' girl, including joining the boys for the opening of bird-hunting season. She also posed for the cover of *Texas Monthly* wearing a black leather jacket and sitting on a Harley-Davidson motorcycle.

★ ★ ★ ★ ★ ★ ★ ★ ★ ★ ★ ★ ★ ★ ★ ★ ★ ★ ★ ★ ★ ★ ★ ★ ★ ★ ★ ★ ★ ★ ★

focused on probusiness legislation rather than problem solving. He was successful in reducing the power of Comptroller Carole Keeton Strayhorn, who had tested the waters for a possible run against Perry in the next Republican primary by lambasting the lack of concern for poor children and their healthcare needs, and in augmenting the power of the governor's office. Perry continued to earn his conservative credentials in the subsequent legislative sessions of 2005 and 2007, pushing business interests, emphasizing tax cuts over solutions to the knotty school finance problem (see Chapter 13), and even enduring criticism from fellow Republicans for letting his industry ties dominate public policy. His major speeches often addressed the concerns of poor people, but his legislative agenda tended to address the desires of business.

Most state officeholders in Texas are conservative, and a candidate for governor needs not only their support but also access to the big campaign money waiting in the pockets of conservative businesspersons, bankers, and attorneys (these last often have state agencies as customers and clients). Although unanimity does not exist in either party, and while urban–rural differences increase yearly, the nominee generally can count on all factions of the party for support in the general election.

Ann Richards served as governor from 1991 until 1995.

## WASP, MIDDLE-AGED MALE

Texas has not had a non-Anglo governor since it became independent of Spain and Mexico. Only two Roman Catholics—Frances (Sissy) Farenthold in the 1972 Democratic primary and Tony Sanchez in 2002—have been serious contenders for the governor's office; Kinky Friedman in 2006 was the only serious Jewish candidate, but he drew only 12 percent of the vote. The religious preferences of the governors elected in the Lone Star State have been confined to the mainstream Protestant churches, such as Methodist and Baptist.

Texas governors have tended to reach the top office shortly after their fiftieth birthday. Of the thirty-one individuals who have served as governor under the 1876 Constitution, only two—Ann Richards and Miriam A. Ferguson—were female. However, among the twenty-five women who had been elected as governors by 2007, only Texas, Arizona, Kansas, and New Hampshire have elected two different women.

## ATTORNEY/BUSINESSPERSON, COMMUNITY PILLAR

Governors, as well as legislators, are often attorneys. Since 1876, sixteen of the thirty-one Texas governors have been lawyers. However, of the five most recent governors in the state, only Mark White was a lawyer. Bill Clements and George Bush were businesspeople. Ann Richards, although she had been a public school teacher, was essentially a professional politician who went to work as a lobbyist for a Washington-based law firm when she left office. Rick Perry is a fifth-generation Texas farmer-rancher with more than twenty years spent as an elected official.

The final personal characteristic that candidates must have is being a "pillar of the community." Governors are members of civic, social, fraternal, and business organizations and seem to be the epitome of stable family life. Richards, being divorced, was something of an exception, but was frequently photographed with her children and grandchildren.

# Roles of the Governor and Limits on Those Roles

The office of governor consists of a repertoire of at least seven roles that the incumbent must play. Five are formal; that is, they are prescribed by the constitution and supplementing statutes. Two are informal and symbolic; that is, they derive from the Texas political setting (see Table 8-3). Governors of all states play similar roles, as does the president, who also has added responsibilities in the areas of diplomacy and economics.

The personality of the governor and the political and economic circumstances that prevail during a governor's administration largely determine which roles are emphasized. As the first opening quotation in this chapter indicates, the governorship is a unique office, with its distinctive qualities further highlighted by the varied approaches taken by different governors.[7] How a governor goes about trying to get policy preferences enacted by the legislature and implemented by the bureaucracy constitutes leadership style. Leadership style is crucial to Texas because the governor so often has to depend on persuasive skills to offset the limitations on the office. Democratic theory dictates that the elected executive be accountable for the executive branch. In Texas, the governor has to rely heavily on informal means to gain the expected control over the state bureaucracy and to achieve his or her policy agenda.

To view the governor in action, this chapter looks briefly at the styles of the governors of the state during the modern era. These brief biographical sketches may help the reader understand the diverse personalities and operating styles of recent Texas governors.

TABLE 8-3

## Roles of the Governor

| Constitutional and Statutory Roles | Informal and Symbolic Roles |
| --- | --- |
| Chief Executive | Chief of Party |
| Chief Legislator | Leader of the People |
| Commander in Chief/Top Cop | |
| Chief of State | |
| Chief Intergovernmental Diplomat | |

Dolph Briscoe (1973–1979) had such a low profile that *Texas Monthly* pictured him on the cover as an empty chair in reference to his spending more time at his Uvalde ranch than at his Austin desk. He personified the quest for the office just to acquire something more for the man who has almost everything. Mark White (1983–1987) inherited a deteriorating economy and emphasized education and economic development as ways to shore up the state financial picture. However, he was accused of being all style and no substance. Bill Clements (1979–1983, 1987–1991) emphasized tax reform, a war on drugs and crime, long-range planning, and better ties to neighboring states and Mexico during his first term. During his second, of necessity he emphasized economic diversification. Clements had a reputation as an obstructionist, making it difficult for public policy to develop, but his legacy was bringing "business principles and discipline to the state budget and government."[8]

The governor acknowledged to be atypical, Ann Richards (1991–1995) was grounded in Travis County politics and got high marks for the quality and diversity of her appointments; for forcing changes in the controversial boards governing some state agencies, especially the State Insurance Board and the Board of Pardons and Paroles; and for exerting executive control over other agencies, such as the Texas Department of Commerce. Richards insisted on high ethical standards, although some of her staff members stumbled later on. She also worked hard at economic diversification. However, Richards's approach to legislative relations was partisan and heavy-handed, and, although she was appreciated for her sense of humor, she sometimes had difficulty pushing her policy agenda through the legislature. Her 1994 bid for reelection was inept, and she also faced the national Republican sweep. Richards lost handily to George W. Bush.[9]

George W. Bush, son of a former president,[10] operated very differently from Richards. The Bush approach to legislators was nonpartisan, low-key, and consensus building. Bush saw himself as a deal maker. He campaigned on four issues: reform of the juvenile justice system, setting limits on civil lawsuits (tort reform), more flexible and better public education, and restrictions on welfare. These issues were common throughout the country in 1994. Once elected, Bush stuck with those issues and pushed each through the 1995 legislature. While he was successful in further expanding public school flexibility in the 1997 legislative session, his push for major changes in the Texas tax system was rebuffed. He had to settle for a proposed constitutional amendment to increase the tax exemptions for homesteads. By the time the Seventy-sixth Legislature met in January 1999, no doubt existed about the governor's political plans. The *Wall Street Journal*, whose political philosophy is closely aligned to that of Bush's "compassionate conservatism," summarized the year by noting the total dominance of the capitol complex by a governor who was out of the state campaigning much of the time. The *Journal* staff noted the Bush "'Yellow Rose Garden' strategy of having potential presidential supporters and advisers, along with world leaders, come to Austin" as overshadowing "anything that was happening across the street at the state Capitol,"[11] including the partial resolution of the state's public school funding issue.

Rick Perry's tenure as governor began on such a low key that *Texas Monthly* magazine rated him as "furniture" after the 2001 session. That designation indicated that he had little effect on the outcome of the session until after it was over. Then Perry surpassed even Preston Smith's and Bill Clements's penchant for using the veto, killing eighty-two bills—some of vital concern to his own party. In 2003, he ended his first session as the elected governor with the huge issue of school finance left unaddressed. Perry let congressional redistricting (see Chapter 6) come to dominate his thinking and expressed more concern about not raising taxes than about resolving the knotty problem of school finance. In 2005, Perry's plan to solve the state's most pressing problem, school finance, was unanimously rejected by the legislature, which finally produced a school finance bill in a special session in 2006. In 2007, Perry used a variety of techniques in an effort to appear as an effective executive suitable for national office, but found great resistance from the legislature, the attorney general, and the public.[12] Table 8-4 illustrates some of the well-publicized controversies between the governor and other policymakers.

Governor Rick Perry seemed to get into difficulty with virtually everyone in 2007 when he tried to accomplish his policy objectives by executive decree, only to be reminded that he did not have such power under the Texas Constitution.

*Courtesy of Ben Sargent.*

TABLE 8-4

## Rick Perry's 2007 Use of Executive Authority and the Challenges

| Governor's Action | Public/Institutional Reaction |
| --- | --- |
| Executive order for all sixth-grade girls to be vaccinated for a sexually transmitted virus causing cervical cancer | Public and lobbyists' negative reaction resulting in legislation prohibiting such a mandate via executive order. Governor Perry allowed the bill to become a law without his signature. |
| Proposal that the state sell the lottery to a private party | Lukewarm reception even among fellow Republicans. |
| Proposal for a Trans-Texas Corridor, to include a new highway that would parallel Interstate 35 and include a series of toll roads | Public and Senate objections to the toll road component and to the awarding of a lucrative contract to a Spanish company; new toll roads were put on hold, except for one North Texas tollway for which bids were in progress. Rural landowners were vocal about their fears that the state would confiscate their property for highway rights-of-way. |
| Support of TXU's desire to build eleven new coal-fired electric generating plants | Strong environmentalists' outcries against dirty fuel source; ultimately, sale of TXU to private investors, who promised only three coal-fired plants, two new nuclear reactors, and operation of a new "green" TXU. |
| Appointing special master to investigate charges of sexual and physical abuse at Texas Youth Commission facilities | Criticism that the governor's office did not take over the TYC as it had earlier taken over the Economic Development and Tourism Office when it fell into corruption; legislation completely revamping the TYC. |
| 2005 executive order that 65% of public school district funds be expended for instruction | By 2007, identification of a loophole that allowed a lesser percentage so long as expenditures were disclosed to the public. |

SOURCES: Christy Hoppe, "Perry's Agenda on Ropes," *Dallas Morning News*, March 12, 2007, 1A, 6A; Christy Hoppe, "Opinion Trims Perry's Power," *Dallas Morning News*, March 13, 2007, 1A, 9A; Kelley Shannon, "Texas Governorship Weak, but Perry Presses Big Plans," *Denton Record-Chronicle*, February 25, 2007, 3A; Tony Hartzel, "Put the Brakes on Toll Roads, Critics Say," *Dallas Morning News*, March 2, 2007, 1A, 12A; Karen Ayres, "Districts Benefit from Loophole," *Dallas Morning News*, March 8, 2007, 1A, 2A; Emily Ramshaw, "TYC Board to Quit," *Dallas Morning News*, March 15, 2007, 1A, 16A; "An Accounting of Notable Issues of the 2007 Legislature," prepared by the *Austin American-Statesman* and available at http://www.statesman.com/news/content/gen/ap/TX_XGR_Did_Didnt .html?COXnetJSessionIDbuild35c=7NBmGcLPYQ8JkhCyndpvTQG0f5QRwG1Lcph0fhhwLw6322TbPc1!-424220207 &UrAurth=%60N\ NUOaNJUbTTUWUXUVUZTZUbUWU_U_UZU\U^UcTYWYWZV &urcm=y.

# Formal Roles and Limitations

The Texas Constitution was written at a time when concentrated power in the hands of a single state official was viewed with great apprehension. E. J. Davis, the last Republican governor before Clements, held office from 1870 to 1874, and his administration was characterized by corruption and repression. Consequently, when the 1876 Constitution was drafted, the framers reacted against the Davis administration by creating a constitutionally weak governor's office (see Chapter 2).

Today, the governor must still cope with a highly fragmented executive branch that results in a plural executive. The executive branch includes not only the governor but also five other elected executives, two elected boards, and a complex system of powerful policymaking boards and commissions. Recent governors have sought greater institutional power with modest success, and Rick Perry made substantial progress toward modernization of the Texas governor's office with a series of bills passed by the Seventy-eighth Legislature in 2003. These bills resulted in control of economic development, health and human services, and the chairmanship of many state boards.[13]

## CHIEF EXECUTIVE

News stories frequently describe the governor as the "chief executive," referring to gubernatorial control over the state bureaucracy and **appointment and removal,** budgeting, planning, supervisory, and clemency powers. Although this is one of the governor's most time-consuming roles, it traditionally has been one of the weakest, as the following discussion illustrates.

★ ★ ★ ★ ★ ★ ★ ★ ★ ★ ★ ★ ★ ★ ★ ★ ★ ★ ★ ★ ★ ★ ★ ★ ★ ★ ★

### *How a Governor Can Get Things Done*

George W. Bush, elected in 1994, observed that "the way to forge good public policy amongst the leadership of the legislative branch and executive branch is to air our differences in private meetings that happen all the time. . . . The way to ruin a relationship is to leak things and to be disrespectful of meeting in private."

★ ★ ★ ★ ★ ★ ★ ★ ★ ★ ★ ★ ★ ★ ★ ★ ★ ★ ★ ★ ★ ★ ★ ★ ★ ★ ★

SOURCE: R. G. Ratcliffe, "Away from the Spotlight, Governor Makes His Mark," *Houston Chronicle*, April 15, 1995, 10A.

### APPOINTMENT

Texas is said to have a long ballot because a large number of state officials are elected by the people rather than appointed by the governor. The list of officials elected on a statewide basis includes the lieutenant governor, whose major role is legislative; the attorney general; the comptroller of public accounts; the commissioner of the General Land Office; and the agriculture commissioner. In addition, members of the Texas Railroad Commission and the State Board of Education are elected. They are elected independently, so they feel no obligation to the governor, and because they may want the governor's job, they may even wish to make the incumbent look bad. Absent direct influence on these elected officeholders, the governor must be highly skilled in the art of persuasion.

The most visible executive appointments that the governor makes are those of secretary of state, commissioner of education, commissioner of insurance, commissioner of health and human services, and the executive director of the Economic Development and Tourism Division. The governor also appoints the director of the Office of State–Federal Relations and the adjutant general, who heads the state militia. He or she also fills any vacancy that occurs in one of the major elected executive positions, such as railroad commissioner. In the event of a vacancy, the governor appoints someone to fill the office until the next election. She or he also appoints all or some of the members of about two dozen advisory councils and committees that coordinate the work of two or more state agencies.

Most state agencies are not headed up by a single executive making policy decisions. The result is a highly fragmented executive branch; power is divided among both elected executives and appointed boards. Nevertheless, the governor has a major effect on state policy through approximately 3,000 appointments to more than 100 policymaking, multimember boards and commissions. Examples include the University of Texas System board of regents, the Public Utility Commission, and the Texas Youth Commission. Rick Perry sought much greater control over the chairs of state boards, and in the third called legislative session of 2003, he succeeded in gaining greater control by being able to appoint the presiding officer as long as the appointee had received Senate confirmation.[14]

The members of these boards are usually appointed for a six-year term but with the following limitations:

1. **The terms of board and commission members are overlapping and staggered to prevent the governor from appointing a majority of the members until late in his or her first term of office.**

2. **The statutes establishing the various boards and commissions are highly prescriptive and often specify both a certain geographic representation and occupational or other background characteristics of the members.**

3. **Appointments to some boards and commissions must be made from lists supplied by members of professional organizations and associations.[15]**

One other important use of the appointment power is filling vacancies in the judiciary. Although Texas has an elected judiciary, every legislature creates some new courts, and vacancies occur in other courts. The governor makes appointments to these benches until the next election. Indeed, many district court judges in the state are first appointed and subsequently stand for election.

The governor must obtain a two-thirds confirmation vote from the Texas Senate for appointments; the president needs only a simple majority from the U.S. Senate. As in national politics, there is the practice of "senatorial courtesy": The Senate will usually honor the objection of a senator from the same district as the nominee for appointment by refusing to approve confirmation.

Texas's short biennial legislative session, however, permits the governor to make many interim appointments when the legislature is not in session. This practice gives these appointees a "free ride" for as long as nineteen months. These recess appointments must be presented to the Senate within the first ten days of the next session, whether regular or special.

Another aid to the governor is incumbency. If a governor is reelected, he or she will be able to appoint all members of the board or commission by the middle of the second term, perhaps earlier if some members resign. The governor may then have considerable influence over policy development within the agency, albeit with little time left in office.

## REMOVAL

The governor has only limited removal power in Texas. The governor can remove political officials he or she has appointed, with the consent of the Senate, a power in effect only since a 1980 constitutional amendment. He also can remove personal staff members and a few executive directors, such as the one in the Department of Housing and Community Affairs. However, the governor cannot remove members of boards and commissions whom he did not appoint and obviously cannot remove state executives who were elected in their own right. This lack of removal power deprives the governor of significant control over the bureaucrats who make and administer policy on a daily basis. In turn, the governor's job of implementing policies through the state bureaucracy is made more difficult.

The three general methods for removing state officeholders are

1. **Impeachment,** which involves a formal accusation—the impeachment—by a House majority and requires a two-thirds vote for conviction by the Senate

2. **Address,** a procedure whereby the legislature requests the governor to remove a district or appellate judge from office (a two-thirds vote of both houses is required)

3. **Quo warranto proceedings,** a legal procedure whereby an official may be removed by a court

Because Article XV of the Texas Constitution stipulates the right to a trial before removal from office, impeachment is likely to remain the chief formal removal procedure because it does involve a trial by the Senate. However, even its use is quite rare.

## BUDGETING

By law, the governor must submit a biennial budget message to the legislature within five days after that body convenes in regular session. This budget is prepared by the governor's Division of Budget, Planning, and Policy. The executive budget indicates to the legislature the governor's priorities and signals items likely to be vetoed. With the exception of the item veto, the Texas governor lacks the strong formal budgetary powers not only of the president but also of many state executives (see Chapter 13). The governor has one additional financial power, that of approving deficiency warrants of no more than $200,000 for the biennium for agencies that encounter emergencies and/or run out of funds.

Traditionally, the Legislative Budget Board (LBB), which also prepares a budget for the legislature to consider, has dominated the budget process. The legislature always has been guided more by the legislative budget than by the governor's. A significant exception occurred in the regular 2003 legislative session when the governor's staff was heavily involved in developing the final budget for floor consideration. This concession by legislative leaders, along with reorganization measures, was one of several signals that the Republicans—usually known as the party opposed to strong government powers—were willing to consider greater executive authority in Texas.[16] In addition, the legislature gave the governor $295 million to spend on economic development in fiscal years (FY) 2004–2005 and another $182 million for 2006–2007.

## PLANNING

Both modern management and the requirements of many federal grants-in-aid emphasize substate regional planning, and the governor directs planning efforts for the state through the Budget, Planning, and Policy Division. When combined with budgeting, the governor's planning power allows a stronger gubernatorial

★ ★ ★ ★ ★ ★ ★ ★ ★ ★ ★ ★ ★ ★ ★ ★ ★ ★ ★ ★ ★ ★ ★ ★ ★ ★ ★ ★

### *Budget Growth in a Conservative Era*

A lthough Rick Perry frequently called for conservative revenue measures and restrictions on state spending, he saw the budget continue to grow during his administration, including a 10.3 percent increase from FY 2006–2007 to $152.5 bil-
lion for FY 2008–2009. This period also saw the state swing from a deep shortage to a
generous surplus. Per person spending actually declined in terms of national rankings.

★ ★ ★ ★ ★ ★ ★ ★ ★ ★ ★ ★ ★ ★ ★ ★ ★ ★ ★ ★ ★ ★ ★ ★ ★ ★ ★ ★

SOURCE: "Five Years of Change with Perry," *Austin American-Statesman*, September 4, 2006, B1.

hand in the development of new programs and policy alternatives. Although still
without adequate control over the programs of the state, the governor has had
a greater voice in suggesting future programs over the past two decades, mainly
because many federal statutes designated the governor as having approval power
for federal grants.

Especially in his first term, Bill Clements approached the governor's office
from the planning perspective, including the development of the Texas State Government Effectiveness Program to make state agency management more efficient
and the creation of the Texas 2000 Commission to look at issues that would become increasingly more pressing as the next century neared. During the Richards
administration, Comptroller John Sharp—in part at the request of the governor
to allow a more rational appropriations act for fiscal years 1992–1993—developed an elaborate system for monitoring the performance of state agencies. This
system, known as the Texas Performance Review (TPR), requires state agencies
to engage in strategic planning. The TPR has continued as a vital part of state
government. In 2003, Governor Rick Perry and the legislative leaders, following
disputes over the budget process, removed this function from the office of Comptroller Carole Keeton Strayhorn and moved it into legislative staff agencies.

## SUPERVISING

The state constitution charges the governor with the responsibility for seeing that
the laws of the state are "faithfully executed" but provides few tools for fulfilling this function. The governor's greatest supervisory and directive powers occur
in the role of commander in chief (see "Commander in Chief/Top Cop" section).
Governors can request reports from state agencies, appoint board chairs, remove
their own appointees, and use political influence to force hiring reductions or
other economies. But lack of appointment power over the professional staffs of
state agencies and lack of removal power over a predecessor's appointees limit
the governor's ability to ensure that the state bureaucracy performs its job.

The governor thus must fall back on informal tactics to exercise any control
over the administration. In this respect, the governor's staff is of supreme importance: If staff members can establish good rapport with state agencies, they
may extend the governor's influence to areas where the governor does not have
formal authority. They are aided in this task by two factors of which agency personnel are well aware: the governor's leadership of the party and veto powers
(both discussed in the "Chief Legislator" section).

## CLEMENCY

The governor's power with regard to acts of clemency (mercy) is restricted to one thirty-day reprieve for an individual sentenced to death. In cases of treason against the state (a rare crime), the governor may grant pardons, reprieves, and commutations of sentences with legislative consent. The governor also may remit fines or bond forfeitures and restore driver's licenses and hunting privileges. In addition, the governor has the discretionary right to revoke a parole or conditional pardon. Beyond these limited acts, the state's chief executive officer must make recommendations to the Board of Pardons and Paroles, which is part of the Department of Criminal Justice. Although empowered to refuse an act of clemency recommended by the board, the governor cannot act without its recommendation in such matters as full and conditional pardons, commutations, reprieves, and emergency reprieves.

★ ★ ★ ★ ★ ★ ★ ★ ★ ★ ★ ★ ★ ★ ★ ★ ★ ★ ★ ★ ★ ★ ★ ★ ★ ★ ★ ★ ★ ★

### Ma Ferguson and Clemency

The governor's clemency power was not always so restricted. Under the Constitution of 1876, it was actually quite extensive. During the 1920s and 1930s, however, Governor Miriam "Ma" Ferguson was suspected of selling pardons, in combination with other financial shenanigans. Critics complained that "Ma pardons criminals before they're indicted." In response to this perceived abuse of the governor's power, in 1936 the state adopted a constitutional amendment establishing the Board of Pardons and Paroles and severely limiting the governor's authority to pardon, especially in the area of prisoners condemned to die. Now, the only action the governor can take without the written recommendation of the board is to give a death row inmate one thirty-day reprieve.

★ ★ ★ ★ ★ ★ ★ ★ ★ ★ ★ ★ ★ ★ ★ ★ ★ ★ ★ ★ ★ ★ ★ ★ ★ ★ ★ ★ ★ ★

SOURCE: Dave McNeely, "What Bush Could and Couldn't Have Done," *Austin American-Statesman*, June 24, 2000, A15.

## CHIEF LEGISLATOR

Although the legislature tends to dominate Texas politics, the governor is a strong chief legislator who relies on three formal powers in carrying out this role: **message power, session power,** and **veto power.**

### MESSAGE POWER

The governor may give messages to the legislature at any time, but the constitution requires a gubernatorial message when legislative sessions open and when a governor retires. By statute, the governor must also deliver a biennial budget message. Other messages the governor may choose to send or deliver in person are often "emergency" messages when the legislature is in session; these messages are a formal means of expressing policy preferences. They also attract the attention of the media and set the agenda for state government. Coupled with able staff work, message power can be an effective and persuasive tool. In both 2003 and 2007, Governor Perry declared insurance rates and medical malpractice reform as emergency measures, an indication that he had not achieved his policy objectives. A governor also often delivers informal messages at meetings and social gatherings or through the media.

## SESSION POWER

As discussed in Chapter Six, the legislature is constitutionally forbidden to call itself into special session; only the governor may do so. Efforts to modify this power via constitutional amendment did not survive in the 2007 legislative session. Called sessions are limited to a maximum duration of thirty days, but a governor who wants to force consideration of an issue can continue calling one special session after another.

The governor also sets the agenda for these sessions, although the legislature, once called, may consider other matters on a limited basis, such as impeachment or approval of executive appointments. As the complexity of state government has grown, legislators sometimes have been unable to complete their work in the short biennial regular sessions. When they fail to complete enough of the agenda, they know they can expect a special session. However, any governor contemplating a special session must consider whether she or he has the votes lined up to accomplish the purpose of the session.

Special sessions offer a way around the restricted biennial legislative session of 140 days. The eight governors before Bush called a total of thirty-four special sessions. Bill Clements called six; Ann Richards called only two. Bush called none, a reflection on the one hand of his ability to get along with the legislative leadership and on the other hand of budget surpluses. Rick Perry, in part because of his party's dominance of state government, used the session power extensively, calling seven special sessions in the 2003–2006 time period, including three in 2003 to deal with congressional redistricting and government reorganization and four (2003, two in 2005, and 2006) to address the state's method of funding public schools.[17]

★ ★ ★ ★ ★ ★ ★ ★ ★ ★ ★ ★ ★ ★ ★ ★ ★ ★ ★ ★ ★ ★ ★ ★ ★ ★ ★ ★ ★ ★ ★ ★

### *The Veto Record Book*

Governor Rick Perry holds the record for the most bills vetoed in a single session—82—and for the most bills vetoed in the shortest time—132 in three years. Bill Clements holds the overall record for the most bills vetoed—190 in eight years. Perry is a Republican governor with a Republican legislature; thus, he vetoed the bills of his own party. He also used the veto to discipline wayward legislators—for example, his annulment of four noncontroversial bills sponsored by fellow Republican Charlie Geren, who failed to support his reorganization efforts. Clements was a Republican governor with a Democratic legislature who was trying to transform the state in terms of both policy and procedure.

★ ★ ★ ★ ★ ★ ★ ★ ★ ★ ★ ★ ★ ★ ★ ★ ★ ★ ★ ★ ★ ★ ★ ★ ★ ★ ★ ★ ★ ★ ★ ★

# VETO POWER

The governor's strongest legislative power is the veto. Every bill that passes both houses of the legislature in regular and special sessions is sent to the governor, who has the option of signing it, letting it become law without signing it, or vetoing it.[18] If the legislature is still in session, the governor has ten days—Sundays excluded—in which to act. If the bill is sent to the governor in the last ten days of a session or after the legislature has adjourned, the governor has twenty days—including Sundays—in which to act. If the governor vetoes a bill while the legislature is still in session, that body may override the veto by a two-thirds vote of both houses.

Because of the short legislative session, many important bills are often sent to the governor so late that the legislature has adjourned before the governor has had to act on them. In such instances, the veto power is absolute. The legislature cannot override if it is not in session, and consideration of the same bill cannot be carried over into the next session. Short biennial sessions thus make the governor's threat of a veto an extremely powerful political tool. Also, the override of a veto takes a two-thirds vote in both houses of the legislature, a majority that is not easy to get. As an indication of how rare an override is, thirty-eight years separated the last two: W. Lee O'Daniel had twelve vetoes overridden in 1939–1941, and Bill Clements had a veto of a local bill overridden in 1979.

The governor has one other check over appropriations bills: the item veto.[19] The governors in forty-three other states have a similar power. This device permits the governor to delete individual items from a bill without having to veto it in its entirety. The item veto may be used only to strike a particular line of funding, however; it cannot be used to reduce or increase an appropriation.

The item veto illustrates a reality of gubernatorial power in Texas. The governor's power over legislation is largely negative—he or she often finds it easier to say no than to get his or her own legislative agenda adopted. This truism particularly describes the budget process. Yet the timing of the appropriations act and the number of items that the legislature can cram into one line item are

Governor Rick Perry vetoed a record eighty-two bills passed by the legislature in 2001, including several important to his own Republican Party. In 2003, he vetoed 50, and in 2005, another 19. Results were pending for 2007 when this book went to press.

*Courtesy of Ben Sargent.*

factors that affect the governor's use of the item veto as a fiscal tool to control spending.[20]

The line-item veto power has been blunted somewhat since the first term of Bill Clements. Reacting to a Clements veto of special appropriations for higher education in 1983, the legislature passed lump-sum appropriations for each higher educational institution when Clements returned to office in 1987 to prevent use of the item veto on special line items. Clements still vetoed several other bills favoring higher education. The legislature has continued to pass lump-sum appropriations acts.

## COMMANDER IN CHIEF/TOP COP

The state of Texas does not independently engage in warfare with other nations and thus would seem to have no need for a commander in chief. However, the governor does have the power to declare martial law—that is, to suspend civil government temporarily and replace it with government by the state militia and/or law enforcement agencies. Although seldom used, this power was invoked to

★ ★ ★ ★ ★ ★ ★ ★ ★ ★ ★ ★ ★ ★ ★ ★ ★ ★ ★ ★ ★ ★ ★ ★ ★ ★ ★ ★

### *Ranger Bush*

Before George W. Bush ran for public office, he was the managing owner of the Texas Rangers baseball team. When he was sworn in as governor, he became the commander of the Texas Rangers state police force. He is thus the only human being in history to go from being the head of the Texas Rangers to being the head of the Texas Rangers.

★ ★ ★ ★ ★ ★ ★ ★ ★ ★ ★ ★ ★ ★ ★ ★ ★ ★ ★ ★ ★ ★ ★ ★ ★ ★ ★ ★

quell an oil field riot in East Texas in 1931 and to gain control of explosive racial situations in East Texas in 1919 and on the Gulf Coast in 1943.

Additionally, the governor is commander in chief of the military forces of the state (Army and Air National Guard), except when they have been called into service by the national government. The head of these forces, the adjutant general, is one of the governor's important appointees. The governor also has the power to assume command of the Texas Rangers and the Department of Public Safety to maintain law and order. These powers become important during disasters such as floods or tornadoes, when danger from the aftermath of the storm or from unscrupulous individuals such as looters may be present. In addition, following the national tragedy of terrorist attacks on the United States on September 11, 2001, the national government created a Department of Homeland Security and mandated security responsibilities for state and local governments in addition to their traditional function of disaster management. The Texas homeland security office, the Division of Emergency Management, reports to the governor, but is operationally attached to the Texas Department of Public Safety. Chapter Fifteen discusses the consequences and implications of the terrorist threat.

In routine situations, the governor is almost wholly dependent on local law enforcement and prosecuting agencies to see that the laws of the state are faith-

★ ★ ★ ★ ★ ★ ★ ★ ★ ★ ★ ★ ★ ★ ★ ★ ★ ★ ★ ★ ★ ★ ★ ★ ★ ★ ★

## *The Governor in Command*

Governor Mark White used the commander-in-chief powers in a controversial way in 1985. First, he authorized the state militia to participate in a military training exercise in Honduras, which borders on the politically volatile countries of Nicaragua and El Salvador. Then White joined the troops and oversaw the delivery of Texas barbecue to the militia over the Easter weekend—just as the legislature began to discuss the state budget.

In 1999–2000, Governor George Bush also used the commander-in-chief powers in an unusual way. In his bid for the Republican nomination for president, he traveled across the United States. During these campaign tours, he was protected by the Texas Department of Public Safety, which always guards the governor. Thus, for a change, a few state troopers and Texas Rangers got to see much of the country.

In 2005 Governor Rick Perry announced that Texas would need to guard its own borders because the federal government had failed to do so. He emphasized reducing crime along the Texas-Mexico border, training the National Guard to respond to emergencies, and generally relying on law enforcement for safety. Like President George Bush at the national level, he endorsed a sponsored immigrant worker program. In 2006 Perry used the commander-in-chief powers again to mobilize the evacuation of Texas coastal cities threatened by Hurricane Rita.

★ ★ ★ ★ ★ ★ ★ ★ ★ ★ ★ ★ ★ ★ ★ ★ ★ ★ ★ ★ ★ ★ ★ ★ ★ ★ ★

fully executed. When there is evidence of wrongdoing, the state's chief executive often brings the informal powers of the gubernatorial office to bear on the protection problem, appealing to the media to focus public attention on errant agencies and officeholders. Such was the case in 1992, when Governor Richards received considerable media coverage for joining nursing home inspectors in on-site visits to both poorly run and well-run nursing homes.

## CHIEF OF STATE

Pomp and circumstance are a part of being the top elected official of the state. Just as presidents use their ceremonial role to augment other roles, so also do governors. Whether cutting a ribbon to open a new highway, leading a parade, or serving as host to a visiting dignitary, the governor's performance as chief of state yields visibility and the appearance of leadership, which enhance the more important executive and legislative roles of the office. In the modern era, the governor is often the chief television personality of the state and sets the policy agenda through publicity. Ann Richards, for example, was a national TV celebrity, sometimes more popular outside the state than inside. George Bush was a presidential candidate and in demand outside the state, too.

More and more, Texas governors are using the ceremonial role of chief of state, sometimes coupled with the role of chief intergovernmental diplomat, to become actively involved in economic negotiations such as plant locations. Efforts are directed toward both foreign and domestic investments and finding new markets for Texas goods. In such negotiations, the governor uses the power and prestige of the office to become the state's salesperson. Mark White and Bill

Clements both made significant use of this role to attract businesses to the state, and Rick Perry traveled from Austin to New York to Italy touting the benefits of business relocation to Texas. Ann Richards strongly pushed for U.S. Senate approval of the North American Free Trade Agreement (NAFTA) because of the likelihood of expanded Texas–Mexico trade.

A savvy governor uses the chief of state role to maximize publicity for himself and his program. Because Texas is the second largest state in the country, the actions of the Texas governor often make national as well as state headlines.

## CHIEF INTERGOVERNMENTAL DIPLOMAT

The Texas Constitution provides that the governor, or someone designated by the governor, will be the state's representative in all dealings with other states and with the national government. This role of intergovernmental representative has increased in importance for three reasons. First, federal statutes now designate the governor as the official who has the planning and grant-approval authority for the state. This designation has given the governor's budgeting, planning, and supervising powers much more clout in recent years, and federal budget philosophy (see Chapter 13) further enhances the governor's role.

Second, some state problems, such as water and energy development, often require the cooperation of several states. For example, in 1981–1982, Governor Clements and five other governors tried to plan solutions for the water problems of the High Plains area. Additionally, although the U.S. Constitution precludes a governor from conducting diplomatic relations with other nations, Texas's location as a border state gives rise to occasional social and economic exchanges with the governors of Mexican border states on matters such as immigration and energy. The box earlier in this chapter outlines the aggressive international role of the two largest American states, California and Texas.

Third, acquiring federal funds is always important because they relieve the pressure on state and local government revenue sources. Often, the governor works in concert with other governors to try to secure favorable national legislation, including both funding and limits on unfunded federal mandates (see Chapter 12). Thus, the governor is an active member of the National Governors Association and a participant in the National Governors Conference. He or she also is active in regional and political party groups. Texas governors, like their counterparts in other states, are proactive representatives.

A more traditional use of the governor's intergovernmental role is mandated by Article IV of the U.S. Constitution, which provides for the rendition (surrender) of fugitives from justice who flee across state lines. The Texas governor, like other governors, signs the rendition papers and transmits them to the appropriate law enforcement officials. Law officers are then in charge of picking up the fugitives and returning them to the appropriate state.

# Informal Roles and Limitations

In addition to the five "hats" just described, there are at least two others that the governor must wear. They have no basis in law, but they are nevertheless important to the job. The degree of success with which the governor handles these informal roles can greatly affect the execution of the formal roles.

## YOU DECIDE

### Does the Texas Governor Need More Power?

The powers of the Texas governor used to be ranked almost at the bottom of gubernatorial powers in the fifty American states. More recently, the Texas governor's institutional powers—those established by constitution and statute—rank just about in the middle. Indeed, the powers of the governor of California are considered less than those of the Texas governor, although the New York governor has greater power. Thus, even among the very largest states, Texas stands in the middle.

| PRO | CON |
|---|---|
| Texas should, by statute or constitutional amendment, increase the power of the governor because: | Texas should not, by statute or constitutional amendment, increase the power of the governor because: |
| ▲ Bureaucrats have far too much discretion to act when there is no clear executive authority. | ▼ The personal power of the governor—based on margin of electoral victory and personal persuasion—is already great. |
| ▲ The public is confused by the number of elected officials in Texas (the long ballot). | ▼ The veto power is virtually absolute. |
| ▲ Texas needs someone with greater authority to show mercy to convicted felons facing the death penalty. | ▼ Dispersion of power is a good way to keep one person from gaining too much control. |
| ▲ A governor needs to be able to control all boards and commissions soon after election to implement policies he or she favors. | ▼ The governor's clout is obvious when one considers the salary, the size of the staff, and the lack of effort over the years to remove the governor from office. |
| ▲ A more powerful governor would mean that the legislature's power could be reduced. | ▼ Democracy is better served when the legislature is the more powerful institution because the people are closer to their elected representatives than to the governor. |
| ▲ Texas needs its governor to have meaningful budget authority. | ▼ The dual budgeting system encourages Fiscal control. |

# CHIEF OF PARTY

As the symbolic head of the Democratic or Republican Party in the state, the governor is a key figure at the state party conventions and usually is the leader of the party's delegation to national conventions. A governor may, however, have to compete with his or her party's U.S. senator. Governors are able to use their influence with the party's state executive committee and at party conventions to gain a subsidiary influence over candidates seeking other state offices. An active, skilled governor can thus create a power relationship with state legislators and bureaucrats that the more formal roles of the office do not permit. The governor also wins some political influence by campaigning for other party candidates who are seeking state or national offices.

Governor Bill Clements, the first modern Republican governor of Texas, used the party role extensively to extend Republican influence through the appointment power. He appointed enough Democrats to maintain the goodwill of the majority leadership at the time. Governor Ann Richards made key executive and judicial appointments from her Democratic Party colleagues, but worked with the minority party on other issues. For example, she showed some willingness to deal with the Republicans on redistricting in exchange for GOP support for legislation, such as a state lottery, that she and the Democrats wanted.

One of the most interesting contrasts is that between the state's two most recent Republican governors. In 1995, George Bush operated on a nonpartisan basis and secured the support of both members and leaders of the Democratic majority legislature for his legislative program. He also made his own Republican Party angry by cooperating with the Democrats and by having a moderate position on a number of issues. For example, Governor Bush and Speaker of the House Pete Laney worked especially well together, and Bush told the state party bigwigs to back off from trying to defeat Laney in his 1996 reelection bid. He also battled the party establishment to insist on the inclusion of Senator Kay Bailey Hutchison in the delegation to the presidential nominating convention in 1996 (social conservatives wanted to exclude her because of her moderate position on the abortion issue). In 1997, he fared somewhat less well with the legislature even though the Senate had become Republican, in part because of resistance to his tax plan by conservative members of the GOP. He had also become staunch friends with Democratic Lieutenant Governor Bob Bullock. By the time the delegation was formed for the 2000 national convention, Bush was the assured presidential nominee of the party. Even with the obvious presidential bid, Bush continued to work well with Democrats, who realized the advantages that having a Texas president could bring.

Rick Perry's approach was more combative, both with members of his own party and with the state's Democrats. In 2001, the legislature was split between a Republican Senate and a Democratic House, and Perry had come to office by succession when Bush ran for president. Perry was not a significant factor in the legislative session until he angered his GOP colleagues by vetoing some of their pet bills after the session had ended. In 2003, Perry was emboldened by having been elected to office and by the Republican control of all branches of government.

He took a particularly partisan approach by forcing congressional redistricting and continued to demonstrate that Republicans were sparring among themselves, especially when he led the attack on the comptroller to reduce her power—and thus her possible vantage point as a contender against him in 2006.

Reelected by a plurality of less than 40 percent in 2006, Perry stormed into the 2007 legislative session with policy positions at variance not only from those of Democrats but also his fellow Republicans (see Table 8.4).

## LEADER OF THE PEOPLE

Most Texans, unaware of the limitations on formal gubernatorial powers, look to the chief executive of the state for the leadership necessary to solve the state's problems and to serve as their principal spokesperson on major issues. A skilled governor can turn this role to substantial advantage when bargaining with other key figures in the policymaking process, such as the presiding officers, legislators, and top bureaucrats in the state's administration. For example, through the media, the governor can rally public support for programs and policies. Choosing to accept invitations to speak is another way a governor can gain public exposure and thus support for programs and plans, including the budget. Public appearances usually serve as occasions for emphasizing gubernatorial accomplishments. They also allow a governor to show concern for ordinary citizens with extraordinary problems, such as visits to areas damaged by tornadoes or floods. In keeping with the traditionalistic tenor of the state, some governors use this role to show that they are "active conservatives." Coupled with the strong legislative role, this informal role is critical to a governor's success. Leadership has been depicted as consisting of two parts: the ability to "transact" (that is, to make things happen) and the ability to "transform" (that is, to decide what things should happen).[21] The successful Texas governor is one who can both make things happen and decide what policies ought to happen.

A populist approach is consistent with the values of democracy. So also is a more conservative approach that addresses issues that the public reiterates with each opinion poll. Thus, although they held different positions—except that both wanted to improve public education—and used different styles, Ann Richards and George Bush both demonstrated leadership, which is extremely important in a plural executive system. Perry has pushed to strengthen the office of governor while at the same time limiting the powers of government in general; thus, his leadership skills seem more dedicated to a personal agenda than to a public one.[22]

## Summary

The governor of Texas shares many of the characteristics attributed to members of the legislature in Chapter Six. Generally, the governor is a conservative White male attorney or businessman. Since 1974, the Texas governor has had the advantage of a four-year term and is paid fairly well. Nevertheless, the office is constitutionally weak, and the approval and successful implementation of gubernatorial budgetary and programmatic policies depend more on the governor's adroitness in developing leadership skills than on formal powers. Some movement toward increasing gubernatorial powers by legislative action has taken place in recent years.

The Texas governor has many important functions to perform, which are embodied in the various roles that make up the office of chief executive for the state. These roles, however, are restricted in the following major ways:

1. There are five other elected executives, an elected state policy board, and an elected regulatory commission. Thus, the state has a plural executive.

2. The state bureaucracy is largely controlled by multimember boards and commissions, with the result that the state administration is fragmented.

3. Senatorial confirmation of appointees requires a two-thirds vote.

4. The governor's power to remove appointed officials other than personal staff is still restricted in spite of recent statutory increases in the removal power.

5. The state has both a legislative and an executive budget.

On the other hand, the governor does have some constitutional and statutory strengths, and gubernatorial powers have increased substantially with the New Federalism concept of federal funding for state programs and the subsequent prominence of the governor's role in planning and interstate problem solving. The major strengths of the governor's office are the following:

1. Effective control over regional planning and federal grant applications

2. An item veto over appropriations and a general veto over legislation that, because of timing, is often absolute

3. Command over the militia and law enforcement agencies in time of crisis

4. Party, personal, and ceremonial leadership opportunities

5. Control over the presiding officers of appointed boards and commissions

The description of state bureaucracy in the next chapter should help the reader gain a greater understanding of the governor's difficulties when trying to control state agencies.

## Glossary Terms

appointment and removal

impeachment

message power

plural executive

populist

session power

veto power

## Study Questions

1. What are the formal qualifications to be governor of Texas? What personal characteristics do governors tend to have? Which of the personal characteristics do you think is most likely to change and why?

2. What powers does the governor have in the chief executive's role? What are the limitations?

3. Why do you think many analysts regard the role of chief legislator as the governor's most significant role?

4. What formal roles other than chief executive and chief legislator does the governor perform? What does the governor do in these other roles? Which one(s) do you see as growing most in importance?

5. What informal roles are played by the governor? How do these roles help the governor perform his or her formal roles?

6. From your reading of this chapter, how important do you think the personality and "style" of a governor are? Why?

7. Do you think Texas should have a cabinet system such as exists in the national government? Why or why not?

8. Would you like to work in the governor's office? In which part? What specifically would you like to do?

## Surfing the Web

Readers are urged to visit the companion site for this book:

**http://academic.cengage.com/polsci/Kraemer/TexasPolitics10e**

# The Administrative State

Solicitor General Ted Cruz and Attorney General Greg Abbott are shown en route to a federal court hearing on the Texas congressional redistricting plan.

> Many people consider the things which government does for them to be social progress, but they consider the things government does for others to be socialism.
>
> EARL WARREN, CHIEF JUSTICE OF THE UNITED STATES, 1953–1969

> The public's right to know is essential to accountability in government. We have the right to know what occurs in government meetings and what is contained in public records.
>
> INTRODUCTION TO THE OPEN MEETINGS ACT TRAINING VIDEO. TEXAS ATTORNEY GENERAL'S OFFICE, 2006

# Introduction

Few of us need an introduction to the administrative state because public administration is part of our daily lives. Traffic police, public school principals, highway workers, college registrars, clerks in state and federal offices—we all have seen, or been involved with, public employees who apply and enforce public policy.

All of us have also heard considerable criticism of government policies and administration. Earl Warren's observation in the opening quote summarizes the dilemma of democratic government. As citizens seek more programs, any given individual's preferred program is social progress, but a contrary preference by someone else is suspect. Given the conservative mood of the United States during the last years of the twentieth century and the early years of the twenty-first, calling attention to this dilemma is particularly appropriate. We simultaneously want less government but more programs that benefit us.

The political culture of a state directly affects what government programs the state provides. In states with a moralistic culture, greater emphasis is placed on programs for the common good such as environmental protection, education, and social services. In states such as Texas, with a heritage of individualistic-traditionalistic political culture, policymakers focus more on cost avoidance and its corollary, tax cutting, and on providing a business environment with minimum regulations and impediments. In turn, the state administration reflects those policy preferences.

This chapter begins with a description of the state administrative agencies. To help the reader gain a clearer understanding of the complexities of modern **bureaucracy** and how our state public administration works, this chapter then discusses why and how "big government"—the administrative state—became so big. Bureaucracy is a type of organization associated with red tape, specialization, and **hierarchy**. Hierarchy refers to an arrangement that puts few people but maximum power at the top of the organization, and many people with little power at the bottom of the organization. Finally, the chapter examines efforts to control the bureaucracy and ensure that it performs as the public and elected officials intend.

A few definitions are in order at the outset. *Public policy* is the strategy or philosophy behind individual government decisions. These decisions come to us in forms such as laws, judicial rulings, and federal and state programs. Public policies are carried out, or implemented, by public administrators. Legislators determine what is to be done in general. Bureaucrats determine what is to be done specifically because it is their job to *implement* policy—that is, to translate policy into action. Thus, some bureaucratic decisions are in themselves operational public policy—for example, determining the student activities fee on a campus in pursuit of a broader statewide policy that those who benefit from higher education should have a substantial role in paying for it. Policy is not always implemented successfully. For example, Texas state government coupled with local school districts run a large establishment, the purpose of which is to educate young people; yet, tests show that many of the state's young people never learn to read above a very rudimentary level.

*Public administration* has several different but related meanings. It refers not only to the activities necessary to carry out public policy but also to the various agencies, boards, commissions, bureaus, and departments that are responsible for these activities and collectively to the employees who work in the various agencies. The term *agency* itself refers to any department, agency, commission, board, bureau, or other public administrative organization. Both *administrator* and *executive* refer to top-level individuals in public administration. Any state employee may be a *bureaucrat*, but the term most commonly is limited to administrators, executives, and lower echelon white-collar office employees who are appointed politically or, especially, selected because of some test of their merit. Members of the traditional professions and also of the professions peculiar to government are more usually referred to by their professional titles, such as teacher, nurse, attorney, or game warden.

Implementing or executing the law is formally the responsibility of the executive branch of government; thus, the bureaucracy is nominally headed by the chief executive—in Texas, the governor. This chapter shows, however, that the bureaucracy permeates all branches and that its interests and powers crisscross the entire fabric of governmental structure. Furthermore, as the previous chapter demonstrated, the governor is a constitutionally weak chief executive who lacks the full set of tools required to control the bureaucracy in spite of significant recent increases in statutory power. In fact, many politicians and political scientists consider the administrative state so powerful as to constitute a fourth branch of government.

Woven throughout this chapter is a concern for the democratic legitimacy of the administrative state. In a democracy, the participation of the citizens legitimates government action. However, administrators, or "bureaucrats" as they are frequently called, are not elected. Often, they cannot be removed by the governor, who is, of course, elected by the people. Yet they often wield great power in Texas politics. What can justify such power?

# State Administrative Agencies

Although we must concede that a state bureaucracy is necessary to carry out government policy, we might be happier if the Texas administration were easier to understand. Even for the experienced observer, state administration in Texas is confusing; for the novice, it is perplexing indeed. Three essential characteristics of the state administration cause this confusion.

1. No single, uniform organizational pattern exists.

2. Texas administration features numerous exceptions to the traditional bureaucratic characteristic of hierarchy.

3. The number of state agencies depends on one's method of counting.

There are at least five different types of top policymakers in state agencies: (1) elected executives, (2) appointed executives, (3) an elected commission and an elected board, (4) ex officio boards and commissions, and (5) appointed boards and commissions (see Table 9-1). Agencies headed by an elected or appointed executive follow traditional hierarchical principles in that a single individual clearly is the "boss" and thus is ultimately responsible for the operation of a particular department or office. But the agencies that are headed by a multimember board or commission have three or six or even nineteen bosses—whatever the number of members on the board. Although there also is a hierarchical organization in these agencies, it begins with the professional staff of the agency, the level below that of the policy-setting board.

Another complication is that one office, board, or commission may be responsible for the general policies of a number of separate agencies. For example, the Board of Regents of the University of Texas is the policymaking board for the entire University of Texas System, which includes fifteen agencies that are separately funded. As of fiscal years 2006–2007, at least 231 agencies, institutions, and independent programs are funded by general appropriations.[1] This list is not all inclusive, however, because not all agencies appear in the state budget.

For example, the fifty community college systems are listed as a single entity but not as individual systems or campuses. A rough count of just the budgeted policymaking boards, commissions, departments, and offices—excluding the courts and related agencies, the legislature and its staff agencies, and the offices of elected executives—yields a count of about 110 agencies. Community/junior colleges are excluded from this number because they have locally appointed boards.

Perhaps the reader is beginning to see why the number of state agencies is usually expressed in approximate terms. In the space allotted here, there is no way to name, much less describe, even those agencies with which the authors are very familiar. A few of the most important state agencies are used to illustrate the various bureaucratic arrangements in the state.

## AGENCIES WITH ELECTED EXECUTIVES

Five state officials, in addition to the governor, are elected on partisan ballots for four-year terms. They are, in theory at least, directly accountable to the citizenry for their performance and their integrity in office. One of these, the lieutenant

## TABLE 9-1
## Types of Administrative Agencies in Texas

| Agencies Headed by Elected Executives |
| --- |
| Office of the Attorney General |
| Department of Agriculture |
| Office of the Comptroller of Public Accounts |
| General Land Office |
| **Agencies Headed by Appointed Executives** |
| Office of the Secretary of State |
| Health and Human Services Commission |
| **Multimember Boards and Commissions** |
| Elected Board and Commission |
| • State Board of Education |
| • Texas Railroad Commission |
| Ex Officio Board |
| • Bond Review Board |
| Appointed Boards and Commissions |
| • Texas Higher Education Coordinating Board |
| • Public Utility Commission |

governor, David Dewhurst, who was profiled in Chapter Six, presides over the Texas Senate and does not head any executive office. The lieutenant governor performs as an executive only when the governor is away from the state or upon succession to the governorship. The other four are department heads. The incumbents named here were those elected in 2006 to serve until 2010.

## ATTORNEY GENERAL

Along with the governor, the lieutenant governor, and the speaker of the House, the attorney general is one of the most powerful officers in Texas government. Although candidates for the position often run on an anticrime platform, the work of the office is primarily civil. As the attorney for the state, the attorney general and staff represent the state and its agencies in court when the state is a party to a case. The Office of the Attorney General also is responsible for such varied legal matters as consumer protection, antitrust litigation, workers' compensation insurance, organized-crime control, and environmental protection.

The attorney general's greatest power, however, is that of issuing opinions on questions concerning the constitutionality or legality of existing or proposed legislation and administrative actions. These opinions are not legally binding, but they are rarely challenged in court and thus effectively have the same importance as a ruling by the state's Supreme Court. Because the attorney general's opinions often make the headlines, and because the attorney general works with all state agencies, the office is second only to the governor's office in the public recognition it receives. Because the position is regarded as one of the stepping-stones to the governor's office, attorneys general often encourage publicity about themselves, their agency, and their support groups with an eye to possible future election campaigns. Republican Greg Abbott, a former Texas Supreme Court justice, was first elected in 2002, stressing his philosophy of political restraint. He demonstrated the influence of his office in 2007 when he honored the request of legislators to rule on the governor's use of the executive order, saying that such orders were advisory not mandatory.

Elected Bureaucrats in 2007: Comptroller of Public Accounts Susan Combs presents her revenue estimates to the legislature.

## COMPTROLLER OF PUBLIC ACCOUNTS

The comptroller (pronounced con-TROL-ler) is responsible for the administration of the state tax system and for performing preaudits of expenditures by state agencies. In addition, as part of the budget process, the comptroller certifies to the legislature the approximate biennial income for the state. The Texas Constitution precludes the legislature from appropriating more funds than are anticipated in state revenues for any biennial period. Texas, like most other states, must have a balanced budget. Since the phase-out of the treasurer's office in 1996, the comptroller is also the state's banker. As such, the comptroller is the custodian of all public monies and of the securities that the state invests in or holds in trust. The comptroller's office also issues the excise tax stamps used to indicate the collection of taxes on the sale of alcoholic beverages and cigarettes in the state. In short, the comptroller takes in the state's revenues, safeguards them, and invests them. The merger of the comptroller's and the treasurer's offices made the comptroller's position even more powerful than it already was.

Susan Combs, who previously served as commissioner of agriculture, was elected as comptroller in 2006. One of the hallmarks of her campaign was transparency in government; she immediately

APPARENTLY, THE BOYS HAD NEVER HEARD THE OLD TEXAS EXPRESSION: "IF MAMA AIN'T HAPPY, AIN'T NOBODY HAPPY..."

Angry at Comptroller Carole Keeton Strayhorn's original budget estimates and then at her railing at the governor and the legislature for failing to take care of children's healthcare needs in 2003, Rick Perry and the Seventy-eighth Legislature stripped her office of a number of powers. Strayhorn was being whispered as a possible rival to Perry in the next Republican gubernatorial primary. She subsequently ran as an Independent and lost.

*Courtesy of Ben Sargent.*

began to post the expenditures of state agencies on her Web site to keep the public informed. Combs had the luxury of certifying $14.3 billion in available revenue beyond the previous budget to the legislature for 2008–2009, but took office with somewhat reduced powers. Carole Keeton Strayhorn, the previous comptroller who resigned to run as an independent candidate for governor, had angered Governor Rick Perry and his supporters, who reduced the role of the office in performance reviews.

## COMMISSIONER OF THE GENERAL LAND OFFICE

Only Texas and Alaska entered the Union with large amounts of public lands, and only they have land offices. About 22.5 million Texas acres are administered by the commissioner of the General Land Office. This acreage includes 4 million acres of bays, inlets, and other submerged land from the shoreline to the three-league marine limit (10.36 miles out). The land commissioner's land-management responsibilities include

1. Supervising the leasing of all state-owned lands for such purposes as oil and gas production, mineral development, and grazing (over 14,000 leases)

2. Administering the veterans' land program, by which veterans may buy land with loans that are backed by state bonds

3. Maintaining the environmental quality of public lands and waters, especially coastal lands

Republican Jerry Patterson was first elected as commissioner in 1998 and reelected in 2002 and 2006. Like all land commissioners, he must try to balance environmental interests with land and mineral interests. Patterson is a former state senator.

## COMMISSIONER OF AGRICULTURE

Farming and ranching are still important industries in the state, even though only about 1 percent of the population is engaged in agriculture. The Texas Department of Agriculture, like its national counterpart, is responsible both for the regulation and promotion (through research and education) of the agribusiness industry and for consumer protection, even though these functions may sometimes be in conflict. Departmental activities are diverse—for example, enforcing weights and measures standards, licensing egg handlers, determining the relative safety of pesticides, and locating export markets for Texas agricultural products. Pesticides illustrate the conflicting nature of the roles assigned to this office: Requiring that pesticides be safe for workers, consumers, and the environment may be detrimental to the profits of farmers.

Election to this office is specified by statute rather than by the state constitution. Republican Todd Staples, whose experience cuts across many functions of the department he now heads, has been a cattleman, owned a plant and landscape business, owned a real estate company, and served three terms as a state representative. He was elected as commissioner for the first time in 2006.

★ ★ ★ ★ ★ ★ ★ ★ ★ ★ ★ ★ ★ ★ ★ ★ ★ ★ ★ ★ ★ ★ ★ ★ ★ ★ ★ ★ ★

### *E-Snail*

Trying to make state government accessible electronically has proved daunting. While both elected officials and administrative agencies have Web sites with links to many types of information, getting the state ready to "do business" on the Web has been a slower process. Three priorities are

- the issuance of driver's licenses—temporarily limited by the need for such information as eye tests

- filing of taxes—limited by security concerns and small-business owner reluctance

- public assistance—limited by the fact that most welfare families are not part of the computer society

★ ★ ★ ★ ★ ★ ★ ★ ★ ★ ★ ★ ★ ★ ★ ★ ★ ★ ★ ★ ★ ★ ★ ★ ★ ★ ★ ★ ★

SOURCE: "Government of the Future," *Wall Street Journal*, January 5, 2000, T1.

## AGENCIES WITH APPOINTED EXECUTIVES

One example of an agency headed by an appointed executive is the Office of the Secretary of State. The state constitution stipulates that the governor shall appoint the secretary of state, whose functions include safeguarding the great seal

Elected Bureaucrats in 2007: Commissioner of Agriculture Todd Staples takes a strong stance against watered gas.

of the state of Texas and affixing it to the governor's signature on proclamations, commissions, and certificates. In addition to this somewhat ceremonial duty, the duties of the secretary include certifying elections (verifying the validity of the returns), maintaining records on campaign expenditures, keeping the list of lobbyists who register with the state, administering the Uniform Commercial Code, issuing corporate charters, and publishing the Texas Register—the official record of administrative decisions, rules, regulations, and announcements of hearings and pending actions. The newest duty of the secretary is to serve as the state's international protocol officer. Governor Rick Perry appointed his deputy chief of staff, Phil Wilson, to the office in 2007. Wilson had been the leader of the governor's economic development efforts. The secretary of state's office, though appointive, can sometimes be a springboard to elective office. Former Lieutenant Governor Bob Bullock and former Governor Mark White both held the position, as did former Comptroller John Sharp and former Mayor Ron Kirk of Dallas. Antonio (Tony) Garza, the George Bush secretary of state from 1995 through most of 1997, continued in their footsteps by being elected to the Texas Railroad Commission in 1998; President Bush then appointed him as ambassador to Mexico in 2002.

## BOARDS AND COMMISSIONS

Multimember boards or commissions head most state administrative agencies and make overall policy for them. These boards appoint chief administrators to handle the day-to-day responsibilities of the agencies, including the budget, personnel, and the administration of state laws and those federal laws that are carried out through state governments. Two of these boards and commissions have elected members. The others have appointed or ex officio members.

# ELECTED BOARD AND COMMISSION

As previously mentioned, the Texas Railroad Commission (TRC) is one of the most influential agencies in the state, and its three members are powerful indeed. The commission has tremendous political clout in the state because of its regulation of all mining and extractive industries, including oil, gas, coal, and uranium. Of growing importance is its control of intrastate road transportation—buses, moving vans, and trucks, including tow trucks—because of the importance of trucking rates to economic development. (Trucking is the number one method by which goods are conveyed to market.) The TRC also regulates intrastate railroads. Its members are chosen in statewide elections for staggered six-year terms. In 1995, the TRC became all Republican for the first time and has remained so. The commissioners are Elizabeth Jones, Michael Williams, and Victor Carrillo. Williams is the first African American to hold a statewide nonjudicial position; Governor Bush appointed him to fill out Carole Keeton Strayhorn's term when she became comptroller, and he was elected in 2002 for a six-year term. Carrillo is the third Mexican American to serve on the TRC. Originally appointed in 2003 to fill the term of Tony Garza when he was named an ambassador, Carrillo was elected to a full term in 2004. Jones, a three-term legislator, was appointed by Governor Perry in 2005 to fill the unexpired term of Charles Matthews when he was named chancellor of the Texas State University System, and was elected in her own right in 2006.

The fifteen-member State Board of Education was originally created as an elected body. As part of the public school reforms of 1984, it was made an appointive board. In 1987, the voters overwhelmingly approved returning it to elective status. Its fifteen members are chosen by the voters from districts across the state. A majority of the board's members are conservative Republicans, a

Elected Bureaucrats in 2007: Michael Williams, the senior member of the Texas Railroad Commission, advocates tax credits for oil exploration.

The State Board of Education, which oversees the Texas public schools, is an elected board that is well known for controversies arising over textbook selections. Science and history textbooks are particularly liable to argument.

*Courtesy of Ben Sargent.*

fact that has reintroduced a longstanding controversy about the board's selection of textbooks for public schools.

## EX OFFICIO BOARDS AND COMMISSIONS

There are many boards in the state administration whose members are all ex officio; that is, they are members because of another office they hold in the administration. When these boards were created, two purposes were served by ex officio memberships: The members usually were already in Austin (no small matter in pre-freeway days), and they were assumed to have some expertise in the subject at hand. An example is the Bond Review Board, which includes the governor, lieutenant governor, comptroller, and speaker of the House and ensures that debt financing is used prudently by the state.

## APPOINTED BOARDS AND COMMISSIONS

Administration of most of the state's laws is carried out by boards and commissions whose members are appointed rather than elected and by the administrators the boards then appoint. The members of many boards are appointed by the governor, but some other boards have a combination of gubernatorial appointees, appointees of other state officials, and/or ex officio members. These boards vary in size and, as a rule, have general policy authority for their agencies. Members serve six-year overlapping terms without pay.

There are three broad categories of appointed boards and commissions: (1) health, welfare, and rehabilitation; (2) education; and (3) general executive and administrative departments. Examples of each category are (1) the Health and Human Services Council, (2) the Texas Higher Education Coordinating Board, and (3) the Parks and Wildlife Department and the Public Utility Commission, respectively.

## APPOINTED BOARDS AND CITIZENS

**The Case of the Public Utility Commission** How do the 110 or so policymaking boards affect the ordinary citizen? One example is the Public Utility Commission of Texas (PUC), which fosters competition and promotes a utility *infrastructure* (the basic physical structure for delivery of public utilities such as pipelines, cables, and transformers). PUC has been very busy since the legislature deregulated the electric industry in 1999, both overseeing procedures for deregulation and trying to ensure the availability of adequate and reliable electric power. A second focus is overseeing the telecommunications industry. Any Texas citizen can contact PUC's Office of Customer Protection to complain about unreliable electric or telecommunications service or seeming misdeeds on the part of providers of those utilities. For example, if a Texas college student has been "slammed" (had her telephone service switched without authorization from one carrier to the next), "crammed" (had unauthorized charges on his telephone bill), or is unable to resolve a dispute with the manager of an apartment complex due to the submetering of electric service, the PUC represents a possible solution to the problem.

**The Case of the College Governing Board** Whether one is in a public community college, a private university, or a public university, that institution has a board of trustees or a board of regents. These board members set policy for the college and appoint the president. In the case of a university system, such as University of Texas or Texas A&M, the board is responsible for all institutions in the system. At a typical board of regents meeting, the board members (1) renewed the president's contract, (2) approved a resolution increasing the amount of local tuition, (3) granted tenure to twenty faculty members, (4) approved the hiring of a new liberal arts dean, and (5) approved a contract for construction of additional classrooms in the environmental sciences building. Each of these actions affected students—directly in the case of tuition increases and classroom space and indirectly in the case of the three types of personnel actions.

**The Case of the Parks and Wildlife Board** If a person is "outdoorsy" and likes to camp, fish, or hunt, the annual decisions of the Parks and Wildlife Board (TPW) on what fees will be levied for each of these activities are of interest. Texas traditionally has had very low parks and wildlife fees compared with other states. If that fishing license suddenly costs $100 instead of $28, the outdoors person might have second thoughts about this form of recreation. Sports people also are affected by decisions of this board as to what type of fish it will release into the lakes of the state and how well state and sometimes local parks are managed. (TPW often operates local parks such as a lakeside recreational area by agreement with the local government.) TPW became very controversial in 2006–2007 when the sorry state of most state parks became frequent topics in the media; both underfunding and poor spending habits had led to the decline of the parks system.

# Big Government: How Did It Happen?

Our country changed from an individualistic society that depended on government for very little to an urban, interdependent nation supporting a massive governmental structure. How did this change come about? And why?

The many, and complex, answers to these questions involve the Industrial Revolution, the mechanization of farms and ranches, and the technological revolution. These changes in turn led to urbanization. When workers followed job opportunities from farms to factories, much of the nation's population shifted from rural to urban areas. The American business philosophy was *pseudo laissez faire*—that is, commerce and industry should be allowed to develop without government restraint but with governmental aid, and government's responsibility for the well-being of its citizens was minimal. The American social philosophy was social Darwinism, which holds that the poor are poor because they are "supposed" to be that way due to their "naturally" inferior abilities and that the rich are rich due to their "naturally" superior abilities. American barons of industry—individuals earlier in our history and now usually corporate owners—grew rich and powerful, controlling not only the economy but also the politics of the nation.

Eventually, the conditions resulting from these two philosophies, principally an unpredictable boom-and-bust economy and widespread poverty, caused a number of political developments. The expansion of voting rights, big-city ward politics, and a Populist movement that insisted on protection for workers and farmers are only a few examples. The outcry against the economic conditions brought about by pseudo laissez faire finally became so great that the national government stepped in to curb the worst excesses of big business and to attempt to protect citizens who could not protect themselves. For example, the railroads so controlled state legislatures in the last quarter of the nineteenth century that state governments were powerless to protect their citizens. The Interstate Commerce Commission (ICC) was created in 1887 to regulate the railroads, which had been pricing small farmers out of business by charging exorbitant freight rates.

The creation of the ICC illustrates the beginning of an activist national government. During the thirty years just before and just after the turn of the twentieth century, the focus was on regulation of the economy. The second growth thrust came in response to the Great Depression of the 1930s, with the expansion of both government services and the administration necessary to implement them. For example, the Social Security, farm price support, and rural electrification programs all began in the 1930s. This expansion represented a major shift in political ideology from a conservatism that held, in the words attributed to Thomas Jefferson, that "that government is best which governs the least, because its people discipline themselves," to a liberalism that held government intervention to be the best route to the betterment of the individual.

## POSTWAR GROWTH

After World War II, government continued to expand in scope. There were social concerns such as civil rights, newly recognized industrial problems such as environmental pollution, and technologies such as nuclear power, all requiring oversight. The federal government not only entered areas that traditionally had been left to state and local governments—education and healthcare, for example—but also fostered social change through such policies as equal opportunity and affirmative-action employment. By channeling funds for new programs at the state and local levels through state agencies, the federal government has served as the major catalyst for the increased role of the public sector.

The scope of government grew for two basic reasons. First, once politics ceased to be solely the domain of the social and political elite, newly enfranchised and politically active citizens demanded government intervention to improve the quality of their lives. The elderly wanted security when they retired from the workforce. Veterans returning from World War II wanted an education and jobs. Minority groups wanted better housing, economic opportunity, and political rights. In an urbanized, interdependent society, neither the church and charities nor individuals themselves could provide a better quality of life. Only government, with its resources and its power, could do so.

Second, the complex society created a need for governmental expansion. How could the private sector deal with chemical wastes that forced the closing of a whole town or with the Three Mile Island nuclear accident? How could individuals or businesses cope with unemployment created by complicated forces such as spiraling production costs, interest rates, and world oil markets? How could private citizens and business corporations tackle issues such as immigration, right to life/abortion, or the chronic cycle of poor education/limited job

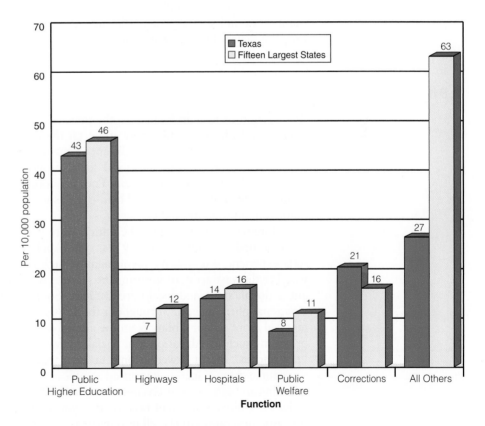

**FIGURE 9-1 State Employment in Texas and Fifteen Largest States, per 10,000 Population, by Function**

SOURCE: Fiscal Size-Up, 2006–2007 Biennium (*Austin: Legislative Budget Board, 2005*), 49.

possibilities/poverty? Modern issues simply transcend both private-sector and limited-government solutions.

The national government continued to expand its programs and their associated costs throughout the 1970s. State and local governments grew rapidly to take advantage of available federal dollars for new programs, to respond to mandatory federal initiatives, to promote economic expansion, and to develop new programs and services brought about by citizens' demands for an improvement in the quality of life. Each new service increased the number of people necessary to keep the wheels of government turning. In a state such as Texas, with a high population growth rate, it is inevitable that the combination of more programs and increased population would cause an increase in the size and scope of state and local governments. Figure 9-1 shows the largest program areas in Texas as compared with all of the fifteen most populous states. Texas has fewer employees per 10,000 population than the other states except in the category of corrections.

Because these numbers already take into account the difference in population among the states, one is left to conclude that either Texas has proportionately more criminals than other states or more of a lock-'em-up attitude. The following two chapters help to explain that the reason for the large number of corrections employees is the lock-'em-up attitude.

In all the other major categories of expenditures—higher education, highways, hospitals, and public welfare—Texas has fewer employees. Those lower numbers do not signal greater efficiency. Rather, they signal that Texans receive proportionately fewer government services than citizens in the other large states.

# 1980 ON

The election of Ronald Reagan to the presidency in 1980 signaled a shift away from liberal ideology and a new stress on the role of the states in the American federal system. It also brought about cuts in funding for federal programs, forcing reductions in state and local social programs that had previously been funded by the national government. Poor economic conditions in both the Midwestern industrial states and "oil belt" states such as Texas also brought about a reduction in programs and services.

Moreover, citizens across the nation were beginning to doubt what liberal ideology had wrought. In the 1970s, states such as California and Massachusetts experienced a citizens' revolt against high taxes as the voters questioned whether the vast array of government services was worth the costs, namely, giant national, state, and local bureaucracies. Soon, the taxpayers' revolt became a national phenomenon. Throughout the 1980s, citizens and elected officials demanded more accountability from the administrative state. At the national level, programs such as education and social welfare were cut back or capped, and "tax reform" meant lower income taxes, particularly for the affluent. At the same time, defense spending went up significantly. The gap between government spending and government revenue was filled by borrowing. By the end of the decade, the United States had become the world's largest debtor nation while its domestic programs largely fell into disarray.

During the early 1990s, the economy faltered all across the country. The largely Anglo middle class was more concerned about the economy and its role in it than about social issues. Economic and political distance between the mainly White suburbanites and the basically minority lower economic class in the central cities increased. Because the lower class tends not to vote, governments at all levels tended to listen to the suburbanites, a phenomenon that meant even more emphasis on accountability, greater demands for tax ceilings and spending cutbacks, and more emphasis on economic development and less on the welfare state. However, major problems that only government could address remained—crime, environmental pollution, and the educational system, for example. Moreover, the national government began to impose requirements such as clean air and water upon the states in the form of mandates. The states then passed problems and mandates such as the need for better education to the local governments.

Therefore, state and local governments began to grow in size, programs, and expenditures, much to the regret of many taxpayers, who preferred less government and an end to state and local tax increases. Texas has the additional burden of being a high population-growth state through the 1990s and 2000s. Figure 9-2 shows relatively steady growth since 1980, with a higher growth rate for local government, which includes public schools. Even when the economy is in the doldrums, government employment often holds steady or even grows as government responds to the needs of the people. The best example is the Great Depression of the 1930s.

In Texas and many other states, a review of bureaucratic performance began, especially on the criterion of efficiency—the least expenditure of dollars and other resources per unit of output–in the early 1990s. President Bill Clinton assigned Vice President Al Gore to begin a similar initiative in the national government based on the models set by Texas and a half-dozen other states. These activities are known as *reinventing* or *reengineering government.*

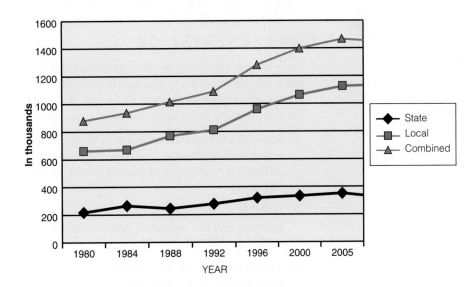

**FIGURE 9-2  State and Local Government Employment in Texas, 1980–2005 [in 000s]**

SOURCE: Texas Almanac, *1982–1983, 1986–1987, 1990–1991, 1994–1995, 1998–1999, 2002–2003, 2006–2007 eds. (Dallas: A. H. Belo/*Dallas Morning News, *1981, 1986, 1989, 1993, 1997, 2001, 2006), 410, 597, 502, 467, 548, 576, respectively.*

Citizen dissatisfaction was nowhere more evident than in the election of 1994, with the national sweep of elections by conservative Republicans. Candidates for the U.S. Congress, especially the House of Representatives, had campaigned on a "Contract with America" platform that included major federal governmental cutbacks among its many provisions. Although some cuts occurred, with emphasis on gaining control of various social programs such as welfare, a booming economy as the new century dawned allowed a combination of debt repayment, program expansion, and tax cuts. Thus, the Contract with America, although well publicized, was not carried out.

However, in 2000 nationally and in 2002 in Texas, the Republican Party captured the executive branch and a majority of both houses of the legislative branch. As a result, policy preferences shifted again. At the national level, domestic programs were secondary to defense, and the budget deficit was allowed to balloon. At the state level, policymakers showed more concern for reducing taxes and constraining social programs than for addressing citizen needs, especially when dollars were short (see Chapters 13 and 14).

# Characteristics of Bureaucracy

Of the many ways to organize human activities—committees, commissions, task forces, and so forth—the form most often used is bureaucracy, not only in government but also in businesses, clubs, churches, and many other organizations. The bureaucratic structure is traditionally viewed as the most efficient way to organize human endeavors so as to assure competent, quick, and expert problem solving. As so often happens, however, the ideal differs considerably from the reality. Indeed, experts on governmental organization and management frequently suggest alternatives to a strict bureaucratic organization.[2]

## TRADITIONAL CHARACTERISTICS

Early in the 1900s, Max Weber, considered the father of modern sociology, listed the main characteristics of a bureaucratic organization as part of his examination of the phenomenon of authority. Weber's list is important because it has been the starting point for subsequent discussions of bureaucratic structures.

1. Authority is hierarchical; an organization chart of a bureaucracy looks like a pyramid. At the top, there are the fewest people but with the greatest authority. At the base of the pyramid are the most people but with the least authority.

2. Individuals are assigned specific tasks to perform, and a combination of training and the continual performance of these tasks results in expertise in the specific area.

3. Bureaucracies have defined jurisdictions; that is, they are created to accomplish definite and limited goals.

4. There are extensive rules and regulations to ensure that policy is implemented uniformly and consistently.

5. Bureaucrats, because they follow comprehensive and detailed rules that depersonalize administration, are politically neutral.[3]

★ ★ ★ ★ ★ ★ ★ ★ ★ ★ ★ ★ ★ ★ ★ ★ ★ ★ ★ ★ ★ ★ ★ ★ ★ ★ ★

## *Pushing the Cost of Government Downward*

Citizens see the cost of government as rising even when one level of government brags about tax cutting. Examples of what happens when a high-level government begins to retrench are seen all over Texas in the very practical matters of water runoff and solid waste (garbage) disposal. At one point, the national government provided considerable assistance with the costs of laying new sewer lines and acquiring landfill sites. The assistance is no longer forthcoming, but environmental standards have risen higher and higher. Small cities can ill afford the costs of disposing of their own wastes under the new standards and are dependent on contracts with larger communities to provide all or some of these services, as is the case, for example, with Graham and Fort Worth or Krum and Denton. While the higher-level government can boast of budget slashing and program reduction, citizens don't pay any less; they just transfer their dollars from one government to another. The situation for small cities and their residents has not changed.

★ ★ ★ ★ ★ ★ ★ ★ ★ ★ ★ ★ ★ ★ ★ ★ ★ ★ ★ ★ ★ ★ ★ ★

## MODERN CHARACTERISTICS

Today's American bureaucracies deviate considerably from the classic European organizations that Weber observed. Boards and commissions, rather than a single chief executive, are often at the power peak of agencies; authority (and accountability) is thus diffused. Jurisdictions are so broadly defined (as in the national Department of Health and Human Services) that limits on goals and authority are obscured; confusion and competition result from overlapping jurisdictions and authority. Agency staffers, especially executives and sometimes minor bureaucrats, far from being politically neutral, are very much involved in political processes. Moreover, bureaucracies hire, fire, and promote from within. It is often very difficult even for bureau managers to fire someone and usually impossible for the chief executive to dismiss an employee. This feature of modern bureaucracies means that they are largely divorced from outside control.

The public interest sometimes becomes lost in the shuffle. We seemingly are overwhelmed by the administrative state, which Emmette Redford defines as a society in which "we are affected intimately and extensively by decisions in numerous organizations, public and private, allocating advantages and disadvantages to us."[4]

The cumulative effect of these deviations from Weber's model is that the bureaucracy is relatively free from outside control: Administrators enjoy a substantial amount of independence. Politicians in most democracies complain about the difficulty of getting bureaucrats to do anything they don't want to do. When administrators do not fear being fired for refusing to cooperate with politicians, they may evade and even disobey the orders of the people they are supposedly working for. In the twenty-first century, we must consider how the power of government agencies that are not accountable to the people's representatives can be considered legitimate. Conversely, we have to consider that bureaucrats may be dedicated to professional standards that transcend the politics of the moment; thus, the recipients of public services may continue to receive benefits even while politicians running for office call for an end to various social programs.

★ ★ ★ ★ ★ ★ ★ ★ ★ ★ ★ ★ ★ ★ ★ ★ ★ ★ ★ ★ ★ ★ ★ ★ ★ ★ ★ ★ ★

## Up a Tree

Why do citizens rail against bureaucracy so often? One answer is that bureaucrats often have to enforce laws that were not well conceived. In Highland Village northwest of Dallas, one family tangled with the city because of their children's tree house for which they had not sought a zoning variance or building permit. A city ordinance placed a number of restrictions on structures that were not part of the main house. Although the city manager and the public works director worked with the family, helping whenever they could, they still had to enforce the law and insist on relocation of the tree house.

★ ★ ★ ★ ★ ★ ★ ★ ★ ★ ★ ★ ★ ★ ★ ★ ★ ★ ★ ★ ★ ★ ★ ★ ★ ★ ★ ★ ★

SOURCE: "Bird House Dwellers, You're Next," an item in *Select List*, May 4, 2000, published for subscribers by Lewis F. McClain.

The rules designed to ensure consistency and fairness sometimes contradict one another. Equal opportunity requires absolutely equal treatment of all candidates for a job, for example, but affirmative action requires special measures for protected classes of citizens. Other rules create problems while trying to solve them. For example, regulations of the federal Occupational Safety and Health Administration (OSHA) require roofers to be tethered to the roof to avoid falling, but roofers contend that many injuries can occur because of tethering. However, rules or "red tape" have always been a nuisance to citizens. In fact, the term red tape goes back to the days of a powerful British monarchy when orders from the king were bound in packets by red ribbons.

Today, we also are unsure of what the role of the expert should be. Traditionally, the expert was to carry out detailed functions—whether issuing a driver's license or testing water purity in the city's laboratory. But increasingly, experts, who often disagree with one another or have narrow views, dominate our organizations. Lawyers and accountants are prime examples in both business and government.

Another characteristic of modern bureaucracies is their reliance on managers not only to oversee policy implementation but also to serve as brokers between citizens and elected officials. In both business and government, layers of management isolate the citizen-customer from key decision makers.

In the United States, size also is of concern, especially the relationship between the number of government employees and the numbers of citizens served. The number of federal civilian employees—about 182,000 of whom work in Texas—has changed little since the 1960s. In fact, state and local governments, contract employees, nonprofit organizations, and consultants administer many national programs. For forty years, major shifts in the numbers of federal government personnel have occurred only when the military was engaged in a buildup or in a downsizing. In the 1990s, government reorganization and the quest for a balanced budget resulted in the elimination of about 300,000 federal jobs. Calls for more limited government in the early 2000s have resulted more in a redeployment of government workers than in a reduction in force. Much of the redeployment has been directed to Homeland Security.

An economy of scale exists in the states. Generally, the larger the state, the lower is the ratio of state employees to citizens. As Figure 9-3 shows, this relationship is approximate. California, the most populous state, has the third lowest number of full-time equivalent (FTE) employees per 10,000 population (110) and is ranked forty-seventh. Illinois, the fifth largest state, and Florida, the fourth largest, both have 105 employees per 10,000 population and rank fiftieth and forty-ninth, respectively. However, Texas and New York, the second and third largest states, respectively, seem to have some inefficiencies, because they rank only forty-fourth and forty-second, respectively, with 119 and 128 employees per 10,000 population. Still, they look very efficient indeed when compared with the 448 and 376 employees per 10,000 population of Hawaii and Alaska, respectively. Hawaii is a series of islands and Alaska is huge in land mass but

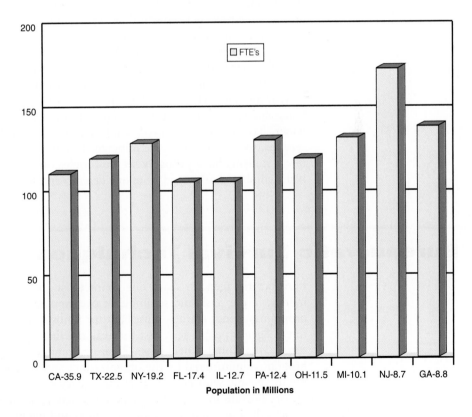

**FIGURE 9-3 Number of Full-Time Equivalent Employees per 10,000 Population, Ten Largest States**

SOURCE: Fiscal Size-Up, 2006–2007 Biennium (*Austin: Legislative Budget Board, 2005*), 37, 49.

★ ★ ★ ★ ★ ★ ★ ★ ★ ★ ★ ★ ★ ★ ★ ★ ★ ★ ★ ★ ★ ★ ★ ★ ★ ★ ★

### *Employee Turnover*

In addition to greater efficiency that results in fewer full-time equivalent employees per 10,000 population, the number of state workers has been affected both by program cuts (some of which are described in Chapters 13 and 14) and a number of factors leading to higher turnover among Texas public employees. Chief among those factors are low pay and modest retirement benefits.

★ ★ ★ ★ ★ ★ ★ ★ ★ ★ ★ ★ ★ ★ ★ ★ ★ ★ ★ ★ ★ ★ ★ ★ ★ ★ ★

SOURCE: Jason Embry, "Turnover Among State Workers Has Inched Up in '05," *Austin American-Statesman*, December 24, 2005, B1.

sparsely populated, making service delivery difficult for both states. Texas may appear slightly inefficient because it has a similar problem in the western part of the state. However, the number of FTEs in Texas has been going down.

A final characteristic of modern bureaucracy is frequent reorganization. In trying to find the most efficient means of carrying out policies and at the same time coping with increased numbers of employees and the proliferation of programs, governments keep shuffling their internal organization. President Jimmy Carter drew up a major reorganization plan for the federal bureaucracy that was approved by Congress in 1978. In the 1990s, President Bill Clinton assigned Vice President Al Gore the task of government reorganization. Many states, Texas among them, have enacted legislation that calls for periodic evaluations of state agencies. The Sunset Law, for example, is discussed later in this chapter. Some major agencies in Texas, such as those dealing with health, welfare, and water, have been reorganized, with an emphasis on consolidating fragmented services. Other agencies have initiated their own reorganizations. For example, many students have probably seen examples on their campuses of departments being combined or moved from one dean to another.

## Bureaucratic Survival Techniques

Bureaucratic agencies share one characteristic with the rest of us: They need money. In the push and scramble of overlapping jurisdictions, authorities, and programs, agency staffers must fight for funds if they want their agency to continue. Agency people seek first survival and then growth for three principal reasons: (1) personal—their jobs; (2) programmatic—genuine commitment to the program administered by the organization; and (3) clientele—a sincere concern for the people who benefit from the agency's programs. Because the administrators operate in the arena of political activities, they use political tactics to achieve their goals, just as state legislators and the governor do. Administrators must develop their own sources of political power if they want policies favorable to them enacted into law, and they have done so.[5]

# SOURCES OF BUREAUCRATIC POWER

## CLIENTELE GROUPS

The cornerstone of an agency's political clout is its relationship with its **clientele (interest) group** or groups. This relationship is mutually beneficial. The agency and its clientele have similar goals, are interested in the same programs, and work together in a number of ways, including sharing personnel, information, and lobbying strategies. The greater the economic power of the clientele groups, the stronger the political ties between them and "their" agencies—so strong in fact that "regulation" often becomes promotion of the clientele group's interests.

Among the better known agency–clientele relationships are those between the oil, gas, and transportation industries and the Texas Railroad Commission; the Texas Good Roads and Transportation Association (an interest group) and the Texas Department of Transportation; and the banking industry and the State Banking and State Depository Boards. The ties are not always economically motivated, however, as for example, in the case of the support given to the Parks and Wildlife Department by local chapters of the National Rifle Association or to Texas Tech University by its alumni. During a legislative session, the competition for as large a share as possible of the state's financial resources can be fierce indeed, with phalanxes of agency–clientele group coalitions lined up against one another.

## THE LEGISLATURE

Agencies' relationships with legislators are of two types: direct and indirect. First, agencies directly attempt to influence legislation and their budgets by furnishing information in writing and through testimony to legislative committees. In addition, agency executives work hard to get to know the speaker of the House, the lieutenant governor, and the members of the Legislative Budget Board and the Legislative Council, all of whom operate year-round, even when committee chairs and other legislators have gone home. Second, agencies use their clientele groups to try to influence legislation, budgets, and the selection of legislative leaders. During budget shortfalls in recent years, a number of state agencies—including higher education—became adept at finding powerful groups such as chambers of commerce and specially formed support groups to try to ward off agency budget cuts.

## THE CHIEF EXECUTIVE

As previously noted, the governor's power over state agencies has been strengthened, but bureaucrats also want gubernatorial support. The governor usually appoints the agency head or members of the board or commission that oversees the agency, and for many agencies, he or she appoints the board chair. A governor who is a skillful chief legislator can help an agency get its budget increased or add a new program. The chief executive can also referee when an agency does not have the support of its clientele group and give an agency visibility when it might otherwise languish in obscurity. The governor's legislative and party roles can be used to influence neutral legislators to look favorably on an agency, and the governor can greatly affect an agency's success or failure through appointments to the policy board or commission that oversees it. To state administrators, the chief executive is more powerful than the formal roles of the gubernatorial office would suggest. For example, in 1991, Governor Ann Richards forced the reorganization of the Texas Department of Commerce, ending its practice of making expensive foreign "economic development" trips.

In 1995, Governor George Bush pushed legislation that would benefit insurance companies by making it harder to sue and to gain large dollar amounts from a suit. He then put the Insurance Commission (now Department) on notice to begin looking at lowering insurance rates because the companies would be more profitable in the absence of big settlements against them. Despite more regulatory legislation later, Texas continues to have high rates, particularly for homeowners insurance.

In 2003, Governor Rick Perry gained control of the economic development function while seeing to the end of the Department of Economic Development. Although that move may seem hostile, in reality, he rescued an important state function from a corrupt agency and immediately began to push for more international trade. In 2007, he had to contend with a corrupt Texas Youth Commission, which, by a combination of gubernatorial and legislative actions, was essentially reconstituted.

## THE PUBLIC

Some bureaucratic agencies enjoy considerable public recognition and support. Among these are the Texas Rangers (perhaps the most romanticized bureaucracy in the state), the Texas Department of Transportation, and the Parks and Wildlife Department. The Rangers are well known, of course, because of many dramatic incidents in the early days of bringing "law and order" to the state. The latter two agencies use the technique of news and information for gaining public attention: road maps, carefully labeled highway projects, mapped-out camping tours, and colorful signs. In fact, the photograph on the cover of this book was supplied without charge after having been chosen from the many hundreds available in the photographic library of the Department of Transportation in Austin. However, generally favorable opinion toward Parks and Wildlife has not saved the agency from disastrous budget reductions that have resulted in the closing of some state parks and related facilities.

Usually, however, agencies have little, if any, public support to help them gain legislative or gubernatorial cooperation. The public, diverse and unorganized, often is unaware of the very existence of many agencies, much less able to give them the concerted support necessary to influence top-level elected administrators. Such support, when forthcoming, depends largely on the public's awareness of the importance of the agency's programs to the general welfare.

## EXPERTISE AND INFORMATION

Expert information is a political commodity peculiar to bureaucrats, who enjoy a unique position in state government through their control of the technical information that the governor and legislators must have to develop statewide policies. Although all bureaucracies have this advantage, it is particularly strong in Texas because the state's legislative committee system does not produce the same degree of legislative expertise as do the seniority system and continuous sessions of the U.S. Congress. Usually, the only alternative source for the legislator who does not want to use the information from an agency is the agency's clientele group. For example, if the legislature is trying to determine whether the state is producing enough physicians, the Board of Medical Examiners and the Department of State Health Services, as well as the Texas Medical Association and the Texas Osteopathic Medical Association, are all ready to furnish the information. The public's ideas on the subject are seldom considered. The more technical an agency's specialty, the greater is that agency's advantage in controlling vital information.

## LEADERSHIP

Another factor that determines the political power of bureaucracies is the caliber of leadership within the agency. Agency heads must be able to spark enthusiasm in their employees, encourage them toward a high level of performance, and convince elected officials and clientele groups that their agencies are performing effectively. A competent chief administrator will usually be retained by the members of the agency's governing board or commission, even though the board or commission membership changes over the years. The department benefits from continuity and stability at the top, and there is minimal disruption in the agency's relationship with clientele groups and legislators.

## INTERNAL ORGANIZATION

Some agencies have a **civil service system** that protects agency workers from outside influence. In a civil service system, workers are hired on merit—that is, their performance on written tests and other forms of examination—and are evaluated on job performance. Agencies with a merit-based personnel system can resist the influence of, for example, a legislator trying to get his nephew hired for the summer or an aide to the governor who wants an agency employee fired because the two had a disagreement. The adoption of a civil service system for hiring and promoting state workers introduces a paradox into the democratic nature of Texas government. The point of the "merit system" is to insulate agency workers from undue interference by politicians and from having to make decisions on a partisan basis. Yet those politicians are the people's representatives. When they cannot control state administrators, the people's will is obstructed. Part of the hostility that private citizens often express against bureaucrats may be due to this recognition on their part that "civil servants" are paid with taxes, yet are at best imperfectly accountable to the people. At the same time, we must consider the consequences if every administrative agency was forced to bend to the partisan will of elected officials.

# BUREAUCRATIC INVOLVEMENT IN THE POLICYMAKING PROCESS

## IMPLEMENTATION OF THE LAWS

The primary task of state bureaucrats is to implement the laws of Texas. In carrying out this task, however, they have considerable **administrative discretion**; that is, they are relatively free to use their own judgment as to how the laws will be carried out. Regulatory boards illustrate most clearly the power of administrative agencies. When the Texas Railroad Commission determines the monthly oil allowable (the number of barrels of oil that can be pumped during a particular month), it is making (administrative) rules that, like legislative statutes, have the force of law. It is, therefore, performing a quasilegislative function. When the Alcoholic Beverage Commission decides who will be issued a license to sell beer, wine, and distilled spirits, it is performing a quasijudicial function by determining whether a person has the right to go into business.

Often, a statute passed by the legislature creates a general framework for implementing a service or regulatory program, but state agencies have considerable discretion in interpreting statutes. Consequently, the 110 or so policy-making boards, commissions, and authorities are very important in determining what government actually does. Especially in a state like Texas, which lacks a cabinet system and an integrated executive branch, the average citizen is affected on a daily basis by what these boards do, but that citizen may have little understanding of how they work or how to approach them. Recent changes that resulted in making the board chairs accountable to the governor may help because the public can more nearly determine "who's in charge here." The board and commission structure makes public participation more difficult. Moreover, these boards usually appoint an executive director or college president to carry out their policies, and that executive officer has considerable influence over board policies.

★ ★ ★ ★ ★ ★ ★ ★ ★ ★ ★ ★ ★ ★ ★ ★ ★ ★ ★ ★ ★ ★ ★ ★ ★ ★ ★ ★ ★

## *Reorganization, Texas Style*

I n 2003, Governor Rick Perry sought legislative approval of a major state reorganization that would move Texas toward a cabinet-style government by giving him power over the heads of state agencies. The legislature responded by reorganizing the comptroller's office, eleven health and human services agencies, the pardon and paroles board, and economic development and by giving the governor control over the heads of appointed state boards and commissions.

★ ★ ★ ★ ★ ★ ★ ★ ★ ★ ★ ★ ★ ★ ★ ★ ★ ★ ★ ★ ★ ★ ★ ★ ★ ★ ★ ★ ★

For example, a Texas State University student may wish to protest the abolition of a popular major. Determining how to make a protest requires information about how the decision was made. Was the change made by the system's board of regents on its own or upon recommendation of the president, or was it forced by policies of the Texas Higher Education Coordinating Board in Austin? Were the students consulted before the decision was made?

Although it can obscure how a decision was made, administrative discretion can be a positive factor in effective government. A common example is the decision of a Department of Public Safety law enforcement officer to allow one suspect to go free in the hope that he will lead criminal-intelligence agents to a more important suspect. Another example is that of professors at state universities, who have considerable freedom to design their classes. The professor decides on the balance between lecture and discussion, textbooks, whether to show videotapes, what the mix of multiple choice/essay tests will be, whether to require work on the World Wide Web, and the basis of grading. Thus, by interpreting laws, making rules, and making judgments, administrators make public policy.

## INFLUENCING LEGISLATION

Bureaucrats directly influence the content and meaning of statutes that are passed by the legislature, and they do so in three principal ways: by drafting bills, furnishing information to legislators, and lobbying.

During its short session, the Texas legislature is under great pressure to draft, consider, and dispose of needed legislation. State bureaucrats are eager to aid the lawmakers, and two ways in which they do so are mutually beneficial: furnishing specialized information to legislative committees and drafting bills that individual legislators may then present as their own. Legislators thus gain needed assistance, and administrators are able to protect their agencies by helping to write their own budgets and develop their own programs.

Bureaucrats also influence legislation by lobbying legislators for or against proposed bills. State employees cannot legally act as lobbyists, but they can furnish information. For the average citizen, it's splitting hairs to make that distinction. Agencies usually work closely with their clientele group or groups in the lobbying endeavor. The governor is also lobbied not only for support of legislation that is favored by agencies and their clients but also for agency appointments that are acceptable to them and their clients. If successful, both these lobbying activities can greatly influence the decisions of legislators as well as the policies set by boards and commissions. Furthermore, over 336,000 state employees, through such organizations as the Texas Public Employees Association, are an active lobby at budget time on matters of salary and fringe benefits.

# What Happens to the Public Interest?

Public administration originally was created to serve and protect the public interest. Sometimes, however, the public interest can be forgotten in the shifting, complex kaleidoscope of hundreds of agencies, bureaus, departments, and commissions constantly striving for more money, more personnel, more programs, and more power. Bureaucrats are no more evil, incompetent, or venal than employees of privately owned companies. However, the bureaucracy is funded with public money—tax dollars—so people naturally are a little more concerned with the honesty and efficiency of the state's administration than with that of Texas Instruments or Tenneco, for example.

Administrative scandals such as the mistreatment of people with mental retardation at state schools or public employees benefiting from state travel in the name of economic development heighten that interest. Sixty years ago, Paul Appleby drew the distinction between government and private administration by noting that the public administrator is continually subject to "public scrutiny and outcry" by "press and public interest in every detail of his life, personality, and conduct."[6] In short, public administrators live in the proverbial goldfish bowl. For people who are worried about democratic accountability, of course, it is a good thing to put administrators into a goldfish bowl. Constant publicity may not be as effective in instilling democratic accountability into administrators as it is with elected politicians, but it is better than nothing.

# BUREAUCRATIC ORIENTATION

It is a fact of organizational life that the longer one remains in one agency or company, the more one's perspectives narrow to those of the organization. After a while, one begins to support that organization's way of doing things. In a public agency, this orientation often leads to a loss of concern for more general public goals and an inability to see different points of view. This shifting of bureaucratic orientation is known as *goal displacement*—that is, the replacement of one goal by another. In this case, the public interest is forgotten and the agencies' interests and those of their clientele groups become paramount. Many complex factors are involved in the displacement of publicly stated goals in agency priorities: (1) the rapid, piecemeal creation of new agencies that have overlapping jurisdictions and authorities; (2) the co-optation of regulatory agencies by their clientele groups; (3) the fact that most top-level administrators are appointed by an executive who has no power to remove them from office and that most career bureaucrats are protected in their jobs by tenure; (4) the fact that the public is generally bewildered about which government official or body is responsible for what governmental action or program; and (5) the fact that the publicly stated goals may not have been the "real" goals to begin with.

One agency that overstepped the law was the Texas Youth Commission, which underwent a considerable overhaul in 2007 after sexual abuse and physical violence against the young inmates in its charge were revealed.

*Courtesy of Ben Sargent.*

The vast majority of public managers and bureaucrats are conscientious, and many of them have a keen sense of public interest. Nevertheless, the authors share with democratic theorists a concern about reconciling bureaucracy and democracy. The growth in the size and scope of government brings with it a need for adequate controls. Even if the controls are not needed all the time, citizen participation in government requires their presence.

## OVERSTEPPING THE LAW

In addition to the bureaucratic orientation that develops over time, some state administrators are further tempted toward inappropriate bureaucratic activities. In Texas, these temptations are due to (1) extremely strong special-interest groups, (2) weaknesses in the governor's office, and (3) the handicapped legislature. State agencies and bureaucrats have run afoul of the law in a variety of ways, such as using state funds for personal travel, assigning contracts without bids, awarding six-figure consulting contracts as a means of hiring "unseen" staff, and causing injuries and deaths through failure to enforce safety regulations. These incidents involved irregularities, not simply inefficiencies.

How, then, do we go about the job of ensuring that the state bureaucracy performs honestly, efficiently, and effectively? How do we ensure that public trust is warranted and that legislative intent is satisfied? In short, how do we ensure accountability on the part of the state administration?

# Harnessing the Administrative State

As part of the state's system of checks and balances, the governor has a veto over legislative acts, and the legislature can impeach a governor or refuse to confirm gubernatorial appointments. As well as controlling various offices and agencies that report directly to them, all three traditional branches of government—executive, legislative, and judicial—have means of holding the bureaucracy, sometimes called the "fourth branch of government," in check. Democratic theory posits that government should be elected by the people, but most administrators are not. The governor and other elected officials have legitimacy (popular acceptance). State administrators must derive as much legitimacy as they can from these elected officials.

During the 1980s, the issue of bureaucratic accountability to the people through their elected representatives became increasingly important at both the state and the national levels because of tight budgets, public desire to maximize each tax dollar, and a strong, conservative, antigovernment trend. The importance of accountability was brought home in 1991 when the governor and the legislature agreed that a budget would not be forthcoming for the 1992–1993 biennium until all state functions were audited to determine if money was being wasted. From that agreement sprang the nationally recognized Texas Performance Review (TPR) system administered first by John Sharp, later by Carole Keeton Strayhorn, and then by the Legislative Budget Board. TPR requires that, before agencies can submit their budget proposals, they must prepare strategic plans that emphasize quality of service, access to programs, and measures of agency performance. Citizen demand for accountability and government's response to it illustrate that both citizens and elective officials play a role in harnessing the administrative state.

★ ★ ★ ★ ★ ★ ★ ★ ★ ★ ★ ★ ★ ★ ★ ★ ★ ★ ★ ★ ★ ★ ★ ★ ★ ★ ★

## *The Budget Is Made Up of a Lot of Little Things . . .*

In the Texas Performance Review prior to the 1995 legislative session, the comptroller's office discovered that the state had spent $70,000 in tax money over the previous three years just to provide copies of the mileage chart to state agencies. The mileage chart is the official table of how many miles a state employee can claim when traveling from one city to another on state business. As a result, the Seventy-fourth Legislature in 1995 mandated that this information be transmitted electronically. One can multiply this small example by hundreds to get a sense of what TPR does.

★ ★ ★ ★ ★ ★ ★ ★ ★ ★ ★ ★ ★ ★ ★ ★ ★ ★ ★ ★ ★ ★ ★ ★ ★ ★ ★

## HOW MUCH ACCOUNTABILITY TO THE CHIEF EXECUTIVE?

It would seem logical to make the bureaucracy accountable to the governor, who is the chief executive and nominal head of the state administration. But the governor's powers were limited intentionally to avoid centralizing government power in any one office.

1. Appointment powers are restricted and removal powers are limited.

2. There is no true executive budget, although the Seventy-eighth Legislature acted as if there was one in 2003.

3. The executive branch is fragmented: Four departments, a major commission, and a major board are headed by elected officials, and many separate agencies deal with related functional areas—more than 30 policymaking boards are involved in the area of education alone. Instead of single-headed agencies, about 110 multimember boards and commissions officially make policy for their agencies. In reality, the executive director of the agency, who administers the affairs of the agency, is usually the most powerful person connected with the organization—and is partially insulated from elected officials by the board.

Even if there were a complete reorganization of the executive branch, including consolidated departments headed by officials who constituted a governor's cabinet—such as thirty-nine other states have—the sheer size and diversity of the bureaucracy, coupled with other demands on the governor's time and staff, would make executive control loose and indirect. Just as it is difficult to hold a president responsible for the actions of a Social Security clerk in Laramie, Wyoming, it would be difficult to hold a governor responsible for the actions of a college professor in Canyon or a welfare caseworker in El Paso. Some agencies have responded to the governor's urging to use an *ombudsman*—grievance person—to hear public complaints against administrative agencies in an effort to increase executive responsiveness to citizen problems.

Stronger supervisory control would allow the governor to exercise greater influence over major policy decisions. With a consolidated executive branch, unen-

# YOU DECIDE

## Does the Texas Governor Need Cabinet Government in the Executive Branch?

Thirty-nine other states have an executive branch that is organized like that of the U.S. government—that is, a chief executive who heads a cabinet made up of directors or secretaries of a limited number of broad-based departments. Possible departments include Public and Higher Education, Public Safety and Criminal Justice, and Health and Human Services, for example.

| PRO | CON |
|---|---|
| Texas should pass the necessary statutory and constitutional provisions to establish a cabinet system because: | Texas should not pass the necessary statutory and constitutional provisions to establish a cabinet system because: |
| ▲ Citizens could more easily understand a government that was organized like that of the United States. | ▼ "Supersized" departments would concentrate power in the hands of too few people. |
| ▲ Greater economy and efficiency could be achieved with broad-based departments that could operate with economy of scale. | ▼ Many smaller programs that serve useful purposes—for example, medical help for children with kidney disease—would get lost in the bureaucracy of large departments. |
| ▲ The heads of the broad-based departments would be clearly associated with their agencies, could more easily be held accountable, and would more likely carry out the governor's policy preferences. | ▼ The governor already has enough to do without directly supervising a cabinet. |
| ▲ The fact that a majority of states have a cabinet system is evidence in and of itself of the value of this type of organization. | ▼ There is almost no chance that voters would approve a constitutional amendment supporting cabinet government; thus, efforts to make this major change would be better aimed at improving state programs. |

cumbered by other elected administrators, and with managerial control over the state budget, the chief executive would have more hope of implementing policy. The advantage of having a strong chief executive as the head of a more truly hierarchical administration would be having overall responsibility vested in a highly visible elected official who could not be so easily dominated by special interests.

Texas has been moving slowly toward a more integrated executive branch, at least with regard to agencies headed by appointed executives or appointed boards. Nevertheless, the governor relies heavily on the roles of chief legislator, chief of state, and leader of the people to influence state agencies. However, all the modern governors have succeeded in adding some clout to their chief executive role—more removal power, more appointments to the executive director positions in state agencies and to the chairmanships of boards, more budget clout, and mandatory strategic planning. They are aided by the Division of Budget, Planning, and Policy.

# HOW MUCH ACCOUNTABILITY TO THE LEGISLATURE?

## LEGISLATIVE OVERSIGHT

Legislatures traditionally have been guardians of the public interest, with powers to oversee administrative agencies. These powers include budgetary control, the postaudit of agency expenditures to ensure legality, programmatic control through the statutes, investigation of alleged wrongdoing, and impeachment of officials. Although traditional legislative oversight is somewhat effective in Texas, several factors militate against its total success. One is the tripartite relationship among legislators, bureaucrats, and special-interest groups. Legislators may be reluctant to ruffle the feathers of groups that supply them with campaign contributions by pressing their oversight vigorously. These groups in turn often have strong connections to the bureaucracy. Another is the high turnover of legislative committee personnel. A third is the lack of ongoing supervision because legislators are on the job only part time as a result of Texas's short biennial legislative sessions. Much of the burden of oversight falls on the Legislative Budget Board, the Legislative Council, and the Legislative Audit Committee, although historically none of these has adequate staff or time for a thorough job, and none is well known to the general public. The reorganization that took place in the fall of 2003 may result in better staffing and more visibility for these agencies.

A substitute for direct legislative oversight is legislation that micromanages an agency or set of agencies and requires some other agency to be the control force. A good example is the highly specific legislation passed in the 1997 session that dictates the core curriculum, the admission standards, and the maximum number of credit hours at publicly assisted colleges and universities. The Texas Higher Education Coordinating Board was put in charge of enforcing these statutes, which affect every student at a public college or university in the state.

## SUNSET ACT

With the passage of the Sunset Law by the Sixty-fifth Legislature in 1977, Texas established a procedure for reviewing the existence of all statutory boards, commissions, and departments—except colleges and universities—on a periodic basis. More than 150 agencies and advisory committees are included, and new ones are added as they are created. These sunset reviews are conducted by a twelve-member Sunset Advisory Commission composed of five senators and five representatives appointed by their respective presiding officers, who also appoint two citizen members. The chairmanship rotates between the House and the Senate every two years. The Sunset Commission can determine the list of agencies to be reviewed before the beginning of each regular legislative session as long as all agencies are evaluated within a twelve-year period. The agencies must submit self-evaluation reports, and the Sunset Commission coordinates its information gathering with other agencies that monitor state agencies on a regular basis, such as the Legislative Budget Board, legislative committees, and the offices of the state auditor, governor, and comptroller. Following sunset review, the legislature must explicitly vote to continue an agency and may reorganize it or force it to modify its administrative rules and procedures.

By the time of the 2005 legislative session, the sunset process had resulted in the following:

- Creating a new structure for workers' compensation

- Strengthening of the Public Utility Commission's authority to oversee the Electric Reliability Council of Texas

- Public membership on most state boards and more public participation

- Stronger prohibitions against conflicts of interest

- Improved enforcement processes

- Elimination of overlap and duplication

- Abolition of thirty-one agencies

- Abolition of nineteen additional agencies, with functions transferred to other agencies

- Merger of eleven agencies

- About $737 million in savings and increased revenues to the state since the inception of the process.[7]

The Sunset Commission's 2008–2009 agenda includes a mixed bag of forty general government, health and human services, public safety and criminal justice, business and economic development, and regulatory licensing agencies and programs.

★ ★ ★ ★ ★ ★ ★ ★ ★ ★ ★ ★ ★ ★ ★ ★ ★ ★ ★ ★ ★ ★ ★ ★ ★ ★ ★ ★

## *Oops!*

Although most of the agencies abolished through the sunset process had outlived their usefulness, such as the Pink Bollworm Commission, the State Board of Dental Examiners was eliminated in 1993 when the legislature failed to pass the statute authorizing its renewal. Its function of testing and licensing dentists and other dental personnel was taken over by the Texas Department of Health for two years until the board was recreated.

★ ★ ★ ★ ★ ★ ★ ★ ★ ★ ★ ★ ★ ★ ★ ★ ★ ★ ★ ★ ★ ★ ★ ★ ★ ★ ★ ★

# HOW MUCH ACCOUNTABILITY TO THE PUBLIC?

## ELECTIVE ACCOUNTABILITY

American government is based on the premise that it will be accountable to the people it governs. If accountability cannot be achieved directly—all citizens of a political division meeting to vote directly on laws and policies—theoretically, it can be achieved through elected representatives who meet in government and report back to their citizen-constituents. But voters encounter difficulty when they try to make intelligent decisions regarding the multitude of names on the long ballot in Texas. Long ballots tend to lead to confusion, not accountability. Additionally, the vastness of the bureaucracy and the reality that incumbents can usually count on being reelected simply because the voters recognize their names mean that the elective process has become an unsatisfactory method of ensuring responsible administrative action. In view of these problems, Texas citizens need some way to check on the activities of particular administrators and agencies on which public attention, for whatever reason, is focused. Until recently, however, there has been no easy way to do this.

## OPEN RECORDS AND MEETINGS

Under the Texas Open Records Act, originally passed in 1973, the public, including the media, has access to a wide variety of official records and to most public meetings of state and local agencies. The importance of this access in a democracy is reinforced by the second quotation opening this chapter. Sometimes called the **Sunshine Law** because it forces agencies to shed light on their deliberations and procedures, this act is seen as a way to prevent or expose bureaucratic ineptitude, corruption, and unnecessary secrecy. An agency that denies access to information that is listed as an open record in the statute may have to defend its actions to the attorney general and even in court.

The 1987 Open Meetings Act strengthened public access to information by requiring government bodies to certify that discussions held in executive sessions were legal or to tape-record closed meetings. Closed meetings are permitted when sensitive issues such as real estate transactions or personnel actions are under consideration, but the agency must post an agenda in advance and submit it to the secretary of state, including what items will be discussed in closed session. Since 1981, the legislature has also required state agencies to write rules and regulations in understandable language. In recent years, the Texas Open Records Act has been frequently amended to permit exceptions. For example, many search committees looking for city managers, executive directors of agencies, and college presidents were being foiled by premature disclosure of the names of individuals under consideration and sought some protection from the act.

In 1999, the legislature strengthened open meetings provisions by placing firm restrictions on staff briefings that could be made before governing bodies at the state and local level. Two new types of exceptions emerged from the Seventy-sixth Legislature—economic development and utilities deregulation—but these were seen as protections on behalf of the public when a government was in a competitive situation.[8] That is, while Texas government became even more open following the 1999 session, governments were allowed to have closed meetings when competitive issues were the topic of discussion.

In 2005, the Seventy-ninth Legislature mandated that not only public officials but members of all boards, including local ones, receive training in open government. The second quotation at the beginning of this chapter is drawn from the materials made available to those required to receive training. The formats include online instruction, DVDs, and organized classes.

## WHISTLE-BLOWER PROTECTION

The 1983 legislature passed an act affording job security to state employees who spot illegal or unethical conduct in their agencies and report it to appropriate officials. The national government established the precedent for whistle-blower legislation in 1978. The term whistle-blower comes from the fact that employees who report illegal acts are "blowing the whistle" on someone. The implementation of this act has not been promising, as the situation described in the box indicates.

★ ★ ★ ★ ★ ★ ★ ★ ★ ★ ★ ★ ★ ★ ★ ★ ★ ★ ★ ★ ★ ★ ★ ★ ★ ★ ★ ★

### *Whistle-Blower Protection?*

In 1991, George Green, a former Department of Human Services architect, was awarded $13.6 million under the Texas whistle-blowing protection legislation. Green had repeatedly complained to supervisors that the state welfare department was being cheated by building contractors. Ultimately, the department fired Green and tried to prosecute him on the petty charge of making a $0.13 telephone call to his father.

In 1995, legislators finally voted to pay the judgment—the Senate at the full value, the House at less. No compromise was reached, and Green had to wait until November to receive a $13 million payment.

★ ★ ★ ★ ★ ★ ★ ★ ★ ★ ★ ★ ★ ★ ★ ★ ★ ★ ★ ★ ★ ★ ★ ★ ★ ★ ★ ★

SOURCE: "Fired Whistle-Blower Wins $13.6 Million in DHS Suit," *Dallas Morning News*, September 25, 1991, 1–18; Christy Hoppe, "Senate Backs Payment to Fired Whistle-Blower," *Dallas Morning News*, May 25, 1995, 20A.

## IS THERE ACCOUNTABILITY?

The passage of sunshine and sunset laws in recent years has enabled the public, the press, and the legislavture to harness the worst excesses of bureaucracy more successfully. In addition, routine audits often turn up minor violations, a forceful governor or attorney general can "shake up" a state agency, and the state budget can be a means of putting a damper on any agency that seems to be getting out of hand. Top-level officials also have to file financial disclosure forms as a check on potential conflicts of interest. These devices help guard against serious wrongdoing on the part of state officials and help ensure accountability.

Serious wrongdoing is not usually the problem. Much more frequently, we see indifference or occasional incompetence. How can we minimize the indifference and incompetence that citizens sometimes encounter in state, federal, or local agencies? How can we reduce the amount of time-consuming red tape? There seem to be few formal means of ensuring that bureaucratic dealings with citizens are competent, polite, and thorough—until citizen reaction demands them. What little political attention is given to the administrative state is aimed primarily at the federal bureaucracy rather than at state or local bureaucracies. Yet, public managers may have come up with their own solution: the Citizens as Customers Movement. This approach requires that public employees treat citizens as customers in the same way that a business treats its customers as valuable resources. State and local governments also have implemented Raising the Bar campaigns to signify a commitment to higher standards of service.

Thus, we find that elected officials, with the assistance of the media, can ensure a fair measure of bureaucratic accountability and that they continue to seek ways to control the appointed bureaucracy. The current emphasis on government performance is merely the latest of these ways.

# Suggested Reforms

The Texas administrative structure is difficult for the average individual to understand. Overhauling it is not easy because a major package of constitutional amendments and statutes would be required. Perhaps the most important suggestion is also the most obvious: to create a cabinet-type government. The 231-plus total agencies could be consolidated into a series of executive departments reporting to the governor. The only elected executives would be the governor and the lieutenant governor. The new departments might include the following:

- Public and Higher Education
- Health and Human Services
- Natural Resources
- Highways and Public Transportation
- Public Safety and Criminal Justice
- Commerce and Economic Development
- Administrative Services
- Professional and Occupational Licensing

This scheme, similar to the organization of the national government, would still leave the biggest regulatory commissions as independent agencies—the Texas Railroad Commission and the Public Utilities Commission, for example.

The likelihood of such a sweeping change is almost zero. However, minor steps toward consolidation have occurred, most noticeably in the creation of a single office responsible to the governor to oversee health and human service activities.

# Summary

A combination of the Industrial Revolution, public reaction against a pseudo laissez faire philosophy and social Darwinism, urbanization and the development of a mass society, and the enormous amount of federal funds that have been made available to the states in the past few decades contributed to the rise of big government. Big government means big bureaucracy: the administrative state.

The Texas bureaucracy, like administrations everywhere, has had to develop its own sources of political support and power. Having done so, it influences the development of state policy not only in the day-to-day execution of the state's laws but also through providing information and influencing legislation. A major problem, then, is to harness the powerful state administration, a task that is far from easy. Two measures, however—the Open Records Act and the Sunset Law—have made strides in the direction of giving Texas citizens a responsible bureaucracy. Since 1991, the combined efforts of the governor, the comptroller, and the legislative leadership to insist on a budget based on planning and on quantitative measures of agency performance—the Texas Performance Review—have been another important step. Traditional controls such as the legislative audit and the legislature's power to investigate agency activities also help promote accountability on the part of the administration.

Nevertheless, major problems continue. The fragmented structure of the state's administration—231 agencies, including four department heads and a commission and a board that are completely independent of the governor—permits the bureaucracy considerable flexibility in carrying out legislative mandates according to its own priorities.

For the present, the growth of government—prompted by public demand for services, business demands for programs, and bureaucratic survival tactics—seems destined to continue in a hodgepodge fashion. On the one hand, such a system means that citizens can gain access to their government through many points. On the other hand, it means that it is very difficult to tell "who's in charge here" and to place responsibility. To some extent, then, the state's bureaucracy represents the proverbial twin horns of a dilemma. The goal of representativeness may be achieved by the administrative state in Texas; the goal of responsiveness may not be. Yet democratic theory demands that government not only represent its many constituents but also respond to their needs.

Chapters 13 and 14 cover the state budget and major policy issues in Texas. Together they provide a picture of state elected officials and state administration in action.

## Glossary Terms

| | |
|---|---|
| administrative discretion | hierarchy |
| bureaucracy | sunset review |
| civil service system | Sunshine Law |
| clientele groups | |

## Study Questions

1. What were the two key factors in the growth of the administrative state?

2. What are the sources of bureaucratic power?

3. How are bureaucrats involved in the policy process?

4. What devices are available to both elected officials and the public to keep the bureaucracy in check?

5. What are the five types of policymakers in Texas administrative agencies? What do each of the elected executives do? What do the Texas Railroad Commission and State Board of Education do?

6. Can you think of state agencies other than the Public Utilities Commission, the Higher Education Coordinating Board, and the Parks and Wildlife Department that regularly affect you? In what way does each agency you considered impinge on your life?

7. What changes do you think should be made in the Texas executive branch? Why? What would you hope to accomplish?

8. Have you had an especially bad experience with a state agency? What was it? Have you had an especially good experience? What was it? What factors do you think may have caused the differences between the two experiences?

## Surfing the Web

Readers are urged to visit the companion site for this book:

**http://academic.cengage.com/polsci/Kraemer/TexasPolitics10e**

# The Judiciary

The building in Austin where the Texas Supreme Court interprets the state constitution.

> Nothing can contribute so much to [the judges'] firmness and independence as permanency in office.
>
> ALEXANDER HAMILTON, *FEDERALIST 78*, 1787

> If I asked you to design a criminal justice system and you came up with one like we have here in Texas, we'd have to commit you to Austin State Hospital because you'd be a danger to yourself and society.
>
> JIM MATTOX, ATTORNEY GENERAL OF TEXAS, 1988

> The law, in its majestic impartiality, forbids the rich as well as the poor to sleep under bridges, to beg in the streets, and to steal bread.
>
> ANATOLE FRANCE (JACQUES THIBAULT), FRENCH NOBEL-PRIZEWINNING AUTHOR, *LE LYS ROUGE*, 1894

# Introduction

A discussion of the **judiciary**—the system of courts, judges, lawyers, and other actors in the institutions of justice—brings up several problems for democratic theory. Judges are the arbiters of conflicts within society and the interpreters of the rules by which we govern ourselves. Many people think that judges should be able to hold themselves above the dirty struggles of the political process. As a consequence, there have always been those who followed Alexander Hamilton in arguing that judges should be as independent as possible from the democratic necessities of elections, interest groups, and money. Many other people have pointed out, however, that democracy requires important decision makers to be accountable to the public and therefore made to stand for election.

As a consequence, a democratic political system faces troubling questions: Are judges part of the political process or not? If they are, how can they be installed in office in a manner that ensures they will be fair and impartial but still accountable to the public? In Texas, the customary answer has been to come down firmly on the side of democracy and to make judges answerable to the people. It turns out, however, that when judges are treated like other politicians, they become vulnerable to the same suspicion that they are allowing private interests to corrupt their views on public affairs.

Furthermore, the importance of money in the judicial system has another disquieting aspect: It creates doubts as to whether the courts are fulfilling the democratic ideal that they provide equal justice to all. If access to legal representation is expensive, and if the outcome of trials depends on adequate representation, do poor people have a fair chance in a courtroom? Because of these suspicions and doubts, the Texas judiciary is a troubled democratic institution.

The first subject of this chapter is an examination of the political nature of judges, followed by a summary of the important features of the judicial branch of government in Texas. The focus then shifts to a consideration of the players in the state system of justice. The remainder of the chapter is devoted to discussions of some of the vexing problems facing the state judiciary from the perspective of democratic theory. The output of the judicial system—the substance of justice—is discussed in the next chapter.

# The Myth of the Nonpolitical Judiciary

"There ought to be a law . . ."

This expression is sometimes heard in America and reflects the faith many of our citizens have in laws as solutions to social problems. When a law is enacted, Americans tend to believe that the problem has been solved and promptly forget about it. The fact that the many laws already on the books have not solved our society's problems does not seem to shake our faith that a few more will do the trick.

Hand in hand with this faith goes the American perception of **judges**—the government officials who preside over a courtroom and rule on the application of the laws—as men and women who are somehow "above" the political process. Professor Geoffrey C. Hazard Jr. of Yale Law School describes this perception: "Scratch the average person's idea of what a judge should be and it's basically Solomon. If you had a benign father, that's probably what you envision. We demand more from them, we look for miracles from them. . . . It's romantic, emotional, unexamined, unadmitted, and almost undiscussable."[1]

Over the centuries, most judges in Texas and elsewhere have attempted to live up to the romantic ideal of the wise rule giver. They do so because they know that people are more likely to comply with the decisions of judges if those judges are perceived as nonpolitical. Judges wear black robes, are addressed as "Your Honor" in the courtroom, write opinions in a specialized language that is beyond the understanding of most citizens, and in general try to speak and act in a way that indicates they are not part of the messy business of governing.

This performance is not entirely insincere. In the long history of the development of our legal system, great jurists in England and the United States have developed—and are developing—neutral, impersonal criteria to use in making decisions. The hope is that a judge can become like a surgeon operating on a patient or a scientist examining evidence to support or contradict a hypothesis: impartial and incorruptible, above passion and prejudice. The ideal judge will rule on evidence and procedure purely on the basis of fairness and established principles. Common observation suggests that this ideal has some basis in reality and that judges are less moved by personal idiosyncrasy and outside influence than are legislators or governors.

But the notion that what judges do is not political is a well-polished myth. Whenever judges apply a statute, and especially when they interpret a constitution, they make choices among competing rules, individuals, and groups. When a judge makes a decision, somebody wins and somebody loses. Those somebodies can be very large groups of people who win or lose a great deal and care intensely about the outcome of the decision. As a result, the coalitions of interests that tend to oppose each other in political parties also tend to adopt differing philosophies of judicial interpretation. Republican judges, in perfectly good faith, usually interpret words so as to favor the interests displayed in Table 4-2 in Chapter Four. Democratic judges, also in good faith, generally interpret words so as to favor a conflicting set of interests. Therefore, judges make laws, and the constitution, in the process of interpretation. This crucial activity of interpretation makes Texas judges, and especially members of the Supreme Court and Court of Criminal Appeals, central components of the state's political system.

Former Texas Judge W. A. Morrison, a justice of the Texas Court of Criminal Appeals, made no bones about his personal contribution to the state's system of laws. "I have engrafted into the law of this great state my own personal philosophy," he stated. Claiming that every appellate judge does much the same thing, he explained that during his first day on the bench as a young man, the other two judges—both of whom were "at least seventy years old"—could not agree on more than a dozen cases, and so Morrison cast the deciding vote in each one. He attributed his having "engrafted" his personal philosophy into the state's law to a greater degree than most other judges to the fact that he came to the bench early in life and remained longer than most.[2]

Another Texas jurist, district judge John Dietz, clearly acknowledged the political aspect of his job in 2002: "I redistribute wealth. I decide whether someone can keep theirs or [must] give it to someone else."[3]

The fact that Texas judges are elected makes the political nature of their work even more obvious. As one state jurist proclaimed in the early 1970s, "This job is more politics than law; there's no two ways about it. Hell, you can have all kinds of dandy ideas, but if you don't get yourself elected, you can sell your ideas on a corner somewhere. Politics isn't a dirty word in my mouth."[4]

Although judges from the rival political parties frequently split in judicial philosophy, they can also strongly disagree with others of the same party in their analysis of individual cases. A case in point is a verbal brawl that erupted in the Texas Supreme Court in 2000 over the proper interpretation of a law requiring a doctor to notify the parents of a girl under the age of eighteen before performing an abortion on her.[5] All nine of the justices were Republicans, but the case reveals the important differences over judicial principles that can exist between nominal allies.

In 1999, the legislature had passed the "parental notification" bill, and Governor George W. Bush had signed it. Mindful of federal courts' history of voiding state antiabortion laws, however, the legislature had put in a "judicial bypass" clause, allowing an underage girl to get an abortion without informing her parents if she could convince a state judge that she met certain criteria. Among the criteria were that she was mature and well informed. In early 2000, a pregnant teenager ("Jane Doe" in court discussions) had asked a judge to give her a judicial bypass and had been turned down. She appealed, and the problem quickly landed on the docket of the state's highest civil court.

The case brought up important questions of interpretation. What did "mature" and "well informed" mean when applied to a teenager? Had the legislature intended to make judicial bypass a relatively easy and common process or something difficult and rare? By a six to three vote, in March 2000 the Court ruled that the legislature had intended the criteria to be relatively easy to meet and, overruling the lower appeals court, granted permission to "Jane Doe" to have an abortion.

Although all nine justices were members of the same party, the partisan unanimity masked an ideological divide. The three dissenters expressed their outrage. "The plain fact is that the statute was enacted to protect parents' right to involve themselves in their children's decisions and to encourage that involvement as well as to discourage teen-age pregnancy and abortion," fumed Justice Nathan Hecht. "The court not only ignores these purposes, it has done what it can to defeat them." The majority's "utter disregard" for legislative intent was "an insult to those legislators personally, to the office they hold and to the separation of powers between the two branches of government." No less annoyed, Justice Priscilla Owen charged that the majority had "manufactured reasons to justify its action" and "acted irresponsibly." (A year later, after President Bush had nominated her to be a federal judge, this allegedly "extremist" antiabortion opinion caused Democrats in the U.S. Senate to filibuster against Owen's confirmation. She was not finally confirmed until 2005.) Justice Gregg Abbott accused the majority of practicing "interpretive hand-wringing."

In response, several members of the majority criticized Hecht's "explosive rhetoric," accusing him of having "succumbed to passion." To interpret the law as the dissenters urged, argued Justice Alberto Gonzales (later to be appointed U.S. Attorney General by President Bush), would be to misunderstand the new law and "would be an unconscionable act of judicial activism."

In this one episode, the true nature of the judiciary stood revealed. Fair-minded or not, judges bring as many preconceptions and differences of outlook to their work as do legislators or executives. They have ideological commitments. They have no Olympian detachment from the issues they decide. They are politicians in black robes.

# The Players in the System of Justice

The judiciary is part of an entire system that attempts to interpret and apply society's laws. A summary of the parts of this system, and some of its subject matter, follows.

## THE ATTORNEY GENERAL (AG)

The attorney general is an independently elected executive (see Chapter 9) who has important functions within the judicial system. Indeed, although the popular image of the governor is that he or she is the most important single politician in Texas, the attorney general is more directly relevant to the judicial functions of the state. As Texas's chief lawyer, the attorney general (helped by many assistant AGs) represents state agencies when they sue a private individual or another agency or when they are sued. The AG also represents the state as a whole when it becomes involved in the federal courts.

In addition, the AG has a highly significant, if somewhat informal, power: the authority to issue **advisory opinions**. The constitution established the attorney general not only as Texas's chief legal officer but also as legal adviser to the governor and other state officials. The legislature later expanded the scope of the AG's advisory activity. Out of this expansion has arisen the now firmly established practice that the legislature, agencies of the executive branch, and local governments will seek advice on the constitutionality of proposals, rules, procedures, and statutes. In 2006, Greg Abbott handed down 106 "Attorney General's Opinions" dealing with the constitutionality of proposed government laws or actions, and his office supplied various state and local governments with 15,159 Open Record Letter Rulings, answering their requests for advice on whether to release specific information.[6] Rather than filing a court action that is expensive and time consuming, Texas officials who go to the attorney general obtain a ruling on disputed constitutional issues in a relatively brief period of time and at almost no expense. The Texas judiciary and virtually everyone else in the state have come to accept these rulings, albeit sometimes with a good deal of grumbling.

The most publicized attorney general's ruling of modern times, and perhaps in history, dealt with the divisive subject of affirmative action. For some years prior to 1996, the University of Texas Law School had been favoring African American and Latino applicants in its admissions process; that is, minority applicants were judged by a lower set of standards than were Anglo applicants. An Anglo woman, Cheryl Hopwood, had been turned down for admission to the law school despite the fact that her qualifications (grades and Law School Aptitude Test scores) were higher than those of some minority applicants who had been admitted. Hopwood sued in federal court. In 1996, the fifth circuit federal appeals court ruled in Hopwood's favor, deciding that such "reverse discrimination" against Anglos was unconstitutional.[7]

The federal fifth circuit court's decision was significant as it stood because it applied to the state's premier law school. Nevertheless, its scope did not extend to other schools. On February 5, 1997, however, Attorney General Dan Morales dismayed Texas's university community by issuing Letter Opinion 97-001, in which he decreed that the federal court's ruling had outlawed race as a consideration in any admissions process or financial aid decision at any public school. Affirmative action was therefore forbidden in all Texas public colleges.[8]

In 1999, Morales's successor as attorney general, John Cornyn, issued another opinion that called Morales's ruling too broad and rescinded it. Cornyn stopped short of actually claiming that Morales's reasoning was wrong, merely stating that colleges should wait and see how an appeal of the Hopwood decision to the U.S. Supreme Court turned out.[9] Although the Supreme Court declined to hear Texas's appeal, in 2003 it in effect reversed the Hopwood decision when it upheld the affirmative action program at the University of Michigan. After seven years, therefore, Texas universities were again free to consider race in their admissions policies.[10]

The issue of affirmative action is still a highly controversial one and can be expected to generate more litigation. Nevertheless, the important point here is that in one of the most important and intensely conflict-ridden issues in Texas, policy has been set neither by the state legislature nor the governor but by the attorney general. Such is the power of this institution in state government.

# LAWYERS

Law is a "profession," meaning that not just anyone can claim to be an attorney. Everyone who practices law for money must have passed the state bar examination and received a license; the overwhelming majority of licensed lawyers have also attended law school. In the winter of 2007, the state was home to 71,170 licensed attorneys. The legal profession differs substantially in socioeconomic and other characteristics from the population in general. Most lawyers are White males who come from relatively wealthy families. In 2007, 28 percent of Texas lawyers were women, 3.8 percent were African American, and 6.4 percent were Hispanic. The pool of attorneys is presently being broadened, however, and is becoming more diverse in its ethnic and gender background.[11]

## THE STATE BAR OF TEXAS

All lawyers who practice within the state are required to maintain membership in the State Bar and pay annual dues. The State Bar occupies a unique position: It is an agency of government, a professional organization, and an influential interest group active in state politics.

# The Court System

In 1972, the Texas Chief Justice's Task Force for Court Improvement wrote,

> The Texas Constitution prescribes the basic organizational structure of the Texas court system. That structure is essentially the same today as it was under the republic of Texas. The rigidity of the constitutional structure has led to the development, of necessity, of one of the most complex and fragmented judicial systems of all the states.[12]

Nineteen years later, the Texas Research League opened its study of the state's court system with the words, "The Texas judiciary is in disarray with the courts in varying parts of the state going their own way at their own pace. . . . Texas does not have a court *system* in the real sense of the word."[13] These are not the only reformers' panels to have been dismayed by the Texas court system. As the chapter-opening quotation from former Attorney General Jim Mattox suggests, almost anyone who has looked closely at the state judicial system has concluded that its tangled organization prevents it from functioning efficiently. Critics complain about the duplication of jurisdiction between types of courts, about the fact that not all courts keep records of their proceedings, about the fact that a single court may both try cases and hear appeals, and about the lack of standardization within the system, so that the jurisdiction of the sundry types of courts varies from county to county. Whether it functions well or badly, however, the court system does function.

The following sections present a brief description of the activities of Texas's system of 2,676 courts and 3,240 judges from its lowest to its highest levels (see Figure 10-1).[14]

## MUNICIPAL COURTS

City courts are authorized by the state constitution and by state laws to handle minor criminal matters involving a fine of no more than $500 with no possibility of imprisonment (Class C misdemeanors), where they have **concurrent jurisdiction** with justice courts. They also have **exclusive jurisdiction** over municipal ordinances and can impose fines of up to $2,500. Municipal courts have no **civil**

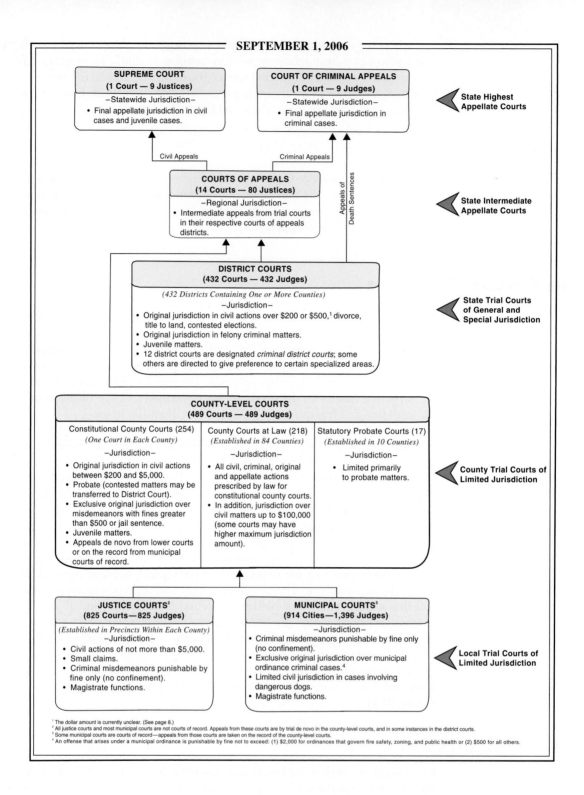

**SEPTEMBER 1, 2006**

**SUPREME COURT**
**(1 Court — 9 Justices)**

–Statewide Jurisdiction–
• Final appellate jurisdiction in civil cases and juvenile cases.

**COURT OF CRIMINAL APPEALS**
**(1 Court — 9 Judges)**

–Statewide Jurisdiction–
• Final appellate jurisdiction in criminal cases.

State Highest Appellate Courts

Civil Appeals

Criminal Appeals

Appeals of Death Sentences

**COURTS OF APPEALS**
**(14 Courts — 80 Justices)**

–Regional Jurisdiction–
• Intermediate appeals from trial courts in their respective courts of appeals districts.

State Intermediate Appellate Courts

**DISTRICT COURTS**
**(432 Courts — 432 Judges)**

*(432 Districts Containing One or More Counties)*
–Jurisdiction–
• Original jurisdiction in civil actions over $200 or $500,[1] divorce, title to land, contested elections.
• Original jurisdiction in felony criminal matters.
• Juvenile matters.
• 12 district courts are designated *criminal district courts*; some others are directed to give preference to certain specialized areas.

State Trial Courts of General and Special Jurisdiction

**COUNTY-LEVEL COURTS**
**(489 Courts — 489 Judges)**

Constitutional County Courts (254)
*(One Court in Each County)*

–Jurisdiction–

• Original jurisdiction in civil actions between $200 and $5,000.
• Probate (contested matters may be transferred to District Court).
• Exclusive original jurisdiction over misdemeanors with fines greater than $500 or jail sentence.
• Juvenile matters.
• Appeals de novo from lower courts or on the record from municipal courts of record.

County Courts at Law (218)
*(Established in 84 Counties)*

–Jurisdiction–

• All civil, criminal, original and appellate actions prescribed by law for constitutional county courts.
• In addition, jurisdiction over civil matters up to $100,000 (some courts may have higher maximum jurisdiction amount).

Statutory Probate Courts (17)
*(Established in 10 Counties)*

–Jurisdiction–

• Limited primarily to probate matters.

County Trial Courts of Limited Jurisdiction

**JUSTICE COURTS[2]**
**(825 Courts—825 Judges)**

*(Established in Precincts Within Each County)*
–Jurisdiction–
• Civil actions of not more than $5,000.
• Small claims.
• Criminal misdemeanors punishable by fine only (no confinement).
• Magistrate functions.

**MUNICIPAL COURTS[3]**
**(914 Cities—1,396 Judges)**

–Jurisdiction–
• Criminal misdemeanors punishable by fine only (no confinement).
• Exclusive original jurisdiction over municipal ordinance criminal cases.[4]
• Limited civil jurisdiction in cases involving dangerous dogs.
• Magistrate functions.

Local Trial Courts of Limited Jurisdiction

[1] The dollar amount is currently unclear. (See page 8.)
[2] All justice courts and most municipal courts are not courts of record. Appeals from these courts are by trial de novo in the county-level courts, and in some instances in the district courts.
[3] Some municipal courts are courts of record—appeals from those courts are taken on the record of the county-level courts.
[4] An offense that arises under a municipal ordinance is punishable by fine not to exceed: (1) $2,000 for ordinances that govern fire safety, zoning, and public health or (2) $500 for all others.

**FIGURE 10-1 Court Structure of Texas**

jurisdiction and deal mainly with violations of traffic laws. They generally do not keep records of trials. In fiscal 2006, there were 1,396 municipal court judges in 914 cities, who disposed of 7,101,848 cases.

Qualifications for municipal judges are decreed by the governing body of the city. Most municipal judges are appointed by the governing body, although in a few cities they are chosen in nonpartisan elections. Terms of office are usually two years. Their salaries are paid entirely by the city and are highly variable.

## JUSTICE COURTS

Until recently known as "Justice of the Peace" courts, these are **original trial courts** with both civil and **criminal jurisdiction.** JP courts deal with misdemeanor criminal cases when the potential punishment is only a fine. They have exclusive jurisdiction over civil cases where the amount in controversy is $200 or less and concurrent jurisdiction with both county and district courts when the amount in controversy is between $200 and $5,000. Their judges preside over small claims courts, act as notaries public and, like other Texas judges, are authorized to perform marriages. In all but the largest counties, they may function as coroners, and in this role they may be required to certify cause of death, despite the fact that few if any justices have any medical training. In fact, there are no constitutional or statutory qualifications for justice court judges, who may therefore come from any background. As a result, only about 6 percent of Texas's justice court judges are lawyers.

Justice court judges are elected by the voters of the precinct and, like other county officials, serve for four years. Salaries range from practically nothing to over $60,000 per year depending on the size of the precinct, the volume of activity, and the generosity of the county commissioners. Texas's 825 justice courts disposed of 2,195,249 criminal cases and 2,265,547 civil cases in the fiscal year ending August 31, 2006.

## COUNTY COURTS

The Texas Constitution requires each county to have a *court of record*—that is, a court where a complete transcript is made of each case. Judges of these 254 "constitutional" courts need not be lawyers but only "well-informed in the law of the state." They are elected for four-year terms, and their salaries are paid by the counties and are highly variable. County court judges in urban areas can be paid more than $100,000 per year. At the other end of the scale, judges in rural counties can bring home closer to $10,000. Vacancies are filled by appointments made by the county commissioners court. Not all constitutional county courts exercise judicial functions. In large counties, the constitutional county judge may devote full time to the administration of county government.

When county courts do exercise judicial functions, they have both original and **appellate jurisdiction** in civil and criminal cases. Their **original jurisdiction** extends to all criminal misdemeanors where the fine allowed exceeds $500 or a jail term may be imposed. County courts also hear appeals in criminal cases from justice and municipal courts. In civil matters, constitutional county courts have concurrent jurisdiction with justice courts when the amount in controversy is between $200 and $5,000.

The volume of cases in approximately thirty of the state's larger counties has moved the legislature to establish a number of specialized county courts, with jurisdiction that varies according to the statute under which they were created. Some exercise jurisdiction in only civil, criminal, probate, or appellate matters, while others are in effect extra, generalist county courts. Judges for these 233 "statutory county courts" and "statutory probate courts" must be attorneys. They are paid the same amount as the judges in the constitutional county courts.

Appellate jurisdiction from the decisions of county courts rests with the courts of appeals. County courts disposed of 154,448 civil, 616,862 criminal, and 8,635 juvenile cases in fiscal year 2006.

## STATE TRIAL COURTS: THE DISTRICT COURTS

In Texas, district courts are the principal trial courts. There were 432 of these busy courts as of 2006. Each has a numerical designation—for example, the 353rd District Court—and each court has one judge. Most district courts have both criminal and civil jurisdiction, but in the metropolitan areas, there is a tendency for each court to specialize in either criminal, civil, or family law cases.

District court judges must be attorneys who are licensed to practice in the state and who have at least four years' experience as lawyers or judges prior to being elected to the district court bench. The basic salary of $125,000 paid by the state is supplemented by an additional sum in most counties. Terms are for four years, with all midterm vacancies filled by gubernatorial appointment.

Cases handled by district court judges are varied. The district courts usually have jurisdiction over felony criminal trials, divorce cases, suits over titles to land, election contests, and civil suits in which the amount in controversy is at least $200. They share some of their civil jurisdiction with county courts depending on the relevant state statute and the amount of money at issue. An additional complication for the allocation of jurisdiction is that at least one court in each county must be designated as the **juvenile court** to handle Texans younger than seventeen who are accused of crimes. These courts can be district, county courts at law, or constitutional county courts.

District court cases are appealed to a court of appeals, except for death-penalty criminal cases, where appeal is made directly to the Court of Criminal Appeals. In fiscal year 2006, district courts disposed of 547,813 civil, 258,991 criminal, and 38,074 juvenile cases.

## INTERMEDIATE STATE APPELLATE COURTS: THE COURTS OF APPEALS

The courts of appeals have intermediate civil and criminal appellate jurisdiction. Unlike the lower courts, appellate courts—the courts of appeals, the Court of Criminal Appeals, and the Supreme Court—are multi-judge courts that operate without juries. Appellate courts consider only the written records of lower court proceedings and the arguments of counsel representing the parties involved.

Texas's fourteen courts of appeals, each of which is responsible for a geographical district, have from three to thirteen justices per court, for a total of eighty judges statewide. In each court, the justices may hear cases *en banc* (together) or in panels of three. All decisions are by majority vote. Justices are elected for staggered six-year terms and must have the same qualifications as justices of the state's Supreme Court: Each must be at least thirty-five years of age and have ten years' legal experience either as a practicing attorney or as a practicing attorney and judge of a court of record. Associate justices receive an annual salary of $137,500, and the chief justice, elected as such, receives $140,000. Within each district, counties are authorized to supplement the basic salary up to $145,000 and $147,500, respectively.

Jurisdiction of the courts of appeals consists of civil cases appealed from district courts, county courts, and county courts at law and of criminal cases, except for capital murder, appealed from lower courts. They both review the decisions of lower court judges and evaluate the constitutionality of the statute or ordinance on which the conviction is based. Decisions of the courts of appeals are usually final, but some may be reviewed by the Court of Criminal Appeals or the Texas Supreme Court. The courts of appeals disposed of 5,440 civil and 6,344 criminal cases in fiscal year 2006.

# HIGHEST STATE APPELLATE COURTS

Texas and Oklahoma are the only states to have split their highest appellate jurisdiction between two courts: a **Supreme Court** that hears only civil cases and a **Court of Criminal Appeals** for criminal cases. Each has responsibility not only for reviewing the decisions made by lower court trial judges but also for interpreting and applying the state constitution. It is this last power of constitutional interpretation that makes these courts of vital political importance.

## THE COURT OF CRIMINAL APPEALS

This is the state's final appeals court in criminal matters, although in rare instances its decisions may be appealed to the U.S. Supreme Court. It considers *writs of error*, filed by losing attorneys who contend that their trial judge made a mistake in applying Texas law and who wish to have the verdict overturned, and *writs of habeus corpus*, in which attorneys claim that a certain person has been unlawfully detained and should be released. In fiscal year 2003, this court disposed of 269 cases, in the process writing 486 opinions. Those dispositions included a review of 26 death-penalty appeals, of which the court affirmed 24 sentences and reversed 2.

Qualifications for judges of the Court of Criminal Appeals and the justices of the Supreme Court are the same as those for justices of the courts of appeals. The nine judges of the Court of Criminal Appeals are elected on a statewide basis for six-year staggered terms, and the presiding judge runs as such. Vacancies are filled by gubernatorial appointment. Cases are normally heard by a three-judge panel. The salary is $150,000 per year, and the presiding judge receives $152,500.

## THE SUPREME COURT

Like its counterpart at the national level, the Texas Supreme Court is the most prestigious court in the system. Unlike its national counterpart, it hears only appeals from civil and juvenile cases.

Qualifications for Supreme Court justices are the same as those for the judges of the courts of appeals and Court of Criminal Appeals. There are nine justices on the bench, including a chief justice who campaigns for election as such. All are elected for six-year staggered terms, with three justices elected

Solicitor General Ted Cruz presents the state's position to the Texas Supreme Court on Wednesday, July 6, 2005, in Austin, Texas. Supreme Court justices, at left, heard oral arguments from both sides in the ongoing court battle over how Texas pays for public education.

every two years. Salaries are the same as those for the Court of Criminal Appeals.

The Supreme Court has no authority in criminal cases. Its original jurisdiction is limited, and most cases that it hears are on appeal from the courts of appeals. Its caseload is somewhat lighter than the caseloads of other state courts; it disposed of only 133 cases in fiscal 2006, writing 145 opinions in the process.

However, the Supreme Court also performs other important functions. It is empowered to issue *writs of mandamus*—orders to corporations or persons, including judges and state officials other than the governor, to perform certain acts. Like the Court of Criminal Appeals, it spends much of its time considering applications for *writs of error*, which allege that the courts of appeals have ruled wrongfully on a point of law. It conducts proceedings for removal of judges and makes administrative rules for all civil courts in the state. Thus, the court "acted upon" 2,940 matters in fiscal 2006.

The Supreme Court also plays a unique role within the legal profession in Texas. It holds the power of approval for new schools of law; it appoints the Board of Law Examiners, which prepares the bar examination; it determines who has passed the examination; and it certifies the successful applicants as being entitled to practice law in Texas.

# Juries

Ordinary citizens have an important part to play in the judicial system. There are two institutions that temporarily recruit Texans from their jobs and pastimes to participate in the functioning of the courts.

## GRAND JURIES

**Grand juries** meet in the seat of each county and are convened as needed. Grand jurors are chosen from a list prepared by a panel of jury commissioners—three to five persons appointed by the district judge. From this list, the judge selects twelve persons who sit for a term, usually of three months' duration. Grand jurors consider the material submitted by prosecutors to determine whether sufficient evidence exists to issue a formal **indictment,** that is, an official accusation.

Normally, the cases considered are alleged **felonies**—serious crimes. Occasionally, persons are indicted for **misdemeanors**—minor crimes—as was Speaker of the House of Representatives Gib Lewis in December 1990. In Texas, grand juries are frequently used to investigate such problems as drug trafficking within the community, increasing crime rates, alleged misconduct by public officials, and other subjects. As mentioned in Chapter Three, in 2005 a Travis County grand jury indicted U.S. House majority leader Tom DeLay and two of his political associates on charges of violating Texas's campaign finance laws.

★ ★ ★ ★ ★ ★ ★ ★ ★ ★ ★ ★ ★ ★ ★ ★ ★ ★ ★ ★ ★ ★ ★ ★ ★ ★ ★ ★

### Citizenship Pays Better Now

Although it is the duty of every citizen to help run the state judicial system by serving on juries, the government recognizes that time is money, and that therefore it is appropriate to pay jurors for their participation. Nevertheless, until 2005 jurors were reimbursed at the rate of only $6 a day, an amount that could often not even compensate them for the price of their lunches. A 2003 study on jury participation rates reported that only 19 percent of those summoned to jury duty in Dallas and Houston actually showed up, and argued that the low pay was a major reason for the cities' inability to motivate those called to serve.

Spurred by the report, and urged to action by some of the state's prominent judges and attorneys, the 2005 state legislature upped jurors' pay for the first time since 1954. As of January 1, 2006, jurors still receive $6 for the first day of work, but are paid $40 for each subsequent day.

★ ★ ★ ★ ★ ★ ★ ★ ★ ★ ★ ★ ★ ★ ★ ★ ★ ★ ★ ★ ★ ★ ★ ★ ★ ★ ★ ★

SOURCE: Steve Quinn, "Texas Jurors Getting $34-a-day Raise," *Denton Record-Chronicle*, December 30, 2005, A2.

## TRIAL JURIES

**Trial juries** make actual decisions about truth and falsehood, guilt and innocence. Under Texas law, defendants in civil cases and anyone charged with a crime may demand a jury trial. Although this right is frequently waived, thousands of such trials take place within the state every year. Lower court juries consist of six people, and district court juries have twelve members. The call to duty on a trial jury is determined through the use of a jury wheel, a list generated from the county voter registration, driver's license, and state identification card lists.

## Police

The state maintains an extensive organization primarily for the enforcement of criminal law. In addition to the judiciary and various planning and policymaking bodies, Texas has about 50,000 law enforcement officers staffing state and local police agencies. Principal among these is the Texas Department of Public Safety (DPS). The DPS, with headquarters in Austin, employed 3,496 commissioned officers in 2005.[15] It is one of only eight state police agencies across the nation empowered to conduct criminal investigations. The other law enforcement officers are employees of the 254 county sheriff's departments and more than 1,000 local police departments. Coordination and cooperation among these police agencies are sometimes haphazard and sometimes effective.

# Removal and Reprimand of Lawyers and Judges

The Texas State Bar is authorized by the legislature to reprimand or disbar any practicing attorney in the state for fraudulent, dishonest, or unethical conduct. Grievance committees have been established in each congressional district to hear complaints and to act against offending attorneys. In practice, however, reprimand and disbarment are uncommon and usually occur only after the offending lawyer has been convicted on some serious charge.

District and appellate court judges may be removed from the bench by impeachment after a vote of two-thirds majority of the legislature. District judges may also be removed by the Supreme Court, and lower court judges may be removed by action of a district court. A 1965 constitutional amendment established a thirteen-member Texas State Commission on Judicial Conduct that is authorized to hear complaints against any judge in the state and to censure, reprimand, or recommend removal by the Texas Supreme Court. But again, as with the disbarment of lawyers, punishment of judges is a rare occurrence.

# Issues Facing the Texas Judiciary

## TOO MUCH CRIME, TOO MANY CRIMINALS

Even if the Texas court system were perfectly organized, it would still be having major problems. There are simply too many accused criminals being arrested for any system to handle. From 1982 to 1992, the state's crime rate increased 12 percent so that its citizens suffered 44,583 reported robberies, 9,424 reported rapes, 86,196 reported aggravated assaults, and 2,239 reported murders in the last of those years.[16] In the early 1990s, however, the crime rate began to decline and continued to fall through the decade. Although the crime rate ticked up slightly in the early years of the new millennium, in 2005 it still remained 31 percent below its level of 1992. Nevertheless, even with the dramatically lowered crime rate, the police still made 1,106,887 arrests in 2005.[17]

Further, while the crime rate as a whole was moderating, the number of offenses by juveniles—especially of a violent nature—remained dismayingly high. In Texas, arrests of those between the ages of ten and sixteen for violent crime increased 282 percent from 1984 to 1993. Although the growth in juvenile violence leveled off after that, the long-term trend was still alarming. Whereas only 3 percent of those arrested for murder in 1977 had been juveniles, in 2005 juveniles contributed more than 5 percent.

The high levels of street crime, leading to large numbers of arrests, have swamped the courts, making Texas's 3,240 judges, the most of any state, still not enough. Not only are the courts dangerously overcrowded, but so also are the prisons. In 2006, 110 state prisons in Texas held about 156,000 inmates. One out of every 151 Texas residents was incarcerated. Despite having spent billions for new prison construction during the 1990s, state officials discovered in 2006 that their facilities were nearly full and might soon require expansion.[18]

Members of the public, justifiably outraged over the threat of murder, rape, assault, robbery, and drug dealing in their neighborhoods, demand that officials "lock 'em up and throw away the key." But the truth is that there are few places to put today's criminals, let alone tomorrow's.

Given this impossible situation, judges do what they can to keep the system functioning by accepting **plea bargains**. A defendant pleads guilty to a lesser charge—say, manslaughter instead of murder—and receives a lesser penalty (less time in prison or a probated sentence), and a trial is avoided. More than nine of ten criminal trials in Texas end in a plea bargain.[19]

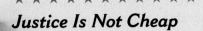

## Justice Is Not Cheap

The sheer number of crimes is a burden not only to the state as a whole but also to its individual parts. For example, in 2003, Hidalgo County in South Texas was struggling with the responsibility of conducting sixteen murder trials. Eleven of the accused killers were indigent, so the county had to appoint, and pay for, their defense counsels.

State law required that two lawyers be appointed to represent such defendants. To be qualified to handle a death penalty case, the lead attorney had to have practiced in fifteen felony jury trials and tried two death penalty cases as first or second defense counsel. Only eleven lawyers in Hidalgo County were qualified to handle such cases. Furthermore, because court-appointed attorneys were paid $40 an hour for out-of-court work and $70 for in-court work, much less than the standard $200-per-hour fee schedule that prevailed among lawyers in 2003 for private representation, competent attorneys were often reluctant to take on such cases.

As a result, Hidalgo County was scrambling, first to find attorneys willing and able to defend accused murderers, and second to pay for them.

SOURCE: "Murder Cases Try County's Resources," *Austin American-Statesman*, May 12, 2003, B6.

Because a plea bargain puts the criminal back on the streets quickly, it does almost nothing to make society safer. Ordinary citizens are often appalled at the swiftness with which violent criminals are recycled into their neighborhoods, but the courts cannot handle the twin problems of a crushing caseload and overstuffed prisons in any other way.

And so, despite the somewhat lower crime rate it has enjoyed over the past decade, Texas still suffers from a plague of criminals. As a result, its judicial system continues to deal unsuccessfully with an impossibly large workload.

# JUDICIAL SELECTION

The job of a judge is an inherently ambiguous one in a democratic society. Many people believe, with Alexander Hamilton, that judges serve society best if they are *independent*—that is, if they are at least partly insulated from outside pressures. The best way to insulate judges is to have them appointed for life. Yet democratic theory requires that all public officials be *accountable* to the public, which would seem to demand that they all be subject to frequent review through regularly scheduled elections. Although some scholars have tried to argue that judges should be both independent and accountable, the two concepts are inherently contradictory.[20]

In practice, various levels of government have tried to compromise the two desirable but incompatible goals in different ways. At the federal level, judges are appointed by the president and serve for life, whereas in many states, including Texas, their jobs must be periodically ratified by the voters in partisan elections. Whatever compromise is chosen, it is never satisfying to everyone. National politicians frequently argue that federal judges must be made more accountable, but in Texas, there are always some prominent people arguing that state judges should be granted more independence. There is no easy answer to the dilemma of accountability versus independence; citizens must make up their own minds. Here is a discussion about two of the ways the argument has surfaced in Texas.

## PARTISAN ELECTIONS?

In the fifty states, six methods are used to select judges:[21]

1. Partisan elections. Judges are chosen in elections in which their party affiliation is listed on the ballot. This is the system employed in Texas and fourteen other states.

2. Nonpartisan election. Judges are chosen in elections, but no party labels appear on the ballot (nineteen states).

3. Appointment by legislatures. The state legislature chooses the judges, although the governor often influences its choices (four states).

4. Appointment by the governor. The chief executive appoints judges, sometimes with the consent of the legislature. Various interest groups—legal, political, and economic—attempt to influence the governor's choice (seven states).

5. Merit plan. The governor makes the appointments from a list submitted by a nominating commission. At regular intervals, judges must be approved by the voters in a referendum. If they fail to win a majority of the votes, they must leave office, and the governor appoints someone else (twenty-two states).

6. Combination. There are various combinations of the first five methods, meaning that judges at different levels may be chosen by different methods in the same state. Because a state may thus fall under more than one category, the numbers listed above for each method sum to sixty-seven rather than fifty.

In Texas, all judges except municipal judges are popularly elected in a partisan contest. Trial court judges serve for four years before having to face the voters again, and appellate judges enjoy a six-year term. The consequence of the state's system is that judges are like other politicians in that, although they do not campaign all the time, they must always be thinking about the next election. Like other politicians, they are aware that what they do or say today may affect their chances for reelection tomorrow. Unlike other politicians, however, judges are supposed to be fair and impartial when trying cases and to pay no attention to the possible partisan consequences of their decisions.

This task is too difficult for imperfect humans. With the next election always just over the horizon, partisanship comes to permeate a courthouse, and the struggle for advantage may taint the quest for impartial decisions. After her defeat in the 1994 Republican landslide, Democratic District Judge Eileen O'Neill wrote a sad analysis of the impact of Texas's judicial electoral processes on its justice system.

> As the campaign season approaches at the courthouse, lines get drawn. Sitting judges join in the search for contenders for open, and sometimes occupied, benches. Judges become guarded in their comments to colleagues and suspicious of their staffs. . . . By November, most everyone belongs to a side, willingly or otherwise, with some perceived stake in the outcome.[22]

It would be placing too much faith in human self-restraint to expect justice to be blind under such circumstances.

★ ★ ★ ★ ★ ★ ★ ★ ★ ★ ★ ★ ★ ★ ★ ★ ★ ★ ★ ★ ★ ★ ★ ★ ★ ★ ★ ★ ★ ★ ★

## Robed Debaters?

While some reformers are trying to make Texas judges less like other politicians, federal courts have been issuing rulings that must make them more like the others. Until July of 2002, state judicial candidates were required to follow Canon 5(I) of the Texas Code of Judicial Conduct, which stated, "A judge or judicial candidate shall not make statements that indicate an opinion on any issue that may be subject to judicial interpretation by the office which is being sought or held . . ." In other words, judicial candidates were forbidden to discuss the issues they might be required to decide. In *Republican Party v. Minnesota*, however, the U.S. Supreme Court struck down a state restriction almost identical to the one in Texas. Writing for the five to four majority, Justice Antonin Scalia enunciated the principle that "We have never allowed the government to prohibit candidates from communicating relevant information to voters during an election." Two months later, the Texas Supreme Court issued a new code, which still prevents candidates from promising to decide a specific case in a specific manner but permits them to indicate a general attitude on a question that might come before their court.

In January 2006, the U.S. Supreme Court affirmed its *Minnesota* ruling. Later the same year, a federal appeals court issued another ruling about judicial campaigns, in which it held that the state of Kentucky could neither forbid candidates for judgeships to personally solicit campaign funds, nor prevent them from advertising their partisan affiliations.

*(continued)*

★ ★ ★ ★ ★ ★ ★ ★ ★ ★ ★ ★ ★ ★ ★ ★ ★ ★ ★ ★ ★ ★ ★ ★ ★ ★ ★ ★ ★ ★ ★

(continued)

The result of these federal court rulings will certainly be that judicial candidates will campaign on issues, personally ask for donations, and advertise their party membership more than ever. One can anticipate a future campaign in which candidates for the Supreme Court or Court of Criminal Appeals debate each other on television.

SOURCES: David Rottman, "The State Courts in 2005: A Year of Living Dangerously," *The Book of the States*, Vol. 38 (Lexington, Ky.: Council of State Governments, 2006), 238; Christy Hoppe, "Ruling Likely to Change Texas Judicial Elections," *Dallas Morning News*, June 28, 2002, A20; "Texas Judges Can Now Opine Publicly," *Austin American-Statesman*, August 23, 2002, B7; Adam Liptak, "Judges Can Solicit Election Funds, Court Rules," *Austin American-Statesman*, October 12, 2006, A19.

People who want to change the way Texas chooses its judges argue that circumstances such as the one sketched by Judge O'Neill are unavoidable in a selection system that rests upon partisan elections. But others are less eager to throw out the democratic baby with the partisan bathwater. All systems have flaws, and the democratic appeal of partisan elections is strong. As David Willis, an adjunct law professor at the University of Houston, wrote in a defense of Texas's system,

> Judicial candidates, like everyone, have philosophical preferences. Choosing a partisan label suggests a whole cluster of attitudes toward the role of government in addressing social challenge It is an inexact science, but why deprive us of this crucial information about a candidate?[23]

Scholarly research supports Professor Willis's point. Studies show that the most important factor in allowing citizens to predict how judges will decide cases is their political party. Republican judges tend to favor business and people with power and wealth; Democrats tend to favor labor unions, the poor, and social underdogs in general. In other words, Texas has the perfect system for allowing its citizens to select judges who share their ideologies.[24] Moreover, as the findings summarized in the box illustrate, there is no good evidence that a different system of choosing judges would produce a more honest system than the one Texas has now. An appointive or nonpartisan system might not create a better judiciary and would be less democratic.

## IS JUSTICE FOR SALE?

The practice of electing judges is thus in line with democratic theory. When judges must run for office at periodic intervals, they are kept accountable to the people's wishes. However, there is a problem with elections, a problem common to all offices but particularly troubling in regard to the judiciary. When judges have to run for office like other politicians, they also have to raise money like other politicians. When lawyers who practice in judges' courtrooms or others with a direct interest in the outcome of legal cases give judges campaign contributions, it raises the uncomfortable suspicion that those judges' court rulings might

★ ★ ★ ★ ★ ★ ★ ★ ★ ★ ★ ★ ★ ★ ★ ★ ★ ★ ★ ★ ★ ★ ★ ★ ★ ★ ★ ★ ★

## Is Reform Needed?

In 2001, political scientist Melinda Gann Hall published a systematic evaluation of the consequences of Supreme Court selection processes in the fifty states. Her conclusion was, "Court reformers underestimate the extent to which partisan elections have a tangible substantive component and overestimate the extent to which nonpartisan and retention races are insulated from partisan politics." In simpler language, state high court judges who are appointed are not, as a group, more independent from the political process than are judges who are elected in partisan races.

In short, the available evidence suggests that the way Texas chooses its judges is not an unusually bad way, and there is no reason to think that some other way would be better.

★ ★ ★ ★ ★ ★ ★ ★ ★ ★ ★ ★ ★ ★ ★ ★ ★ ★ ★ ★ ★ ★ ★ ★ ★ ★ ★ ★ ★

SOURCES: Melinda Gann Hall, "State Supreme Courts in American Democracy: Probing the Myths of Judicial Reform," *American Political Science Review*, Vol. 95, no. 3, June 2001, 326.

be affected by the money. Wealthy special interests may taint the administration of justice just as they deform the public policy made by other institutions.

James Andrew Wynne Jr., is a judge in the North Carolina Court of Appeals. The North Carolina judicial system is similar to the one in Texas, with partisan elections for almost all levels. In 2002 Judge Wynne used a vivid metaphor to summarize the uneasiness of those who suspect that justice may be for sale in such judicial systems. Suppose, he mused, that major-league baseball umpires had to run for office, and the players were allowed to contribute money to their campaigns: "Under that scenario, how can anyone have the confidence in the strike calls of an umpire if you know the pitcher contributed $10,000 to select that umpire to call the game?"[25] It is a fair question. Wealthy private interests may taint the administration of justice just as they deform the public policy made by other institutions. (Perhaps Judge Wynne's argument had some effect. Before the 2004 election, North Carolina instituted partial public financing of state judicial campaigns.)[26]

Texas, however, continues to require its judicial candidates to finance their election campaigns with private funds. Not surprisingly, one of the chief sources of campaign contributions to judicial candidates is the very lawyers who will be practicing in their courts if they win office. In 2003, for example, Texans for Public Justice analyzed the campaign finances of eighty-seven winning candidates for the intermediate courts of appeals. TPJ concluded that attorneys contributed 72 percent of the total funding for those successful races.[27] In a preliminary analysis of the funding of the reelection races of the five justices on the supreme court running for reelection in 2006, TPJ concluded that 51 percent of their total funding had come from attorneys and law firms.[28] It is difficult to imagine that judges would be able to forget the source of their campaign resources when arbitrating the cases of attorneys and groups that have supported them.

In an analysis of the decisions of the Ohio supreme court aimed at addressing this very question, reporters for the *New York Times* compared the behavior of those justices to the sources of the funds for their campaigns. They came to two conclusions. First, Ohio supreme court justices almost always failed to

★ ★ ★ ★ ★ ★ ★ ★ ★ ★ ★ ★ ★ ★ ★ ★ ★ ★ ★ ★ ★ ★ ★ ★ ★ ★ ★ ★ ★ ★ ★

## *Money and Justice*

I t is not only in raising campaign funds that judges become beholden to attorneys who may practice in front of them. In 2005, the state Commission on Judicial Conduct rebuked Texas Supreme Court Justice Nathan Hecht for his vocal advocacy of Harriet Miers, President Bush's nominee to the U.S. Supreme Court. (Miers later withdrew her name from consideration.) Hecht objected to the official criticism, and filed suit against the Commission, which meant, of course, that he had to hire lawyers. Hecht won his case, and the rebuke was withdrawn, but meanwhile he had amassed a debt of $340,000.

Not a wealthy man, Hecht could not pay his debt himself. Instead, he turned to his list of campaign contributors, and asked for financial assistance. In 2007, the same lawyers who had helped get him into office gave him enough cash to pay his legal bills. Hecht would be superhumanly virtuous if he did not feel very grateful to his benefactors, both in and out of the courtroom.

★ ★ ★ ★ ★ ★ ★ ★ ★ ★ ★ ★ ★ ★ ★ ★ ★ ★ ★ ★ ★ ★ ★ ★ ★ ★ ★ ★ ★ ★ ★

SOURCE: Chuck Lindell, "Proposals to Reimburse Justice Moot," *Austin American-Statesman*, March 21, 2007, B1.

withdraw from hearing cases in which lawyers and interests who had contributed to their campaigns appeared. Second, over the course of twelve years, supreme court justices voted in favor of those contributors 70 percent of the time.[29] There is no reason to think that Texas judges behave any differently.

Responding to the public perception that justice might be for sale, in 1995 the legislature passed the Judicial Campaign Fairness Act (JCFA). This legislation limited individual contributions to statewide judicial candidates to $5,000 each election and prohibited law firms from contributing more than $30,000 to individual Supreme Court candidates. Judicial candidates were also forbidden to accept more than a total of $300,000 from all political action committees.

Although the intent of the JCFA was clearly to stop the contamination of the Texas judiciary by money, events almost immediately proved it to be ineffective. In 1996, Texas Supreme Court Justice James A. Baker allowed an attorney with a case pending before him to participate in his fund-raising efforts.[30] When journalists reported this obvious conflict of interest, the bad publicity forced Baker to withdraw from the case. His withdrawal solved the immediate concern about one questionable case, but it did not address the basic problem. As long as attorneys are allowed to raise campaign funds for judges and to contribute money themselves, there will be public doubts about the impartiality of the judiciary. The JCFA, while it was well intentioned, does not address this fundamental problem.

In 2000, two consumer-advocacy groups filed suit in federal court, arguing that when Texas allows judges to solicit campaign contributions from lawyers who may appear in their courts, the state violates its citizens' constitutional rights to fair trials. They lost the case, with U.S. District Judge James Nowlin writing, "The issue of limiting campaign contributions and/or potential contributions are questions for the citizens of Texas and their state representatives, not a federal court." Given this decision, if the Texas system of financing judicial elections is to be changed, the impetus must come from inside the state.[31]

As with elections to other offices, the suggestion is sometimes made that both the appearance and the reality of impropriety could be avoided if judicial campaigns were publicly, as opposed to privately, financed (see Chapter 5). Public financing, it is argued, would permit judges to be held democratically accountable, yet would soften the impact of special interests. Former Chief Justice Tom Phillips of the Texas Supreme Court, for one, has advocated this change in the state's judicial elections. Phillips points out that no additional tax money need be used for this reform because judicial campaigns could be bankrolled using an existing $200 lawyer occupation tax that raises $10 million annually.[32] So far, however, this suggestion has found no support among lawmakers.

## EQUAL JUSTICE?

The dilemmas of too much crime and of judicial selection are not the only serious problems facing the Texas system of justice. The state has for some time been in the midst of another argument over the way it affords legal representation to poor people accused of crimes. Before people are put in prison, they must be tried and convicted. Because one of the most important ideals of democracy is that everyone is equal before the law, Texans would like to think that all accused persons are treated fairly and impartially in this process. A well-functioning democracy features a judiciary that rigorously but fairly judges the guilt of everyone brought to trial. Nevertheless, there is substantial evidence that the Texas criminal justice system does not affect all citizens equally. It imposes severe burdens on the poor and particularly on members of ethnic minorities—the same groups who are at a disadvantage in other areas of politics. Legal fees are expensive—in 2007, the standard lawyer's fee was $300 per hour—and the system is so complex that accused people cannot defend themselves without extensive and expensive legal help.

The result is that the prisons, and death row, are full of poor people. Wealthier defendants can afford to hire attorneys to help

Cartoonist Ben Sargent satirizes the dilemma of a judiciary that must run in partisan elections: As is the case with elections to the legislator or executive offices, candidates become dependent on the people who give them campaign contributions, which creates the suspicion that their decisions are not impartial.

*Courtesy of Ben Sargent.*

# YOU DECIDE

## At-Large or Single-Member District Elections?

State district judges in Texas are selected in **at-large elections**. All candidates receive their votes from the whole district, which in a metropolitan area is typically a county. Such elections tend to make it difficult for minorities to be elected. If, for example, a quarter of the population of a county is Hispanic, and there is more-or-less bloc voting by each ethnic group, then Hispanic candidates will be outvoted three to one every time. Although Hispanics represent 25 percent of the population in a given county, they will have 0 percent of the judges in that county.

Consequently, minority representatives almost always prefer single-member **district elections** to at-large elections. If the county is carved into a number of geographic districts, with each district electing a single judge, then (assuming that people of different ethnic groups tend to live in different areas) the proportion of judges from each group should be roughly proportional to that group's representation in the population of that county. Minority leaders, therefore, often argue that Texas should adopt a system of electing county judges in which all candidates run from single-member districts.

| PRO | CON |
|---|---|
| ▲ The 1965 Voting Rights Act forbids systematic discrimination against the voting rights of minorities. Because at-large districts make minority candidates unelectable, they are illegal. | ▼ The Voting Rights Act forbids discrimination against *voters*. It does not guarantee that minority *candidates* must win. |
| ▲ In many counties, the proportion of minority judges is far below the proportion of minority citizens in the county. | ▼ The lack of minority judges is mainly caused by the lack of qualified minority attorneys. It is there for not evidence of discrimination. |
| ▲ Ever since 1994, very few minority judges have been elected in Texas. This fact is evidence that Anglo citizens refuse to vote for minority candidates. | ▼ The lack of minority success at the polls is caused by the fact that almost all minority candidates are Democrats. Where Democrats do well, as in Dallas County in 2006, minority candidates do well. |
| ▲ When minority citizens see that there are no minority judges, it undermines their faith in the justice system; such a lack of faith cannot be good for society as a whole. | ▼ Granted, this is a problem. The solution is for minorities to become Republicans, thereby increasing their chance to be elected. |
| ▲ Minorities should be guaranteed some representation on the bench by the deliberate creation of some "minority–majority" districts. | ▼ Such a plan would amount to a "Democrat-protection scheme," which the Constitution does not oblige Republicans to endorse. |
| ▲ Putting aside questions of minority politics, single-member districts provide better representation for discrete areas of a city or county. | ▼ At-large election plans ensure that each candidate must consider the welfare of the entire county, whereas district plans create a system of jealous, quarreling pieces. |

*(continued)*

(*continued*)

▲ Minorities should keep suing in federal court until Texas is forced to create a single-member district judicial election system.

▼ In *Houston Lawyers' Assoc. et al.* v. *Attorney General of Texas et al.* (501 U.S. 419, 1994) the federal courts already settled this question; more lawsuits would be futile.

SOURCES: James Cullen, "Lawyers Protect Their Own," *Texas Observer*, September 17, 1993, 4; Suzanne Gamboa, "Judicial Elections Proposal Rejected," *Austin American-Statesman*, August 25, 1993, A1; Lani Guinere, *The Tyranny of the Majority: Fundamental Fairness in Representative Democracy* (New York: Free Press, 1994); David Lubin, *The Paradox of Representation: Racial Gerrymandering and Minority Interests in Congress* (Princeton, N.J.: Princeton University, 1997); David T. Canon, *Race, Redistricting, and Representation: The Unintended Consequences of Black Majority Districts* (Chicago: University of Chicago, 1999).

them try to "beat the rap," and in any case, they are often offered plea bargains that allow them to stay out of prison. But until recently, Texas lacked a system of *public defenders* to provide free legal assistance to accused criminals who were too poor to pay a lawyer, except in the case of defendants who had been convicted of capital murder and sentenced to death. Judges, using county rather than state funds, appointed private attorneys to represent indigent defendants. Frequently, they were inexperienced or already busy with paying clients.

In 1999, journalist Debbie Nathan spent time observing the way county-appointed attorneys interacted with their indigent clients. Her summary had to be troubling to citizens who thought that the poor, too, should be entitled to competent legal counsel when they are accused of a crime.

> What I witnessed was low-grade pandemonium. Attorneys rushed into court, grabbed a file or two, and sat down for a quick read; this was their first and often most lengthy exposure to their new client's case. Confused-looking defendants, mostly Hispanic or African American, met their counsel amid a hubbub of other defendants, defendants' spouses, and defendants' squalling babies.[33]

Reformers argued that if justice was to be done, Texas should have a system of public defenders equal in number and experience to the public prosecutors. Without such procedures, the system inevitably discriminated against poor defendants, who tended to be minority citizens. For example, in 1993, the Texas Bar Foundation sponsored a study by the Spangenberg Group of the state's system of appointing attorneys for indigents accused of murder. The group's conclusions about Texas justice were consistent and unambiguous.

> In almost every county, the rate of compensation provided to court-appointed attorneys in capital cases is absurdly low . . . the quality of representation in these cases is uneven and . . . in some cases, the performance of counsel is extremely poor.[34]

If such deficient legal representation was common for citizens accused of murder, which is a high-profile crime, then the representation afforded people accused of lesser crimes must have been even worse. It stood to reason that defendants who received inferior public legal representation would be convicted more often, and be given harsher sentences, than defendants who could afford to hire private attorneys. Indeed, a study in the early 1990s concluded that a White person convicted of assault had a 30 percent chance of drawing a prison sentence, while a Hispanic with a similar record had a 66 percent chance and an African American had a 76 percent chance.[35]

In short, the reality of unequal justice was a challenge to the democratic ideal of the Texas judicial system. Responding to such persistent criticism of the way the state's legal system treated the poor, the 2001 legislature moved to make it more equitable. The Texas Fair Defense Act, sponsored by Senator Rodney Ellis of Houston, was designed to standardize and better fund indigent defense in felony cases. Although the law left counties, not the state, with primary responsibility for providing lawyers for poor defendants, it required prompt appointment of counsel, mandated quick attorney–client contact, ordered the counties to create a standard of qualification for attorneys, charged them with setting a fee schedule for defense attorneys, and imposed other requirements. Just as important, it appropriated $19.7 million in state funds each year to supplement the $90 million the counties typically spend on indigent defense.

In 2003, the Texas Defender Service and the Equal Justice Center cooperated to study how the Fair Defense Act was being implemented. Their conclusions were disturbing. Studying the thirty-three counties that had accounted for 87 percent of those sent to death row since 1976, they reported that only Lubbock and Brazoria Counties were fully complying with the law. The thirty-one others were failing in their obligation to provide adequate counsel to indigent defendants for various reasons, including insufficient compensation for attorneys, low standards, or unsatisfactory or complete lack of standards for defense lawyers. The actual facts are somewhat ambiguous because in a follow-up report by National Public Radio, county officials claimed that they were in fact implementing the law but had merely failed to report their activities to authorities in Austin. The best that can be said, therefore, is that troubling questions remain about the adequacy of the defense that the state provided to its accused indigent citizens.[36]

The problem of unequal justice is especially acute because Texas is a state with the death penalty. From the year 1982, when Texas resumed executions following a hiatus ordered by the U.S. Supreme Court, through the end of 2006,

The democratic ideal of equal justice for all citizens faces a severe test when poor people are accused of crimes. If they cannot pay a private attorney, and the state refuses to provide them with competent counsel, they stand little chance of receiving an adequate defense.

*Courtesy of Ben Sargent.*

the state executed 379 people, including three women.[37] In Chapter Eleven, the issue of whether capital punishment is defensible will be examined. Whether the death penalty is justifiable, however, it would seem to be inflicted unequally on poorer and wealthier defendants. The problems of unequal justice for the poor continue up the judicial ladder to the most serious crime.

The fact that poor defendants probably have a greater chance of being incarcerated, and executed, would not be so worrisome if there were reasons to have confidence in the fact that they were all guilty. However, recent history is not reassuring to partisans of the state's criminal justice system on that issue.

As detailed in the box, there is good reason to think that some of the people convicted of capital crimes in Texas have actually been innocent, the victims of a criminal justice system that often fails to ensure them an adequate trial. Further, there are numerous examples of people who have been convicted of crimes and sentenced to prison, only to have later advances in investigative science prove them

★ ★ ★ ★ ★ ★ ★ ★ ★ ★ ★ ★ ★ ★ ★ ★ ★ ★ ★ ★ ★ ★ ★ ★ ★ ★ ★ ★ ★ ★ ★ ★

## Does Texas Execute the Innocent?

Theoretically, the state maintains an elaborate system of safeguards to ensure that defendants who have been convicted of murder and sentenced to die for their crime are actually guilty. There is an automatic appeal filed by the defendant's lawyer, and reviewed by the staff and justices of the court of criminal appeals. At the same time, the original trial judge appoints a second attorney to investigate the conditions of the trial, try to find additional evidence or indications of official misconduct, and then file a "writ of habeas corpus" asking the court of criminal appeals to overturn the conviction or the death sentence.

In practice, as Chuck Lindell discovered when he reviewed eleven years of writs for the *Austin American-Statesman* in 2006, the court of criminal appeals tolerates such shoddy work from its habeas corpus lawyers that the system is often a fraudulent substitute for real justice. "Lawyers appointed to handle appeals for death row inmates routinely bungled the job," Lindell wrote in a series of articles, "submitting work that falls far below professional standards . . . Some appeals are incomplete, incomprehensible or improperly argued. Others are duplicated poorly from previous appeals." Lindell found examples of cases in which "Witnesses lied, prosecutors hid evidence or scientists flubbed their analyses." His articles described an underfunded system that routinely had to employ the worst lawyers in the state to provide a sham review of the convictions of the state's poorest defendants.

Although Lindell did not state the implied conclusion directly, others made the obvious deduction from his investigation. "Texas has sent a number of innocent people to death row and has executed several with strong claims of innocence. . ." wrote Dave Atwood shortly after the series ran in the paper. And indeed, Atwood's conclusion from Lindell's evidence is inescapable. It only remained to point out that those who have been wrongly put to death have tended to be the state's poor and minority citizens.

★ ★ ★ ★ ★ ★ ★ ★ ★ ★ ★ ★ ★ ★ ★ ★ ★ ★ ★ ★ ★ ★ ★ ★ ★ ★ ★ ★ ★ ★ ★ ★

SOURCES: Chuck Lindell, "Sloppy Lawyers Failing Clients On Death Row," *Austin American-Statesman*, October 29, 2006, A1; Chuck Lindell, "When $25,000 Is The Limit On A Life," *Austin American-Statesman*, October 30, 2006, A1; Dave Atwood, "We Are All Guilty of Homicide," *Austin American-Statesman*, November 27, 2006, A9.

innocent. The ability of geneticists to analyze DNA, in particular, has led to the overturning of a remarkable number of convictions. From 1989 to May 2007, 200 people nationwide were released from prison after DNA tests led to the nullification of their sentences, 28 of them in Texas.[38]

A remarkably large number of these wrongfully convicted people have been in Texas. In 1997, Governor Bush pardoned Ben Salazar, who had spent five years in prison, and Kevin Byrd, who had been incarcerated for twelve years, both for rape. In 2000, Roy Wayne Criner was also pardoned on the basis of new DNA evidence. He had served ten years of a life sentence for a rape and murder he did not commit. In 2003, Josiah Sutton, serving twenty-five years for a 1998 rape, was freed when the Houston Police Department crime lab admitted that it had botched his DNA test.[39] In 2006 Governor Perry pardoned Greg Wallis and Billy Wayne Miller for similar reasons. They had been in prison eighteen and twenty-two years, respectively, and, if the ability to analyze DNA had not come along, would be there still.[40]

Even more unsettling is the case of Delma Banks.[41] In 1980, Banks, who is Black, was arrested, tried, and convicted of the shooting murder of a sixteen-year-old White boy, Richard Whitehead, in Nash, near Texarkana. Banks, who had no prior criminal record, was sentenced to death, and the appeals process began. Over the next few years, his case attracted the attention of the NAACP, which furnished him with a lawyer. Through a strenuous and lengthy process of prying loose suppressed and ignored facts, his attorney, George Kendall, managed to bring several types of evidence to public attention.

1. There was no physical evidence linking Banks to the murder, no DNA, no fingerprints, no blood, and no murder weapon. On the contrary, forensic evidence strongly suggested that the boy's death occurred when Banks was indisputably in Dallas, three hours away. Some observers have suggested that the significance of this fact was not made clear to the jury because Banks's court-appointed attorney provided an "inattentive defense."

2. It has also been suggested by numerous observers that the jury was not inclined to notice the weakness of the prosecution's case because it consisted entirely of White citizens. Prosecutors dismissed African Americans from the jury pool.

3. The case against Banks rested entirely on the testimony of two men. One, Robert Farr, concealed from the jury the fact that he was a paid police informant, hired specifically to incriminate Banks, when he testified that Banks had confessed to him that he had killed someone. Years later, just before he died of cancer, Farr signed an affidavit affirming that he had lied on the stand about his knowledge of the crime. The second witness, Charles Cook, testified during the trial that Banks had also confessed to him that he had murdered Whitehead and stolen his Ford Mustang. Police have never found the car, but they did finally recover the murder weapon, *at Cook's house.* Nineteen years after the crime, George Kendall persuaded a federal judge to issue an order that forced Bowie County prosecutors to turn over the transcript of the police interrogation of Cook, a document they had withheld from the original defense lawyer. The transcript reveals the police "coaching" Cook in his testimony. Cook later stated that he had lied at the trial because he was told that his own pending arson charge would be dismissed if he performed "well" while testifying against Banks.

As these bits of dismaying evidence of prosecutorial misconduct dribbled out over the years, they gradually stimulated a movement to have Banks retried. Various journalists, in and out of Texas, took up his cause. Two former federal judges and a former federal prosecutor, all supporters of the death penalty in general, filed *amicus curiae* ("friend of the court") briefs in appeals to both the federal and Texas courts. As execution day approached in March 2003, twenty-four Republican and Democratic state legislators, twelve each from the House and Senate, signed letters to Governor Perry urging him to grant Banks a thirty-day reprieve.

The various facts, doubts, and suspicions about the Banks case did not move the Texas Court of Criminal Appeals, however. The day before the scheduled execution, it rejected all appeals for a new trial. In her majority opinion, Judge Cathy Cochran wrote, "After 23 years of litigation review and re-review by this court and the federal courts, applicant (Banks) has had his fair share of due process in our state criminal justice system."

On March 12, 2003, Banks, having finished his last meal of cheeseburgers and French fries, was ten minutes away from being strapped to a gurney in the death chamber at Huntsville prison when the news came that the U.S. Supreme Court had issued a stay of execution. The Court had not ordered a new trial or overturned his conviction but simply stopped his execution while it considered the issues. In February 2004, the same Court threw out Banks's death sentence and ordered the fifth federal circuit court to consider the issue of whether he deserved a new trial. At long last, it had begun to look like Banks might be given justice, but as this book went to press, Delma Banks still did not know his fate.

Such examples of possible miscarriages of justice must make observers wonder how many other people are in prison or on death row in Texas because they were too poor to pay a lawyer, were in the wrong place at the wrong time, made an enemy of some county prosecutor, or happened to be assigned an indifferent or incompetent defense attorney. After an execution, of course, it is too late to help the person who has been wrongly convicted.

## Summary

The judiciary is an uncomfortable part of the political system. There is a sense in which what judges do is neutral and nonpolitical, and jurists play up this aspect of their job. It is a myth, however, that the judiciary handles every problem in a nonpolitical manner. Especially in the higher appellate courts, which are responsible for interpreting the state constitution, the act of judging is an intensely political process. The conflict between functioning as neutral arbiters and functioning as political adjudicators creates problems for all judges, and it does so especially in Texas, where judges are part of the partisan system of state governance.

Many individuals function together to make the state judicial system what it is. The most important single official is the attorney general, but judges, attorneys, the State Bar, the police, and members of juries also play important roles. The state's judicial system is inadequately organized, which makes its other problems worse.

Over the last quarter century, many observers have concluded that the Texas judiciary does not function well. Besides its inefficient organization, its problems are caused, first, by the fact that there is simply too much crime for the system to process effectively. Second, the system of partisan elections runs the risk of forcing judges to worry about the next campaign instead of applying themselves to impartial evaluation. Third, the system forces judges to rely on campaign contributions from people affected by judicial decisions, which creates many opportunities for impropriety. There is controversy over whether there is a fourth problem: At-large districts have the effect of making the election of minority judges less likely.

The disadvantage that poor people experience when dealing with the judicial system mirrors their disadvantages in the rest of the political system, but the problem is particularly troublesome because equal justice under law is one of the most cherished ideals of democracy. Unequal justice, which appears to result in the conviction of innocent people in Texas, is especially disturbing because the state enforces capital punishment on many of its convicted murderers.

## Glossary Terms

| | |
|---|---|
| appellate jurisdiction | indictment |
| at-large election | judge |
| attorney general's advisory opinion | judiciary |
| civil jurisdiction | juvenile court |
| concurrent jurisdiction | misdemeanor |
| Court of Criminal Appeals | original jurisdiction |
| criminal jurisdiction | original trial courts |
| district election | plea bargain |
| exclusive jurisdiction | Supreme Court |
| felony | trial jury |
| grand jury | |

## Study Questions

1. How are elected judges politicians in the same way that legislators and members of the executive branch are? How are they different?

2. Describe briefly the organization and jurisdiction of the Texas judiciary.

3. Why is the attorney general such an important component of the state's judicial system?

4. How many "supreme courts" does Texas have? In two words, what is the jurisdiction of each?

5. Why do so many people object to the fact that judges may accept campaign contributions from attorneys who practice in their courtrooms? Do you agree with the criticism?

6. What are the advantages and disadvantages of filling judgeships by partisan elections?

7. Why do minorities generally object to at-large judicial elections? What are the advantages of such a system? What are the disadvantages?

8. What causes the Texas judicial system to discriminate against poorer citizens? Can you think of any reforms that might change the situation?

# Surfing the Web

Readers are urged to visit the companion site for this book:

**http://academic.cengage.com/polsci/Kraemer/TexasPolitics10e**

# The Substance of Justice

The gurney in Huntsville state prison where condemned murderers are strapped prior to being executed.

The majority, in that country [the United States] . . . exercise a prodigious actual authority, and a power of opinion which is nearly as great; no obstacles exist which can impede or even retard its progress, so as to make it heed the complaints of those whom it crushes in its path. . . . I know of no country in which there is so little independence of mind and real freedom of discussion as in America.

ALEXIS DE TOCQUEVILLE, FRENCH VISITOR TO THE UNITED STATES, *DEMOCRACY IN AMERICA*, 1835

# Introduction

The output of the judicial system is extraordinarily important to all of us. The system protects—or fails to protect—our rights in a democratic society and processes our case in the event we are accused of a crime. It also allocates large amounts of money and power by arbitrating between various conflicting interests, especially those of a business nature.

The subject of the previous chapter was the structure and behavior of the Texas judiciary. On the whole, it earned rather low marks for democratic virtue. That being so, it might be expected that the products of the system—the substance of justice—would similarly fail to stand up under scrutiny. Somewhat surprisingly, however, close examination reveals that justice in Texas is a good deal more complicated, and in some cases more admirable, than a knowledge of the judiciary's institutional weaknesses might lead us to believe.

The first topic of this chapter is an examination of the Texas judiciary's record on civil liberties and civil rights, followed by an evaluation of the manner in which it deals with accused criminals, and then a discussion of some of the issues surrounding the cry for "tort reform" in the area of lawsuits against business. The conclusion is that the system's record is uneven. In some areas, such as civil rights and liberties, it is dishearteningly backward. In other areas, especially the manner in which it has forced the state to equalize education, it is surprisingly progressive. When measured against the standards of democratic theory, Texas justice provides cause for both pessimism and optimism.

# Civil Liberties

The phrase **civil liberties** refers to the basic individual freedom from government interference that is crucial to sustaining a democratic government. Democracy requires that citizens be free to speak, read, and assemble so that they may choose in an independent and informed manner among competing ideas, candidates, and parties. In addition, because a democratic society must respect individual autonomy of thought and conscience, government must not be allowed to interfere with freedom of religious choice.

The First Amendment to the U.S. Constitution declares that Congress may neither abridge the people's freedom of speech or of the press, nor their right to assemble peaceably, nor to petition the government for a redress of grievances. It also forbids Congress to "establish" religion—that is, support it with money and coercive laws—or prohibit its free exercise. The Fourteenth Amendment, passed after the Civil War in the 1860s, has gradually been held by the U.S. Supreme Court to apply most of these protections to the states—a process known as "incorporation."

In addition, the states have similar guarantees in their constitutions. Article I, Section 8 of the Texas Constitution assures us that "no law shall ever be passed curtailing the liberty of speech or of the press," and Section 27 promises that the state's citizens may assemble "in a peaceable manner" and petition the government "for redress of grievances or other purposes." Individual liberties are thus acknowledged in Texas, as in the federal government, to be of fundamental importance to a democratic society.

Given this apparent unanimity, we might think that there would be little disagreement about how these freedoms were to be protected. If so, we would be mistaken. The words in both constitutions seem evident enough in their protection of individual freedoms, but the history of the documents teaches us that the meaning of any political guarantee must be fought over. In the South, especially, the traditionalist political culture has never been eager to grant the individual freedoms promised by constitutions. Majorities in the South have been especially resistant to the idea that African Americans and Mexican Americans should enjoy the same personal liberties as Anglos. For all of the nineteenth and most of the twentieth century, Texas was quite reluctant to give its citizens the freedom its constitution guarantees. Even in the twenty-first century, there are hot disagreements about which exercises of government authority are legitimate and which violate someone's civil liberty.

Furthermore, there are always politicians and private citizens who either do not understand the importance of civil liberties or do not value them. Individual rights are therefore frequently under siege somewhere, in Texas or other states. The ambiguous but very serious war that began with the terrorist attacks of September 11, 2001, has only sharpened disagreements about the balance between government authority and personal freedom. Sometimes the battle over civil liberties is fought in the legislature. Just as frequently, however, the struggle takes place in court.

## FREEDOM OF EXPRESSION

Although "freedom of speech and press" seems to be an unambiguous phrase, only a little thought can create a variety of difficult problems of interpretation. Do constitutional guarantees of freedom of speech protect those who would incite a mob to lynch a prisoner? Teach terrorist recruits to make bombs? Tell malicious lies about public officials? Wear a T-shirt lettered with obscenities to high school? Spout racist propaganda on a local cable TV access program? Publicly burn an American flag? Falsely advertise a patent medicine? These questions and others like them have sparked intense political and intellectual conflict.

In 1925, in *Gitlow* v. *New York*, the U.S. Supreme Court for the first time held that the freedom of speech and press guarantees of the First Amendment to the federal Constitution were binding on state and local governments through the "due process of law" clause of the Fourteenth Amendment.[1] In the more than eight decades since the *Gitlow* decision, the Court's interpretation of the meaning of "freedom of speech and press" has constantly evolved so that American liberties are never quite the same from year to year. Since the 1960s, the First Amendment has come to contain protection for a "freedom of expression" that is larger than mere speech and press. Citizens may engage in nonspeech acts that are intended to convey a political communication.

For example, at the 1984 Republican National Convention in Dallas, Gregory Lee Johnson and others protested the Reagan administration's policies by burning an American flag while chanting, "America the red, white, and blue, we spit on you." Johnson was arrested and charged with violating a Texas law against flag desecration. Johnson's attorneys argued that his act was "symbolic speech" protected by the First Amendment.

The U.S. Supreme Court agreed. In its 1989 decision in *Texas* v. *Johnson*, the majority held that "Johnson's burning of the flag was conduct sufficiently imbued with elements of communication to implicate the First Amendment,"[2] thus overturning the Texas law and freeing Johnson from the threat of jail time.

This decision caused a national furor. A large majority of Americans, while they supported freedom of expression in the abstract, were not willing to grant it to someone whose ideas they found so obnoxious. In this way, they showed the inconsistency that people sometimes display when they discover that they dislike the specific consequences of general principles they otherwise endorse.

The majorities in the United States and in Texas did not realize that it is despised expressions of opinion such as Johnson's that most require First Amendment protection. Democracy requires not only majority rule but also minority rights. Fashionable opinion does not need protection because its very popularity renders it immune from suppression. But the expression of a political idea that the great majority finds agreeable is not "freedom of expression" at all. Freedom comes into play only when there is some danger to the speaker for expressing his or her thought—that is, when the thought is disagreeable to the majority. The American—and Texas—public missed this point. The clamor to outlaw flag burning was an example of the "tyranny of the majority" that Alexis de Tocqueville, quoted at the beginning of this chapter, warned would be the dark side of American democracy.

The public being so aroused, the U.S. Congress was not about to stand in its way. Congress quickly passed the Flag Protection Act of 1989, mandating a one-year jail sentence and $1,000 fine for anyone who "knowingly mutilates, defaces, physically defiles, burns, maintains on the floor or ground, or tramples upon, any flag of the United States." A federal court quickly struck down this law for the same reason that the Supreme Court had invalidated the Texas statute. In doing so, it exercised the independence that Alexander Hamilton, quoted at the beginning of Chapter Ten, argued was crucial to the judiciary. Because federal judges could not be removed, they were free to protect the liberty of an unpopular person such as Gregory Lee Johnson.

An anti-war protest in Austin on March 20, 2003, the day after the United States invaded Iraq, created a superficially similar question of the right to protest. Reacting against President Bush's attack on that Middle Eastern country, several hundred peace activists staged a demonstration in Austin that began on the University of Texas campus. Marching down Congress Avenue to the bridge crossing the Colorado River, the protestors stopped in a mass and sat down in a circle, blocking all traffic. After warning the sitters to disperse, police arrested about fifty.

The protestors seemed to see themselves as latter-day Gregory Lee Johnsons. One claimed to a reporter that by obstructing the city's transportation, they were exercising their "right to civil disobedience."[3] But the differences between Johnson and the antiwar activists were instructive. Although Johnson had deliberately chosen to express his opinions in a manner that was offensive to most Texans in 1984, he had not interfered with the rights of other people to go about their business. In contrast, the 2003 protestors had intentionally blocked the bridge precisely because such an action would hinder the activities of thousands of city residents. In arresting Johnson, Dallas police had done nothing but squelch his political statement. In arresting the antiwar protestors, Austin police had protected the city's residents from disruption of their lives. While Johnson did have a right to express his unpopular opinion, the more recent protestors were mistaken when they thought that they had a "right to civil disobedience." Argument is one thing; imposition on other people is another.

**As Ben Sargent dramatizes in this cartoon, preventing people from expressing their opinion by burning the flag violates the freedom for which the flag stands.**

*Courtesy of Ben Sargent.*

Similar confrontations everywhere often call for such subtle distinctions. Always, protestors are apt to exaggerate their rights to self-assertion while government officials are apt to exaggerate their authority to protect the public peace. In these disputes judges are often needed to decide where the rights of individuals end and the rights of the community begin.

## FREEDOM OF RELIGION

The First Amendment provision that forbids Congress to pass laws "respecting an establishment of religion" has been interpreted to mean both (1) that there should be a "wall of separation" between church and state and that government may not help or even acknowledge religion in any way, and (2) that government may aid religion, at least indirectly, as long as it shows "no preference" among the various religious beliefs. Although the U.S. Supreme Court frequently talks "wall of separation," in practice it has allowed the states to provide a variety of aids to religion—for example, school lunches and public facilities for church-run schools and tuition grants for church-run colleges—as long as government agencies do not show a preference for one church over another.

A First Amendment provision regarding religion that is frequently misunderstood forbids Congress to prohibit the "free exercise" of faith. The freedom to believe in a supreme being necessarily involves the freedom to disbelieve. The freedom to worship requires the freedom not to worship. As U.S. Supreme Court Justice David Souter wrote for the majority of the court in 2005, "the touch-

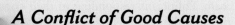

## A Conflict of Good Causes

Conflicts over religion involve more than the civil rights of individuals. They also impinge upon such profane subjects as city zoning ordinances.

In 1999 the Texas legislature passed the Religious Freedom Restoration Act. Under that law, local governments must show that they have a compelling interest, such as protection of public health or safety, before they can limit the practice of religion.

Also in 1999, Rick Barr, pastor of Grace Christian Fellowship in Sinton, near Corpus Christi, set up a faith-based rehabilitation center for nonviolent parolees across the street from his church. Shortly afterward, Sinton officials passed an ordinance prohibiting parolees from living within 1,000 feet of a church or school, thus effectively outlawing the program. Barr sued, arguing that the law was specifically intended to prevent him from operating his faith-based program, and was therefore a violation of the Religious Freedom Restoration Act. City attorneys argued that the zoning change did not limit the Grace Christian Fellowship's religious practice, and that they had the authority to protect the community from parolees.

In late 2006 the Texas Supreme Court agreed to hear the case. As this book went to press, the court had not rendered its judgment.

SOURCE: Jim Vertuno, "High Court To Hear Religious Freedom Case," *Austin American-Statesman*, December 27, 2006, B2.

stone for our analysis is the principle that the First Amendment mandates government neutrality between religion and religion, and between religion and non-religion."[4] Under the U.S. Constitution, therefore, the atheist and the believer are equally protected. Thus, the provision of the Texas Constitution—Article I, Section 4—that requires persons holding public office to "acknowledge the existence of a Supreme Being" is contradicted by the nation's fundamental law and is no longer enforced.

Because of the passion and prejudice that surround the subject of faith, government officials sometimes follow momentary convenience rather than timeless principles when making decisions about religious questions. As a result, the politics of religious freedom is often characterized by inconsistency and hypocrisy.

Nevertheless, courts have devised some tests with which to bring a measure of rationality to their decisions. On the one hand, the courts usually do not permit a general law protecting the public welfare to be violated in the name of religious freedom. For example, early in the twentieth century, Texas courts ruled that parents could not refuse to have their children vaccinated against smallpox on the grounds that it was contrary to their religious convictions.[5] In a similar vein, Texas courts ruled that members of a church were not denied their freedom of religion by a zoning ordinance that restricted use of property surrounding the church to single-family dwellings.[6] (This particular principle may be due for a rethinking—see the box).

On the other hand, laws conflicting with religious beliefs may sometimes be overturned if the public interest is not seriously threatened. For example, in 1938, a Texas appellate court, anticipating a similar U.S. Supreme Court ruling five years later, held that a parent who refused to salute the flag as a matter of religious conviction could not be deprived of custody of his or her child.[7]

In Texas as in other states, religious belief can be intense, and religious people can sometimes be intolerant of others who do not share their particular doctrinal enthusiasm. Politicians responding to their constituencies sometimes take actions that threaten the religious rights of people whose views happen to be in the minority. When they do so, they come into conflict with the federal Constitution, and religious fervor is translated into political tension.

A major issue of this sort is the question of religious recitation in public schools. In 1962 and 1963, the U.S. Supreme Court ruled that a nondenominational prayer used in public schools[8] and the reading of the Bible and the recitation of the Lord's Prayer[9] were unconstitutional. The basis of the decisions was that the prayer was a Christian ritual imposed upon all children of a school, many of whom might be non-Christian. Because the prayer takes place in a public school, it is an example of the "establishment" of religion outlawed by the First Amendment.

Although the reasoning of these decisions is difficult to refute, they nevertheless caused a great public outcry, and even today, a large majority of Americans would support a constitutional amendment to permit prayer in the schools.[10] In the absence of such an amendment, local politicians and school boards in many areas try to evade the Court's pronouncements by sneaking in prayer under some other name. As a result, the courts still deal with school prayer cases.

A good example is the situation in Santa Fe, on the Texas mainland north of Galveston. The population of this small town is about 90 percent Protestant, and mainly Baptist, with a significant representation of fundamentalists (who believe that every word of the Bible is literally true). In the 1990s, encouraged by the Santa Fe school board, teachers and students began pushing their variety of religion in the classrooms. Among other instances of official advocacy of a particular faith, a teacher handed out flyers advertising a revival, schools invited representatives of the Gideon Bible society to campus to proselytize, and a Protestant chaplain was recruited to read Protestant prayers at school ceremonies.

Two sets of parents, one Catholic and the other Mormon, objected to such spiritual propaganda aimed at their children and in 1995 filed suit. Realizing the legal threat, the Santa Fe school board forbade most of the objectionable activities. It retained, however, the practice of allowing one student, elected by majority vote of the student body, to recite a "brief invocation and/or message" over the stadium's public address system before each high school football game. The parents sued again, pointing out that a majority of the student body would always pick a Protestant to speak the "message" and that the chosen person would invariably select a prayer as the message. Moreover, because the district's public address system was employed to broadcast the prayer, this state institution was being used to subject their children to a religious message they did not want to hear. In other words, the parents argued, the Texas government was imposing an establishment of religion on their children, an action that violated the First Amendment. They were victims of the tyranny of the majority.

Texas's Republican establishment, part of a political coalition that includes the Christian Right (see Chapters 3 and 4), supported the school board. The fact that a public opinion survey showed that 82 percent of Texans agreed that students should be allowed to lead prayers over public address systems before sporting events no doubt encouraged the politicians to endorse the Santa Fe majority.[11]

"Have we actually reached the point as a society where saying a prayer for the health and well-being of the players and the safe return home of the visiting team is no longer acceptable in Texas?" asked party chair Susan Weddington. Attorney General John Cornyn and Governor George W. Bush filed a "friend of the court" brief supporting Santa Fe's position. "The Santa Fe district's students have a constitutionally protected right to free speech, including the right to offer a prayer before football games," wrote Cornyn.[12]

Because it dealt with a First Amendment issue, the Santa Fe lawsuit was decided by federal rather than Texas courts. And federal judges, not subject to the same pressure to cater to majority values as are Texas politicians, did not think that the majority in Santa Fe had a right to impose its particular religious beliefs on the minority. In June 2000, by a six to three vote, the U.S. Supreme Court upheld a lower appeals court ruling that the Santa Fe pregame "message" was unconstitutional. At their next meeting, the school board eliminated the policy, and that particular squabble over civil liberties was over.[13]

The general issue, however, showed no sign of exiting from Texas politics. In 2003, the Texas legislature passed a law requiring that all the state's schoolchildren must begin the day with a quasi-religious ritual. First they must recite the Pledge of Allegiance to the American flag, then the Texas Pledge, and then observe a minute of silence (during which, presumably, most of them would pray, although that activity was not required in the statute). The law was certainly intended to instill patriotism in children; it may have been intended as a first step in the reintroduction of prayer in the state's schools.[14]

In 2006 a couple who were the parents of children in the Carrollton-Farmers Branch school system filed suit against this law, contending that there was no **secular** (that is, nonreligious) purpose for the moment of silence. "This is just a ruse to get prayer in school," argued David Croft, one of the parents. "Is there any study showing a moment of silence helps education?"[15]

As this book went to press, the courts had as yet rendered no decision in the particular lawsuit filed by Mr. Croft. Whichever way the courts finally decide the particular case, however, it is certain that the general issue will not be settled. There will be many more laws, and many more lawsuits, on the subject of church and state in the future of Texas.

## A RIGHT TO KEEP AND BEAR ARMS?

Crime has become one of the most important political issues in the United States in general, and Texas in particular, and arguments about how to control it are part of contemporary political discussion. One of the suggested ways of reducing the number of homicides is to restrict access to guns. On the one hand, because firearms kill about 30,000 people in the United States each year, including about 14,000 homicides (1,405 of them Texans in 2005) annually, it is not implausible to argue that crime would be less of a problem if fewer people had guns.[16]

On the other hand, there are about 14 million hunters in the country and millions more who own firearms for target practice or self-defense, so there is also a great resistance to the idea of gun control. Many people agree with the opposite of the gun-control argument; they believe that law-abiding citizens would be safer from crime if they were allowed to carry concealed weapons for self-defense. Although there were only 163 justifiable homicides (defense of persons or property) by private citizens in the United States in 2003, *protective* uses of guns against burglary, assault, and robbery have been estimated to be as high as two million a year.[17] There are thus rational arguments both for and against an armed citizenry.

It is not the purpose of this chapter to examine the entire political issue of whether government should attempt stricter control over firearms. As part of a discussion of civil rights and liberties, however, it will be useful to evaluate one important part of the argument: the claim that Americans have a personal right, guaranteed by both the United States and Texas Constitutions, to own guns.

The Second Amendment to the U.S. document reads in its entirety, "A well regulated Militia, being necessary to the security of a free State, the right of the people to keep and bear Arms, shall not be infringed."[18] Millions of Americans believe that this part of the Bill of Rights prohibits government from interfering with their gun ownership. The National Rifle Association, an organization with a 2005 membership of 4 million, is particularly tireless in arguing this position. Any issue of the NRA's magazine, *The American Rifleman*, contains numerous assertions of an individual "right to keep and bear arms" as promised by the Second Amendment. Although public opinion surveys consistently show that two thirds of the American people, and depending on the question, from three fifths to three quarters of Texans, favor stricter gun control, many politicians echo the claim that the Second Amendment prohibits all regulation of firearms.[19]

Furthermore, a significant proportion of Texans evidently believe that they have a constitutional guarantee to own anything from a purse pistol to an assault rifle and that government does not have the legitimate authority to do anything about it. They agree with former Republican state Representative Rick Green, who wrote in 2000 that "The Second Amendment prevents federal interference with the citizen's right to keep and bear arms for personal defense."[20] (This is an argument about "rights," but it falls under the category of civil "liberties" because its subject is individual freedom from government intrusion.)

Citizens can, of course, interpret the Constitution as they see fit. There is no magic person or institution that can say for certain what the document "means."

If some people want to argue that the Second Amendment gives them a right to own guns, that is their right under the First Amendment.

Nevertheless, a consultation of both the historical and judicial records makes it clear that, under the normal rules of logic and language, the Second Amendment does not create an *individual* right to keep and bear arms. The amendment was created in 1789 to protect state militias—that is, official state military organizations, not private clubs or vigilante groups—from being disbanded by the federal government. It was not intended to guarantee the right to firearm ownership to private citizens. Beginning in the nineteenth century, the U.S. Supreme Court has been unvarying in applying this historical understanding to gun control laws whenever these have been challenged. In the most important case, decided in 1939, the U.S. Supreme Court held that the "obvious purpose" of the Second Amendment was to protect militias, not individuals.[21]

The notion that Americans have a constitutional right to bear arms individually, as private citizens, thus has no historical or legal support. Nevertheless, because millions of people continue to believe the opposite, the argument over the federal government's authority to regulate firearms will not be resolved soon.

The Texas Constitution would at first seem to be clearer in its creation of a personal right to own guns than the U.S. document. Section 23 of the Bill of Rights (Article I) guarantees that "Every citizen shall have the right to keep and bear arms in the lawful defense of himself or the State, but the Legislature shall have power, by law, to regulate the wearing of arms, with a view to prevent crime." Although the wording of the guarantee evidently establishes the right to keep a gun in the home, the right to any other use of firearms is highly ambiguous. Because the legislature can regulate the "wearing" of a gun, it can in effect prevent citizens from "bearing arms" outside their homes. Therefore, private citizens have no constitutional *right*, in a realistic sense, to carry weapons. Their ability to do so is subject to the decisions of the legislature. Although the section on bearing arms is placed in the Bill of Rights, as a practical matter the subject is not about rights, but about ordinary law and, thus, ordinary politics. In other words, the question of citizen ownership and use of firearms, under both the American and Texas Constitutions, is a question of public policy, not a question of civil liberties.

Because the opinion articulated by Representative Green is strong in Texas, the state's public policy has long been permissive of private gun ownership.[22] In 1995, the armed-citizen attitude carried the day in the state legislature, which passed a law allowing Texans who have undergone ten hours of training to carry concealed handguns, and affirming the right of a citizen to defend his or her home against intrusion (this is known as the "castle doctrine"). Many local governments, however, continued to ban firearms from various areas within their jurisdiction, such as city buses, libraries, and senior citizen centers. In 2003, pro-gun groups persuaded the legislature to pass a law preempting local authority to regulate concealed weapons. Under this law, only the state can designate areas where weapons are banned.[23] (It may be of interest to students that schools and colleges are among the places designated by the state as areas where handguns are not permitted.)

The 1995 law was explicit in permitting citizens to defend their homes with deadly force. It was ambiguous, however, about the extent to which they might defend their property outside the home. In 2007 the legislature clarified this point. It passed a law extending the castle doctrine to defense against unlawful entry of a vehicle or workplace.[24]

# ABORTION

Today, in Texas and in the United States as a whole, abortion joins race at the top of the list of divisive and inflammatory political issues. People do not even agree on what they are arguing about. Supporters of legal abortion maintain that the issue is whether a woman should have the right to control her own body. Opponents insist that the issue is whether the born should be allowed to kill the unborn. Because those on each side feel deeply, discussion of the issue never produces agreement; it only creates division and anger. Sometimes it results in violence.

Until 1973, there was no national abortion policy. For the first two thirds of the twentieth century, most states either discouraged or forbade private citizens to have abortions. In that year, however, the situation was radically changed by the U.S. Supreme Court's decision in the case of *Roe* v. *Wade,* a case arising from the Texas courts.[25] Building on the notion of a personal right to be free of government intrusion that it had been expanding since the mid-1960s—a right grounded in the freedoms granted by the First, Third, Fourth, and Fifth Amendments to the Constitution—the Court wrote that the Bill of Rights protected sexual privacy, including the right to have an abortion. All state antiabortion laws were overturned.

After the *Roe* v. *Wade* decision, abortion became a common medical procedure, in Texas as elsewhere. There were about 79,000 legal abortions performed in the state in 2003.[26]

It also, however, ignited an emotional national political debate that continues today. People who support the Court, who call themselves "pro-choice," argue that the decision to terminate a pregnancy should be made by the woman and her doctor; government has no business interfering. Those who disagree, styling themselves "pro-life," argue that to terminate a pregnancy is to commit homicide and that government has every obligation to prevent such a crime.

One of the arguments of the pro-choice forces is that no court, federal or otherwise, should have the authority to intervene in an area of public policy that impinges on such deeply held personal values as the nature and beginning of human life. Pro-life activists make the opposite argument from Alexander Hamilton's, quoted at the beginning of Chapter Ten. They say that an "independent" judiciary that preempts the legislature—the people's representatives—from creating policy in an area of passionately felt moral opinions is short-circuiting democracy. Pro-life citizens therefore believe that in this area, unelected judges have no legitimacy. Pro-choice advocates, looking to the courts to protect what has become, to them, an important civil liberty, agree with Hamilton and support the concept of an independent judiciary.

The abortion debate is as fierce in Texas as in any other state. The Christian Right, in particular, is fervently antiabortion. In 1994, it captured the state's Republican Party and wrote an uncompromising "pro-life" plank into the platform at the state convention. (The state Republican platforms of 1996 through 2006 repeated this call for a "Human Rights Amendment" to the U.S. Constitution—see Chapter 4.) Although statewide Republican candidates have sometimes tried to distance themselves from the party's official position on this issue, the pro-life position is endorsed by most members of the majority Republican delegations in both houses of the state legislature. Meanwhile, the wing of the state Democratic Party that is liberal on social issues, as exemplified by former Governor

Ann Richards and 2002 gubernatorial candidate Tony Sanchez, is staunchly pro-choice. (Chris Bell, the 2006 Democratic candidate for governor, avoided discussion of the issue.) The party as a whole contains many different views on this topic.

The 1999 legislature passed a "parental notification law," which required that, before a girl under the age of eighteen could get an abortion, her physician must inform her parents. Although the parents could not stop the operation, they would have forty-eight hours to counsel the girl about her choices. A public opinion poll showed that 73 percent of Texans supported this law, but the minority who opposed it felt their opposition strongly.[27] The judicial wrangle that resolved a dispute about the interpretation of this law, already discussed in Chapter Ten, is only too typical of the ill-feeling aroused by this issue.

If there is a single lesson to be learned from the history of the abortion debate, it is that political conflicts that derive from strongly held, clashing moral convictions cannot be resolved by judges. Perhaps they cannot be resolved at all.

Whether pro-life or pro-choice positions dominate Texas government in the future, the state's judges will have their hands full attempting to apply the law in an impartial manner.

For the present, the tenor of state policy is strongly pro-life. The 2003 legislature passed three laws that were intended to discourage or obstruct women from having abortions. First, the Women's Right to Know Act's main provision required that any woman must sign a statement at least twenty-four hours before the termination of her pregnancy affirming that she had been given access to photos of fetal development and information regarding the risks of abortion and pregnancy. Second, an amendment to the state's general appropriations bill cut off all public funding to any organization that provides abortions—a provision that applied mainly to Planned Parenthood. (This organization immediately sued, and federal Judge Sam Sparks quickly suspended the law on the grounds that much family planning money that the state administers comes from the federal government, and the state does not have the legal authority to cut off such funding.) Third, the Prenatal Protection Act amended the state's penal code to define an "individual" as beginning at the moment of fertilization and allowing criminal charges or civil lawsuits to be filed when an unborn child is killed.[28]

In 2005 the legislature passed a law that severely restricted the ability of doctors to perform abortions during the last three months of pregnancy, and required them to get the written permission of a girl's parents before performing an abortion on her at any stage of her pregnancy. The representatives who voted for this law appear not to have realized that, when combined with the Prenatal Protection Act, it created the possibility of criminal charges against doctors.

But the Texas District and County Attorneys Association immediately perceived the implication in the intersection of the two laws. In a guide to newly-enacted state statutes it published after the legislature adjourned, it anticipated that if a doctor performed such a procedure on a girl without her parents' permission, or performed the procedure during the third trimester on even an adult woman, the doctor could be charged with murder. Although everyone denied that such a prosecution had been the intention of the 2005 law, it did seem that such a doctor could potentially be facing capital punishment. Moreover, it was not hard to imagine that some county attorney, ambitious for higher political office, might seek to enhance his or her reputation as an antiabortion crusader by putting a doctor on trial for capital murder. Mindful of this potential development, in 2006 David Swinford, chair of the House State Affairs Committee, formally asked Greg Abbott for an Attorney General Opinion (see Chapter 10) exploring the possibilities in the combination of the two laws.[29]

In early 2007 Abbott rendered his opinion. Although the document is written in obscure legalese, the bottom line is that a doctor could not be charged with a capital crime for violating the state's abortion laws. According to Abbott, such an action would make a doctor subject to the state Occupations Code, not the Penal Code. The OC provides for civil and administrative penalties—that is, a fine or the revocation of a license to practice—but does not permit jail time or execution.[30] Although this opinion prevented the state courts from having to render an opinion that would surely have made a large proportion of the state's population unhappy no matter how the issue was decided, the episode illustrated the passions underlying the abortion debate, and the way they can generate unintended consequences for citizens and the judiciary.

# Civil Rights

Broadly speaking, civil liberties refer to citizens' rights to be free of government regulation of their personal conduct, whereas **civil rights** refer to the claims the members of all groups have to be treated equally with the members of other groups. Generally, if government harasses individual people because of something they have said or done, it may have taken away a civil liberty. If government oppresses groups of people because of some ethnic, gender, or other category to which they belong, it has violated their civil rights.

Historically, the domination of Texas by the traditionalist political culture inhibited state courts from actively protecting the civil rights of Blacks and Mexican Americans. Jim Crow laws, Black Codes, poll taxes, and other infringements on rights and liberties existed undisturbed by the state judicial system for decades. These blights on democracy were overturned by federal, not state, courts.

## SCHOOL SEGREGATION

In 1954, the U.S. Supreme Court rendered one of the landmark decisions of its history. In a unanimous verdict, the Court ruled in *Brown* v. *Board of Education* that public schools that were segregated on the basis of race were in violation of the "equal protection of the laws" clause of the Fourteenth Amendment.[31] This decision was intensely disagreeable to the ruling Anglos in Texas and the sixteen other states that had segregated schools, and, at first, sparked a great deal of obstruction and evasion. In 1970, for example, Sam Tasby, an African American, sued the Dallas Independent School District (DISD) in federal court because his son was unable to attend a White school near his home. The DISD was in almost continuous litigation for more than thirty years thereafter, spending millions of tax dollars to draw up unsatisfactory desegregation plans and then contest the adverse rulings of the courts. In 2000, long after Mr. Tasby's son was grown and out of school, DISD officials decided that compliance was a better strategy than resistance and hired Mike Moses, deputy chancellor of Texas Tech University, to lead the district toward integration. In 2003, U.S. District Judge Barefoot Sanders decided that "the segregation prohibited by the United States Constitution, the United States Supreme Court and federal statutes no longer exists in the

★ ★ ★ ★ ★ ★ ★ ★ ★ ★ ★ ★ ★ ★ ★ ★ ★ ★ ★ ★ ★ ★ ★ ★ ★ ★

## *Similar But Different*

C ivil liberties refer to those actions that government is forbidden to take. Civil rights refer to those actions that government must take to ensure equal citizenship to everyone.

★ ★ ★ ★ ★ ★ ★ ★ ★ ★ ★ ★ ★ ★ ★ ★ ★ ★ ★ ★ ★ ★ ★ ★ ★ ★

DISD" and ended federal court supervision. By that time, the composition of the district's students had declined from 59 percent White to 7 percent, the percentage of Hispanic students had risen to 59 percent, and the percentage of African Americans had held steady at a third of the population.[32]

As with school prayers and Bible reading, schools occasionally still attempt to defy the federal courts by segregating their students by ethnicity. For example, although North Dallas's Preston Hollow Elementary School was officially integrated, in practice the principal assigned White students to one set of classes, and minority students to another set. In 2006 an Hispanic parent sued, and federal judge Sam Lindsay found for the parent. Preston Hollow's principal, wrote Lindsay in his opinion, was "in effect, operating at taxpayers' expense, a private school for Anglo children within a public school that was predominantly minority." The judge ordered the school district to pay the Hispanic parent $20,200, and immediately stop segregating the students.[33]

Despite such attempts to bring back the Old South, the great majority of school districts, the great majority of the time, are now legally integrated. The major problem today is not that school districts deliberately separate students but that economic class separates them. Because poor people and middle-class people tend to live in different areas, and especially because the poorer tend to make their homes in the cities while the wealthier often live in the suburbs (Dallas and its environs are a good example), citizens of different economic classes are served by different school districts. And because poorer districts cannot afford to supply adequate schooling, economic disparity is turned into educational inequality. This is one of the major civil rights problems of the twenty-first century. For many states, Texas included, it has raised the question of whether education should be considered a civil right.

## EDUCATION: A BASIC RIGHT?

In 1987, Texas District Judge Harley Clark shocked and outraged the Texas political establishment by ruling in the case of *Edgewood* v. *Kirby* that the state's system of financing its public schools violated its own constitution and laws. Clark's ruling referred to Article VII, Section 1, which requires the "Legislature of the state to establish . . . an efficient system of public free schools," and part of Article I, which asserts that "All free men . . . have equal rights." Additionally, Section 16.001 of the Texas Education Code states that "public education is a state responsibility," that "a thorough and efficient system [is to] be provided," and that "each student enrolled in the public school system shall have access to programs and services that are appropriate to his or her needs and that are substantially equal to those available to any similar student, notwithstanding varying local economic factors." The state's educational system, however, did not begin to offer equal services to every child. During the 1985–1986 school year, when the *Edgewood* case was being prepared, the wealthiest school district in Texas had $14 million in taxable property per student, and the poorest district had $20,000. The Whiteface Independent School District in the Texas Panhandle taxed its property owners at $0.30 per $100 of value and spent $9,646 per student. The Morton ISD, just north of Whiteface, taxed its property owners at $0.96 per $100 evaluation, but because of the lower value of its property was able to spend only $3,959 per student.[34]

Gross disparities such as these made a mockery of the constitutional and statutory requirements, as well as the demands of democratic theory for equal educational funding. An estimated 1 million out of the state's 3 million schoolchildren were receiving inadequate instruction because their local districts could not afford to educate them. Democracy requires only equality of opportunity, not equality of result. But inequality of education must inevitably translate into inequality of opportunity. The courts were following the dictates of democratic theory in attempting to force the rest of the political system to educate all Texas children equally. (It is worth noting that since 1971 twenty state supreme courts have likewise held that their state's school funding system unconstitutionally discriminates against poor districts.)[35]

The appropriate remedy was to transfer some revenue from wealthy to poorer districts. But, given the distribution of power in Texas, and especially the way it is represented in the legislature, this strategy was nearly impossible. As explained in Chapters Four and Five, because of the lack of voting participation by the state's poorer citizens, its wealthier citizens are overrepresented in the legislature.[36] Despite the fact that a badly educated citizenry was a drag on the state's economy and therefore a problem for everyone, taxpayers in wealthier districts resisted giving up their money to educate the children of the poor in some other district. Their representatives refused to vote for some sort of revenue redistribution, regardless of what the court had said.

In October 1989 the Texas Supreme Court unanimously upheld Clark's ruling that the system was unconstitutional, and told the legislature to fix it. There followed four years of stalling, blustering, and complaining by the House and Senate. Several times the courts threw out laws that made cosmetic changes in the state's school system without addressing the central problems of unequal funding.

Finally, in 1993 the legislature passed a law that would take about $450 million in property taxes from ninety-eight high-wealth districts and distribute the money to poor districts. (The media instantly dubbed this the "Robin Hood Law," after the twelfth-century English bandit who allegedly robbed from the rich and gave to the poor.) In January 1995 the Texas Supreme Court upheld the new law by a bare 5 to 4 majority.

The 1995 decision was not the end of the issue. Wealthy citizens continued to complain about the Robin Hood law and to file lawsuits against it. Beginning in 2001 several school districts challenged the plan on the grounds that it violated the state constitution. In order to fulfill their obligations both to their own and to other districts' children, they argued, they were forced to peg their property-tax rates at the constitutional ceiling of $1.50 per $100 of assessed evaluation. Therefore, by in effect forcing all districts to tax at the same top rate, Robin Hood violated the constitution's ban on a statewide property tax. The slow movement toward a state supreme court decision in this case through 2005 undoubtedly encouraged legislatures to adopt a wait-and-see attitude and thus not do anything to upset the tax applecart (see Chapters 6 and 13).

In November 2005, the state supreme court declared the Robin Hood law unconstitutional on the narrow grounds that it forced school districts into a statewide property tax. The court did not address the larger issue of whether redistribution of wealth between rich and poor districts was itself constitutional. The justices gave the legislature until June 1, 2006 to reform the system.[37] Governor Perry called a special session of the legislature for the spring of that year.

Although the entire Texas political establishment was under the gun during the May 2006 special session, its task was greatly eased by the state's $10.5 billion surplus. With so much extra money to spread around, the governor, the lieutenant governor, and the speaker of the house were able to give something to both rich and poor school districts (for the financial details, see Chapter 13). Essentially, they increased the amount of money the state would give to poor districts—the state's share of funding public education went up from 38 percent to about half—while cutting property taxes for wealthier citizens and reducing the amount that wealthy districts had to share. The whole agreeable scheme depended on the continued generation of a surplus by a roaring state economy. As long as the economic boom lasted, everyone would be willing to live with the results.[38]

Nevertheless, nearly two decades of litigation and political struggle have made one thing clear. The state judiciary, at least in this one area, have become the champion of the underdog. There never would have been a Robin Hood law in 1993 or a special legislative session in 2006 if the courts had not held the feet of the legislature and the governor to the fire. Texas courts missed the boat on civil rights and civil liberties, but they are ahead of the curve in educational equity. In this one area, Texas judges have somehow risen above the burdens of history and are attempting to force the people of Texas to live up to their democratic ideals.

## CIVIL RIGHTS IN MODERN TEXAS: JASPER AND TULIA

Although the civil rights atmosphere in Texas is very different from what it was a few decades ago, there are still problems to overcome before everyone is treated equally under the law. Two of the most intense confrontations between the attitudes of the Old South traditionalist culture and progressive racial policies occurred in the towns of Jasper in 1998 and 1999 and Tulia in the first years of the new century.

Jasper is a small city near the Louisiana border in the piney woods of East Texas. In June 1998, three White men chained an African American named James Byrd Jr. by his ankles to the bumper of a pickup truck and then dragged him three miles down country roads, leaving his mangled corpse by the gate of a traditionally Black cemetery. This horrendous murder, which raised collective memories of the days when dozens of southern Black men were lynched every year, shocked the nation and attracted enormous media attention. For a few distraught hours, it almost seemed to people of goodwill that no progress had been made in Texas race relations in a century.[39]

Soon, however, the differences between the old and new Texas became clear. Only two days after the crime, Jasper County Sheriff Billy Rowles, who is White, arrested three White men. The evidence against them was overwhelming; among other things, Byrd's blood was found on their clothing. All three men were

John William King, front, and Lawrence Russell Brewer are escorted from the Jasper County courthouse Tuesday, June 9, 1998, in Jasper, Texas. King, Brewer, and Shawn Allen Berry were convicted of first degree murder in the death of James Byrd Jr., who was tied to a truck and dragged to his death along a rural East Texas road.

uneducated and had criminal records. Two were avowed racists. By February 1999, one of the men had been tried, convicted, and sentenced to death by an integrated Jasper jury. This was only the second time in Texas history that a White man had been given capital punishment for the murder of an African American. Soon, the other killers had been convicted, one also receiving the death penalty and the other a life sentence. Meanwhile, at James Byrd's funeral, citizens of every color had mourned together.

The Jasper murder and its aftermath illustrated the truth that racism is still virulent in Texas, but it is neither dominant nor respectable. The killers were on the fringes of society; indeed, two were virtually career criminals. All public statements by Texas officials showed them to be as outraged as general opinion in the rest of the country. In Jasper, there was no one who attempted to justify the actions of the three killers. The citizens of the community treated the murder as a shared calamity.

While the Jasper drama was unfolding, a different kind of civil rights outrage was beginning in Tulia, a small town between Amarillo and Lubbock.[40] In January 1998, the Panhandle Regional Narcotics Task Force hired Thomas Coleman, a former law enforcement officer in several cities, as an undercover agent. Regional drug task forces, financed by federal money but answerable to the governor's office, are special law enforcement agencies that span jurisdictional boundaries and traditionally operate without much outside scrutiny. The members of this one evidently did not bother to discover that Coleman had left many of his jobs under an ethical cloud and that he was, as one journalist would later summarize, "a racist, a liar, and a thief."[41] Working with the Swisher County prosecutor's office (which was also apparently uncurious about his background), Coleman began conducting undercover "sting" operations in Tulia, looking for drug pushers.

In July 1999, police and sheriff's officers arrested forty-six people, most of them African American, but a few Hispanic, whom Coleman accused of having sold him illegal drugs. In a series of trials and plea bargains, by the spring of 2000, thirty-eight of these people had been convicted of various drug charges. Several later explained that they had accepted plea bargains because, having seen the sentences handed down after the first convictions—60, 99, and 434 years—they were convinced by their lawyers that their best strategy was to plead guilty

★ ★ ★ ★ ★ ★ ★ ★ ★ ★ ★ ★ ★ ★ ★ ★ ★ ★ ★ ★ ★ ★ ★ ★ ★ ★ ★

## *Thought-crime or Emotion-crime?*

In the 1999 legislature, Senator Rodney Ellis, an African American from Houston, sponsored a bill that attempted to clarify Texas's 1993 hate crime law. Because of its vagueness, this law had been employed to prosecute criminals only twice since it had been passed, despite the occurrence of more than 300 hate crimes a year in Texas.

Supporters of the bill contended that the Byrd murder highlighted the need for additional measures to protect people from being assaulted because they happened to belong to an unpopular group. The bill passed the House but failed in the Senate. There were several arguments made against the measure. Some critics pointed out that, without a new law, Byrd's killers had been swiftly brought to justice and given the ultimate penalty—why was another law necessary? Others expressed discomfort with the idea of punishing criminals for the thought behind their crime rather than for the crime itself. Still others argued that to punish criminals based on the identity of their victim would be to deny the equal protection of the laws to victims who were not included under the law's protection. Finally, some politicians refused to vote for a law extending special protection to homosexuals, asserting that such a consideration would be tantamount to endorsing their behavior.

By 2001, however, the temper of the state had changed. The legislature passed, and Governor Perry signed into law, the "James Byrd Jr. Hate Crimes Act" in May. It increased penalties for crimes that were motivated by hostility to race, color, disability, religion, national origin or ancestry, age, and gender and sexual orientation.

★ ★ ★ ★ ★ ★ ★ ★ ★ ★ ★ ★ ★ ★ ★ ★ ★ ★ ★ ★ ★ ★ ★ ★ ★

SOURCES: Nathan A. Kracklauer, "The Crusade against Hate: A Critical Review of Bias Crime Legislation," Plan II honors thesis, University of Texas at Austin, May 1, 2000; *Crime in Texas 1998* (Austin: Department of Public Safety, 1999), 61; Terence Stutz, "Hate Crimes Bill Fails," *Dallas Morning News*, May 14, 1999, A1; The Power of 1 Web site: www.powerofone.org/.

and accept a lesser sentence, even though they were innocent. Coleman's testimony was the only evidence against any of these people. He never produced any drugs or drug paraphernalia to substantiate his accusations, and no drugs were found when any of the defendants were arrested. Nevertheless, Coleman was named "Outstanding Lawman of the Year" by the Texas Narcotics Control Program.

But soon after the Tulia defendants went to prison, journalists in Texas and elsewhere, and the national NAACP, began to raise public doubts. For one thing, it did not seem to make sense that Tulia, a town of about 5,000 residents, could support so many drug pushers. For another, investigations into Coleman's past turned up plenty of people willing to testify to his habitual disregard for the truth, his tendency to take things that did not belong to him, and his hostility to Black citizens.

Further, solid evidence surfaced as to the unreliable nature of Coleman's testimony in these specific cases. One woman produced bank records proving that she was in Oklahoma at the time Coleman testified he was buying drugs from her. A man had a timecard showing that he was at work when Coleman claimed that the two of them were engaging in a transaction. Another man, who was short and bald, pointed out that Coleman had identified him in testimony as tall

★ ★ ★ ★ ★ ★ ★ ★ ★ ★ ★ ★ ★ ★ ★ ★ ★ ★ ★ ★ ★ ★ ★ ★ ★ ★ ★

### *Better Late Than Never?*

S ometimes, efforts to rectify past injustices take strange turns. In 1921 the City of Denton condemned an entire African American neighborhood, called "Quakertown," to create Civic Center Park, and moved the residents to another part of town. In 2007, the city council voted to rename the park Quakertown Park as a sort of perpetual apology to its former residents.

★ ★ ★ ★ ★ ★ ★ ★ ★ ★ ★ ★ ★ ★ ★ ★ ★ ★ ★ ★ ★ ★ ★ ★ ★ ★ ★

and bushy-haired. As the evidence mounted of something rotten in Tulia, the state's judicial system was persuaded to act.

In early 2003, the Texas Court of Criminal Appeals assigned retired state judge Ron Chapman to investigate the case. After hearing from a variety of witnesses, including Coleman, the judge, prosecutors, and defense attorneys agreed that, in the words of Chapman's opinion, "Coleman's repeated instances of verifiably perjurious testimony render him entirely unbelievable under oath."

By the end of 2003, all the Tulia defendants had been released from prison, and been pardoned by Governor Perry. In March 2004, the city of Amarillo agreed to pay $6 million to the forty-five Tulia defendants in return for their agreement to drop lawsuits (an average of $133,000 each). By the end of 2004, Tom Coleman had been convicted of aggravated perjury and imprisoned, and Swisher County district attorney Terry McEachern had lost his bid for reelection and had been sanctioned by the state bar association.[42]

From a civil rights perspective, the Tulia case is both different from and similar to the Jasper case. In Jasper, three White individuals inflicted a terrible crime on another individual because he was Black, but the community responded as one civilized entity. In Tulia, the community power structure itself—the county district attorney's office, in league with the drug task force—was so indifferent to the civil rights of the local minority citizens that it was virtually an accomplice in a crime against them. Nevertheless, in a large sense, the two cases are similar: Eventually, justice was done. For much of the history of Texas, crimes against minorities, official and individual, were everyday occurrences in the state. Texas officials did not concern themselves with injustices to African Americans or Latinos and did not respond to accusations that their rights had been violated. In that sense, Jasper and Tulia, for all the residual racism they revealed, also show us how far Texas has progressed in granting equal rights to all its citizens.

## CIVIL RIGHTS FOR CONVICTED CRIMINALS

People convicted of crimes are still citizens, and although they lose many of their civil rights, they retain others. The Eighth Amendment to the U.S. Constitution forbids "cruel and unusual punishments," and most people, upon reflection, would probably agree that, however much we may fear and dislike criminals, there is something unseemly about subjecting them to torture or bestial conditions while they are incarcerated.

For most of the twentieth century, however, state prison systems, especially in the South, were places where criminals were subjected to treatment that, if not unusual, was certainly cruel. A number of states even passed laws declaring the inmates of correctional institutions to be legally dead during their confinement. They might sue the state for violation of their rights after being released—being returned to life—but the chances of receiving justice months or years after the fact were remote.[43]

In the 1960s, however, as federal courts became more receptive to civil rights cases, literally hundreds of suits were brought in areas such as access to courts, mail censorship, medical care, solitary confinement, racial discrimination, work programs, staff standards and training, and a host of other aspects of a prisoner's existence. A glance at the legal record indicates that more cases were being filed against Texas jails and prisons than against those of any other state.[44]

The most important case of this type, and one that attracted national attention, began in 1972. An inmate brought suit against the Texas Department of Corrections (TDC), alleging cruel and unusual punishment of the 15,700 inmates in Texas prisons. In *Ruiz* v. *Estelle*, David Ruiz accused the TDC of violating prisoners' constitutional rights in the following five areas:

1. **The physical security of prisoners**

2. **Living and working conditions**

3. **Medical care**

4. **Internal punishment administered by TDC**

5. **Access to courts of law**

Testimony in the case revealed horrific differences between the ideal system portrayed by top TDC officials and the actual conditions that existed within the prisons. Among the more chilling revelations was the fact that guards rarely entered the prisoners' cell blocks. Internal security was maintained by "building tenders"—privileged prisoners—who maintained order by terrorizing other inmates with lead pipes and other weapons.

Federal Judge William Wayne Justice ruled in favor of Ruiz, finding the TDC guilty of violating the Eighth Amendment. He ordered the organization to make a series of changes in its housing and treatment of prisoners. State officials reacted by "stonewalling"—denying that poor conditions existed, criticizing Judge Justice's "interference," and stalling on reform. The case dragged on for years before Governor Clements and other officials finally agreed to spend the money to make an effort to bring the TDC up to minimum standards.[45]

In 1992, Judge Justice approved a partial settlement of the Ruiz case, and the state was put back in charge of most of its prison functions. He warned Texas authorities, however, that the federal government would be monitoring its treatment of prisoners. In 2002, when David Ruiz was sixty years old, and the state prison system housed 145,000 inmates, Justice approved an agreement ending the lawsuit.[46]

As with any social change, the recognition that prisoners and others in state custody are human beings and have constitutional rights came about only with difficulty. The state resisted, and the federal courts had to step in. But much progress has been made. Official attitudes and programs today are more enlightened than those of three decades ago.

# Capital Punishment

Texas is one of thirty-eight states that imposes **capital punishment**—the death penalty—for specific types of murder. The state reserves the ultimate punishment of lethal injection for "capital felony"—criminal homicide associated with one or more of eight aggravating circumstances.[47] Some examples of those circumstances would be murder of a peace officer or firefighter, murder for hire, and murder of a child under six.[48]

Capital punishment is a highly controversial issue in Texas, in the United States, and internationally (see the "You Decide" box). The great majority of Texans approve of imposing the death penalty for criminals who have been convicted of capital felony (see Table 11-1). An ancient Greek definition of justice is "getting what one deserves." The majority of citizens believe that some people have committed crimes so terrible that they "deserve to die." Yet many scholars and people of conscience argue that the death penalty does not deter crime and only adds a public, official murder to the private, unauthorized murder committed by the criminal. Both sides in the debate feel strongly. As with other emotional social issues such as abortion, the courts are not able to resolve the dispute.

In 1972, the U.S. Supreme Court stopped the states from carrying out capital punishment because, it ruled, the death penalty was capriciously applied and, especially, racially biased.[49] In 1976, after the states had taken steps to meet the Court's objections, it allowed executions again, subject to a number of rather stringent rules. The state must ensure that whoever imposes the penalty—judge or jury—does so after careful consideration of the character and record of the defendant and the circumstances of the particular crime. States are not allowed to automatically impose capital punishment upon conviction for certain crimes, such as murder of a peace officer. The capital sentencing decision must allow for consideration of whatever mitigating circumstances may be relevant. Capital punishment may be imposed only for crimes resulting in the death of the victim, so no one may be executed for rape, for example.[50]

**TABLE 11-1**

## Texas Public Opinion about Capital Punishment, 2003

| Issue | Percent Supporting |
|-------|:---:|
| **Death Penalty for Murder** | 76 |
| **Life without Parole Option** | 72 |
| **Execution of Those Who Murder at 17** | 60 |
| **Ban on Execution of the Mentally Retarded** | 58 |

SOURCE: Texas Poll, results reported in David Sedeno, "In Search of Alternatives," *Dallas Morning News,* March 16, 2003, A3.

## YOU DECIDE

### Is Capital Punishment Justified?

Large majorities of citizens in the United States as a whole and Texas in particular support capital punishment, but there is a vocal minority that strongly opposes the practice. The arguments for and against capital punishment are both moral and practical:

| PRO | CON |
|-----|-----|
| ▲ Executions are expensive because they are delayed by frivolous appeals. Eliminate those appeals and the cost will fall. | ▼ It costs more than $2 million to execute a criminal, about three times the cost of imprisoning someone for forty years. |
| ▲ Not executing people costs lives also. Convicts escape and kill, and they kill while in prison. No executed person has ever committed murder again. New scientific techniques, such as DNA testing, make the system less mistake-prone. | ▼ No matter how careful the judicial system, some innocent people are bound to be executed. |
| ▲ Social science studies are inconclusive as to whether capital punishment deters. Besides, a main purpose of capital punishment is retribution, not deterrence. | ▼ The death penalty does not deter criminal behavior. |
| ▲ Forcing a murderer to pay for his crimes with his life is not wrong; it is justice. | ▼ Two wrongs do not make a right. |
| ▲ The great majority of Americans believe that killing is sometimes justified, as in defense of the country or to punish murderers. | ▼ Killing is always wrong, whether done by an individual or the state. |
| ▲ Statistical studies show that Black murderers are no more likely to be executed than White murderers. | ▼ The system of capital punishment is racially biased. |

SOURCES: Thomas R. Dye, *Understanding Public Policy*, 8th ed. (Upper Saddle River, N.J.: Prentice Hall, 2008), 86–87; Hugo Adam Bedau, ed., *The Death Penalty in America: Current Controversies* (New York: Oxford University, 1997), passim; Audrey Duff, "The Deadly D. A.," *Texas Monthly*, February 1994, 38; Jim Mattox, "Texas' Death Penalty Dilemma," *Dallas Morning News*, August 25, 1993, A23; Thomas Sowell, "The Trade-Offs of the Death Penalty," *Austin American-Statesman*, June 15, 2001, A15; "Death No More," editorial in *Dallas Morning News*, April 15, 2007, P1.

Texas resumed executions in 1982. Of the states that now allow capital punishment, it has been the most efficient in killing convicted criminals. The Lone Star State executed 379 people convicted of murder—376 men and 3 women—from 1982 through the end of 2006, far more than its share of those who were put to death nationally. It executed 24 in 2006.[51]

Although capital punishment draws persistent criticism (see the "You Decide" box and the story of Delma Banks in Chapter 10), its overwhelming popularity virtually assures that it will remain the law of the state. Within that overall truth there are smaller issues that confront the state's policymakers. Until recently, one of these was the question of whether Texas should create a sentencing category of "life without parole." Until 2005, there were two possible sentences for those convicted of murder: life and the death penalty. Those sentenced to life were eligible for parole after having served forty years. Opponents of the death penalty believed that juries would sentence more killers to life if they could be assured that the criminal would never be paroled; consequently, they support the addition of the new sentencing category. Supporters of capital punishment shared that analysis of the situation, and consequently, they opposed the reform.

As Table 11-1 illustrates, the life without parole option enjoyed almost as much support among Texas citizens as did capital punishment itself. Each legislative session in the recent past, civil liberties groups, anti-capital punishment organizations, and some prosecutors endorsed a bill that would make the change in the state's laws. Each session, however, the bill would be strongly opposed by some big-city prosecutors and victims-rights groups, and would fail.

Nevertheless, in 2005, the tide was running against the hard-line position on the death penalty. An awareness of the results of DNA testing, already discussed in chapter 10, had tended to take the wind out of the sails of those who argued that states do not make mistakes in their judicial processes. Moreover, a series of Supreme Court decisions had made it clear that the justices were losing patience with state judiciaries that seemed too ready to ratify the results of sloppy court processes.[52]

As a result, in 2005 a bill filed by Eddie Lucio, a Democrat from Brownsville, passed the House and Senate and was signed by Governor Perry. In order to persuade enough legislators to back his measure, Lucio was forced to drop a provision in the bill that retained the old "life-with-parole-after-forty-years" possibility. Now, a "life" sentence in Texas means just that; convicted murderers cannot expect to ever get out of prison. But they will probably be less likely to be sentenced to the ultimate penalty.[53]

Another recent issue associated with the death penalty debate is the question of how young a killer must be before he or she is too young to execute. In the history of crime, people as young as six years old have purposefully killed other people, but no one argues that children who become murderers that young should be executed. Yet, if not at six, then at what age does a criminal become executable by the state? Traditionally, the official Texas answer was that people who become murderers at seventeen were mature enough to pay the ultimate penalty, and the state put its policy into practice. In 2002, for example, three men who had committed murder at the age of seventeen were given lethal injections in Huntsville.[54]

Nevertheless, even many people who supported capital punishment in general were given pause by the thought of holding seventeen-year-olds to a mortal standard. In virtually every other area, state law considered someone of that age to be a child and too immature to be trusted with the responsibilities of adulthood. In Texas, people of seventeen years were too young to vote, to buy alcohol, or to enter into a contract. To consider them mature enough to forfeit their lives for a crime seemed to many people to be a large contradiction. As Table 11-1 illustrates, while a significant majority of Texans supported the idea of executing someone who killed as a juvenile, it was a noticeably smaller majority than supported capital punishment as an overall policy. The American Bar Association, which took no position on the issue of capital punishment itself, opposed the execution of juvenile offenders. The Inter-American Commission on Human Rights, a judicial committee of the Organization of American States, periodically appealed to Texas and other states to end the execution of those who committed their crimes while they were children.[55]

Texas lawmakers, however, seemed content to leave the seventeen-year-old minimum alone. The question of the execution of underage murderers was seldom even discussed in the legislature. No doubt this lack of interest in the question was caused by most politicians' determination to be known as "tough on crime," and their fear that, if they voted for any leniency toward murderers, their opponent in the next electoral campaign would label them "soft on crime." Texas judges, also being subject to campaign criticism, were similarly reluctant to hand their prospective opponents such a potential accusation, and seemed reluctant to intervene.

The justices of the U.S. Supreme Court, however, not being under the necessity of defending themselves during election campaigns, had no such fear. In 2005 they struck down the execution of criminals who were younger than eighteen when they committed their crimes. The ruling in effect commuted the sentences of seventy-two convicted murderers nationwide—twenty-eight of whom were in Texas—to life imprisonment, and forbid the capital sentencing of others in the future.[56]

In these two important issues surrounding capital punishment, therefore, Texas policy changed significantly in 2005. The political disagreement over the death penalty remains, however, and is certain to supply abundant controversy in the future.

# Torts and Tort Reform

A **tort** is a private or civil wrong or injury resulting from a breach of a legal duty that exists by reason of society's expectations about appropriate behavior rather than a contract. The allegedly injured party sues the alleged wrongdoer to receive compensation for his or her losses. Because tort actions are civil, not criminal, the losing party does not go to jail but must pay money to the injured party. The loser may also sometimes have to pay "punitive damages," compensation in excess of the actual damages. These are awarded in the case of willful and malicious misconduct. A doctor whose negligence causes health problems to a patient may be the object of a tort action, as may a company whose defective product causes injury to its customers, a business whose unsafe premises cause an accident among its shoppers, a city that fails to warn of a washed-out road, and so on.

Up to 1995, business in Texas had been complaining for years that it was being stifled by unjustified litigation. Doctors joined business leaders in asserting that "pain-and-suffering" awards in malpractice suits had gotten so out of hand that many physicians were being forced to stop treating patients. The tort

★ ★ ★ ★ ★ ★ ★ ★ ★ ★ ★ ★ ★ ★ ★ ★ ★ ★ ★ ★ ★ ★ ★ ★ ★ ★ ★ ★ ★ ★ ★

## *Hurry Up and Go Out Of Business*

At the same time that state lawmakers severely restricted the ability of patients to sue their doctors for malpractice in 2003, they created an institution that was supposed to protect and inform consumers about the behavior of health professionals. The Office of Patient Protection was supposed to monitor thirty-five boards that oversee and regulate more than a half-million doctors, nurses, dentists, dietitians, and others.

But the OPP never got off the ground. By the time its first chairman, Harry Whittington, had been appointed by the governor, rented an office, purchased furniture, hired a staff, created a Web site, developed a complaint form, and visited with the heads of the thirty-five boards under his authority, it was time for the 2005 legislature. Searching for ways to save the state money, and perhaps responding to the health professionals' doubts about regulation of their behavior by a state office, senators refused to fund the commission. It folded up and went out of business in August, 2005, without having acted on a single consumer complaint. The extra five dollars that health professionals were made to pay for licensing fees, which was supposed to fund the OPP, now goes into general state revenue.

★ ★ ★ ★ ★ ★ ★ ★ ★ ★ ★ ★ ★ ★ ★ ★ ★ ★ ★ ★ ★ ★ ★ ★ ★ ★ ★ ★ ★ ★ ★

SOURCE: Mary Ann Roser, "Patient Protection Office Shut; Fee Goes On," *Austin American-Statesman*, October 13, 2005, A1.

reform movement thus originated in the opinion of important, wealthy interests that the Texas judicial system was dominated by the wrong values and had to be reined in. "Tort reform" is really "court system reform," in that it consists largely of taking power out of the hands of judges and juries, limiting their discretion, and denying them jurisdiction.

Meanwhile, lawyers and many consumers' groups argued that there was no "litigation crisis" and that the whole tort reform movement was the result of a business–physician political alliance that was misleading the public in order to get away with abuse of consumers. Tim Curtis, executive director of Texas Citizen Action, argued, "Remember that these defendants include: insurance companies who cheat their policyholders; manufacturers of dangerous and defective products that have killed and maimed children; inexperienced, careless, or drug impaired doctors who commit medical malpractice on trusting patients; even unscrupulous lawyers . . . Legal concepts like joint and several liability and punitive damages have removed countless dangerous products from store shelves. Professionals who abuse their trust have been forced to change their practices or leave the profession."[57]

The antitort reform coalition is thus pro-courts. Its purpose is to defend the power and discretion of judges and juries by endorsing the intelligence and justice of their actions in regard to civil litigation.

Whatever was the reality behind the clashing perceptions of the American, and Texas, litigation systems, in the early 1990s business (especially the insurance industry) and doctors launched a massive and well-financed campaign to persuade both state legislatures and Congress to enact comprehensive tort law reform. In Texas, the trend of history was on their side in this endeavor. Traditionally, business and doctors are part of the coalition of the Republican Party, while lawyers and consumer groups are part of the Democratic coalition (see Chapter 4). As Republicans partially took over Texas government in the 1994 election, and then wholly took it over in 2002, they became increasingly able to enact legislation that pleased their core constituency.

Tort reformers wanted to change several aspects of Texas's laws regulating civil suits.

1. Punitive damages. Reformers wanted to change the law to make a litigant prove that not just "gross negligence"—the wording under the state's statute until 1995—but actual malice was involved before punitive damages could be awarded. Also, they wanted to limit the amount of punitive damages. Doctors were particularly determined to cap the size of any amounts that a jury could award a plaintiff beyond actual medical damages.

2. Joint and several liability. Under the law prevailing to 1995, anyone who participated in as little as 11 percent of the cause of the injury could be held liable for the actions of others. This meant that if company A was found to be 11 percent at fault, and the other companies were bankrupt or otherwise unreachable, company A had to pay 100 percent of the award to the plaintiff. Reformers hoped to eliminate this responsibility of the richest, most available company.

3. Venue. Attorneys filing tort cases had been able to "shop around" for a judge who was known to be sympathetic to plaintiffs. Reformers wanted to restrict filings to the geographical area where the injury occurred.

4. Deceptive Trade Practices Act. Texas's consumer protection act provided triple damages for things such as deceptive real estate or stock deals. Reformers wanted to make a consumer prove that a deceptive act occurred knowingly.

In 1995, with Republican Governor George W. Bush lobbying hard for tort reform but Democrats holding on to shrinking majorities in both houses of the legislature, the result was a compromise. Some of the highlights of new laws passed that year were

1. Punitive damages were limited to the greater of $200,000 or the sum of two times economic damages, plus $75,000.

2. The joint and several liability rule was changed so that a defendant would have to be more than 50 percent responsible to be held liable for all damages.

3. To eliminate venue shopping, the legislature decreed that a business can be sued only in the county in which an injury occurred or in a county in which it has a principal office.

4. Judges were given more power to punish plaintiffs who file frivolous suits.

5. Plaintiffs who sue doctors or hospitals were required to post a $5,000 bond; if the claim proved baseless, the plaintiff was made to forfeit the bond.

In 2003, after achieving majorities in both houses of the legislature, Republicans finished the job of revamping Texas's tort laws. They limited citizens' ability to file class-action suits, conferred immunity from suits on companies whose products meet government standards, limited the fees of trial lawyers in some cases, established penalties for plaintiffs who rejected settlements before trial even if they won the case, and capped "pain-and-suffering" awards in medical malpractice suits at $250,000.[58]

As a result of the tort reform movement, therefore, Texas civil courts are markedly less important and have much less freedom of choice than they enjoyed prior to 1995.

Reactions to the legal changes have been predictably different from different sides of the political fence. Supporters of the 1995 and 2003 reforms argue that patients now have more access to healthcare because doctors who were leaving the state or retiring due to increasing insurance costs are staying in practice now that insurance rates have moderated.[59] Opponents of the reforms counter that malpractice insurance rates rose in the late 1990s and early 2000s, and fell after 2003, because of changes in the insurance market, and had nothing to do with tort reform. Meanwhile, patients who have been the victim of negligent doctors or dishonest hospitals have no recourse because they have been frozen out of the legal system.[60] Likewise, the pro-reformers boast that the "New Era of Pro-Business Leadership Is Good for Texas,"[61] while anti-reformers lament that the members of Texans for Lawsuit reform "have remade the world in their image, one in which there is no recourse for wrongdoing, one in which the powerful simply get their way."[62]

Like the arguments over abortion, capital punishment, and other controversies discussed in this chapter, the disagreement over the value of tort reform will never die because on the issues of lawsuits there is a permanent conflict between

Ben Sargent here expresses the point of view of those who opposed tort reform in 1995 and 2003: It is a means by which rich special interests maintain their privileges at the expense of ordinary citizens.

*Courtesy of Ben Sargent.*

people who are likely to sue and those who are likely to be sued. Unlike those other issues, however, torts do not involve constitutionally protected rights. As a result, on this subject, federal courts are reluctant to intervene in the Texas political process. Whatever the legislature, the governor, and the state Supreme Court endorse will be Texas law. Given the Republican alliance with anti-tort interests, and that party's ascendancy in state politics, Texas policymakers can be expected to remain hostile to "frivolous" lawsuits. For the time being, tort reformers have won, and as a result, the Texas civil justice system is greatly diminished in authority.

# Conclusion

Overall, a survey of the products of the state court system suggests that it works better than its chaotic organization and controversial system of judicial selection might lead us to expect. Although Texas courts are not perfect examples of democracy in action, they have sometimes been ahead of the rest of the state's political system in dealing with the substance of justice. The state's judicial system, troubled as it is, gives some hope that it will be able to cope with the challenges of the future.

Meanwhile, courts will continue to be asked to resolve the unresolvable social conflicts of our time.

## Summary

The output of the Texas system of justice has improved in some ways in recent years. Whereas Texas courts used to be inhospitable to claims that people's civil rights and liberties had been violated, they are now more open to such claims. As incidents in Jasper and Tulia illustrate, Texas still contains hardcore racism, but the state judicial system is working to mitigate its effects.

Although there is an argument about whether citizens have a right to keep and bear arms, upon inspection this issue turns out to be a dispute over ordinary public policy, and thus a problem for the legislature, rather than over a civil liberty that must be defended by the courts.

The Texas courts have courageously taken on the rest of the political establishment, including especially the legislature, in ordering a more equitable distribution of school revenues. They have not completely succeeded in introducing educational equality into Texas public schools, but they have forced the legislature to make the educational system at least somewhat more equitable.

Arguments are ongoing over some questions of rights and liberties. Although the national and state courts participate in social struggles over abortion, prayer in the schools, and personal expression, these issues provoke so much disagreement that they cannot be settled judicially. In two areas, however—the rights of criminals in Texas prisons and school segregation—the federal courts have been very active over the past three decades in forcing the reform of the system.

In recent years, many businesses became convinced that the outcome of Texas's tort laws were damaging the state's economy. They complained that the courts were too tolerant of frivolous suits that sometimes cost businesses so much money that they were forced to close down. In 1995 and 2003, the legislature, at the urging of Governors Bush and Perry, rewrote many of the tort laws so as to take discretion away from the civil judiciary. It is now much more difficult to file, and to win, a civil lawsuit in Texas. This change made consumer representatives unhappy, but as long as the Republican Party controls most state offices, the changes are unlikely to be undone.

## Glossary Terms

capital punishment

civil liberties

civil rights

secular

tort

## Study Questions

1. Why is freedom of expression important in a democracy? Do you think the rules of freedom of expression should be different during a war?

2. What is the practical difference between freedom *of* religion and freedom *from* religion?

3. Is the right to keep and bear arms guaranteed by the U.S. Constitution? To whom? Is that same right guaranteed by the Texas Constitution?

4. Why do you think the issue of abortion is so divisive? Could you imagine a way to resolve it, either legislatively or judicially?

5. Discuss the facts and issues in *Edgewood* v. *Kirby*. Do you agree with the way the courts handled the problem of school funding or do you agree with the legislature? Since the Texas Constitution was written in 1876, why do you think it took until 1989 for the state Supreme Court to declare the system of school funding unconstitutional?

6. Do you think it matters whether people convicted of committing crimes have rights? What is the recent record of Texas in granting such rights?

7. Do you support the death penalty? Why or why not?

8. What recent changes have been made in the tort laws of Texas? Who wanted the changes and why? Who opposed the changes and why?

## Surfing the Web

Readers are urged to visit the companion site for this book:

**http://academic.cengage.com/polsci/Kraemer/TexasPolitics10e**

# Local Government

Solid waste collection is a basic local government service, whether it is provided by the city, as this photo in Denton depicts, or by a private agency with which the city or county contracts.

All politics is local.

OLD ADAGE IN AMERICAN POLITICS

The new city manager is (1) invisible, (2) anonymous, (3) nonpolitical, and (4) none of the above. Increasingly, modern city managers are brokers, and they do that brokering out in the open.

ALAN EHRENHALT, DEPUTY EDITOR, *GOVERNING: THE MAGAZINE OF STATES AND LOCALITIES*, 1990

State-versus-local tension is getting worse. Locals fear state budgets will be balanced at their expense. They may be right.

ALAN GREENBLATT, *GOVERNING: THE MAGAZINE OF STATES AND LOCALITIES*, 2002

# Introduction

When the Texas Constitution was being written in 1875, only 8 percent of the state's population lived in urban areas. By the 2005 federal census estimates, Texas was almost 87 percent urban based on the proportion of the population living in places with a population of 2,500 or more. The U.S. Bureau of the Census and the Texas State Data Center forecast that Texas will have 66 percent more people in 2025 than it had in 2000, although the current population growth rate indicates that the projection is an underestimate. Much of this population growth will be among people who have specific problems—Hispanics and the elderly in particular—and most of it will be in urban areas. Much of the state's history and many of its problems are linked to urbanization and population growth.

Once one of the most rural states, Texas is now one of the most urban. Most of the change has taken place since 1950, when the development of such industries as petrochemicals and defense began luring rural residents into cities. Like most American cities, Texas cities have been unplanned until very recently. Growth patterns are largely determined by developers, who give little thought to the long-range effects of their projects on the total community. Only in the past thirty years has community planning come to be taken seriously. In Texas and elsewhere, the nation's domestic problems—racial strife, unemployment, inflation, storm damage, delinquency, crime, substance abuse, inadequate healthcare, pollution, inadequate transportation, taxation, and the shortage of energy—seem to be focused in the cities. But before examining city government and its problems, this chapter steps back in time and looks at the first unit of local government: the county.

Local government is an especially rich field for exploring whether the tests of democratic government outlined in Chapter One have been passed. Americans have long viewed local government as the government that is closest and most responsive to them. As one of the opening quotations notes, "All politics is local." Political careers begin at the local level; even national issues are translated into their prospective effect on the local community; the local paper—whether daily or weekly—provides in-depth information about local government doings. Local government in Texas reflects more of a moralistic culture than does the Texas state government, in that local government traditionally offers an array of tools for general citizen involvement and control. In looking at the organization, politics, and finance of Texas's local governments, this chapter closely examines whether citizens take advantage of the opportunity for involvement at the local level and whether differences exist between general-purpose local governments (cities and counties) and special-purpose local governments (special districts).

# Counties: One Size Fits All?

## HISTORICAL AND LEGAL BACKGROUND

The county is the oldest form of local government in America, and in rural Texas it is still the most important.[1] Today, there are 3,043 counties in the 47 states that have this form of government. Texas has the largest number of counties—254—of any state in the nation. Across the nation, counties vary enormously in size and importance. The largest in area is San Bernardino County in California, with 20,131 square miles. Arlington County, Virginia, is the smallest, with only 2 square miles. The largest county in Texas is Brewster, with 6,028 square miles; the smallest is Rockwall, with 147 square miles. Even more striking contrasts exist in population size. The 2004 population of Loving County in West Texas was a grand total of 52 people and continuing to decline. Harris County, which includes Houston, had 3.7 million, a figure that represented continuing growth.[2]

In Texas, as in other states, the county is a creation of state government. In the days before automobiles, citizens could not be expected to travel to the capital to conduct whatever business they had with the state; therefore, counties were designed to serve as units of state government that would be geographically accessible to citizens. Indeed, the size of Texas counties was limited by how far a citizen could travel in a day on horseback. Until city police departments assumed much of the role, the county sheriff and the sheriff's deputies were the primary agents for enforcement of state law. County courts still handle much of the judicial business of the state, and they remain integral to the state judicial system. Many state records, such as titles, deeds, and court records, are kept by the county; many state taxes are collected by the county, and counties handle state elections. Counties also distribute large portions of the federal funds that pass through the state government en route to individuals, such as welfare recipients. Thus, most dealings that citizens have with the state are handled through the county. Yet, strangely, state government exercises virtually no supervisory authority over county governments. They are left to enforce the state's laws and administer the state's programs pretty much as they choose.

County officials are elected by the people of the county and have substantial discretion in a number of areas. For example, they can appoint some other county officials and set the tax rate. The result is a peculiar situation in which the county is a creation of state government, administering state laws and programs—with some discretion on the part of its officers—but county officials are elected by the people of the county and are in no real way accountable to the state government for the performance of their duties. Not surprisingly, county officials view themselves not as agents of the state but rather as local officials. One result is that enforcement of state law varies considerably from county to county.

## ORGANIZATION AND OPERATION OF COUNTY GOVERNMENT

The Constitution of 1876, which established the state government, also set out the organization and operation of county government. The same concerns and styles are manifest for both governments, and there are close parallels in their organization and operation. For example, the decentralized executive found at the state level is reproduced at the county level in the county **commissioners court**,[3] the governing body in all Texas counties, and in semi-independent county agencies.

### STRUCTURE

Another distinctive feature of Texas counties is the absence of **home rule**, which allows local governments to adopt their own charters, design their organizations, and enact laws within limits set by the state. Texas had a county home-rule provision of sorts between 1933 and 1969, but it was unworkable and was finally amended out of the constitution. Because the county is the creation of the state and has no home-rule authority, the organization and structure of county government are uniform throughout Texas. Tiny Loving County and enormous Harris County have substantially the same governmental structure. Unlike counties in many other states, Texas counties do not have the option of having a form of government with an appointed professional administrator, such as the council-manager type described later in this chapter. Nor can they choose a form of government with an elected chief executive similar to the strong mayor-council form of city government.

Counties have often found themselves saddled with unnecessary offices, such as treasurer, school superintendent, or surveyor. In November 1993, Texas voters were asked once again to vote on eliminating the position of county surveyor in two specific counties (McLennan and Jackson). But they also got to vote on whether, in the future, only residents of the county involved would need to vote to abolish an office. The vote was more than six to one in favor of eliminating the need for the whole state to vote on the business of one county.

Figure 12-1 illustrates the organization of Texas county government. The county is divided into four precincts, each of which elects a commissioner to

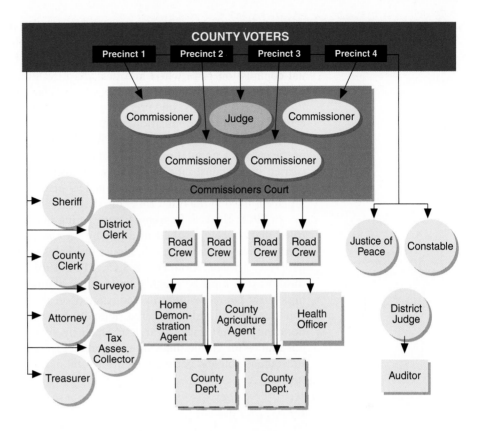

**FIGURE 12-1  Organization of County Government in Texas**

*SOURCE: George D. Braden,* Citizens' Guide to the Texas Constitution, *prepared for the Texas Advisory Commission on Intergovernmental Relations by the Institute of Urban Studies, University of Houston (Austin, 1972), 51.*

the commissioners court. The presiding officer of the commissioners court is the county judge. The county commissioners and the administrative agencies constitute the executive branch of county government, but the commissioners court performs as a legislature as well. Figure 12-1 also illustrates that counties have a large number of elected officials, ranging from a sheriff to constables to an attorney.

Each of the four commissioners is elected from a precinct, but the county judge is chosen in an **at-large election**—that is, one in which all registered voters in the county are eligible to participate. County officials are chosen in partisan elections; that is, candidates run as Democrats, Republicans, or minor party candidates.

## APPORTIONMENT

In the past, when county commissioners drew county precinct lines, they drew those lines on some basis other than population. Unlike **gerrymandering**, where the objective is to perpetuate the position of the dominant party or faction, county precinct apportionment was for the purpose of reelecting incumbent commissioners and dividing the county road mileage on an equal basis. Roads, a major county function, were often more important than people. Not only were roads the lifeline for the state's rural population, which was once in the majority, but also contracts for roadwork represented the best opportunity for individual commissioners to wheel and deal. As a result, county commissioners often created precincts with great disparities in population.

During the 1960s, one precinct in Travis County contained almost 60 percent of the county's population, including most of the African Americans, Mexican Americans, and poor Whites. Another precinct contained only 6 percent of the county's population, mainly upper-middle-class Whites. Midland County carried bias against city dwellers to the ultimate extreme: One precinct, composed of the City of Midland, contained 97 percent of the people. The remaining 3 percent lived in the other three districts.

In 1968, the U.S. Supreme Court, acting in a case against Midland County, ruled that all counties had to abide by the *one-person, one-vote* rule that had been applied earlier to the U.S. House of Representatives and to state legislatures (*Avery v. Midland County*, 88 S.Ct. 1114, 1968). This rule requires that electoral districts must be roughly equal in population. After this ruling, some commissioners courts voluntarily redistricted on the basis of population; in other counties, federal judges ordered population-based redistricting. County apportionment has resurfaced as an issue in recent years in disputes over adequate opportunities for ethnic minorities to contend for county offices, in counties with substantial political party competition, and in urban counties with fast-growing suburbs.

## COMMISSIONERS COURT

The term *commissioners court* is a misnomer. It is not a judicial body but an executive (policy-administering) and legislative (policymaking) body for the county.

Although technically the county is nothing more than an administrative arm of the state, the commissioners court does have functional latitude in several areas. In addition to setting the tax rate for the county (a legislative function), it exercises discretion in the administration of state programs (an executive function). Some of these state programs are mandatory, but the county may choose among others and may determine the amount of money allocated to each. For example, the state and counties are responsible for healthcare for the indigent, including care for individuals who are not qualified for the federally funded Medicaid program, and counties must ensure that hospital service is provided. An individual county, however, may elect to operate a public hospital, pay a public hospital in an adjacent county for services, or pay a private hospital for care of the indigent. Counties also are responsible for building and maintaining county jails, generally for providing health and safety services in rural areas, and for subdivision regulation in unincorporated areas. Perhaps the most important power of the commissioners court is that of controlling the county budget in most areas of county government. If it chooses, it can institute a variety of different programs, many of which are major undertakings, such as county hospitals, libraries, and various welfare programs. Counties are also active in economic development activity.

The county commissioners court has the responsibility for conducting general and special elections. The court also has the power to determine the precinct lines for the justice of the peace precincts as well as for the precincts of the four commissioners themselves. This power is a potent political weapon that can be used to advance the cause of some individuals and groups and to discriminate against others. When these lines are not drawn fairly and equitably, malapportionment results, as was the case in the Midland situation noted earlier.

## COUNTY OFFICIALS

The *county commissioners* also perform important functions as individuals. Each is responsible for his or her own precinct, including the establishment of road- and bridge-building programs, which represent a major expenditure of county funds. Since 1947, counties have had the authority to consolidate the functions of building and maintaining roads and bridges. About 10 percent of Texas's 254 counties have established a countywide unit system, enabling commissioners in those counties to take advantage of volume purchasing, share heavy road equipment, and so on. When she was a Travis County commissioner, former Governor Ann Richards led an unsuccessful campaign for statewide adoption of the unit system. In the other 90 percent of Texas's counties, individual commissioners still tend to roads and bridges in their individual precincts. One reason is the importance of these transportation facilities to residents in outlying areas and thus the potential effect on reelecting the commissioner. Another reason is that individual commissioners simply like the power implicit in hiring personnel and letting contracts for road and bridge work. They also like the political advantage to be gained from determining the locations of new roads and which existing roads and bridges will be improved.

The *county judge* performs many functions. As a member of the commissioners court, the judge presides over and participates fully in that body's decision making. As a member of the county election board, the county judge receives the election returns from the election judges throughout the county, presents the returns to the commissioners court for canvassing, and then forwards the final results to the secretary of state. In counties with a population of fewer than 225,000, county judges also serve in an administrative capacity as county budget officer. They have the authority to fill vacancies that occur on commissioners courts. They are notaries public, can perform marriages, and issue beer, wine, and liquor licenses in "wet" counties. Many citizens see the county judge as a representative of the people and ask him or her to intervene with other elected officials and county bureaucrats. Many county judges have strong countywide power bases and are influential politicians.

The county judge also presides over the county court, although the position does not require legal credentials other than "being well informed in the law." County judges devote time to such matters as probate of wills, settlement of estates, appointment of guardians, and in many counties, hearing lawsuits and minor criminal cases. However, in larger counties, the county commission usually relieves the judge of courtroom responsibilities by creating one or more county courts at law.

One of the most visible legal officers is the *county sheriff*, who is elected at large. The sheriff has jurisdiction throughout the county but often also makes informal agreements involving a division of labor with the police of the municipalities in the county. Particularly where large cities are involved, the sheriff's office usually confines itself to the area of the county outside the city limits. A major exception is that the sheriff is sometimes in charge of a joint crime task force, for example, a specialized group created to address illegal drug manufacturing and sales. The county sheriff has comprehensive control of departmental operations and appoints all deputies, jailers, and administrative personnel. In fact, the principal function of the sheriff is to serve as administrator of the county jail system. County jails house defendants awaiting criminal trial, individuals convicted of a misdemeanor and sentenced for a term up to a year, and felony (serious crime) convicts waiting to be transported to a state prison. Some counties have found it profitable to build larger jails than they require and rent space to the state and to other counties. Depending on the size of the county, the sheriff's department may be quite complex and may have a substantial annual budget. A 1993 amendment to the state constitution authorizes the legislature to impose qualifications on sheriffs, such as mandatory training as a peace officer.

★ ★ ★ ★ ★ ★ ★ ★ ★ ★ ★ ★ ★ ★ ★ ★ ★ ★ ★ ★ ★ ★ ★ ★ ★ ★ ★

## *Where There's Smoke*

County governments tend to be very loose in their operations—sometimes even in counties that are considered to have modernized county government. In Denton County, the road and bridge department created a couple of giant barbeque smokers (valued together at almost $10,000 not counting the labor of county employees), one for itself and one for the sheriff's department. One high-level official resigned and another was indicted on three misdemeanor charges in the wake of an investigation about the smokers and the possible misuse of county funds. The sheriff's department claimed the smokers were necessary for its substance abuse programs. Following an investigation, the county commissioners court ordered the smokers to be sold to the highest bidder at the next auction of surplus equipment. Meanwhile, the resigned official applied for a less important job with the county, which turned down the application.

★ ★ ★ ★ ★ ★ ★ ★ ★ ★ ★ ★ ★ ★ ★ ★ ★ ★ ★ ★ ★ ★ ★ ★ ★ ★ ★

Another prominent county official is the *county attorney*, also elected at large. As the head of the county's legal department, the county attorney provides legal counsel and representation of the county. The attorney also prosecutes misdemeanors in the justice of the peace and county courts.

Another of the important elective offices in the county is that of *county clerk*, who is also elected at large. The county clerk is the recorder of all legal documents (such as deeds, contracts, and mortgages), issues all marriage licenses, and is the clerk of both the county court and the commissioners court. Many of the responsibilities for the conduct of elections, which formally rest with the commissioners court, actually are performed by the county clerk. For example, absentee voting is handled by the county clerk.

The *assessor-collector of taxes* collects the ad valorem (general property) tax for the county, collects fees for license plates and certificates of title for motor vehicles, and serves as the registrar of voters. This last duty is a holdover from the days of the poll tax, which was a fee paid to register to vote. The assessor-collector's job has been changed in recent years by the creation of the uniform appraisal system, to be discussed later in this chapter. In counties of 10,000 or more population, a separate assessor-collector is elected at large; in smaller counties, the sheriff serves as assessor-collector.

Other legal officers of the county are the *justices of the peace* (JPs) and the *constables*. In most but not all counties, there is at least one justice of the peace and one constable for each of the four precincts. Larger counties may have as many as eight JP districts. In the largest counties, numerous deputy constables assist the elected constables. The justice of the peace is at the bottom of the judicial ladder, having jurisdiction over only minor criminal cases and civil suits. The constable has the duty of executing judgments, serving subpoenas, and performing other duties for the justice of the peace court. Like the commissioners, the constables and JPs are elected for four years on a partisan basis by district.

Another elected official is the *county treasurer*, who is the custodian of public funds. Some counties have a *county school superintendent* to oversee rural schools.

The county has a number of other officers, some of whom perform important functions. In larger counties, a *county elections coordinator* is appointed to supervise elections. In counties with a population of more than 35,000, the state law requires that an *auditor* be appointed by the district judge having jurisdiction in the county for the purpose of overseeing the financial activities of the county and assuring that they are performed in accordance with the law. A *county health officer* to direct the public health program is also required by state law and, in most counties, a *county agricultural agent* and a *home demonstration agent* are appointed by the commissioners court for the purpose of assisting (primarily) rural people with agriculture and homemaking. The last two officers are appointed in conjunction with Texas A&M University, which administers the agriculture and home demonstration extension programs.

## COUNTY FINANCE

The financing of local government varies a great deal depending on the type of government. Counties depend heavily on local property taxes and on intergovernmental transfers, chiefly welfare money that is passed down from the national government to the Texas Health and Human Services Commission to the counties. The intergovernmental money is beyond the control of the local government.

The state legislature determines the maximum tax rates that local governments can set. For counties, the property tax rate may not exceed 80 cents per $100 of assessed valuation for general government purposes. However, for specific purposes such as farm-to-market roads and flood control, the county property tax rate can go up to $1.25 if authorized by the legislature and approved by the voters of the county. Within these limits, the commissioners court annually sets the specific rate.

Counties also receive funding from federal grants other than welfare and from various state programs. State maintenance of rural farm-to-market roads and state highways is an important financial aid to Texas counties. Counties get miscellaneous income from local charges collected from hospitals, toll roads, and recreation facilities and from fines, special assessments, and interest earned. Selected counties have also been authorized to collect a sales tax.

Figure 12-2 illustrates revenues and expenditures for a hypothetical Texas county. As the chart shows, a typical Texas county spends the largest share of its budget on health and welfare programs. Not only are counties the "pass-through" agencies for implementing welfare programs, but they are also responsible for indigent healthcare. One factor that will cause a variance in the percentage

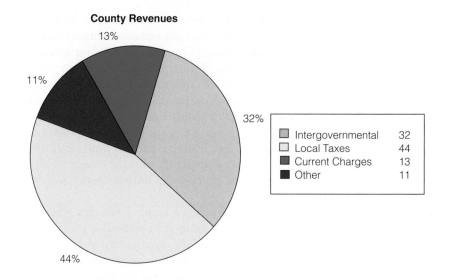

**County Revenues**

| | | |
|---|---|---|
| ▨ | Intergovernmental | 32 |
| ☐ | Local Taxes | 44 |
| ▨ | Current Charges | 13 |
| ■ | Other | 11 |

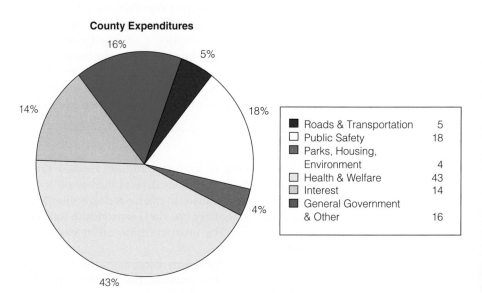

**County Expenditures**

| | | |
|---|---|---|
| ■ | Roads & Transportation | 5 |
| ☐ | Public Safety | 18 |
| ▨ | Parks, Housing, Environment | 4 |
| ☐ | Health & Welfare | 43 |
| ▨ | Interest | 14 |
| ▨ | General Government & Other | 16 |

**FIGURE 12-2 Typical Texas County Revenues and Expenditures**

SOURCE: *Data were drawn from a variety of census reports and budgets. No one specific county is represented.*

of expenditure from one county to another is whether the county maintains its own public hospital or pays another county for hospital services. Another cost that has risen over the past decade is that of jails, as counties struggle to meet court-imposed minimum jail standards. County law enforcement costs depend on how much unincorporated land there is in the county. For example, in Dallas County, little unincorporated land exists, thereby minimizing the sheriff's enforcement range. In rural counties and even in heavily populated Harris County, much of the county is unincorporated and dependent on the sheriff's office. Decisions about program and budget priorities are made by the county commissioners.

Of course, individual Texas counties vary greatly in both revenue and expenditures depending on whether they are rural or urban, rich or poor, large or small. They also vary according to the services demanded by the residents.

## COUNTY POLITICS

County politics is characterized by three interrelated qualities: partisanship, precincts, and a long ballot. With the exception of the professional appointments noted earlier, such as a home demonstration agent and health officer, all the county officials discussed earlier in this chapter are elected. The key electoral units are the four commissioners' precincts, which also serve as the electoral base for constables and JPs. All contenders run under a political party banner and are elected during general elections when major officials such as president, governor, and members of Congress are elected. Because the form of government is the same in all counties, so also are the electoral arrangements. Thus, to a great extent, a description of state parties and elections also describes county politics (see Chapters 4 and 5).

## AN EVALUATION OF COUNTY GOVERNMENT

When industrial firms experience problems, they call in teams of management consultants, who make a searching examination and a critical evaluation of the firm's operation. If one could arrange for a management consulting firm to make a thorough examination of county government in Texas, its report would very likely include the following topics.

### STRUCTURE AND PARTISANSHIP

The county in Texas is a nineteenth-century political organization struggling to cope with the twenty-first century—hence, the "one size fits all" title of this main section. In many states, counties have the same flexibility as cities to choose a *form of government* that is appropriate for the size and complexity of that particular jurisdiction. In Texas, all county governments have the same structure, and the emphasis is on *party politics* because all officials are elected on a partisan basis. The positive aspect of partisanship is that the average voter can understand more clearly what a candidate's approximate political position is when the candidate bears the label Republican or Democrat than when there is no identifying tag.

Nationally, although most counties operate with a commission, urban counties serving the majority of the nation's citizens operate with a county manager or appointed administrator.[4] California, Florida, and North Carolina are examples of states in which counties are professionally managed. Texas, of course, does not provide formal authority for counties to vary the form of government, but the largest Texas counties increasingly are hiring experienced local government managers to tend to administrative functions. Although the current structure is uniform and simple, it also makes it difficult to produce decisions for the benefit of all or most county residents because of the emphasis on precincts. Commissioners tend to see themselves as representing their precinct rather than the county as a whole. In turn, the precinct focus makes it difficult to enjoy economies of scale, such as purchasing all road-paving materials at one time.

PRESIDIO COUNTY COURTHOUSE

JEFF DAVIS COUNTY COURTHOUSE

VAL VERDE COUNTY COURTHOUSE

LLANO COUNTY COURTHOUSE

Texans enjoy roaming through historic Texas county courthouses, many of which have been restored to their nineteenth and early twentieth century glory.

The partisanship and restrictive structure can lead to governance problems. Commissioners often squabble over petty matters. Citizens have difficulty deciding whom to blame if they are dissatisfied with county government, because the commissioners serve as a collective board of directors for the county. For example, a troublesome sheriff—a not uncommon situation—may be re-

★ ★ ★ ★ ★ ★ ★ ★ ★ ★ ★ ★ ★ ★ ★ ★ ★ ★ ★ ★ ★ ★ ★ ★ ★ ★

## *Corralling Sheriffs*

Sheriffs and county commissioners often tangle. Although the sheriff is elected independently of the commissioners court, the county's chief law enforcement agent still must depend on the governing body for a budget. Sheriffs tend to view the law enforcement and jail budgets as sacrosanct, but the commissioners have to fund the budgets and tend to pare down sheriffs' requests for dollars.

Sometimes the conflicts are more colorful. In one North Texas county, the sheriff decided to "encourage" a high level of participation in local elections by requiring that all employees of the sheriff's department vote in the 2000 party primaries. The requirement was even included in the departmental personnel manual. Following widespread negative publicity, the sheriff recanted. Employees were allowed to decide for themselves whether to vote.

★ ★ ★ ★ ★ ★ ★ ★ ★ ★ ★ ★ ★ ★ ★ ★ ★ ★ ★ ★ ★ ★ ★ ★ ★ ★

elected while the voters blame the county commissioners for the sheriff's behavior. Similarly, the voters may focus on the county judge, who has one vote on the commissioners court just like the other members, when other members of the court should be the object of attention. Such confusion can happen in any government, but the large number of elected officials—mirroring the state pattern—compounds the problem.

A plus for counties is that they are less bureaucratic than other governments; thus, the average citizen can more easily deal with a county office. One reason may be that, unlike the state government, county government does not have a clear-cut separation between legislative and executive branches and functions. The merger of executive and legislative functions, which is called a unitary system, also is found in some city and special district governments. It can sometimes produce a rapid response to a citizen problem or request.

One county judge assessed county government by noting that many county officials are highly responsive to public demands when they must face competitive elections. In fact, he argued that counties are the last true bastions of *grassroots politics*, whereby government is close to all the people in the county. Although the court sets much of the policy and the tone for the conduct of county operations, it lacks the authority to give explicit orders to subordinate officials. Nevertheless, this county judge pointed out, by controlling the budget, the commissioners court can often dictate the behavior of other elected officials. Additionally, counties have the lowest tax rates of all the governments in Texas.[5] Another county judge put it this way: "We do meat-and-potatoes government . . . not flashy, press-release government, but good government."[6]

Thus, the evaluation of county organization and politics is mixed. The public often shows little interest in county government. Voter turnout is low, and even the media tend to ignore county government and focus instead on big city, state, and national political events. The county is a horse-drawn buggy in structure. It is often highly democratic, especially when it advocates the interests of groups ignored by other governments, because the commissioners must secure support for reelection. However, the willingness of commissioners and other elected officials to attend to the needs of individuals and to deal with details can easily lead to corruption.

## MANAGEMENT PRACTICES

With the exception of a few of the larger counties, county government in Texas is one of the last bastions of the **spoils system** in which people are appointed to government jobs on the basis of whom they supported in the last election and how much money they contributed. A spoils system may help to ensure the involvement of ordinary citizens in government by allowing a highly diverse group of people to hold government jobs. When such a dispersion of jobs occurs, the result is *pluralism*—that is, a reflection in public employment and public policy of the cultural diversity in society. However, a spoils system can also lead to the appointment of unqualified people, especially in jobs requiring specialized training. It can contribute to a high turnover rate if the county tends to usher new elected officials into office on a regular basis. For example, a common practice is for a newly elected sheriff to fire several deputies and bring in his or her own people. Finally, a spoils system may create not pluralism but *elitism;* those persons appointed to public office may represent only a narrow spectrum of society and reflect only the upper crust of the dominant political party. Democratic government demands that citizens not only be willing to obey the law but also be able to count on public officials being scrupulous in their own behavior and not merely partisan. Therefore, most experts think a spoils system has more risks than advantages.

From a management standpoint, a merit system—a *civil service* or a *merit system* of recruitment, evaluation, promotion, and termination is one based on qualifications—and a pay scale that would attract and hold competent personnel would help improve governmental performance. These also would be fair to employees for their labors and to taxpayers as a return on their dollars. The larger counties have made significant strides toward developing professional personnel practices such as competitive hiring, merit raises, and grievance processes, but 90 percent of the counties have a long way to go. In a larger county, commissioners also appoint a wide array of professionals, such as a budget officer, personnel director, and economic development coordinator.

Two other features of county government illustrate its tendency toward inefficient management: decentralized purchasing and the road and bridge system. *Decentralized purchasing* means that each department and each commissioner make separate purchases. Quantity discounts, which might be obtained with a centralized purchasing agent, are unavailable on small-lot purchases. Also, the opportunity for graft and corruption is real. To be sure that they will get county business, sellers may find themselves obligated—or at least feel that they are—to do a variety of favors for individual officials in county government. This situation is not unknown in the other governmental units but becomes more widespread in highly decentralized organizations.

Unless a Texas county belongs to the elite 10 percent that have a *unit system for countywide administration of the roads and bridges*, individual commissioners may plan and execute their own programs for highway and bridge construction and maintenance at the precinct level. The obvious result is poor planning and coordination and also duplication of expensive heavy equipment. These inefficiencies are important because counties, like other local governments, must cope with taxpayer resistance to providing more funding for government. Thus, efficient performance is a must.

★ ★ ★ ★ ★ ★ ★ ★ ★ ★ ★ ★ ★ ★ ★ ★ ★ ★ ★ ★ ★ ★ ★ ★ ★ ★

## *Consequences of No County Ordinance Power*

In unincorporated areas, the lack of county ordinance power manifests itself in many ways. Fireworks stands inevitably are erected a few feet outside a city's jurisdiction; contractors frequently take more liberties with sound construction principles in rural areas; and controversial establishments such as topless bars, noisy gun ranges, and polluting cement plants find homes in unincorporated county areas. In Williamson County, just north of Austin, a property management company even erected a 120-foot-high billboard that violated both state signage regulations and the rules of the homeowners' association for the apartments themselves. In all of these cases, counties are powerless to act.

★ ★ ★ ★ ★ ★ ★ ★ ★ ★ ★ ★ ★ ★ ★ ★ ★ ★ ★ ★ ★ ★ ★ ★ ★ ★

## LACK OF ORDINANCE POWER

Texas counties have no general power to pass ordinances—that is, laws pertaining to the county. They do have authority to protect the health and welfare of citizens, and through that power, they can regulate the operation of a sanitary landfill and mandate inoculations in the midst of an epidemic. They can regulate subdivision development in unincorporated areas, sometimes sharing power with municipalities and, for flood control, the federal government. However, the lack of general ordinance power means that, for example, they cannot zone land to ensure appropriate and similar usage in a given area, and they have trouble guarding against rutted roads and polluted water supplies when land developers or gas drillers start to work.[7]

## RECOMMENDATIONS

Having reviewed Texas county government, our mythical management consultants probably would recommend

- **Greater flexibility in this form of government, particularly in heavily populated areas, to encourage more professional management of personnel, services, purchasing, and all other aspects of county government**

- **Taking advantage of economies of scale by centralizing purchasing and adopting a unit system of road and bridge construction and maintenance**

- **Cooperative delivery of services**

However, they probably would not yet explore any of the forms of city–county cooperation that exist in areas such as San Francisco, Honolulu, or Nashville because counties in Texas are not yet ready to function as cities. The exceptions are El Paso County, where the county and city have explored consolidation, and Bexar County, where the county judge has advocated merger. The *Austin American-Statesman* has also urged some consideration of "government modernization" on the Travis County commissioners.[8]

Texas counties have no authority to pass general ordinances that could, for example, regulate land use in rural areas. The *colonias* on the outskirts of Texas cities along the Mexican border are an example of unregulated growth.

*Courtesy of Ben Sargent.*

## PROSPECTS FOR REFORM

Given the obvious disadvantages of the current structure, what are the prospects for changing county government in Texas? County commissioners, judges, sheriffs, and other county officers, acting individually as well as through such interest groups as TACO (Texas Association of County Officials), are potent political figures who can and do exercise substantial influence over their state legislators. Unfortunately for the taxpayers, most county officials have shown little willingness to accept change in the structure and function of county government. The exceptions are usually county commissioners in more heavily populated counties, who have taken a number of steps to professionalize government, including the appointment of personnel and budget experts. They are outnumbered ten to one by commissioners in less populous areas. Thus, substantially more citizen participation will be necessary if change is to occur. If city residents, who tend to ignore county politics, were to play a much more active role, reform might be possible because of the sheer numbers they represent when approaching legislators.

# Cities: Managed Environments

Unlike the county, the city has a long history of independence and self-government. The power of Greece was concentrated in city-states such as Athens and Sparta, which as early as 700 B.C. were centers of culture and military might. In the Middle Ages, European cities received crown charters that established them as separate and independent entities. One of their major functions was to protect their citizens from external danger; for this reason, the cities of the period were surrounded by high walls, and the citizens paid taxes for this protection. In America, this tradition continued, and early American cities sought charters initially from the British crown and later from the state legislatures. In Texas, San Fernando de Béxar (now San Antonio) was the first city. Its settlement was ordered by the king of Spain and began with fifteen families in 1731.

State legislatures traditionally have been less than sympathetic to the problems of the cities, partly because of rural bias and partly because they wished to avoid being caught in the quagmires of city politics. Therefore, in the nineteenth century, the states (including Texas) established **general laws**—statutes that pertained to all municipalities—for the organization of the city governments, to which municipalities were required to conform. But these general laws were too inflexible to meet the growing problems of the cities, and around the turn of the century, there was a movement toward *municipal home rule*. The home-rule laws permitted the cities, within limits, to organize as they saw fit.[9]

In Texas, the municipal home-rule amendment to the constitution was adopted in 1912. It provides that a city with a population of more than 5,000 is allowed—within certain procedural and financial limitations—to write its own constitution in the form of a city charter, which would be effective when approved by a majority vote of the citizens. A city charter is the local equivalent of a constitution. Home-rule cities may choose any organizational form or policies as long as they do not conflict with the state constitution or the state laws. General-law cities may organize according to any of the traditional forms of municipal government discussed later in this chapter, but with a number of restrictions due to the complex statutory categorization of general-law cities based on combinations of population and land area.

Traditionally, municipalities were organized into one of three types of governments: *mayor-council, commission*, and *council-manager*. Within these categories were a variety of subtypes. In the modern era, the commission form is rarely used, but hybrid forms of government that combine mayor-council and council-manager are growing in popularity; at least seven modern forms of municipal government have been identified.[10] Thus, it is sometimes difficult to slot an individual city into a particular category. This chapter looks at the three basic types, noting the most frequent variations on each.

In addition to home rule, two other legal aspects of city government in Texas are *extraterritorial jurisdiction* (ETJ) and *annexation*. ETJ gives cities limited control over unincorporated territory contiguous to their boundaries; that is, cities get some control over what kind of development occurs just outside the city limits. The zone ranges from a half-mile in distance for cities under 1,500 in population to five miles for those over 100,000. Within these zones, municipalities can require developers and others to conform to city regulations regarding construction, sanitation, utilities, and similar matters. In this way, cities can exercise some positive influence on the quality of life in the immediate area around them.

Socially irresponsible individuals and businesses sometimes locate outside both city limits and a city's extraterritorial jurisdiction for the dual purposes of avoiding city taxes—usually higher than the county's—and city regulation such as building codes. The lack of county ordinance power encourages such behavior, while ETJ helps to correct it.

Annexation power allows cities to bring adjacent unincorporated areas inside the municipal boundaries. Doing so helps prevent suburban developments from incorporating and blocking a large city's otherwise natural development. It also allows a city to expand its tax base. In the 1950s and 1960s, municipalities could make great land grabs without any commitment to providing services, but over the years, annexation powers have been curbed. The legislature in 1999 tightened requirements considerably with the passage of SB 89. Effective September 1, 1999, cities have more restrictions about notifying individuals in the area to be annexed. Beginning in 2002, they must immediately provide fire, police, and emergency services to the annexed area and must improve infrastructure such as roads, water supply, and sewer systems within two-and-a-half years. Exceptions are areas with fewer than 100 residents and areas that have asked for annexation.

★ ★ ★ ★ ★ ★ ★ ★ ★ ★ ★ ★ ★ ★ ★ ★ ★ ★ ★ ★ ★ ★ ★ ★ ★ ★ ★ ★ ★ ★

## Life Downtown: A View of Five Cities

Although Easterners have realized the advantages of living downtown rather than in the suburbs, Texans are only recently coming to realize pluses such as elimination of rush hour traffic woes and proximity to sports venues and entertainment centers. Austin, Dallas, Fort Worth, Houston, and San Antonio have paid special attention to downtown redevelopment and to attracting residents to the downtown area. One of the biggest drawbacks has been the lack of grocery stores. Indeed, early in 2004, when a major grocery chain announced plans to build a store in downtown Dallas, the news received prominent coverage in both the print press and the broadcast media; ultimately, by 2006 the grocery store required almost $600,000 in subsidies from the city to stay open.

★ ★ ★ ★ ★ ★ ★ ★ ★ ★ ★ ★ ★ ★ ★ ★ ★ ★ ★ ★ ★ ★ ★ ★ ★ ★ ★ ★ ★ ★

SOURCES: Dave Harmon, "Livable, Workable, Playable: Five Texas Cities Have Seen the Future, and It's an Urban Center That Is Livable, Workable, Playable," *Austin American-Statesman*, January 1, 2004, A5, A12–13; Dave Levinthal, "Grocery for City's Center," *Dallas Morning News*, January 6, 2004, 1A, 9A.

The old annexation law required notification by public announcement, not by apprising individual residents, and it required provision of services but over a four-and-a-half-year period. The new law set off an explosion of annexations, particularly in the Dallas–Fort Worth area, prior to the notification provision going into effect in 1999.

Annexation laws in Texas help prevent a phenomenon that is very common in other states' cities, such as Cleveland and Denver. There, more affluent residents have fled to upscale suburbs in what is often called "White flight." They leave the inner cities with inadequate tax revenues and decaying facilities. They no longer pay city taxes but continue to use and enjoy such services as airports, libraries, utilities, and museums, which city residents pay taxes to support. When a city exercises its annexation powers, it can protect its tax base somewhat as well as preserve space for future development. Although Texas's larger cities are surrounded by suburbs, many of which are upscale, they have been somewhat successful in counteracting White flight and the erosion of their tax bases and are even experiencing new development in downtown areas. Houston is the best (or worst) example of a city using annexation to protect itself. In

★ ★ ★ ★ ★ ★ ★ ★ ★ ★ ★ ★ ★ ★ ★ ★ ★ ★ ★ ★ ★ ★ ★ ★ ★ ★ ★

## A Zoning-Free City

Houston has long been known as the only major American city without zoning ordinances that dictate what can be built where—homes, offices, factories. In the past, city leaders have used such terms as a "Communist plot" and "socialized real estate" to describe zoning. Voters have explicitly and repeatedly rejected it, most recently in 1993. As a result, a church, an office tower, and a home can be found adjacent to one another.

Houston, with more than 2 million people at the time of the 2005 census estimate, is the fourth largest city in population in the United States. It is the second largest city in terms of land area, but its 579.4 square miles don't approach the huge 1,697.2 square miles of Anchorage, Alaska, which has only 261,000 people. Nevertheless, a growing, sprawling American megacity without zoning is rare.

★ ★ ★ ★ ★ ★ ★ ★ ★ ★ ★ ★ ★ ★ ★ ★ ★ ★ ★ ★ ★ ★ ★ ★ ★ ★ ★

SOURCES: See, for example, "'Anything Goes' Houstonians May Go the Limit: to Zoning," *New York Times*, October 27, 1993, 1; Patrick Barta, "To Limit Growth, Houston Turns to Deed Restrictions," *Wall Street Journal*, May 12, 1999, T1, T3. Comparative statistics are from "Incorporated Places with 100,000 or More Inhabitants in 2000—Population, 1970 to 2000, and Land Area 2000," *Statistical Abstract of the United States* (Washington, D.C.: U.S. Department of Commerce, Bureau of the Census, 2003), Table 33, p. 36, accessed at http://www.census.gov/prod/2003pubs/02statab/pop.pdf and "Incorporated Places with 150,000 or More Inhabitants in 2005—Population, 1980 to 2005," Table 31 of the *Statistical Abstract* (2006) accessed at http://www.census.gov/compendia/statab/population/.

1995, Houston, along with Austin, Nederland, and Longview, was the target of special legislation advocated by suburbanites to limit annexation power. Again, the cities prevailed.

## ORGANIZATION OF CITY GOVERNMENT

Home-rule cities have overwhelmingly opted for the council-manager plan of government. Of the 313 cities for which information was available,[11] 282 (90 percent) used the council-manager form, another 15 had created a hybrid mayor-administrator form, and only 16 operated under the mayor-council plan. None used a straight commission form, although some city councils call themselves "commissions." Among general-law cities, only 47 (5 percent) were recognized council-manager or mayor-administrator cities.[12] The basic forms of local government are described next, with emphasis on the two most popular forms: council-manager and mayor-council.

### THE COUNCIL-MANAGER FORM

San Antonio and Dallas are two of the largest cities in the country—along with Phoenix and San Jose—using this organizational model (Figure 12-3), but smaller cities such as Beeville, Gainesville, and Yoakum also operate with the *council-manager* form of government. Under this system, a city council of five to fifteen members is elected at large or by districts and in turn appoints a city manager who is responsible for the hiring and firing of department heads and for the preparation of the budget. A mayor, elected at large or by the council, is a member

**FIGURE 12-3 Council-Manager Form**

*SOURCE: Adapted from* Forms of City Government *(Austin: Institute of Public Affairs, University of Texas, 1959), 23.*

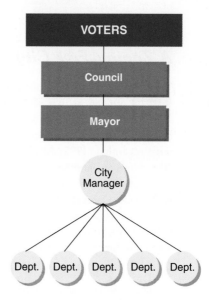

of the council and presides over it but otherwise has only the same powers as any other council member.

Proponents of council-manager government, including many political scientists, traditionally have argued that this form of government allows at least some separation of politics and administration. They believe that the council makes public policy and that, once a decision is made, the manager is charged with administering it. In reality, however, politics and administration cannot be separated: The city manager must make recommendations to the council on such highly political matters as tax and utility rates and zoning,[13] as the brokering role cited by Alan Ehrenhalt in the chapter-opening quotation indicates. Nevertheless, some citizens claim to perceive a distinction in this type of government between politics and policymaking on the one hand and administration on the other, and many are convinced that it is the most efficient form of city government. States with a large number of council-manager cities include Texas, California, Maine, and Michigan, among others.

For all its efficiency and professionalism, council-manager government does have some problems. First, because council members are part-time and often serve short tenures, they may rely heavily on the manager for policy guidance. Because the manager is not directly responsible to the voters, this practice makes it more difficult for the average citizen to influence city hall, and many citizens react negatively to reading in the local newspaper about the city manager's policy recommendations, even though the council must approve them. Second, the comparison is frequently drawn between council-manager government and the business corporation because both involve policymaking "boards" and professional managers. When coupled with the emphasis on efficiency, this image of a professionally trained "business manager" also tends to promote the values of the business community. The result is that festering political problems, especially those involving ethnic minorities and the poor, may not be addressed in a timely manner. However, district elections and direct election of the mayor in council-manager cities have reduced this problem somewhat, as representation on city councils has become more diversified. Also, city managers are now trained to

★ ★ ★ ★ ★ ★ ★ ★ ★ ★ ★ ★ ★ ★ ★ ★ ★ ★ ★ ★ ★ ★ ★ ★ ★ ★ ★ ★

## *On Becoming a City Manager*

How does one become a city manager? A city manager usually has a master's degree in public administration, public policy, or public affairs. The most common route is an internship in a city while still in school, followed by a series of increasingly responsible general management positions: administrative assistant, assistant to the city manager, assistant city manager, and then city manager. Alternatively, an individual may begin in a key staff area—for example, as a budget analyst, then budget director, and then director of finance—or in a major operating department—for example, as an administrative assistant in the public works department, then as an assistant director, and then director. Usually, the individual must move up through these positions in several municipalities to reach the top job. The Web site of the International City/County Management Association (www.icma.org) provides other information for the individual seeking a local government career, as does the Web site of the National Association of Schools of Public Affairs and Administration (http://www.naspaa.org/students/careers/careers.asp).

★ ★ ★ ★ ★ ★ ★ ★ ★ ★ ★ ★ ★ ★ ★ ★ ★ ★ ★ ★ ★ ★ ★ ★ ★ ★ ★ ★

be sensitive to all citizens. As the executive director of the International City/County Management Association put it, "For nearly 90 years, the council-manager form has successfully adapted to American community needs."[14]

## THE MAYOR-COUNCIL FORM

In the *mayor-council* form of municipal government, council members are elected at large or by geographic districts, and the mayor is elected at large. At large means citywide. The mayor-council form has two variants: the *weak mayor-council* form and the *strong mayor-council* form. In the weak mayor-council form, other executives such as the city attorney and treasurer also are elected, whereas in the strong mayor-council form, the mayor has the power to appoint and remove other city executives. In the strong mayor-council form, the mayor also prepares the budget, subject to council approval. In both mayor-council forms, the mayor can veto acts of the city council, but typically fewer council votes are needed to override the mayor's veto in a weak mayor-council city than in a strong mayor-council city. An individual city charter may combine elements of both strong mayor-council and weak mayor-council government—for example, giving the mayor budget control while also allowing for some other elected positions. Figure 12-4 illustrates the strong mayor-council form. A diagram of a weak mayor-council form would be very similar, except that a series of other elected officials would be specified, such as the city attorney, police chief, and parks and recreation director.

The words *strong* and *weak* are used in reference to a mayor's powers in the same way that the word *weak* is applied to the Texas governorship. The terms have to do with the amount of formal power given to the chief executive by the city charter. An individual mayor, by dint of personality, political savvy, and leadership skills, can heavily influence local politics regardless of restrictions in the city charter.

**FIGURE 12-4 Strong
Mayor-Council Form**

*SOURCE:* Forms of City
Government *(Austin: Institute
of Public Affairs, University of
Texas, 1959), 10.*

*\*In a number of strong mayor-
council cities, the chief of police
and some other department
heads are elected, although that
is not the case in Texas.*

*\*\*Common departments
are fire, police, streets and
sanitation, utilities, parks and
recreation.*

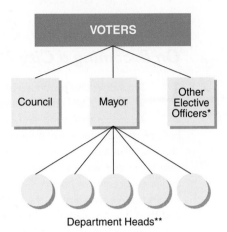

Department Heads**

The strong mayor form is most common among the nation's largest cities, whereas the weak mayor form prevails in smaller communities. In Texas, none of the state's largest cities have pure mayor-council government, although Houston comes closest because it uses a hybrid mayor-council form with a chief administrative officer. Small-city examples include Hitchcock and Robstown.

Because mayor-council government is what is called an "unreformed" or a "political" model,[15] it may experience more efficiency problems than a professionally managed city and have less ability to arrive at consensus on policy. To overcome some of its problems, mayor-council cities—particularly larger ones—often have a deputy mayor or chief administrative officer appointed by the mayor who tends to the internal business of the city while the mayor tends to political matters.[16] The leading character in a popular television show at the turn of the century, *Spin City*, was a deputy mayor.

Many political scientists favor the strong mayor-council form of government because they think it seems most likely to provide the kind of leadership needed to cope with the growing problems of major urban areas and it focuses on an elected, not an appointed, official. One reason for this opinion is that the mayor and council members, especially in larger cities, are full-time paid officials who can devote their time to the development of public policy and oversight of government services. Thus, policy proposals come directly from elected officials. If these officials represent a broad public interest, as opposed to narrow interest groups, democracy is well served.

## MAYOR-MANAGER FORM

The *mayor-manager* form of government, also called the *chief administrative officer* (CAO) form, is growing in popularity nationwide.[17] This plan has generated interest because it combines the overt political leadership of a mayor-council plan with the professional management skills identified with council-manager government. Typically, it arises when the mayor recognizes a need for managerial assistance. In this form of government, the city manager reports only to the mayor, not to the council as a whole, and focuses on fiscal/administrative policy implementation. The mayor provides broad policy leadership in addressing major problems such as crime and economic development. In Texas, some smaller cities such as Argyle and Mathis use a city administrator plan, but often the smaller communities use the hybrid only until a charter election can be held to adopt council-manager government. Elsewhere, mayor-manager government is often practiced in consolidated city–county governments such as Lexington-Fayette County, Kentucky, and some cities, such as San Ramon, California.

A variant of mayor-manager government is arising in larger municipalities. In Texas and across the country, large cities using the council-manager plan have seen disputes develop among the mayor, council members, and managers as assertive mayors try to carve out a larger role for themselves. The growing interest of big-city mayors in controlling both the political and the administrative aspects of city government is illustrated by events in Dallas. In 1987–1991, Mayor Annette Strauss imposed strong political leadership on the city with her "Honey, do it for Dallas" approach that masked behavior at times more reminiscent of a strong mayor than the mayor of a council-manager city. Then, in 1992–1993, Mayor Steve Bartlett, a former U.S. congressman, and City Manager Jan Hart struggled for control, with Hart ultimately leaving in 1993 to enter the private sector. In 1997, Mayor Ron Kirk struggled more with the Dallas City Council, which resisted his bid for greater power, than he did with City Manager John Ware, but his intent was the same as Bartlett's: to gain control of the city's executive establishment. In 2002, a charter review commission initiated by Dallas Mayor Laura Miller began studying stronger formal powers for the mayor and perhaps the possibility of eliminating the city manager position. Two different elections on the issue of a strong mayor-manager form for Dallas were held in 2005; both resulted in retention of the traditional council-manager form. More cooperative mayor-manager relationships *can* exist in large cities, as for example in Fort Worth.

Table 12-1 summarizes the form of government used in the nation's and the state's largest cities. It also provides information on population size, the percentage of population change between the 1990 and 2000 censuses, and the physical size of the cities.

## THE COMMISSION FORM—A HISTORICAL FOOTNOTE

The *commission* form of city government is said to have originated in Galveston. In 1900, the city lost 7,200 persons in a disastrous storm surge that swept the Texas coast in the wake of a fierce hurricane. The city then applied for and received permission from the state legislature to adopt a commission form of government to meet its emergency needs.

Under this type of organization, the elected commissioners collectively compose the policymaking board and, as individuals, are administrators of various departments such as public safety, streets and transportation, finance, and so on. They are usually elected at large. Although widely copied initially, the commission system has more recently lost favor because many think that the commissioners tend to become advocates for their own departments rather than public interest advocates who act on behalf of the entire city. Also, the city commission is subject to many of the same problems as the county commission, including corruption and unclear lines of responsibility. Although some cities still call their city councils commissions, Texas home-rule cities have abandoned this form of government. Galveston itself was recognized by the International City/County Management Association as a council-manager city in 1961. Some general-law cities still have commission government.

**TABLE 12.1**

## Basic Facts about America's Ten Largest and Texas's Seven Largest Cities, as of the 2005 Census Estimate

| City with Rank in Population | 2005 Population | % Population Change 2000-2005 | Land Area in Square Miles | Type of Governance |
|---|---|---|---|---|
| 1. New York City | 8,143,197 | +1.7 | 303.3 | Mayor-Council |
| 2. Los Angeles | 3,844,829 | +.04 | 469.1 | Mayor-Council |
| 3. Chicago | 2,842,616 | −1.8 | 227.1 | Mayor-Council |
| 4. Houston, TX | 2,016,582 | +.03 | 579.4 | Mayor-Council with Chief Administrative Officer (CAO) |
| 5. Philadelphia | 1,463,261 | −3.6 | 135.1 | Mayor-Council |
| 6. Phoenix | 1,461,575 | +10.7 | 474.9 | Council-Manager |
| 7. San Antonio, TX | 1,256,509 | +9.5 | 407.6 | Council-Manager |
| 8. San Diego | 1,225,540 | +20.6 | 324.3 | Mayor-Council with Chief Operating Officer (COO) |
| 9. Dallas, TX | 1,213,825 | +2.1 | 342.5 | Council-Manager |
| 10. San Jose | 912,331 | +1.9 | 175 | Council-Manager |
| 16. Austin, TX | 690,252 | +5.1 | 251.5 | Council-Manager |
| 19. Fort Worth, TX | 624,067 | +16.7 | 292.5 | Council-Manager |
| 21. El Paso, TX | 598,590 | +6.2 | 249.1 | Council-Manager |
| 50. Arlington | 362,805 | +9.0 | 99.5 | Council-Manager |

NOTE: This information is for the city alone, not the metropolitan area, which may be double or triple the population size and several times the land area of the central city.

SOURCES: "Top 50 Cities in the U.S. by Population and Rank," *Infoplease.com* found at http://www.infoplease.com/ipa/A0763098.html, plus individual city pages; "Directory of ICMA-Recognized Local Governments," *Who's Who in Local Government Management* (Washington, D.C.: International City County Management Association, 2007), accessed at www.icma.org but available only to members.

## FORMS USED IN GENERAL-LAW CITIES

Texas has about 850 general-law cities—cities whose population is fewer than 5,000 or somewhat larger cities that, for one reason or another, have not opted for home rule. These cities can organize under any of three basic forms of government: aldermanic (a variant of the mayor-council type), council-manager, or commission. However, state law limits the size of the council, specifies other mu-

San Antonio, with its Riverwalk, is often considered Texas's most distinctive city.

nicipal officials, spells out the power of the mayor, and places other restrictions on matters that home-rule cities can decide for themselves.[18]

Because of their small size, most of the general-law cities have chosen the aldermanic model—basically, mayor-council government. The council-manager form, calling for the hiring of a professional city manager, is thought to be too expensive and unnecessary in a small city. There is also the problem of finding a trained city manager who is knowledgeable about small-town issues. However, many smaller cities, such as Anthony and Nolanville, have designated the city clerk as the chief administrative officer without bothering to adopt council-manager government formally. A few have hired a part-time manager—usually a graduate student in a nearby public administration program—or have banded with other small communities to hire a "circuit-riding" city manager. Whatever their official title—city manager, city clerk, city secretary, or assistant to the mayor—administrators in smaller cities more than earn their salaries. They usually serve as general managers, personnel directors, tax assessor-collectors, and so forth because they are often the only full-time professional in the city's government.

Local government is responsible for most police work. Here, a Houston mounted police officer directs traffic.

A shrimper unloads the Lady E at the Port of Brownsville. The sea is an important part of the economy of Texas.

Sports are important in Texas, but especially in a small town like Pilot Point where G.A. Moore became Texas's winningest high school football coach.

## WHAT FORM IS PREFERABLE?

The only clear answer is that city size seems to have some effect on the type of municipal government that works best. For small cities, the type of government does not seem to matter much. Smaller cities that can afford a city manager often do well with that form, but most use a mayor-council form, often relying on the city secretary to coordinate administrative affairs. Mid-size cities (from 25,000 to 250,000 in population) can afford to hire a manager, and because they tend to be suburban and relatively homogeneous in terms of class and ethnicity, they experience fewer intense political conflicts than larger cities. As a result, they often adopt the council-manager form of government because

YOU DECIDE

## Should the Largest Cities (Dallas, San Antonio, Austin, Fort Worth, for Example) Abandon Council-Manager Government in Favor of a Strong Mayor-Council Form?

I t is not uncommon across the country for cities to switch from council-manager government to mayor-council or mayor-manager (mayor-administrator) government once they near or exceed a half-million people in size. In Texas, Dallas has struggled bitterly with the issue of possible change, while El Paso moved from mayor-council to council-manager government. What do you think the very large cities in the state should do?

| PRO | CON |
|---|---|
| Any large city should adopt a new municipal charter calling for a strong mayor-council form because: | A large city that has council-manager government should keep its present governmental form because: |
| ▲ It needs a strong chief executive as leader, someone elected to provide political and policy direction for the city. | ▼ A strong mayor would just divide the community because mayors must spend more time tending their electoral bases, to ensure that their friends win and their enemies lose, than focusing on making city government work efficiently and effectively for all citizens. |
| ▲ The mayor and the manager disagree publicly too much. | ▼ The mayor can provide leadership even in a city manager form of government. |
| ▲ The city has district council elections. Only the mayor can represent the whole city (except Austin, which has at-large elections). | ▼ The city manager is bound by a national code of ethics that requires him/her to stay out of politics and focus on making sure things run right. |
| ▲ City managers tend to favor business interests. | ▼ The mayor and individual council members would be more likely to jockey for political position in a different form of government. |
| ▲ It is too easy for the city manager and the rest of the bureaucracy to perform poorly without anyone knowing. | ▼ Day-to-day operations are so complicated in a big city that a professional manager needs to be in charge of them. |
| ▲ More citizens would vote if the mayor's race mattered more. | ▼ A strong mayor is more likely to "break the bank" in giving away political favors. |
| ▲ The city could address its out-and-out political problems better. | ▼ Large cities with mayor-council or mayor-manager government still have major political problems. |

it allows for relatively efficient operation and permits the city administration to maintain a distance from party politics and from state and national political issues. In big cities, however, where it is impossible to escape from class and ethnic tension, the overtly political mayor-council or mayor-manager form is often a better choice because of the need for the political focus provided by the elected mayor.[19]

# CITY FINANCE

## REVENUES AND EXPENDITURES

The most important sources of municipal funding are the property tax, general and selective sales taxes, borrowing through bonds, and user fees, especially for utilities such as water, solid waste pickup, waste water, and electricity. Fees can be collected for almost any service, from playing a round of golf at the municipal course to airport landing fees. Other sources include intergovernmental transfers and miscellaneous fees and fines, such as liquor licenses and traffic fines collected by the municipal court. Figure 12-5 shows how a typical Texas city raises revenue and then spends it.

Cities spend their money on diverse services. For most cities, the largest areas of expenditure are utilities (laying all those water lines costs a lot of money!); parks, recreation, and environmental compliance—a category that includes solid waste disposal—and police and fire protection. Other categories of spending include streets, general government, and health and welfare. Interest on debt is significant in many municipal budgets, especially in areas of high growth, where the city can never seem to catch up on construction needs.

## FISCAL PROBLEMS

Municipalities, like the state, have had to adapt to changing economic conditions and shrinking sources of income coupled with burgeoning population growth. In the thirty-five year period since 1970, the state has gone through a boom-bust-boom cycle. At the beginning of the twenty-first century, cities were most concerned about keeping up with growth in the face of limited options on how to pay for it.

What are the causes of fiscal stress in Texas municipalities?[20] There are at least six, as follows:

1. **Public aversion to rising property (real estate) taxes. In Texas, this aversion includes the Texas 8 percent rollback, which stipulates that any combination of an increase in tax rate or tax base of 8 percent or more is subject to an election to roll back the increase if the revenue is to be used to support regular government operations. Tax rate is the amount per $100 of property valuation due in taxes; tax base is the real estate that is assessed and assigned a value. This provision applies to all local governments.**

2. **Changes in national priorities and responsibilities. Political conservatism has resulted in a redistribution of aid to cities. Today, for example, less money is available for the physical rebuilding of cities, and more money is available to meet potential terrorist threats.**

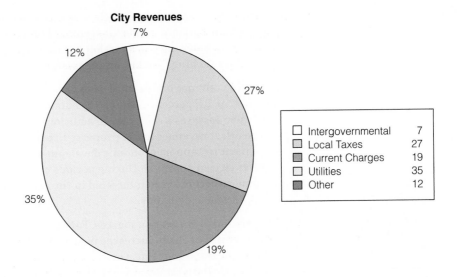

**City Revenues**

| | |
|---|---|
| ☐ Intergovernmental | 7 |
| ☐ Local Taxes | 27 |
| ☐ Current Charges | 19 |
| ☐ Utilities | 35 |
| ☐ Other | 12 |

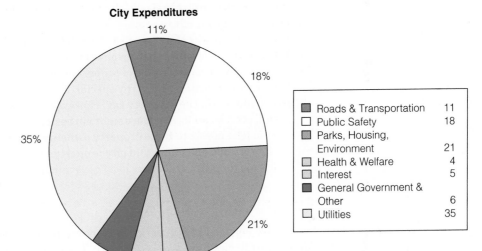

**City Expenditures**

| | |
|---|---|
| ■ Roads & Transportation | 11 |
| ☐ Public Safety | 18 |
| ☐ Parks, Housing, Environment | 21 |
| ☐ Health & Welfare | 4 |
| ☐ Interest | 5 |
| ■ General Government & Other | 6 |
| ☐ Utilities | 35 |

**FIGURE 12-5 Typical Texas City Revenues and Expenditures**

*SOURCE: Data were drawn from a variety of census reports, budgets, and certified annual financial audit reports. No specific city or town is represented.*

3. Shifting of service burdens to the cities by both the national and state governments. These shifts are as varied as requiring cities over 50,000 to maintain state highway rights-of-way inside city limits and rigorous clean water standards without financial assistance to meet them. The notion of **mandates**—requirements imposed by a higher level of government upon a lower one—is troublesome when a mandate comes without monetary assistance. The chapter-opening quote by Alan Greenblatt reflects this concern.

4. Changes in federal fiscal policy. The 1986 federal income tax reform made it less attractive to purchase municipal bonds, which are the primary means of funding major local projects. Subsequent spikes and dips in the stock

market have made it, respectively, less attractive and more attractive to purchase government bonds. Government bonds do not pay as well as the returns on a booming stock market but offer security when the market is in decline and earnings are low or nonexistent.

5. Increasing reliance on the local sales tax. Cities can assess a 1 percent retail sales tax, or 1.5 percent if the city is outside a metropolitan transit district, which also assesses a sales tax. In addition, cities can add another 0.5 percent to offset revenues lost if property taxes are lowered, and yet another 0.5 percent to support economic development. Any sales tax authorization requires citizen approval. During periods of economic decline, municipalities tend to become very interested in the additional sales tax possibilities to meet revenue demands.

6. Competition over revenue sources. For example, most citizens are particularly resentful of sharp increases in property taxes; indeed, property tax resentment is the root cause of taxpayer revolt. Cities often find themselves particularly constrained with regard to the property tax, not because of their own sharp increase in the tax rate, but because of school district increases that affect basically the same people and because of state officials who like to boast of tax cuts—but the cuts are in local property taxes, not state taxes, as was the case with the 2007 cuts in school property taxes. Today, cities often find that revenues from sales taxes and utility fees are greater than revenue from the property tax. Municipalities are more fortunate than counties and many special districts because they are not quite so dependent on the property tax. However, as the 2007 legislative session began, attacks on local government authority to use the power of *eminent domain* (the power to force property owners to sell to government) and threats of caps on county and city property tax increases loomed as further problems for cities and other local governments.

## FISCAL SOLUTIONS

Cities have engaged in six tactics in response to the tightening revenue picture. All these strategies have worked in part. The problem for municipalities is how to respond to a disaster—such as the tornadoes that plague Texas, a major economic upheaval such as the closing of a military base, or yet more federal and state mandates for, say, clean air—when they are just holding their own.

1. They have placed greater emphasis on *public–private cooperation* in everything, from joint funding of arts centers to private sponsorship of Fourth of July celebrations.

2. Cities have turned to *privatization*—that is, turning some services over to the private sector. The most frequent example is solid waste disposal. Instead of the city hauling away garbage, the homeowner or business pays a private company to dispose of solid wastes.

3. Cities are *asking citizens to volunteer* to perform some services that were formerly provided by paid employees. Examples include picking up litter and supervising and even constructing playgrounds.

4. Municipalities have turned to *productivity enhancement*, a package of management techniques ranging from flexible scheduling of employees' time

to workload standards and pay-for-performance, to make scarce financial resources stretch further.

5. Cities have sought *new revenue sources*. One is user fees—charges paid directly by the consumer of services. Although municipalities have long had user fees for services such as water, they are charging new or higher fees for other services, such as recreational facilities. The other is special fees, including so-called impact fees charged to developers for the effect that land development has on streets, utilities, and other basic services.

6. Municipalities have simply *terminated certain services*; the most obvious example is the refusal to accept grass clippings at the local landfill in an effort to extend the life of the landfill.

★ ★ ★ ★ ★ ★ ★ ★ ★ ★ ★ ★ ★ ★ ★ ★ ★ ★ ★ ★ ★ ★ ★ ★ ★ ★ ★ ★ ★

## Who Says Reading Is Fundamental?

Local government revenue shortfalls have particularly affected public libraries. Some cities have slashed their library budgets to increase funding for services such as fire and police. Others have looked to privatization of library services. Others still have considerably increased the fees to out-of-town users, for example, rural users of city libraries, following cuts in county allocation of library funds to cities.

★ ★ ★ ★ ★ ★ ★ ★ ★ ★ ★ ★ ★ ★ ★ ★ ★ ★ ★ ★ ★ ★ ★ ★ ★ ★ ★ ★ ★

## CITY POLITICS

The discussion of forms of city government and city finance provided a substantial amount of factual information about the operation of the city but has said little about how city government really works. Who gets the rewards, and who is deprived? Which individuals and groups benefit most from city government, and which groups bear the burdens?

The electoral system used by Texas cities is an indication of how the rewards and deprivations are distributed. Although the partisanship of candidates is well known in cities such as Beaumont and El Paso, all Texas cities hold **nonpartisan elections**. The irony is that the municipalities are surrounded by counties with highly partisan elections. In most Texas cities, municipal elections are held during the spring in a further attempt to separate city government from party politics.

In this electoral setting, a private interest group such as a local realtors' association or homeowners may sponsor a slate of candidates for municipal office, just as a political party would, under the guise of a civic organization that purportedly has no goals of its own except efficient and responsive government. Such a claim is misleading, however. These groups do have goals and are highly effective in achieving them. In some cities, a charter association or good government league exists; these organizations inevitably reflect the interests of conservative business elements in the community. In other cities, environmentalists or neighborhood advocates or antitax groups may launch well-organized single-issue campaigns. In addition, a number of more or less ad hoc groups usually appear at election time to sponsor one or more candidates, and in all Texas cities, independent candidates also come forth with their own campaigns to seek public office.

Closely associated with nonpartisan elections is the system of electing candidates for the city council at large. All voters select all the members of the council and vote for as many candidates as there are positions on the council. In another practice widely followed in Texas cities, the **place system**, the seats on the council are designated as Place One, Place Two, and so on. In this type of election, candidates who file for a particular place run only against other candidates who also file for that place. Voting is still citywide. The at-large, by-place system predominates in smaller cities.

★ ★ ★ ★ ★ ★ ★ ★ ★ ★ ★ ★ ★ ★ ★ ★ ★ ★ ★ ★ ★ ★ ★ ★ ★ ★ ★ ★ ★

## *Urban Diversity*

Changes in Texas politics are most evident in the major cities where leaders and interest groups reflect newer interests and where the sacrosanct principle of non-partisanship is sometimes violated.

Austin, San Antonio, Houston, Dallas, El Paso, Fort Worth, and Galveston have had women mayors, as have more than 200 smaller communities. El Paso and San Antonio have elected Mexican American men as mayors, and Dallas and Houston have elected African American men. Austin, Houston, and Dallas have become the homes of large groups of politically active homosexuals. In all three cities, politicians of many ideological persuasions seek the support of the Gay and Lesbian Political Caucus, and in 2006, Dallas launched a major initiative to attract gay and lesbian tourists.

In the big cities, the importance of neighborhood representation and ethnic representation has intensified to such an extent that it is difficult to gain a workable consensus for establishing public policy. Instead, individual council members sometimes advocate the needs of their districts to the exclusion of concerns about the city as a whole.

★ ★ ★ ★ ★ ★ ★ ★ ★ ★ ★ ★ ★ ★ ★ ★ ★ ★ ★ ★ ★ ★ ★ ★ ★ ★ ★ ★ ★

Increasingly, however, Texas cities with populations of 50,000 or more are amending their charters to provide for a **district system**, wherein candidates are required to live in a particular geographic area within the city and run against only those candidates who also live in the district. Voters choose only among candidates within their district, although the mayor is usually elected at large. In other cities, some council members are elected by district and some at large.

Often, the change to district elections occurs as the result of a successful court suit alleging discrimination against minorities, who find it difficult to win election in a citywide race. Running in districts costs less money and has the advantage of allowing minority candidates to concentrate their campaigning in neighborhoods with large numbers of individuals who share the candidate's ethnic background. Often, additional council seats are created when a city switches to district elections.

Advocates of at-large and by-place elections argue that the council focuses on citywide concerns, but district elections result in a fragmented council whose members concentrate on only the problems of their electoral district. They also think district elections are incompatible with council-manager government, which predominates in the state's home-rule cities, because they make local elections "too political." Advocates of district elections think the council is more representative when members are elected by wards or districts because minorities, spokespersons for citizens' groups, and individuals without personal wealth have a better opportunity to be elected and will be more inclined to address "local district" problems. They believe government by its very nature is political, and so all political viewpoints should be represented.

Questions about the organization of elections and the nature of representation are at the heart of the democratic process. One measure of a city's democratic morality is the extent to which the council represents the city's ethnic, economic, and geographic diversity. Thus, democratic theorists sometimes recommend district over at-large elections except in small municipalities where all candidates are likely to be known by most voters.[21]

Controversy also exists over whether elections should be nonpartisan. One argument is that nonpartisan elections rob the voters of the most important symbol that they have for making electoral choices: the party label. Without knowing whether a candidate is a Democrat, a Republican, or a member of some other party, how does the voter decide how to vote?

In answering this question, critics of nonpartisan elections say that voters depend on personalities and extraneous matters. For example, television personalities and athletes frequently win elections simply because they are better known than their opponents. These critics also think that nonpartisan elections rob the community of organized and effective criticism of the government in power. Because most candidates win as individuals rather than as members of an organized political party with common goals and policies, such criticism is sporadic and ineffectual, and meaningful policy alternatives seldom are stated. Texas political parties are not well organized. The blame for weak party organizations is often placed on nonpartisan local elections because the parties have no strong grassroots input. Another criticism is that nonpartisan elections encourage the development of civic organizations that are in essence local political parties whose purposes and policy proposals are not always clear to the voters.

Advocates of nonpartisan elections obviously disagree. They think the absence of a party label allows local elections to focus on local issues and not on national issues about which the municipal government can do little or nothing— for example, whether President Clinton should have been impeached or whether President Bush should have invaded Iraq. They note that television personalities, athletes, and actors are also elected under party banners. Moreover, they point to the fact that local civic groups clarify, not confuse, local issues. Homeowners, taxpayers, and consumers have become political forces that stand in contrast to the traditional, business-oriented civic associations. As a result, participation is enhanced, although resolving political disagreements has become more difficult.

At-large elections, nonpartisan voting, and holding elections in the spring apparently do contribute to low voter turnout. A municipal election in which as many as 25 percent of the eligible voters participate is unusual. Many local elections are decided on the basis of the preference of only 5 or 10 percent of the eligible voters. Moreover, statistics on voting behavior for all elections show that older, affluent Whites vote more frequently than do the young, the poor, and ethnic minorities. The structure of municipal elections in Texas, particularly when those elections are at large, tends to perpetuate the dominant position of the White middle-class business community. Thus, when one examines municipal government against the criteria for a democratic government, one finds some problems of participation, especially among the less affluent and ethnic minorities.

# Special Districts: Our Hidden Governments

Perhaps the best way to introduce the topic of special districts is to look at the changes in Texas local government shown in Table 12-2. The number of counties has been stable for almost a century; the number of school districts has steadily declined as districts consolidate to gain greater economy and efficiency. The number of municipalities has increased largely because unincorporated suburbs on the edges of central cities have become incorporated cities. The big increase is in nonschool special districts, which doubled in number in a thirty-year period; their growth has finally slowed.

## WHAT IS A SPECIAL DISTRICT?

A special district is a unit of local government created by an act of the legislature to perform limited functions. Its authority is narrow rather than broad, as in the case of the city or the county. Any further definition is almost impossible; special districts vary enormously in size, organization, function, and importance.

There are about two dozen different types of special districts in Texas. Approximately one fourth of these are housing and community-development districts, while another fourth are concerned with problems of water—control and improvement, drainage, navigation, supply, and sanitation. Other frequently encountered types of special districts are airport, soil conservation, municipal utilities, hospital, fire prevention, weed control, and community college districts.

**TABLE 12-2**
## Number of Units of Local Government in Texas, 1972–2002

| Type of Government | 1972 | 1982 | 1992 | 2002 | % Change 1992–2002 |
|---|---|---|---|---|---|
| Counties | 254 | 254 | 254 | 254 | 0 |
| Municipalities | 1,000 | 1,121 | 1,171 | 1,196 | +2.1 |
| School districts | 1,157 | 1,125 | 1,101 | 1,090 | −1 |
| Other special districts | 1,215 | 1,692 | 2,266 | 2,245 | −.09 |
| TOTAL | 3,626 | 4,192 | 4,792 | 4,785 | −.01 |

NOTE: One of the school districts is classified as dependent on another local government, most likely a county.

SOURCE: U.S. Department of Commerce, Bureau of the Census, *2002 Census of Governments*, vol. 1, no. 1, *Government Organizations* (Washington, D.C.: December 2002), Tables 1, 3, and 5.

No single state or county agency is responsible for supervising the activities or auditing the financial records of all these special districts. Such supervision depends on the type of district involved. For example, community college districts are supervised by the Texas Higher Education Coordinating Board and the Texas Education Agency. Average citizens, however, have a hard time keeping track of the many special districts surrounding them. The lack of uniformity and resulting confusion are caused in part by the various ways in which special districts can be created: through special acts of the legislature or under general laws, by general-purpose governments (cities and counties) in some instances, and even by state agencies.

## WHY SPECIAL DISTRICTS?

Why does Texas have so many special districts? Are they really necessary?

### INADEQUACY OF ESTABLISHED GOVERNMENTS

First, our established governments—the cities and counties—are inadequate to solve many of the increasingly diverse problems of government. The problem of flood control can seldom be solved within a single city or county, for example; in fact, it frequently goes beyond state boundaries, thus requiring an interstate authority. Cities and counties may find it difficult to finance needed projects. Hospital and community college districts are sometimes created because the debt limitations on established governmental units make taking on a major new activity all but impossible. Then, too, local units may be incapable of coping with governmental problems for other reasons, such as poor organizational structure and a lack of personnel. Special districts are part of the price paid for governmental institutions such as counties that were fashioned a century ago and are not always capable of addressing complex modern problems.

★ ★ ★ ★ ★ ★ ★ ★ ★ ★ ★ ★ ★ ★ ★ ★ ★ ★ ★ ★ ★ ★ ★ ★ ★ ★ ★ ★ ★

### Central Appraisal Districts

Every county has a central tax appraisal district that is responsible for assessing property and providing up-to-date tax rolls to each taxing jurisdiction—county, municipalities, school districts, and other special districts. This system began in 1982 to eliminate the confusion caused by different taxing jurisdictions setting different values on property. In addition to assessment, the uniform appraisal district may have a formal agreement with one or more of the taxing jurisdictions to collect the taxes.

★ ★ ★ ★ ★ ★ ★ ★ ★ ★ ★ ★ ★ ★ ★ ★ ★ ★ ★ ★ ★ ★ ★ ★ ★ ★ ★ ★ ★

These inadequacies make the creation of a new unit of government an attractive solution. Perhaps nowhere does one see the need for, and advantages of, special districts more than in the various water supply districts. The Lower Colorado River Authority, for example, owns and operates six of the seven lakes in the Austin area.

## EASE OF ORGANIZATION AND OPERATION

Part of the attraction of special districts is that they are *easy to organize and operate*. Political leaders of cities and counties frequently promote a special district as a solution to what might otherwise become "their problem," and the legislature is willing to go along. Creating a hospital district, for example, means that the city and the county don't have to raise their taxes. Indeed, the cost may be spread over several cities or counties included in the special district. Hunt Memorial Hospital District (Greenville and Commerce areas) is illustrative.

## PRIVATE GAIN

In a few instances, *special districts have been created primarily for private gain*. Land speculators and real estate developers create special districts called municipal utility districts (MUDs) on the outskirts of urban areas to increase the value of their holdings. Once enabling legislation has been obtained from the state, it requires only a handful of votes in the sparsely settled, newly created district to authorize a bond issue for the development of water, sewer, and other utilities. This development increases the value of the property in the district to the benefit of the developers. Ultimately, of course, the taxpayers pay for the bonds, sometimes through very high utility rates. MUDs are a good example of the consequences of a lack of effective state regulation of special districts. Economic development districts created by counties have the ability to collect taxes that are used mainly for private benefit. Examples include a district in Bexar County created to establish a golf course resort, one in Smith County that allowed a builder and his employees to constitute the board governing a district created to fund a truck stop, and a Hays County water control and improvement district that benefited only one California-based home builder.[22] Denton County became so profligate in creating special taxing districts to help the developers of luxury housing additions that the attorney general in 2001 announced new rules for approving bond elections affecting such districts.

## FLEXIBILITY

*Special districts offer great flexibility to government organizations* and have the added attraction of rarely conflicting with existing units. A two-city airport such as Dallas–Fort Worth International is the result of a flexible airport authority. In 1997–2000 and again in 2006, however, DFW proponents did find themselves in conflict with airlines that wanted to expand operations at Dallas's Love Field.

## APOLITICAL APPROACH

With highly technical problems such as flood control, the *special district offers the opportunity to "get it out of politics."* In other words, it is possible to take a businesslike approach and bring in technical specialists to attack the problem. The Wise County Water Control and Improvement District #1 is an example. Such districts really are not apolitical but they do allow the focus to remain on the task at hand. Of course, other types of special districts—most notably, those whose purpose is economic development—tend to be highly political.

★ ★ ★ ★ ★ ★ ★ ★ ★ ★ ★ ★ ★ ★ ★ ★ ★ ★ ★ ★ ★ ★ ★ ★ ★ ★

### Easy or Not?

Lawmakers in the Seventy-eighth Legislature in 2003 quickly disagreed over special taxing districts. Senator Ron Wilson (a Houston Democrat) introduced, without success, legislation to make it even easier to create such districts. A longtime foe of the districts, Senator Jane Nelson (a Denton County Republican), immediately revealed the proposal to the public, saying, "It just means we're going to have to be more careful, more vigilant, for a longer time."

★ ★ ★ ★ ★ ★ ★ ★ ★ ★ ★ ★ ★ ★ ★ ★ ★ ★ ★ ★ ★ ★ ★ ★ ★ ★

SOURCE: Pete Slover, "Taxing Districts May Be on Fast Track," *Dallas Morning News*, January 17, 2003, 16A.

## ASSESSMENT OF SPECIAL DISTRICTS

Special districts other than school and appraisal districts are *profoundly undemocratic*. They are "hidden governments," with far less visibility than city or county governments. It is not an exaggeration to say that every reader of this book is under the jurisdiction of at least one special district, yet it will be a very rare reader who knows which districts affect her or him, how much they cost in taxes, who the commissioner or other officials of each special district are, whether they are elected or (as is more frequently the case) appointed, and what policies they follow. Special district government is unseen by and frequently unresponsive to the people. Thus, when one applies the test of democratic morality, one finds that special districts fail to meet the standards of participation and public input. Indeed, they are sometimes an unfortunate reflection of Texas's traditionalistic and individualistic political culture.

Most special districts are small in size and scope. Therefore, they are *uneconomical*. Their financial status is often shaky, and so the interest rates that taxpayers must pay on the bond issues used to finance many types of special dis-

★ ★ ★ ★ ★ ★ ★ ★ ★ ★ ★ ★ ★ ★ ★ ★ ★ ★ ★ ★ ★ ★ ★ ★ ★ ★

### Taxation without Representation?

The Denton County Development Districts No. 6 and 7 illustrate the problem with special districts. These districts built and operate Lantana, a large upscale housing development. The commissioners were elected by three voters, who also created the districts in the one election held in 2000. Commissioners meet on a weekday in Dallas, posting meeting notices on a tree along a busy street that is partially obscured by shrubbery. They have authorized $137 million in bonds; they are paid $150 per meeting; and none of the three live in Lantana. Public outcry led to more formal notices and elections in November 2006.

★ ★ ★ ★ ★ ★ ★ ★ ★ ★ ★ ★ ★ ★ ★ ★ ★ ★ ★ ★ ★ ★ ★ ★ ★ ★

SOURCE: Peggy Heinkel-Wolfe, "Tree Stumped," *Denton Record-Chronicle*, February 19, 2006, 1A, 10A.

trict projects are exceptionally high. Economies such as large-scale purchasing are impossible. Finally, one of the most serious consequences of the proliferation of special districts is that they *greatly complicate the problems of government, particularly in urban areas*. With many separate governments, the likelihood is greater that haphazard development, confusion, and inefficiency will occur. No single government has comprehensive authority, and coordination among so many smaller governments becomes extremely difficult. Texans have been reluctant to experiment with a comprehensive urban government. Their individualism demands retention of the many local units, although other states' metropolitan areas, such as Miami and Nashville, have succeeded with comprehensive government. Instead, Texans rely on one of the twenty-four *regional planning councils*, also known as *councils of governments* (COGs), to provide coordination in metropolitan areas. These voluntary organizations of local government provide such functions as regional land-use and economic planning, police training, and fact-finding studies on problems such as transportation.

Given the inadequacies of comprehensive planning and periodic revenue shortfalls at the local level, special districts will surely continue to proliferate. Under current conditions, they are too easy to create and operate as short-range solutions to governmental problems. Such continued proliferation, without adequate planning and supervision, will result not in solution, but rather in worsening, of the problems of local and particularly urban government.

## SCHOOL DISTRICTS

School districts are an exception to much of the foregoing discussion of special districts for several reasons. First, school board members are publicly elected, most commonly in an at-large, by-place system. Second, their decisions are usually well publicized, with the local newspapers and broadcast media paying careful attention to education decisions. Third, the public has considerable interest in and knowledge about school-district politics. Indeed, although county or city public hearings sometimes fail to attract a crowd, as soon as a school board agenda includes a topic such as determining attendance districts—basically, who gets bused and who doesn't—or sex education, the public turns out for the debate. Fourth, the number of school districts has been steadily declining for fifty years. Finally, although the local boards have a substantial amount of control over such matters as individual school management, location of schools, and personnel, the state is the ultimate authority for basic school policies and shares in the funding of public schools.

Public school finance has been a dominant issue in Texas politics at several points in the state's history but particularly since 1987. The fact that more than 1,000 school districts exist is one of the factors contributing to considerable unevenness in the quality of education provided from one district to the next. That unevenness in turn creates inequities in funding public education. School districts depend on two revenue sources: property taxes and state assistance. However, in Texas, state aid pays for only about half the cost of public education, thereby putting considerable pressure on the unpopular tax. The two largest differences in spending in richer versus poorer districts is in facilities (posh buildings, full computerization versus bare bones) and enrichment activities (choir trips to Europe versus a poor-quality field for athletics and band). The issue of school finance is addressed throughout this book.

## School Board Elections

L arge urban school districts have had the same struggles over district versus at-large elections as have cities. At-large proponents argue that "children" not "politics" should prevail. District proponents argue for "representation." In Dallas, the board is elected by district and has been sharply divided. Bill Rojas, a new superintendent hired in the fall of 1999, had already grown crosswise with several board members before Thanksgiving. By July, he had been fired after quarreling with the board over everything from bringing in the for-profit Edison Project to pump up the district's low-performing campuses to personality clashes with individual board members to allegations of serious expense account abuses. Amarillo has used an experimental voting procedure to try to find a compromise between district and at-large elections.

# Local Government: Prospects for the Future

The trends toward urbanization and suburbanization no doubt will continue, with the result that local government problems will become more acute than they are today. What are the prospects for local governments in Texas under these circumstances?

## The Austin Example

N owhere is the problem of rapid growth and dealing with a sprawl that even cuts across county lines more obvious than in the Austin Metropolitan Area, which topped 1 million in population in 1996. The city of Austin grew from 254,000 in 1970 to 657,000 by 2000 and to almost 700,000 by 2005. All of the authors of this book have lived in Austin. They can recall a smooth flow of traffic that always led to arriving within twenty minutes at any destination. Now, it can take twenty minutes to go from the University of Texas at Austin campus just to a main thoroughfare.

There are several developments worth noting. As urban problems and local finance problems become more acute, national and state governments are being forced to pay more attention to them. One major consideration in the 1999 legislative struggle over utility deregulation was the recognition that the legislature would have to find a way for both cities and private companies to retire their debt on power plants. This recognition came about in part because the *legislature is becoming more "citified."*

Another significant development occurred in August 1978, when the voters of Houston and six of its suburbs approved the creation of a Metropolitan Transit Authority with taxing power and authority to establish transit systems as alternatives to Houston's increasingly congested freeways. As expected, other Texas major metropolitan areas have followed suit, and even mid-size areas such as Denton County have approved transit authorities. It has long been obvious that the practice of virtually every person using his or her own motor vehicle for personal and business travel is incompatible with increasing urbanization. Smog, congestion, and even rush-hour gridlock do not make for a high quality of life. *Mass transit systems* must be established if the trend toward further urbanization is to continue, especially given the inability of the state to build roadways fast enough to move traffic at peak times or to clean the air sufficiently to meet federal standards.

Another development is that of *strategic planning,* a type of planning that focuses on identifying a mission and pursuing it in an opportunistic manner by taking advantage of any favorable situation that comes along. For example, a community that strives to attract high technology might aggressively seek to persuade electronics plants to locate there, perhaps even ignoring some of their environmental problems.

## Metropolitan Areas

Exactly what constitutes a metropolitan area is confusing. The U.S. Bureau of the Census recognizes metropolitan statistical areas (MSAs); consolidated metropolitan statistical areas (CMSAs), which are very large metro areas often encompassing several cities that, if located elsewhere, would be metro areas in and of themselves; and primary metropolitan statistical areas (PMSAs), which are components of CMSAs. Complicating matters is the fact that the U.S. Bureau of the Budget added its own category of micropolitan area for federal budgeting purposes. The twenty-seven recognized metropolitan statistical areas in Texas are Abilene, Amarillo, Austin–San Marcos, Beaumont–Port Arthur, Brazoria, Brownsville–Harlingen–San Benito, Bryan–College Station, Corpus Christi, Dallas, El Paso, Fort Worth–Arlington, Galveston–Texas City, Houston, Killeen–Temple, Laredo, Longview–Marshall, Lubbock, McAllen–Edinburg–Mission, Odessa–Midland, San Angelo, San Antonio, Sherman–Denison, Texarkana (Texas and Arkansas combined), Tyler, Victoria, Waco, and Wichita Falls. Dallas–Fort Worth and Houston–Galveston–Brazoria are recognized as consolidated metropolitan areas.

A fourth area of concern for the future is *interlocal cooperation.* COGs are one example of an arrangement that allows the many kinds of local governments—counties, cities, special districts—to work together to solve their common problems. Cooperative ventures such as city-county ambulance service, city-school playgrounds and libraries, and multiple-city purchasing are other examples. Indeed, interlocal agreements are the most dynamic element of modern intergovernmental relations and can help overcome some of the negative effects of the growing number of governments.

A fifth area of concern is *ordinance-making power for counties*. The lack of ordinance-making power is developing into a serious problem for safety, environmental, and aesthetic standards as well as other matters. For example, an issue of growing concern is the lack of control over adult bookstores and massage parlors that set up shop just outside a municipality, where control of them becomes a problem for the county. Counties want and need ordinance-making power but have thus far been denied it, primarily because of the opposition of real estate businesses and developers, who can, for example, create developments in unincorporated areas outside the extraterritorial jurisdiction of the cities that do not have to meet rigorous city building codes.

A sixth major problem that will continue to plague local governments is *funding*. With an improved economy, some of the financial strains have been alleviated, but unlike those of many enterprises, the costs of local government are not subject to economies of scale. In manufacturing, for example, producing more cars or soap bars results in lowered unit costs—the cost of one car or bar of soap. This principle doesn't hold true for picking up more bags of garbage or cleaning more streets or teaching more children. Burgeoning populations that move farther and farther away from the central city make delivery of services more costly.

# Leadership in Local Government

Historically, genuine differences have existed between county leadership and the leadership of other local governments. Elected officials in county government hold full-time positions that pay decent salaries and represent starting points in party politics. In most other local governments, a strong tradition of amateurism prevails: Elected officials are paid parking-and-lunch money and give their time as merely an extension of the same service orientation that leads them to accept office in Kiwanis or Rotary or the Business and Professional Women's Club. The decentralized nature of county governments has often led to rural fiefdoms of commissioners or sheriffs, but in urban counties, candidates as diverse as ethnic minority candidates with major social agendas and young conservatives contemplating a lifetime in politics are beginning to seek county office. As previously noted, Former Governor Ann Richards began her political career as a county commissioner. In large cities, serving on the city council also can be a step into big-time politics, and mayors have gone on to both the state and national capitols. City councils and school boards are becoming increasingly diversified in terms of gender, ethnicity, and viewpoint.[23]

The Texas Association of County Officials continues to be dominated by rural interests, although there is a block of urban counties interested in more than roads and bridges. Municipalities are more consistently aided by the Texas Municipal League, which has divisions for both elected officials and professional personnel. In addition, a variety of specialized organizations such as the Texas Public Power Association address other local interests. All of these groups also lobby for local interests with the legislature.

★ ★ ★ ★ ★ ★ ★ ★ ★ ★ ★ ★ ★ ★ ★ ★ ★ ★ ★ ★ ★ ★ ★ ★ ★ ★

## *Hurricane Force*

Texas cities in 2005 and early 2006 were severely impacted by Hurricanes Katrina and Rita. The former resulted in tens of thousands of persons, especially New Orleaneans, fleeing Katrina in favor of Houston, Dallas, and many other Texas cities. The latter caused major damage to the Texas Gulf Coast, especially in the Golden Triangle (Beaumont–Port Arthur–Orange and surrounding towns). Houston hosted more evacuees than any other city. Because of its successful response to the crisis, the city was named "Texan of the Year" for 2005 by the *Dallas Morning News*.

★ ★ ★ ★ ★ ★ ★ ★ ★ ★ ★ ★ ★ ★ ★ ★ ★ ★ ★ ★ ★ ★ ★ ★ ★ ★

## Summary

Local governments are the governments most likely to have a daily impact on citizens, and much of this effect is critical to the quality of life. Will our children get a good public school education, or should we save to send them to private school? Is our neighborhood safe, or will we have to live behind triple-locked doors with a guard dog for a companion? Will we enjoy a reasonably efficient and economical transportation system, or will we have to fight dangerous and congested freeway traffic two or three hours a day to get to and from our jobs?

★ ★ ★ ★ ★ ★ ★ ★ ★ ★ ★ ★ ★ ★ ★ ★ ★ ★ ★ ★ ★ ★ ★ ★

## *How to Get Involved in Local Government*

Local government is the logical starting point for exercising your democratic rights and becoming involved as a participant in government. Here are a few suggestions for how to go about getting involved.

■ **Go to the party precinct conventions, held immediately after the primary elections (see Chapter 4).**

■ **Attend a public hearing and speak out.**

■ **Organize a petition drive on a matter of importance to you—saving the trees along a planned freeway route, for example.**

■ **Attend a neighborhood meeting.**

■ **Attend a meeting of the city council, county commission, or school board.**

■ **Talk to the city clerk or the county clerk to find out how to volunteer for an advisory committee or citizen task force.**

■ **Volunteer to work for a local candidate during an election.**

★ ★ ★ ★ ★ ★ ★ ★ ★ ★ ★ ★ ★ ★ ★ ★ ★ ★ ★ ★ ★ ★ ★ ★

The answers to these and a hundred other critical questions are given by the units of local government. Texas counties, cities, special districts, and COGs are not fully prepared to provide optimum solutions. County governments must cope with modern problems despite having an inflexible, outmoded organizational structure. City governments are better organized and have more comprehensive powers, yet they too are burdened by a variety of factors, including the rapid increase in urban population, the proliferation of independent special districts, and the limited and frequently reluctant cooperation of state and national government. COGs, as voluntary organizations, provide only very limited solutions to problems of organized, coordinated planning. All local governments will face serious revenue problems for the foreseeable future.

This chapter has examined how the general units of local government—counties and cities—are organized and financed and what the major political features are. It has looked at the reasons for and the problems created by special districts, singling out school districts as not fitting the pattern of other special districts. It suggests that Texas, like most states, will undoubtedly continue to become more and more urbanized. Consequently, problems such as congestion, poor housing, inadequate schools, and crime will grow. It is imperative that local governments both represent the diversity of the state and govern effectively. Democracy is about both participating and getting things done.

## Glossary Terms

| | |
|---|---|
| at-large elections | home rule |
| commissioners court | mandates |
| district system | nonpartisan elections |
| general laws | place system |
| gerrymandering | spoils system |

## Study Questions

1. Why do you think the authors of this book as well as other analysts criticize county government as an anachronism with its "one-size-fits-all" government? Do you agree or disagree with that label and its implications?

2. What is a home-rule city? What are the forms of government used in home-rule cities? Why do you think most home-rule cities have council-manager government?

3. Imagine that you are consultant to a city of 250,000 people. Your advice is sought on how to structure municipal elections. How would you advise this city with regard to the time when city elections should be held and whether to have nonpartisan candidates and at-large elections? Why?

4. Why does Texas have so many special districts, and what are some of the problems associated with them?

5. Based on what you have read, what do you think life will be like in a Texas city in the year 2020? Why?

6. Which type of local government do you think is truly at the "grass roots"—that is, which type more nearly represents all the citizens and works hardest to solve human problems?

7. Attend a meeting of your local city council, school board, or county commission. Then describe for your fellow students what you learned by attending the meeting.

8. Would you consider a career in local government management? Why or why not?

## Surfing the Web

Readers are urged to visit the companion site for this book:

**http://academic.cengage.com/polsci/Kraemer/TexasPolitics10e**

# The State Economy and the Financing of State Government

**13**

*Many states reap a substantial portion of state revenues from gambling, but conservative Texans have protested against an expansion of gambling in the state.*

> Texas has an economy that is the second largest in the nation and the 15th largest in the world based on GDP (PPP) figures. [GDP/PPP are database acronyms.]
>
> WIKIPEDIA: THE FREE ENCYCLOPEDIA, 2007

> . . . most officeholders would rather handle rattlesnakes than vote for an income tax.
>
> DAVE MCNEELY, LONG-TIME WRITER ON TEXAS POLITICS, IN STATE LEGISLATURES, 2007

> I will be proud to sign this plan that will reward teachers and reform our schools, provide a record property tax cut that will make home ownership more affordable, reduce the net tax burden on Texans by nearly $7 billion, and improve our tax system so it is fairer because it is broader.
>
> GOVERNOR RICK PERRY
> FOLLOWING THE 2006 SPECIAL SESSION

# Introduction

The ability of any government to generate the revenues needed to provide the programs and services that citizens want is directly tied to the economy. Are most people working? Are wages good? Are profits high? Is money available for loans to finance business expansion and home ownership? This chapter begins by sketching the boom-and-bust economy of the state and the resulting difficulties the state has in producing a budget.

Texas emerged from the economic troubles that began in 1983 when oil prices plummeted, wreaking havoc on the Texas economy and on state finance. The state enjoyed sizable surpluses in the three legislative sessions from 1997 to 2001, making it possible to address a number of program needs. By the time the 2003 legislative session began, Texas, along with the rest of the nation, was in deep economic doldrums and facing a $10 billion deficit. By 2006, when the state finally addressed the issue of school finance, a key means of paying for the schools was a budget surplus. Even with $6.1 billion reserved for the property tax relief that was a part of property tax cuts associated with school funding, for fiscal years (FY) 2008–2009 the state had $2 billion in surplus funds to dedicate to economic stabilization and another $5 billion for general expenses. At the same time, Comptroller Susan Combs was warning that economic slowdown was likely, thus beginning another downturn in the economic cycle. This up-and-down situation of deficit and surplus is complicated by the fact that the state, unlike the national government, is "pay-as-you-go"; it cannot just go into debt to finance government services, and services often suffer, as Chapter fourteen points out. The three quotations that open this chapter neatly summarize the dilemmas that the legislature constantly faces—a boom-and-bust economy, big spending needs, and a reluctance to increase taxes.

Another major issue concerning the revenue system is its fairness. Citizens always seek fairness. Yet, as we shall see, the poor in Texas pay a higher proportion of their incomes in taxes than do the wealthy. This fact raises questions about how democratic the state revenue system is and constitutes a major theme of this chapter.

The chapter also looks at how the state spends its money, including how elected officials struggle to agree on what the budget will be. Because the budget is the best guide to policy priorities, it is a practical test of how well citizens' interests are accommodated in state spending.

Texas has grown from 16.7 million people in 1988 to about 24 million people in 2007, an increase of almost 44 percent in just nineteen years. During that same period, the state budget has increased from $20.9 billion for **fiscal year** (FY) 1989 to $68.8 billion for FY 2007—an increase of 229 percent. However, when adjusted for population growth (more people require more services) and for **inflation** (that is, increases in what things cost), the Texas budget was relatively flat across this period according to the Legislative Budget Board, as Figure 13-1 shows. Budget growth has been only about 1.6 percent a year, less than the population growth and inflation rates for the period as a whole. Indeed, the adjusted budget for FY 2006–2007 shows a proportionate decrease in spending from the previous biennium.[1]

★ ★ ★ ★ ★ ★ ★ ★ ★ ★ ★ ★ ★ ★ ★ ★ ★ ★ ★ ★ ★ ★ ★ ★ ★ ★ ★

### Fiscal Years

All governments and businesses operate on fiscal years, a phrase that refers to the budget year. Sometimes the fiscal year is the same as the calendar year, but often, particularly for governments, the year is different. In Texas, the fiscal year is September 1 until August 31 of the following year. The year in which the fiscal period ends is designated as the fiscal year. Thus, FY 08 covers September 1, 2007, until August 31, 2008. Forty-six states use a fiscal year that runs from July to June. The other exceptions besides Texas are New York (April to March), Alabama, and Michigan. The latter two states have the same fiscal year as the national government, October to September.

★ ★ ★ ★ ★ ★ ★ ★ ★ ★ ★ ★ ★ ★ ★ ★ ★ ★ ★ ★ ★ ★ ★ ★ ★ ★ ★

# The Texas Economy

## HISTORY

Historically, the Texas economy has been based on natural resources, chiefly oil, land, and water. Indeed, Texas has been characterized as the state where "money gushes from the ground in the oil fields and grows on the citrus trees in

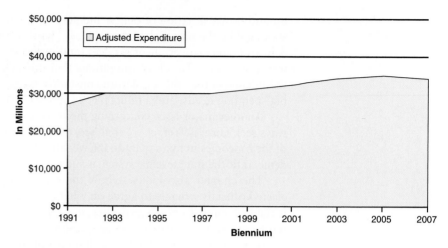

**FIGURE 13-1 Trends in Texas Government Expenditures, FY 1991–FY2007, Adjusted for Inflation and Population**

SOURCE: *Legislative Budget Board, Fiscal Size-Up, 2006-2007 (Austin: LBB, 2005), 8.*

the irrigated orchards."[2] Texas is still an important producer of oil and gas, and listings of its principal products include petroleum, natural gas, and natural gas liquids.[3] Chemicals, cotton, and cattle also contribute their share of wealth.

The state's natural resources are bountiful but not endless—that is, once used, they cannot be replaced. Furthermore, the Texas economy is shifting from one based on natural resources to one based on information and technology. In 2006, the overall Texas economy was slightly over a trillion dollars a year, according to the Business and Industry Data Center, which concluded that the state's economy would rank as the eighth largest in the world if the state were an independent nation.[4] Of that, slightly less than 1.4 percent came from agriculture, forestry, and fisheries. Although the percentage of the state economy derived from agriculture has declined, only California has a larger agribusiness economy. At the same time, mining, which includes oil and gas production—once 27 percent of the state's economy—had shrunk to 6.5 percent.[5] Both of these figures are somewhat misleading because manufacturing, construction, and wholesale and retail trade all include some elements of agriculture and mining, such as petrochemical plants, drill sites, and agricultural processing factories. Yet, one cannot ignore that the oil fields no longer represent the chief revenue source for the state. Indeed, gas drilling has shown more promise than oil.

Although the state's recent economy has moved away from one based solely on natural resources, it still has been subject to the ups and downs of resource-based components such as oil and agriculture. Indeed, the erosion of the natural-resource-based economy meant that thousands of Texans found themselves out of work. In June 1986, the state unemployment rate reached 9.6 percent, compared with a national rate of 7.3 percent. The collapse of financial institutions made the problem worse. In 1988–1990, Texas led the nation in the number of banks and savings and loans that failed. Also at that time, the defense industry was depressed by the end of the Cold War in the early 1990s.

State government worked to shore up the shaky economy by consolidating economic development programs, developing aggressive marketing campaigns for farm and ranch products, and selling the high-technology capability of the state through industry–university partnerships. By the turn of the century, Texas was second only to North Carolina in business relocations, and the employment rate was going up, although with some concern that too many of the new jobs were at the lower end of the pay scale. College-educated workers who found jobs in the high-technology and dot.com firms were doing well, but the economic distance between highly skilled and unskilled workers seemed to be growing.[6]

## THE EARLY TWENTY-FIRST CENTURY

Beginning in the spring of 2000, the high-tech sector of the U.S. economy began to plummet. NASDAQ, the index that reflects technology stocks, lost almost three quarters of its value, and large layoffs in telecommunications, computer, and Internet firms led to prolonged unemployment in "new economy" industries.

On September 11, 2001, terrorists attacked the United States by hijacking four airliners and using them as weapons. Two of these planes brought down the twin World Trade Towers in New York and a third destroyed a section of the Pentagon in Washington, D.C. The horror of lost lives and the surprise of the attack coupled with actual economic damages, particularly to the travel industry, further shook confidence in the U.S. economy. A series of corporate scandals made matters worse, especially because they involved the top corporate officers growing very rich while the pensions and ultimately the jobs of ordinary workers were squandered. The largest scandal of all was Houston-based Enron. Military action that began in Afghanistan in 2001 and Iraq in 2003 followed the 9/11 attack. Coupled with two national tax cuts, the costs of war sent the country into significant debt and rattled the economy further.

Texas and other states were in no way immune to these national and international events.[7] Although Texas exports more products for sale than any other state, border cities failed to realize the economic hopes they had based on the North American Free Trade Agreement of 1993 (NAFTA).[8] Two prolonged droughts in the first six years of the new century damaged the agrarian economy. Tourism, important to many areas of the state, was reeling from the public's reluctance to travel, and all the airlines other than Southwest were losing money until 2006–2007. All states were having trouble meeting new obligations for homeland security in the wake of budget deficits.[9]

Texans' confidence in the economy was steadily eroding due to the lack of job growth and the sluggish economy. The state's unemployment rate was above 6 percent throughout 2003. The state had banked on high technology as an answer to the waning of the old natural-resource-based economy, but the high-tech crash led to tens of thousands of job layoffs and foreclosures on thousands of homes. The feeling of malaise was not improved by national news that some of the "new economy" jobs based on information and technology were being exported permanently to other countries with lower wage scales.[10]

However, some bright spots began to emerge. Houston's low unemployment rate signaled recovery in the oil and petrochemical industries. Texas also profited from heightened military activities because of its many defense contractors, although individual families lost ground when reservists were called up from better paying jobs into military service. Generally, higher unemployment rates cause a demand for more government services. The "bottom line," however, was that the legislature began its 2003 session with a $10 million deficit, a situation not unfamiliar in other state capitals.

The 2005 and 2007 legislatures both began with surpluses as the economy improved. Thus, once again, the boom-and-bust cycle had made its will known. Texas reemerged as the No. 1 state in the country for corporate relocation and expansion.[11] By 2007, unemployment was down to 4.1 percent, and 239,000 jobs had been created in twelve months, in part due to robust foreign trade. Dallas–Fort Worth, Austin, and Houston ranked in the top 30 global cities in the country, which is a designation given to cities with a strong orientation toward international business. Texas had moved to No. 2 in the country as a desirable retirement spot. Even agriculture was improving because the 2005–2006 drought had ended.[12] This rosy picture is tempered by the fact that the funding of state government, as we shall see later in this chapter, has become heavily dependent on surpluses created in 2004–2006, and many Texans, like other Americans, were finding themselves mired in debt even to the point of losing their homes in foreclosures and lacking in basic protections such as health insurance.

## ANALYSIS

At least six reasons help to explain the ups and downs of the Texas economy and the growth in the state budget over the past quarter century.

1. Overproduction of oil worldwide in the early 1980s, and again in the 1990s, led to price slides that placed a strain on the Texas economy, especially in the earlier period. However, oil prices experienced a resurgence in 1999, in 2003–2004, and especially in 2006–2007. Rising prices help oil companies and increase severance tax dollars, but they are problems for ordinary citizens and energy-hungry businesses.

2. A number of federal policy changes—including tax policy, prohibition of sales taxes on Internet sales, failure to provide a remedy to state and local governments in disputes over taxes on catalog sales, unfunded or underfunded mandates (requirements) such as No Child Left Behind, and the growing cost to states for Medicare and Medicaid expenses—have cost states $100 billion for FY 2004 through 2007, according to the National Conference of State Governments.[13] National policy is likely to continue to put pressure on state governments, in part because of the *devolution* of government—that is, the passing down of authority to state and local government from the national government, often without economic support.

3. Texans responded to the challenges posed by the economic doldrums of the 1980s and diversified the economy. However, the new technology-based economy was the hardest hit by the national economic slump that began in 2000, and the exporting of jobs from this sector has made full recovery difficult.

4. At times during the 1970s, double-digit inflation prevailed; both public and private spending increased in proportion to the inflation rate. During the 1980s and 1990s, the nation continued to experience some inflation but at a much lower rate. In the early years of the twenty-first century, the fear was that the reverse economic condition—deflation—might occur; that is, prices and wages might continue to go down, not up.

5. The Texas revenue system, particularly its tax structure, lacks **elasticity;** that is, it is not easily adjusted to ups and downs in the economy. The in-

elastic revenue structure coupled with spending demands and federal cutbacks proved to be a problem in the new century when the economy sagged. Indeed, states that rely heavily on sales tax revenues have been hit particularly hard by federal policy changes.

6. When state government enjoyed a surplus in 1997, it chose to rebate the money to taxpayers in the form of reduced local school taxes; the 1999 surplus partly went for improved services but also included tax cuts. This action was in line with strong conservative trends to reduce taxes rather than increase spending. By 2003, demands for services were up, but the no-new-taxes philosophy was strongly entrenched, leading to extraordinary pressures on the state budget. Texas policymakers followed their long tradition of spending surplus as a way to fund the schools in 2006–2007 and even general government functions for 2008–2009.

# Where Does the Money Come From?

State finance consists of raising and spending money. For most of those involved in government, the budget is the bottom line, as it is for the rest of us. Policy decisions regarding state financing are made in the glaring light of political reality—what political scientist Harold Laswell called "Politics: Who Gets What, When, and How" back in 1911. Whenever money is raised, it comes from someone; whenever it is spent, someone gets it. Struggles over who will pay for the government and who will receive dollars from it are at the heart of politics in Texas, as elsewhere.

Part of the struggle over revenues comes from philosophical disagreements about revenue sources and who should bear the burden of taxation (see the later section on "Ability to Pay"). Both the traditionalistic and individualistic political cultures are rather antitax overall and in favor of regressive taxes when money must be raised. (More will be said about ability to pay later in this chapter.)

Figure 13-2 gives an approximate idea of the sources of state revenue for FY 2008–2009. It shows that 51.1 percent of all revenues come from taxes; 31.2

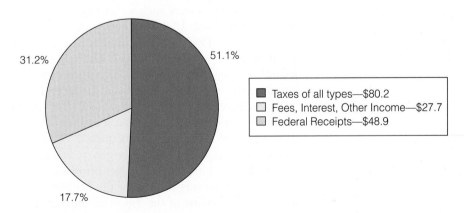

31.2%  51.1%

- Taxes of all types—$80.2
- Fees, Interest, Other Income—$27.7
- Federal Receipts—$48.9

17.7%

**FIGURE 13-2  Projected Texas State Revenues by Source, 2008–2009 Biennium, in Percentages (in Billions)**

SOURCE: Biennial Revenue Estimate, 2008-2009 (Austin: Texas Comptroller, 2007), passim.

TABLE 13-1
## Patterns of Change: Texas State Revenue Sources over Time in Percentages

| Source | 1982–83 baseline | 1986–87 | 1990–91 | 1994–95 | 1998–99 | 2002–03 | 2006–07 | 2008–09 |
|---|---|---|---|---|---|---|---|---|
| Taxes | 62.2 | 64.3 | 60.0 | 50.9 | 49.9 | 49.5 | 45.7 | 51.1 |
| General sales | 24.3 | 24.7 | 33.5 | 27.7 | 27.6 | 28.3 | 26.3 | 35.1 |
| Severance | 18.4 | 7.5 | 4.9 | 3.2 | 2.0 | 2.1 | 2.5 | 3.7 |
| Other | 19.5 | 32.1 | 21.6 | 20.0 | 20.3 | 19.1 | 16.9 | 12.3 |
| Federal funds | 21.4 | 19.4 | 24.6 | 30.1 | 29.1 | 31.3 | 35.5 | 31.2 |
| Licenses, fines, fees, other receipts, surplus* | 5.2 | 5.4 | 9.1 | 10.9 | 11.5 | 12.7 | 12.1 | 13.6 |
| Leases, interest, investments | 11.2 | 10.9 | 6.3 | 5.7 | 4.4 | 4.4 | 4.2 | 2.5 |
| Lottery | — | — | — | 2.3 | 5.1 | 2.1 | 2.5 | 1.6 |

*The "other" category of revenue was calculated differently in earlier years so that the categories of "licenses, etc." and "leases, etc." are directly comparable beginning only in 1990–1991.

SOURCE: *Fiscal Size Up, 1982–83, 1986–87, 1990–91, 1994–95, 1998–99, 2002–03, 2006–07* (Austin: Legislative Budget Board), Chapter 2 on revenue, and *Biennial Revenue Estimate* (Austin: Office of the Texas Comptroller, 2007), 1-3, 11, 34.

percent from federal grants; and 17.7 percent from all other sources, including fees, fines, and penalties, interest, investments, land leases, the lottery, the surplus, and other sources such as lawsuits. Figure 13-2 is best considered in conjunction with Table 13-1, which provides a view of the changing revenue picture since FY 1982–1983, which is used as baseline because those were the last years when oil ruled the Texas budget. The table also shows the ups-and-downs of federal funding, with emphasis on the considerable importance of federal dollars since the mid-1990s. However, the federal contribution must be considered in the context of what the funding can be spent for (homeland security, roads, Medicaid, for example) and what it cannot be spent for (little for environmental compliance or education, for example). The table shows further fluctuation in revenue sources over time due largely to economic downtrends and uptrends as well as the changing federal budget priorities.

The table reflects the rise of the Middle East as a major supplier of petroleum and the decline of the Texas oil industry both in the relentless loss of revenues from the severance tax—the tax on the production of oil, gas, and other minerals—and in the downward trend of leases, interest, and investment income. As the oil business slacked off, interest in leasing state land to explore for oil or gas also declined, although gas mining has picked up considerably in recent years, particularly in the northern part of the state. Texans historically enjoyed low taxes because of the oil and gas revenue, which was an especially appealing tax source because out-of-state purchasers paid for much of it.

Other revenues paid directly by individuals—for example, licenses and fees—showed steady increases as politicians attempted to offset the loss of severance tax dollars. The two most recent sets of fiscal years also reflect the use of a budget surplus to help fund state government. Seeking to avoid tax increases, the legislature has frequently turned to charges such as the fee paid for a professional license or charges such as college tuition to augment the state treasury. The table also reveals that hoped-for infusions of cash from nontax sources such as the lottery have not been forthcoming, even after legislators decided in 2003 to participate in the multistate Mega Millions lottery to boost gambling revenue.

Always of importance is the proportion of state revenues generated by the general sales tax—the added cents on every hamburger and spiral notebook—because this tax tends to hit the poor the hardest. The sales tax actually has declined in percentage of revenues generated, although not in dollars, over the period from FY 1982–1983 to FY 2008–2009 because of the increase in nontax revenues and federal dollars.

Economic growth, higher and more expensive fees, and requiring local governments to fund some activities previously paid for by the state have generated sufficient dollars for the state to operate even in the wake of changes in traditional revenue sources. This chapter examines each major source of state income.

## COLLECTION AND ADMINISTRATION

State revenues are collected in many ways by many people. Monies from federal grants may be sent directly to the state agency responsible for administering the program being funded. The general retail sales tax is collected by retail merchants and then forwarded to the state comptroller. Other taxes, such as the inheritance tax, may be forwarded directly from the individual to the state comptroller. The two officials most concerned with state financial administration are the comptroller, who is responsible for tax collection, investments, and the safeguarding of public funds, and the auditor, who oversees state agencies to ensure the legality of their expenditures.

Once collected, state revenues are channeled into various funds, some of which are designated to supply monies for the general operation of government, while others are dedicated to (reserved for) specific services. The five major funds in Texas are

1. **The General Revenue Fund, which supports the majority of state programs**

2. **The Omnibus Tax Clearance Fund, which is allocated in part to two other funds, the General Revenue Fund and Available School Fund, and in part to such specific functions as the construction of farm-to-market roads, parks, and teachers' retirement**

3. **The Available School Fund, which underwrites public school textbooks and part of the Foundation School Program, the major source of state aid for local school districts**

4. The Highway Motor Fuel Fund, one fourth of which is allocated to the Available School Fund and the remainder to highways and roads

5. The State Highway Fund, which is used for highway and road construction and maintenance, right-of-way acquisition, and related purposes

Other funds set aside for particular purposes include those dedicated to parks and wildlife, county and district roads, and teachers' retirement.

## NONTAX SOURCES OF REVENUE

The state has sources of revenue other than the checks oil producers write to the state comptroller and the pennies, nickels, and dimes that citizens dig out of their pockets to satisfy the sales tax. These revenues include federal grants, borrowing, and several other sources, including fees such as college tuition. Together, these sources account for just under half (48.9 percent) of state revenues.

### FEDERAL GRANTS

The largest nontax source of money is federal grants. Beginning in the 1960s, state and local governments became heavily dependent on national budgetary policies that distributed monies to the treasuries of states, cities, and other local governments. Originally, these dollars came to states in the form of **categorical grants-in-aid** that could be used only for specific programs such as community health centers. **General revenue sharing** was then enacted; it was distributed by formula and could be used by state and local governments for whatever projects these governments wanted—police salaries, playground equipment, home care for the elderly. General revenue sharing ended for states in 1979 and for cities in 1986.

In addition, the federal government began to fund **block grants**, which ultimately became the principal vehicle for distributing dollars for general use in broad programs such as community development. States gained more control under block grants because many funds were no longer channeled directly to local governments but rather "passed through" a state agency. This flexibility came at a price, however, as the amount of funding for many programs, especially those affecting the poor and urban development, was reduced. For the first time in a third of a century, states had a dollar drop in federal aid in 1982 as a result of Jimmy Carter–Ronald Reagan fiscal federalism.

Recent increases in federal funding were attributable initially to interstate highway construction and maintenance spending following the increase in the national motor fuels tax in 1983. Subsequently, federal aid to the states increased because of the rising costs of social programs that are largely or completely funded by the national government, especially medical care for the poor, which is discussed in Chapter Fourteen. National welfare reform legislation signed shortly before the 1996 presidential election resulted in the states' being asked to take over new responsibilities for health benefits for the poor and to emphasize job placements instead of cash assistance as the focus of welfare programs.[14] At the same time, the national government passed along funding to help support public assistance programs. However, critics of state policy processes have continued to chide Texas officials for not taking full advantage of national programs and even being willing to sacrifice considerable federal funds to avoid spending a smaller amount of state funds. Most recently, some federal funds have been made available to help meet the requirements of post-9/11 homeland security. Altogether, the states and localities agree that costs of meeting the many federal mandates have exceeded the revenues provided. Nationally, the fiscal relationship between the national government and the states is seen as "fractured," indeed "at an all-time low."[15]

## BORROWING

Governments, like private citizens, borrow money for various reasons. Political expediency is one. Borrowing allows new programs to be implemented and existing ones to be extended without increasing taxes. A second reason is that borrowing allows future beneficiaries of a state service to pay for that service. Students who live in residence halls, for example, help pay off the bonds used to finance those halls through their room fees.

State government indebtedness is highly restricted in Texas, however. The framers of the state constitution strongly believed in "pay-as-you-go" government. A four-fifths vote of the legislature is needed to approve emergency borrowing, and the state's debt ceiling originally was limited to $200,000. A series of amendments has altered the constitution to allow the issuance of state bonds for specific programs, particularly land for veterans, university buildings, student loans, parks, prisons, and water development. In FY 2005, outstanding state indebtedness was $18.2 billion. Although this figure was the twelfth highest absolute level of indebtedness among the fifty states, Texas was ranked forty-ninth in terms of per capita state indebtedness.[16]

## OTHER NONTAX SOURCES

Because taxes are unpopular in Texas and elsewhere, government inevitably looks to nontax revenue sources whenever possible. The prospective budget deficits that began in 1985 have resulted in a pattern of raising money by increasing fees for almost everything, looking to gambling as a source of public revenue, and even manipulating state pension funds. An excellent example is college tuition, a type of **user fee**—that is, a sum paid in direct exchange for service.

Although current students may find this fact hard to believe, senior college tuition was only $4 per credit hour in 1984, plus about that much more in fees. Tuition and fees have risen steadily since 1984, both as a reflection of inflation and of state policymakers' desire for students to pay a higher proportion of the costs of their own education. At first, fees increased far more sharply than tuition to make up for the relatively low state-set tuition. Indeed, the universities charged a fee for "anything and everything"—for each course, for publications, for building use, and so on—in their desperate attempt to overcome inadequate state funding and deal with the privatization of higher education—that is, the steady erosion of public support. The picture changed in 2004 after boards of regents were given discretion to set tuition locally, and the governing boards took advantage of their new authority and raised tuition sharply. As a result, for fall 2007, tuition and fees combined at state universities ranged from about $144 to $256 a credit hour for an undergraduate student who is a Texas resident—a far cry from the $8 or so of twenty years earlier. Tuition was much higher for students in graduate and professional schools and for out-of-state students. Each community college district sets its own rate because two-year colleges are financially supported not only by state revenues but also by local taxes. Originally, the community colleges kept tuition on the low end, but by 2007, most community/junior colleges were charging $39 to $65 per credit hour.

Other fees—for everything from driver's licenses and car inspections to water permits, from personal automobile tags to daycare center operator licenses—have continued to increase. Fines for various legal infractions have risen. Even the cost of fishing licenses has gone up.

Other nontax sources of state revenue include the interest on bank deposits, proceeds from investments, and sales and leases of public lands. Having a surplus increases investment income. The doldrums of the oil industry decrease income from land leases; higher prices encourage exploration and thus more leasing of land.

The 1987 legislature proposed a constitutional amendment, approved by the voters in November of that year, that permitted parimutuel betting on horse races and, in three counties, on dog races on a local-option basis. By 1991, however, track betting had contributed virtually nothing to state coffers because the state's share of the proceeds—5 percent—was so high that track developers declined the opportunity to invest. Even though the 1991 legislature lowered the state's share to a graduated rate beginning at 1 percent, first-class tracks have been slow in coming.

A state lottery also was debated in 1987, 1989, and 1991 but was not approved by the legislature. Ann Richards and her Democratic primary opponent Jim Mattox had both campaigned on a pro-lottery platform in 1990. Governor Richards apparently was able to work out a deal with enough legislators—allegedly supporting their redistricting concerns—to get a lottery on the November 1991 ballot. Voters approved the lottery, which began in summer 1992. Since then, whether the revenues were to be dedicated to education has been an issue. The 1997 legislature did dedicate the revenues but moved other funds that had previously been earmarked for education back to the general fund. Administrative scandals and some falloff in betting have resulted in the lottery's not meeting revenue expectations. Consequently, in 2003, the legislature authorized the state's participation in the Mega Millions multistate lottery to try to improve revenues. Various schemes, such as legal slot machines, to expand gambling as a revenue source have not succeeded because of public objections.

Gas drilling in the Barnett Shale has become a profitable source of revenues for the state and for local governments, especially those in the northern part of the state.

## TAXATION

Taxes are the most familiar sources of governmental revenue and the most controversial. Since colonial days and James Otis's stirring phrase "no taxation without representation," citizens have sought justice in the tax system. The conservative heritage of Texas has not always made justice easy to find.

Taxes are collected for two principal reasons. *Revenue taxes*—for example, the general sales tax—are the major source of government income. They make it possible for government to carry out its programs. *Regulatory taxes*—for example, the taxes on tobacco and alcohol—were originally designed primarily to control the individuals and/or organizations subject to them and to either punish undesired behavior or reward desired behavior. However, they are also easier taxes to raise because any given regulatory tax affects only part of the population, and other citizens are willing to support the increase.

Both individuals and businesses pay taxes. Certain taxes, such as the retail sales tax, are paid directly by the consumer, and others, such as the tax on insurance transactions, are paid directly by businesses. Some would contend, however, that in the final analysis private citizens pay both types of taxes because business passes its tax expenses on to the consumer. Only a tax on profits works to slow or stop this pass-through of tax costs.

Although our discussion focuses on **tax equity** (fairness), another great concern with the Texas tax system is the lack of elasticity, which was discussed earlier in this chapter as one of the key factors resulting in periodic **revenue shortfalls**—insufficient funds to cover spending. A system based so heavily on sales and excise taxes runs into problems when the economy sours because the lower and middle classes, on whom such taxes depend, curtail their spending. With that curtailment comes a tailing off of tax revenues tied to consumer spending.

The tax policies of individual states reflect their economic resources, their political climates, and their dominant interest groups. Forty-three of the fifty states levy a personal income tax, although in two, the income tax is limited to interest and dividends. Forty-five states levy a corporate income tax. Texas has no personal income tax, and, instead of a true corporate income tax, levies a complex business franchise tax that is based on the gross receipts of the business minus either the cost of goods sold or the total personnel costs—the individual business decides which each year. Smaller businesses with gross receipts under $300,000 are exempt. The franchise tax has been altered several times in recent legislative sessions to broaden the base and produce more revenue, most recently in the third called session of 2006.[17] The state of Washington levies a similar tax.

Texas relies heavily on the general sales tax and other forms of sales taxes, such as the one paid at the pump for motor fuels. The result is a disproportionately high taxpaying burden on poor and middle-income taxpayers and an unevenness of the tax burden among different types of businesses. Each revenue shortfall brings with it debate over the need for a broader and more elastic tax system, but the state's traditionalistic-individualistic political culture is readily apparent in the usual results of these discussions—namely, finding ways to reduce the property tax and increase general and selective sales taxes, which both individuals and businesses pay.

Discussions about taxation, whether at the national, state, or local level, are seldom objective. One's own political philosophy and tax status inevitably color one's comments on the subject. Indeed, when government talks about taxes, its noble-sounding phrases such as "the public interest" do not always ring true. Today's citizens are sophisticated enough to realize that extensive campaigning, heated debates, and vigorous lobbying have formed our tax policies and that the public interest usually has been construed so as to benefit the influential. One of the least successful aspects of American democracy is the tax system, which at both the national and state levels tends to favor those who are better off. Modern-day proposals to eliminate the federal income tax and move to a system of a very large (over 20 percent) national sales tax exemplify how tax systems can be made to benefit the wealthy, because such schemes include taxes on clothing, cars, and washing machines but not on the purchase of stocks, bonds, or real estate investment trusts.

Texas professes fiscal conservatism and practices that philosophy by limiting state and local debt and by operating on a pay-as-you-go basis. The state budget reflects the political conservatism of Texas in its taxing and spending practices. An analysis of who pays, who does not pay, and who benefits from Texas taxes reveals not only the political and economic philosophy behind taxation in the state but also which special-interest groups most influence the legislature.

## WHO PAYS?

The question of who pays which taxes raises two issues. The first is ability to pay, and the second is whether individuals and businesses both really pay.

**Ability to Pay** A matter of some importance to taxpayers is whether the tax system is progressive or regressive. Progressive taxation is characterized by a rate that increases as the object taxed—property, income, or goods purchased—grows larger or gains in value. As noted earlier, progressive taxation is based on ability to pay. The best-known example is the federal income tax, which progresses from relatively low rates for those with small incomes to increasingly higher rates for those with larger incomes. Note, however, that loopholes in the federal tax laws and ceilings on special taxes such as Social Security still result in a proportionately heavier tax burden for the middle class than for the wealthy.

Although technically a tax system that involves a higher rate with a declining base, **regressive taxation** has come to refer to a system in which lower income earners spend larger percentages of their incomes on commodities subject to flat tax rates. The best example of Texas's reliance on regressive taxes is the general retail sales tax, which provides almost one third of total state revenue and over 60 percent of the tax revenue. The general sales tax is assessed at 6.25 percent on a wide variety of goods and services at the time of sale, regardless of the income or wealth of the purchaser. Municipalities also can levy a 1 percent additional tax, as can mass transit districts and county economic development districts. Municipalities can also add sales tax percentages of a half percent each for economic development and in lieu of reduced property taxes. The result is that most Texans pay a sales tax of 8.25 percent.

The additional selective sales (excise) taxes—those levied on tobacco products, alcoholic beverages, and motor fuels, for example—also are regressive. The $20,000-a-year secretary and the $200,000-a-year executive who drive the same distance to work pay the same 20 cent a gallon tax on gasoline, but who is better able to bear the tax burden? Figure 13-3 shows the major taxes in Texas.[18]

Citizens for Tax Justice (CTJ), a Washington, D.C.-based research and lobbying group, examined the tax structures in all fifty states in 2002. Ten states, including Texas, were dubbed "the terrible 10" for the regressivity of their tax structures. Only Washington, Florida, Tennessee, and South Dakota were rated as having higher tax rates for their poorest citizens than did Texas. According to CTJ, in 2002 the poorest Texans paid 11.4 percent of their income in state taxes, while the richest paid only 3.5 percent.[19] The gap, while large, had narrowed somewhat during the 1990s. Also, Texas, unlike some states, does not yet

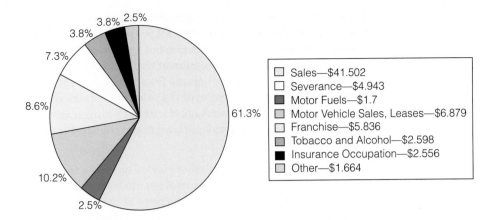

**FIGURE 13-3  Estimated State Tax Collections by Major Tax, 2008–2009 Biennium, in Percentages (in Billions)**

*SOURCE:* Biennial Revenue Estimate, 11. *Total taxes: $67.678 billion. Chart uses rounded numbers.*

tax "lifeline items"—food purchased at a grocery store, prescription medicines, or work clothes. CTJ has subsequently focused on national tax policy and has not repeated its analysis of the states.

At this stage, Texas cannot claim to have a progressive tax system. The restructuring of the corporation franchise tax in 2006 produced greater equity in business taxes and closed the loopholes that allowed major corporations to escape paying the tax. Nevertheless, the state has passed a constitutional amendment making institution of a personal income tax very difficult. Yet, a fair tax system is a value associated with democratic government. Many observers believe that a progressive income tax would be fairer than the general sales tax and could replace all or part of it. But the state's conservatism and the dominance of business lobbies in the state government have thus far precluded the adoption of a progressive tax policy. Moreover, in the early years of the twenty-first century, resentment against the U.S. Internal Revenue Service and the federal income tax has carried over into state politics and made tax reform virtually impossible.

**Taxes Paid by Individuals** A number of taxes are levied directly against individuals, for example, the inheritance tax, collected at the time beneficiaries inherit estates; the motor fuels tax, paid each time a motorist buys gasoline; and the ad valorem property tax, collected on real property, buildings, and land by local governments. (The state ad valorem property tax was abolished by a 1982 constitutional amendment, but the property tax remains a mainstay for local governments.) Businesses also pay the motor fuels tax and local property taxes, of course, but by increasing prices they let their customers pick up the tab.

Some authorities would include all sales taxes in the category of taxes paid by individuals, on the assumption that businesses pass them on to the consumer just as they do local ad valorem and state vehicle registration taxes—whether that is the intention of the law or not. There are two types of individual sales taxes

1. The *general sales tax* is a broadly based tax that is collected on most goods and services and must be paid by the consumer. It is illegal for a business to

absorb the tax—for example, as a promotional device. This familiar tax was first adopted in Texas in 1961, with a 2 percent rate. Nationally, Mississippi was the first state to have a sales tax, but twenty-nine other states adopted the tax during the Great Depression of the 1930s. Originally, many exemptions existed, but these have become fewer and fewer with each legislative session except for an expansion of the sales tax holiday that allows Texans to purchase school clothes in August without paying a sales tax. Indeed, the tax is now paid on many services (lawn maintenance, for example) as well as goods (hamburgers, jeans).

2. *Selective sales taxes* (excise taxes) are levied on only a few items, comparatively speaking, and consumers are often unaware that they are paying them. These taxes are included in the price of the item and may not even be computed separately. Tobacco products, alcoholic beverages—tobacco and alcohol taxes are sometimes called "sin taxes"—automobiles, gasoline, rental of hotel rooms, and the admission price for amusements (movies, plays, nightclubs, sporting events) are among the items taxed in this category.

General and selective sales taxes account for more than four fifths of the state's tax revenue. Business initially pays about half of these taxes before recouping them in their pricing.

Taxes Levied on Businesses    Taxes levied on businesses in Texas produce considerable revenue for the state but are often regulatory in nature. One example is the *severance taxes* levied on natural resources, such as crude oil, natural gas, and sulfur, that are severed (removed) from the earth. Their removal, of course, depletes irreplaceable resources, and part of the tax revenue is dedicated to conservation programs and to the regulation of production; thirty other states have similar taxes. Severance taxes once were the backbone of the state's revenue system. They then declined for twenty-five years, only to make a modest comeback for FY 2008–2009 due to the price of oil and the burgeoning natural gas drilling business. They are expected to yield 7.3 percent of the tax revenue for FY 2008–2009.

The major Texas business tax today is the *franchise tax*, which is assessed against corporations, partnerships, business trusts, professional associations, business associations, joint ventures, holding companies, and other legal entities. Excluded are sole proprietorships and general partnerships. This tax is a revenue tax that reflects the cost of doing business in the state. Some people regard it as a type of corporate income tax because the business pays taxes based on its gross receipts. This tax was overhauled substantially in 1991 and 2006 to make it fairer. It originally emphasized taxes only on capital-intensive businesses such as manufacturing and collected little from labor-intensive businesses such as computer software firms, financial institutions, and even the big downtown law firms. The 1991 version also left a loophole that let big corporations such as Dell, Inc. (the computer company) declare themselves to be partnerships and thus not covered by the tax. The more comprehensive 2006 version of the tax is expected to provide at least 8.6 percent of the tax revenue for FY 2008–2009.

In addition to the franchise tax, there are special *gross receipts taxes* levied on specific businesses, most notably utilities. Among other taxes levied directly on businesses in Texas is the *insurance premium tax*, levied on gross premiums collected by insurance companies. Miscellaneous *special taxes and fees* for such varied activities as chartering a corporation, brewing alcoholic beverages, and selling real estate also exist. Whenever possible, businesses pass these taxes along to consumers in the form of higher prices. Together, they account for about 6.3 percent of the state's tax revenue.

Because it is difficult to determine exactly what business taxes are passed on to consumers, one can only guess at who pays. Roughly 48.9 percent of the state's income comes from nontax sources. Of the revenue that comes from taxes, businesses directly pay at least 18 percent of the total. However, many taxes are paid by both individuals and businesses, making it difficult to assess

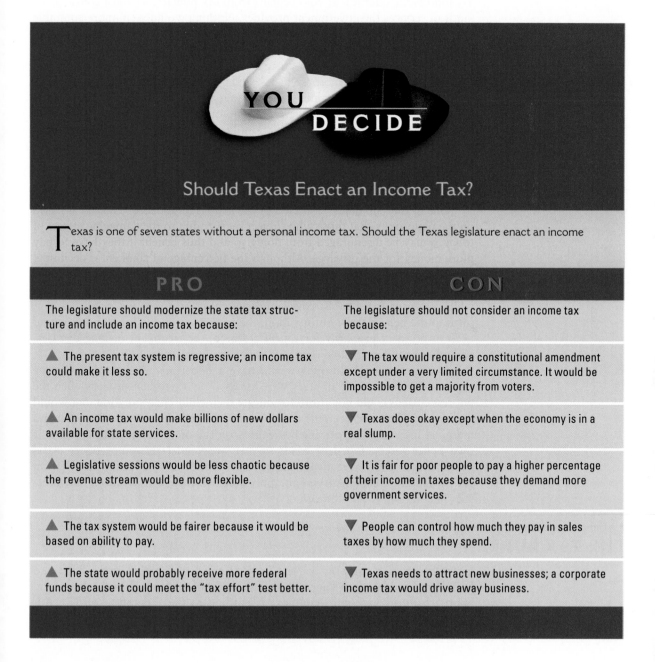

## YOU DECIDE

### Should Texas Enact an Income Tax?

Texas is one of seven states without a personal income tax. Should the Texas legislature enact an income tax?

| PRO | CON |
|---|---|
| The legislature should modernize the state tax structure and include an income tax because: | The legislature should not consider an income tax because: |
| ▲ The present tax system is regressive; an income tax could make it less so. | ▼ The tax would require a constitutional amendment except under a very limited circumstance. It would be impossible to get a majority from voters. |
| ▲ An income tax would make billions of new dollars available for state services. | ▼ Texas does okay except when the economy is in a real slump. |
| ▲ Legislative sessions would be less chaotic because the revenue stream would be more flexible. | ▼ It is fair for poor people to pay a higher percentage of their income in taxes because they demand more government services. |
| ▲ The tax system would be fairer because it would be based on ability to pay. | ▼ People can control how much they pay in sales taxes by how much they spend. |
| ▲ The state would probably receive more federal funds because it could meet the "tax effort" test better. | ▼ Texas needs to attract new businesses; a corporate income tax would drive away business. |

what proportion of the taxes businesses and individuals actually pay. Examples of these latter taxes include those on motor fuels, motor vehicle sales and rentals, and utilities. Texas businesses actually contribute a higher percentage of state revenues than businesses nationally contribute to federal revenues. The federal corporate income tax, for example, produces slightly less than 8 percent of the national government's revenue. The most significant federal revenue sources are the personal income tax and the Social Security and Medicare taxes.

## WHO BENEFITS?

To address the question of who benefits from tax policies, we must consider the kinds of services the government provides. Nothing would seem more equitable than a tax structure resulting in an exact ratio between taxes paid and benefits received, and in Texas, some taxes are levied with exactly that philosophy in mind. The motor fuels tax, 20 cents per gallon on gasoline and diesel fuel, is paid by those who use motor vehicles, and three fourths of the revenues from this tax are spent on maintaining and building highways and roads. The remainder goes to public schools. However, the motor fuels tax also points up a problem with the "benefit theory" of taxation. People who do not own automobiles and who do not buy gasoline also benefit from those big trucks hauling goods to market over state highways. The owners of an ambulance that transports an accident victim to a hospital buy the gasoline but may benefit far less from it than do the victim and her or his family and friends.

One of the "sin taxes" collected by the state is on tobacco. This tax is based on the philosophy that those who subject their bodies to the damaging effects of tobacco may be discouraged from doing so and thus benefit if they have to pay more money for the privilege. Although the percentage of smokers is declining, the decline is not particularly due to this tax, which has become, in effect, a use tax. Those who smoke receive no special benefits from revenues from this tax, which are used for schools, parks, and general government functions. To conform to the benefit theory of taxation, the revenue from the tobacco tax would need to be spent primarily for cancer research, the treatment of lung diseases, and other programs related to the effects of smoking.

A strict benefit philosophy would have a disastrous effect on low-income citizens. For example, if all taxes were assessed on a pay–benefit basis, then the poorest citizens could not afford to educate their children, a situation that would only entrap them further in the cycle of minimal education, low-paying jobs, and marginal incomes. The extremely wealthy, on the other hand, could have their own police forces, four-lane roads to their weekend farms, and college classrooms with five-to-one student–teacher ratios. Society would hardly benefit from such a situation. Clearly, trying to apply a benefit theory of taxation, like all issues in taxation, is very difficult.

## THE TAX BURDEN IN TEXAS

Texas has prided itself on being a low-tax state, and both George Bush and Rick Perry had legislative agendas that pushed tax relief—a popular short-term approach during a boom economy. According to the Federation of Tax Administrators, an organization dedicated to improving state tax administration, Texas ranks fortieth in per capita state and local tax revenue and forty-second in the percentage of personal income paid in state taxes.[20] The Tax Foundation, a Washington think tank that caters to business organizations, reported that Texas ranked fortieth in combined state and local taxes for 2007.[21] The slight difference in the state-only and combined state and local rankings indicates that the state may not be so supportive of its local governments as other states, causing local taxes to be proportionally higher. However, the state's 2006 change in school finance methodology has brought the state only and combined state-and-local rankings more into line (see the case study on school finance). The Tax Foundation ranks Texas twenty-seventh when federal taxes are also included. That ranking is a measure not only of business activity in the state and sizable personal wealth held by a minority of Texans but also of the population size of the state and of the fact that the state has no personal income tax so that only a portion of the general sales tax can be used to offset the federal income tax whenever Congress authorizes such deductions.

One irony of the Texas tax situation is that the state does not fare well under many federal grant formulas, which include tax effort—the tax burden already borne by citizens—as a criterion. The state does least well on matching grants for social services and welfare. Although Texas ranked second in individual income taxes paid and fourth in corporate taxes paid, the state was ranked only thirty-first in terms of per capita federal spending.[22] In short, Texans contribute more in federal taxes to get back a dollar in federal grants than residents of most other states.

# CONTEMPORARY ISSUES

## PERSPECTIVES FROM THE PAST

For a half-century, Texas relied on oil and gas production taxes as the major source of state revenue, with most of these being paid by out-of-state purchasers. How good were the good old days? "Texas went from 1971 to 1984 . . . without an increase in state tax rates, or new taxes" while the population was growing 42 percent.[23] After the world oil market crashed, Texans were ill prepared to develop a responsible and responsive revenue policy to provide funds for state services. As the boxed item shows, the state got better at revenue measures and benefited subsequently from a booming economy and some additional federal funds.

## WHAT'S NEXT?

Texas will be no different from other governments in its need to find adequate and equitable revenue sources to support the services needed by a rapidly growing citizenry and to make up for periodic revenue shortfalls that have a major effect on all states. One strategy that the state will pursue is *performance evaluation and management*, including cutbacks to funding that are recommended in the biennial Texas Performance Review and in human service spending. The importance of the Texas Performance Review can only grow. The TPR originated with John Sharp when he was comptroller and was pursued relentlessly by his successor, Carole Keeton Strayhorn. Strayhorn's approach, coupled with her refusal to certify the budget, led the 2003–2004 legislature to reduce her powers and grant the performance review authority to the Legislative Budget Board. The performance evaluation/cutback approach is grounded in a national movement to "reinvent government."[24] This demand emerged from strategic planning and quality management movements in the private sector as sluggish industries had to downsize—or in the new terminology, "rightsize."

Performance reviews speak not only to "smaller" but also to "smarter." About every two years *Governing* magazine examines management and/or fiscal policies in the states. The magazine published a fifty-state report on taxation early in 2003. The report began with the observation that "The vast majority of state tax systems are inadequate for the task of funding a 21st-century government."[25] A top rating was four stars. Texas got one star on the adequacy of its revenue, one on the fairness of the system to taxpayers, but three on management of the system. In 2005, *Governing* graded the states again to see how they had weathered national economic downtrends and responded to state needs.[26] Those ratings gave Texas an overall grade of "B," with individual grades of "B" for money (revenue), people (personnel practices), and information (Web sites, technology) and "B−" for infrastructure (roads, bridges).

★ ★ ★ ★ ★ ★ ★ ★ ★ ★ ★ ★ ★ ★ ★ ★ ★ ★ ★ ★ ★ ★ ★ ★ ★ ★ ★ ★ ★ ★

## The Cycle of Bust and Boom: State Budgets over Twenty Years, FY 1990–1991 to FY 2008–2009

▪ **FY 90–91:** legislative authorization of a 12 percent spending increase by fiscal sleight-of-hand tricks such as using the money reserved to settle lawsuits against the state; another tax study that was ignored

▪ **FY 92–93:** initiation of the Texas Performance Review (TPR), leading to $382 million in budget cuts—not all of which materialized—and to other cuts in agency budgets for FY 93; thirty new revenue measures, including a major restructuring of the corporation franchise tax, totaling $2.6 billion; voter approval of a state lottery

▪ **FY 94–95:** $2 billion in increased revenues without any tax increase due to measures such as TPR savings on Medicaid and changes in tax collection schedules; voter approval of a constitutional amendment limiting the possibility of an income tax to simultaneous local property tax relief

▪ **FY 96–97:** $9.8 billion in increased revenues without any tax increase due to an improved economy, more federal contributions, more lottery revenues

▪ **FY 98–99:** constitutional amendment to triple the homestead tax allowance for school districts to lower individual taxes; more than a $7 billion spending increase due to a strong economy, federal funds, and a big surplus; failure to produce a bill incorporating recommendations from the governor's tax study

▪ **FY 00–01:** $506 million in tax breaks for both business and consumers; continuing pressures on local governments to raise the property tax to make up for a lack of state revenues allocated to them; also, an $11 billion spending increase due to the continuing strong economy

*(continued)*

★ ★ ★ ★ ★ ★ ★ ★ ★ ★ ★ ★ ★ ★ ★ ★ ★ ★ ★ ★ ★ ★ ★ ★ ★ ★ ★ ★ ★ ★

★ ★ ★ ★ ★ ★ ★ ★ ★ ★ ★ ★ ★ ★ ★ ★ ★ ★ ★ ★ ★ ★ ★ ★

*(continued)*

▪ FY 02–03: a session more dedicated to spending than to tax breaks, although there were minor revenue reductions; some improvement in social programs in the $12.2 billion in added spending

▪ FY 04–05: a nasty legislative session because of $9.9 billion revenue shortfall, later reduced to $9.3 billion at the last minute because of increased federal funds; spending up about $3 billion due to federal social program dollars; general revenue expenditures reduced for the first time since World War II; many user fee increases but legislative resistance to a tax bill; highlight was comptroller's refusal to certify that revenues were available to fund the budget

▪ FY 06–07: restoration of a number of social program cuts made in the previous biennium in a $138.2 billion budget; new business, cigarette, and used car taxes, coupled with a reduction in local school property taxes, as a means of funding public education in special session of 2006

▪ FY 08–09: Record $152.5 billion budget, funded partially with surplus funds to allow further cuts in local school property taxes; noticeable pork barrel funding for pet projects of members of the House speaker's team followed by $650 million in line item vetoes by the governor; improvements in funding for children's health, the youth corrections program, and pay for public employees

★ ★ ★ ★ ★ ★ ★ ★ ★ ★ ★ ★ ★ ★ ★ ★ ★ ★ ★ ★ ★ ★ ★ ★

Another strategy that all states, including Texas, and the national government will use is *privatization*. Two examples are the private prisons that now serve the state—the state contracts with them for services—and the increasing rate of tuition and fees paid by college students. The first is direct private provision of service; the second is passing along the cost to private citizens rather than burdening the revenue system.

A third strategy is to *change the revenue structure* to avert the revenue shortfalls that plagued the state in the 1980s and early 2000s. Change would focus on making the system more elastic and better able to fund state services consistently. The major change to date is the restructuring of the corporate franchise tax discussed earlier in this chapter. The dominant issue of the 1997 and 2005–2006 legislative sessions was revenue restructuring to lower school property taxes, but the lower property taxes did not stem entirely from a new revenue system. Instead, the difference between the revenues formerly raised by the school districts and what they raise now was to be made up by state surpluses, with uncertainties about what happens when there is not a surplus.[27]

Another aspect of revenue structure is the competition among governments for tax sources. National and state governments both tax motor fuels, tobacco, and alcohol, for example, and both levels of government keep increasing tax rates. Both the state and local governments have general sales taxes. The upshot is that the combined tax rates begin to vex citizens after a while. Ironically, cuts in federal income tax rates since the 1980s enhance the state income tax as a logical new source of state revenue.

★ ★ ★ ★ ★ ★ ★ ★ ★ ★ ★ ★ ★ ★ ★ ★ ★ ★ ★ ★ ★ ★ ★ ★ ★ ★ ★

## *Shooting Oneself in the Foot?*

One of the more bizarre aspects of Texas government finance occurred in 2007. In 2006 the legislature authorized major tax cuts in local property taxes, with the funding difference made up by surplus revenues. However, a quirky provision added to the state constitution in 1978 stipulates how much the state can spend out of the pot of money not designated for a specific purpose at the time it is collected. Although the state had a huge budget surplus in 2007, over $14 billion for the 2008–2009 biennium, this provision limited spending to only about $2.1 billion of that surplus. Legislators had to work hard to find a way around the spending cap to avoid cuts in major state programs that badly needed a restoration of funding after the cuts during the last budget deficit and to fund the cuts in local property taxes by providing support for the schools in part through the surplus. Smoke and mirrors always works in politics, however, and a combination of a legislative vote to exceed the cap, coupled with throwing a number of popular measures to the voters in the form of constitutional amendments (no voter approval, no spending) was used.

★ ★ ★ ★ ★ ★ ★ ★ ★ ★ ★ ★ ★ ★ ★ ★ ★ ★ ★ ★ ★ ★ ★ ★ ★ ★ ★

For tax restructuring to occur, state politics would have to change. Businesses, including partnerships, would have to accept some sort of business activity tax that functions as a true corporate income tax, whatever it is called. Ultimately, private citizens would have to be willing to accept a personal income tax. Businesses have accepted major changes in business taxes in 1991 and 2006, with the result that business taxes are broader and fairer than in the past. However, only about one third of private citizens now file an itemized federal tax return; thus, one argument that in the past has favored a personal income tax—the ability to deduct state income taxes but not sales taxes from one's federal income tax return—may be dead. Changes in public attitude are critical to legislative action because the mere advocacy of an income tax is a sure ticket out of office.

Democratic theory recognizes the equality of the citizenry, and many people think that a revenue system that extracts more from people the poorer they are seriously compromises equality. Since 1991, business has paid a greater share of taxes, but as previously noted, the tax system in Texas is still regressive, placing a proportionately heavier burden on those with the lowest incomes. The reality is that without an income tax, the state will always have difficulty meeting its revenue needs in anything other than a booming economy. Historically, Texas attracted businesses because they found a favorable tax structure in the state. However, the experience of other states with economic development indicates that many modern industries are also concerned about the stability of state services. Such stability is difficult in the absence of a flexible tax structure.

The difficulty of revenue restructuring is illustrated by the 1997 legislature's failed debate over tax reform. Similar frustration occurred in the failure of the legislature to address school finance problems in the 2003 regular session or the fruitless special session of April 2004, postponing the solution until the last moment in a 2006 special session. The Ben Sargent cartoon compares legislative inertia in the face of inadequate funding for state services to Nero's playing his fiddle while Rome burned.

Liberals like Ben Sargent compared the 2003 legislature's refusal to raise taxes to meet the state's budget crisis to Emperor Nero's fiddling while Rome burned in A.D. 64.

*Courtesy of Ben Sargent.*

★ ★ ★ ★ ★ ★ ★ ★ ★ ★ ★ ★ ★ ★ ★ ★ ★ ★ ★ ★ ★ ★ ★ ★ ★ ★ ★ ★ ★ ★

## Case Study: The 2006 Special Session on School Finance

Push finally came to shove for state policymakers in 2006 when the state was faced with a June 1 Texas Supreme Court mandate to fix the school finance problem or risk a shutdown of the public school system. The governor and legislature had failed to reform school finance in the 2003 and 2005 regular sessions or three previous special sessions called for that purpose.

Issues included finding a replacement for the "Robin Hood" method of having wealthier school districts send money to poorer districts, gaining business support for new taxes, reducing local school property taxes, and perhaps improving the spending power of public schools. When legislators convened on April 17, armed with recommendations from a bipartisan tax commission appointed by the governor, advocacy of the plan by the governor, support of the business community, and a general public concern about the fate of the schools, they were able to produce a solution. To do so, they laid aside the extreme partisanship of the other legislative sessions from 2003 to 2005; the leaders agreed to agree; and they had the advantage of an $8.2 billion budget surplus. Five bills were necessary to effect a new funding system. These bills

*(continued)*

★ ★ ★ ★ ★ ★ ★ ★ ★ ★ ★ ★ ★ ★ ★ ★ ★ ★ ★ ★ ★ ★ ★ ★ ★ ★ ★ ★ ★ ★

★ ★ ★ ★ ★ ★ ★ ★ ★ ★ ★ ★ ★ ★ ★ ★ ★ ★ ★ ★ ★ ★ ★ ★ ★ ★ ★ ★ ★

*(continued)*

1. Replaced some school property taxes with $2.4 billion of the budget surplus (and the likelihood that the rest of the surplus would be absorbed over a four-year period); included teacher pay raises and some additional school funding

2. Changed the corporate franchise tax to make it applicable to most businesses in the state through a gross receipts tax

3. Changed the method of calculating the value of used cars in order to maximize the sales tax on them

4. Added $1.00 additional tax to the cost of a package of cigarettes, making the tax $1.41

5. Specified that the tax changes in the business, cigarette, and vehicles sales taxes would be used to cover the losses from reductions in local school property taxes and provided that, once the school property tax rate for maintenance and operations drops to $1 per $100 property valuation (it was $1.50), the revenue from new taxes would not only fund the difference but the rest would be used to lower property taxes further

Almost immediately, questions began about the adequacy of the measures for the long run. Certainly, the schools would open for the 2006–2007 academic year, but the dependence on the surplus and the general dependence of the whole plan on a booming economy made analysts wonder how permanent the fix was. There was some flexibility that would allow local districts to enact a small property tax rate increase. Public school advocates had been vocal about the emphasis placed by the governor on reducing property taxes, but the governor also understood the political reality that Texas ranked fourteenth in the nation in individual payments of property taxes.

★ ★ ★ ★ ★ ★ ★ ★ ★ ★ ★ ★ ★ ★ ★ ★ ★ ★ ★ ★ ★ ★ ★ ★ ★ ★ ★ ★ ★

SOURCES: Terrence Stutz and Christy Hoppe, "Industry Girds for Special Session," *Dallas Morning News*, March 18, 2006, 1A, 4A; Terrence Stutz, "Lawmakers Head Home Feeling Victorious," *Dallas Morning News*, May 16, 2006, 3A; Claire Cummings, "Perry: Tax Bill Aids Economy," *Dallas Morning News*, May 24, 2006, 3A; Christy Hoppe, "School 'Fix' Plan: Is It Sufficient?" *Dallas Morning News*, May 14, 2006, 1A, 2A.

Chapter Eleven lays out the constitutional and other legal issues that are part of the public school finance crisis in Texas. This mini-case study focuses purely on the financial issues associated with the schools.

# Where Does the Money Go?

Occasionally, an argument is heard in the state's legislative chambers that reflects serious concern about budgeting a particular program—who will benefit from it, whether it is needed by society, and how it will be financed. More generally, however, whether funds are allocated for a proposed program depends on which interests favor it and how powerful they are, who and how powerful the

Although businesses spent years finding ways to avoid the old corporate franchise tax, basically saying "tax anybody but me," in the fall of 2006 it was agreement among the state's businesses that led to a broad-based business activity tax that is the backbone of public school funding.

*Courtesy of Ben Sargent*

opposition is, and what the results are of compromises and coalitions between these and "swing vote" groups. The political viewpoints of the legislators, the governor, and the state bureaucracy also have an impact on budgetary decisions. In short, decisions about spending public money, like decisions about whom and what to tax, are not made objectively. Rather, they are the result of the complex relationships among the hundreds of political actors who participate in the state's governmental system. The biases of the political system are thus reflected in the biases of state spending.

This section outlines the stages in the budgetary process and then describes the state's major expenditures.

## PLANNING AND PREPARATION

The budgetary process consists of three stages: planning and preparation, authorization and appropriation, and execution (spending). Budget planning and the preparation of the proposed budget are functions of the chief executive in the national government and in forty-four states, but Texas has a **dual-budgeting system.** The constitution makes the legislature responsible for the state budget. The legislature is aided in this task by the Legislative Budget Board (LBB) and its staff, which prepare a draft budget. Four senators and four representatives compose the LBB, which is cochaired by the lieutenant governor and the speaker of the House. Figure 13-4 depicts the workings of the LBB.

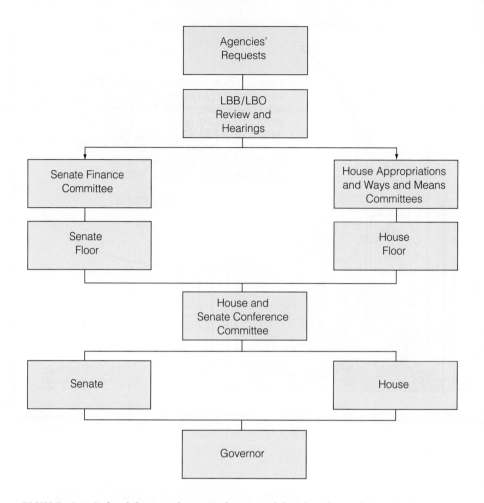

FIGURE 13-4  Role of the Legislative Budget Board (LBB) and Legislative Budget Office (LBO) in the Texas Budget Process

Modern governors have understood the importance of the budget as a political tool, and so, with the aid of the Budget, Planning, and Policy Division, the governor also prepares a budget. This duplicate effort is wasteful, but it does allow different political perspectives on state spending to be heard. In 2003, the legislature took a most unusual approach to budgeting by involving the governor as an equal participant with legislators themselves. By 2007, legislators were trying to find ways around gubernatorial vetoes once again.

The two budgets agree in one respect: Both tend to be *incremental*—that is, both propose percentage increases or decreases for existing programs and the addition of new programs by way of feasibility studies and pilot programs. The recent emphasis on performance may at least give lawmakers a better picture of the real priorities of state agencies and how costs relate to benefits to the state.

Budget planning ordinarily begins in the spring of the even-numbered year before the year in which the legislature meets in regular session. Since 1992, strategic planning has been integrated with budgeting so that the LBB, the governor's office, and the agencies have a compressed time period for preparing budget proposals. State agencies submit their requests for the next biennium on forms prepared jointly by the governor's and the LBB's staffs. Then, at joint hearings, the two staffs try to obtain sufficient information from agency representatives about agency needs to make adequate evaluations of the requests from the agencies. These hearings are usually held in the early fall and are the final joint effort of the two staffs. At this time, individuals and outside groups—the state's dominant interest groups—also provide input. Each staff then prepares a set of budget recommendations that reflects the priorities of its office. When completed, each document is almost two inches thick and provides summary information as well as an agency-by-agency breakdown by specific budget categories. Both are submitted to the appropriate legislative committees for consideration.

Both budgets outline state expenditures for a two-year period. Completed in time for the opening of the legislature in January of one year (for example, 2009), they must project state spending through August two years later (2011), regardless of any changes in the economic outlook that may take place during that thirty-two-month period. Consequently, shifts in the funding of state programs may be needed. Certainly, when we realize that the constitutional directive for biennial legislative sessions means that the funding of state programs must be planned almost three years in advance, we more easily understand why the state budget planners lean toward incrementalism rather than rationalism.

## AUTHORIZATION AND APPROPRIATIONS

The authorization and appropriation stage consists of the authorization of programs to be provided by the state and the passage of a bill appropriating money—the state budget. The House Ways and Means (revenues), House Appropriations (spending), and Senate Finance (both revenues and spending) committees are the key legislative players. Agency representatives, the governor's staff, interest-group representatives, and private citizens testify on behalf of the particular agency or program of concern to them. There is considerable forming and re-forming of coalitions as legislators, lobbyists, and committee members bargain, compromise, trade votes, and generally endeavor to obtain as much for "their side" as possible. Past campaign contributions begin to pay off at this stage, and the relative power of different interest groups is reflected in the state budget. For example, political campaigns frequently include a call to "get tough on crime" and to build more prisons; in turn, prisons are typically well funded. The four main teachers' groups in the state expend considerable effort in trying to influence legislators, and schoolteachers usually get raises, albeit often small ones. The success of the business lobby is the most problematic. In 1995, business got virtually everything it wanted. In 1997, business buried the tax bill it did not want but also found itself on the receiving end of a lot of negative legislation. In 1999, business got some tax breaks and the ability to shop for competitive electric rates. In 2003, the business lobby was so dominant that the visitors' gallery where corporate lobbyists sat while legislators were meeting was dubbed "the owner's box." In 2006 the business lobby accepted new taxes in order to fund public schools, and, in terms of fiscal policy, was virtually left alone in 2007.

The authorization and appropriation stage is a lengthy one, and the Appropriations and Finance committees submit their reports—the two versions of the appropriations bill—near the end of the session. Speaker Pete Laney and Lieutenant Governor Bob Bullock improved the process considerably, beginning in 1993, when they insisted on adequate time for review of the proposed state spending plan. The two versions are never identical; so, a ten-member conference committee composed of an equal number of senators and representatives carefully selected by the presiding officers must develop a single conference report on the budget, including adequate revenue measures to fund the proposed spending, because Texas has a balanced-budget provision that requires the state comptroller to certify that expected revenues are sufficient to fund expenditures. The two houses must accept or reject the report as it stands. Usually, this approval comes fairly late in the session, often at the proverbial "eleventh hour." The approved appropriations bill then goes to the governor for signature.

The governor has a very powerful weapon, the line-item veto, which allows the striking of individual items from the appropriations bill if he or she disagrees with the spending provision. However, the governor cannot add to the budget or restore funding for a pet project that the legislature rejected. Throughout this chapter the reader will see slightly different dollar totals reflected in various tables and charts because the information was based on different documents—estimates at the beginning of the Eightieth Legislature in 2007, the appropriations act passed by legislators, and the amount available after Governor Rick Perry vetoed $650 million in individual budget items, chiefly special items the legislature appropriated for use by community colleges, universities, health science centers, and prisons.

## EXECUTION/SPENDING

The actual disbursement of the state's income is rather technical and less interesting as a political process. It includes such details as shifting money into various funds, issuing state warrants and paychecks, internal auditing of expenditures by agency accountants, and external auditing by the state auditor's staff to ensure the legality of expenditures.

The major political issue involving budget execution has been efforts by several governors to gain greater control over spending between legislative sessions. In 1980 and 1981, voters defeated constitutional amendments that would have increased the governor's authority. The 1987 special legislative session resulted in some increase in the governor's authority to slow down expenditures. In 1991, the legislature not only empowered the LBB to move money from one agency to another agency based on performance but also created a new tripartite body—the governor, the lieutenant governor, and the speaker—to deal with spending and reallocation.

A second political issue in budget execution concerns auditing. The state auditor, a legislative appointee, monitors state agencies and for many years has issued management letters directing agencies both to abandon and to implement different management practices. In 1988, Attorney General Jim Mattox issued an attorney general's advisory opinion that a legislative appointee could not constitutionally tell an executive agency head how to run the agency. However, with new powers granted in the tidal wave of performance-oriented reforms in 1991, the state auditor is now mandated to perform management audits.

Because the services delivered through state budget expenditures are of more interest to the average citizen than the technicalities of how the budget is executed, this section emphasizes a summary of spending on major state services. Figure 13-5 shows that health and human services plus education account for almost three fourths of the FY 2008–2009 Texas budget of $152.5 billion (before the line item vetoes). Many of the program areas summarized here as objects of expenditure are discussed throughout the book as significant political issues.

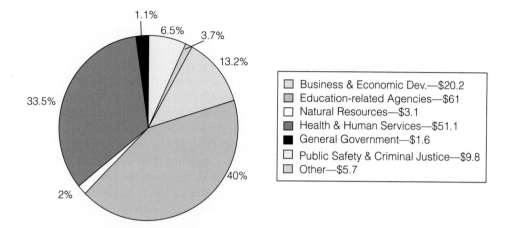

Business & Economic Dev.—$20.2
Education-related Agencies—$61
Natural Resources—$3.1
Health & Human Services—$51.1
General Government—$1.6
Public Safety & Criminal Justice—$9.8
Other—$5.7

**FIGURE 13-5  Texas State Spending by Function, 2008–2009 Biennium (in Billions)***

*Before any gubernatorial vetoes.*

SOURCE: *Robert T. Garrett, "House Passes Budget," Dallas Morning News, May 28, 2007, 1A, 3A. Total equals $152.5 billion, rounded.*

In 2006, after two regular sessions and four special sessions, the legislature finally produced a package of legislation to change the method of financing public schools. There was little confidence among policy analysts that the plan offered a permanent solution because it depended on the use of budget surpluses.

*Courtesy of Ben Sargent.*

# EDUCATION

For FY 2008–2009, 40 percent of the state budget was slated for public schools and higher education. More than two thirds of the education budget of $61 billion was for elementary and secondary schools in the state's 1,090 (as of the 2002 Census of Governments) independent school districts and for state schools for the deaf and visually impaired. The state provides textbooks as well as special services such as programs for disabled children and vocational courses, the Texas Assessment of Knowledge and Skills (TAKS) achievement tests—to be replaced by end-of-course exams—school buses, operating costs, and teacher salaries. The state does not pay the total costs of public education, however. Local school districts share the cost and also are responsible for buildings and other school facilities. Those that can afford it provide supplements to attract the best teachers, buy additional library books, develop athletic programs, and offer students enrichment opportunities. As was summarized in Chapter Eleven, financial equality is the dominant issue affecting public schools. As of 2004 Texas ranked thirty-sixth among the states in combined state and local per capita spending for public education.[28] Table 13-2 shows how the fifteen most populous states spend their money for various major categories of state services and allows a comparison of Texas with the other fourteen states, as well as providing the ranking for Texas among all fifty states. The figures are on a per capita basis—that is, dollars expended per person. In overall education expenditures, the table shows that Texas ranked tenth among the fifteen most-populated states and fortieth among all fifty states for all education expenditures.

The other large slice of the education dollar pie—about $21 billion after the governor's vetoes—supports higher education: the operations of general academic institutions and community colleges, the technical college system, health science centers, and extension programs, plus retirement systems and debt payments on buildings. For both junior and senior colleges, a formula based on such factors as semester credit hours determines the basic level of state support, with the formula funding supplemented by special program funding and affected by performance norms originally adopted in 1992. One positive piece of legislation in 1997 was the

The Dallas Mavericks' outstanding "sixth man," Jerry Stackhouse, is shown visiting an elementary school to encourage the students to take their studies seriously. Education is one of the two largest categories of state spending.

## TABLE 13-2
## Per Capita State Government Expenditures for Selection Functions, Fifteen Most Populous States, 2003, in Order of Overall Per Capita Expenditures

| State | Total | Education | Highways | Hospitals | Public Welfare | All Other |
|---|---|---|---|---|---|---|
| New York | $6635 | $1416 | $202 | $190 | $2024 | $2303 |
| California | 5765 | 1733 | 202 | 142 | 1367 | 2321 |
| Washington | 5317 | 1745 | 311 | 175 | 1018 | 2067 |
| New Jersey | 5201 | 1298 | 296 | 162 | 811 | 2634 |
| Massachusetts | 5095 | 1055 | 378 | 79 | 824 | 2758 |
| Michigan | 5060 | 1911 | 276 | 166 | 906 | 1801 |
| Ohio | 4930 | 1428 | 278 | 120 | 1095 | 2010 |
| Pennsylvania | 4642 | 1179 | 407 | 157 | 1300 | 1518 |
| North Carolina | 4080 | 1470 | 323 | 125 | 928 | 1235 |
| Illinois | 4055 | 416 | 303 | 71 | 907 | 1652 |
| Virginia | 3955 | 1327 | 351 | 256 | 711 | 1309 |
| Georgia | 3749 | 1469 | 212 | 79 | 929 | 1059 |
| Indiana | 3724 | 1394 | 276 | 46 | 867 | 1141 |
| **Texas** | **3313** | **1221** | **238** | **128** | **837** | **1031** |
| Florida | 3313 | 960 | 291 | 13 | 788 | 1260 |
| 50-state Average | $4683 | $1416 | $295 | $132 | $1083 | $1755 |
| **Texas as % of** | **73.8** | **86.2** | **80.7** | **96.9** | **77.8** | **58.8** |
| **Average and Ranking** | **49** | **40** | **44** | **20** | **37** | **48** |

*Numbers rounded.

SOURCE: *Fiscal Size-Up, 2006-07*, 46, based on U.S. Bureau of the Census data.

creation of a greatly simplified funding formula. Local tuition and fees account for a sizable portion of campus funding and was a matter of considerable debate during the 2007 session. The community/junior colleges also are supported by local districts. In 2003, the legislature deregulated university tuition, thereby permitting the institutions to begin charging whatever they needed to charge in 2004. One comparative measure of higher education in Texas is that the state ranks twenty-ninth in the number of persons age twenty-five or older who hold a bachelor's degree. Another measure is that, of all students enrolled in higher education, in Texas 86.9 percent are in public institutions, considerably above the national ranking of 76.8 percent.

## HEALTH AND HUMAN SERVICES

Some $51.1 billion—33.5 percent of the budget—is allocated for human services programs, including welfare, unemployment compensation, employment services, workers' compensation, services for special groups such as the blind and the elderly, and health programs such as mental health and retardation programs, treatment of substance abuse, contagious-disease control, and treatment for catastrophic illnesses such as AIDS, cancer, and kidney failure. About 60 percent of the funding comes from the national government. Chapter Fourteen will discuss the welfare system.

Although expenditures for health and human services are the second largest segment of the state budget, Texas ranked thirty-seventh among the fifty states in per capita expenditures for welfare services and twentieth in hospital services. The state has generally improved in the these rankings over the past twenty years, but the rankings fluctuate because Texas has a tendency to cut social services first when the budget is tight.

★ ★ ★ ★ ★ ★ ★ ★ ★ ★ ★ ★ ★ ★ ★ ★ ★ ★ ★ ★ ★ ★ ★ ★ ★ ★ ★ ★ ★ ★

### Bad to Worse

During the 2003 legislative session, when health and welfare services were being slashed as they were in a number of other states, Governor Rick Perry advised the public "not to worry" because Texas would not become "another Mississippi," a state traditionally ranked toward the bottom in social services and also a very poor state. The Mississippi governor was quick to point out that Texas was already ranked below Mississippi in such services.

★ ★ ★ ★ ★ ★ ★ ★ ★ ★ ★ ★ ★ ★ ★ ★ ★ ★ ★ ★ ★ ★ ★ ★ ★ ★ ★ ★ ★ ★

## BUSINESS AND ECONOMIC DEVELOPMENT

Texas's expenditures for business and economic development for FY 2008–2009 are $20.2 billion, or 13.2 percent of the total budget. This category includes transportation, economic development to promote the state's economy, the efforts of the Housing and Community Affairs Department on behalf of local governments, and employment and training services. Just under one half of the expenditures in this category come from federal funds, particularly highway matching funds to maintain and upgrade the 3,233 miles of federal interstate highways in Texas. In 1977, the legislature capped highway expenditures, with the result that the transportation portion of the state budget has declined from 21 percent to about 9 percent. Texas ranks forty-fourth among the states in per capita spending on highways. Rankings are not available for other services in this category.

## OTHER MAJOR EXPENDITURES

The next largest category of expenditures is public safety, at just over $9.8 billion, or 6.5 percent of the total budget. This category includes law enforcement, prisons, and related programs. Texas is third in the actual dollars spent for prisons but last in per-prisoner expenditures.[29] The remainder of the budget, $10.4 billion, accounts for 6.8 percent of state expenditures. Services, programs, and agencies in this category include general government—the legislature, the judiciary, the governor, and various management offices—as well as parks, natural resources, and regulatory agencies. This category also includes the set-asides of any surplus for future expenditures.

## Summary

Economic conditions, the political climate, and power plays are all part of the game of generating revenues for state government and determining how that income will be spent. Both taxing and spending are usually incremental, with major changes rarely occurring. However, the state's boom-and-bust economy over the past twenty-five years meant more tax and fee increases than usual and less budget growth. That "downer" scenario periodically reverses itself when the economy is in the boom part of the cycle, such as FY 2008–2009, when both revenue and spending decisions were attributable to a robust economy.

In comparing Texas with other states, we find that the combined state and local tax burden is relatively low, with Texas ranked in the bottom fifth of all states. These rankings are based only on taxes, not total revenues. We also note the significant absence of any personal or corporate income tax, although business has been asked to pay a larger share of the tax burden through the revamped franchise tax. The fundamental difference in the Texas revenue system from that of many other states is the disproportionate burden borne by the poorest citizens. This regressive system raises serious questions about how democratic the tax system is in the state.

Democracies are also responsive to the citizenry. The state's spending may not meet the needs of all its citizens, particularly when one considers that it ranks in the bottom fifth of all states in its per capita spending for education, highways, and many functions of general government and only slightly better for welfare, for which the federal government pays a large portion.

The Texas budget process differs procedurally from the ones used by most other states. Those differences include the dual-budgeting system, the extraordinary dominance of the presiding officers in the appropriations process, and the virtually absolute veto power of the governor as a result of the short legislative session.

Important aspects of state finance in Texas are

1. The reliance on taxes paid directly or indirectly by the individual

2. The reliance on regressive taxes such as the sales tax as a major revenue source for the state

3. The restrictions on borrowing

4. The importance of federal funds in the state budget

5. The extent to which the budgetary process is dominated by the legislature and to which the legislature in turn is dominated by the presiding officers

6. The obvious need for diversified revenue sources

7. The seemingly endless problem of school finance

The largest expenditure category is education, followed by health and human services, business and economic development, public safety and criminal justice, and "other," which includes everything else. Critical issues affecting some of these state service areas are discussed in the next chapter and in earlier chapters.

## Glossary Terms

| | |
|---|---|
| block grants | inflation |
| categorical grants-in-aid | progressive taxation |
| dual-budgeting system | regressive taxation |
| elasticity | revenue shortfalls |
| fiscal years | tax equity |
| general revenue sharing | user fee |

## Study Questions

1. What are the different sources of nontax revenue in Texas? How have these changed in recent years?

2. Think about business taxes in Texas. Do you think that business pays its fair share of taxes? Do you think Texas will adopt a true corporate income tax in your lifetime?

3. This chapter has criticized both the regressiveness and the lack of elasticity in the Texas revenue system. What does each of those terms mean? Give and discuss an example of each; then indicate what some of the revenue considerations are as we begin the twenty-first century.

4. What pitfalls do you think exist because of the dual-budgeting system? Do you think there are any advantages to such a system?

5. Throughout this chapter, the authors have made comparisons with other states. What similarities and differences can you identify?

6. If you could increase spending in any one of the seven categories shown in Figure 13-5, which would it be? What if the total amount available had to remain the same? Would you still increase spending in that category? If so, in what category would you decrease expenditures to offset this increase? Discuss the likely effects on services in both the increased and the decreased categories of expenditure.

7. How a government gets money (revenue) and how it spends money are reflections of the political culture of that government. Texas has a traditionalistic-

individualistic political culture, not a moralistic one. Explore how state finance reflects that political culture.

## Surfing the Web

Readers are urged to visit the companion site for this book:

**http://academic.cengage.com/polsci/Kraemer/TexasPolitics10e**

# Issues in Public Policy

Sometimes it floods, but sometimes extreme drought leads to destructive grass fires, such as the one that leveled Cross Plains in 2005.

Here's a forecast of the hot policy issues facing legislatures . . .
planning for emergencies, closing the energy gap, tax and spending
limits, defining "public use," funding education, examining
immigrant rights, GPS for sex offenders, dealing with real ID
[authentic documents], contemplating stem cell research,
and it's a campaign year.

NICOLE CASAL MOORE, *STATE LEGISLATURES*, JANUARY 2006

Do your share for cleaner air.

SLOGAN OF THE TEXAS CLEAN AIR ROUNDTABLE

Water is like sex. Everybody thinks that there's more of it around
than there really is and that everybody else is getting
more than his fair share.

OLD WYOMING SAYING

# Introduction

Texas, like all other states, has an agenda of programs and services that it needs to address. These constitute the policy agenda for the state. When elected officials develop **public policy**, they are establishing priorities for programs that benefit the public. However, agreement on what those priorities should be rarely exists. People even argue, sometimes intensely, about whether government should address some problems at all. Consequently, many controversial issues confront state policymakers. This disagreement and debate are part of a democratic society. In Texas, the backdrop of a traditionalistic-individualistic political culture that runs headlong into a newer moralistic culture among a vocal minority in the state makes the disagreements sharper. Also, even when people agree that a particular problem needs to be addressed, they may disagree about the best way to deal with it. Furthermore, the fiscal health of the state can complicate the policy agenda considerably. Rarely does the state have enough money to fund all the desired programs, and so state finance itself becomes a major policy issue.

The development of public policy begins with the emergence of a problem that needs to be addressed. When someone in government recognizes the need to deal with a problem, it is placed on the policy agenda. One way in which a prospective program or service makes its way onto the policy agenda is through the efforts of the governor and key legislators (see especially Chapters 7 and 8). Often, gubernatorial and legislative viewpoints conflict. This clash was highlighted in 2007 when Governor Rick Perry, Speaker of the House Tom Craddick, and Lieutenant Governor David Dewhurst agreed on virtually no major policy issues, and the disputes during the legislative session were both across and within party lines. Perry's efforts to use the executive order to avoid the legislative process were special irritants.[1]

A second way in which a prospective program or service gets onto the policy agenda is through the political processes that involve interest groups and lobbyists, who make known the priorities they think the state should set. These individuals and groups work through elected officials, the bureaucracy, and the media, but they are especially vigorous in pursuing legislative support for their policy emphases. The water policy discussed later in this chapter is an example of the coming together of legislative, bureaucratic, and interest-group concerns. The business lobby was fundamental to the solution of public school finance. After the governor and legislators battled from 2003 until 2006, the issue was resolved temporarily—part of the funding depends on having a surplus—when the business community agreed to a revamped franchise tax and openly supported the change.

Another avenue for setting the policy agenda is through the *intergovernmental* system—the complex relationships among federal, state, and local governments—and through the *intragovernmental* system—the relationships that cut across the different branches of government. Often, these relationships result in a **mandate**, a term that refers to an action of one government or branch of government that requires another government to act in a certain way. National clean air standards that must be implemented by state and local governments are an example. Intergovernmental and intragovernmental mandates help policymakers identify and define issues even when they would prefer to ignore them. Mandates are often burdensome to the lower level of government, which is required to act even though it receives no funding to help implement the new program. Nationally, the fiscal impact on the states from federal mandates for FY 2004–2007 was over $100 billion, and the National Conference of State Legislatures commented on the poor shape of American federalism.[2]

Mandates have several possible sources. These include the courts, administrative regulations, legislation, and/or highly publicized shifts in national priorities. For example, changes in Texas public school finance began in 1973 with a federal court order and continued with a 1987 state court order to provide a more equitable and "efficient" system of funding public schools.[3] The issue was not settled until 2006. Similarly, the state prison system was tied up in a long-running court suit that began in 1971, with the federal courts not relinquishing supervision until 2002.[4] The suit stemmed from historic problems such as overcrowding, abuse of prisoners, and poor healthcare facilities.

The welfare system in Texas is a product of the state's emphasis on efficiency, national budget cutting, and changing national priorities, and state efforts to gain administrative approval from the federal bureaucracy as well as the traditionalistic-individualistic political culture. All states are struggling to provide adequate welfare services in the midst of federal changes. The transition from welfare to workfare is discussed in this chapter.

An example of intergovernmental influence through administrative regulations is environmental standards. Across the country, states are trying to deal with provisions of the Clean Water Act, the Safe Drinking Water Act, and the Clean Air Act. As we shall see in this chapter, Texas is one of the states that is furthest from meeting the national standards. Despite less pollution of its ground and streams in recent years, Texas continues to be listed among the states that release the most toxic **pollutants** into the air, and the two largest metropolitan areas—Dallas–Fort Worth and Houston—appear on the "bad guy" lists developed by organizations such as the American Lung Association and the federal Environmental Protection Agency. One price the state pays for housing the largest petrochemical industry in the country, as well as having an attitude that results in little public transportation and lots of individual vehicles, is a large volume of pollutants. Other industries produce different toxic wastes, such as those polluting the Ogallala aquifer from the Pantex weapons plant in the Panhandle and agricultural use of pesticides and fertilizers.

Highway construction also shows a sensitivity to changing national priorities. For example, the state's spending on highways was intentionally decreased in 1977 but rose temporarily in the 1980s because of federal funds made available to refurbish and complete the interstate highway system. Federal funding was held back for years, although a reliable transportation system is fundamental to economic development. Today, as this chapter demonstrates, the Texas Department of Transportation (TX-DOT) can address only a fraction of the need for new roads and highway improvements and has decided that adequate roads can be provided only by assessing tolls to travel on them. Local governments are then challenged to find other funding for costly surface transportation without adequate state or national government help.

Another example of how public policy gets set is the intragovernmental example of state-assisted higher education in Texas. A public university is a state agency, just as is the Department of Human Services or the Department of Parks and Wildlife. For example, the 1997 legislature, after years of ignoring higher education, enacted rules governing a number of procedures that had previously been regarded as local business for the institutions. In doing so, the legislature was giving explicit instructions to executive branch agencies. The legislature also has dictated diversity goals and called for greater excellence in higher education, but in doing so, it has indirectly mandated that colleges and universities raise tuition sharply to generate funds to achieve curriculum, diversity, and excellence targets. In 2007 many legislators, ruing the cost of education for the students, began to question the tuition rates and briefly considered a number of measures to clamp down on various institutional practices, such as allowing faculty members to change textbooks when they see the need, before turning to larger issues.

Although the mandates may be difficult to implement, they are not the causes of society's problems. Urbanization, industrialization, inflation, economic downturns, depletion of natural resources, the world oil market, citizen demand, and the curtailment of federal funds to state and local governments are among the causes. Because new and different problems constantly emerge, we cannot even conceive of all the problems that are on the Texas policy agenda. Complicating virtually every issue in Texas is the high rate of population growth. Texas and its local governments simply have trouble keeping up with growth.

This chapter cannot explore even all the major items on the policy agenda. Some issues—the state budget, local government politics and finance, campaign finance, redistricting, civil liberties, abortion, education funding, higher education diversity, and tort reform, for example—have been discussed elsewhere in this book. Other issues that are not discussed here include the need for further deinstitutionalization of the mentally retarded, childcare and child abuse, care of the elderly, illegal aliens, substance abuse, and acquired immune deficiency syndrome (AIDS). The chapter-opening quote of the list of ten issues prominent nationally applies to Texas, too. Simply put, this chapter discusses a sample of four diverse issues on the agenda—*economic development (the business of business), poverty and welfare, saving the environment, and transportation*—to illustrate policymaking in the nation's second largest state. In some measure, these issues are paired opposites: business development and poverty, a clean environment and more transportation.

Some of these issues, such as poverty and welfare, are favorites of progressives and liberals. Others, such as economic development, have traditionally been of greater interest to conservatives but are becoming more important for everyone. Still others, such as education, create widespread concern. The reader who keeps track of what the governor requests and what the legislature does every two years can get an idea of which political forces are dominant at any given time. Certainly, state policymakers find it more to their liking to deal with economic issues, which fit the conservative culture of the state, than with social issues, which they often address only by trying to "reform" current policies and practices that deal with social problems or by trying to gain "accountability" by slashing revenues.

Readers are also reminded that, through the early 1990s, the Senate was more progressive than the House and kept issues such as education, the environment, and social programs on the agenda. Since 1992, the Senate has grown more conservative, and the two houses are more nearly alike. Also, the House has become prone to bickering as it has grown more partisan. Indeed, an agenda for the future is the constitutional challenge to the power of the speaker of the House that must be settled before the 2009 legislative session. For all the issues, the cast of characters is constantly changing. It includes elected officials—the governor and other state executives, legislators, and judges, as well as their national counterparts—plus bureaucrats, representatives of various general and special interest groups, the media, local governments, business, and industry. In addition, public opinion changes as interpretations of any given situation become known.

The issues the state chooses to address and how state policymakers attempt to solve public problems permit another examination of how democratic the Texas political system is. Do policymakers try to deal with a wide variety of issues affecting all citizens? Or do they mainly look at issues placed on the agenda by political elites? Can they solve contemporary problems in the context of a conservative political culture when many of the issues stem from the needs of the "have-nots" of society, who traditionally have been supported by liberals? Do they consider alternative viewpoints? Can their policies be implemented effectively, or are they merely "smoke and mirrors" that only seem to address the problem?

Overall, state policymakers have coped reasonably well. It is true that Texas, when compared with other states, tends to rank toward the bottom in many service areas. It is equally true that the state is sometimes slow to respond to issues such as adult healthcare, failures of electric deregulation, and campaign finance.[5] However, state officials cannot proceed at a pace faster than that at which the public is willing to move and to fund. One of the awkward aspects of democracy is that following majority opinion does not always lead to wise or swift policy decisions.

# The Business of Business

Chapter Thirteen reviewed the Texas economy since the mid-1980s and its effect on state finance. The state slid from boom to bust, in part because of depressed oil and agricultural prices and fluctuations in the American dollar that heavily influenced the state's ability to market its agricultural products abroad. All of these factors were beyond the state's control. Once oil and agriculture weakened, spin-off effects included sharp declines in banking, the savings and loan industry, real estate, and construction. While the national focus shifted away from the oil states in the early 1990s as the troubled economy in New England and on the West Coast became more evident, Texas was still struggling to right the economic ship that had capsized in the 1980s. However, by the late 1990s, the Texas economy was booming again until the state was confronted with the economic slump that plagued the entire nation after the September 11, 2001, attacks on the World Trade Center and Pentagon. By 2004, some recovery was evident, but critical sectors such as high technology were still slumping. By 2007, the state had a robust surplus that was built on revenues collected from 2004 to 2006.

When Texas or any other state attempts to rebuild its economy, two basic strategies are available: recruiting major new industries or government installations and retaining and even expanding existing businesses, particularly small businesses. Sometimes relying on major new industries or government installations can create problems. For example, after the national government partially completed the superconducting supercollider in Ellis County, Congress killed the project in 1995, leaving the state with essentially nothing to show for its recruiting efforts. All recent governors have stressed job creation, with Republicans George W. Bush and Rick Perry also stressing creating a more favorable business environment. Overall, 1995, 2001, and 2003 were considered as particularly probusiness legislative sessions by observers of Texas politics. In 2005–2006 business got a revamped workers' compensation law but also new taxes to pay. The results of the 2007 legislative session were mixed for business: no lowered utility rates, an upgraded water plan that affects everyone, a moratorium on most privately financed toll roads, and corrections to the franchise tax overhauled in the 2006 special session.

Toward the end of the first decade of the twenty-first century, Texas has had some successes with its business policies. Part of the revenue forecast that the state comptroller of public accounts prepares for the legislature before each regular session is a review of the Texas economy. In 2007, Comptroller Susan Combs observed that for 2008–2009, "This is a great time in Texas. . . . Our state's economy is continuing to produce revenue growth to serve Texans' needs. However, it is my duty as Comptroller to point out that I do expect a cooling of the economy in the months ahead."[6] The comptroller's office specifically pointed to increases of 7.4 and 6.7 percent in personnel income for FY 2006–2007, more oil and gas rigs than at any time since 1985, and one of the strongest housing markets in the county. However, she expressed concerns about energy costs—while oil and gas producers and related industries may profit from rising prices, other businesses and residential consumers suffer—and the likelihood that slumps in the housing market were forthcoming. Nevertheless, the forecast was for an additional 412,000 jobs during 2008–09. The Business and Industry Data Center, which is part of the Economic Development and Tourism Division of the governor's office, further pointed to the strength of the state in international trade (number one in export revenues), national leadership in job growth, and the breadth of transportation available in Texas.[7]

Economic prosperity is an issue for everyone in the state. It is supported by ethnic minorities and Anglos, by men and women, by Republicans and Democrats, by urbanites and rural interests. If the number of jobs is insufficient, if the markets for manufacturing and agricultural products are inadequate, if businesspeople cannot secure loans that enable them to expand, we are all affected. As is so often the case, however, tactics for achieving prosperity are open to debate. Conservatives think government's role should be to create conditions that allow business and industry to grow, and if business is healthy, prosperity will "trickle down" to the ordinary citizen. Liberals think government should intervene more directly and ensure that ordinary workers are aided by such policies as a minimum wage, mandatory benefits, and health and safety programs.

# MODERN POLICY INITIATIVES

Texas developed a number of policy initiatives to promote the return to prosperity and then to continue economic vitality. The measures described in the next section are policies that pertain directly to business. However, equally important are measures described elsewhere in this chapter and this book to improve education, provide more adequate transportation, and improve the quality of life of Texans. Indeed, as the reader will see, Texas does not always rate well nationally because, despite a favorable business climate, its weaknesses in education, research, highways and other fundamentals are viewed negatively.

## ECONOMIC DEVELOPMENT

The state began to rebuild the economy in 1987 when the legislature created a Texas Department of Commerce (TDC) to integrate most of the twenty-one separate programs, funds, offices, and commissions dedicated to economic development and related activities. TDC activities included workforce development and job training grants, block grants made for community development, tourism development, loans for exporters, small and minority-owned business programs, general business development, business expansion services, fine arts programs, advanced technology funds, and international trade and foreign office representation.

The TDC developed a reputation for spending money in ways that mainly benefited the governing board and key administrators but not the state of Texas. One of Governor Ann Richards's first acts after she was inaugurated in January 1991 was to tackle the reorganization of the commerce department. Ultimately, she gained control of the executive director's position so that the agency head was appointed by the governor.

The agency was reorganized again in 1997 and its name changed to the Department of Economic Development (TDED). The 1997 changes mainly got rid of archaic provisions in the enabling law and created a name that made the agency's purpose clearer. The 2003 legislature once again reconfigured the economic development function, eliminating the separate department. A new Texas Economic Development and Tourism Office (TEDTO) was created in the office of the governor. Additionally, the governor was given $295 million in economic incentive funds over and above the TEDTO budget, and the incentive funding has been forthcoming from subsequent legislatures.

In addition to TEDTO, the Texas Workforce Commission, the Department of Housing and Community Affairs, the Texas Lottery Commission, the Office of Rural Community Affairs, and the Department of Transportation are all classified as agencies dealing with business and economic development. Also, Texas has thirty-five regulatory agencies that oversee individual businesses and professions. Most prominent among these are the Department of Insurance, the Department of Banking, and the Public Utility Commission.

## WORKERS' COMPENSATION

Workers' compensation is a program to provide medical, income, death, and burial benefits for workers who are injured, become ill, or are killed on the job. The program has existed largely in its present form since 1917. The procedures and especially the costs of the program affect businesses of all sizes, from the local "Making the Cut" lawn-mowing service to the giant Exxon-Mobil Corporation, which is headquartered in Irving. Texas is unique among the states in allowing employers to choose whether to provide workers' compensation, although public employers and employers who accept a public construction contract must provide workers' comp. Employers who are not participants in the program must notify both the Texas Workers' Compensation Commission and all employees. These employers have a number of options to the workers' compensation program, including private insurance and setting aside reserve funds ("self-insurance").

A major policy initiative affecting business was the revamping of the workers' compensation program in 1991. The 1991 reforms were designed to move Texas away from a system that resulted in the state's having simultaneously the highest costs and the lowest benefits of any U.S. state. The complex 1991 legislation covered such diverse issues as mandatory safety programs, fraud, self-insurance, and a source of revenue for the insurance fund. Yet, evolving a workable workers' comp program has not been an easy task.

By 1994, the state had returned to a situation of high costs and low benefits, although the costs were still lower than in 1991. Texas was not unique in its workers' compensation problems,[8] and the state took further steps to lower the

Michael Dell announces an expansion of Dell Computers while Governor Rick Perry looks on. Economic development is one way to enhance state revenues.

costs to industry. Organized labor then brought a court challenge to the system, complaining that the lowered costs were directly at the expense of workers and their benefits. In 1995, the Texas Supreme Court ruled against the workers. By late 1996, not only was the system solvent, but also the workers' compensation fund had become a big moneymaker. Even after the payouts to workers, the fund rebated $600 million to insurance companies. In 2003, Texas businesses received a bonus in the form of new limits on workers' comp medical costs coupled with a prohibition against the use of preinjury waivers of liability in lieu of workers' compensation coverage. Individual workers' benefits were enhanced at the same time. The program has not been particularly newsworthy in recent years, but it is one that is of constant interest to employers, especially small employers who do not have the resources to use one of the private options. Benefits are based on the statewide average weekly wage, which is the maximum that the program will pay. For 2007, the maximum is $674 a week, the minimum is $101. These amounts apply to both temporary and lifetime benefits. The maximum for impairment and supplemental income benefits is $472; the minimum is the same.[9]

## LEGISLATIVE HIGHLIGHTS, 1995–2007

In some legislative years, business receives so many benefits that the purpose of the governor and the legislature appear to *be* business. In 2003, for example, when the Republicans took full command of state politics, they openly placed the business agenda at the top of their priority list. Although the business lobby didn't get everything it wanted, Austin observers joked about the visitors' gallery being called the "owner's box" because of all the business lobbyists and the lack of attention to other issues. In other years, the legislature may turn more to school finance or children's health and do little for business. For example, in 2007, the big agenda item for business was reduction in electric utility rates; business got nothing.

The list below summarizes modern Texas legislative sessions and their effect on business in the state.

- 1995: tort reform, including limits on frivolous lawsuits and the amount of damages corporations might have to pay; protection of favored longtime Texas telephone carriers against the big national long-distance carriers; continuation of the "phantom tax" on utilities that allowed power and telephone companies to pass along "taxes" that are really nothing more than devices to increase corporate profits; postponement of a required conversion of trucks from petroleum fuel to propane or natural gas; and restrictions on the City of Austin's environmental regulations in favor of high-powered developers.

- 1997: authorization for banks to make home equity loans (after a constitutional amendment); business proprietors were saddled with being the enforcers for new restrictions on teenage smoking and drinking

- 1999: electric deregulation, which was a national issue;[10] although Texas learned some lessons from two dozen other states that were already engaged in deregulation, the statute ultimately proved to be ridden with loopholes that did not result in a lowering of electric rates and produced a very complex regulatory environment for setting prices; the first sales tax holiday to allow families to make their back-to-school dollars go further and bolster shopping in the state; an increase in highway speeds to seventy miles per hour, a boon to truckers; more restrictions on suits against business corporations; consumer protection against cramming—charging for unwanted services—and slamming—unauthorized switching of a customer from one carrier to another—by telecommunications firms; legislation stabilizing local and long-distance telephone rates

- 2001: additional tort reform legislation; big insurance company benefits when legislation limited homeowners' claims, provided new rate structures for automobile and homeowners insurance, and created greater controls on the medical liability associated with workers' compensation coverage

- 2003: an agenda dedicated to saving business from more taxes, which resulted in failure to resolve school finance and left 80 percent of Texas businesses not subject to the franchise tax with loopholes to escape inclusion; public approval of a constitutional amendment that allows the legislature to set the maximum dollar amounts that can be awarded in lawsuits and provides other relief that makes it more difficult for a plaintiff to win a damage case; approval of another amendment that allows homeowners to secure a line of credit based on the equity in their homes (and lenders to reap the interest); a new governor's economic development fund, initially capitalized at $295 million

- 2005–2006: revamping of workers' compensation in the regular session, followed by a special session in 2006 that resulted in a complete overhaul of the corporation franchise tax, which not only increased state revenues to pay for public schools but also made the tax applicable to virtually all businesses in the state with at least $300,000 in gross profits

- 2007: electric industry escape of a number of proposed major changes, resulting in no rate relief for either business or citizens and no environmental clean-up of coal-fired generating plants; two-year moratorium on most new toll roads but not abandonment of Governor Rick Perry's controversial Trans-Texas Corridor (see discussion later in this chapter)

## ONGOING CONCERNS

Texas constantly shifts from the economic doldrums to economic prosperity. Not only are such swings difficult for business, but they also cause great unpredictability in state revenues that can be used for a variety of programs. When state policymakers focus only on trying to help business, especially big business, in the state, they often fail to provide an adequately educated workforce and amenities that lead to a high quality of life. As a result, those businesses that the state hopes to attract may not find the state all that attractive after all. In 2007, the Corporation for Enterprise Development (CFED), a Washington, D.C., research firm, ranked all the states on the basis of sixty-seven factors that collectively provided grades for business performance, business vitality, and development capacity.[11] Overall, Texas was ranked as a non-honor roll state.

The Texas grades were

- Performance: F. This category included employment, income, stewardship of natural resources, equity (the gap between rich and poor), and social conditions. Many jobs are low paying and foster a widening of the gap between rich and poor citizens. (The state has failed in this category since 1999.)

- Business Vitality: A. This category included the robustness of businesses, ability to operate within the global economy, business leadership, venture capital, and available labor. The number of business starts and job growth in new companies as well as the state's trade volume in the international market helped the state earn the A grade, which it has held since 2003.

- Development Capacity: D. This category included the education system, vision toward twenty-first century development, physical infrastructure, and financial, natural, and technological **infrastructure** (roads, water systems, and other expensive public installations). A major factor in the mediocre rating was the quality of the educational system. (This grade is worse than in 2003.)

This sort of mixed report card would find the average schoolchild in considerable trouble with his or her parents. The pluses for Texas were job growth, electronic public services, manufacturing investments, initial public offerings, employment growth, infant mortality, and basic educational skills especially in math. However, the minus list was longer than the plus list. Texas stays in perennial trouble with the CFED because of its poverty rate, employer health coverage, voting rate, income distribution, high school completion, uninsured low-income children, and higher education attainment, among other factors. These factors are all significant when the state tries to expand its economy by recruiting new industries or new corporations to the state.

The weakness of the state's educational system and problems with its job training programs are examples of the negatives the state encounters in business recruitment. As of 2003–2004, the state ranked twenty-ninth in the percentage of the population graduating from college and in the pupil–teacher ratio in public schools, thirty-first in classroom teacher salaries, twenty-fifth in the average salary of college associate professors, and thirty-sixth in per-pupil elementary and secondary school expenditures and in high school graduation rates.[12] These statistics make the state more attractive to service industries requiring minimal skills than to high-paying, high-technology and financial businesses.

On the other hand, Texas fares very well in national rankings concerning small businesses, according to the Small Business and Entrepreneurship Council, a Washington, D.C.-based organization that lobbies for small businesses. Texas was ranked ninth nationally, with emphasis on factors such as its lack of an income tax, its status as a right-to-work (basically anti-union) state, its regulatory environment, and having one of the lower ratios of government employees to citizens.[13]

These various rankings point out how interrelated major issues are and why the governor and legislative leaders cannot address one issue without addressing others. The 2007 legislature, for example, continued the tax breaks associated with the school funding solution of 2006 but did not provide for teacher raises, and the governor used his line item veto mainly against colleges. However, the biggest issue left unresolved in 2007 and waiting attention in 2009 is cleaning up the electric deregulation legislation. The focus of the "dereg" dispute was over TXU, a huge power company whose rates were "the price to beat," that is, whose rates were not to be exceeded by other power providers. The fight began with TXU's desire to build eleven new coal-fired generating plants (see the section on clean air later in this chapter), moved to the state's trying to get a piece of the action when a buy-out offer was made for TXU, and ended with no change.

# Poverty and Welfare

Conservative agendas have dominated national and state politics since the mid-1990s, and they have long shaped Texas politics. In short, for reasons that were discussed throughout this book, the viewpoints of individuals in upper income brackets often dominate public policy, and the predominant traditionalistic-individualistic political culture underlies this approach to politics. These political facts of life are particularly important when we examine the issues of poverty and welfare. Whenever the government attempts to improve the quality of life for the poor, it is producing **redistributive public policy**[14]—that is, policy that redistributes wealth from those who have the most to those who have the least. Inevitably, then, poverty and welfare politics produces strong emotions and sharp political divisions. In Texas, as elsewhere, some policymakers and ordinary citizens think that poor people could be more effective at helping themselves through job training, education, and looking for work. Even when compassion exists for those too ill or infirm to work, it does not spill over into sympathy for individuals deemed to be shirkers. Other people think that people are poor because they have never been given an opportunity to have a good education or relevant job training. In truth, all these opinions are correct. The reasons for poverty are many. The task at hand is to determine how the state of Texas addresses poverty issues. Any state's role in combating poverty and seeing to the welfare of its citizens is a mix of both state policy and federal programs. Because of changes in national policy, Texas, which has traditionally relied on federal funds for its welfare programs, has had to make changes in its own welfare system.

## POVERTY IN TEXAS

The **poverty threshold** for a family of three was $17,170 for fiscal year 2007.[15] This guideline is often stated for a family of three because a typical poor family consists of a mother and two children; an additional family member increases the line by $3,480. The guideline allows for much higher living costs in Alaska and Hawaii but makes no allowance for the higher living costs in major cities as compared with small towns and rural areas.

Poverty statistics are census-based and are reported after general population figures are made available. Thus, there is some lag time between the current year and the most recent year for which comparative statistics are available. The *Texas Fact Book 2006* includes data for 2003–2004. It reports that Texans were thirty-second in personal income, first in the percentage of the population not covered by health insurance, and sixth in the percentage of the population living in poverty. The median family income in Texas in 2003 was $40,934, leading to a ranking of thirty-three in the country.[16] Ironically, even though Texas is a leader in the number of new jobs created annually, many of those jobs are low paying.

The National Center for Children in Poverty at Columbia University reports that 23 percent of all Texas children live in poverty—that is, the household

The Seventy-eighth Legislature in 2003–2004 provided the governor with a slush fund to attract new business to the state but left basic services such as education, welfare, children's health, and medical assistance underfunded. The Seventy-ninth and Eightieth Legislatures did a better job with human services while preserving economic development funds.

*Courtesy of Ben Sargent.*

income is below the poverty guideline—and another 26 percent are low income, that is, their family income is less than 200 percent of the poverty threshold. These figures were above the national averages of 18 percent and 21 percent, respectively.[17] Seventeen of the 200 poorest counties in the United States are in Texas, including nine—Starr, Maverick, Willacy, Hudspeth, Presidio, La Salle, Dimmit, Hidalgo, and Zavala—in the twenty-five very poorest.[18] The per capita income in Starr County was only $7,069, less than a quarter of that for the state as a whole. Slight shifts in the various poverty rankings occur from year to year, but Texas rarely varies its relative position by more than one place.

Statistics for Medicaid (the program that provides health insurance for the poorest individuals) enlighten the poverty figures. Over 71 percent of the recipients of Medicaid are children; three quarters of them live in households where at least one parent works. Seventeen percent of all Texas children receive Medicaid, but estimates are that another 1.4 million are not covered by any insurance program.[19] Rural south and southwest Texas and the ghettos and *barrios* of the largest cities have the highest number of poor people.

One question that arises when the stark numbers of Texas poverty are stated is "what about the homeless?" Neither the state nor the national government has a very accurate measure of the number of homeless people because the homeless are a mix of people who sometimes have work, sometimes do not, and include a substantial number of mentally ill people. When adequate help is provided, the majority of homeless move into housing and find a job, according to the U.S. Bureau of the Census.[20] The bureau conducted a large-scale study of homeless persons and providers of services to the homeless in 1995 and 1996 and estimated almost 2 million homeless persons nationwide. It determined that "overall the homeless were deeply impoverished and most were ill." Two thirds had some type of chronic illness, with more than half of these beset with mental illness. According to the Texas Department of Community Affairs, Texas has an estimated 180,000 to 200,000 homeless persons.[21] More than a quarter of the homeless have a childhood history of living in an institution or being in foster care. Given the population size of Texas and the entrenched poverty in some parts of the state, one can safely assume a sizable homeless population.[22]

## THE PLAYERS AND THE MAJOR PROGRAMS

HB 2292 passed by the legislature in 2003 resulted in a major reorganization of health, welfare, and social services in Texas. Twelve health and human services agencies were consolidated into four departments that are part of a large, umbrella agency known as the Health and Human Services Commission. The super-departments, which split up and reassigned services offered by their predecessors, are

- **Department of State Health Services (DSHS), which includes broad-based health services, healthcare information, mental health, and alcohol and drug abuse programs.**

- **Department of Aging and Disability Services (DADS), which includes services for the mentally retarded and community care, nursing home, and aging services.**

- **Department of Family and Protection Services (DFPS), which includes child and adult protective services and childcare regulatory services.**

- **Department of Assistive and Rehabilitative Services (DARS), which includes rehabilitation, services for the blind and visually impaired, services for the deaf and hard of hearing, and early childhood intervention.**

Each of these departments is headed by a commissioner who reports to the executive commissioner of health and human services, who in turn reports to the governor. A nine-member Health and Human Services Council assists the executive commissioner in policy development. In addition, the Health and Human Services Commission determines eligibility for and administers a number of significant programs that cut across the departments. These programs include accreditation, welfare, Medicaid/CHIP, and nutrition, among others. Employment services and benefits are handled through the Texas Workforce Commission.

In Texas, programs to help needy citizens long have been funded primarily with federal dollars supplemented by whatever additional funds the state was obligated to provide to be eligible for the federal dollars. The Texas Constitution places a ceiling on welfare expenditures. Since a 1982 amendment, that ceiling has been 1 percent of the state budget for general public assistance, as long as the state ceiling did not conflict with federal welfare program requirements. However, this provision is more flexible than the previous one, which was expressed in dollar amounts.

The national Social Security Administration provides direct case assistance for aged, disabled, and blind Texans through the Supplemental Security Income (SSI) program, and the U.S. Department of Health and Human Services channels funds to the consolidated Texas Health and Human Services Commission (HHSC) for the Temporary Assistance to Needy Families (TANF) program, which replaced the old Aid to Families with Dependent Children (AFDC) program. TANF is a program for families with needy children under age eighteen who have been deprived of financial support because of the absence, disability, unemployment, or underemployment of both parents. The U.S. Department of Agriculture administers the food stamp program, passing dollars through the HHSC. Medicaid, a program of medical assistance for the needy, is a joint federal–state program administered through the HHSC. Medicaid's principal programs are for children, the aged, the blind and disabled, and maternity care.

TANF, food stamps, and Medicaid are the largest welfare programs. They all work with one another so that a person eligible to receive help from one program is *sometimes* eligible to receive help from one or more of the others, although the formulas determining eligibility vary with each program. Although most states supplement these programs, Texas historically has chosen to provide "bare bones" programs. Figure 14-1 illustrates for FY 2005 the assistance that

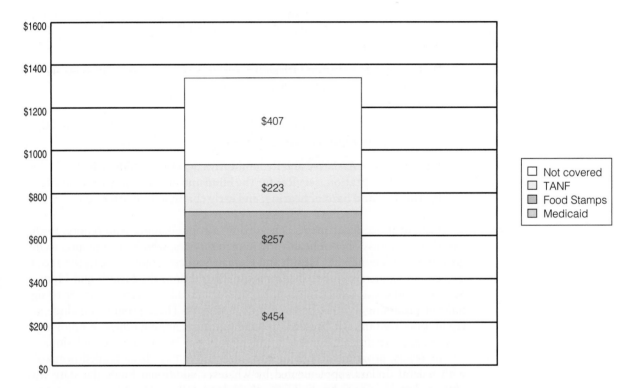

**FIGURE 14-1  Cash Value of Typical TANF Family's Monthly Benefits and Services, Fiscal Year 2005**

NOTE: *The typical Temporary Assistance for Need Families (TANF) family in Texas consists of a single female caregiver and two children who receive no child support. The federal poverty level for a family of three was $1,341 in FY 2005, the last year for which figures were available for all three programs.*

SOURCE: *Fiscal Size-Up, 2006–07 (Austin: Legislative Budget Board), 164–166; Texas Medicaid in Perspective, Sixth Edition (Austin: Texas Health and Human Services Commission, 2007), 5–11.*

## TABLE 14-1
### Texas TANF, Food Stamp, Medicaid, and CHIP Recipients, Fiscal Years 2003–2007

| Program | 2003 | 2004 | 2005 | 2006* | 2007* |
|---|---|---|---|---|---|
| TANF | 367,893 | 273,520 | 224,284 | 228,427 | 232,171 |
| Food stamp | 1,885,000 | 2,287,000 | 2,449,000 | 2,452,000 | 2,459,000 |
| Medicaid/ acute care | 2,466,119 | 2,659,892 | 2,758,730 | 2,986,661 | 3,114,218 |
| CHIP | 506,968 | 409,865 | 333,707 | 362,175 | 382,175 |

*estimated

SOURCE: *Fiscal Size-Up, 2006–2007* (Austin: Legislative Budget Board, 2005), 113, 163, 166.

a typical welfare family received monthly—$454 for Medicaid, $257 for food stamps, and $223 for TANF. This typical family consisted of a mother and two children who receive no child support. Thus, the typical Texas payment of $934 to a qualifying family left the family $407 short of moving to the breakpoint for the poverty level.

Table 14-1 shows the fluctuating dependence of many Texans on various forms of assistance during the early years of the twenty-first century. The state's approach was to cut back on funding by tightening eligibility rules for these programs when the state faced shortfalls and to increase funding during times of surplus. The victims of this approach have been mainly children who in most states would be covered by the Children's Health Insurance Program (CHIP).

Indeed, the two programs that serve adults as well as children (food stamps and acute Medicaid) show increased numbers of recipients, whereas the two programs targeted mainly to children (TANF and CHIP) show mainly declines. TANF is "welfare," basically for families without a working adult. Recipients of both food stamps and Medicaid, including CHIP, often include the working poor. The number of TANF recipients peaked in FY 1993, while the number of food stamp recipients peaked in FY 1994, although it is slowly rising again. CHIP did not begin until FY 1999 and peaked in FY 2003. Medicaid has been the subject of serious debate among national and state policymakers in recent years because of the growing cost of healthcare. Nationally and in Texas, almost two thirds of all health assistance goes to children, but the highest costs are associated with the disabled and the elderly.

Other social services include day care, foster homes, energy assistance for low-income persons (to help with heating bills), child protective services, and job training. Healthcare is, of course, a problem affecting everyone, and problems shared by persons from all social classes tend to have a higher degree of political support than problems that afflict only the poor.[23] State services range from programs for children with physical disabilities and for individuals with devastating diseases, such as cancer and tuberculosis, to rehabilitation of trainable people with mental retardation and the control of rabies in skunks. Although such programs are not restricted to the poor, their existence eases the burden of medical costs for less well-off Texans. Additionally, a joint state–county system of indigent healthcare has existed since 1985.

Changing federal and state policy, economic conditions, and population changes contribute to the variations in the numbers from year to year, but overall the numbers indicate that Texas does not do a particularly good job in helping poor people. Texas for years has ranked in the bottom quarter of states with regard to social services. It is a state of contrasts between rich and poor, and although the stereotype of Texas is a state filled with rich oil tycoons, the state is, in fact, the fifth poorest in the United States.[24] Complicating this picture is the fact that Texas is now a state with a majority of ethnic minorities, a fact that adds political fuel to the debate over social policy.

Another related service is unemployment compensation—that is, payments to unemployed workers. This program is one that cuts across programs affecting business and those affecting the poor. It is administered by the Texas Workforce Commission, which also assists individuals in finding jobs and keeps records of employment in the state. Unemployment compensation is a joint federal–state effort. The basic funding method is a tax on wages paid by employers, plus any surcharge needed to make the system fiscally sound, and reimbursements from governmental units for any unemployment benefits drawn by their former employees. If a state has its own unemployment compensation program and an agency to administer it, the employers can charge off most of the tax on their federal tax returns. If the federal government administers the program directly, employers cannot take advantage of the tax writeoff. In Texas, unemployment benefits vary according to previous wage and disability status. For FY 2007, the minimum weekly unemployment benefit was $56, and the maximum was $364 (the disabled received about twice that amount). Benefits are payable for a period up to twenty-six weeks except when the federal government extends the period as it usually does during periods of prolonged unemployment.

A related program is workers' compensation, which provides medical support for workers injured on the job or made ill by the job environment. This program was discussed earlier in the chapter.

# RECENT POLICY DEVELOPMENTS

Early in the 1990s, many states, including Texas, had addressed the issue of welfare reform, all of them with emphasis on converting welfare to workfare, forcing "deadbeat dads" and "misanthrope moms" to provide child support, and employing modern electronics to aid in tracking those in the welfare system. In 1996 Congress passed and President Bill Clinton signed the Personal Responsibility and Work Opportunity Reconciliation Act, otherwise known as welfare reform. Fundamentally, this legislation followed the lead of the states in getting people off welfare and onto payrolls.

The *workfare* approach carried with it not only such positive values as helping welfare recipients regain their self-esteem by becoming better trained and gainfully employed and freeing up money for other programs but also such negatives as more rules and regulations. The federal reform allowed five years of welfare support, but the time clock begins to tick from the first date a recipient receives a check even though the person might have extensive training to

## The New "Down and Out"

The recession of 2001–2003 produced some strange side effects. Social service agencies in counties heavily populated by previously high-salaried individuals in the telecommunications industry—Collin County, for example—were receiving requests for financial assistance for out-of-work telecom executives and engineers. Case workers reported in the spring of 2003 that some of the applicants needed a "reality check." Unwilling to let go of their big houses, expensive cars, or club memberships, they were applying for assistance to continue their upscale life style. They were not successful.

undergo. Texas provides for only three years of assistance although the average time on welfare is less than two years. The federal requirement is that the individual be working within two years, without the flexibility of the earlier Texas plan that includes job training, parenting or life skills training, and education or literacy training within the definition of work.[25]

In their concern for reducing welfare fraud, putting people to work, and generally moving one step away from Big Government, the politicians initially failed to address the fundamental reality of welfare reform—namely, that the legislation forces single mothers of dependent children to go to work and may cost their children healthcare through Medicaid. Because workfare means that their children will either be left alone all day or placed in daycare, this consequence would seem to contradict the much-touted "family values" espoused by many politicians. Less parental care is also likely to have the further consequences of more juvenile crime, poorer school performance, and thus, paradoxically, even more welfare dependency. Welfare reform illustrates how complex social issues are. In trying to fix one set of problems, it is all too easy to create another set. The healthcare aspect of the problem was addressed in the federal Balanced Budget Act of 1997, which created the Children's Health Insurance Program (CHIP) for low-income children. Child care has proved more elusive and is heavily dependent on local nonprofit and community programs. In fact, the administration of President George W. Bush preferred faith-based programs to solve many social problems, including child care. (Faith-based programs are those provided by churches and other religious organizations rather than by public agencies.)

The 1996 federal act created a "cafeteria-style" welfare system for the states, with each state receiving a block grant for welfare support, which it could apportion among programs that the state judged as having the highest priority. Proportionately less money now flows from Washington, and the states are allowed under the national legislation to slash their own welfare payments by 20 percent with no loss of federal funds.

Because budget surpluses in 1999 and 2001 allowed the state to fund social services, the legislature softened eligibility requirements and broadened some programs in those years. But with a faltering economy producing fewer tax revenues and more need for social services, by 2003 social service funding once again became a focal point of the legislative session. Medicaid expenses nationally were growing 7 to 8 percent a year, a major problem for Texas and many other states that were already facing deficits. State officials across the country

The Dallas "Hunger Buster Van" offers food to the homeless after the city passed a number of restrictions on where homeless persons could be fed.

Migrant workers in El Paso reflect another aspect of poverty in Texas.

found themselves having to decide among many well-deserving programs such as healthcare, higher education, highways, and high schools.[26] The opening ploy of the Texas legislative session was a House plan to deal with the budget shortfall via massive cuts in social services; part of this strategy was to pare back social services that House conservatives detested. That plan was unfeasible not only because it lacked Senate support but also because cutting state services meant cutting federal dollars. Nevertheless, the combination of revenue shortfalls coupled with an unwillingness to raise taxes led to significant cuts, even though the cuts were not so deep as the House wanted.

The Seventy-ninth Legislature in 2005 moved to shore up the health and human services programs somewhat. Financial supplements were made to cover Medicaid and CHIP costs and the application and operations aspects of these programs were modified, although to the great confusion of clients.[27] Some of the people cut from services in 2003 were restored to the rolls in 2005. In 2007, the legislature took a similar tack, with another 100,000 children added to the CHIP program for FY 2008–2009, but more than 1 million needy children still were left without healthcare.

## ANALYSIS

The off-again/on-again support for social services results in muddled signals. One reading is that despite a set of elected officials even more conservative than those of the past, the state had developed a social conscience with regard to the needy. An alternative interpretation is that the state was mainly interested in money—finding ways not to spend state dollars on the poor and finding ways to get a bigger piece of the federal welfare pie. Beyond dispute is the fact that Texas has a welfare problem that is tied to social divisions that rest on ethnic conflicts and struggles between the haves and the have-nots.

A combination of stringent qualifications for recipients and a booming economy resulted in one effect desired by state and federal welfare reformers—namely, a drop in the number of aid recipients, a fact displayed in Table 14-1. Generally, the number of those receiving assistance was starting down in all categories in spite of rapid population growth until economic recession began to take hold in 2001. Medicaid recipients even dropped slightly in 2000. The same figure also shows the effect of a poor economy in 2002–2003 when the caseloads in all three major social programs—Medicaid, TANF, and food stamps—began to grow until the legislature further tightened eligibility requirements in the 2003 legislative session.

The second effect was that Texas, like other states, is not spending all the money to which it is entitled by federal programs. According to *State Legislatures* magazine, the states with the highest poverty rates, Texas included, were spending less than 69 percent of their allotted funds. The states as a whole were spending only 76 percent of their block grant funds.[28] This publication, which is published by the National Conference of State Legislatures, points out two important facts about the underspending. First, those individuals who remain on welfare will be very difficult to place in jobs for reasons such as domestic violence, little training, lack of transportation, and lack of childcare. Second, innovative states—Arizona, Colorado, Florida, Maine, Michigan, New York, Washington—used the funds not spent on TANF recipients to provide a variety of solutions to hardcore unemployment and chronic welfareism. One of the reasons for the sparring between Comptroller Carole Keeton Strayhorn and Governor Rick Perry and

# YOU DECIDE

## Should Texas Find Ways to Pay for More Social Services?

The Seventy-eighth Legislature in 2003 faced a $10 billion budget shortfall. To deal with the major budget problem, legislators enacted measures that withdrew social services to tens of thousands of Texans. Consequently, Texas continues to rank toward the bottom of all states in its support for programs for the poor, the chronically ill, and children.

| PRO | CON |
|---|---|
| ▲ Many social service recipients are the working poor. They have full-time, but low-paying, jobs that are inadequate to support their families. | ▼ Welfare recipients are lazy and must be forced to find jobs to support themselves and their families. It's not the role of the state to support them. |
| ▲ The biggest cuts have been in children's medical services, but it is far better to offer preventive programs to poor kids than to wait for a serious illness to strike them. | ▼ It is far more important to fund public education than to provide public funding for indigent children's health. |
| ▲ The mentally ill, including many homeless persons, were hit hard by the changes. These persons are basically helpless and deserve state assistance. | ▼ The most expensive medical programs are for mental illness and substance abuse. People get themselves into these messes. Let them get themselves out. |
| ▲ When good jobs are scarce and families are having a hard time making it economically, the state should provide even more social services, not fewer. | ▼ Citizens cannot afford to pay more state taxes and fees to support poor people. If public programs exist, they should be funded entirely by the federal government. |
| ▲ Human resources are the most important resources of all. It's good public policy to invest in them. | ▼ Privatization is a highly desirable public policy. If people need help, they should ask local charities. |

the legislative leadership in 2003–2004 was Strayhorn's frequent criticism that Texas was leaving federal money on the table to avoid spending state money.

Several factors make it likely that social services will be a perennial issue in Texas politics. First, the economy swings between boom and bust, and when the economy is sluggish, the number of aid recipients increases at the same time that the state is less able to pay for the services. Second, the state's immigration rate is among the highest in the country, and many of the immigrants, especially those who are illegal, lack essential job skills. They often constitute the working poor, especially because they are willing to work for inferior wages.[29] Third, disparities between rich and poor seem to be growing, and that difference is exacerbated by a rapidly growing elderly population with more women than men.[30] National tax policy intensified the phenomenon of the rich getting richer and the poor getting poorer. Fourth, the conservativism of Texans is becoming even more evident in a Republican-dominated state in which many, not all, elected officials have an inherent dislike of social programs.

# Saving the Environment

For Texans, environmental issues are particularly important. The state lived off the environment—land, water, air, and minerals—for much of its history but increasingly finds that environment deteriorating (land, water, air) or being used up (minerals). The situation is made worse by the booming population of the state. In addition, Texas is a place where nature is often hostile—tornadoes, flash floods, droughts, wildfires, hurricanes, even occasional earthquakes confront its citizens, not to mention rattlesnakes, killer bees, and fire ants. Moreover, Texans, as the proud inheritors of a frontier past, remain unclear on whether to nurture the environment or conquer it.

Furthermore, the national government has required a cleanup of the environment. Texas, like other states, is finding environmental cleanliness to be another one of those well-intentioned but costly federal programs. Three key pieces of national legislation are the Safe Drinking Water Act of 1974, the Clean Water Act of 1977, and the Clean Air Act of 1990. These laws include standards that are expensive to implement. The federal government was not forthcoming with funding adequate to assist state and local governments in meeting the new criteria, although these laws are examples of the mandates discussed earlier in the chapter. The twenty-first century dawned with the state facing environmental issues that affect the priority probably dearest to state policymakers—economic expansion.

## IS THERE ANY WATER? IS IT SAFE TO DRINK?

Texas has three basic kinds of water problems: water quality, water supply, and water damage. All remain perennial contenders for the policy agenda.

Under average rain conditions, the rule of thumb is that for every twenty miles one moves westward in the state, average annual rainfall diminishes by an inch. Texas is a very wide state indeed, so by the time one reaches El Paso, the average rainfall is only eight inches a year, compared with fifty-five inches in the southeastern part of the state. Consequently, West Texas politicians have kept the issue of *water supply* in the forefront for thirty years. They made water a critical issue in seven legislative sessions between 1969 and 2001, and the state produced various schemes and plans for providing water and engaged in extensive water planning. Texans are very conscious of that old Wyoming saying that opens this chapter.

Drought plagued parts of the state in 1996, 1998–2000, 2003, and 2005–2006.[31] The drought of 1996 made water supply a focal point of the 1997 legislative session, even though 1997 proved to be an extraordinarily wet year, with severe spring floods. Lawmakers came prepared to deal with water, and they produced a comprehensive 220-page bill covering most aspects of water in the state. The exception was the 400 or so inadequate dams in the state. In 2001, the legislature placed on the ballot a constitutional amendment expanding the authority of the Texas Water Development Board and providing additional bonding authority for the TWDB to help build water projects. In 2002, the TWDB published *Water for Texas—2002*, a three-volume fifty-year plan for the development of water resources in the state. This plan was amended in 2006 to become the *2007 State Water Plan*.[32] In 2003, the legislature passed seven water conservation bills, the most notable being those that created an ongoing task force to monitor and make recommendations about water conservation in the state and that spelled out five- and ten-year requirements for water savings, including percentage reductions in the average daily water use per person. Two major water supply bills were passed in 2007. One bill focused on construction of new reservoirs; the locations are designated, but there is no assurance that the reservoirs will actually be built. The other bill stressed public awareness. A fundamental reality of the Texas water supply is that Caddo Lake on the Louisiana border is the only natural lake in the state. This forcing of the state into a constant building program to create reservoirs to hold rain runoff validates the chapter-opening quote about a fair share of water. As the state becomes more densely populated, resentment grows, especially from water-rich East Texans who are tired of their land being gobbled up and turned into giant reservoirs to serve areas farther west.

## *Wild Fires and Flash Floods*

Oene of the chapter-opening photographs shows a wildfire of the type that gutted small Texas towns such as Cross Roads and Ringgold, while the other shows low-lying Houston suffering from the ravages of the periodic flash floods that afflict the state. In late 2005 and early 2006, the severe drought led to extensive fires that resulted in both loss of life and property damage. On just two days in March 2006 eleven lives and 700,000 acres were lost to fires. At the same time, Texas leads the nation with almost a half-million properties insured against flood; Houston and Harris County lead the state. The year 2007 saw the adage "When it rains, it pours" holding true in Texas. Early summer rains did $27 million worth of damage to the small city of Gainesville (north of Denton) in one morning and deluged Marble Falls (near Austin) with nineteen inches of rain in twenty-four hours. Indeed, after the extreme drought of 2005–2006, 2007 was extremely wet. Texas's infamous thunderstorms and the deluges that come from them are the reason that Texas ranks far higher than any other state in the number of deaths from flash floods. More than half of flash flood deaths are vehicle related: People try to cross flooded roadways.

SOURCE: "Flood Damage and Fatality Statistics," *Flood Safety,* available at http://www.floodsafety.com/national/life/statistics.htm; David McLemore, "It's Just a Tinderbox," *Dallas Morning News,* March 14, 2006, 1A, 15A; Holly Yah, "Fire Victims Assess Losses," *Dallas Morning News,* January 3, 2006, 1A, 4A.

Another persistent issue is *water quality.* The oft-cited bottom line for water and for air quality in Texas is that, since 1988, Texas has ranked toward the top in the country in the millions of tons of toxic **pollutants** it spewed into the air, let seep into the ground, and dumped into the water. Everything from runoff of fertilizer used in agriculture to inadequate storm water control can cause water quality problems. A series of state agencies has overseen environmental quality. The most recent one to emerge is the Texas Commission on Environmental Quality (TCEQ) in 2002. TCEQ is the new name for the Texas Natural Resource Conservation Commission (TNRCC), which was created in 1993 as the result of a merger between the Texas Water Commission (TWC) and the Texas Air Control Board. TNRCC (called "ten-rack" or sometimes "trainwreck") was sometimes heavyhanded in the way it regulated Texas communities to force compliance with the standards of the Environmental Protection Agency, which administers the national policy. Consequently, in 2001, the legislature passed sunset legislation (see Chapter 9) requiring a name—and presumably an image—change.[33] One 2007 bill concerned the environmental health of the state's waterways. Taking the necessary steps to avoid toxic pollutants such as pesticides, heavy metals, and raw sewage is up to communities.

## IS THE AIR SAFE TO BREATHE?

The Texas Commission on Environmental Quality also sets standards and emission limits for the abatement and control of air pollution. This agency is responsible for state compliance with the national Clean Air Act, part of which

Barton Springs, a natural swimming hole, is almost hallowed water in Austin. It has been menaced by developers since the early 1990s. In 2003, the *Austin American-Statesman,* the city of Austin, and the state health department concluded that some clean-up was in order because the sediment at the bottom of the springs contained a carcinogen, though the three did not agree on the degree of danger in the Barton Springs mud.

*Courtesy of Ben Sargent.*

★ ★ ★ ★ ★ ★ ★ ★ ★ ★ ★ ★ ★ ★ ★ ★ ★ ★ ★ ★ ★ ★ ★ ★ ★ ★ ★

## In Case the Bluegills Are Blue

The media constantly report strange and dangerous items found in waterways, including everything from industrial chemicals to birth control pills. In 2004, a Baylor University scientist found concentrations of Prozac, a medicine used to treat clinical depression, in bluegills, a type of fish living in Dallas's Pecan Creek near a water treatment plant.

★ ★ ★ ★ ★ ★ ★ ★ ★ ★ ★ ★ ★ ★ ★ ★ ★ ★ ★ ★ ★ ★ ★ ★ ★ ★ ★

SOURCE: "Fish Pharm Redux," *Fly Rod & Reel*, March 2004, 14.

is moving the public to do its share for cleaner air, as the chapter-opening quotation says. The national legislation, originally passed in December 1990 and modified in 1996, regulates emissions that cause acid rain and affect the quality of air in metropolitan areas, and also controls the release of toxic pollutants into the air. Much work must be done to clean up the state's air, particularly in major metropolitan areas, where motor vehicles emit a large volume of toxic gases, and in areas where the petrochemical industry operates. The basic standards for clean air are set by the U.S. Environmental Protection Agency (EPA).

Although in 2002 EPA lessened the stringent requirements it adopted in 1997,[34] Texas still had 12 million residents living in smog, and the numbers were growing. As of 2007, Texas "nonattainment areas" (areas that do not meet federal air quality standards because of excessive amounts of carbon monoxide, particulate matter, and/or ozone) are Houston–Galveston–Brazoria, Dallas–Fort Worth, Beaumont–Port Arthur, San Antonio, and El Paso. Austin–San Marcos and Northeast Texas are on the edge because of high ozone content.[35] In June 2007 the U.S. Department of Energy announced that Texas not only ranked No. 1 in harmful gases but also spewed out more harmful pollutants than the next two biggest offenders, Calfiornia and Pennsylvania, combined.[36]

Texas, like everywhere else in the world, faces the various effects of global climate change, holes in the ozone layer, and the "greenhouse" effect in general. (The *greenhouse effect* is the buildup of gases that retain heat reflected from the earth's surface; this heat retention then causes climatic changes.) Moreover, densely populated states and states with large amounts of square miles dependent on cars and trucks—such as Texas and California—continue to see their urban areas listed as having dirty air. The state has faced the vehicle pollution problem even more intensely since 2004, after the U.S. Supreme Court removed the last barrier against Mexican trucks freely using U.S. roadways.[37] Environmentalists have long had serious reservations about these trucks because of the lower environmental standards held by the government of Mexico and because the average age of a Mexican truck is sixteen years.

Also, Texas is a high-population and highly industrialized state and needs electric power, but like the other states, power plants are a frequent source of air pollution. Considerable time was spent in the 2007 regular legislative sessions debating whether tighter regulations on power companies, especially TXU, were needed, but in the end, only two minor air quality bills were passed.

Meanwhile, TXU, while "threatening" to build eleven new coal-fired plants, agreed to build only three after being bought out by a "greener" holding company. Soon after the session ended, TXU announced the possibility of going national, thus avoiding Texas's efforts to re-regulate electric power to the extent of trying to tell TXU what kind of generating plants to build. The state is caught in the proverbial "no win" situation with regard to power plants because Texas is facing a power shortage, and coal plants[38] are faster and cheaper to build than nuclear plants. Texas has only two nuclear power plants on line—Comanche Peak south of Dallas and South Texas near Houston—though national power companies in 2007 expressed an interest in building as many as six more.[39]

Although the EPA sets standards, the national government has not wanted to be a major player in the clean-up effort, leaving that chore to the states.[40] In December 1999, TNRCC published prospective air quality regulations in the *Texas Register*. These regulations stressed industrial clean-ups, a move toward California standards of motor vehicles' anti-pollution devices, and even restrictions on the times of day when heavy construction equipment could be operated. In 2001 the legislature closed a loophole that allowed older industrial plants to pollute, passed but did not fund the Texas Emissions Reductions Plan, and generally was more environmentally conscious than its immediate predecessors. By 2003 funding the emissions program was critical because the nonattainment areas faced federal sanctions in 2005 that could severely limit industrial growth and highway construction. Very late in the regular session, the Seventy-eighth Legislature funded the emissions abatement plan with revenue that would come from an increase in the vehicle title transfer fee that Texans pay when they buy a car or truck. However, the legislation passed in 2005 was limited to administrative matters. The Eightieth Legislature in 2007 only passed an extension of the assistance program for low-income people to repair vehicles that do not meet emission standards and a statute strengthening permitting for construction of any source producing air emissions.

A few days after the close of the 2007 session, the TCEQ approved a plan for smog reduction in the DFW area to meet a 2009 EPA target, but EPA officials were already muttering some doubts about the rigor of the plan.[41] EPA repeatedly has warned the most seriously polluted areas—Dallas–Fort Worth and Houston–Galveston–Brazoria—that they have only until 2010 to "clean up their act," lest they face such draconian measures as limited hours of construction, limits on new industries, and even the closing of drive-through windows at restaurants.

## THE LAND: IS IT SAFE TO WALK HERE? IS THERE ROOM?

Where does one put solid waste, whether that waste is toxic chemicals, radioactive byproducts, or just simply the paper, plastic, bottles, and cans that are the residue of everyday living? Four possible solutions are recycling, composting, incineration, and landfill disposal. In Texas, landfills are by far the most common solution because they are the cheapest. Consequently, the municipalities of the state are facing major problems with their landfills, both because of the amount of land needed to dispose of wastes—and the resistance of citizens to having a landfill in their part of town—and the need to meet stringent federal regulations first adopted in 1991 pertaining to such matters as methane gas, which is a landfill byproduct, and control of toxic substances that might be leeched into the soil.

The federal regulations evolved from the Resource Conservation and Recovery Act. The TCEQ has jurisdiction over solid waste disposal in the state.

One of the reasons the state has such a problem with wastes is that Texas has so many "dirty" industries. For example, Texas is a major producer of petrochemical products such as fertilizers, paints, and motor fuels, all of which have hazardous byproducts. It is a big mining state, with the slag from mineral production a danger in itself. These same industries intensify the water pollution problem because of the runoff of toxic materials into the storm water drains and waterways of the state. As the discussion about the economy in Chapter Thirteen indicated, Texas has also become a high-technology state, and one of the worst pollution programs for landfills comes from electronic waste.[42]

★ ★ ★ ★ ★ ★ ★ ★ ★ ★ ★ ★ ★ ★ ★ ★ ★ ★ ★ ★ ★ ★ ★ ★ ★ ★ ★ ★

## Going Green

Two municipalities that operate municipal power programs have encouraged "going green." Austin is providing substantial rebates for residents who install a solar energy system. Denton provides a "green sense" option to electric customers, who can choose to be supplied only by renewable energy sources such as solar, wind, geothermal, and water.

★ ★ ★ ★ ★ ★ ★ ★ ★ ★ ★ ★ ★ ★ ★ ★ ★ ★ ★ ★ ★ ★ ★ ★ ★ ★ ★ ★

SOURCES: Erik Rodriguez, "Council OKs Solar Rebates," *Austin American-Statesman*, May 28, 2004, B1, B5; "Green Sense," on the Web site of Denton Municipal Electric, available at http://www.dmepower.com/GreenSense.cfm.

A special problem is that in dealing with radioactive materials such as those from power plants, medical facilities, and defense plants, the state must be concerned with disposal of its own radioactive materials. The national government periodically has looked to the state as a potential national storage site for radioactive wastes. Texas for years tried to deal with this problem in isolation, ignoring other states, but burying one's head in the sand doesn't work when an eighteen-wheeler carrying nuclear waste is speeding along a Texas highway. Lobbyists tried to gain passage of bills in four sessions of the legislature beginning in 1995 to open the state to private companies in the nuclear waste disposal business. They were finally successful in 2003, when the legislature created two privately run, state-licensed disposal facilities,[43] one to handle wastes generated by states participating in an interstate compact agreement and one to handle federal wastes. One state senator protested, "This makes Texas the dumping ground of the United States and the world."[44] People in Nevada might disagree, with Congress in 2002 choosing Nevada's Yucca Mountain as the official disposal site for high-level waste from all the nation's nuclear reactors.

## ANALYSIS

Operating dirty industries and dirty municipal waste facilities is cheaper than operating clean ones, yet the real problem is not a venal unwillingness to protect the environment but, rather, the very high costs of doing so. Anyone who has watched the haze settle in over Houston or Dallas or Austin in the afternoon rush hour knows that there is a problem, as does anyone who has seen dead fish floating belly up in the state's rivers or read about the latest controversy of drilling for natural gas almost anywhere and everywhere. However, environmental policymaking often tends to produce diametrically opposed views and make compromise difficult. Interests from ranches to factories that lower their costs of production by polluting air and water resist government attempts to order them to clean up their operations, as do small business such as dry cleaners that often produce pollutants. And as explained in Chapter Three, because these polluting interests tend to be organized and well represented among Austin lobbyists, they can often put up a serious resistance to pro-environmental forces. Environmental policymaking is thus an issue well suited to illustrate the difficulties encountered by democracies in achieving the public interest. In Texas, the politics of special interests often dominate land, water, and air policy to the detriment of society as a whole. Thus, Texas state environmental policy often does not meet the test of democratic theory. It frequently is the embodiment of the state's traditionalistic-individualistic political culture and the antithesis of a moralistic political culture. The seriousness of lobby involvement in environmental regulation was made evident in the December 2003 audit of TCEQ, which criticized the agency's policies for being weak and ineffective against polluters. The governor (and the businesses that support him) was quick to defend the agency.[45]

★ ★ ★ ★ ★ ★ ★ ★ ★ ★ ★ ★ ★ ★ ★ ★ ★ ★ ★ ★ ★ ★ ★ ★ ★ ★ ★

## Willie and the Veggies

What do Willie Nelson, a private partnership in Galveston Bay now tied in with Chevron, and the City of Denton with its industry partner have in common? They are all producing biodiesel fuel. Agricultural products such as soybeans or used vegetable oil from restaurants are converted to fuel; the fuel is then blended with regular diesel fuel to make a much cleaner burning fuel. In Denton, for example, the entire fleet of solid waste vehicles as well as many of the local school district buses now run on biodiesel.[46]

Other local governments, even in small towns such as Feris and Stephenville, are converting waste, manure, and the like into methane gas. The gas in turn is then used to provide fuel for power plants.

★ ★ ★ ★ ★ ★ ★ ★ ★ ★ ★ ★ ★ ★ ★ ★ ★ ★ ★ ★ ★ ★ ★ ★ ★ ★ ★

Nevertheless, Texas is still spending considerable money on environmental matters—an apparent reflection of its size and the magnitude of its problems. The TCEQ budget alone for FY 2008–2009 is almost $900 million although it is less than the previous biennium. Local governments are also spending considerable money through their wastewater and solid waste operations.[47] In addition, there is positive evidence of cooperation among state officials, private interests, environmental organizations, and scientists in the matter of water policy. In 2004, a Study Commission on Water for Environmental Flows, a Scientific Advisory Committee, a Water Conservation Task Force, and a Select Committee on Water Policy were all at work addressing water supply and water quality,[48] and municipal utilities throughout the state were "taking on" polluters whether they were private industries or even the Army Corps of Engineers. The 2007 legislature followed through with modifications to the state's water plan that tentatively approved sites for new water reservoirs. However, the state's innate conservatism is unlikely to make Texas a model for environmental policymaking; change will come slowly.

# Highways and Byways

## THE SITUATION

As has been stated repeatedly throughout this book, Texas is a large state, both in land area and in population, and the number of people in the state continues to grow. As a big urban state, Texas needs jobs for its citizens, and it needs to be able to transport people and goods on its highways and roads. Those highways and roads were once a source of immense pride to Texans—smooth, wide roads traversing the terrain of Texas. Today, besides their general popularity, one reason trucks and sports utility vehicles dominate even city traffic may be the fear that a smaller vehicle could disappear into the chuckholes that mar federal and state highways as well as local streets. Four basic issues surround the highway system: (1) traffic flow—that is, being able to get from point A to point B in a reasonable amount of time; (2) safety—that is, as much protection as possible from everything from faulty vehicles to drunk drivers; (3) environmental issues discussed in the previous section, including air pollution and floods; and (4) alternative modes of transportation, ranging from mass transit to using waterways, rail, and air instead of roads.

Altogether, Texas has more than 301,989 miles of highways, roads, and streets[49] and 48,720 bridges.[50] In any given year, 14–15 percent of the road miles and about 3 percent of the bridges are resurfaced or rebuilt. However, the Texas Department of Transportation (TX-DOT) can only respond to about 10 percent of the legitimate needs for roadway construction and repairs in the state. As examples of roadway shortcomings in Texas, the U.S. 59 and I-45 interchange and the 610 Loop at I-10 interchange in Houston both ranked in the top twenty for freeway congestion in the United States, and the Dallas–Fort Worth area ranked sixth nationally in the amount of time commuters sat in traffic. Overall, Houston ranked fifteenth and Dallas–Fort Worth ranked eighteenth in the nation in time spent in commuting.[51]

Nowhere is the plight of the state's highways and byways more evident than on Interstate 35 (I-35), which begins in Laredo and goes to Duluth, Minnesota—the state's North American Free Trade Alliance (NAFTA) highway. A ride on I-35, which is always under repair and often being expanded, too often includes stop–start traffic and bumpy pavement, particularly around the biggest cities along its path. A growing concern—and a spinoff of the state's being an entry point for NAFTA traffic—is the condition of the roadways in border areas.

Throughout the state, the general safety of truck traffic is an issue. It is often easy for truckers to avoid rules such as load weights and safety checks, and a quarter of the drivers involved in fatal crashes have been convicted of crimes. The *Dallas Morning News* cited statistics that 502 people died in truck accidents in 2005 and 9,807 were injured, while only 632 state highway patrol officers tried to enforce the rules with 344,000 trucks. Only California has more trucks than Texas, and no state has more border crossings.[52]

## ACTIONS AND ANALYSIS

Why have the state's highways (and bridges) become a problem rather than a matter of state pride? First, population growth has been accompanied by increased use of the roadways. Second, the erratic Texas weather—drought and flood, warm winters followed by icy ones—takes a tremendous toll on highways, roads, and streets. Third, road construction once consumed 21 percent of the state's budget; now, only about 11 percent of the budget is dedicated to highways, roads, and bridges. Texas is forty-fourth among all states in its per capita expenditures for highways, having chosen to spend more of its funds on other programs. Fourth, although the motor fuels taxes at both the national and state level were hiked in 1983 and 1984, respectively, highway funding is insufficient to meet needs, especially in a fast-growing state.

One problem is that the federal government chose to put the national highway trust fund "on budget." That term means that monies in the trust fund can be used for general expenditures, and the increase in federal funds for highways and bridges has been far less than anticipated. Beginning in 1998, governors of the fifty states began to pressure Congress for better highway funding, and highway allocations have improved in the twenty-first century via the Transportation Equity Act for the 21st Century (TEA-21) and particularly under the Highway Funding Restoration Act of 2003, which gave Texas almost 300 million additional highway dollars. Still, Texas was receiving only 87 cents in highway funds for every dollar it contributed in federal gasoline sales taxes.[53]

The other major problem, of course, is that the state has struggled with its own budget. Demands for allocations exceed available revenue. The prevailing political philosophy opposes new taxes; thus, finding new sources of state dollars has been difficult. Roads and bridges, though, are popular with most segments of Texas society. Business and industry need them to transport goods and workers. Ordinary citizens want better and faster means to reach their destinations.

Consequently, Governor Rick Perry followed through on his promise to improve the transportation system in Texas. In 2002, Perry directed the Transportation Commission to develop a new highway plan. The commission produced an ambitious plan entailing 4,000 miles of new roads that would loop around major urban areas and divert traffic from existing roadways. The estimated costs were staggering, between $145 and $183 billion, with a timetable of as much as fifty years.[54] Traditional highway funding sources (federal funds, motor fuels tax, motor vehicle registration fee, and sales tax on vehicle lubricants) would not be sufficient to fund the system. Toll roads and private partnerships were recommended as alternatives, along with a heavy reliance on local entrepreneurship to produce "bids" offering local participation to entice state dollars. The idea was to find creative means to meet the state's growth-induced transportation needs.[55] Other states have taken a similar approach.[56] Environmentalists, farmers and ranchers, and municipal officials (who thought the plan would not help city traffic) voiced opposition to the plan. Implementation of the first stages of the plan was announced in May 2004 when TX-DOT revealed a $9 billion plan to maintain the transportation system. The 2007 legislative session included vigorous debate over whether to defer implementation of toll roads as a means of financing new highways. (There was a two-year deferral except for Highway 121 in the Dallas–Fort Worth area, for which bids had been solicited.) The debate followed in the wake of controversies over awarding toll road contracts to foreign venders and over the proposed Trans-Texas Corridor that would parallel Interstate 35 but require the acquisition of private homes, farms, and ranches. Complicating the picture was the rigidity of Transportation Commission Chair Ric Williamson, a highly knowledgeable and very powerful ally of the governor.[57]

Texas highway expenditures have been capped as a percentage of the budget since 1977. Combined with the federal policy of diverting highway trust funds to cover other programs, this cap means that the Texas Department of Transportation can fund only a fraction of the projects that TX-DOT itself has evaluated as worthwhile. Officials of general-purpose local governments—cities and counties—talk more about roads than anything else, recognizing that clogged traffic arteries mean an inability to attract new industry, ineffective movement of people to their places of work and play, and, because of the greater air pollution created by cars idling in traffic, more difficulty in meeting air quality standards. Recent policy developments in the early years of the twenty-first century promise to improve the situation, but road development and maintenance are slow processes. No "overnight" cures exist for transportation problems.

Motor vehicles traveling on highways and roads obviously are not the only way of getting from place to place. Texas has other transportation issues, too. While the largest cities have done well under airline deregulation, smaller communities had their air service reduced or terminated. The state tried to encourage a high-speed rail system and authorized private development in 1989, but the

Family farmers and small-town residents throughout the central part of the state protested plans for the Trans-Texas Corridor, a new superhighway paralleling Interstate 35, that would gobble up agricultural property and family homes in its wake. The TTC was also controversial because the first contracts awarded were to foreign firms.

*Courtesy of Ben Sargent.*

company could not develop the line without public support. Meanwhile, passenger trains serving Texas have not been particularly successful. The state lacks sufficient navigable waterways to consider watercraft as a transportation alternative. The development of mass transit systems, whether bus or light rail, has been slowed in the major cities both by local political squabbles and a lack of the federal funding that once supported mass transit.

Texas must find a way to meet its transportation needs, both to keep its formidable economic engine running smoothly and to meet its obligations to clean up the air. The state has yet to find the right combination, although better highway funding is a beginning.

# Conclusions

The state has shown stinginess in trying to mitigate poverty, a cavalier approach toward the environment, and even an inconsistent policy toward business, fostering big business but not always considering smaller businesses or the importance of infrastructure such as highways. In each of the issues examined in this chapter, powerful interests dominate the outcome, and the average citizen's perspective is not always considered. When judged by standards of democratic theory, Texas often falters. However, there are signs of improvement—creating a consolidated environmental agency with real clout, for example—and public policy can only be improved by the further democratization of the state. Moreover, solutions to major state problems are often compounded and confounded by the inter- and intragovernmental nature of public policy.

The resolution of each issue is important to the future of Texas, and each is linked not only to the others discussed here but also to other significant issues that are not outlined in this chapter. Without addressing the considerable poverty of the state, Texas may find it difficult to resolve other policy issues such as economic diversification and sound public education. But without economic growth and the infrastructure to support it, finding jobs for those with limited skills will be impossible. Moreover, abject poverty tends to foster crime. Education has long been seen as the key to the proverbial better future. However, Texas has allowed its higher education system to lag behind that of the nation as a whole, and its economic future depends on catching up. Everyone needs clean water, air, and land, and environmental quality also is tied to the need for economic diversity to avoid further expansion of high-pollution industries. None of these issues is new. All are costly to deal with—so much so that solving one problem may worsen another. Many hold the possibility of legal action by individuals favoring or opposing a particular course of action.

## Summary

Texas policymakers have dealt with all the issues described in this chapter to some extent, but problems remain on the public policy agenda.

1. The Texas economy regularly cycles through the highs of booms and the lows of busts. The revenue implications of these cycles were discussed in the previous chapter. This chapter has indicated that such shifts result in varying periods of attention on business development. The legacy of the traditionalistic-

individualistic political culture is a tendency to try to fulfill the wishes of the business community even if state services go unfunded.

2. The transformation of the welfare system into workfare is a national priority with which Texans can agree. However, the change in philosophy and the reduction in federal social spending are both boon and bane to Texas. Texas will have greater flexibility in making decisions on what programs to offer its neediest citizens. It will not enjoy having to spend more state money to pay for those programs. In addition, the state probably will continue to have one of the highest proportions of poor people in the country for the foreseeable future and will also continue to use cuts in social programs as a way to balance the budget in lean financial times.

3. Texas has always been proud of its resources, but it has materially damaged those resources. Now the state must find an integrated, comprehensive approach to environmental quality. It keeps trying to find a workable solution and has emphasized clean industry in its economic development efforts. Since 1997, the state has taken a comprehensive approach to water management, both quality and supply. It mainly follows the federal lead with regard to land use. It postponed dealing with clean air standards until the proverbial eleventh hour and still has a long way to go to meet federal standards.

4. Texas, both by itself and in concert with other states, must find a solution to the problems with its highways, roads, and bridges. Transportation is an element not only in economic development but also in air quality and even in education, with regard to moving students from home to school and back again. Public transportation is a vital element in the transition from welfare to work because low-income workers often do not own automobiles.

The issues discussed in this chapter affect all citizens, albeit in different ways. They bring to mind the haves and have-nots of our society, disparities among ethnic groups, and even problems of mortgaging our children's future by failing to address current problems.

## Glossary Terms

| | |
|---|---|
| infrastructure | public policy |
| mandate | redistributive public policy |
| pollutants | workers' compensation |
| poverty threshold | |

## Study Questions

1. This book argues that Texas public policy has long been dominated by special interests. Do you agree or disagree with this notion? Why? What effect would domination by upper income groups have on state policy toward the poor? On state policy toward economic development? What effects do you think the conservative political culture has?

2. Put on your "creative thinking cap." What suggestions can you think of to address the childcare and child health problems associated with putting welfare mothers to work? Try to imagine solutions that will not require huge expenditures of public dollars.

3. Do you agree or disagree with the arguments made about highways and bridges in Texas? What has been your personal experience? Has that experience changed as you moved from home to campus? How?

4. How do you think Texas political conservatism has affected Texans' attitudes toward the environment? What evidence have you personally seen that reflects an attitude that the environment is something to conquer or subdue? What evidence have you seen that reflects an attitude that the environment is something to be treasured and preserved?

5. Try to get a sense of what it is like to be poor. Assume that you work full time and make $5.15 an hour in an unskilled job, or about $865 a month. You are the sole support for yourself and two young children. Assume that you also qualify for a combination of $435 a month in welfare benefits such as food stamps and CHIP. Now, make a budget for how you will spend the $1,300, including taxes, Social Security, housing, food, clothing, healthcare, and transportation. (Although many college students live on far less than this amount, you must also assume that you have no family help and no reservoir of resources.) What was the toughest thing about making the budget? What couldn't you do that you would like to have done?

6. Think back to what you have learned about the revenue system and revenue shortfalls in Texas. Given the revenue problems of the state, which of the issues discussed in this chapter—economic growth, poverty and welfare, the environment, and highways—would you address first? Should the state find new revenue sources to solve all the problems?

7. Consider any one of the four major issues discussed in this chapter. How well do you think democratic ideals such as participation, diversity, and concern for the general welfare are reflected in state policy?

8. How have other governments helped to shape the public policy agenda of Texas?

## Surfing the Web

Readers are urged to visit the companion site for this book:

**http://academic.cengage.com/polsci/Kraemer/TexasPolitics10e**

# The Future of Texas Politics

**1**

The past, as symbolized by a cattle drive, and the future, as symbolized by NASA's space shuttle, are both part of the Texas in which today's students must live.

The outstanding fact of history is that it is a succession of events that nobody anticipated before they occurred.

LUDWIG VON MISES, AUSTRIAN ECONOMIST, *THEORY AND HISTORY*, 1969

The future is Texas: If you want to see where America is heading, start by studying the Lone Star State.

HEADING ON AN ARTICLE IN THE BRITISH PUBLICATION *THE ECONOMIST*; REPRODUCED IN THE *AUSTIN AMERICAN-STATESMAN*, JANUARY 5, 2003

# Introduction

Most readers of this book are in their late teens or early twenties. Many, perhaps most, will spend the next half-century or so living in Texas. What will Texas and the Texas political system be like in the first half of the twenty-first century?

Any attempt to anticipate the next several decades of Texas politics requires great caution. As Ludwig von Mises points out, people do not have a good track record when it comes to forecasting the future. Nevertheless, it is possible to call attention to conditions and trends that are likely to be important in shaping the next few years of the state's history. Indeed, the attempt to foresee is important in itself. One of the purposes of knowledge is to help citizens anticipate and react intelligently to the changing world in which they live. And if the editors of *The Economist* are correct, understanding the present and future of Texas will help in understanding the present and future of the United States.

Prediction of the future can be based only on knowledge of the past and present. This final chapter summarizes the reality of the Texas political system as it currently exists and then suggests how some present historical trends might play themselves out during the coming years. Finally, it evaluates the extent to which Texas government measures up to the ideals of democracy now and is likely to measure up in the future.

# The Texas Political System

## POLITICAL CULTURE

Texas's history and the political culture that grew out of it are distinctive. Texas has a mystique unequaled by any of the other forty-nine states, born of the nature of the people who settled it, its size, and the fact that for over a decade it was an independent nation. It also has a unique political culture.

As discussed in the first chapter, the Texas political culture is a combination of the traditionalistic and individualistic strains. The traditionalistic culture, dominant in the southern history of Texas, deemphasized participation of all the citizens and emphasized domination of society by an Anglo elite. The individualistic culture, dominant in the business history of the state, emphasized allowing as many people as possible (again with an Anglo bias) to get rich by taming the land. In the twenty-first century, the blend of the two cultures has produced a system of political values that is pro-development, unsympathetic toward those who fail to achieve material success, and intensely conventional in regard to such subjects as religion and sexual behavior. Combined, the modern blend of traditionalistic and individualistic cultures produces a dominant Anglo population that is strongly conservative on both economic and social issues.

Because Mexican Americans and African Americans, despite having made major strides in overcoming the prejudices and discriminations of past decades, are still not fully participant in the state's politics, Texas government is still usually dominated by Anglo values. As a result, Texas political culture produces a voting population that dislikes and distrusts government. In general, Anglo Texans' main request of government has usually been that it keep taxes low. Consequently, the state's human services and economic regulatory programs pale beside those of the other large, populous states. Texas entrepreneurs have long worked successfully to minimize effective governmental regulation by influencing legislators and co-opting agencies. They also have succeeded in establishing a system of state taxation that is both low in rate and highly regressive. But they have never been above using government to protect and enhance their interests—for example, land grants of millions of acres to railroads or regulation of petroleum production to stabilize markets and protect state producers from competition. The result is a pseudo laissez faire economic culture. Dominant economic interests ask for government action when it is useful to them, and resist government action when it might be inconvenient, regardless of how helpful that action might be to poor and powerless Texans or the natural environment.

Akin to pseudo laissez faire is social Darwinism, the argument that those "at the top" deserve to be there, and those "at the bottom" deserve their place as well. Because the poorer classes turn out to vote at such low rates, Texas politicians usually see their chief constituency as those at the top. Thus, as the British observers in *The Economist* summarize, "This is a land of low taxes, weak labor unions, a shriveled public sector and a paltry welfare state."[1] There are individual exceptions to the *The Economist*'s summary, but its portrait of Texas politics as serving those at the upper end of the social scale rather than those at the lower end is accurate most of the time.

# THE INPUTS TO THE POLITICAL SYSTEM

The party system is one area in which prediction of the short-term future seems relatively unrisky. The state is clearly moving in the direction of having ideologically homogeneous parties, with a conservative Republican Party taking most elections from a liberal Democratic Party.

Texas provides a nearly ideal setting for the exercise of interest-group influence, and the state's political system, despite its increasing size and diversity, remains heavily influenced by the dominant economic interests. Interest-group power is facilitated by the state's traditionally low voter turnout, especially among Mexican Americans and African Americans. Interest-group influence is also enhanced by a system of privately funded campaigns and by the short legislative sessions coupled with small staffs who need help in drafting bills. Wealthy individuals and groups are able to use the state's interest-group and electoral systems to rent the loyalty of politicians so that private power often dominates public authority.

# THE CONSTITUTION

The Texans who wrote the Constitution of 1876 created a document that was so long, restrictive, complicated, and detailed that it permitted only a very inefficient and weak state government. The Texas Constitution not only disperses power and impedes development of effective government but makes it nearly impossible to determine who is responsible for developments when they occur. When Texas voters go to the polls on election day, they can never be certain whom to reward, whom to punish, or why. This lack of clear responsibility for public policy adds to the advantages that wealthy individuals and interest groups have in exercising influence behind the scenes.

Despite the inadequacies of the Texas document, however, constitutional reform is not a top priority. The many special-interest groups that benefit from the protections and opportunities afforded them by the current state constitution are in no hurry to see a new, streamlined document created. Moreover, ordinary citizens are skeptical about reform and fear that they might get something worse than what they have now. Thus, those who defend the status quo invariably have an advantage over those who try to bring about change.

# THE INSTITUTIONS OF GOVERNMENT

Texas government reflects the provisions of the state's constitution and the purpose of its authors. The legislature, meeting in regular session for only 140 days every two years, is marked by extremely low salaries, insufficient research and committee staff support, and intermittent high turnover. Under these conditions, legislators are almost compelled to follow the lead of the powerful presiding officers and their usual allies, the dominant economic interest groups. The governorship is deliberately hampered by the constitution, with many of its functions carved up and distributed to other elected executives. Beginning in 2003, the capture of both the legislature and the governor's mansion by a Republican majority served to quiet discord and make the task of running the state go more smoothly, at least for a while. By the 2007 legislative session, however, the governor was fighting various rebellions within his own party, which illustrates the structural weakness of his office. And the Republican ascendancy did not change the essential nature of a political system dominated by wealthy interest groups and a socially conservative electorate.

State administration consists of more than 200 agencies that have no common bond. Neither the governor nor the legislature is in command, and each agency seems to be responsive primarily to its own goals and clientele groups. Although a variety of reforms in the 1990s and 2000s have probably made administration more efficient, power relationships have not changed. Special interests still work with administrative agencies to continue business as usual, and demands for efficiency and budgetary responsibility must be vigorous and perpetual.

Until the defeat of many Democratic judges in the elections beginning in 1994, the judiciary had maintained a certain distance from the other institutions of government. That independence had allowed Texas judges to force policy improvements on the legislature, most notably in the area of school finance. It will be worth watching to see if the judiciary persists in its progressive path, given the new electoral reality. Whatever its party balance, responsiveness to the people's wishes, or courageous independence, however, the judicial system will not be able to rid itself of major problems. The poor will still be at a comparative disadvantage when they attempt to get justice, the system will still be choked by more criminals than it can process, and its organization will still be complex and confusing. Because of Governor George W. Bush's quest for the presidency, the campaign of 2000 brought a great deal of often critical national attention to the Texas judicial system. Texas's habit of executing prisoners who were convicted on patently frail or tainted evidence came in for much harsh comment. Yet the election came and went, and the system remained unchanged.

Local government in Texas is also consistent with the constitution and other state institutions. County government, reflecting the values of 1876, is ill conceived and poorly organized for a twenty-first century urban state. Municipal government, characterized by nonpartisan politics and increasingly by appointed professional staffs, sometimes leaves citizens in a quandary as to how to solve political conflicts. Moreover, the state has become less supportive of the cities in its policies. It has imposed more mandates and has cut into the cities' most important source of revenue by passing various sales-tax holidays. Even more importantly, state government has encroached on both the cities' authority and their revenue base by imposing its own rules on areas of governance that formerly belonged to the local areas (see the discussion of the 2005 telecommunications law in Chapter 3 for a good example).

In sum, the state government that functions under the Constitution of 1876 does not provide Texans with all they might hope for in the way of efficient and public-spirited management of their social problems.

# The Coming Challenges

Despite its imperfections, modern Texas government has functioned tolerably well in many areas. Texans have been able to build roads and bridges, educate a significant proportion of their children, lower the state's crime rate, and provide various kinds of services for themselves. If Texans seem reluctant to change their structure of government and habits of behavior, it may be because they believe that government always falls short of the ideal and that reform may only make things worse.

They may be right. However, a political system that has worked adequately for the past and present may not be sufficient for the future. As the twenty-first century progresses, Texans face a set of challenges that will greatly test their capacity to respond. They have to ask themselves if the political culture and institutions that are good enough now will be good enough in the future.

# THE ECONOMY

Economically, Texas has historically been a lucky state. For most of the twentieth century, both its citizens and its government were able to live off the petroleum that nature stored under the surface of the land. The oil and gas are not gone, and they will play an important role in the state's economy for decades to come. But they no longer dominate the Texas economy and government as they once did. Once contributing at least a third of state government's total revenue, by 2007 petroleum's share was under 3 percent.[2] Ironically, as the state's reliance on natural resources taxes has diminished, local governments in many areas of the state have been growing more dependent on the royalties provided by gas drilling. Nevertheless, as a whole, Texas government now relies on a diversified economy rather than on the extraction of oil and gas. By the 2007 legislature, these new industries were providing a firm foundation for state government. The state's lawmakers were presented with the agreeable task of writing a budget amid a state surplus that had reached several billion dollars, and seemed to grow with each new estimate.

★ ★ ★ ★ ★ ★ ★ ★ ★ ★ ★ ★ ★ ★ ★ ★ ★ ★ ★ ★ ★ ★ ★ ★ ★ ★ ★ ★ ★ ★

## *Too Much and Not Enough*

One of the ironies of hunger in the twenty-first century was that it often seemed to coexist with overeating. Thus, although Texas, when measured against the situation in the other forty-nine states, contained an unusually high percentage of poor people at risk for hunger, it also scored near the top on a scale of the fattest populations. More than a quarter of its residents were obese, placing it tenth on the scale of plumpness, according to a report by the Trust for America's Health. Most of the most obese states, like Texas, were in the southern part of the nation, with Mississippi earning the unenviable distinction of containing the highest percentage of citizens who had succumbed to what one journalist termed our collective "porkiness plague."

★ ★ ★ ★ ★ ★ ★ ★ ★ ★ ★ ★ ★ ★ ★ ★ ★ ★ ★ ★ ★ ★ ★ ★ ★ ★ ★ ★ ★ ★

SOURCE: Bob Dart, "What We Weigh Down South in Dixie Has Us Topping the Nation's Chunky Chart," *Austin American-Statesman*, August 30, 2006, A11.

Despite the fact that the state's economy had escaped its dependence on oil and gas, however, by the middle 2000s it still had a long way to go to pull many Texans out of dire straits. The poverty rate was 17.6 percent in 2005, fifth highest of the fifty United States.[3] Almost one Texas child in four lived in poverty.[4] Texas ranked first among the states in the percentage of its population "at risk for hunger."[5]

Although the future of any economy is one of the most difficult things to predict, if Texans are to continue to progress they must try to anticipate and plan for the employment situation that their children will face. In 1992, Robert Reich, a Harvard economist and later President Clinton's secretary of labor, published *The Work of Nations*, a useful look into the future of the workforce, which has become highly influential.[6] Reich argued that the increasing globalization of every nation's economy is tending to stratify national workforces into three classes of workers.

The members of Class One, suggests Reich, do the repetitive, simple tasks needed to manufacture products—assembling toasters, for example—that are increasingly sold on the international market. Because almost anyone can do these tasks, and because it is now easy to ship products long distances cheaply, the workers in one country are nearly interchangeable with those in another. If a corporation is dissatisfied with workers in the United States—because they join a union, for example—it can ship their jobs to Mexico; if Mexicans are not satisfactory, it can move the jobs to Singapore, and so on. The ability of employers to manufacture anywhere tends to depress the wages of workers everywhere to the lowest possible level. In other words, Class One workers in the United States can in the future expect to earn no more than similar workers in Third World countries, if they have jobs at all.

Class Two jobs consist of the provision of services that are also relatively simple and easy but that require the provider to be in the physical presence of the consumer. Examples would be counter servers in fast-food restaurants, temporary workers, taxi drivers, childcare providers, secretaries, retail clerks, and security guards. Although these jobs cannot be sent overseas, there are very many people who want them and are able to do them. Class Two workers therefore have relatively little market power and thus receive low wages and few benefits. According to Reich, an increasingly large number of Americans are employed in Class Two jobs. This scenario is disturbing because many Class Two workers will be without health insurance or retirement benefits.

Reich argues that Class Three workers will be the winners in the economy of the future. These are highly educated "symbolic analysts" who have technical skills that the emerging "enterprise net" corporations will need. Examples of those workers who will be in demand are scientists, engineers, bankers, accountants, computer programmers, advertising executives, writers, and various kinds of consultants. These workers will have high incomes, adequate benefits, and a fulfilling, comfortable lifestyle.

Reich's general framework does not take into account swings in the business cycle, as the thousands of unemployed Texas engineers and computer programmers during the mid-2000s would have attested. Nevertheless, over the long run, Reich's prediction that the higher the percentage of the American workforce that is employed in Class Three jobs, the better off the country will be, is surely accurate.

As a consequence, the number of Americans—and Texans—prepared to take their place in the new economy will depend on their educational level. Independent research has often reinforced Reich's point that the key to a prosperous population in a vibrant economy is education. It is not that there will be no demand for workers of limited skills in a service economy. Much of the job growth in recent years has been among Class Two workers, who only need health and motivation, not high education, to find employment. But the jobs that are thus created are frequently below the customary standard of wages and benefits. In the country as a whole in 2000, for example, the average income for a household in which the main breadwinner had a high school education was $45,368. The average income for a household in which the main breadwinner was a college graduate was $84,029.[7] Education is the foundation of prosperity for the individual and for society.

Therefore, the major means of creating a prosperous Texas in the twenty-first century will have to be building a first-rate state educational system. At present, it seems clear that some Texans are getting the right training, but there is legitimate doubt that the state is doing all it can to maximize the number of its citizens who will be Class Three workers in the future (see Chapter 14). For example, a 2006 study based on data from the 2002–2003 school year concluded that Texas ranked 35th among the states in the percentage of high school students who graduated in four years.[8] One-third of high school students in the Lone Star State fail to graduate with their class. Most of those are doomed to live their work lives in Reich's Classes One or Two.

Even if Texas manages to improve its educational system enough to prepare an optimal percentage of its workers for the years ahead, there will still be a significant number left behind. Reich argues on humanitarian grounds that national and state governments will have to provide social services—health insurance, for example—to Class One and Two workers to prevent their falling into wretchedness and despair. As of 2007, Texas was not doing all it could to meet the social challenges of the new century. The structure of state government, the low voter turnout by poor citizens, and the dominance of conservative political values all conspired to prevent Texas from doing much to improve the lives of its less wealthy residents. The future does not look bright for those who lack the skills and savvy to advance in a pseudo laissez faire economy and a conservative political culture.

One possibility for Texas society over the next several decades, then, is a growing disparity between the income levels of those at the top and bottom of the social scale. A substantial number of Texans will have access to all the comforts and toys of the future economy, but a considerable, and perhaps growing, portion of the population will sink further into poverty and hopelessness. If the present distribution of wealth and education remains unchanged, another result would be that most of those on the top of the pyramid would be Anglo, and most of those on the bottom would be Latino and Black. It is by no means certain that such ethnic stratification will intensify, because there has been a surge of minority citizens into the middle classes in recent years. Whether or not the present ethnic divisions increase, however, there is a clear trend toward widening economic inequality. Moreover, not only the economy, but also the population of Texas is evolving. Changes in what scientists call the **demographics** of the Lone Star State have the potential to make as big an impact on its future as anything that could happen to its economy.

## POPULATION

In late 1994, Texas passed New York and became the second most populous state, with more than 19.5 million residents. By 2000, it had added another million people, and by July 2006, three million more.[9] The news that Texas was growing rapidly would not have surprised its citizens, who had become used to new subdivisions and shopping malls springing up around every city and former suburbs seeming to mutate into metropolises. A prediction that even von Mises would have to endorse is that the Texas population will continue to increase.

A team of demographers at Texas A&M University has projected various consequences for the state's society if present population trends continue. The "if" clause in the previous sentence is important. No one knows now if the future

Demonstrators gather in downtown Dallas on Sunday, April 9, 2006, in support of immigration reform laws.

will be approximately like the present or, if not, in what ways it will differ. No one knows, for example, if the stream of poor, uneducated Mexican migrants into Texas, many of them "undocumented," will continue at present rates. When demographers paint a statistical picture of the future, they must always keep their fingers crossed, hoping that their assumptions are more or less correct. Furthermore, putting people into the traditional demographic categories of Anglo, Black, and Hispanic becomes more difficult all the time as an ever-increasing percentage of the population falls either between or outside those categories. Nevertheless, smoothing over some of the difficulties with statistics and definitions allows demographers to project alternative futures so that professors and students can talk about them.

If, then, we assume that demographers' calculations and definitions are about right, we can examine their findings and consider their implications. The Texas A&M estimate, based on the assumption that the state's population—including its injection of illegal immigrants—will continue to expand at recent rates, projects that Texas may have a population of more than 32 million by the year 2020.[10] Perhaps developers and construction workers view this prospect with delight, but the rest of the state's residents may feel more like the passengers on the hurtling bus in the motion picture *Speed,* unable to stop as the vehicle rushes toward destruction. The state is already wrestling with many problems caused by an expanding population. As more people move to Texas and are born here, the problems will get worse.

For example, in 1999, median household income for Texas Anglos was about $47,000, and for both Blacks and Hispanics it was slightly above $29,000.[11] Although minority income actually grew *faster* during the 1990s than Anglo income, the disparity was still considerable at the end of the decade. Minorities differ in other ways from Anglos. As groups, they are younger, less well educated, less likely to have jobs, more likely to be on welfare (TANF), and more likely to be in prison.[12] If demographic trends continue unaltered, then Texas as a whole will become poorer (that is, the average income will fall) and less educated (the average number of years of schooling completed will fall), and the state will be required to supply more government services such as welfare, schooling, and unfortunately, prisons. It goes without saying that the state government is not preparing itself for such imminent future challenges.

Demographic trends promise other political problems, also. Because both the Anglo and Black populations are growing much more slowly than the Hispanic population, they are also aging. In the next several decades, Texas will become a state with, on average, relatively old Anglos and Blacks and relatively young Hispanics. Among other implications, this means that there will be a quickly growing demand for health services. The Texas A&M study concludes that by 2040 the state will have to add 276,840 healthcare professionals, an increase of 142.6 percent.[13]

Whether the exact trends anticipated by demographers are the ones that come to fruition, the population is certain to grow. Other states—California is the model here—have demonstrated what happens to quality of life when population mushrooms. Pollution, for one, is a problem that becomes worse with increasing population. The state's efforts to deal with environmental problems—especially the controversy over the proposals by an electric utility to build more coal-fired generating plants—have already been discussed in Chapter Fourteen. But it will be worthwhile to glance over the issue again within the context of Texas's ever-rising number of inhabitants.

As each Texas family buys an automobile, and then perhaps a second car, and as ever more families want transportation, the noxious stuff that comes out of tailpipes builds to intolerable levels. One group of scholars has calculated that, under moderate assumptions of population growth, by 2020 each Lone Star motorist will have to reduce his or her driving by 37.5 percent to avoid worsening the already unclean air of the state's cities.[14]

Given Texas's traditional love affair with driving—often, of course, in a pickup truck rather than a car—and given the state government's lackadaisical attitude toward pollution, it is unlikely that much will be done to keep Texas's air breathable. In 1999, Houston passed a dubious milestone by overtaking Los Angeles as the American city with the most polluted air.[15] Not coincidentally, according to a 2001 study, Houston was home to the fourth most clogged roadways in the country in terms of hours lost in traffic jams, ranking behind Los Angeles, Atlanta, and Seattle. (Dallas was tied for fifth, Austin was seventh; Fort Worth, San Antonio, and El Paso were relatively jam-free.)[16] In 2004, Houston unveiled its solution to smoggy air and gridlocked streets: a seven-and-one-half mile "light rail" train that runs through the downtown area. City leaders hailed the new form of public transportation as the beginning of the city's rebound into healthful breathing and hassle-free commuting. Their optimism seems to have been justified, for by 2007 Houston had dropped to fifth in the ranking of metropolitan areas with the worst ozone pollution (Los Angeles was again first; the Dallas–Fort Worth area was tenth).[17] Eventually, if it develops as planned, by

Automobiles have always symbolized personal freedom to Americans in general and Texans in particular. When they become too numerous and concentrated, however, they stop being the servants of human beings and become their masters. When that happens, they can become symbols of servitude rather than of freedom.

*Courtesy of Ben Sargent.*

2019 the light rail system will run for forty-seven miles and, incidentally, cost $8 billion.[18]

The wildly different rates of growth in the Anglo, African American, and Hispanic communities, besides their consequences for the Texas economy and environment, can be expected to make a significant impact politically. According to the U.S. Census, in 2005 the percentage of Anglos in the Texas population dropped to 49.8 percent, making the state's traditional majority population an actual minority, although they were still the largest minority. If present immigration and birth/death trends continue, however, Hispanics will almost certainly be a majority of the Texas population by 2040.[19]

An increasingly Hispanic and decreasingly Anglo Texas is certain to experience major cultural dislocation. Mexican Americans are different from the traditional southern Anglo citizen of Texas in several ways. Whereas most Anglo Texans are Protestant, Mexican Americans are largely Roman Catholic. Whereas most Anglos speak only English, most Mexican Americans are bilingual; a significant minority speak only Spanish. Whereas the great majority of Anglos identify themselves only as citizens of the United States, an important proportion of Mexican Americans—especially, of course, immigrants—retain at least some loyalty to Mexico.

These differences have produced a great deal of cultural friction in the past and will probably continue to do so in the future. Cultural differences inevitably translate into political conflict. Given the Anglo population's customary conservatism, the relative poverty of the Mexican American population, and that population's growing size and more liberal political leanings (see Table 5-4 in Chapter 5), the future will most likely hold many clashes between Anglo and

## TABLE 15-1
## Projections of the Texas Population

| Estimate | Year | Anglo | Black | Hispanic | Other |
|---|---|---|---|---|---|
| | 2000 | 53.1% | 11.6% | 32.0% | 3.3% |
| Low | 2010 | 49.9 | 11.5 | 35.2 | 3.4 |
| High | 2010 | 45.2 | 11.1 | 39.2 | 4.5 |
| Low | 2020 | 47.0 | 11.3 | 38.3 | 3.4 |
| High | 2020 | 37.5 | 10.2 | 46.4 | 5.9 |

NOTE: Low refers to low projections of immigration from Mexico; high refers to high projections of immigration.

SOURCE: Steve H. Murdock, Steve White, Md. Nazrul Hoque, Beverly Pecotte, Xuihong You, and Jennifer Balkan, *The New Texas Challenge: Population Change and the Future of Texas* (College Station: Texas A&M, 2003), 27.

Mexican American political values. Indeed, Latino voters will probably present Texas's customary political conservatism with its strongest challenge in history.

African Americans are unlikely to be bystanders in this political struggle. Texas liberals have long dreamed of a "rainbow coalition" in which Anglo liberals, Mexican Americans, and African Americans would unite to seize power from the conservative Anglo establishment. Although this coalition has occasionally come together successfully—behind Ann Richards in 1990, for example—more often it has been defeated. It was defeated resoundingly in the 2002 elections, as Anglo conservative Republicans bested the carefully crafted Democratic ticket of a Mexican American candidate for governor, a Black candidate for U.S. Senate, and an Anglo candidate for lieutenant governor.

But the Democrats can be expected to continue to try to entice minorities to polls with rainbow candidates. Sooner or later, this strategy is likely to be successful. As the minority population expands, the prospects for rainbow victory will improve. The prospects for this grouping's dominating Texas politics are uncertain, but they improve every year into the future.

Texas politics is thus potentially far more open and complicated than it has often seemed in the past. The right political leader, arguing the right set of issues, could change the complexion of the state's public policy debates and scramble its customary voter coalitions. And the emergence of strong, imaginative leaders is an occurrence no political scientist has been able to predict.

# URBAN TEXAS

In the course of the twentieth century, Texas evolved from one of the most rural states to one of the most urban. While many rural attitudes still prevail, Texans live in cities, and more and more will face the realities of urban existence. The rapid growth of the state primarily means the rapid growth of the cities. In the 1990s, Austin, Laredo, and McAllen were all among the ten fastest growing metropolitan areas in the country. In 2006 the Census reported that thirteen of the nation's fastest-growing counties were in Texas.[20] Predictions are that at some point in the mid decades of the twenty-first century, some 10 million Texans will inhabit a continuous urban strip along Interstate 35 from a point north of Dallas–Fort Worth southward through Waco, Temple, Austin, San Marcos, and New Braunfels to a point well south of San Antonio. A few years later, this megalopolis will extend farther south to Laredo and into Mexico. Another urban strip may extend from the Beaumont–Port Arthur–Orange area west through Houston to a point well beyond the western edge of San Antonio. Whether urban growth happens in precisely this way is unimportant. But it will happen.

What will life be like in urban Texas thirty or forty years from now? There are hints available from the older cities of the nation, particularly those of the northeast. Many have experienced decay of the central city and a declining tax base, a movement of those who can afford it to the suburbs, problems of congestion and pollution, crime, unemployment, inadequate healthcare, abuse of drugs, and gang warfare, to mention only the most obvious. Surely, this is a long way from the American—and Texas—dream of people owning their own land and living a semi-rural life, free, clean, and healthy. Yet it is the reality of life for many millions of Americans.

The traditional Texas attitude is that if government is kept small enough and taxes are low enough, then things will follow their beneficial natural course and all will be well. The cities of the northeast, however, suggest that more thought and planning are needed to preserve urban livability. Will Texans learn from the mistakes of others and prepare for the problems of urbanization?

The answer to that question cannot be found in this book. But this survey of Texas society and politics should suggest that Texans must think hard about the future of their cities and what can be done now to change the course of their development.

# Preventing the Worst of All Possible Futures

The first eight editions of this book contained no mention of terrorism. In this lack of foresight the authors were no more inadequate than other scholars, journalists, and politicians. The terror attacks of September 11, 2001, were graphic illustrations of Ludwig von Mises's cautions about human inability to see around the next historical corner.

As with citizens in other parts of the nation, the new reality of terrorism has forced Texans to adapt, maneuver, and invest resources in a manner that is sometimes creative and sometimes painful. In the post-9/11 years there were many examples of terrorism's relevance to the Texas polity.

1. In Washington in 2005, Texas's U.S. Senator John Cornyn united with senators from other large, industrial states such as California, New Jersey, New York, and Florida to sponsor a bill that would mandate that funding from the federal homeland security budget be spent on the basis of the threat of attack. Congress had been allocating homeland security money on the basis of the influence of the representative, doling out billions of dollars to rural areas that faced little risk, while underfunding the coastal urban areas that might actually be a target. Despite the reasonableness of their bill, it did not pass, and Texas, second in population among the states, was only fifth

in the amount of anti-terrorism money it received from the federal budget in 2006.[21]

2. In Austin in 2003, the legislature passed HB 9, directing the governor's office to establish a homeland defense strategy, centralizing communications and coordination efforts in his office, and defining homeland security for the state Government Code. The governor's office now maintains a Web site informing citizens about the "Homeland Security Advisory System," containing specific instructions about how to "remain vigilant and report suspicious activity" and "volunteer to help" and offering "additional resources for communities, schools, and businesses."[22]

   The new state office formulated its first "Homeland Security Strategic Plan" in 2004, and revised it in 2005. As revised, the plan calls for building a statewide intelligence capability, formulating a strategy for dealing with vulnerable groups of people during an emergency, and making sure that all law enforcement and first responders personnel have the technological capabilities (that is, the same types of radios operating on the same frequencies) to communicate with one another when the phone lines are down.[23]

3. In Lexington, Kentucky, in 2007, a private company was maintaining a massive database on Texans. Under the 2003 law discussed above, the state department of homeland security, headquartered in the governor's office, had constructed the Texas Data Exchange, an all-encompassing intelligence database designed to centralize information that might be useful to either catch criminals or identify potential terrorists, and awarded a contract to Appriss, Inc. of Lexington, to watch over it. The governor's office was therefore privy to all the information Texans provided the state when they applied for a driver's license, or a concealed-weapons permit, or a vehicle registration, or a voter registration. Department of homeland security director Steve McCraw justified the activity by saying that "What we are trying to build is an intelligence capability or intelligence-sharing capability" that would protect Texans from crime and terrorism. But civil libertarians were skeptical. "Criminal intelligence data should be in the hands of a professional law enforcement agency that has distance from the political pressures on elected officials," said Rebecca Berhhardt of the Texas American Civil Liberties Union. "How can we be sure that we will never have a governor who will misuse this power?"[24]

4. In Houston in 2003, city officials were embarrassed by a report in the *Chronicle* exposing slack security at its port and ship channel, areas that service 7,000 ships annually, are densely populated, and are home to several petrochemical plants. Prodded by a call from Texas Homeland Security Chief Jay Kimbrough, Harris County officials immediately moved to tighten surveillance and oversight.[25]

5. In College Station in 2006, Texas A&M University created three new degree programs for students wishing to specialize in the terrorist threat—a bachelor's degree in forensic science and a master's and doctorate in homeland security. David McIntyre, director of A&M's Integrative Center for Homeland Security, announced that "We will make a robust effort to coordinate the curriculum with existing elements of the [federal] Department of Homeland Security, the Department of Defense and state and local agencies nationwide," adding that "the deans have made it clear

## YOU DECIDE

### Is Terrorism Different?

The prospect of facing an invasion, not of uniformed soldiers employing conventional weapons, but of people in street dress willing to commit suicide while using highjacked airplanes, fertilizer bombs in panel trucks, biological and chemical agents, or in the worst scenario, a nuclear device, has presented a challenge to American democracy. Can America, and Texas, continue to permit freedom of movement, freedom of information flow, and freedom from government observation when the potential costs of another terrorist attack could be catastrophic? Should Texans be willing to tolerate severe restrictions on their customary personal liberty in return for increased security?

| PRO | CON |
|---|---|
| ▲ Terrorism poses an unprecedented threat to public safety. It requires a dramatic rethinking of our tradition of personal freedom. | ▼ No doubt some changes will have to be made, as at airports. But the United States has faced severe crises before—the Civil War comes to mind—without sacrificing most democratic freedoms. |
| ▲ The possibility of infiltration by murderous zealots is a threat that demands constant surveillance of movements, activities, and searches for information within the population. | ▼ The same argument was made during the anti-Communist hysteria of the 1940s and 1950s. The United States managed to weather that threat without jettisoning its democratic liberties. |
| ▲ Those who object to government efforts to make the country and the state safer are consciously or unconsciously aiding the terrorists. | ▼ Again, the same argument frequently cropped up in the 1940s. We are not made safer by public discourse that insults critics of government policy. |
| ▲ Government officials will be held accountable if there is another terrorist attack. Therefore, they must be given the tools to combat terrorism. | ▼ "Tools" are one thing; elimination of personal liberty is another. It is the responsibility of government to fight terror without destroying the nature of the society it is supposedly trying to protect. |

SOURCES: Edward S. Greenberg, "Will Things Ever Be the Same? The 'War on Terrorism' and the Transformation of American Government," 31–33 and Robert L. Lineberry, "Public Policy After September 11," 158–162, both in *American Government in a Changing World: The Effects of September 11, 2001* (New York: Longman, 2003); and numerous print and electronic media reports.

that they want a program that will meet the highest standards of academic quality." [26]

6. In the Metroplex in 2003, forty business and university organizations formed the Dallas–Fort Worth Homeland Security Alliance, a nonprofit col-

laboration to attempt to identify and fix security weaknesses. The alliance brings people from different professions together to study protection of the "critical infrastructure" of North Texas, including banking and finance, utilities, transportation, telecommunications, and the petroleum industry. The leaders of the new institution hoped to make the Metroplex one of the "centers of excellence in homeland security."[27]

7. In Austin in 2007, the state senate planned to install metal detectors on the rotunda of the institution's third-floor gallery and the hall at the main entrance. Signs were posted warning visitors not to enter the gallery with weapons. The change was motivated by a letter from Senator Kim Brimer, chair of the Senate Administration Committee, after a meeting with the State Preservation Board, consisting of the governor, speaker of the House, lieutenant governor, Brimer, and others. Brimer's letter stated that the committee "feels that this is the appropriate time to consider Capitol security in light of the current world situation."[28]

8. On the Llano Estacado in 2006, the South Plains Association of Governments coordinated a regional exercise to test the ability of officials to respond to a "weapons of mass destruction incident." Authorities from the cities of Lubbock and Levelland, Texas Tech University, and Hockley, Brownfield, Terry, Plainview, and Hale counties participated.[29]

All over the state, in private life, in the economy, and in politics, millions of Texans were adjusting to the new reality of potential terrorist attacks. Some consequences of the shift in emphasis can be identified. The governor has more power and responsibilities. The state's economy has been put under a strain, both because individuals, groups, and governments have been forced to spend fortunes to attempt to head off possible attacks and because restrictions on travel put a crimp on trade. Other consequences are more difficult to anticipate, but they will be significant. How the post-9/11 Texas polity will interact with the changing Texas population is a question that will keep textbook writers employed for many decades.

# The Future of Texas Democracy

There have been many comparisons in this book of the ideal of the democratic polity to the reality of Texas politics. In summary, in a perfect democracy, all adult citizens participate in regularly scheduled elections contested by programmatic parties offering the voters clashing visions of the ways that public policy can solve the state's problems. During the campaigns preceding these elections, the candidates discuss the problems facing the state and debate possible policies for dealing with them, the media fairly report the debate, and the citizens listen to it, using it as the basis for their own choices in the polling booth. This debate is not distorted by extremely unequal financing for the various points of view and is enhanced by complete freedom of speech and of the press. Once in office, the winners of the election carry out their pledges as a team, without being deflected from their purposes by wealthy special interests or an impossibly convoluted system of political institutions. Citizens pay attention to the performance of politicians in office and the effects of the policies they enacted, evaluate the incumbents, and take those evaluations into account during the next electoral cycle.

As a consequence, the policies that emerge from the governmental system, while they are not necessarily either liberal or conservative, are at least a reflection of the well-considered preferences of the majority of the citizens. That is the ideal.

The Texas reality, as we have seen, is somewhat different. Barely half of Texas's eligible citizens can be counted on to vote even in major national elections, with sometimes less than 10 percent fulfilling their civic duty in municipal elections. This low turnout rate strongly favors the wealthier Anglo population. Much of Texas's minority population is conspicuous by its absence from the polling booth. The campaigns are noteworthy for the conservative bias of the media that report them and the distorting effect of campaign contributions on candidate behavior. Once in office, the winners have difficulty functioning as a policymaking team because of the fragmented nature of the constitutional system and the distracting effect of special-interest lobbies that surround them, although the unified party government that prevailed after the 2002 election went a long way toward softening some of the kinks in the Texas system. The output of this actual system is often a caricature of the preferences of the majority of Texans. It is biased—not always, but frequently—toward the conservative values of upper-class Anglos and the interests of corporations.

Texas democracy, as it stands, is therefore greatly flawed. As observers have pointed out during all of history, however, all human institutions are imperfect.

★ ★ ★ ★ ★ ★ ★ ★ ★ ★ ★ ★ ★ ★ ★ ★ ★ ★ ★ ★ ★ ★ ★ ★ ★ ★ ★ ★ ★ ★

## Yes, Things Do Change

Within the context of examining the many cultural and political areas in which Texas has not changed much in the last 100 years, it is also useful to notice some of the ways in which it is dramatically different now. A good example that illustrates the transformation of the status of women is recounted in a 2002 book about the state attorney general and the oil industry.

It seems that in 1908 the attorney general was suing the Waters-Pierce Oil company for violation of the state's antitrust laws. One of the charges against the president of the company, Henry Pierce, was that he had sworn in a notarized affidavit in 1900 in Texas that Waters-Pierce was not part of the Standard Oil trust. In a 1906 deposition in a Missouri antitrust suit, however, he had sworn that his company was controlled by Standard. Had he committed perjury in 1900?

Pierce's defense attorney argued that because the notary who took the original affidavit was female, and because women were not allowed to vote in Texas, therefore they could not hold the position of notary public. If Pierce had sworn to an ineligible notary, claimed the lawyer, the document was invalid, and he could not be accused of having lied.

Although Pierce was eventually exonerated on an unrelated technicality, the judge in the case rejected the argument that women were not capable of serving as public officials in Texas. The fact that an attorney could make such an argument with a straight face, however, and that a judge could take it seriously approximately 100 years ago, demonstrates the massive changes in some Texas cultural attitudes that occurred during the twentieth century.

★ ★ ★ ★ ★ ★ ★ ★ ★ ★ ★ ★ ★ ★ ★ ★ ★ ★ ★ ★ ★ ★ ★ ★ ★ ★ ★ ★ ★ ★

SOURCE: Jonathan W. Singer, *Broken Trusts: The Texas Attorney General Versus the Oil Industry, 1889–1909* (College Station: Texas A&M, 2002), 206–207.

To conclude that Texas institutions fall short of the ideal is not very helpful. A better question would be: Is Texas democracy moving closer to or further from the ideal?

Looking back over the last century, there is reason to feel optimistic, for the Texas political system is far more defensible now than it was in, say, 1908. Then, African Americans, Mexican Americans, and poor Anglos were discouraged from political participation by a web of laws and informal practices that kept the ballot box a wealthy Anglo preserve. The reigning Democratic Party suppressed rivals and limited freedom of expression by potential dissenters. State government was so small that it had little ability to meet the challenges of the coming century. Corporations, particularly the railroads, dominated state policymaking. The state scarcely deserved to be called a democracy. Compared with the Texas of 1908, the Texas of 2008 is practically a utopia.

Much of the improvement that has occurred in Texas over the past century is not the result of the efforts of Texans themselves but was imposed on the state by the federal government. Still, whatever the reason, Texas is a better democracy than it was. It is unlikely that the changes will be undone.

The Texas of 2008 thus has the potential to improve as much in the twenty-first century as it did in the twentieth. Although voting turnout is low, that is the result of lethargy among the citizens, not suppression by the powers that be. Turnout could rise at any time, and in fact it has been increasing slowly and fitfully in recent years. An increase in the turnout rate could be a first step in an improvement in the quality of state government. The increased party competition of recent years may also lead to better government. Once political competition is established, it has a tendency to involve everyone. As Republicans and Democrats struggle over each election, both parties will see the need to appeal to more and more citizens. As a larger percentage of the people becomes involved, they may demand a state government that is more responsive to them and less to special interests. They may even decide to change the state constitution so that coordinated government action is possible. Once all varieties of citizens begin to vote, it could happen.

## Summary

As it does in most polities, democracy in Texas falls short of the ideal. Although Texas is now a two-party state, its very strong interest-group system ensures that private power often overbalances public policymaking. Its constitution disperses power, thus impeding the development of effective and responsible government. Voter turnout, especially among Mexican Americans and African Americans, is low, although it has been rising somewhat in recent decades. When measured against the standards of democratic theory, Texas government seems to be unsatisfactory, although not intolerable.

This imperfect political system will face a series of challenges in the future. The economy will need to continue diversifying. To help it do that, the state's educational system, which shows some signs of improvement but is still generally inadequate, will have to be improved. The population, which may reach 32 million by the year 2020, will generate many problems of pollution, water supply, and cultural conflict. The burgeoning cities will have to be managed so that they do not turn into cesspools of social pathology. The ambiguous challenge of potential terrorism will create many difficulties and costs for Texans in their private and public capacities.

Judging Texas only in relation to ideal standards of democracy creates pessimism that the state can deal with its future. On the other hand, there is also evidence that Texas will be able to handle the opportunities and challenges that will come its way. Some trends in public opinion, voter turnout, and party competition hint that the state's political potential is more open and complicated than it often appears. Moreover, an evaluation of Texas in historical time makes it clear that the state has improved greatly over the past century. This conclusion suggests that the potential for improvement in the present century is equally great.

## Glossary Term

demographics

## Study Questions

1. Looked at from the perspective of democratic theory, what are the most discouraging aspects of Texas politics? What are the most encouraging aspects?

2. Over the last two decades, what aspects of Texas politics have changed the most? Has the change been for the better?

3. Over the last two decades, what aspects of Texas politics have changed the least? Is this stability good or bad?

4. Does the evidence seem to suggest the conclusion that the threat of terrorism will be handled by Texas without fundamental changes in its institutions and political practices?

5. On a scale of 1 to 10, with 10 being perfect, rate Texas government in relation to democratic theory. On the same scale, rate the Texas of 1908. Are the two ratings similar or far apart? What explains the differences?

6. What trends make you most pessimistic about the future of Texas politics? What trends make you most optimistic? On balance, do you come down on the side of optimism or pessimism?

## Surfing the Web

Readers are urged to visit the companion site for this book:

**http://academic.cengage.com/polsci/Kraemer/TexasPolitics10e**

# Notes

## CHAPTER 1

1. Much of this account draws on material in *The Texas Almanac 1964–1965* (Dallas: A. H. Belo, 1963), 35–54; *The Texas Almanac 1986–1987* (Dallas: A. H. Belo, 1985), 163–224; *The Texas Almanac 1992–1993* (Dallas: A. H. Belo, 1991), 27–54, 324; and other footnoted material.

2. Alwyn Barr, *Black Texans: A History of African Americans in Texas 1528–1995* (Norman: University of Oklahoma Press, 1996), 17.

3. David Montejano, *Anglos and Mexicans in the Making of Texas 1836–1986* (Austin: University of Texas Press, 1986), 54, 58; Louis L'Amour, *North to the Rails* (New York: Bantam Books, 1971).

4. Jonathan W. Singer, Broken Trusts: The Texas Attorney General versus the Oil Industry, 1889–1909 (College Station: Texas A&M, 2002), 5.

5. Barr, *Black Texans*, op. cit., 134–135; Montejano, *Anglos and Mexicans,* op. cit., 143–144.

6. "Texas a Net Loser from Falling Oil Prices, Economist Reports," *Energy Studies,* vol. 11, no. 5 (May/June 1986), 1 (newsletter of the Center for Energy Studies at the University of Texas at Austin).

7. Calculated from tables on page 14 of *Crime in Texas 1992* (Austin: Texas Department of Public Safety, 1993).

8. Robbie Morganfield, "Texas Passes NY," *Houston Chronicle,* December 28, 1994, 1A.

9. Duwadi Megh, "Study: No. 2 'Cyberstate' Texas Lost the Most Jobs in Tech Bust," *Austin American-Statesman,* June 26, 2002, D1.

10. Suzannah Gonzales and Carrie MacLaggan, "Texas Is Fifth-Poorest State, Data Show," *Austin American-Statesman,* August 30, 2006, B1.

11. Sam Dillon, "States Are Relaxing Standards on Tests to Avoid Sanctions," *New York Times,* May 22, 2003, A1.

12. Information in the following account comes from Michael Graczyk, "Parole Board Refuses to Stop Man's Execution," *Austin American-Statesman,* August 14, 2002, B6; Susan Ferriss, "Execution Leads Fox to Scrap Trip," *Austin American-Statesman,* August 15, 2002, A1; Toby Sterling, "World Court: U.S. Must Stay 3 Executions," *Austin American-Statesman,* February 6, 2003, F1; Linda Greenhouse, "Treaty Doesn't Give Foreign Defendants Special Status in U.S. Courts, Justices Rule," *New York Times,* June 20, 2006, A15.

13. The following discussion is based on Daniel J. Elazar, *American Federalism: A View from the States,* 3rd ed. (New York: Harper & Row, 1984), 109–173; Ira Sharkansky, "The Utility of Elazar's Political Culture: A Research Note," 247–262; Robert L. Savage, "The Distribution and Development of Policy Values in the American States," 263–286, and Appendices A, B, and C, 287–294 in Daniel J. Elazar and Joseph Zikmund II, eds. *The Ecology of American Political Culture: Readings* (New York: Thomas Y. Crowell, 1975).

14. Sharkansky, "Utility," op. cit., 252.

15. For a description and evaluation of social Darwinism in American culture, see Carl N. Degler, *In Search of Human Nature: The Decline and Revival of Social Darwinism in American Social Thought* (New York: Oxford University, 1991) and David F. Prindle, *The Paradox of Democratic Capitalism: Politics and Economics in American Thought* (Baltimore: Johns Hopkins University, 2006), 107–122.

16. Kendra A. Hovey and Harold A. Hovey, CQ's State Fact Finder 2006 (Washington, D.C.: CQ Press, 2006), 45, 44.

17. Suzannah Gonzales and Corrie MacLaggan, "Texas is Fifth-Poorest State, Data Show," *Austin American-Statesman,* August 30, 2006, B1.

18. Steve Brown, "Texas No. 2 on List of Best Business Sites," *Dallas Morning News,* October 2, 1996, D1.

19. Doug Wong, "*Forbes* Magazine Ranks Austin No. 1 for Business," *Austin American-Statesman,* May 9, 2003, D1.

20. Hovey and Hovey, op. cit., 71.

21. The CED's state rankings and a discussion of how they were created can be found on its Web site: www.cfed .org; all states that made the honor roll in 2002 also made it in 2006.

22. "Texas Leads in Population Growth," *Austin American-Statesman,* December 22, 2006, A1.

23. Alicia A. Caldwell, "Census: More Than Half of Texans Are Minorities," *Austin American-Statesman,* August 11, 2005, B1.

24. Mark Babineck, "Hispanic Majority Seen in Texas by 2030s," *Austin American-Statesman,* January 12, 2002, B6

25. Steve Murdock, Steve White, Md. Nazrul Hoque, Beverly Pecotte, Xuihong You, and Jennifer Balkan, *The New Texas Challenge: Population Change and the Future of Texas* (College Station: Texas A&M, 2003), 7; *Latinos in Texas: A Socio-Demographic Profile* (Austin: Tomas Rivera Center, 1995), 66, 84, 111.

# CHAPTER 2

1. Martha Derthick, in "American Federalism: Half-Full or Half-Empty," *Brookings Review*, Winter 2000, 24–27, examines the status of federal–state relations at the turn of the century.

2. See http://tlo2.tlc.state.tx.us/txconst/toc.html for the complete text of the Texas Constitution.

3. Texas was governed by Mexico from 1821 to 1836. Beginning in 1824, the Mexican Congress, acting under the Mexican Constitution, joined Texas and Coahuila, with Saltillo as the capital. That arrangement prevailed until independence in 1836. Thus, Texas was also governed by a seventh constitution, albeit as a colony, not as an independent nation or a state.

4. See, for example, Fred Gantt Jr., *The Chief Executive in Texas: A Study in Gubernatorial Leadership* (Austin: University of Texas Press, 1964), 24.

5. The Jacksonians supported slavery and the brutal treatment of Native Americans.

6. Jim B. Pearson, Ben Procter, and William B. Conroy, *Texas, The Land and Its People*, 3rd ed. (Dallas: Hendrick-Long, 1987), 400–405; *The Texas Almanac, 1996–1997* (Dallas: Dallas Morning News, 1996), 499.

7. Historical perspectives are based on remarks of John W. Mauer, "State Constitutions in a Time of Crisis: The Case of the Constitution of 1876," Symposium on the Texas Constitution, sponsored by the University of Texas Law School and the *Texas Law Review*, October 7, 1989.

8. The Grange originated in Minnesota in the 1860s in protest to farmers' grievances about low prices and the actions of big business—namely, the railroads and the grain companies—with which they had to deal. The organization reached its peak of power and membership in the 1870s.

9. Wilbourn E. Benton, *Texas Politics: Constraints and Opportunities* (Chicago: Nelson-Hall, 1984), 51.

10. Because of its length, the entire Texas Constitution is rarely reproduced. However, the *Texas Almanac and State Industrial Guide* (published every two years by the Dallas Morning News) included the full text with all amendments until the 2000–2001 edition, and continues to summarize proposed amendments and to track their passage. As previously noted, the complete document can be found online at http://tlo2.tlc.state.tx.us/txconst/toc.html.

11. A full discussion of poorly organized sections and provisions in conflict with federal law can be found in *Reorganized Texas Constitution without Substantive Change* (Austin: Texas Advisory Commission on Intergovernmental Relations, 1977).

12. The Alabama Constitution had approximately 340,136 words as of early 2006. This and other comparative information can be found in *The Book of the States, 2006 Edition*, vol. 38 (Lexington, Ky.: Council of State Governments, 2006), 7.

13. The definitive study of the Texas Constitution is Janice C. May, *The Texas State Constitution, A Reference Guide* (Westport, Conn.: Greenwood Publishing Group, 1996).

14. Article I, Section 4 stipulates acknowledgment of the existence of a Supreme Being as a test for public office; however, this provision is not enforced because it violates the U.S. Constitution.

15. Todd J. Gillman, "Bill of Rights Might Face Tough Ride Now," *Dallas Morning News*, August 22, 1992, 12F.

16. As long as citizens were legally perceived to be citizens of the state first and of the nation second, state guarantees were vital. In recent years, state courts have begun to reassert themselves as protectors of rights because the federal courts have begun to be less assertive in their own decisions.

17. See, for example, David Westphal, "Homeland Security Plan Spurs Liberties Concerns," *Sacramento Bee*, August 9, 2002, posted at http://foi.missouri.edu/ terrorandcivillib/homelandsecplan.html; "Numbers," *Time* magazine, December 23, 2002, 21; and "USA Patriot Act," *Wikipedia, the Free Encylopedia*, posted at http:// en.wikipedia.org/wiki/Patriot_act, February 1, 2006.

18. Article XV specifies the grounds for impeachment of judges but not for the impeachment of executive officers; only the power to impeach the latter is given.

19. Thad Beyle, "The Governors," in Virginia Gray, Russell L. Hanson, and Herbert Jacob, *Politics in the American States*, 7th ed. (Washington, D.C.: CQ Press, 1999), 210–211. Beyle's chapter is the basis for other comments about ranking. In the 4th edition of Virginia Gray, Herbert Jacob, and Kenneth N. Vines, eds., *Politics in the American States* (essentially an earlier edition of the 1999 book), Beyle rated the Texas governor in the weakest six in their formal powers.

20. Even with all the modern cases dealing with the rights of the criminally accused, no national prohibition exists on the state's right to appeal in criminal cases. See *Palko* v. *Connecticut* (302 U.S. 319, 1937) for the Supreme Court's position on the issue. Texas allowed no appeal by the state until 1987.

21. Contrary to popular opinion, a justice of the peace without legal training cannot become a judge on a superior (appeals) court. Qualifications for these courts include ten years as a practicing lawyer or a combination of ten years of legal practice and judicial service.

22. Some years ago, *Forbes* magazine reported that Texas and Alabama have the most expensive judicial elections in the country. With major amounts of money—as much as $2 million for a Texas Supreme Court seat—on the line, vote-getting skills become especially important. See Laura Casteneda, "D.C. Worst, Utah Best on Litigious List," *Dallas Morning News*, January 3, 1994, 1D, 4D.

23. Although many small school districts have consolidated, Texas continues to be among the national leaders in the number of special districts. The state had 3,335 special districts when the most recent Census of Governments was taken in 2002, almost three times the number of municipalities.

24. The National Municipal (now Civic) League of Cities State Constitutional Studies Project last produced its *Model State Constitution*, 6th ed., in 1968 (New York: National

Civic League). Web searches reveal a variety of other "models," all of which seem to be partisan versions of constitutions from states where constitutional revision has been active.

25. For example, a majority of states, including Alabama, New York, Pennsylvania, South Carolina, and Texas, do not have a provision allowing citizens to initiate a constitutional amendment. California, Illinois, Michigan, and Montana are among the eighteen states that provide for the citizen initiative. *The Book of the States, 2006*, 13.

26. A detailed analysis of the 1975 document is available in George Braden, *Citizen's Guide to the Proposed Constitution* (Houston: Institute of Urban Studies, University of Houston, 1975). The University of Houston served as a research and information center during the revision efforts and published numerous reports beginning in 1973. Scholars from across the state were involved in the Houston research. One, Janice C. May, published a book-length study, *Texas Constitutional Revision Experience in the 70s* (Austin: Sterling Swift, 1975). A summary of the general literature on the revision efforts and of voting behavior can be found in John E. Bebout, "The Meaning of the Vote on the Proposed Texas Constitution, 1975," *Public Affairs Comment*, vol. 24 (February 1978), 1–9, published by the Lyndon B. Johnson School of Public Affairs at the University of Texas at Austin.

27. Draft resolution and "Comparison of Current and Proposed Constitutions" provided by the office of Senator John Montford, January 1992.

28. Sam Attlesey, "Texas Constitution Outlasts Plan for Rewrite," *Dallas Morning News*, April 25, 1999, 54A.

29. See, for example, "Member Update: Texas Constitutional Revision," *The Texas Voter* 40 (Winter 2005), insert., and Heber Taylor, "It's Time to Draft a New Texas Constitution," *Galveston County Daily News* (November 9, 2005), originally available at http://galvestondailynews .com/story.lasso?ewed52df9eea56de051ec.

# CHAPTER 3

1. Texas Ethics Commission Web site, www.ethics.state .tx.us/main/lobbyist.htm, accessed January 13, 2007.

2. Karen Brooks, "Selling Lobbyists on Ethics," *Dallas Morning News*, September 16, 2006, A1.

3. Dave McNeely, "After Agitating Cyclists, Senator Revises Bike Bill," *Austin American-Statesman*, March 29, 2001, B1; and state legislative Web site: www.capitol.state .tx.us/.

4. Sherri Deatherage Green, "Lewis Forges Alliance with Burson for Lobbying Efforts," *PR Week*, April 28, 2003, 4.

5. Paul Burka, "Is the Legislature for Sale?" *Texas Monthly*, February 1991, 118.

6. Information on the TRMPAC/TAB scandal comes from the following sources: Andrew Wheat, "Taylor-Made Election Law," *Texas Observer*, March 18, 2005, 13; Jake Bernstein, "TRMPAC in its Own Words," *Texas Observer*, April 1, 2005, 6; Laylin Copelin, "Eight Corporations Added to 2002 Campaign Lawsuit," *Austin American-Statesman*, August 19, 2005, A5; Philip Shenon and Carl Hulse, "DeLay Is Indicted in Texas Case and Forfeits G.O.P. House Post," *New York Times*, September 29, 2005, A1; Anne E. Kornblut, "How a Tested Campaign Tool Led to Conspiracy Charge," *New York Times*, September 29, 2005, A3; Molly Ivins, "DeLay's Pattern: Taking It All a Step Too Far," *Austin American-Statesman*, October 1, 2005, A15; Laylin Copelin, "DeLay Indicted on 2 New Counts," *Austin American-Statesman*, October 4, 2005, A1, 10 Laylan Copelin, "Election Ad Indictment Thrown Out," *Austin American-Statesman*, June 30, 2006, A1.

7. James A. Garcia, "Lobbying Group Subsidiary Will Gather Insurance Data," *Austin American-Statesman*, August 27, 1996, B1; information updated by authors.

8. Laylan Copelin, "Ethics Legislation Passes in Overtime," *Austin American-Statesman*, June 2, 2003, B1.

9. Articles in the *Austin American-Statesman* are the source for this discussion of the telecom conflict: "Cable Industry Sues Again over Law," January 28, 2006, F2; Bruce Meyerson, "Sprint Joining Cable Providers to Battle SBC," November 3, 2005, B1; Claudia Grisales, "SBC Asks to Provide TV to San Antonio," October 11, 2005, D1; "Cable Firms Sue to Stop Telecom Law," September 9, 2005, C1; "Perry Approves Changes to Telecom Laws," September 8, 2005, C2; Bruce Mehlman and Larry Irving, "On Telecom, Texas Is Set to Bring on Competition," August 31, 2005, A13; Tim Morstad and Gus Cardenas, "Texas Needs to Stand Up to Big Phone Companies," August 18, 2005, A13; Claudia Grisales, "Phone Lobby Spent Big to Outmaneuver Cable Rivals," August 18, 2005, A1; Claudia Grisales, "Phone Companies Gain TV Win," July 18, 2005, B1; Phil King, "On Telecom, Legislature Lost a Chance to Help Consumers," June 30, 2005, A13; Jaime Martinez, "Bill Would Only Widen Digital Divide in Texas," May 17, 2005, A13; Claudia Grisales, "Legislative Battle over Television Looms," May 7, 2005, A1; Claudia Grisales, "Ad War Erupts in Fight over Telecom Reform," April 28, 2005, D1; Gary Chapman, "To Ensure Texas' Future, We Must Rewrite the Rules on Telecom," March 5, 2005, A15.

10. Diane Renzulli and The Center For Public Integrity, *Capitol Offenders: How Private Interests Govern Our States* (Washington, D.C.: Public Integrity Books, 2002), 95, 100.

11. Testimony of J. Robert Hunter before the Committee On Commerce, Science and Transportation of the U.S. Senate, October 22, 2003, available on the Web site of the Consumer Federation of America: www .consumerfed.org/; accessed September 23, 2006 (type "insurance industry" into site's search engine; pp. 3, 2.

12. Elyse Gilmore Yates, "Insure Integrity in the Insurance Industry," *Texas Observer*, February 8, 1991, 11.

13. Renzulli, *Capitol Offenders*, op. cit., 105.

14. Ibid., 97.

15. Bruce Hight, "Runaway Rates Have Consumers Seeing Red," *Austin American-Statesman*, September 1, 2002, H2; Shonda Novak, "Consumer Groups Call For Regulation of Home Insurers," *Austin American-Statesman*, September 7, 2002, G1.

16. Carlos Guerra, "Insurance Money Trail," *Austin American-Statesman*, August 7, 2002, A11.

17. Ibid.; Shonda Novak, "Insurers Ordered to Retool Pricing," *Austin American-Statesman*, August 14, 2002, A1.

18. Claudia Grisales, "Insurers Join Forces to Lobby Lawmakers," *Austin American-Statesman*, July 27, 2002, A1.

19. Dave Harmon, "Insurers Face New Scrutiny under Law," *Austin American-Statesman*, June 11, 2003, B1; Shonda Novak, "Insurers Ordered to Slash Rates," *Austin American-Statesman*, August 9, 2003, A1; Shonda Novak, "Insurers Must Cut Rates, Official Says," *Austin American-Statesman*, September 13, 2003, F1.

20. W. Gardner Selby, "Despite Changes, Home Insurance Priciest in Texas," *Austin American-Statesman*, April 24, 2007, A1; Editorial: "False Claims," *Texas Observer*, January 27, 2006, 2.

21. Clive S. Thomas and Ronald J. Hrebenar, "Interest Groups in the States," in Virginia Gray and Russell L. Hanson, *Politics in the American States: A Comparative Analysis*, 8th ed., (Washington, D.C.: Congressional Quarterly, 2004), 122.

22. Ibid., 119.

23. Tom Craddick, "Reining in a Civil Justice System Gone Wild," *Austin American-Statesman*, August 29, 2003, A15; Jake Bernstein and Dave Mann, "The Rise of the Machine," *Texas Observer*, August 29, 2003, 8.

24. "Money Limits," *Texas Observer*, December 15, 2006, 5.

25. "History in the Making," *PR Newswire*, June 2, 2003, 1.

26. Dick Weekley, "Texas Ranks 'Best in the Nation' in Tort Liability Index but Report Shows More Reforms Are Needed" on Web site of Texans for Lawsuit Reform, www.tortreform.com/dick_weekley_oped.asp; information taken from Pacific Research Institute, www.pacificresearch.org; both sites accessed September 23, 2006.

27. The information in this section is based on Mary Flood, "Doctors Orders: Medical Lobby Becomes a Powerhouse in Austin," *The Wall Street Journal*, May 19, 1999, T1; Osler McCarthy, "Doctor, Lawyer Groups Bury the Hatchet," *Austin American-Statesman*, February 28, 1999, J1; Laylan Copelin, "Influence Is Name of Game for an Army of Lobbyists," *Austin American-Statesman*, January 12, 2003, E3; "Texas Docs Led by Old Political Hand," *Modern Healthcare*, April 21, 2003, 32; R. G. Ratcliffe, "Perry Signs Prompt Pay Legislation," *Houston Chronicle*, June 18, 2003, A17; David Pasztor, "Doctors' Lobbying Stirs Concern," *Austin American-Statesman*, September 2, 2003, B1; news release, Texans For Public Justice, "Prop. 12 Proponents Gave $5.3 Million To Perry, Dewhurst and Lawmakers in 2002," August 29, 2003, 2.

28. "Memo to TMA Members After New Tax Bill Passed," on TMA Web site: www.texmed.org/, addressed September 24, 2006.

29. This section is based on information in Charles P. Elliott, Jr., "The Texas Trial Lawyers Association: Interest Group under Siege," in Anthony Champagne and Edward J. Harpham (eds.), *Texas Politics: A Reader* (New York: W.W. Norton, 1997), 162–176; Terry Maxon, "Lawyers Top Doctors in Fund Raising for Prop. 12," *Dallas Morning News*, August 21, 2003, D1; David Pasztor, "Prop. 12 Fight Has Silenced Lawyers," *Austin American-Statesman*, September 4, 2003, A1.

30. Laylan Copelin and David Pasztor, "Limits on Damages Narrowly Approved," *Austin American-Statesman*, September 14, 2003, A1; Jake Bernstein, "Bustin' Labels," *Texas Observer*, September 26, 2003, 6.

31. The information in this section is based on William Martin, *With God on Our Side: The Rise of the Religious Right in America* (New York: Broadway Books, 1996); Chuck Lindell, "Pulpit to Polls Movement Gathers Steam," *Austin American-Statesman*, March 6, 1994, A1; Ken Herman, "Education Board Cuts Disney Ties," *Austin American-Statesman*, July 11, 1998, A1; Paul Burka, "The Disloyal Opposition," *Texas Monthly*, December, 1998, 117; "Christian Coalition Loses Tax Status Fight," *Austin American-Statesman*, June 11, 1999, A2; Laurie Goldstein, "Christian Coalition Reported in Crisis," *Austin American-Statesman*, August 2, 1999, A1; Molly Ivins, "State Board of Obfuscation," *Austin American-Statesman*, November 3, 1999, A17; A. Phillips Brooks, "'Bush Backlash' Sways Education Race," March 1, 2000, B1; Harvey Kronberg, "Ratliff Behind the Scenes of Race," *Austin American-Statesman*, April 25, 2000, A11; Mark O'Keefe, "Religious Right Buckling under Success," *Austin American-Statesman*, December 16, 2001, H1; Matt Curry, "In Texas, Appealing to Churchgoers Is an Integral Part of Campaigning," Associated Press news release, July 24, 2002, 1.

32. DeLay quoted in Jim Lobe, "Another Toxic Texan Rises to the Top," Inter Press Service news release, November 16, 2002, 2.

33. This summary is based on the information in Emily Ramshaw, "Fruitful Year for Christian Right," *Dallas Morning News*, May 17, 2007, A1.

34. Molly Ivins, "Compassion Eases Pain for Oil Bidness," *Austin American-Statesman*, February 20, 1999, A11.

35. All figures from U.S. Bureau of Labor Statistics *News*, January 20, 2006, from the BLS Web site: www.bls.gov/news.release/pdf/unions2.pdf; accessed September 24, 2006

36. A *secondary boycott* occurs when one union boycotts the products of a company being struck by another union. The *checkoff system* is a method of collecting union dues in which an employer withholds the amount of the dues from workers' paychecks. *Mass picketing* occurs when so many people picket a firm that traffic is disrupted and the firm cannot conduct business. A *closed shop* is in effect when workers must already be members of a certain union in order to apply for work in a given firm. A *union shop* is in effect when workers do not have to be members of the union to apply for work, but must join if they get a job.

37. Steven Greenhouse, "Labor Movement Dusts Off Agenda as Power Shifts in Congress," *New York Times*, November 12, 2006, A13.

38. The information in this section is based on Benjamin Marquez, LULAC: *The Evolution of a Mexican-American Political Organization* (Austin: University of Texas, 1993); Lori Rodriguez, "LULAC Turning Puerto Rican," *Houston Chronicle*, July 9, 1994, A25; James E. Garcia, "Latino Politics: Up to LULAC to Reform or Be Left Behind," *Houston Chronicle*, September 9, 1999, OUTLOOK, 1; Lori Rodriguez, "LULAC's Leaders Speech at Convention First Ever," *Houston Chronicle*, July 11, 2002, A1; Lori Rodriguez, "LULAC Role Evolves, But Equity Still Focus," *Houston Chronicle*, July 23, 2002, A1; Amber Novak, "Up in Smoke," *Texas Observer*, May 23, 2003, 4; Scripps Howard Austin Bureau, "LULAC Sponsors Students' Trip to Austin to Oppose School Cuts," *Corpus Christi Caller-Times*, May 4, 2003, C4; "LULAC Questions GOP Tax Plan," *La Prensa San Diego*, May 23, 2003 Online Edition, 1; U.S. Labor Department news release, "Labor Dept. Enforcing Laws to Protect Most Vulnerable Workers," June 19, 2003, 1; Meena Thiruvengadam, "CAFTA Proves Divisive for LULAC Chapters," *San Antonio Express-News*, July 8, 2005, B8

39. Thomas and Hrebenar, "Interest Groups," 119.

40. Kendra A. Hovey and Harold A. Hovey, *CQ's State Fact Finder 2006* (Washington, D.C.: Congressional Quarterly, 2006), 43, 48.

41. Dan A. Lewis and Shadd Maruna, "The Politics of Education," in Virginia Gray, Russell L. Hanson, and Herbert Jacob, eds. *Politics in the American States: A Comparative Analysis*, 7th ed. (Washington, D.C.: Congressional Quarterly, 1999), 404; Hartman quoted in Jenine Zeleznik, "Lobbyists Warn Texas Teachers about Upcoming Special Session," *The Monitor*, September 10, 2003, 1.

42. Whiteker quoted in Jason Embry and Robert Elder, "Fed Up, Pro-Education Candidates Step Up," *Austin American-Statesman*, October 23, 2005, A1.

43. Donna New Haschke, "Short Term 'Fix' Will Test the Future of Texas Public Schools," *Advocate*, Fall 2006, 2; accessed on September 24, 2006, from TSTA Web site: www.tsta.org/news/current/06FallAdvocate.pdf

# CHAPTER 4

1. The customary assignment of liberals to the left side of the political spectrum and conservatives to the right side derives from the seating of parties in the French Parliament. Royalists, Gaullists, and others of a conservative persuasion always sit to the right of the center aisle, while socialists, communists, and others of more "progressive" persuasion sit to the left.

2. Figures from statewide Texas poll conducted by the Texas Credit Union League between September 5 and 18, 2006, accessed on its Web site on October 1, 2006: www.tcul.coop/

3. Robert S. Erickson, Gerald C. Wright Jr., and John McIver, "Political Parties, Public Opinion, and State Policy in the United States," *American Political Science Review*, vol. 83, no. 6 (September 1989), 729–750, especially 737.

4. Douglas E. Foley, *Learning Capitalist Culture: Deep in the Heart of Tejas* (Philadelphia: University of Pennsylvania Press, 1990), 110.

5. Quoted in Molly Ivins, "Political Writing—A State of Lazy Journalism," *Texas Humanist*, November-December, 1984, 14–15.

6. Donna St. George, "Americans Are Using Talk Radio to Carry Their Voices to Congress," *Austin American-Statesman*, November 6, 1994, D1.

7. For a theoretical analysis of the evolution of party positions during the twentieth century, see Gary Miller and Norman Schofield, "Activists and Partisan Realignment in the United States," *American Political Science Review*, vol. 97, no. 2 (May 2003), 245–260.

8. Figures from statewide Texas poll conducted by the Texas Credit Union League between September 5 and 18, 2006, accessed on its Web site on October 1, 2006: www.tcul.coop/

9. The four largest counties—Bexar, Dallas, Harris, and Tarrant—are so populous that they are entitled to more than one state senator. In these counties, each state senatorial district holds its own district convention rather than a countywide convention.

10. Dave McNeely, "Party Politics in the Precincts," Austin American-Statesman, March 4, 2000, A15.

11. Ken Herman, "Perry Not Standing on GOP Party Platform," Austin American-Statesman, June 12, 2002, A9.

12. Molly Ivins, "Texas Elephants Look to Ostracize the RINOs," Austin American-Statesman, June 12, 2002, A17; Jake Bernstein, "Elephant Wars," Texas Observer, Jule 5, 2002, 16.

13. 2006 Republican state platform, page 12.

14. John F. Bibby and Thomas M. Holbrooke, "Parties and Elections" in Virginia Gray and Russell L. Hanson, eds. Politics in the American States: A Comparative Analysis (Washington, D. C.: Congressional Quarterly, 2004), 74.

15. Gerald C. Wright and Brian Schaffner, "The Influence of Party: Evidence from the State Legislatures," American Political Science Review, vol. 96, no. 2, (June 2002), 376-377.

16. Dave McNeely, "Bipartisanship: The Road Not Taken in '03," Austin American-Statesman, January 4, 2004, H1.

17. Sean Theriault, "Party Polarization in the U.S. Congress: Member Replacement and Member Adaptation," Party Politics, vol. 12 (July 2006), 483-503.

18. Dave McNeely, "For Incumbent Democrats, Some Heads Are Starting to Roll," Austin American-Statesman, March 10, 2004, A12; Ken Herman, "Wilson Pays Price for Siding with GOP," Austin American-Statesman, March 11, 2004, A1.

19. Laurie Goodstein, "Issuing Rebuke, Judge Rejects Teaching of Intelligent Design," New York Times, December 21, 2005, A1; W. Gardner Selby, "Perry: Add Intelligent Design to Classes," Austin American-Statesman, January 6, 2006, A1.

20 "Populist Party Platform," in Michael B. Levy, ed. Political Thought in America: An Anthology (Chicago: Dorsey Press, 1988), 356-359.

# CHAPTER 5

1. "White primary" laws and rules prevented voting in primary elections by anyone who was not Caucasian. Although the 15th Amendment to the U.S. Constitution, passed in 1870, guaranteed the right of all citizens of any race to vote in general elections, it did not apply to primaries. The poll tax law required a citizen to pay a tax months in advance of election day in order to register. Unless registered, citizens were not legally qualified to vote. Poor people, of whom many were minority citizens, were often unable to pay the tax and thus became ineligible to vote. The U.S. Supreme Court invalidated Texas's white primary law in 1944 in *Smith v. Allwright*, 321 U.S. 649. The 24th Amendment to the Constitution, adopted in 1964, forbid the poll tax in federal elections. Under threat of federal action, Texas repealed its state poll tax law in 1966 by amendment of its constitution. The state legislature, however, adopted a severe registration law that was, in effect, a poll tax under another name. A federal court struck down this law in *Beare v. Smith*, 321 F. Supp., 1100 (1971).

2. *Beare v. Smith*, 321 F. Supp., 1100 (1971).

3. Suzannah Gonzales and Corrie MacLaggan, "Texas Is Fifth-Poorest State, Data Show," *Austin American-Statesman*, August 30, 2006, B1.

4. U.S. Census Bureau, *Statistical Abstract of the United States, 2003* (Washington, D.C.: U.S. Government Printing Office, 2003), 269; U.S. Census Bureau, "Voting and Registration in the Election of November 2002: Detailed Tables for Current Population Report," at www.census.gov/prod/2004pubs/p20-552.pdf, accessed December 4, 2006.

5. From a state survey by the Texas Credit Union League, accessed on its Web site on October 1, 2006: www.tcul.coop/

6. Colleen McCain Wilson, "For Sanchez, More Wasn't Better," *Dallas Morning News*, November 7, 2002, A1; Laylan Copelin, "Costs Soar in Race to Be Governor," *Austin American-Statesman*, October 29, 2002, B1; Wyne Slater and Pete Slover, "For Sanchez, Perry, the Well Isn't Dry Yet," *Dallas Morning News*, October 13, 2002, A1; Pete Slover, "Political Checks and Balances," *Dallas Morning News*, January 16, 2003, A1.

7. Wilson, ibid.; Laylan Copelin and David Elliott, "Williams Outspending Richards 2–1," *Austin American-Statesman*, October 30, 1990, A1.

8. Keith E. Hamm and Gary F. Moncrief, "Legislative Politics in the States," in Virginia Gray and Russell L. Hanson, eds., *Politics in the American States: A Comparative Analysis*, 8th ed., (Washington, D.C.: Congressional Quarterly, 2004), 168.

9. Texans for Public Justice, *Keeping Texas Weird: The Bankrolling of the 2006 Gubernatorial Race*, September, 2006, accessed on TPJ's Web site on October 2, 2006: www.tpj.org/

10. Laylan Copelin, "Few Fans of Campaign Changes," *Austin American-Statesman*, April 22, 2007, B1.

11. Mike Ward, "65% of Politicians in Poll Favor Public Favor Public Financing of Campaigns," *Austin American-Statesman*, March 11, 1990, B8.

12. Quoted in Jeff South and Jerry White, "Computer Network Tracks Politicians' Funds," *Austin American-Statesman*, August 16, 1993, B1.

13. Laylin Copelin, "Ethics Panel's Future Hanging in the Balance," *Austin American-Statesman*, April 24, 2002, A1; Jake Bernstein, "A Dog Not Allowed to Hunt," *Texas Observer*, April 12, 2002, 3.

14. Copelin, "Campaign Changes," op. cit.

15. Julia Malone, "Campaigns Take Low Road," *Austin American-Statesman*, October 26, 2006, A7.

16. Kim Fridkin Kahn and Patrick Kenney, "Do Negative Campaigns Mobilize or Suppress Turnout? Clarifying the Relationship between Negativity and Participation," *American Political Science Review*, vol. 93, no. 4 (December 1999), 877–778; Stephen D. Ansolabehere, Shanto Iyengar, and Adam Simon, "Replicating Experiments Using Aggregate and Survey Data: The Case of Negative Advertising and Turnout," ibid., 901–909.

17. Thanks to Joe Kulhavy of the Texas Secretary of State's office for supplying us with this information.

18. David Pasztor, "Millions Pour into Proposition 12 Fight," *Austin American-Statesman*, September 6, 2003, A1; Laylin Copelin and David Pasztor, "Limits on Damages Narrowly Approved," *Austin American-Statesman*, September 14, 2003, A1.

19. John M. Broder, "Growing Absentee Voting Is Reshaping Campaigns," *New York Times*, October 22, 2006, "National Report" section, 14.

20. Christy Hoppe, "At 'Halftime,' State Candidates Continue Smash-Mouth Politics," *Dallas Morning News*, September 1, 2002, A1.

21. "Judge Says Perry Took Ruling Out of Context in Ad," *Austin American-Statesman*, July 31, 2002, B3; Molly Ivins, "The Summer of Our Discontent," *Denton Record-Chronicle*, August 10, 2002, A6.

22. Ken Herman, "Perry Uses DEA Murder in New TV Ad," *Austin American-Statesman*, October 26, 2002, B1.

23. Jeff Zeleny and Megan Thee, "Exit Polling Shows Independents, Citing War, Favored Democrats," *New York Times*, November 8, 2006, A1.

24. Barry Schwartz, "Mr. Bland Goes to Washington," *New York Times*, November 7, 2006, A14.

25. "Watkins: 'A New Day in Dallas County,'" www.WFAA.com, accessed November 8, 2006; Dan Felstein and Chase Davis, "Warning for GOP in Harris County," *Houston Chronicle*, November 9, 2006, A1; Thomas

Korosec, "Democrats Turn Dallas County a Shade of Blue," *Houston Chronicle*, November 9, 2006, B4.

# CHAPTER 6

1. See www2.state.id.us/legislat/citizen.html and http://legisweb.state.wy.us/leginfo/guide98.htm.

2. See, for example, Ernest Callenbach and Michael Phillips, *A Citizen Legislature* (Berkeley/Bodega, Cal.: Banyan Tree Books/Clear Glass, 1985).

3. In studies involving six other states, about one third of the legislators indicated that casework is their most important function, and three fourths reported spending at least one quarter of their time on favors for constituents. See Patricia K. Freeman and Lilliard E. Richardson Jr., "Casework in State Legislatures," *State and Local Government Review*, vol. 16 (Winter 1994), 21–26; Richard C. Elling, "The Utility of State Legislative Casework as a Means of Oversight," *Legislative Studies Quarterly*, vol. 4, no. 3 (1979): 353–380. Also see Keith E. Hamm and Gary F. Moncrief, "Legislative Politics in the States," in Virginia Gray and Russell L. Hanson, eds., *Politics in the American States: A Comparative Analysis*, 8th ed. (Washington, D.C.: Congressional Quarterly Press, 2004), especially 174–176.

4. The U.S. Constitution provides for a maximum of one representative for each 30,000 people. If no ceiling were statutorily set and this limit were actually attained, the U.S. House of Representatives would have about 9,948 members. The Texas Constitution sets a maximum membership of 150 in the House, although it allows one representative for each 15,000 citizens within that limit. If legislators represented only 15,000 constituents, the Texas House would have more than 1,523 members.

5. Information on the legislatures of other states has been summarized from *The Book of the States, 2006*, vol. 38 (Lexington, Ky.: Council of State Governments, 2006), 61–134.

6. See Dawson Bell, "Reducing Rancor in Michigan," *State Legislatures*, December 1999, 22–24, especially the sidebar analyzing term limits on p. 23, and Stanley M. Caress et al., "Effect of Term Limits on the Election of Minority State Legislators," *State and Local Government Review*, vol. 35 (Fall 2003), 183–195.

7. According to census estimates for July 2005, Texas has a population of 22,859,968 persons. Dividing that figure by 31 for senatorial districts yields the ideal district size of 737,418; dividing by 150 for representatives, the figure is 152,400. Obviously, citizens move in and out of districts, so the numbers are not exact, and they change as the population increases.

8. A county was entitled to a maximum of seven representatives unless its population exceeded 700,000; then one additional representative could be districted for each additional 100,000 in population.

9. 369 U.S. 186 (1962).

10. 377 U.S. 533 (1964).

11. A multimember district is one in which two or more representatives are elected by all the people in that district. All the representatives represent all the people of the district. Multimember districts tend to reduce considerably the ability of ethnic minorities to win election, and the citizens tend not to be sure which representative is truly theirs.

12. See Steven Bickerstaff, "Legislative and Congressional Reapportionment in Texas: A Historical Perspective," *Public Affairs Comment*, vol. 37 (Winter 1991), 1–13, for a good review of early redistricting developments.

13. See Arturo Vega, "Gender and Ethnicity Effects on the Legislative Behavior and Substantive Representation of the Texas Legislature," *Texas Journal of Political Studies*, vol. 19 (Spring/Summer 1997), 1–21.

14. See, for example, *Shaw* v. *Reno* (509 U.S. 630, 1993), which dealt with standards of racial equality in redistricting, and *Hunt* v. *Cromarite* (526 U.S. 541), which resulted in a requirement that overt racial gerrymandering had to be present to overturn district lines.

15. A good account of the Republican feuding can be found in Patricia Kilday Hart, "Party Poopers II," *Texas Monthly*, December 2001, 60, 62, 64.

16. Comparative data come from *The Book of the States, 2006*, 84–87. For background information, see Karen Hansen, "Legislative Pay: Baseball It Ain't," *State Legislatures*, July/August 1997, 20–26; "Legislator Pay Inches Up," *State Legislatures*, May 1999, 5; and "State Legislators' Salaries Down 6%," *PA Times*, March 2007, 1, 10.

17. "State Stats, *State Legislatures*, February 2004, 5.

18. See "80th Legislature (2007) Statistical Profile" (Austin: Legislative Reference Library of Texas, 2007), available at http://www.lrl.state.tx.us/legis/profile80.html; D'Ann Petersen and Laila Assanie "The Changing Face of Texas: Population Projections and Implications" (Dallas: Federal Reserve Board, October 2005), available at http://www.dallasfed.org/research/pubs/fotexas/fotexas_petersen.html; and Steve H. Murdock, "The Population of Texas: Historical Patterns and Future Trends Affecting Education" (February 2007), available at http://209.85.165.104/search?q=cache:IvYJNGjqD5AJ:txnp.org/seminar/2007_02_07_Education_Summit_SA.ppt+The+Population+of+Texas:+Historical+Patterns&hl=en&ct=clnk&cd=1&gl=us&client=firefox-a.

19. Karen Brooks, "Lawmakers Plan to Put More Religion in Your Life," *Dallas Morning News*, April 22, 2007, http://www.dallasnews.com/sharedcontent/dws/dn/latestnews/stories/042207dntexlegegod.3959ab1.html and Karen Brooks and Staci Hupp, "House: Allow Religion in School," *Dallas Morning News*, May 1, 2007, 1A, 2A.

20. See expenditures for all state offices at http://www.followthemoney.org.

21. See Emily Ramshaw, "Do Campaign Funds Bankroll a Cushy Lifestyle?" *Dallas Morning News*, December 17, 2006, 1A, 13A.

22. See, for example, Paul Burka, "Uncivil Union," *Texas Monthly*, June 2005, 8, 10, 12, and Christy Hoppe, "Whose Political Style Will Win in Austin?" *Dallas Morning News*, May 20, 2005, 1A, 8A.

23. Paul Burka, "A Giant Void," *Texas Monthly*, January 2004, 14–16. See also "Bye-bye, Big Guys," *Dallas Morning News*, March 7, 2004, 1H, 6H.

24. Karl T. Kurtz, "Custodians of American Democracy," *State Legislatures*, July-August 2006, 28–35.

25. In the U.S. Congress, seniority is more narrowly defined as continuous service on a committee. The congressional reforms of the 1970s modified the selection of committee chairpersons to allow some departure from the practice that the most senior member of the committee who is a member of the majority party always serves as chair. Seniority is more important in the U.S. Senate than in the U.S. House of Representatives.

26. Alexander Heard, ed., *State Legislatures in American Politics* (Englewood Cliffs, N.J.: Prentice-Hall, 1966), 3.

27. Christopher Z. Mooney concludes that Texas defies the national pattern that states with large populations and a high degree of heterogeneity tend to be more professionalized than small, more homogeneous states. See "The Political Economy of State Legislative Professionalism," paper presented at the annual meeting of the Southwestern Political Science Association, March 19–21, 1992, Austin. Mooney examined thirty years of measurements of the professionalism of legislative bodies in "Measuring U.S. State Legislative Professionalism: An Evaluation of Five Indices," *State and Local Government Review*, vol. 26 (Spring 1994), 70–78. This article is a methodological note, but a table showing the fifty states indicates that Texas does not fare well on professionalism measures. The situation has not changed much in the intervening years.

# CHAPTER 7

1. An excellent account of the nastiness of the legislature in 2003 can be found in Paul Burka, "Ruthless People," *Texas Monthly*, December 2003, 14–18.

2. See http://www.lrl.state.tx.us/ and click on "Bill Statistics" to see a statistical summary of bills and resolutions introduced, passed, and vetoed in recent legislative sessions.

3. The Legislative Reference Library provides detailed information about the legislative process in Texas at http://www.lrl.state.tx.us/citizenResources/LegProcess.html.

4. The lack of public support for the legislature is not unique to Texas or to state legislatures. See "The Poor Public Attitude toward the Legislature," *State Legislatures*, April 1995, 5; John R. Hibbing and Elizabeth Theiss-Morse, *Congress as Public Enemy: Attitudes Toward American Political Institutions* (Cambridge: Cambridge University, 1995).

5. The *Texas Observer* analysis is published in June and the *Texas Monthly* rankings in July following the regular legislative session.

# CHAPTER 8

1. Two exceptions to this tradition were (1) Richard Coke, the first governor under the 1876 Constitution, who served only one term and (2) Ross S. Sterling, who was not reelected in 1932. James E. Ferguson was reelected in 1916 but was impeached and removed from office in 1917. His wife, Miriam A. Ferguson, was later elected twice to nonconsecutive terms.

2. The constitution does spell out the grounds for removing judges, however. Other officials subject to impeachment include the lieutenant governor, the attorney general, the commissioner of the General Land Office, the comptroller, and appellate court judges. The grounds stipulated for impeachment of judges include partiality, oppression, official misconduct, incompetence, negligence, and failure to conduct the business of the court. See Fred Gantt Jr., *The Chief Executive in Texas* (Austin: University of Texas, 1964), 123.

3. Ferguson was impeached and convicted for mishandling public funds, conduct brought to light because funds for the University of Texas were involved.

4. *The Book of the States, 2006*, vol. 38 (Lexington, Ky.: Council of State Governments, 2006), 175.

5. Ibid., 154.

6. The Web site of the Texas governor (www.governor.state.tx.us/divisions) provides an up-to-date list of the various divisions of the governor's office.

7. Thad L. Beyle, "Being Governor," *The State of the States* (Washington, D.C.: CQ Press, 1996), 77–107, discusses how governors might be evaluated, including the index developed by the National Governors Association.

8. An interesting assessment of the Clements years can be found in George Bayoud and James Huffines, "25 Years Later: Clements' Texas Legacy Stands Tall," *Austin American-Statesman,* November 6, 2003, A15.

9. For an excellent look at the career of Ann Richards, see Jan Reid, "Ann: An Appreciation," *Texas Monthly*, November 2006, 177–179, 278–280.

10. As of 2007, Texas claimed three former U.S. presidents—Dwight Eisenhower, who was born in the state; Lyndon Johnson, who was a lifelong resident; and George H. W. Bush, who moved to Texas during an oil boom when he was a businessman, not a politician—as well as the sitting president. George W. Bush.

11. "The Big Winners and Losers of 1999: The Governor Had a Banner Year, While Local Education Lost Out," *Wall Street Journal*, December 29, 1999, T1.

12. Laylan Copelin and Jason Embry, "Lawmakers Rising against Perry Policies," *Austin American-Statesman*, March 18, 2007, A1. See also Arnold Garcia, Jr., "Commentary: After a Series of Political Setbacks,

Perry's Skidding on the Ice," *Austin American-Statesman*, March 11, 2007, H3.

13. See the following bills passed in 2003: HB 2292, regular session; HB 7, third called session; and SB 2, third called session.

14. SB 2, Article 7, third called session, Seventy-eighth Legislature, exempts river authorities, junior college districts, agencies headed by one or more statewide elected officials, agencies with a majority of board members not requiring Senate confirmation, and agencies reporting to one or more elected officials. Purely local boards are also exempted.

15. This practice is most common with the licensing and examining boards in various healthcare fields.

16. See Paul Burka, "Behind the Lines: Altered State," *Texas Monthly*, July 2003, 6, 10, 12.

17. E. Lee Bernick, "Special Sessions: What Manner of Gubernatorial Power?" *State and Local Government Review* 26 (Spring 1994), 79–88, reports that special sessions tend to be cyclical and somewhat responsive to national events that force the states to enact new legislation. Bernick studied special sessions in all fifty states for 1959 through 1989.

18. Unlike the president, the governor does not have a "pocket veto." The governor must send a veto message to block a bill; laying a bill aside without a signature results in the bill's becoming law, even if the legislature adjourns.

19. Congress granted the U.S. president the item veto in 1996; the president used the power eighty-two times before the U.S. Supreme Court declared it unconstitutional in 1998.

20. Pat Thompson and Steven R. Boyd, "Use of the Item Veto in Texas, 1940–1990," *State and Local Government Review*, 26 (Winter 1994), 38–45, provide perspective on the history of the item veto.

21. James McGregor Burns, *Leadership* (New York: Harper & Row, 1978), 42–45.

22. See, for example, Paul Burka, "So Far, So Bad," *Texas Monthly*, May 2003, 6, 10, 12.

# CHAPTER 9

1. The numbers in this paragraph are based on an actual count of entries in Appendix B, *Fiscal Size-Up, 2006–07 Biennium* (Austin: Legislative Budget Board, December 2005).

2. See, for example, Grover Starling, *Managing the Public Sector*, 5th ed. (Fort Worth: Harcourt Brace, 1998), Chapter 7

3. See "Bureaucracy" in *From Max Weber: Essays in Sociology*, translated, edited, and with an introduction by H. H. Gerth and C. Wright Mills (New York: Oxford, 1946), 196–244.

4. Emmette S. Redford, *Democracy in the Administrative State* (New York: Oxford, 1969), 3.

5. An excellent study of bureaucratic power at the national level is Francis Rourke, *Bureaucracy, Politics, and Public Policy*, 4th ed. (Boston: Little, Brown, 1986). Rourke's framework is adopted here.

6. Paul Appleby, *Big Democracy* (New York: Alfred A. Knopf, 1945), 7.

7. *Sunset Process Report Card* (Austin: Sunset Advisory Commission, February 2003 revision), and *Report to the 80th Legislature* (Austin: Sunset Advisory Commission, May 2007).

8. See Alan J. Bojorquez, "New Open Government Legislation," *Texas Town & City*, October 1999, 11–14.

# CHAPTER 10

1. Quoted in Donald Dale Jackson, *Judges* (New York: Atheneum, 1974), 7.

2. "Gin, 'Barbed' Cases Make Morrison Fun," University of Texas *Daily Texan,* February 19, 1964, 1.

3. Dietz quoted in Arnold Garcia Jr., "Do You Know Who Your Judges Are? Maybe You Should Find Out," *Austin American-Statesman*, September 14, 2002, A11.

4. Jackson, *Judges,* op. cit., 98.

5. Most of the information in this discussion comes from Bruce Hight, "Justices Bickering over Abortion Law," *Austin American-Statesman*, June 23, 2000, B1; the court case is *Re: Jane Doe*, number 00-0024, June 22, 2000; on Owen's confirmation, see John Council and T. R. Goldman, "Senate Showdown Ends with Owen Confirmation," *Texas Lawyer*, vol. 20, no. 13, May 30, 2005, 5.

6. Texas Attorney General's Office Web site, www.oag .state.tx.us/, accessed January 13, 2007.

7. *Hopwood v. State of Texas* (78, E.3rd 932, 5th Cir. 1996).

8. Attorney General's Letter Opinion 97–001, February 5, 1997.

9. Attorney General's Letter Opinion JC-107, September 3, 1999; Juan B. Elizondo Jr., "Cornyn Rescinds Hopwood Opinion," *Austin American-Statesman,* October 12, 1999, A1.

10. *Grutter v. Bollinger et al.* (539 U.S. 2003); *Gratz et al. v. Bollinger et al.* (539 U.S. 2003).

11. Statistics from State Bar of Texas Web site: www .texasbar.com/, accessed January 13, 2007.

12. *Justice at the Crossroads: Court Improvements in Texas* (Austin: Chief Justice's Task Force for Court Improvement, 1972), 11.

13. *Texas Courts: A Study by the Texas Research League*, Report Two: "The Texas Judiciary: A Proposal for Structural-Functional Reform" (Austin: Texas Research League, 1991), xi.

14. *Annual Statistical Report for the Texas Judicial System, Fiscal Year 2006* (Austin: Office of Court Administration, 2006), 4, 7–10 and passim.

15. *Crime In Texas* 2005 (Austin: Department of Public Safety, 2006), 67.

16. *Crime in Texas 1992* (Austin: Department of Public Safety, Crime Records Division, 1993), 14.

17. *Crime In Texas* 2005 (Austin: Texas Department of Public Safety, 2006), 15.

18. Mike Ward, "Proposal in the Works for 2 New Texas Prisons," *Austin American-Statesman,* August 7, 2006, A1.

19. *Texas Crime, Texas Justice* (Austin: Comptroller's Office, 1994), 51.

20. Bruce Fein and Burt Neuborne, "Why Should We Care about Independent and Accountable Judges?" *Journal of the American Judicature Society,* vol. 84, no. 2 (September/October), 2000.

21. Henry R. Glick, "Courts: Politics and the Judicial Process," in Virginia Gray and Russell L. Hanson, eds., *Politics in the American States: A Comparative Analysis,* 8th ed. (Washington, D.C.: Congressional Quarterly, 2004), 239.

22. Judge Eileen F. O'Neill, "Judicial Lottery Snakes-Eyes for Texas," *Houston Chronicle,* November 20, 1994, C1.

23. David J. Willis, "Separate Myth, Fact on the Judicial Process," *Houston Chronicle,* February 5, 1995, C1.

24. Glick, "Courts," op. cit., 249.

25. Wynne quoted in Michele Mittelstadt, "Political Money Eroding Trust in Judicial System," *Dallas Morning News*, February 22, 2002, A6.

26. David B. Rottman and Roy A. Schotland, "2004 Judicial Elections," in *The Book of the States*, Vol. 37 (Lexington, Ky.: Council of State Governments, 2005), 305–308.

27. Texans for Public Justice, *Lowering The Bar*, available on the TPJ Website: www.tpj.org/index.jsp

28. TPJ Website, ibid..

29. Adam Liptak and Janet T. Roberts, "Campaign Cash Mirrors a High Court's Rulings," *New York Times*, October 1, 2006, A1.

30. Mike Ward, "High Court Justice Leaves Case Involving Campaign Solicitor," *Austin American-Statesman,* April 13, 1996, B6.

31. Connie Mabin, "Suit Fails to Change Judicial Elections," *Austin American-Statesman,* September 28, 2000, B1.

32. Michele Mittlestadt, "Political Money Eroding Trust in Judicial System," *Dallas Morning News,* February 22, 2002, A6.

33. Debbie Nathan, "Wheel of Misfortune," *Texas Observer,* October 1, 1999, 22.

34. The Spangenberg Group, *A Study of Representation in Capital Murder Cases in Texas* (Austin: State Bar of Texas, Committee on Legal Representation for Those on Death Row, 1993), 157, 163.

35. Jeff South, "Inequality Found in Sentencing," *Austin American-Statesman,* September 4, 1993, A1.

36. David Pasztor, "Death Penalty Law Not Being Followed, Study Finds," *Austin American-Statesman,* October 29, 2003, B1; National Public Radio report, October 29, 2003.

37. From the Texas Department of Criminal Justice Web site: www.tdcj.state.tx.us/statistics/stats-mome.htm, accessed January 15, 2007.

38. Robert Tanner, "Time To Mend Justice?" *Austin American-Statesman,* April 29, 2007, G1.

39. "Inmate Freed after DNA Mix-Up," *Austin American-Statesman,* March 13, 2003, B2.

40. Robert Tharp, "Freedom Isn't Easy for Wrongly Convicted Man," *Austin American-Statesman,* August 5, 2006, D7; "Perry Pardons Man Wrongly Convicted," *Austin American-Statesman*, December 21, 2006, B3.

41. Information about the case of Delma Banks is based on the following sources: David Pasztor, "Lawyer, Ex-Judges Fear Texas About to Kill an Innocent Man," *Austin American-Statesman,* March 6, 2003, A1; Bob Herbert, "Countdown to Execution No. 300," *New York Times,* March 10, 2003, A25; Alberta Phillips, "Seek the Truth, and Let It Set a Wronged Man Free," *Austin American-Statesman,* March 9, 2003, E3; Peter T. Kilborn, "Prominent Ex-Judges and Prosecutors Lead Fight against Milestone Execution Today in Texas," *New York Times,* March 12, 2003, A16; David Pasztor, "Justices Suspend Texas Execution," *Austin American-Statesman,* March 13, 2003, A1; David Pasztor, "Texan's Death Sentence Lifted," *Austin American-Statesman,* February 25, 2004, A1.

# CHAPTER 11

1. *Gitlow v. New York* (268 U.S. 652, 1925).

2. *Texas v. Johnson* (491 U.S. 397, 1989).

3. Erik Rodriguez and Tony Plohetski, "Demonstrations Begin Peacefully, End in Arrests," *Austin American-Statesman,* March 21, 2003, B1.

4. *McCreary County v. ACLU*, 03-1693.

5. *New Braunfels v. Waldschmidt* (109 Texas 302, 1918).

6. *Ireland v. Bible Baptist Church* (480 S.W. 2d. 467, 1972).

7. *Reynolds v. Rayborn* (116 S.W. 2d. 836, 1938).

8. *Engel v. Vitale* (370 U.S. 421, 1962).

9. *Abington School District v. Schempp* and *Murray v. Catlett* (374 U.S. 203, 1963).

10. In 1995, the Gallup Poll reported that 71 percent of Americans responded that they would favor a constitutional amendment that would permit prayers in public schools. Although that exact question containing the word "amendment" has not been asked again, large majorities regularly say that they support the idea of Judeo-Christian displays in public institutions; for example, in 2001, 66 percent favored prayers in public schools; see *The Gallup Poll: Public Opinion for 1995 and 2001* (Wilmington, Del.: Scholarly Resources), 50, 107. In 2005, 76 percent of the American public supported the display of plaques featuring the Ten Commandments in county courthouses; see the Associated Press, "Split Rulings on Ten Commandment Displays," www.msnbc.com for June 27, 2005.

11. Kim Sue Lia Perkes, "Survey: Texans Support Prayers in Public Schools," *Austin American-Statesman,* November 21, 1999, B1.

12. Susan Weddington, "A Referendum on Tradition," *Austin American-Statesman,* March 3, 2000; John Cornyn, "Free Speech Means a Right to Prayer," *Austin American-Statesman,* March 31, 2000; Paul Mulshine, "Whose Religion?" *Austin American-Statesman,* April 4, 2000, A1.

13. David Jackson, "High Court Rejects Pre-Game Prayer," *Dallas Morning News,* June 30, 2000, A1.

14. Lorenzo Sadun, "New Texas Pledge Creates More Divides among States," *Austin American-Statesman,* August 30, 2003, A21.

15. "Moment of Silence Sparks Suit By Parents," *Austin American-Statesman*, March 15, 2006, B1.

16. Thomas R. Dye, *Understanding Public Policy*, 12th ed., (Upper Saddle River, N.J.: Prentice Hall, 2008), 73; *Crime In Texas 2005* (Austin: Department of Public Safety, 2006), 19.

17. Number of justifiable homicides from Handgun Control Web site: www.bradycampaign.org, accessed September 12, 2006; estimate of protective use from Dye, *Public Policy* op. cit., 73.

18. Much of this discussion of arguments over the Second Amendment is based on information in Robert J. Spitzer, *The Politics of Gun Control* (Chatham, N.J.: Chatham House, 1995).

19. Jack Manfuso, "Poll: Most Texans Back Gun Limits," *Austin American-Statesman,* June 30, 2000, B3.

20. Rick Green, "The Real Story of the Second Amendment," *Austin American-Statesman,* April 10, 2000, A9.

21. *United States v. Miller* (307 U.S. 174, 1939).

22. Virginia Gray ranks Texas as the forty-fifth most conservative (that is, most permissive of private gun ownership) among the states; see "The Socioeconomic and Political Context of States," in Virginia Gray and Russell L. Hanson, eds., *Politics in the American States: A Comparative Analysis,* 8th ed. (Washington, D.C.: Congressional Quarterly, 2004), 4, Table 1.1.

23. Robert W. Gee, "Gun-Rights Advocates Brace for Battle," *Austin American-Statesman,* August 30, 2002, B1; Michele Kay, "New Concealed Handgun Law Reverses Limits," *Austin American-Statesman,* June 21, 2003, B1.

24. "Governor Signs Off on Self-Defense Law," *Austin American-Statesman*, March 28, 2007, A11; Jeff Wentworth and Patrick Rose, "Criticism of Gun Bill Was Way Off-Target," *Austin American-Statesman*, March 28, 2007, A11.

25. *Roe v. Wade* (410 U.S. 113, 1973).

26. Jason Embry, "Texas Abortion Law Under Scrutiny," *Austin American-Statesman,* July 13, 2006, A1.

27. Suzanne Gamboa, "Most Favor Abortion Notice Bill," *Austin American-Statesman,* March 3, 1997, B1.

28. David Pasztor, "Senate Passes Bill That Defines a Fetus as an Individual," *Austin American-Statesman,* May 23, 2003, A1; Melissa Ludwig, "Law on Abortion Stayed for Now," *Austin American-Statesman,* August 5, 2003, B1; Rachel Proctor, "Your Right to Not Much," *Texas Observer,* August 20, 2003, 4.

29. Kelley Shannon, "Execute Doctors for Abortions? Some Say It Could Happen," *Austin American-Statesman,* August 30, 2005, B3; Jason Embry, "Texas Abortion Law under Scrutiny," *Austin American-Statesman,* July 13, 2006, A1.

30. Attorney General of Texas, Opinion Number GA-0501, January 24, 2007; we are grateful to Charlotte Harper of the AG's office for clarifying the meaning of this opinion for us.

31. *Brown v. Board of Education of Topeka* (347 U.S. 483, 1954).

32. Joel Anderson, "Judge Ends School Desegregation in Dallas," *Austin American-Statesman,* June 6, 2003, B3.

33. Kent Fischer, "Public School, Private Club," *Dallas Morning News,* November 18, 2006, A1.

34. *Edgewood Independent School System v. Kirby* (777 S.W. 2d 391, Tex. 1989).

35. Kenneth K. Wong, "The Politics of Education," in Grey and Hanson, *Politics in the American States,* op. cit., 368.

36. "Wealthy Make More Donations, Study Finds," *Dallas Morning News,* April 15, 2004, A3.

37. Jason Embry, "School Tax System Unconstitutional," *Austin American-Statesman*, November 23, 2005, A1; Maeve Reston, "Taxpayers' Lawsuit Challenges State's School-Finance System," *Austin American-Statesman*, April 6, 2001, B5; Alberta Phillips, "School Finance Gives Robin Hood Bad Name," *Austin American-Statesman*, April 27, 2001, A15.

38. Jason Embry and Corrie MacLaggan, "It's Finished: All of School Finance Plan Goes To Perry," *Austin American-Statesman*, May 16, 2006, A1; Christy Hoppe, "School 'Fix' Plan: Is It Sufficient?" *Dallas Morning News,* May 13, 2006, A1.

39. Most of the information in this account comes from Michael Berryhill, "Prisoner's Dilemma," *The New Republic,* December 27, 1999, 18–23.

40. Information on the Tulia case is based on Adam Liptak, "Texas Cases Challenged over Officer's Testimony," *New York Times,* March 18, 2003, A20; Nate Blakeslee, "Free at Last?" *Texas Observer,* April 25, 2003, 10; David Pasztor, "In Infamous Tulia, 13 to Walk Free Today," *Austin American-Statesman,* June 16, A1; David Pasztor, "DA Faces State Bar Inquiry in Tulia Case," *Austin American-Statesman,* August 2, 2003, B1; Editorial, "District Attorney in Tulia Case Should Be Held Accountable," *Austin American-Statesman,* December 29, 2004, A10.

41. Pasztor, "Infamous Tulia," ibid.

42. David Pasztor, "Amarillo to Pay $5 Million to 45 in Tulia Case," *Austin American-Statesman,* March 12, 2004, A1; Alan Bean, "A Letter From Tulia," *Texas Observer,* February 18, 2005, 29.

43. *Legal Responsibility and Authority of Correctional Officers* (College Park, Md.: American Correctional Association, 1975), 5.

44. See, for example, Frank S. Malone, *Correctional Law Digest 1977* (Toledo, Oh.: University of Toledo, 1978).

45. Frank S. Kemmerer, *William Wayne Justice* (Austin: University of Texas, 1991), 145–149; *Morales v. Turman* (326 F. supp. 577, 1971); 38. *Ruiz v. Estelle* (666 F.2d 854, 1982); one of the authors of this text made several visits to TDC units during the period of litigation and can personally attest the accuracy of many of Ruiz's charges; see also Steve J. Martin and Sheldon Ekland-Olson, *Texas Prisons: The Walls Came Tumbling Down* (Austin: Texas Monthly Press, 1987); "Inside America's Toughest Prison," *Newsweek,* October 6, 1986, 48–61.

46. Mike Ward, "After 30 Years, Ruiz Is Ready for Case's Close," *Austin American-Statesman,* June 12, 2002, A1; Ed Timms, "30-Year Texas Prison Battle Ends," *Dallas Morning News*, June 9, 2002, A1.

47. *The Book of the States 2006* (Lexington, Ky.: Council of State Governments, 2006), 537–538.

48. Ken Anderson, *Crime in Texas: Your Complete Guide to the Criminal Justice System* (Austin: University of Texas, 1997), 73.

49. *Furman v. Georgia* (408 U.S. 238, 1972).

50. *Gardner v. Florida* (430 U.S. 349, 1977); *Woodson v. North Carolina* (428 U.S. 289, 1976); our summary of these death penalty rules is based on J. W. Peltason, *Understanding the Constitution,* 8th ed. (New York: Holt, Rinehart & Winston, 1979), 185.

51. Michael Graczyk, "Death Penalty Use Bucks Trend," *Austin American-Statesman,* January 6, 2007, B8; Web site, Texas Department of Corrections: www.tdcj.state .tx.us/statistics/stats-mome.htm.

52. Robert Tharp, "Is Death Penalty Losing Capital?" *Dallas Morning News*, December 30, 2005, A1.

53. Mike Ward, "Life Without Parole Among 600 Laws Signed By Governor," *Austin American-Statesman*, June 18, 2005, A15.

54. Alberta Phillips, "We Must Draw the Line at Executing Juvenile Offenders," *Austin American-Statesman,* September 1, 2002, H3.

55. Alfred P. Carlton Jr. (president of the ABA), "Executing Juveniles Demeans Our Justice System," *Austin American-Statesman,* August 27, 2002, A9; David Pasztor, "Global Review of Death Penalty," *Austin American-Statesman,* October 28, 2003, A1.

56. Mike Ward, "High Court Spares Juvenile Offenders," *Austin American-Statesman*, March 2, 2005, A1; the case is *Roper v. Simmons* (543 U.S. 551; 125 S. Ct. 1183; 161 L. Ed. 2nd 1, 2005).

57. Tim Curtis, "Tort 'Reforms' Trying to Take Away Your Rights," *Houston Chronicle,* January 19, 1995, A29.

58. David Pasztor, "House Passes Bitterly Fought Tort Reform Bill," *Austin American-Statesman,* March 29, 2003

59. Howard Marcus and Bruce Malone, "2003 Reforms Helping Doctors Do Their Work," *Austin American-Statesman*, April 10, 2006, A9; Jon Opelt, "Contrary to What Study Says, Malpractice Lawsuits Drive Costs," *Austin American-Statesman*, March 18, 2005, A15.

60. Alex Winslow, "The Human Toll of 'Tort Reform,'" *Austin American-Statesman*, April 12, 2006, A11; Bernard Black, Charles Silver, David Hyman, and William Sage, "Hunting Down the Facts on Medical Malpractice," *Austin American-Statesman*, March 14, 2005, A9.

61. Bill Hammond, "New Era of Pro-Business Leadership Is Good For Texas," *Austin American-Statesman*, April 15, 2003, A11.

62. Mimi Swartz, "Hurt? Injured? Need a Lawyer? Too Bad!" *Texas Monthly*, November, 2005, 258.

# CHAPTER 12

1. Discussion of county government in Texas relies in part on Robert E. Norwood and Sabrina Strawn, *Texas County Government: Let the People Choose* (Austin: Texas Research League, 1984). This monograph is the most extensive work available on the subject.

2. See Texas County Population Estimates 2004, Arranged in Descending Order at http://www.tsl.state.tx.us/ref/ abouttx/popcnty42004.html.

3. Although one often sees commissioners court written as "commissioners'" with an apostrophe, Chapter 81 of the *Texas Local Government Code* is explicit in the lack of an apostrophe.

4. Norwood and Strawn, op. cit., 157.

5. Bell County Judge John Garth, in a conversation with one of the authors on February 21, 1991.

6. Travis County Judge Bill Aleshire in "Elected County Officials—Unlike City—Actually Run Government, "*Austin American-Statesman,* September 26, 1996, A15.

7. Robert Elder Jr. and Brad Reagan, "Rural Counties Try to Stay One Step Ahead of Growth," *Wall Street Journal,* July 12, 2000, T1, T3.

8. Richard Oppel (editor of the paper), "Time to Ask Right Questions about County Government," *Austin American-Statesman,* September 22, 1996, E3.

9. Provisions for how both home-rule and general-law municipalities can organize are found in Chapters 9 and 21 to 26 of the *Texas Local Government Code*. An extensive look at the concept of home rule both in Texas and nationally can be found in Dale Krane, ed., *Home Rule in America* (Washington, D.C.: CQ Press, 2000).

10. See Victor S. DeSantis and Tari Renner, "City Goverment Structures: An Attempt at Clarification," *State and Local Government Review,* vol. 14 (Spring 2002), 95–104.

11. *Texas Almanac, 2006–2007* (Dallas: Dallas Morning News*, 2006), 451–464, by count.

12. Additional information on forms of government came from http://www.icma.org in the section entitled "Who's Who: Recognized Local Governments." This section is

accessible only to members of the International City/County Management Association and provides a list of those cities that meet the criteria to be considered either a council-manager government or a government with a professional general administrator.

13. A thorough look at modern council-manager government can be found in John Nalbandian and George Frederickson, eds., *The Future of Local Government Administration: The Hansell Symposium* (Washington, D.C.: International City/County Management Association, 2002); in the monthly issues of *PM: Public Management,* published by ICMA; and the work of James H. Svara, for example, "Conflict and Cooperation in Elected-Administrative Relations in Large Council-Manager Cities," *State and Local Government Review,* vol. 31 (Fall 1999), 173–189.

14. Bill Hansell, "Evolution and Change Characterize Council-Manager Government," *PM: Public Management,* August 2000, 20.

15. See Robert B. Boynton, "City Councils: Their Roles in the Legislative System," *Municipal Year Book 1976* (Washington, D.C.: International City Management Association, 1976), 67–77, for a detailed discussion on the characteristics of the two models.

16. See Jane Mobley, "Politician or Professional? The Debate over Who Should Run Our Cities Continues," *Governing,* February 1988, 41–48, for an excellent discussion of the advantages and disadvantages of mayors versus city managers as executive officers of cities.

17. See *Model City Charter,* 8th ed. (Denver: National Civic League, 2003).

18. See *Texas Local Government Code,* Chapters 22–25.

19. See, for example, Robert B. Boynton, "City Councils: Their Role in the Legislative System"; Tari Renner and Victor S. DeSantis, "Contemporary Patterns in Municipal Government Structures," *Municipal Year Book 1993* (Washington, D.C.: International City/County Management Association, 1993), 57–68; Daniel R. Morgan and Robert E. England, *Managing Urban America,* 4th ed. (Chatham, N.J.: Chatham House, 1996), 58–80.

20. This discussion of municipal finance relies on concepts articulated by Lloyd V. Harrell, then city manager of Denton, in an April 23, 1988, address to political science honors students at the University of North Texas. His framework is still valid.

21. John Nalbandian discusses local representation in "Tenets of Contemporary Professionalism in Local Government," in George W. Fredrickson, *Ideal and Practice in Council-Manager Government* (Washington, D.C.: International City/County Management Association, 1985), 157–171.

22. Reese Dunklin and Brooks Egerton, "'Designer Districts' Benefit Developers," *Dallas Morning News,* July 3, 2001, 1A, 12A.

23. See, for example, Edward C. Olson and Laurence Jones, "Change in Hispanic Representation on Texas City Councils between 1980–1993," *Texas Journal of Political Studies,* vol. 18 (Fall/Winter 1996), 53–74; Laurence F. Jones, Edward C. Olson, and Delbert A. Taebel, "Change in African-American Representation on Texas City Councils: 1980–1993," *Texas Journal of Political Studies,* vol. 18 (Spring/Summer 1996), 57–78.

# CHAPTER 13

1. *Fiscal Size Up, 2006–07 Biennium* (Austin: Legislative Budget Board, 2005), 11, available online at http://www.lbb.state.tx.us/Fiscal_Size-up/Fiscal_Size-up_2006-2007_0106.pdf. *Fiscal Size Up* is an excellent source of information about Texas state finance, and is published about six months after the close of each regular session of the Texas legislature.

2. Wayne King, "Despite Success, Sun Belt Oil Patch Is Finding It's Not Immune to Recession," *New York Times,* June 9, 1981, 11.

3. See, for example, "Texas, The Lone Star State: Business," *Texas Almanac, Millennium Edition* (Dallas: *Dallas Morning News,* 1999), 5.

4. See "Overview of the Texas Economy," Business and Industrial Data Center, U.S. Bureau of the Census, at http://www.bidc.state.tx.us/overview/2-2te.htm.

5. See Office of the Texas Comptroller, *Texas Economic Update,* Fall 2004, at http://www.window.state.tx.us/ecodata/teufall04/, and *Texas Almanac, 2006–2007* (Dallas: *Dallas Morning News,* 2006), 568.

6. See, for example, "Texas Tomorrow," the special section of the *Dallas Morning News* published on December 19, 1999.

7. For the budgetary plight of the states, see Robert E. Pierre, "The Budget Squeeze," *Washington Post National Weekly Edition,* March 25–31, 2002; William McKenzie, "Your Worst Nightmare Is Slithering into Your State," *Dallas Morning News,* January 14, 2003, 11A; "2002 Tax and Budget Review and 2003 Budget Preview," *State Fiscal Brief* (a publication of the Rockefeller Institute of Government at the State University of New York), March 2003.

8. Katherine Yung, "Tattered Trade Hopes," *Dallas Morning News,* April 13, 2003, 1D, 5D.

9. See, for example, John Machacek and Susan Roth, "Split Looms over $4 Billion for Security," *USA Today,* March 26, 2003, 13A.

10. Angela Shah, "Texans' Confidence in Economy Erodes," *Dallas Morning News,* March 17, 2003, 1D, 3D, and "No Job Growth Seen," *Dallas Morning News,* March 7, 2003, 1D, 11D; Jonathan Weisman, "Jobs Gone for Good," *Washington Post National Weekly Edition,* September 15–21, 2003; 65; Greg Schneider, "Another Kind of Homeland Security," *Washington Post National Weekly Edition,* February 9–15, 2004, 18–19.

11. Angela Shah, " Texas Ranked No. 1 for Corporate Locales," *Dallas Morning News*, March 3, 2006, 1D, 5D.

12. Angela Shah, "Texas Jobless Rate Dips to 4.1%," *Dallas Morning News,* June 16, 2007, 1D; Brendan Case, "18% of Jobs Linked to Trade," *Dallas Morning News,*

May 18, 2007, 3D; "Top Global Cities, *Dallas Morning News*, March 27, 2007, 3D; and Bob Moos, "Texas Leaps to No. 2 as Place to Retire," *Dallas Morning News*, May 29, 2007, 1D, 6D.

13. Nicholas Johnson and Elizabeth McNichol, "How Strong Are State Budgets?" National Conference of State Legislatures (April 2007), available at http://www.ncsl.org/standcomm/scbudg/manmon.htm.

14. See, for example, Carl Tubbesing and Sheri Steisel, "Answers to Your Welfare Worries," *State Legislatures,* January 1997, 12–19; Rob Gurwitt, "Cracking the Casework Culture," *Governing*, March 1997, 27–30; William McKenzie, "Texas Tries to Pick Up the Federal Burden," *Dallas Morning News,* May 20, 1997, 13A.

15. Carl Tubbesing and Vic Miller, "Our Fractured Fiscal System," *State Legislatures*, April 2007, 26–28, quotation on p. 26.

16. *Book of the States, 2007 Edition*, vol. 39 (Lexington, Ky.: Council of State Governments, 2007), 401, and *Texas Fact Book 2006* (Austin: Legislative Budget Board, 2006), 23.

17. See H.B. 3, Seventy-ninth Legislature, Third Called Session, and Dave McNeely, Texas-Style Tax Cut," *State Legislatures*, April 2007, 22–25.

18. Comparative information on sales taxes can be found at the Web site of the Sales Tax Clearinghouse, available at www.thestc.com.

19. "Who Pays State and Local Taxes?" *CTJ Update*, March 2003, 1–2. See also Angela Shah, "Texas Has Low Taxes—Depending on Figures," *Dallas Morning News,* January 23, 2003, 1H, 2H.

20. See the section on various aspects of state and local tax revenue available at www.taxadmin.org.

21. "Texas State-Local Tax Burden Compared to U.S. Average (1970–2007), available at http://www.taxfoundation.org/files/sl_burden_texas-2007-04-04.pdf.

22. *Texas Fact Book 2006* (Austin: Legislative Budget Board, 2006), 20, 23.

23. "Bullock's Tax Speech Serves as a Warning for State," *Austin American-Statesman*, January 27, 1991, A8.

24. See, for example, David Osborne and Ted Gaebler, *Reinventing Government* (Reading, Mass.: Addison-Wesley, 1992), especially Chapter 5, "Results-Oriented Government"; Jonathan Walters, "The Cult of Total Quality," *Governing,* May 1992, 38–41; and the many reports stemming from the Texas Performance Review and the National Performance Review. See also Julia Melkers and Katherine Willoughby, "The State of the States: Performance-based Budgeting Requirements in 47 Out of 50," *Public Administration Review*, vol. 58 (January/February 1998), 66–73.

25. Katherine Barrett, Richard Greene, Michele Mariani, and Anya Sostek, "The Way We Tax: A 50-State Report," available at www.governing.com/archive/2003/feb/8p3intro.txt, quotation on p. 1.

26. Katherine Barrett and Richard Greene, with Zach Patton and J. Michael Keeling, "Grading the States '05: The Year of Living Dangerously," *Governing*, available at http://governing.com/gpp/2005/intro.htm. From this overview section, one can examine the report cards of the individual states.

27. Dave McNeely, "Texas-Style Tax Cut," *State Legislatures*, April 2007, 22–26.

28. Comparative data are drawn from "Texas at a Glance," *Texas Fact Book 2006* (Austin: Legislative Budget Board, 2006), 17–23, and from *Fiscal Size-Up, 2006–07,* 46.

29. From a now-vintage report, "State Prisons Expenditures 2001" by the U.S. Department of Justice, available at http://www.ojp.usdoj.gov/bjs/pub/pdf/spe01.pdf.

# CHAPTER 14

1. For excellent overviews of what happened—or did not happen—during the regular session of the Eightieth Legislature, see "The Best & Worst Legislators, 2007," *Texas Monthly*, July 2007, 95–105, and Jake Bernstein, "A Fish Rots from the Head: With These Three in Charge, the Session was a Stinker," *Texas Observer*, June 15, 2007, 4–7.

2. See Carl Tubbesing and Vic Miller, "Our Fractured Fiscal System," *State Legislatures*, April 2007, 26, and William T. Pound, "Fedralism at a Crossroads," *State Legislatures*, June 2006, 18–19.

3. *San Antonio Independent School District, et al. v. Rodriguez* (411 U.S. 1, 1973) and *William Kirby, et al. v. Edgewood Independent School District, et al.* (777 S.W. 2nd 391,1989) are the appellate court opinions.

4. *Ruiz v. Estelle* (666 Fed. 2d, 854, 1982 and 650 Fed, 2d. 555, 5th Circuit, 1981).

5. See, for example, David Pasztor, "Low-hanging Fruit," *Texas Observer*, January 26, 2007, 8–10, 20–21 for critical issues that the state legislature may continue to dodge.

6. "The State of the Texas Economy," *Fiscal Notes*, April 2007, 11–13, quotation on 11.

7. Home page of the Business and Industry Data Center, available at http://www.bidc.state.tx.us/.

8. Brenda Trolin, in "Can Workers' Comp Work?" *State Legislatures,* May 1992, 33–37, examines the problems and attempted solutions in various states, with Texas being prominently mentioned in the report.

9. "Maximum and Minimum Weekly Benefits," Division of Workers' Compensation, Texas Department of Insurance, available at http://www.tdi.state.tx.us.

10. For the national perspective, see Matthew H. Brown's two articles, "Transforming the Electricity Business," *State Legislatures*, April 1999, 14–19, and "Slow Transition to Competition," *State Legislatures,* May 2000, 28–31. For information on Texas state policy, see, for example, Robert Elder Jr., "To Free Power Market, Lawmakers Aim to Cut Utilities Down to Size,"

*Wall Street Journal,* January 27, 1999, T1, T4, and Eileen O'Grady, "Power Suppliers Scramble to Improve Transmission," *Wall Street Journal,* August 25, 1999, T1, T3.

11. Corporation for Enterprise Development, "2007 Overview: Development Report Card for the States: An Annual Economic Development Benchmarking Tool," available at http://www.cfed.org/focus .m?parentid=34&siteid=2346&id=2346.

12. "Texas at a Glance," *Texas Fact Book 2006* (Austin: Legislative Budget Board, 2006), 18–19.

13. "FSB: Who Loves Small Business Best? 2006," *CNNMoney.com,* available at http://money.cnn.com/ magazines/fsb/fsb_beststates/2006/snapshots/9.html.

14. See, for example, the policy discussion of Randall B. Ripley and Grace A. Franklin, *Congress, the Bureaucracy, and Public Policy,* 5th ed. (Monterey, Cal.: Brooks/Cole, 1991), Chapters 1 and 6.

15. See the U.S. Department of Health and Human Services guidelines at http://aspe.hhs.gov/poverty/07poverty.html.

16. "Texas at a Glance," *Texas Fact Book 2006,* 18–22.

17. See the National Center for Children in Poverty Web site at http://www.nccp.org/.

18. "Lowest Income Counties in the United States," *Wikipedia,* available at http://en.wikipedia.org/wiki/ Lowest-income_counties_in_the_United_States.

19. *Fiscal Size-Up 2006–07* (Austin: Legislative Budget Board, 2005), 111; *Texas Medicaid in Perspective* (Austin: Texas Health and Human Services Commission, 2007), 1–1; and "The Cost of Doing Nothing," *Texas Observer,* June 15, 2007, 3.

20. "Study Provides Look at Homeless," *Dallas Morning News,* December 8, 1999, 3A. See also Joel Stein, "The Real Face of Homelessness," *Time,* January 20, 2003, 52–57, and Wendy Cole and Richard Corliss, "No Place Like Home," *Time,* January 20, 2003, 58–61.

21. "Community Services," Texas Department of Community Affairs, available at http://www.tdhca.state.tx.us/cs.htm.

22. See "Census Finds Drop in Dallas' Homeless," *Dallas Morning News,* April 17, 2007, 1B, 8B for a look at homeless issues in one metropolitan center.

23. For an excellent discussion of the importance of middle-class attitudes in the development of social programs, see Robert Morris, *Social Policy of the American Welfare State* (New York: Harper & Row, 1979), Chapters 1 and 2. Morris, along with C. John E. Hansan, also offers useful commentary on welfare philosophy in the United States in *Welfare Reform, 1996–2000: Is There a Safety Net?* (Westport, Conn.: Auburn House, 1999). See also Juan B. Elizondo Jr. and Gary Susswein, "Judge Defers 'Work' Rules," *Austin American-Statesman,* December 2, 2003, B1, for a different sort of middle-class values issue.

24. Suzannah Gonzales and Corrie MacLaggan, "Texas Is Fifth-Poorest State, Data Show," *Austin American-Statesman,* August 30, 2006, B1.

25. "Welfare Reform, Part Two: A Kinder, Gentler Plan for Texas," *Texas Government News,* September 23, 1996, 2. For an excellent explanation of the federal legislation and its consequences, see Carl Tubbesing and Sheri Steisel, "Answers to Your Welfare Worries," *State Legislatures,* January 1997, 12–19.

26. Scott Pattison, executive director of the National Association of State Budget Officers, in a joint meeting of two standing panels of the National Academy of Public Administration meeting on "Social Equity Implications of Local, State, and Federal Fiscal Challenges," held in Washington, D.C., Raleigh, N.C., and across the country via conference telephone on June 13, 2003.

27. Robert T. Garrett, "Changes in CHIP Frustrate Families," *Dallas Morning News,* March 27, 2006, 1A, 4A.

28. Jack Tweedie et al., "Window of Opportunity for Welfare Reform," *State Legislatures,* April 1999, 22.

29. See Daniel Gross, "Reeled In," *Dallas Morning News,* February 4, 2007, 1P, 5P.

30. Bob Moos, "The Gender Gap Endures, Even in Retirement," *Dallas Morning News,* June 18, 2006, 1A, 10A.

31. Christopher Conte, "Dry Spell," *Governing,* March 2003, 20–24, provides a concise account of the national drought problems.

32. *2007 State Water Plan* is available at http://www.twdb .state.tx.us/publications/reports/State_Water_Plan/2007/ 2007StateWaterPlan/2007StateWaterPlan.htm.

33. A history of environmental quality in Texas can be found on the Web site of the Texas Commission on Environmental Quality at http://www.tceq.state.tx.us/ about/tceqhistory.html.

34. The EPA was following the lead of President George W. Bush who wanted less stringent controls. See, for example, Terry McCarthy, "How Bush Gets His Way on the Environment," *Time,* January 27, 2003, 48–50. See also Gregg Easterbrook, "Why Bush Gets a Bad Rap on Dirty Air," *Time,* September 29, 2003, 53.

35. Texas Environmental Quality Commission, "Texas Attainment Status by Regions," available at http:// www.tceq.state.tx.us/implementation/air/sip/siptexas .html#naas.

36. "Texas No. 1 in Harmful Gases," *Dallas Morning News,* June 3, 2007, 1A, 23A.

37. Anne Gearan, "Coming on I-35: Mexican Trucks," *Denton Record-Chronicle,* June 8, 2004, 1A, 11A.

38. See Linda Sikkema and Melissa Savage, "Nuclear Renaissance?" *State Legislatures,* March 2007, 12–15, for problems associated with coal.

39. Sudeep Reddy, "Warmer Reactions," *Dallas Morning News,* January 16, 2007, 1D, 6D.

40. See Rany Lee Loftins, "State Puts D-FW on Smog List," *Dallas Morning News,* June 13, 2003, 1B, 3B; Tom Arrandale, "The Pollution Puzzle," *Governing,* August

2002, 22–26; Larry Morandi, "Winds of Change," *State Legislatures,* May 2003, 26–29.

41. Randy Lee Loftis, "Cleaning Air Gets Harder," *Dallas Morning News,* June 10, 2007, 1A, 29A.

42. David Hosansky, "Buried in E-waste," *State Legislatures,* June 2004, 20–23.

43. Natalie Gott, "Lawmakers Pass Clean Air Bill, Shoot Down Other Measures," *Denton Record-Chronicle,* June 15, 2003, 4A; Amber Novak, "Up in Smoke," *Texas Observer,* May 23, 2003, 4–7, 27–31.

44. Senator Robert Duncan, a Lubbock Republican, quoted in Terrence Stutz, "Radioactive Dump Approved by Senate," *Dallas Morning News,* May 8, 2003, 5A.

45. Lawrence F. Alwin, CPA, *The Commission on Environmental Quality's Enforcement and Permitting Functions for Selected Programs,* Report No. 04-016 (Austin: State Auditor's Office, December 2003); Christy Hoppe, "Auditors Went Too Far, Perry Says," *Dallas Morning News,* December 30, 2003, 3A.

46. For the national perspective on biofuels, see Glen Andersen, "Homegrown Energy," *State Legislatures,* June 2007, 16–19. This article describes various types of biofuels as well as the effect on American agriculture.

47. For an indication of local water and wastewater rates, which are trending upward both to support water development projects and wastewater runoff mandates, see "Water and Wastewater Survey Results," each May in *Texas Town & City* magazine.

48. See "Water Issues Generate Attention Throughout Texas," *Lone Star Sierran,* Summer 2004, 3–5.

49. "Texas at a Glance," *Texas Fact Book 2006,* 23.

50. This paragraph is based on "Texas Observes Transportation Week, May 16–22," Texas Department of Transportation, press release, May 13, 2004, available at http://www.dot.state.tx.us/txdotnews/025-2004.htm.

51. See, for example, "Traffic Congestion and Reliability: Trends and Advanced Strategies for Congestion Mitigation," Federal Highway Administration, available at http://ops.fhwa.dot.gov/congestion _report/chapter3.htm. See "Highway Congestion Levels Out in DFW," *The Chamber Report,* October 30, 2003, available at http://news.dallaschamber.org/ e_article000197598.cfm; "Life in the Stuck Lane," *Dallas Morning News,* June 21, 2002, 21A; "News at Ten," WFAA, Channel 8, September 30, 2003; "Roads and Bridges," *ASCE's 2001 Report Card for America's Infrastructure,* available at https://www.asce.org/ reportcard/pdf/statechartsroadsbridges.pdf.

52. Gregg Jones, Holly Becka, Jennifer LaFleur, and Steve McConigle, "18 Wheels and Countless Dangers," *Dallas Morning News,* September 17, 2006, 1A, 8A-10A, and "Reviews Make Roads Safer but Rarely Happen," *Dallas Morning News,* September 19, 2006, 1A, 4A-8A; Greg Jones and Holly Becka, "Ex-cons and Big Rigs: A Dangerous Mix," *Dallas Morning News,* December 10, 2006, 1A, 23–25A; McConigle, "Many Truckers Skirting the Rules with No Penalties," *Dallas Morning News,* December 12, 2006, 1A, 12A-14A.

53. "Rep. Harper-Brown Rallies Texas Legislators for Improved Federal Transportation Fund," office of State Representative Linda Harper-Brown, press release, May 8, 2003, available at http://www.house.state.tx.us/news/ release.php?id-293.

54. Christopher Keyes, "Taking Its Toll," *Texas Monthly,* May 2004, 76.

55. See Marisa Medrano Perez and Anne O'Ryan, "Growth Puts the Squeeze on Texas Transportation," *Texas Journey,* November/December 2004, 27–30; Robert Tanner, "Open Road, for a Price," *Austin American-Statesman,* June 12, 2005, H1.; Red McCombs, "Let's Keep Texas Moving," *Austin American-Statesman,* March 13, 2007, A11.

56. See, for example, Christopher Swope, "Unloading Assets," *Governing,* January 2007, 36–40, which analyzes the trend for states, including Texas, to explore selling everything from lotteries to bridges, and Matt Sundeen, "The Money Road," *State Legislatures,* May 2007, 12–15, which examines the leasing of public roads for cash and includes a page on actions of the Texas legislature.

57. Christy Hoppe, "King of Roads Known for Giving Little Ground," *Dallas Morning News,* June 26, 2007, 1A, 5A.

# CHAPTER 15

1. "The Future Is Texas," by the editors of *The Economist,* reprinted in the *Austin American-Statesman,* January 5, 2003, H13.

2. *Fiscal Size-Up, 2006-07 Biennium* (Austin: Legislative Budget Board, 2006), p. 19, Table 15.

3. Suzannah Gonzales and Corrie MacLaggan, "Texas Is Fifth-Poorest State, Data Show," *Austin American-Statesman,* August 30, 2006, B1.

4. Corrie MacLaggan, "More Kids in Poverty, Study Says," *Austin American-Statesman,* June 27, 2006, B1.

5. "Texas Leads Nation in Households at Risk for Hunger," *Austin American-Statesman,* October 29, 2005, B5.

6. Robert Reich, *The Work of Nations: Preparing Ourselves for 21st Century Capitalism* (New York: Random House, 1992).

7. Steve H. Murdock, Steve White, Md. Narul Hoque, Beverly Pecotte, Xuihong You, and Jennifer Balkan, *The New Texas Challenge: Population Change and the Future of Texas* (College Station: Texas A&M University, 2003), 215.

8. Jason Embry, "Study Ranks Texas 35th in Rates of Graduation," *Austin American-Statesman,* June 21, 2006, B1.

9. "Texas Leads in Population Growth," *Austin American-Statesman,* December 22, 2006, A1.

10. Murdock, et al., *New Texas Challenge,* op. cit., 24.

11. Ibid., 54–55.

12. Ibid., 127, 130–131, 145, 180–181, 191.

13. Ibid., 109.

14. Leon F. Bouvier and Dudley L. Poston Jr., *Thirty Million Texans?* (Washington, D.C.: Center for Immigration Studies, 1993), 87.

15. "Panel: Cut Speed Limits to Clear Houston's Air," *Austin American-Statesman,* July 20, 2000, A5.

16. Kelly Daniel, "Austin among Worst in Nation for Time Wasted in Traffic Jams," *Austin American- Statesman,* May 8, 2001, B1.

17. Web site of the American Lung Association: www .lungusa.org, accessed February 10, 2007.

18. Ralph Blumenthal, "Houston Inaugurates Mayor and a Long-Awaited Train," *New York Times,* January 3, 2004, A9.

19. Alicia A. Caldwell, "Census: More than Half of Texans Are Minorities," *Austin American-Statesman*, August 11, 2005, B1; Murdock, et al., *New Texas Challenge*, op. cit., 27.

20. Bob Dart, "Travis County Growth Pattern Changes," *Austin American-Statesman*, March 16, 2006, A1.

21. Press release from Senator Diane Feinstein's office, *Congressional Quarterly,* May 12, 2005; Suzanne Gamboa, "Texas Gets $35 Million in Terrorism Grants," *Associated Press State and Local Wire*, May 31, 2006.

22. Armando Villafranca, "Texas Senate Approves Homeland-Defense Bill," *Houston Chronicle,* May 22, 2003; Web site of Texas Homeland Security Office: www.texas homelandsecurity.com, accessed November, 2005.

23. "Gov. Perry Releases Updated Homeland Security Strategic Plan," *US States News*, November 2, 2005.

24. Jake Bernstein, "The Governor's Database," *Texas Observer*, April 20, 2007, 6–19.

25. Polly Ross Hughes, "Port Attack Odds Slim, but Threat Real; Security Expert Warns of Dire Consequences," *Houston Chronicle,* December 5, 2003, A37; Steve McVicker, "Port Security Holes Patched; Eckels Touts Revisions after Problems Exposed," *Houston Chronicle,* December 30, 2003, A1.

26. "Texas A&M To Create Homeland Security, Forensic Science Degrees," *US States News*, December 1, 2006.

27. Bill Miller, "North Texas Urged to Help Assure Homeland Security," *Fort Worth Star-Telegram,* April 1, 2003.

28. W. Gardner Selby, "Senate To Get Metal Detectors," *Austin American-Statesman*, April 12, 2007, B5.

29. "City of Lubbock Participates in Regional Homeland Security Exercise," *US States News*, October 23, 2006.

# Glossary

## A

**administrative discretion**  The freedom that administrators (bureaucrats) have in implementing and interpreting laws (Chapter 9).

**appellate jurisdiction**  The authority of a court to hear cases sent to it on appeal from a lower court. Appellate courts review only the legal issues involved and not the factual record of the case (Chapter 10).

**appointment and removal powers**  The governor's constitutional and statutory authority to hire and fire people employed by the state (Chapter 8).

**at-large elections**  Elections in which each candidate for any given public office must run jurisdictionwide—in the entire city, county, or state—when several similar positions are being filled (Chapters 10 and 12).

**attorney general's advisory opinion**  A legal opinion as to the constitutionality of legislative proposals (bills), rules, procedures, and statutes (laws) (Chapter 10).

## B

**bicameral**  For a legislative body, divided into two chambers or houses (Chapter 6).

**biennial**  Two years. Thus, a biennial legislative session occurs every other year and a biennial budget is one that directs spending for two years (Chapter 6).

**bill**  A proposed law written on a piece of paper and submitted to a legislature (Chapter 7).

**bills of rights**  Sections of constitutions, most famously the U.S. Constitution, that list the civil rights and liberties of the citizens and place restrictions on the powers of government (Chapter 2).

**block grants**  Federal funds that can be used for a broad range of programs; the state or local government recipient can determine specific uses within broad guidelines (Chapter 14).

**bureaucracy**  A type of organization that is characterized by hierarchy, specialization, fixed and official rules, and relative freedom from outside control (Chapter 9).

## C

**campaign**  The activities of candidates and parties in the period of time before an election that try to persuade citizens to vote for them (Chapter 5).

**capital punishment**  The execution of a convicted criminal, normally only imposed on murderers (Chapter 11).

**casework**  A legislator's doing favors for constituents, such as troubleshooting or solving a problem (Chapter 6).

**categorical grants-in-aid**  Federal funds that can be used only for specific purposes (Chapter 13).

**checks and balances**  An arrangement whereby each branch of government has some power to limit the actions of other branches (Chapter 2).

**civil jurisdiction**  The authority of courts that handle non-criminal cases, such as those dealing with divorce, personal injury, taxes, and debts (Chapter 10).

**civil liberties**  Individual freedoms such as speech, press, religion, and assembly. The protection of these liberties is essential to a vital democratic society. Generally, the protection of civil liberties requires forbidding government to take certain actions (Chapter 11).

**civil rights**  The constitutional claims all citizens have to fair and equal treatment under the law. Among the most important civil rights are the ability to vote in honest elections, to run for and serve in public office, and to be afforded a fair trial presided over by an impartial judge if accused of a crime. Civil rights refer to actions that government must take in order to ensure equal citizenship for everyone (Chapter 11).

**civil service system**  A personnel system in a government administrative agency in which employees are hired, fired, and promoted by the agency, rather than by elected politicians outside the agency. Individuals generally are hired and promoted through some sort of written examination. There are often restrictive rules that make firing an individual employee difficult. Often called the "merit system" (Chapter 9).

**clientele group**  The interest group or groups that benefit from or are regulated by an administrative agency (Chapter 9).

**closed primary**  A primary in which only voters who are registered members of that party may participate (Chapter 5).

**coalition**  A group of interests and individuals supporting a party or a candidate for office (Chapters 3 and 4).

**commissioners court**  The administrative and legislative body of a county; in Texas it has four elected members and is presided over by an elected county judge (Chapter 12).

**concurrent jurisdiction**  The authority of two or more different types of courts to hear the same type of case (Chapter 10).

**conference committee**  A temporary joint committee of both houses of a legislature in which representatives attempt to reconcile the differences in two versions of a bill (Chapter 7).

**conservatism**  A political ideology that, in general, opposes government regulation of economic life and supports government regulation of personal life (Chapters 1 and 4).

**constituent function**   The power of a legislative body to propose constitutional amendments and, in the case of a state legislature, to ratify amendments to the national constitution (Chapter 6).

**constitution**   The basic law of a state or nation that takes precedence over all other laws and actions of the government (Chapter 2).

**constitutional amendment**   A change in a constitution that is approved by both the legislative body, and, in Texas, the voters. National constitutional amendments are not approved directly by voters (Chapter 2).

**constitutional reform/revision**   Making major changes in a constitution, often including the writing of an entirely new document (Chapter 2).

**co-optation**   The process by which industries and their interest groups come to dominate administrative agencies that were originally established to regulate the industry's activities (Chapter 3).

**Court of Criminal Appeals**   The highest state appeals court with criminal jurisdiction (Chapter 10).

**criminal jurisdiction**   The authority of courts that handle offenses punishable by fines, imprisonment, public service, or death. These offenses include murder, rape, assault, theft, embezzlement, fraud, drunken driving, speeding, and other acts that have been defined as criminal by the state legislature or municipal authorities (Chapter 10).

# D

**democracy**   The form of government based on the theory that the legitimacy of any government must come from the free participation of its citizens (Chapter 1).

**demographics**   The objective categories into which people fall, irrespective of their individual personalities, such as sex, race or ethnicity, age, religion, education, and so on (Chapter 15).

**district elections**   Elections in which a polity is divided into geographical areas; candidates for public office must run in one small area rather than in the whole polity; each district usually sends one representative. Also called single-member district elections (Chapters 10 and 12).

**district system**   A system in which a candidate is required to live in the particular geographic area in which he or she runs for office (Chapter 12).

**dual-budgeting system**   A system in which both the executive branch and the legislative branch prepare separate budget documents (Chapter 13).

# E

**elasticity**   The flexibility and breadth of the tax system so that state revenues are not seriously disrupted even if one segment of the economy is troubled (Chapter 13).

**equal protection clause**   The clause in the Fourteenth Amendment to the U.S. Constitution that declares that no state may "deny to any person within its jurisdiction the equal protection of the laws." This clause has been frequently used

by the federal courts to protect the civil rights of American citizens, especially African Americans (Chapter 5).

**exclusive jurisdiction**   The sole authority of one court over a given type of case (Chapter 10).

# F

**federal system**   A system of government that provides for a division and sharing of powers between a national government and state or regional governments (Chapter 1).

**filibuster**   An effort to kill a bill in a legislature by unlimited debate; it is possible in the Texas and U.S. Senates, but not in the Houses of Representatives (Chapter 7).

**fiscal year**   The budget year for a government or a corporation; it may not coincide with a calendar year. In Texas, the state fiscal year runs September 1 through August 31. Municipal fiscal years run October 1 through September 31, the same as the federal fiscal year (Chapters 7 and 13).

**formal qualifications**   Qualifications specified by law for holding public office (Chapter 6).

# G

**general election**   An election in which voters choose government officeholders (Chapter 5).

**general laws**   Statutes that pertain to all municipalities that do not have home-rule status (Chapter 12).

**general revenue sharing**   A federal program that allowed state and local governments great flexibility in the use of federal funds. It expired in 1986 (Chapter 13).

**gerrymandering**   The practice of drawing electoral districts in such a way as to advantage one party or one faction (Chapter 5).

**grand jury**   A legal body of twelve or more individuals convened at the county seat. The grand jury considers evidence submitted by prosecutors and determines whether there is sufficient evidence to indict those accused of crimes (Chapter 10).

# H

**hierarchy**   Levels of authority in an organization, with the maximum authority on top (Chapter 9).

**home rule**   The ability of cities of 5,000 or more population to organize themselves as they wish within the constitution and laws of Texas (Chapters 2 and 12).

***Hopwood* v. *Texas***   The case decided in federal court in 1996 that eliminated affirmative action in admissions to the University of Texas Law School and, through subsequent interpretation, in statewide public college admissions and scholarships (Chapters 11 and 14).

# I

**ideology**   A system of beliefs and values about the nature of the good life and the good society, and the part to be played by government in achieving them (Chapter 4).

**impeachment**   The process of formally accusing an official of improper behavior in office. It is followed by a trial, and if the official is convicted, he or she is removed from office (Chapter 8).

**impresario**   In general, a promoter or organizer of an event; in the context of Texas history, a person who brought groups of settlers to Texas when it was Spanish or Mexican territory (Chapter 1).

**incorporation**   A historical activity by the U.S. Supreme Court, in which it makes the protections of citizen rights established in the Constitution applicable to state and local governments (Chapter 2).

**indictment**   An official accusation that a person or organization has committed a crime, normally issued by a grand jury, and normally involving felonies rather than misdemeanors (Chapter 10).

**individualistic political culture**   The culture, historically dominant in the middle tier of American states, in which citizens understand the state and nation as marketplaces in which people strive to better their personal welfare, citizen participation is encouraged as a means of individual achievement, and government activity is encouraged when it attempts to create private opportunity and discouraged when it attempts to redistribute wealth (Chapter 1).

**inflation**   A rise in the general price level, which is the same thing as a fall in the value of the dollar (Chapter 13).

**infrastructure**   The costly government investments in physical, nonhuman resources such as highways, bridges, water lines, and sewer systems; these make possible economic growth and a reasonable quality of life (Chapter 14).

**interest**   Something of value or some personal characteristic that people share and that is affected by government activity; interests are important both because they form the basis of interest groups and because parties attempt to form many interests into an electoral coalition (Chapters 3 and 4).

**item veto**   The governor's constitutional power to strike out individual items in an appropriations bill (Chapter 7).

## J

**judiciary**   A collective term referring to the system of courts and its judges and other personnel (Chapter 11).

**juvenile courts**   Special state courts that handle accused offenders under the age of seventeen (Chapter 10).

## L

**Laissez faire**   A French phrase loosely meaning "leave it alone." It refers to the philosophy that values free markets and opposes government regulation of the economy (Chapter 1).

**legislative oversight**   The legislature's supervision of the activities of state administrative agencies. Increasingly, the emphasis of oversight is on increasing efficiency and cutting back management—doing more with less (Chapters 6 and 9).

**legislative veto**   A provision in a law that allows a legislature, or one of its committees, to review and revoke the actions of a chief executive or other executive officer (Chapter 7).

**legitimacy**   People's belief that their government is morally just, and that therefore they are obligated to obey it (Chapter 1).

**liberalism**   A political ideology that, in general, supports government regulation of economic life and opposes government regulation of personal life (Chapters 1 and 4).

**lobby**   To try to influence government policy through face-to-face contact (Chapter 3).

**lobbyist**   A person who attempts to influence government policy through face-to-face contact (Chapter 4).

## M

**mandate**   Action that the national government requires state and local governments to take or that the state requires cities, counties, and special districts to take (Chapter 14).

**message power**   The governor's means of formally establishing his or her priorities for legislative action by communicating with the legislature (Chapter 8).

**moralistic political culture**   The culture, dominant in the northern tier of American states, in which citizens understand the state and the nation as commonwealths designed to further the shared interests of everyone, citizen participation is a widely shared value, and governmental activism on behalf of the common good is encouraged (Chapter 1).

## N

**nonpartisan election**   One in which candidates bear no party label such as Republican or Democrat (Chapter 12).

## O

**one-party state**   A state that is dominated by a single political party, characterized by an absence of party competition, inadequate debate of public policy, low voter turnout, and usually conservative public policy (Chapter 4).

**open primary**   A primary in which all registered voters may participate, whether or not they are registered members of the party holding the primary (Chapter 5).

**original jurisdiction**   The authority to hear a case first, usually in a trial (Chapter 10).

**original trial courts**   Courts having the authority to consider and decide both criminal and civil cases in the first instance, as distinguished from appellate courts (Chapter 10).

## P

**permanent party organization**   The small, fixed organization that handles the routine business of a political party (Chapter 4).

**place system**   A form of at-large election in which all candidates are elected citywide, but the seats on the council are designated Place One, etc., and each candidate runs only against others who have filed for the same place (Chapter 12).

**plea bargain**   The process in which an accused person agrees to plead guilty to a lesser crime and receives a lighter sentence. He or she avoids having to stand trial on a more serious charge, and the state saves the time and expense of a trial (Chapter 10).

**plural executive**    A system of organizing the executive branch that includes the direct election of multiple executives, thereby weakening the chief executive, the governor. Related concepts include disintegration and fragmentation (Chapter 7).

**political action committee (PAC)**    A group formed by a corporation, trade association, labor union, or other organization or individual for the purpose of collecting money and then contributing that money to one or more political candidates or causes (Chapter 3).

**political culture**    A shared framework of values, beliefs, and habits of behavior with regard to government and politics within which a particular political system functions (Chapter 1).

**political interest group**    A private organization that attempts to influence politicians—and through them public policy—to the advantage of the organization (Chapter 3).

**political party**    An organization devoted to winning public office in elections, and thus exercising control over public policy (Chapter 4).

**political socialization**    The process by which we learn information, values, attitudes, and habits of behavior about politics and government (Chapter 4).

**pollutants**    Substances which are harmful to human, plant, and/or animal life when they are dumped into water supplies, landfills, or the atmosphere (Chapter 14).

**Populist**    Someone who believes in the rights, wisdom, and issues of the common people, and that those people should be protected from exploitation by corporations, rich people, and government (Chapters 4 and 8).

**poverty threshold**    The level of income below which a family is officially considered to be poor. It is established annually as the basis for determining eligibility for a variety of social programs. Also called the federal poverty line (Chapter 14).

**primary election**    An election held within a party to nominate candidates for the general election or choose delegates to a presidential nominating convention (Chapter 5).

**privately funded campaign**    A system in which candidates and parties must rely on private citizens to voluntarily donate money to their campaign chests; except partially at the presidential level and for some offices in some states, this is the system used in the United States (Chapter 5).

**privatizing**    Turning over public programs to the private sector to implement. For example, municipalities often contract with private waste management companies to dispose of solid waste. The state has contracted with a private firm to operate some Texas prisons (Chapter 14).

**progressive tax**    A tax that increases in rate with the wealth of the one paying the tax; the richer the person or institution, the higher the tax rate (Chapter 13).

**pseudo laissez faire**    A phrase referring to the tendency of entrepreneurs to oppose government involvement in the economy at the general philosophical level, but to seek government assistance for their particular business (Chapter 1).

**publicly funded campaign**    A system in which the government pays for the candidates' campaign expenses, either directly or through parties. This system is not used in the United States except partially at the presidential level and for some offices in some states (Chapter 5).

**public policy**    The overall purpose behind individual governmental decisions and programs. It is the result of public officials' setting of priorities by creating the budget, making official decisions, and passing laws (Chapter 14).

# R

**realignment**    A change in the standing decision to support one party or another by a significant proportion of the electorate, resulting in a change in which party has a "normal" majority on election day (Chapter 5).

**reapportion**    To reallocate legislative seats, adding seats to areas with heavy population growth and taking away seats from areas without growth (Chapter 6).

**redistributive public policy**    Laws and government decisions that have the effect of taking wealth, power, and other resources from some citizens and giving those resources to others. Examples would be the graduated income tax and affirmative actions programs (Chapter 14).

**redistricting**    The designation of geographic areas that are nearly equal in population for the purpose of electing legislators—national, state, and local (Chapter 6).

**regressive tax**    A flat-rate tax that is not based on ability to pay; as a consequence, the poorer the payer of the tax, the larger the percentage of income that goes to the tax (Chapter 13).

**revenue shortfall**    A situation in which state revenues are not expected to be adequate to fund programs and services at current levels (Chapter 13).

**revolving door**    A name given by political scientists to the process in which government regulatory agencies hire their personnel from within the industry being regulated; after they leave the agency, employees are typically hired once more by the regulated industry (Chapter 3).

# S

**Select Committee on Higher Education**    A committee created by the legislature in 1985 to examine all aspects of higher education and make recommendations for action in 1987 (Chapter 14).

**seniority**    In a legislative body, the amount of time spent in continuous service in one house or committee (Chapter 6).

**separation of powers**    A phrase often used to describe the U.S. political system; it refers to the assigning of specific powers to individual branches (in Texas, departments) of government. In reality, the powers of the branches overlap, so that "separate institutions sharing powers" would be a more accurate description of the U.S. system (Chapter 2).

**session power**    The governor's constitutional authority to call the legislature into special session and to set the agenda of topics to be considered in that session (Chapter 8).

**single-member district** A designated geographic area from which only one representative is elected (Chapter 6).

**social Darwinism** A philosophy, drawn from the biological theory of evolution, that holds that the rich are superior people and deserve their wealth, while the poor are inferior and deserve their poverty (Chapter 1).

**spoils system** Appointing people to government jobs on the basis of whom they supported in the last election and how much money they contributed (Chapter 12).

**suffrage** The legal right to vote in public elections (Chapter 5).

**Sunset review** The process by which the legislature reviews the performance of administrative agencies, then renews, reorganizes, or eliminates them (Chapter 9).

**Sunshine law** A law that provides for public access to the records of administrative agencies (Chapter 9).

**Supreme Court** The highest state appellate court with civil jurisdiction (Chapter 10).

# T

**tag** A means by which an individual senator can delay a committee hearing on a bill for at least forty-eight hours (Chapter 7).

**tax equity** The inherent fairness of a tax. As the term is used in this book, ability to pay is a factor in fairness (Chapter 13).

**temporary party organization** The organization formed to mobilize the party's potential electorate and win an election (Chapter 4).

**third party** A minor political party that fails to achieve permanence but frequently influences the major parties and, through them, public policy (Chapter 4).

**tort** A private or civil wrong or injury resulting from a breach of a legal duty that exists by reason of society's expectations about appropriate behavior, rather than a contract. The injured party sues the alleged offender in order to receive compensation for his or her losses (Chapter 11).

**traditionalistic political culture** The culture, historically dominant in the southern tier of American states, in which citizens technically believe in democracy but do not encourage participation, and government activity is generally viewed with suspicion unless its purpose is to reinforce the power of elites (Chapter 1).

**trial jury** Six to twelve persons who determine the legal guilt or innocence of defendants in a criminal trial or the liability of defendants in a civil trial (Chapter 10).

**trickle-down theory** A theory of economic development that maintains that government should create a very favorable climate to attract business and industry, and that the prosperity thus created will trickle down to rank-and-file citizens (Chapter 1).

**turnover** The proportion of the legislature that consists of first-term members because previous members retired, died, or were defeated at the polls (Chapter 6).

# U

**user fee** A fee for a specific governmental service charged to the person who benefits from the service; a greens fee at a municipal golf course and college tuition are both user fees (Chapter 13).

# V

**veto power** The governor's constitutional authority to prevent the implementation of laws enacted by the legislature. The item veto allows the governor to delete individual items from an appropriations bill (Chapter 8).

**voter registration** The process used in every democracy to list the residents who are eligible to vote; it is necessary to prevent fraud but also discourages turnout by erecting a barrier between the citizen and the simple act of voting (Chapter 5).

**voter turnout** The proportion of the eligible citizens who actually cast their ballots in an election (Chapter 5).

# W

**workers' compensation** A program that provides income assurance for a worker injured on the job (Chapter 14).

# Index

## A

Abbey, Edward, 2, 23, 25
Abbott, Greg, 70 *table*, 147, 266, 271, 307–308, 344
Ability to pay taxes, 418–419
Abortion, 115 *table*, 306–307, 341–344, 352
Absentee voting, 157
Accountability of administrative agencies, 293–300
Ad hoc committees, 194
Ad valorem property tax, 419
Address, 253
Administrative agencies, 267–301
　accountability, 182–187, 293–300
　with appointed executives, 270 *table*, 274–275
　attorney general, 270–271
　boards and commissions, 270 *table*, 275–277
　bureaucracy, 268, 282–291
　Commissioner of Agriculture, 274
　Commissioner of General Land Office, 273–274
　comptroller, 271–272
　economic development, 446–447
　with elected executives, 269–273, 270 *table*
　employment in, 280–281 *fig.*, 284–286, 285 *fig.*
　essential characteristics, 269
　future prospects, 478
　growth of big government, 278–281
　gubernatorial appointment to, 251–252
　interest groups and, 216–217
　lawmaking by, 232
　legislative oversight of, 170, 296–297
　legislative process, 216–217, 289–291
　policymaking involvement by, 289–290
　power sources for, 287–289
　public interest, 288, 291–292
　regulatory, 83–84
　suggested reforms, 300
　Texas Performance Review (TPR), 293, 423–424
　types of, 269–277, 270 *table*
Administrative discretion, 289
Administrative function of legislature, 170
Administrators, 268

Advisory opinions, by attorney general, 307
AFDC (Aid for Families with Dependent Children), 454
Affirmative action, 115 *table*, 308
AFL-CIO, 56, 94
African Americans. *See also* Civil rights; Minorities
　affirmative action in higher education, 308
　citizenship, 23
　civil rights in Jasper and Tulia, 347–349
　Civil War, 6–7
　as cotton field laborers, 8
　Democratic Party, 128
　election of 2002, 159, 160 *table*
　equal justice, 325–326
　future prospects, 476–477, 482–485, 491
　Great Depression relief, 13
　historically black colleges, 60
　Jim Crow laws, 9
　Ku Klux Klan, 7–8, 12, 112
　in late 19th century, 8–9
　in legislature, 178 *table*
　liberal Democrats, 129
　NAACP, 87, 95, 132
　nonvoting, 143
　political culture, 23
　population, 31–32, 485 *table*
　post-Civil War, 7–8
　public opinion survey, 144 *table*
　redistricting, 175–182
　reform legislation, 23, 129
　Republican Party, 127
　slavery, 4, 6–8, 23, 40, 111
　in statewide office, 15, 124, 126–127
　voting rights, 11, 138
AG (attorney general), 47, 270–271, 307–308, 330, 432
Age of legislators, 186–187, 187 *table*, 188
Agency, defined, 268
Agosto, Rick, 162
Agrarian movement, 9, 42
Agriculture
　Commissioner of Agriculture, 274
　farmer's political interests, 9, 57
　shifting economy, 407–410
　Texas-Mexico Agricultural Exchange, 21
Aid for Families with Dependent Children (AFDC), 454
Air quality issues, 463–465, 470, 472

Airline deregulation, 470
Airlines, 409, 470
Alamo, 5–6
Allen, Alma, 126
Amendment function of legislature, 169–170
American Bar Association, 355
American Lung Association, 443
American Political Science Association (APSA), 125
*The American Rifleman*, 340
Amicus curiae, 329
Anglos
　Democratic Party, 128
　early Texas, 3–4
　election of 2002, 159
　Great Depression relief, 13
　in legislature, 178 *table*
　liberal Democrats, 129
　political culture, 22–25, 125–126
　political socialization, 106–107
　population, 31–32, 485 *table*
　public opinion survey, 145 *table*
　redistricting, 175–182
　Republican Party, 127
　voter turnout, 490
Annexation power of cities, 377–379
Antitrust suits, oil and gas industry, 11
Appellate courts, 312–313
Appellate jurisdiction, 311–312
Appleby, Paul, 291
Appointed boards and commissions, 276–277
Appointment, gubernatorial power of, 251–252
Appointment of judges, 318
Apportionment, county, 365–366
Appraisal districts, 395
Appropriations
　budget process, 225, 431–432
　fiscal year, 223
　item veto, 223, 257
　legislative committees, 431–432
APSA (American Political Science Association), 125
Army Corps of Engineers, 468
Articles of Confederation, 40
Artistic interest groups, 67
Asian Americans, in legislature, 178 *table*
Assessor-collector of taxes, 368
At-large elections, 324–325, 330, 364–365, 387, 392–394, 398–399
Attorney general (AG), 47, 270–271, 307–308, 330, 432

# Credits

## Photos

**1** © iStockphot **5** © Dennis Flaherty /Getty Images **10** © Associated Press **35** © Harry Cabluck/Associated Press Images **65** Courtesy of the Texas Department of Transportation **79** © AP Photo/Harry Cabluck. **101** Courtesy of the Texas Department of Transportation **120** © AP Photo/Paul Sancya **121** © AP Photo/Michael Stravato **135** © Smiley N. Poole/The Dallas Morning News **159** © AP Photo/Harry Cabluck **166** © Harry Cabluck/Associated Press Images **182** © Bob Daemmrich/CORBIS **203** © Harry Cabluck/Associated Press Images **205** © Lon Otero/Associated Press Images **235** © Harry Cabluck/Associated Press Images **245** © Harry Cabluck/Associated Press Images **246** © Eric Miller/Associated Press Images **266** © Harry Cabluck/Associated Press Images **271** © Harry Cabluck/Associated Press Images **274** © Tony Gutierrez/Associated Press Images **275** © Harry Cabluck/Associated Press Images **303** Courtesy of Texas Department of Transportation. **314** AP Photo/Harry Cabluck. **332** © Mark Jenkinson/CORBIS **348** © AP Photo/David J. Phillip **361** Courtesy of Denton Municipal Utilities **372 (bottom left)** © Bob Daemmrich Photography **372 (bottom right)** © Bob Daemmrich Photography **372 (top left)** © Panoramic Image/Getty Images **372 (top right)** © Walter Bibikow/The Image Bank/Getty Images **385 (bottom)** © James Nielsen/AFP/Getty Images **385 (top)** © Gerg Probst/Stone/Getty Images **386 (bottom)** © Paul Buck/Associated Press Images **386 (top)** © Eric Gay/Associated Press Images **405** © Harry Cabluck/Associated Press Images **416** © Donna McWilliam/Associated Press Images **434** © Moses Olmos/NBAE via Getty Images **440** © Tony Gutierrez/Associated Press Images **447** © Bob Daemmrich/CORBIS **458 (bottom)** © J.R. Hernandez/Associated Press Images **458 (top)** © Matt Slocum/ Associated Press Images **474 (left)** © iStockphoto **474 (right)** (and NASA) **482** © AP Photo/ Erin Trieb

## Cartoons

Cartoons on pages **29, 42, 96, 116, 126, 135, 148, 152, 171, 201, 249, 272, 276, 292, 323, 326, 336, 358, 376, 427, 429, 433, 452, 463, 470, 482** Courtesy of Ben Sargent.